The Nile

The Nile
History's Greatest River

Terje Tvedt

I.B. TAURIS
LONDON • NEW YORK • OXFORD • NEW DELHI • SYDNEY

I.B. TAURIS
Bloomsbury Publishing Plc
50 Bedford Square, London, WC1B 3DP, UK
1385 Broadway, New York, NY 10018, USA
29 Earlsfort Terrace, Dublin 2, Ireland

BLOOMSBURY, I.B. TAURIS and the I.B. Tauris logo are trademarks of Bloomsbury
Publishing Plc

First published in Great Britain 2021

Nilen: historiens elv by Terje Tvedt
Translated by Kerri Pierce
Original copyright © H. Aschehoug & Co (W. Nygaard), Oslo, 2012

Cover design by Adriana Brioso
Cover image: Landscape crossed by the Nile, Palestrina, 2nd–3rd century BC (mosaic).
Museo Archeologico Nazionale di Palestrina e Santuario della Fortuna Primigenia,
Palestrina, Italy. (© Bridgeman Images)

A catalogue record for this book is available from the British Library.

A catalog record for this book is available from the Library of Congress.

ISBN: HB: 978-0-7556-1679-4
ePDF: 978-0-7556-1681-7
eBook: 978-0-7556-1680-0

Typeset by RefineCatch Limited, Bungay, Suffolk
Printed and bound in Great Britain

To find out more about our authors and books visit www.bloomsbury.com
and sign up for our newsletters.

I am like one of those old books that ends up moldering for lack of having been read. There's nothing to do but spin out the thread of memory and, from time to time, wipe away the dust building up there.

Seneca the Younger, 4 BCE–65 CE

Contents

Nubia and the Country Where the Rivers Meet

The Nile Wetlands and the New State

The Country with the Great Lakes

The End of the Journey

Plates

Maps

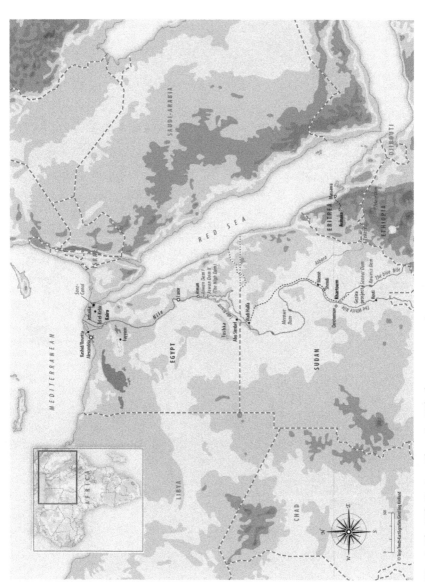

Map 1 The Nile Basin with major Nile dams

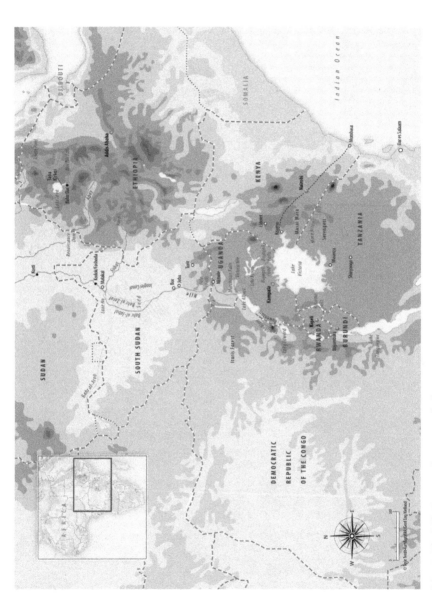

Map 2 The Nile Basin with major Nile dams

1

The Beginning of the Journey

The mosaic outside Rome

On the fourth floor of a modest archaeological museum about 35 kilometres outside Rome can be found the Nile Mosaic. It is about 2,000 years old, almost 6 metres wide, and over 4 metres tall, and depicts vibrantly and from several different vantage points the river and the life along it. At the top, African motifs are represented, and at the bottom Mediterranean scenes are recreated. Although one must view the mosaic from a distance, standing behind ropes to protect it from onlookers, the unusually colourful and clear pattern composed of painted stones attached by mortar comes through. But what is truly original about the Palestrina Mosaic is that the river and the people going about their lives are depicted from an entirely modern perspective, as if the artist saw the Nile from a plane. This work of art is also a prodigiously expressive historical source: it underscores the river's timelessness as society's lifeline and centre, and it illustrates that the Mediterranean receives the history of a continent written in water.

The mosaic depicts the Nile's central place in the lives of the people living on its banks, but also conveys how the river has formed a part of Europe's cultural and religious history. It reminds us of a distant past when the Nile was worshipped as sacred, not only by priests in magnificent temples along the river in Egypt, but also in Europe. The mosaic stems from an epoch when the Nile and Isis cult spread out from Egypt and into the Hellenic and Roman world. The cult was a new, independent religion – a mystery religion that concerned death and rebirth, and that revolved around spectacular processions and rituals in which Nile water played a central role. The British Museum in London holds one of many statues of Isis, patroness of nature and fertility goddess. In her left hand she carries a jar of sacred Nile water, the very medium of salvation. Two thousand years ago, believers could be seen carrying such pitchers of Nile water across plains and up valleys north of the Mediterranean, illustrating a deep historical connection between the jars of Nile water and the later baptismal fonts in European churches.[1]

The mosaic was created several hundred years before the Nile and its Isis cult became a serious competitor of Christianity, the new religion that had spread from the Middle East. The worship of the Nile and its gods continued long into the Christian era, and it was the followers of Isis who lynched Mark the Evangelist when he suffered a martyr's death in Alexandria one Easter a few decades after Christ's death: he was dragged through the streets with a rope around his neck before being decapitated. It was only when Christianity became the state religion of the Roman Empire that the cult surrounding Isis and the Nile was crushed. Having been the cradle of an expansive mystery religion, the Nile Delta now became a centre for early Christianity.

The Nile Mosaic outside Rome represents a long historical thread that subsequent distinctions and borders drawn between continents and nations have rendered indistinct. The river's name is connected to Europe via the Greek poet Hesiod, who lived between 700 and 600 BCE, when Egypt, the Delta and Greece were parts of a common Mediterranean culture. Hesiod called the river *Neilos*, since the numerical value of these Greek letters was 365 – that is to say, everything – as if to underscore that the river was perceived to be *everything*. The mosaic reminds us that the Nile Valley was one of the main routes via which humans wandered out of Africa and peopled the earth; that some of the earliest agricultural societies we know developed along its banks; and that the most impressive and mighty of all the ancient civilizations could emerge thanks to the river.

The mosaic is a topographical depiction of a religious ceremony but can also be interpreted as a celebration of the Nile as a part of Mediterranean culture. The mosaic conveys the same fascination for the river as the Dictator of the Roman Republic, Julius Caesar, must have had, since it has been said he would immediately give away all Egypt if only someone could tell him where the source of the river lay. Where did it come from, all that water that every summer – just when Egypt was at its hottest and driest – flooded out of the burning desert to create one of the most fertile regions on earth? Up until the late Middle Ages in Europe, the river's mystery was shrouded in fantastic, mythical ideas; in the literature it was described as flowing both from Paradise and over a golden stone staircase. The Nile, as such, was long regarded as a divine manifestation. One of the fourteenth century's great chroniclers, Jean de Joinville, summarized the prevailing belief in his *Histoire de Saint Louis*, published between 1305 and 1309: 'No one knows the source of all this water, unless it be the will of God'.[2]

After the triumph of the Enlightenment in Europe, a different and more scientifically based Nile romanticism arose. In the nineteenth century, few geographical questions were discussed more than where the source of the Nile lay. A century and a half ago, the Nile basin became the arena for some of the most fabled scientific surveys in world history, where adventurers and explorers such as Henry Morton Stanley, David Livingstone, John Hanning Speke and the less renowned but wealthy Dutch woman, Alexandrine Tinne, as well as a then-famous Norwegian long-distance runner searched for the river's source. The history of how the Nile was mapped by European geographers, explorers, hydrologists and British water-planners is a history of colonial conquest and of modern science's triumphal march through Africa.

Yet, the river the mosaic captures, frozen fast in a 2,000-year-old moment, has since that time, through every single second, day after day and generation after generation, trickled through impenetrable primeval forests where the sunlight never enters, crashed and roared down volcanic cliffs, forced its way out of gigantic inland lakes, snaked across one of the world's largest swamps, and crossed one of the driest deserts on the planet, all on its course from inner Africa. The river's permanent geography and the water's pulsing rhythm have continued to shape the conditions for society's development and transformation, and the river itself has remained a perpetual object of myth-making and power struggles.

By the time the mosaic was created, the Persians, Alexander the Great and Julius Caesar had, along with their troops, already conquered the Nile Delta – one of the world's most fertile regions. Later, the Arabs conquered the Nile. The Crusaders appeared there. Napoleon rode at the head of his army up the Delta to fight the Battle of the Pyramids. With Cairo as the axis point, the British established their Nile Empire, from the Mediterranean to the river's source, in what was described as the 'heart of Africa', and for the first and only time in history the Nile came under a single power – London. Since the seventh century, those living along the watercourse have been at the centre of the struggle between Islam and Christianity on the African continent. The Nile basin has also been a breeding ground for the international aid system's most classic myths and stereotypes, while some parts of it at the beginning of the third millennium CE are undergoing developments that makes the aid epoch's portrayal of a helpless Africa seem hopelessly outdated.

This book belongs to the same tradition that the Palestrina Mosaic symbolizes: the whole world's fascination for the river's role and significance. It is a history book about the development of civilization and a travel narrative told from the world's longest river. It is, however, also a study of modern hydropolitics and of African development, as well as the way in which these changes reflect, as if in a prism, many of the modern world's most central developmental characteristics. First and foremost, however, the book is the biography of a lifeline that binds almost half a billion people together in a common destiny that none of the eleven countries that share the river today can escape.

I have previously written on the Nile's history, from the period when the river was under British control (*The Nile in the Age of the British*), and during the postcolonial epoch (*The River Nile in the Post-Colonial Age*). I have also published bibliographical surveys on the area (in five volumes) as well as books dealing with the aid epoch in the region. *The Nile: History's Greatest River* has a different focus and a much longer time perspective, and it attempts to connect everything I have learned after countless journeys criss-crossing the entire watercourse, after endless discussions in the late evening hours over café tables from Alexandria to Kigali, after numerous extended interviews with experts, state leaders and ministers, and after spending years in archives on three continents hunting for sources on the region's and the river's history.

What occurs with and along the Nile now and in the coming years will have dramatic consequences for the region and for global politics. As this book is being written, the river, as it courses through both nature and society, is undergoing the most revolutionary transformation it has made throughout its long history. And it is precisely at such dramatic, shifting and inscrutable times that historical knowledge becomes critical; misinterpretation of the present is unavoidable if one does not understand the past.

This narrative is organized as a journey up the Nile, from mouth to source. It is only by following the river *up*, from place to place, as slowly and systematically as the river's own heartbeat, that its secrets can be uncovered and its role and significance for society's development can be understood.

The stream of history

Travelling from Rome, after crossing the Mediterranean I look down on kilometres of sandy beaches; to the west the endless brown desert and below me an immense green garden. I am flying over Egypt and the Nile Delta, my forehead pressed to the window as usual, and while the river appears like a solitary, glistening strip of life surrounded by green, a living protest against the desert's dominance, I notice that my North European blindness to the water's significance falters. I am here to give an opening address on the importance of the history of ideas about water at a conference at the Library of Alexandria. Though having long worked with this subject, I still feel a little nervous – that I, a man from Norway, will be discussing water and the Nile in the Nile's own country. I page again through a classic work on the Nile's geological history, for although the Nile is culture and mythology, romance and nostalgia, Rushdi Said's book, *The River Nile: Geology, Hydrology and Utilization*, underscores that the Nile is fundamentally a physical structure; indeed, one cannot understand its role in society without accounting for its hydrology.[3] On page one of my notebook, which lies on the tray table next to my PC, I write in large characters the most important figures concerning the Nile. I do it almost ritually, as if emphasizing to myself that beneath the thick layer of culture, religion and politics that shapes every contemporary Nile perspective, there runs an actual river with a fixed geographical, hydrological character. The figures I write, of course, are figures with atypical societal significance, just as relevant to the time of the mosaic as they are to today. The Nile we know as a perennially flowing river is the result of relatively recent geological processes 15,000 to 25,000 years ago, when water from Lake Victoria connected with water flowing from Ethiopia and met as the two Niles at present-day Khartoum. The modern Nile is thus a quite young river giving birth to very old civilizations.

I spread out a map of the Nile I always keep with me when I travel here. Because I am a historian and political scientist who also happens to be geographer, it is a reflex action – for maps illuminate connections that often have been of little concern to social scientists. The Nile is more than 6,800 kilometres long, and if you were to stretch it out and shift it using Cairo as the axis point, the river would run across the Mediterranean, through all of Europe, and further north than the northernmost point of Norway. The precipitation area covers around 3 million square kilometres – about a tenth of the area of the entire African continent. Eleven countries share the watercourse and around a thousand different peoples have developed their diverse cultures and societies here over generations. Due to its size and to its variations in climate, topography, flora, fauna and social formations, the Nile basin is, beyond compare, the most complex and varied of all the great rivers, both when it comes to nature and to social relations. The watercourse's extreme political significance is framed by a merciless paradox: though its length is enormous, the river carries very little water. Its annual average has largely been fixed at 84 billion cubic metres, as measured at Aswan in Egypt. That is not much water – around 12 per cent of the Yangtze or the Changjiang, around 6 per cent of the Congo, and around 1 per cent of what the Amazon delivers annually on average to the sea. The reason for this is the Nile's most significant characteristic: long stretches of it run through an entirely precipitation-free zone. In Upper Egypt, the natural annual water flow has been somewhere between 80 and 90 billion cubic metres. Over recent decades, however, that number has been reduced, mainly because about 10 per cent of the water evaporates from large artificial lakes created in the Nubian Desert. And the Nile receives no influx of new water during its almost 2,700-kilometre long journey through one of the world's driest and hottest regions. No other river on earth flows such a distance through desert landscape without receiving contributions from other water sources.

The river's long desert journey is unique. Along its course, two distinct tributary systems with completely different hydrological profiles merge. The main Nile's two principal tributaries, the White Nile and the Blue Nile, converge at Khartoum, the capital of Sudan. Here a remarkable hydrological process takes place, which can also explain why the White Nile has served as Egypt's most important tributary throughout history (up until 1971). In the autumn, the Blue Nile is full of water and acts as a natural barrier to the water in the smaller and weaker White Nile. As the water level in the Blue Nile gradually decreases throughout the spring, the pent-up water from the White Nile runs down to Egypt, and it is this phenomenon that, for thousands of years, made it possible to live and farm during the summer as well.

The Blue Nile flows around 2,500 kilometres from its humble, sacred source on the Ethiopian highlands before it reaches Khartoum. This river, as well as the other tributaries that collect rain in Ethiopia, such as the Atbara (known as the Tekeze and the Setit in Ethiopia and Eritrea) and the Sobat (known as the Baro in Ethiopia), are responsible for almost 90 per cent of the Nile's total water flow. During the autumn, in the flood season, the Blue Nile is utterly dominant. It alone accounts for around 80 per cent of all water flowing into Egypt. Seasonally, however, these tributaries to the main Nile suffer dramatic variations. The Atbara is almost completely dry during the summer, whereas the Blue Nile for three autumn months sends down almost 90 per cent of its entire annual water discharge.

The White Nile is a completely different river. From Khartoum to the most southern point of the swamps – around 1,800 kilometres – the river has a declivity of 1 metre per 24 kilometres, and its water flow varies much less than the Blue Nile throughout the year. There are no tributaries along the entire stretch between Khartoum and Malakal. Then, from the east, comes the Sobat or Baro from Ethiopia, which absorbs several smaller rivers along the way. At this point, the main river turns sharply to the west and flows out of Lake No, a huge lake located downstream of one of the world's largest swamp areas.

This swamp landscape represents the White Nile's most astounding hydrological phenomenon with great economic and political importance: around 50 per cent of the water in Bahr al-Jabal, as the White Nile is known here, never reaches Khartoum or Egypt. A few kilometres north of Juba, the capital of what is now South Sudan, is where the swamps begin. Bahr al-Jabal ('the mountain river' in English, depicting that it originates on the slopes of Central Africa) becomes a massive, slow-moving water body on the level plains of South Sudan. Extending in all directions, its size fluctuates with the season and the Nile's water flow. Other large rivers in South Sudan, like the Bahr al-Arab and the Bahr al-Ghazal (or the Gazelle River, called so because it flows through an enormous park-like area with huge gazelle colonies), never reach the White Nile but terminate in the swamp.

At Juba, the While Nile still has 4,787 kilometres to travel before it reaches the sea. At a point 168 kilometres upstream of Juba, it crosses the Sudan–Uganda border at Fola Rapids after flowing out of Lake Albert, through the swamp-lake Kyoga, after having squeezed itself out of Lake Victoria at Jinja, not far from where Uganda's first hydropower station, known as 'Uganda's beginning', is located today.

These Central African lakes act as the White Nile's immense natural reservoir. They were formed when a wetter climate arrived here, following the retreat of ice in other parts of the globe during the last ice age. Changes in precipitation patterns combined with geological uplift resulted in Lakes Victoria and Albert overflowing with rainwater; this began to stream northwards, thereby forming the perennial Nile. These vast quantities of water, which coursed unimpeded over what was then a dry region, but which today form the huge swamp of South Sudan, reached Egypt, and over a period of several centuries the river gave rise to a number of very exceptional and powerful floods that created the original Nile Delta with its many watercourses.

For the last 10,000 years, Lake Victoria has been predominately stable and is now the world's second largest lake (it has completely dried up in earlier periods). It is the source of heavy precipitation itself, due to evaporation from its enormous surface area, and additionally acquires water from rivers flowing from Burundi, Rwanda, Tanzania, Uganda and, especially, Kenya. The lake is described as the source of the Nile by both encyclopaedias and tourist guides, but the White Nile has many sources – in the east, in Kenya; in the south, in Burundi; and in the west, in Rwanda and in the Democratic Republic of the Congo. The mountains in the west of the basin, the source of some of its most important tributaries, belong to the wettest regions on earth, with rainfall 360 days a year and an annual average of 5 metres. The combination of these fortuitous meteorological and geological conditions has enabled the Nile's continual water flow, even during those times of the year when the Nile rivers in Ethiopia dwindle and some of them practically dry up.

All these figures might seem misplaced, or seem like bean-counting to those who consider a focus on societies to imply limiting oneself to the human realm; that is to say, that a humanistic, human-centred historical narrative should bypass such figures because they are natural science distractions. The opposite is true: these figures summarize in decisive ways not just the framework of societies' development, but they also describe a sustained axis for social development and what is at the heart of societies' existence. It is these measurable geographical traits, furthermore, that give the river its unique regional and local identities, revealing how, all along its banks, it has contributed to societal formation in different ways, creating also various regional possibilities for its exploitation. This book will discuss Nile mythologies and the meaning of Joseph Conrad's *Heart of Darkness* and Herodotus' *Histories*, but it will also show that it is not possible to understand European colonialism's rise and fall, Ethiopia's central role in the prelude to the Second World War, South Sudan's fate and current position, or Egypt's past and future, without bringing the hydrology of the Nile into the story.

The Desert and the Delta

The desert paradise

Just as the value of water only truly becomes clear after experiencing a dry well or a temporary stop in modern, municipal water supply, in order to grasp the Nile's significance for Egypt, one must understand what this desert country would have been without the river.

This Nile biography, therefore, begins with Faiyum, the famous, classic desert oasis west of the river. In the Sahara it is so dry in some places that archaeologists claim to have found unspoiled cigarette paper tossed aside by Allied soldiers during the Desert War in the 1940s. It is here, where the desert changes colour from flecked brown to pure white, that I open my car door to feel the heat, and how it strikes me. I need only walk a few minutes over the nearest sand dunes, away from the asphalt road winding through the brown completely barren landscape, before I see only desert and know that I am alone. Utterly alone. The endless waves of sand, stretching toward the horizon, are reminiscent of the sea, but what really strikes me is the scene's most distinctive feature: a lack of any odours. The feeling of emptiness is strengthened by the wind's brisk, lonely way of blowing. Surrounded by this environment one understands the truth of Egypt – an agricultural desert country depending on water running through ten other countries.

It is at this point, after I climb back into the car and think I hear the motor stall because of the heat, that a city dweller like myself might start developing romantic but frightening fantasies inspired by desert journeys watched on screen: the four-wheeler stranded due to engine trouble, and the wind that slowly but surely buries the vehicle while people seek shelter inside it. The water bottles steadily emptying... But then, abruptly, signs indicating the way to Faiyum come into view.

Known as 'Egypt's Garden' for thousands of years, Faiyum is also called 'the Desert Paradise'.[1] It is a pulsating oasis – with beautiful mosques, old churches and ancient monuments. When standing at the centre of this 692 square kilometre depression and watching the palm trees, all bending in the same direction, donkeys bearing loads of corn and fruit that appear far too heavy for them, water buffaloes studiously contemplating passers-by, and farmers, yes, farmers everywhere, working the small green fields, it is difficult to comprehend that it almost never rains here. What makes this site so intriguing for anyone concerned with humankind's early history is that in prehistoric times it was a fertile paradise. The first permanent Egyptian settlements are estimated to be around 7,000 years old and it is here in Faiyum that they appeared, the result of a migration process with singularly far-reaching consequences. As the Sahara slowly transformed to desert, 'climate refugees', as we would call them today, sought permanent water sources. Thus, gradually, the area east of the Nile Valley was peopled, and from this depression they travelled further to settle on the banks of the perennial river a little to the east, flowing across the Sahara waste.

Faiyum quickly became one of the first true agricultural areas in world history. Its location is due solely to the fact that every year the Nile flooded the low hills separating the river from the oasis. Originally, Faiyum's fertility was the river's natural handiwork. However, the river also demonstrated to humankind the functioning of nature's wonders, or the gods' wonders, since for many they were one and the same thing, and the goal became to imitate them, if on a smaller scale.

Thus almost 4,000 years ago, under the rule of Amenemhet I in the Twelfth Dynasty, the Egyptians had the ingenious idea of controlling the flood with the help of the natural Lake Faiyum as a regulating reservoir.[2] The lake, later described by countless travellers as a divine wonder, as well as a natural one, was quite simply an early Nile dam, presumably one of the first constructions of this type in human history. The nearly 4,000-year-old regulating dam in Egypt's central oasis can be seen as a precursor to the tens of thousands of such structures that make modern society possible. Today, the dam has been expanded to form a massive inland lake that glitters a lazy blue in the middle of a desert, although the water is too dead-looking to seem truly refreshing. From the southern shore, the lake stretches as far as the eye can see; the air is hazy here, it trembles from the heat, and far in the distance arid hills protrude like heads from the lake, silhouetted against the near-white sky with a yellow-red desert hue. Myths tells the story that it was the Biblical Joseph who eventually widened the riverbed that the Nile had created during a violent flood. That is the reason why the canal by some is still called Joseph's Canal. The water system upon which the many date growers, shop owners, restaurants and mosques in Faiyum are wholly dependent is a product of both nature and of humanity's ability to imitate and expand upon the natural. If you walk along the canals winding through the oasis, it is difficult to distinguish where one ends, and another begins. In this way, Faiyum proves a dense, concentrated picture of Egypt – extremely lush, surrounded by desert, built from an amalgam of the Nile's natural character and a water system made and controlled by humans.

Faiyum is Egypt's mirror for another reason as well. Whereas the oasis' water consumption has steadily increased, there is also a growing gap between demand for water and supply of water. Water control in a desert climate is always a two-edged sword, both ecologically and politically, because demand will always keep pace with society's development. It is an indisputable fact that the more that Egyptians become dependent on Nile water, the more vulnerable their society will be to natural and anthropogenic changes to the river's water flow. From a long-term perspective, this can be described as the hydraulic paradox around which Egyptian history revolves.

Scarabs, rebirth and the river of death and life

The desert between Faiyum and Alexandria – nothing but sand and wind. No apparent trace of life, except for a beetle, a scarab, rolling a moist ball of earth up a small mound in the desert sand. At times the ball proves too heavy and rolls back down. The beetle starts afresh, pushing the ball upwards again, centimetre after centimetre. Usually, it is the male beetle that pushes. The female follows behind. They lay their eggs wherever they can find some moist clay or excrement in which to pack them. After that they roll the ball to a safe place in the desert, bury it in the sand and, having thus secured their offspring, they die.

These desert beetles enjoyed sacred status in ancient Egypt. Scarabs evoked and embodied the ancient Egyptian idea of transformation, renewal and rebirth. In Egyptian mythology, Khepri, 'He Who Came Into Being', was the god that symbolized the self-creative ability. He was typically represented as pushing the sun across the sky daily, having already rolled it safely through the Egyptian underworld during the night. Most often Khepri was depicted as a scarab. In some grave paintings, the god who symbolized such creative ability was shown as having the body of a man and the head of a desert beetle.

The ancient Egyptians believed that the beetle, like Khepri himself, came from nothing. Since they also believed that all scarabs were male, the insects creeping out of the balls literally emerged from nothing. They symbolized creative power and eternal life.

The scarabs and Khepri could help explain the natural processes that the Egyptians regularly witnessed: life's rebirth from death, the earth's renewal from lifeless brown to living green, plants appearing from the desert sand as if springing from nothing. Every year the Egyptian farmers, as well as Egyptian society, experienced such miracles. The land was transformed from a place where no life could grow to the world's most fertile region. And nature accomplished this feat on its own. Given the knowledge at the time of how nature operated and functioned, the wonders of the Nile were attributed to the power of gods or, eventually, to the pharaohs as god-kings. Since the Egyptians observed this process every year, it was also natural for them to assume that death was merely a portal to new life.[3] The scarabs that unperturbedly roll their balls of dung or earth up the gentle rise in the desert are nature's history teachers and mythology's harbingers. They are a reminder and exemplification of the ideas surrounding death and life that dominated Egyptian thought, a mode of thinking that coloured and shaped people's world views for much longer than Christian and Islamic perceptions of death and life have dominated Europe's and the Middle East's conceptual universes. In many ways, the Nile's annual miracles set the stage for ideas central to the desert religions that later emerged in its vicinity and that would ultimately impact the world. The beetle, in addition to proving the basis for the first myths, evokes the Nile as a producer of ideas regarding eternal life and as a creator of societal existence.

Religious traditions in ancient Egypt, as in all the major river civilizations in the Middle East and Asia around the same time, arose literally among people who conducted their lives along the banks of the great rivers. This fact obviously stimulated the development of a shrewd administrative system, where the need to calculate taxes based on Nile flood measurements hastened the establishment of fixed measuring units and the advancement of mathematics. The Egyptians were also pioneering when it came to astronomy. This was due to their need to predict not the weather, which remained unvarying, but the flood. The Nile, however, was also central to the people's cosmic universe. When it came to understanding nature and the 'big questions', the river was the great teacher; it shaped those human experiences to which the gods, if their messages were to find fertile ground, had to speak. Its alluvial geography – the river's eternal ambiguity as both life-bringer and death's harbinger, as the source of fruitful irrigation and destructive flooding and drought – naturally shaped conceptions of death and life.

Pyramid texts also show that, for the ancient Egyptians, to cross the Nile was to cross the boundary or connector between states of existence. Social life, earthly life, took place on the river's east bank. By being immediately transported to the west bank after death, the pharaohs could rise from the dead, and it is for this reason that the pyramids, which are, after all, enormous grave monuments, are located there. Immediate crossing of the river westward made reincarnation possible.

The belief that the Nile came from the underworld where death reigned is another illustration of the way in which Egyptian cosmology reflected their environmental and ecological universe. The world was shaped by clear oppositions: between drought and the inundating river, between desert and civilization, between light and dark, between one riverbank and the other, between the earthly river and the divine river of the underworld. Pyramid texts illustrate how the river split Egypt in two between the realms of death and life.[4] The dead travelled west, crossed the underworld and were reincarnated in the east at dawn, after which they traversed the heavens over the Nile to end again in the west, and so on, eternally. The journey in the heavenly world reproduced what daily took place on the Nile. The sun rose, boats crossed the river, the water alternately flooded and subsided, pressed forward and then retreated.

As such, the Nile simultaneously represented a traditional boundary or barrier, as well as a connector or link between two forms of existence. It was logical, therefore, that this river could only be navigated by a supernatural being: the mystical ferryman, Mahaf, who transported the dead. He could travel in both directions because he had two faces, one facing forwards and one behind. Similarly, the river in Egyptian texts acts as both barrier and meeting place between people, worlds, and life and death.[5] As focused as they were on immortality, the ancient Egyptians nonetheless had an optimistic religion: this life was just the beginning of life after death, a passage so to speak, to the next life – like the drought years were a passage, a way-station between the fecundity, the activity, of two Nile floods. It was only in the mid-1800s that the natural, seasonal flows of the Nile were first subjected to human will by big engineering projects. This rendered the river less suitable as raw material for these kinds of religious myth. Now, with the development of mighty dams and reservoirs and massive channels brimming with perennial water kilometres from the river, the foundation was laid for an entirely new type of world view, one based on stories of the triumph of modernity, of the victory of humanity and technology over nature.

Society and the river's rhythm

One of the books I take with me when I travel along the Nile is *The Histories*, written by the Greek scholar Herodotus almost 2,500 years ago. Like all great literature, this book consistently reveals different sides of itself, and its rather intricate yet controlled style and form suits the Nile's nature and social role. Herodotus was a historian – he is often called 'the father of history' – but first and foremost he was a meticulous observer. He travelled to many places in the classical world, the Nile among them, and he talked to the people and priests he met along the way; he listened and took notes; he acted, it seems, as a kind of inquisitive romantic who sought knowledge for knowledge's sake. He was not satisfied simply with what people told him or with what he regarded as inherited truths, however: he wanted to see things himself.

Surrounded by desert on all sides, I am sitting in a restaurant in one of the new cities recently built to the west of the river. I am reading my copy of Herodotus. His descriptions of the ease with which the Egyptians farmed, a fact due to the Nile's natural way of irrigating the ground, capture the heart and character of ancient Egypt:

> It is certain however that now they gather in fruit from the earth with less labour than any other men and also with less than the other Egyptians; for they have no labour in breaking up furrows with a plough nor in hoeing nor in any other of those labours which other men have about a crop; but when the river has come up of itself and watered their fields and after watering has left them again, then each man sows his own field and turns into it swine, and when he has trodden the seed into the ground by means of the swine, after that he waits for the harvest; and when he has threshed the corn by means of the swine, then he gathers it in.[6]

The Egyptians at the time practised basin or flood irrigation. They adapted to the river's natural and very regular fluctuations. In early June, the Nile was a small, modest river. The land and fields had baked in the sun and dried in the Sahara winds until they seemed an extension of the desert. Then, each autumn, the Nile flood arrived. For just a few weeks every year, the river could swell to 400 times what it had been at its narrowest point. During that period, the villages in the Nile Delta were like islands in a brown ocean. After a while the water receded, depositing meanwhile more than 100 million tons of rich, fertile silt as it flooded thick and brown towards the sea. The only thing necessary then was to plant and sow and wait for the crops to grow – larger and faster than they did elsewhere in the world. Egyptians, especially those living in the Delta or in Lower Egypt, did not require a strong state to develop this thriving agricultural production. In Upper Egypt, floodwaters were sealed behind basin walls. When the floods came, the water would be trapped in the basins formed by the walls. This forced the water to stay longer than it would have naturally done. Once the soil was watered, the excess water would be sent down to another basin in need of water.

The Nile's hydrology and ecology posed different challenges of social organization from those of other large civilizational rivers. In Egypt, the state had no need to mobilize tens of thousands or even millions of farmers or forced labourers to build permanent dykes along the river, as did the Chinese state and feudal lords, especially along the Yellow River. Flooding was seldom catastrophic. When the river threatened to rise above the Nilometer level (a means of indicating the height reached by the Nile during its annual floods) to which the population and economy were adapted, an extensive monitoring and safety network was mobilized. A mark on an inner wall at Luxor testifies to an abnormally high flood in the Twenty-Second Dynasty (943–746 BCE) in Upper Egypt. The inscription reads: 'This land was in his power like the sea, there was no dike of the people to withstand its fury. All the people were like [sea] birds [...].'[7]

The Egyptians also implemented huge waterworks, but they did not have the same critical significance as those along the Euphrates and Tigris or along the great Chinese rivers. One of the world's first dams was, however, raised in Egypt *c.* 2600 BCE, the Sadd al-Kefara Dam on Wadi al-Garawi, and it was meant to control the Nile flood. Since it was destroyed shortly after its building, it did not prove decisive for the country's development. The danger of salinization – the build-up of salts in the soil – something that plagued Sumer and perhaps contributed to that civilization's downfall, did not represent the same problem in Egypt due to the flood's annual role. The river regularly washed away salt deposited during the last cultivation season. As such, the character of the Nile decisively aided the fact that Egyptian farmers, for large swathes of the year, simply need do nothing, and so could more easily be mobilized for various types of public works – pyramid building, for example. A widely held belief has long been that Egyptian slaves built the pyramids and other great structures. However, newer research suggests that such theories overlook the river's distinctive hydrology and thereby its role in framing the organizing of agricultural labour. In Egypt, the reality was that for several months every year, farmers simply had nothing to do, since typically the soil was not moist enough in summer to farm. While everyone waited on the next autumn's flood, the population was 'free', and during that time people could be mobilized by their rulers, either by payment or due to their faith in the dominant religion and the pharaoh's divine place within it.

The Egyptians also built canals, although to a much lesser extent than in China and Sumer. That they had the capacity, however, they certainly demonstrated: during the Dynastic Period they constructed long canals from the Nile all the way to the Red Sea, and they also excavated drainage channels in the Delta. After the central government began to assume responsibility for water control, one of the earliest administrative titles given to the local governor was *adj-mer*, canal-digger. The Nile, furthermore, was also relatively easy to navigate. The current carried boats north, while the wind blew largely to the south. By controlling boat transport, state authorities controlled the transfer of wares and people. It was more difficult, in contrast, to navigate the violent Chinese rivers, especially the Yellow River, not to mention the Euphrates and Tigris.

As I approach the Delta, coming from the western oasis, and pass the first small fields on the desert's edge, where men with ox and plough work their artificially watered plots, I again retrieve Herodotus's book: I reread his words and imagine, thanks to his descriptions, that I can see how Egyptians have lived their lives for millennia, eternally striving to adapt to the river's rhythm, to its gifts and to its perils.

Cities and rivers that vanished

If you walk along Alexandria's beaches, where waves crash against kilometre upon kilometre of white sand, and where the sun, with all the typical hallmarks of a triumphant eastern Mediterranean sunset, sinks behind the fortress where the Pharos Lighthouse once stood, it seems unnatural to say that Alexandria is a Nile city. The six-kilometre-long Corniche, the famous beach promenade with its parallel road, insists on turning the city's face to the sea. Much as urban development, road architecture, sewage system aesthetics and changing functions of rubbish dumps must be included in our understanding of societies' history if that history is not to become anaemic and essentially inhuman, so a relevant story of the Nile must extend beyond human ideas and plans. A vital history that strives to place human actions and ideas actively at its centre must also include and integrate nature, ecological processes and technological adaptations; that is to say, it must analyse the varying geographical and hydrological structures of a river that has consistently posed different and changing contexts for the acting individual, whether that person be an army leader, an engineer or a political entrepreneur.

One example of how environmental circumstances have changed was discovered one July day in 1961 by an amateur diver who swam alone in the polluted sea basin just outside Alexandria's promenade. Abruptly, he found himself in an ancient world: he saw a staircase surrounded by white marble columns, a life-sized Roman statue, a gold coin, a sarcophagus and, not far from the mighty fortress that had guarded the city for centuries, two headless sphinxes, more marble columns and a massive statue cleaved in two. Kamel Abul-Saadat, spear fisherman and amateur diver, had uncovered Egypt's buried past.

Only a few stones' throws from where waves crash against Citadel of Qaitbay, and well within sight of the modern library and the promenade, his dive had taken him into an ancient world, silent and submerged. Strange forms were scattered across the sea floor. Alexandria's greatest treasures – the ruins of Cleopatra's palace, among other things – lie 6–8 metres beneath the Mediterranean's surface, undisturbed for thousands of years while, above, the sea strikes unabated against the stone walls surrounding the fortress.

As it stands now, twenty-five ancient cities have been discovered on the sea floor close to the outlets of the present Nile Delta. Though these cities bear witness to many fates and many histories, they first and foremost demonstrate that the Nile, as a river, has its own history, just as the people living along its banks have theirs. Thanks to Herodotus' book, we know that, in his day, there were three rivers located 5–15 kilometres east of Alexandria, whereas today there is only one.[8] There were also four secondary rivers, Saitic, Mendesian, Bucolic and Bolbitine, though the last two were described as being partially artificial, created or influenced by human intervention. As such, Herodotus' meticulous observation ensures that the book continues to speak to us directly, even as other parts of the work belong to a 'foreign country' whose world of ideas completely differs from that of modern rationality. The book's descriptions of the Nile system make it far more relevant and of current importance than many of the articles appearing in yesterday's papers. When Herodotus describes how the river had transformed itself within the Delta, he is speaking to the Modern Age; he is speaking the language of rationality, even though the river as he understood it obviously existed within an entirely different conceptual universe. Herodotus illuminates both these aspects of the Nile's role in human history, as well as how the river has its own history. When he travelled the Delta, the river system had already undergone major changes since 7000 BCE. Back then, what would later become the fertile Nile Delta was swampland cut by a river with indefinite banks where huge papyrus forests provided hippos, crocodiles and birds with fantastic concealment and habitat. By around 3000 BCE, the Mediterranean had risen about 20 metres. The Delta, in prehistoric times, was a gigantic tidal estuary with scattered islands. Throughout the millennia, Nile deposits created land areas that divided the estuary into different branches. Science will probably never be able to determine exactly what occurred during these millennia, but we know that the rivers crossing the Delta changed course, and that parts of the Delta gradually sank into the ocean. Writing around 400 BCE, Herodotus described the cities in the Delta as if they resembled islands in the Adriatic, but located in the midst of a massive, swamp-like area and adapted to the river's natural fluctuations. He also wrote about rivers and cities that by 1000 BCE had completely disappeared.

Underwater archaeologists have now reconstructed where one of the rivers described by Herodotus – the Canopic – met the sea. At its mouth lay Heracleion, named after the classical god Heracles, whom the Greeks (including the Oracle at Delphi) regarded as a descendant of the much older Egyptian Hercules. The Greek historian Diodorus of Sicily relates how Heracles succeeded in damming a flood and forcing the river back to its usual bed. As a result, people built him a temple and named the place after him. Heracleion also contained many temples devoted to Nile gods and, as a religious centre, attracted pilgrims from the entire Mediterranean region. Ancient texts describe the city as a gateway to Egypt. From the city, with the wind blowing north to south you could sail up the Nile to Memphis or Thebes, and down the river with the current.

The Canopic was one of the many rivers that vanished, and the cities along its banks subsequently also disappeared from history. In the pharaonic era, projects to control the river were being implemented and pyramid texts document the digging of transport and drainage canals. Accordingly, this branch of the river was destroyed, not only due to its own relentless ecological logic, but also because the Egyptian rulers dug the Bolbitic canal around 300 BCE. The canal's water-carrying capacity meant there was less water left for the Canopic, something that finally finished it off. Heracleion is one of the cities that underwater archaeologists have discovered, and they have described it as being in many aspects intact, as if frozen in time.

Herodotus' *Histories* has acquired new relevance today. Since he chronicled the city communities he saw and documented where they lay with respect to rivers that no longer exist, archaeologists have something to go on, and people who trust and fear that parts of today's Delta will sink into the ocean can cite historic examples as reference points. From a long Nile-ecological perspective, there are signs that point to an alarming future, a future some believe will prove a reality during the present century. The ancient past has, accordingly, become present in a way that eludes conventional ways of distinguishing between past and present: the past itself is not simply only 'a foreign country'.

The Nile city of Alexander the Great

In the words of E.M. Forster, few cities 'have made so magnificent an entry into history as Alexandria'. And few cities have had a more spectacular and chaotic history, not to mention, many climatologists and ecologists will argue, a more uncertain future.[9] It was Alexander the Great who founded this city not far from the Nile's western estuary, right on the shores of the Mediterranean. The ruler needed a capital city for his newly conquered country. In 331 BCE he ordered the city to be built on the site of what was then a small fishing port. Of the at least seventeen cities Alexander founded and named after himself, today's Alexandria is the only one that has survived the long history of urbanization, a fact due to the Nile's stability as a trade artery and to the city's clever positioning. Namely, attention had been paid not only to existing trade patterns but also to natural processes: to the Nile's hydrology and to the Delta's topography. Instead of building the city in the Delta itself, Alexandria was placed about 30 kilometres to the west. In that way, the Nile's alluvial deposits would not destroy the port, and in addition the city had a bog-like lake as a neighbour to the south.

Due also to the canal commissioned by the young Macedonian ruler, Alexandria remained for centuries the most important trade centre in the evolving Mediterranean economy. The city obtained two good, protected ports that connected trade of diverse wares from two distinct water systems. One port was intended for the transport of Egypt's agricultural wares along the Nile; the Egyptian Delta had for thousands of years already been one of the world's most productive agricultural areas. The second port was equipped for the Mediterranean's new seafaring ships. The city thus became a transit port into Egypt for goods from all corners of the world and for Egypt's products to be shipped out into the world. This Mediterranean hub acquired the reputation early on as a beautiful city with a comfortable climate. Since Egypt was a part of the Hellenic and Roman empire, it attracted numerous Greeks and Romans. Alexander the Great – whom Plutarch claims was not 'so great' but was somewhere between 1.60 and 1.65 metres tall – left behind a city that was perhaps the first to truly warrant the name metropolis.

The more trade the city coordinated, the more it also needed a symbol of its prosperity, not to mention a more effective means of guiding ships through the limestone reefs beyond its coast. Therefore, in 290 BCE, Ptolemy I, who founded the Macedonian Ptolemaic dynasty after Alexander's death, commissioned a lighthouse to be built on Pharos Island in the bay outside the city. When it was completed twenty years later, Alexandria was home not only to the world's first known lighthouse but also to the world's tallest structure: the lighthouse stood at over 120 metres. As a testament to Alexandria's position, *pharos* became the root word for fire in French, Italian, Spanish and Norwegian. Today, looking toward the Ottoman fortress where the lighthouse once towered – whether gazing from one of the balconies of the colonial Cecil House Hotel with its glorious sea views, or sitting and dangling your legs against the wall that curves along the entire promenade, together with some of the hundreds of city inhabitants who always seem to sit there – it is easy to imagine how proud and majestic the Pharos Lighthouse, regarded as one of the Seven Wonders of the World, must have appeared to visitors in the distant past.

Under the Ptolemies, the city became a centre of science, trade and learning throughout the entire Hellenic world. It was a cosmopolitan melting pot where Greek thought, ancient Eastern religions and new mystic cult movements influenced each other. Alexandria was the centre – one of the most remarkable in world history – not for art, as in Athens – but for science. Anatomy, geography, astronomy and mathematics made great strides forward here.

The city's library – the famed Library of Alexandria – attracted the foremost mathematicians, engineers, physicists, architects and geographers. Here, astronomy and mathematics developed in flourishes. Sharp minds drew and debated some of the first world maps. As a result, if there is a place in history that has truly earned the designation *centre of learning*, it is Alexandria during this period. The library built its position by exploiting Alexandria's role as a trade hub. The dynasty's rulers ordered all ships to be searched – for books. Were any found, they must be given to the library. There the books would be copied; the library retained the originals. Such books were catalogued separately, placed under the key word 'from the ships'. The book collection was so extensive that people eventually began making counterfeits, representing works as if they were written by Aristotle, for example, whereas they were written by others. Some have claimed that the library had more than 700,000 documents and that it contained 'all the world's knowledge'. Historians have more lately determined that that number is much exaggerated, although there can be no doubt that, during that period, Alexandria and the Nile Delta were the seat of learning of not only the Nile Valley but also the world.

The economic condition that allowed the city to become a world centre of knowledge 2,000 years ago was the scope of its trade, and what enabled such a thriving trade was Alexandria's location at the most effective point on the line connecting the Nile to the rest of the world. When contact with the Nile system later changed due to hydrological and political reasons, and when the necessary and extensive maintenance work on the transport canals between the Delta and Alexandria was neglected and boats, furthermore, grew larger than the canals could handle, Alexandria gradually declined and, along with it, its great library.

The Nile's significance for Alexandria has, like the city itself, also changed. Little remains of cosmopolitan Alexandria from the era when the library enjoyed its heyday. But here, on the shores of the Mediterranean, is a perfect place to give a talk on the history of ideas about water, discussing, among other things, the importance of Alexandria and the Nile to philosophy's beginnings.

Philosophy's beginnings

I stop the car at one of the palm forests that fill the Delta, wanting to see the forest in the mist of the morning light, before breakfast is served and before the heat becomes unbearable. Alone, I walk along the arrow-straight irrigation canals, in dappled sunlight beneath the palms standing in file, thousands upon thousands of them, like endless alleyways. Occasionally, I encounter a large sand dune, oddly misplaced, the desert here seeming like an interloper in Eden's Garden. The light slants between the palm leaves.

The setting is beautiful and still; even the water flows, or rather trickles, slowly and almost inaudibly at the bottom of the narrow canals. The Qur'an famously says that Allah 'made from water every living thing'. Here, I am a witness to how water shapes everything, albeit with government assistance, for the palms, the green grass, the tiniest plant – all result from the fact that for generations Egyptians have drained and channelled, dammed and directed the water, creating an intricate ecological, economic system under the heading 'water control'.

It was also in this region that one of world history's most famous men wandered around about 3,000 years ago, observing that water was the most elemental of all the basic elements of nature. This man would change the history of philosophy, maybe even the history of ideas. He was Thales of Miletus (624–546 BCE), whom Aristotle later described as the first natural philosopher and of whom Bertrand Russell, in his hugely influential history of philosophy, stated more explicitly: 'Philosophy begins with Thales'.[10]

Thales was interested in everything – philosophy, history, geography, politics and mathematics. He was deeply involved in astronomy, and some claim he was the first to posit the idea of the soul's immortality. Socrates told Plato – and Plato must have found it interesting enough to pass it down – that Thales was once so absorbed in star-gazing that he tumbled into a well, perhaps making Thales the first person to be descried in terms that would become a professional cliché for the absorbed scholar.

Historians have debated for the last 2,000 years how much Thales wrote and what, in fact, he said. Some have claimed that he only wrote 200 lines during his entire lifetime! What immortalized Thales, however, was the statement that water formed nature's basic element, as Aristotle explained several centuries later. In *De Caelo* (*On the Heavens*), Aristotle wrote: 'Others say the earth rests upon water. This, indeed, is the oldest theory that has been preserved, and is attributed to Thales of Miletus'.[11] Thales thought nature was composed of a single material substance – water. The philosopher identified water as being the basis of all things. The earth and everything on it had once been water. Thales, after all, had seen with his own eyes how nature demonstrated and reinforced this truth. On his journeys throughout the Nile Delta he, like everyone else, could see how water, literally speaking, shaped the land and the life, year after year after year. In parts of the year the Delta was a massive swampland but, as the water retreated, rivers, lesser swamps and fertile cultivation areas emerged. The people living along the river and its branches built their houses on pales so they could remain in place when the annual flood came. And every single year the water deposited yet again its inexplicable bonus: a fine layer of natural fertilizer or silt. In Egypt, the question of who or what was responsible for this mysterious annual gift must have been debated for hundreds of generations by poor farmers, by priests and by the rulers whose power depended upon this very process. Back then they had no way of knowing that the Nile carried with it tens of thousands of tons of extremely fertile soil from the Ethiopian highlands, dissolved into small particles in the water that came rushing down for a few months every autumn. Thales offered a tale of water that the Greeks in Athens regarded as a deep philosophical explanation, but what among the farmers in the Egyptian Delta was a well-known observable natural phenomenon. When he pondered what the world was made of, and then answered water, it was an entirely logical, indeed it was a natural, empirical observation based on his travels in Egypt. To his great merit, this observation was reflected upon independent of, or outside, the context of a religious universe that regarded the river and its water to be divine manifestations – and it thus represented philosophy's beginning.

Thales' viewpoint, of course, is also reminiscent of ancient Egyptian ideas. In pharaonic times they believed that the source of life was an inexhaustible, primordial spring, personified by the god Nu, which produced the two holy 'rivers' – the Nile, the life-giver; and the heavens, where Ra, the sun, sails. Within this bottomless, fluid mass floats the seed of all things, as Egyptian priests explained it. This mystical, religious theory on water and earth's creation, for which the Nile provided the basis, was part of the conceptual universe that Thales most likely encountered while in Egypt.

Thales' statement of water's significance occurred at a time when the Nile Delta was by far the most economically productive region of the Mediterranean, as well as its cultural centre. The Nile Delta was part of the region's collective experiential world, also expressed in the connections that existed between the ancient Egyptian and Greek pantheons. If Thales' link to the Nile Delta and its distinctive hydrology and mystical ecology is overlooked or dismissed, and if his claim is analysed as though he concluded that everything was made of water while strolling among the columns of Athens, it is easier to mistake the growth of Western civilization as being more of a European, geographical phenomenon than it actually was.

I ponder this idea while sitting at one of the thousands of pavement cafés located at one of the thousands of small towns in the Delta, where population density is on the rise, even though it already stands at 1,000 people per square kilometre. The local contrasts between lifestyles and lifeworlds is striking – middle-aged men in nice suits and expensive cars, undoubtedly moving between air-conditioned houses and offices; and other middle-aged men who look considerably older and who probably belong to Egypt's 30 per cent illiterate population, standing behind ox carts as farmers have done since the invention of the wheel, trying to convince their oxen to move forward in the noisy chaos, heading, presumably, to the small plots their families cultivate. As I pick up my things and leave a small tip for the waiter, I mutter that everything is definitely not made of water.

Caesar and Cleopatra on the Nile

The year is 47 BCE. Alexandria is still at the height of its power. A gigantic boat progresses slowly up the Nile.[12] On deck stands Cleopatra, Queen of Egypt, and Julius Caesar, Dictator of the mighty Roman Republic. They have left their Alexandria residence to greet the people. Four hundred lesser vessels escort them. The riverbanks throng with crowds. It is a scene from one of world history's most legendary boat tours. As always, myth-making possibilities are strengthened by a lack of actual written sources. Regarding Caesar and Cleopatra's journey up the Nile by boat, there is only one, and it was recorded 150 years after the fact. Appian, who lived in Alexandria, did not write his famous history until the mid-100s. And this lack of precise documentation has given fantasy wings. At the beginning of the 1600s, Cleopatra's drama was immortalized by William Shakespeare in *Antony and Cleopatra*, and countless books have been written and films produced about one of world history's most famous women. Most historians agree that Caesar and Cleopatra did indeed undertake a magnificent journey up the Nile in what at the time seemed an enormous, lavish boat, and that this trip was not simply a romantic cruise but a calculated power play; it was a journey laden with political symbolism.

This 'high-profile' journey, assuming it did occur, must have had a political objective.[13] Since time immemorial the pharaohs had made boat trips along the country's life artery as a display of power and might. Because all life was oriented towards the river and everyone knew that only the mightiest could afford the largest boats, the pharaohs travelled up and down the Nile to evoke and secure their elevated place in society. Along the riverbanks, numerous smaller and larger palaces were erected where the pharaohs could gather their underlings. The connection between receiving homage on a Nile boat and retaining earthly power was obvious and could be repeatably demonstrated. This idea was apparently exploited by Caesar and Cleopatra. After their victory in the civil war against those who supported Cleopatra's brother, Caesar wanted to appear as the powerful, invincible ruler over the Roman Republic's new province. For Cleopatra, it was important to demonstrate that her Roman alliance was to Egypt's advantage and did not signify submission. Whether or not she became pregnant by Caesar while on this boat trip (Caesar was thirty years old at the time), is still debated by historians, despite the fact that Cleopatra herself insisted on it and later gave birth to Ptolemy Caesar, called 'Caesarion' or 'Little Caesar'. The voyage may also have had a religious significance since the Nile was considered to be a holy river and Cleopatra to be the earthly representative of the goddess Isis. Cleopatra was both goddess and queen. As such, the procession up the Nile clearly signified that Caesar and Cleopatra, like other Egyptian rulers before and after them, understood the river's cultural importance, not to mention the political capital to be gained by appearing to be the river's sovereign and divinity. Cleopatra, the Nile goddess, allowed herself to be worshipped on the sacred river. Caesar, Dictator of the world's most powerful state, realized that the Nile was seen as a deity, but he also definitely knew that it was a guarantor of the Roman Republic's grain supply. Even so, what was the historical background for this voyage?

Cleopatra's father, Ptolemy XII, 'the Flute Player', was not recognized as a king by Rome. When he died, Cleopatra, who was eighteen years old, ascended the throne together with her half-brother, Ptolemy XIII, who was six years younger. So total were the ambitions of the royal house that they had adopted a bizarre strategy for retaining power: in order to keep the line pure, the ruler's offspring must marry. As a result, Cleopatra and her twelve-year-old brother were married when they took the throne. The institutionalizing of an incestuous power politics did not remove all rivalry. It helped, however, to concentrate it between brother and sister. It was Ptolemy XIII's adviser who successfully drove Cleopatra from the palace.

Then, on 2 October 48 BCE, Caesar sailed into the bay and seized control of Alexandria. Cleopatra spied her chance to take revenge on her brother and his followers. Caesar was highly ambitious as well and arrived with a force of around

30,000 legionnaires. He installed himself in the palace and began issuing orders as if he ruled Egypt. Cleopatra's younger brother and husband was invited to negotiations.

It is here that Cleopatra enters world history, emerging as a singularly romantic, mystical and tragic figure all at once, familiar particularly through the account written by Plutarch around 150 years later, and which Shakespeare and others have further embellished: Cleopatra had herself smuggled behind enemy lines and was delivered – rolled in a carpet – to Caesar by a Sicilian tradesman. The following morning, Ptolemy and Cleopatra were both summoned before Caesar, who had already fallen for Cleopatra's charms. Her brother immediately realized how things stood and fled the palace, shouting that Cleopatra had betrayed him. In the civil war the following year, Cleopatra and Caesar triumphed over her brother in what is called 'the Battle of the Nile'. Her brother, according to most accounts, was drowned in the river, a traditional way to celebrate a victor's conquest. Caesar awarded Cleopatra the right to the throne, but as a subordinate Roman ally. She accordingly reigned together with another, even younger brother, the eleven-year-old Ptolemy XIV who, in keeping with tradition, became her new husband. Cleopatra has been described by some as the last Egyptian pharaoh to govern Egypt,[14] since her death brought an end to the Ptolemaic dynasty and the Egyptian Empire, and Egypt became part of the new Roman Empire.

The journey upriver underscored that Julius Caesar now ruled Egypt and that the river was the kernel of the Republic's new province. By having Cleopatra at his side, however, Caesar also demonstrated that Rome did not plan to make Egypt Roman, so long as the Dictator got what the Dictator wanted. And what he mainly desired was – lots of grain.

For Rome, Egypt was the crowning jewel, not just due to the country's cultural and religious position but because Egypt proved an increasingly important granary. It has been calculated that around 200,000 tons of wheat were transported to the republican capital every year, and much of that was distributed gratis to the city's numerous poor to prevent uprisings and maintain the workforce. Almost all this grain was watered by the Nile; Egyptian farmers became producers in the Roman economy. Yet for them life remained essentially unchanged: dynasty followed dynasty, regimes came and went, but these events had little consequence for the farmers' lives: the state taxed them as before, mobilized them to build embankments against flooding; and raided them when it served. Meanwhile, both the Ptolemaic and Roman authorities further expanded the irrigation system. They introduced new hoist devices for hauling water from the river to the fields, such as the Archimedes' Screw, and increased the use of both *shaduf* and *sakia*, technological improvements which made it possible to cultivate multiple times a year.

Jesus and Mary's escape up the Nile Delta

According to Christian belief, a few centuries after Thales observed that water had created everything, but not too long after Caesar and Cleopatra accepted the people's homage on their journey up the Nile, a small group that would become even more famous fled up the Nile Delta: the Holy Family.

Egypt and the Nile occupy a central place in the Bible, a fact that underscores the significance in Jesus' day of both country and river for the entire inner Mediterranean region's economy and culture. The Bible is full of detailed descriptions of the Eastern Mediterranean; Egypt is mentioned a total of 659 times. The Nile, one of four rivers flowing through the earthly paradise according to the Bible, is mentioned thirty-seven times, six of these under the name Gihon, which is itself described as the River of Paradise.

The banks of the Nile proved the stage for critical events in Jewish and Christian history. It was Joseph's predictions regarding the river's cycles that made him the Pharaoh's foremost dream interpreter, and it was Joseph's suggestion of how to manage the Nile's seven plentiful years and seven lean ones – storing grain from the good years to use during the poor – that ensured his position as the Pharaoh's most trusted adviser.

The Jewish leader, Moses, was born along the Nile, and it was the rushes in the divine river that saved him from the Pharaoh's persecution. Moses was also 'educated in all the wisdom of the Egyptians'.[15] Aaron, the brother of Moses raised his staff and struck the water of the Nile 'in the presence of Pharaoh and his officials [. . .], and all the water was changed into blood'.[16] It was here that God punished the pharaohs with miserable years. According to the Bible, Abraham dwelt for a time along the Nile's banks and Isaiah promised that God would show himself to the Egyptians in particular, and that they would acknowledge Him on Judgement Day.[17] It was also here, in this relatively affluent and peaceful part of the Roman Empire, that Jesus, Mary and Joseph arrived, finding temporary protection after the family fled Herod's persecutions, including his threat to kill all male children of Jewish origin. The Bible says that God's angel appeared to Joseph, saying: 'Get up, [. . .] take the child and his mother and escape to Egypt. Stay there until I tell you, for Herod is going to search for the child to kill him'.[18] In the Egyptian Coptic Church, 24 June is celebrated as the day that Jesus entered the country. According to Coptic tradition, the Holy Family stayed in Egypt three years and eleven months. Along the river, there are many locations they are said to have visited, sites that later became memorials and pilgrimage destinations, especially for the Coptic Orthodox Church's followers. At the beginning of the 2000s, Atef Obeid, Egypt's prime minister at the time, conducted a ritual with three other ministers and Pope Shenouda III, head of the Coptic Church, as well as Grand Sheik of al-Azhar, the chief cleric of Egypt's Muslim population, at the site where the Holy Family is believed to have arrived at the Nile, in the Maadi suburb of Cairo. From a riverboat, artists sang from a newly composed song and on another boat a tree bowed in homage.[19]

A former pilgrimage site, Tell Basta, is located about 80 kilometres north-east of Cairo on the south-eastern edge of the modern city, Zagazig. Herodotus already described this city – a beautiful temple at its heart surrounded by canals with trees planted along the banks and an annual highlight: the festival of the cat goddess Bastet, daughter of the sun god, a protective mother goddess linked to fertility. Hundreds of thousands of Egyptian pilgrims visited the site yearly. In the same city, however, an old well has also been discovered among the ruins. It is here, according to Coptic tales, that Jesus as a young boy caused water to spring forth from the hill. Just as the Prophet Ezekiel foretold, the idols then crumbled. The population was furious, and Jesus' family was forced to flee. They travelled to what is now called Mostorod, but which was previously known as al-Mahamma or 'the bath'. Supposedly, Mary bathed her child and washed their clothes here. Most of these pilgrimage sites are gone today, swallowed by urbanization and neglect.

The Nile's role in the ancient Israelite and evangelical mythical worlds corresponds to the Nile's central place in the Bible. For this reason, Biblical texts are also a part of the Nile's history, and they have influenced and will continue to impact people's perception of and relationship to the river. The Egyptian Copts keep these stories alive: they are memories of the time when Egypt was still a Christian land; it is a historical narrative that help define their identity. The Copts have also given the Nile a central place in their rituals; among other things, they celebrate the Feast of St Michael, which commemorates the day the archangel prayed to God to make the Nile rise.[20] These myths and stories serve to emphasize that the Nile, in addition to everything else, is a river that many perceive through a religious lens. From this perspective, the present book is nothing less than a biography of God's river.

The Bible: God punishes those who claim they possess the river

As the train speeds through the densely populated Nile Delta on its way from Alexandria to Kafr el-Dawar, crossing countless larger and smaller canals, all of which receive their water from the Nile, I retrieve my copy of the Bible from my bag, lay it on the tray table, and reread those sensational chapters where God punishes the Egyptians for their ideas about and exploitation of the Nile. I want to read this text again while the Delta yet surrounds me, as we whip past fields and I fleetingly glimpse the contours of thousands of impoverished farmers who utterly depend on government control of the river to secure their lifeline. Again, I am reminded of precisely how unfruitful the conception of place is within postmodernism and much contemporary social research. Obviously, it is impossible for everyone to see the Nile Delta as it actually is, independent of any personal filter and perspective, but that does not mean that the Delta can simply be reduced to a social construct: the region is a definite physical setting where people lead their lives defined by it. With this idea as a springboard, it also becomes easier to understand the threat carried by God's words in the Bible.

In the Bible, the Nile as Gihon is the River of Paradise, and although this river, like all rivers, is under God's control, the Nile is the only river that God directly states will be used to punish an entire people. God, it turns out, has a particular idea of how the Nile should be exploited. A strong, literary interpretation of the text implies that anyone who believes that the Nile is theirs, or who thinks 'the Nile is mine', is not only selfish in a social sense, but is in rebellion against God's Word, against His plan for the world.

God's reaction to what He identifies as Egypt's possessive attitude towards the Nile is violent and furious:

Egypt will become a desolate wasteland.
Then they will know that I am the Lord.
Because you said, 'The Nile is mine; I made it',

therefore I am against you and against your streams,
and I will make the land of Egypt a ruin
and a desolate waste from Migdol to Aswan,
as far as the border of Cush.

The foot of neither man
nor beast will pass through it;
no one will live there for forty years.

I will make the land of Egypt desolate
among devastated lands,
and her cities
will lie desolate forty years
among ruined cities

And I will disperse the Egyptians among the nations
and scatter them through the countries.
Yet this is what the Sovereign Lord says:
At the end of forty years
I will gather the Egyptians
from the nations where they were scattered.

I will bring them back from captivity
and return them to Upper Egypt,
the land of their ancestry.
There they will be lowly kingdom.
It will be the lowliest of kingdoms
and will never again exalt itself
above the other nations.
I will make it so weak that
it will never again rule over the nations.[21]

According to the Bible, if taken literally, the Almighty might demonstrate His omnipotence by destroying Egypt. In these verses, the justification is clear: God will do this because the Egyptians have set themselves against Him, and they have set themselves against Him not through adultery, blasphemy or other acts, but by adopting what, in His view, is an unacceptable attitude toward the Nile, because they believe that they have shaped, and so own, the river.

This story in this most best-selling book of all time tells us that the discourse on how the Nile should be controlled is very old, and it provides yet another argument for why it is justified to call the Nile history's greatest river. The Nile is definitely a river running through time both in a physical and social sense, connecting the very distant past with the present in different areas and on different levels. .

I glance out of the window, but since sunset happened in a flash and it is now dark outside, all I see is my face reflected in the glass. Quickly, I put away the book and smile cautiously at the Egyptian passenger next to me, glad he cannot see what I was reading. Studying these Biblical texts on a train through the Nile Delta, however, not only makes it easier to understand the words in their concrete, material actuality, but it serves also as a general reminder of language's precarious position – if one happens to be setting out to write a biography of the Nile. It is a task that demands an extraordinary awareness of the position of the observer, of the outsider, because viewpoint determines how the river is depicted: among the people and the political leaders of the eleven countries that share the river, there are political and ideological disagreements regarding prosaic things, such as how watercourses and drainage basins are to be defined, what constitutes the river's water flow, how much it rains within the basin, what water security means and the nature of water rights. Generally speaking, all agree on cooperation, and cooperation is finding place, but again and again disagreements tend to arise among states and stakeholders when the time comes to define the simplest, most concrete conditions and solutions. This, then, is the challenge of being a nonpartisan biographer of the Nile. I cast another look at my reflection in the window, more self-searching this time.

Islam conquers the Nile Delta

'It's common in the West today to say that the religious war between Christianity and Islam began during the time of the Crusades and Richard the Lionheart. But they completely overlook that Islam crushed Christian Egypt four centuries earlier. We were here first.' The Coptic priest trying to draw me into discussion at the train station regards me through a pair of thick lenses. As he combs his fingers through his long black beard and I am about to ask for more clarification, he continues: 'It's like the warrior Saladin wielded the pen in these politically correct, Western narratives.'

The victory of Islam in Egypt had many consequences, also for Alexandria and Nile control. In 642 Caliph Umar and his army conquered the Delta and Alexandria and overrun the Byzantine forces that still governed there, although Byzantine interest in Egypt was much less than that which Rome had shown. The Islamic army commander described the city seized by the Arabs thus: '4,000 palaces, 4,000 baths, 400 theatres, 1,200 grocers, and 40,000 Jews.' Alexandria was still one of the most important trade centres in the Mediterranean region. Dissatisfaction with Byzantine rule was great, and so in the 600s the Coptic Church's representatives bid their new Arab-Islamic rulers, welcome.[22]

Christianity's power and status had shifted in the centuries prior to the Arab invasion. The Roman Emperor Diocletian, a Croat famous for the palace that characterizes the historic town of Split, had launched a frontal attack on Egyptian Christians. So poorly did the Copts fare here that their calendar starts with the emperor's persecutions. Emperor Constantine, on the other hand, made Christianity the state religion in the 400s. At the same time, a religious-dogmatic schism developed between Egypt's Coptic Church and the Church in Byzantium, the new Church headquarters that were founded by Constantine, helping to undermine the Church's power and Byzantine interests in Egypt. Whereas the Nile Delta had produced a third of the grain for the Roman Empire, the Delta's role for Byzantium was significantly smaller. As a result, the Arab conquerors met little resistance as they marched up the Delta in the middle of the seventh century CE.

When it came to the Arab-Islamic civilization's position, however, control of Egypt and the Nile Delta would prove crucial. The Delta formed a rich bridgehead for further westward expansion into the Maghreb and the Iberian Peninsula, and later into France. It enabled the conquerors to better spread artificial irrigation and new agricultural crops to the arid districts in Europe's south-western regions, thus creating an economic foundation for their success. The Nile Delta remained a granary, but now for the eastern Arab heartlands. One thing the new rulers did almost immediately was to move the capital up the Nile Valley to Fustat or Misr-al-Fustat, close to present-day Cairo. Since Egypt was now subject to the Islamic caliphate, first with its headquarters in Baghdad and then in Damascus, the country's administration, for cultural, historical and power-political reasons, became oriented towards Arabia and the Middle East rather than towards Europe and the Mediterranean, an idea formalized when Arabic became the official language in 706. By moving the capital upstream of the Delta, the Arabs also created a buffer against potential sea attacks. Invading forces might have the upper hand at sea but not on the Delta's canals, according to this strategic military reasoning. As such, Alexandria entered a long decline, bolstered by the neglect of the waterway connecting the Nile and Alexandria.

A popular story in the West has been that Caliph Umar and his army destroyed Alexandria's famous library. According to this version of events, the Arab commander ordered all books to be distributed to the city's 4,000 baths so they could be used to heat the water. And the baths stayed hot for a full six months. The first Western account of this supposed event dates back as far as 1663, in Edward Pococke's translation of *History of the Dynasties*. However, the story was rejected as anti-Islamic propaganda as early as 1713 by Father Eusèbe Renaudot. Many researchers have subsequently drawn the same conclusion. Middle East expert Bernard Lewis, considered by many to be a strong critic of Islam, has also determined that Umar and his soldiers must be acquitted once and for all of this accusation. And all indications unearthed by historical research suggest that, indeed, Umar was not behind the library's destruction. It was instead due to a combination of factors: Caesar's warfare, during which parts of the library were set afire; Christian leaders who considered this seat of learning to be a cultural and religious threat; and, last but not least, Alexandria's general, long-term decline after the Arab's seized it – only to lose interest in this Mediterranean city, as well as in the canals linking it to the Nile.

The Caliph's letter to the Nile

Islamic tradition tells the story of a letter, the first and only to be addressed to a river. It was written by Caliph Umar, also known as Omar al-Faroq or 'the One Who Distinguishes Between Right and Wrong', who succeeded Abu Bakr as the second caliph of the Rashidun Caliphate, directly after Egypt was conquered. The history of this Nile letter is as follows.

When Egypt was conquered, the people approached the commander of the occupying forces, Amr ibn al-As, on the first day of one of their months, and said to him that: 'This our Nile has a certain requirement, and if it is not fulfilled, it will not flow'. He then asked them: 'And what is that?' They answered: 'When eleven nights in this month have passed, we find a young virgin. After her parents have agreed, we adorn her in the finest clothes and jewellery and then cast her into the Nile.' At this Amr replied: 'This will never be in Islam. Islam demolishes what precedes it.'

And the Nile flooded neither little nor much, and thus there were crop failures and people planned to emigrate. When Amr discovered this, he wrote to Umar to tell him what had happened. The caliph wrote back: 'You were right in what you said. Truly, Islam demolishes everything that precedes it.' He placed a note inside the letter and wrote to Amr: 'I have sent you a slip of paper inside my letter, so throw it in the Nile'. When Umar's letter reached Amr, he took the note and read the following: 'From the slave of Allah, Umar ibn al-Khattab Amir al-Mu'minin, to the Nile of Egypt. Now, if you used to flow before, then don't flow! If it was Allah who made you flow, then I ask the Overwhelming One to make you flow.'

Amr threw the slip of paper into the Nile the day before the Festival of the Cross. The people woke in the morning and 'Allah, exalted is He, had made it flow sixteen cubits in one night.' And 'Allah cut off this *sunnah* of the people of Egypt right up to this day.'[23]

In the centuries following the Arab invasion, one foreign dynasty after another seized control of the Egyptian state, even as Egypt evolved into the most central country of the Muslim world. As society at large continued to function as it had for centuries, these frequent changes of state leadership underscore the river's place as a permanent source of riches and stability. Instead of looking to explain such conservatism in terms of 'Egyptian mentality', as has been a common practice among Orientalist historians, it is more fruitful to view this lack of change and mobility in light of the river's behaviour, which year after year had required the same exertion, and brought the same seasonal fluctuations between labour and non-labour. Possibilities for technological innovation were not only limited but largely absent, nor were they, in a certain sense, necessary. During the years the water failed to materialize, or the flood stayed too long, there were crop failures and hardship; dynasties were weakened and sometimes collapsed. Nile water flow had always been the greatest source of uncertainty and apprehension. And Muslims themselves long continued to worship the river, even though Muslim teachings certainly forbade such idolatry.

Napoleon on the march

At the end of the eighteenth century, in July 1798, a political earthquake shook Egypt and with it the Nile Valley's history. The country's technological backwardness was exposed – not just to the rest of the world – but to Egypt itself.

On 1 July 1798, France's expeditionary force, L'Armée d'Orient, led by the then thirty-year-old Napoleon Bonaparte, entered the country at the base of the Nile Delta. For the last 2,000 years it had been the norm rather than the exception that foreign soldiers arrived in Egypt to occupy and exploit the Delta's fertility. However, the fact that Islam's most important and most powerful country could be conquered by a small military contingent from what was, to influential thinking in the Middle East at the time, a barbaric world corner – was humiliating. In the 1700s, the Egyptian elite was composed of Mamluks, a ruling caste of former slave-soldiers who had first seized power almost 1,000 years earlier. Mamelukes were non-Arabic Eurasian slaves, boys sold by their often nomad families, or they were Christians captured in war, taken captive in the Turkish territories and, to some extent, in the Balkans. They had received military training and had been converted to Islam. The first formal Mamluk dynasty was called the Bahri, a name that meant 'sea' or 'river' and referred to their headquarters on Cairo's Roda Island. In 1517, Egypt had been conquered by a regime of Sunni Muslims based in today's Turkey and the country became a junior partner in the great Ottoman Empire. Into the eighteenth century, Egypt steadily acquired more autonomy from Istanbul, and the Mamluks seized the opportunity to recapture their position as Egypt's ruling elite, though still formally subordinate to the Ottomans.

Agriculture remained productive, though pharaonic irrigation methods still dominated, and the rhythm of society was basically as it had been for millennia. After the Nile flooded, earth and clay dams were built to keep the water on the fields for longer than would have been the case naturally. The water was then released back into the river and, meanwhile, the ground had received enough new natural fertilizers and enough water for it to be sown. Extensive maintenance work was undertaken on the canals and earthworks, but no technological advances were made. Both Egypt's people and its rulers were still subject to the whims of the Nile. The waves of famine and epidemics that struck Egypt at the end of the eighteenth century made this very clear and helped to weaken the Mamluk regime.

The typical explanation for this backwardness, or technological standstill, has been to point the finger at religion and culture, adding a blend of 'Egyptian fatalism', 'Islamic conservatism' and even anachronistic illusions of cultural superiority. However, the most significant reason that life in Egypt's numerous rural villages remained largely unchanged cannot be sought solely within such a religious-cultural perspective. The Christian Copts, for example, shared many Muslim values and ideas. The British observer, Edward William Lane related in his famous study first published in 1836, *An Account of the Manners and Customs of the Modern Egyptians*, that Christian women wore veils and disappeared indoors as soon as a man appeared. The veil, in fact, was so common that it was used to express class distinctions: white veils were worn by young, poor women, whereas black was reserved for the more well-to-do.[24] The explanation for Egypt's technological stagnation must, of course, not overlook cultural traditions, religion and ideology, but must go deeper, and also analyse the structuring relations between river and society that over the centuries kept framing human agency. Establishing an alternative farming pattern or rhythms of cultivation unfettered from the seasonal regularity and dominance of the Nile was simply not feasible at the time. Given the topographical and hydrological conditions of the waterscape it was impossible to control the river's water flow in such new and radical ways as to make game-changing agricultural technology a rational alternative. The water–society relationship tended to reproduce itself. The established patterns of adaptive Nile utilization technology that governed both the farming cycle and the manner of labour organization had produced an amazing regularity in economic and social life, and any significant alteration would require a fundamental revolution in Nile control technology that was not available anywhere in the eighteenth century or earlier.

In the years preceding Napoleon's invasion, then, the Mamluk regime had been further weakened by poor Nile years. In August 1791, the flood receded too quickly, the harvest was bad and people were distressed.[25] The general situation deteriorated further during the summer of 1792. In years when the flooding lasted longer than usual, or brought less water than was needed, farmers' incomes were reduced, thereby reducing tax revenues as well. To compensate, the authorities tried to squeeze the farmers in other ways, sometimes resorting to outright armed thievery, thereby increasing conflict between rulers and the ruled and further weakening the Mamluks' position. Napoleon's campaign up the Delta is fascinating from many perspectives. The idea that France should subjugate Egypt had been suggested around a century before by a 26-year-old German diplomat, a man who was later to become a philosopher: Gottfried Leibniz. Leibniz hoped that an Egyptian adventure would turn the Sun King Louis XIV's attention away from any plans or notions of eastward ventures into Europe and so towards the Rhine. By the end of the eighteenth century, however, the geopolitical game was quite different. In Paris, the strategic idea was that French control of Egypt was key to weakening Great Britain as a world power, thus allowing the French to undermine Britain's increasingly stronger ties to India. The need to spread the ideas of the French Revolution – not just to anywhere on the globe but to the very locus where civilization was first born (this was before the remnants and history of the Sumer civilization was discovered) – was something also used to justify the invasion.

At the same time, Napoleon sought to weaken opposition to the French invasion by undertaking political initiatives that undermined the campaign's stated goal of exporting French revolutionary ideas. Napoleon – successor of the French Revolution – sent a proclamation to the Nile shores in Egypt declaring the Qur'an to be the sole road to human happiness and swearing that he, Napoleon, would establish a regime based on the principles of the Qur'an. In a letter to the Egyptians, dated August 1789, he wrote: 'I hope [...] I shall be able to assemble all the wise and learned men of all the countries and establish a uniform government, based on the principles of the Koran, which alone are true and capable of bringing happiness to men.'[26]

He also insisted that Muslim leaders should ask the people to read more than twenty verses in the Qur'an, because it had predicted and described Napoleon's entry into Cairo! He further attempted to pose as a Muslim himself and he participated in Muslim rituals and prayers. Many of his closest officers and political advisers reacted negatively to this tactic, which they thought might well soften resistance in the short term but could create problems in the long term.

Like other great military expeditions and attempts at conquest, Napoleon's campaign was accordingly riddled with conflicts, paradoxes and self-contradictions. To glorify the merits of European civilization in the face of the Islamic world, which had not recognized yet the craft of printing, mythical stories were told about Napoleon, a military leader who rode up the Delta at the forefront of his army while reading a printed book. Every page he read, he tore out and tossed behind him; the pages were collected from the ground, his soldiers imbibing civilization's wisdom and fruits even as they conquered the Orient. Such tales reflect idealized French portrayals of an army leader who staged himself as the representative of a New Age, championing knowledge and rationality to a backward Orient.

Even so, the campaign from Alexandria to Cairo up the Delta was in many ways a military catastrophe. On rations of one water bottle and four biscuits a day, many soldiers died of hunger and thirst; their loads were, additionally, too heavy and their uniforms too hot and tight. They were also basically unprepared for combat in this arena's particular ecology,[27] and the Bedouins either poisoned or filled the wells located on the road from Alexandria to the Nile with sand.[28]

On the outskirts of Cairo, Napoleon's troops clashed with the Mamluks, who occupied both sides of the Nile. Afterwards, with a profound sense for the burgeoning popularity and metaphorical power ancient Egypt now wielded in a Europe that abruptly, and with great curiosity, was preoccupied with all things oriental, Napoleon termed the confrontation 'the Battle of the Pyramids'. In a speech meant to rouse his soldiers, he proclaimed: 'Forty centuries look down upon you.' After two hours, the French troops had obliterated the Mamluk forces. Some 300 Frenchmen and 6,000 Egyptians were killed, a battle that proved the beginning of the end of Mamluk control of Egypt.[29] The Mamluks ultimately surrendered by symbolically handing Napoleon the keys to Cairo. One of the first things Napoleon now did was to create a bridge of boats over the Nile in Cairo and he also ordered a windmill to be built there. Far into the nineteenth century, the few windmills that could be operated in Egypt were called 'Napoleon's windmills'.

Meanwhile, Bonaparte realized, as did Menes and Caesar before him, and Lord Cromer and Gamal Abdel Nasser after, that the legitimacy of any Egyptian leader hinged upon securing adequate water for the fields and protecting the villages from too much flooding. Napoleon now ruled an irrigation economy, or a hydraulic society, where from 17 June onwards, the Nile was observed daily and where 'Nile criers', *Munadee El Nil*, gave everyone continual updates on the status of their lifeline. Napoleon, therefore, immediately declared himself head of the annual festival given in the Nile's honour.

Fath al-Kjalij, or 'the Festival of the Opening of the Canal', had been Egypt's largest annual celebration for many centuries. For the entire summer season, the Khalij Canal was blocked by an earthwork barrier. When the Nile's water level reached a certain point, it was removed and the river water flooded into the canal and, quite literally, life returned after months of drought and scorched fields. As countless Egyptian rulers had done before him, Napoleon himself inspected the Nilometer on Cairo's Roda Island. The water height on the measuring stick determined when the festival would start.

On the morning of the festival, and because Egyptians had been commanded to participate as if the country's situation had normalized, Napoleon commanded the riverboat *Aqaba* to be decorated. He encouraged people to gather along the river and wanted to create the impression that with Napoleon came stability, law and order. As Bonaparte called for the barrier blocking the canal to be removed, people threw offerings of all sorts into the Nile, so Allah would bless the fertility of both women and earth. Workers cast a clay statue called 'the betrothed' into the canal, a practice that

French observers described as a relic dating from the pharaonic custom of tossing a living woman, a virgin, into the Nile as an offering. For Bonaparte, the entire spectacle was an attempt to gain the necessary religious and symbolic charisma required to be accepted as the Great Sultan.

It turned out, however, that staging himself as the Nile's guardian and guarantor through ritual ceremonies was not enough to bolster the legitimacy of the occupation. After just three months, the occupation was met with riots and rebellion. Rebels who killed French officers were accordingly beheaded, their heads stuffed into sacks and then dumped in one of Cairo's central locations. When Jean-Baptiste Kléber, the officer Napoleon had left in command after he himself had returned for France, was murdered in his own headquarters by a young student, the murderer was executed according to what was described as Islamic law. First, he watched as his fellow conspirators were beheaded. Then the hand that took the life was burned to the elbow. Finally, he was impaled on a stake to ensure a slow death. The fight to spread such French revolutionary ideas as freedom, equality and brotherhood demanded drastic measures, but still the days of France as occupier were numbered.

Following Kléber's murder, the French occupation was commanded by General Abdulla Jacques-François Menou, a French convert to Islam. The occupation itself was finally ended by an Anglo-Ottoman invading force. French troops in Cairo surrendered on 18 June 1801, and Menou capitulated at Alexandria on 3 September. The French were forced to withdraw from Egypt and from the Nile Delta after around three years in power, due to internal resistance but particularly due to the alliance between the Ottoman Empire, with its headquarters in Istanbul, and Great Britain, and their joint blockade. This prevented both reinforcements from, and regular contact with, Paris.

Nonetheless, Napoleon's short campaign had truly long-lasting consequences, particularly in two arenas. In the first place, France and its exports became linked to Egypt, a development that in subsequent decades would lead to proposals for digging a new canal joining the Mediterranean and the Indian Ocean, as well as a dam built across the Nile in the Delta. Also, very importantly, Napoleon's Nile expedition organized research efforts and produced stories that have shaped Western concepts of the Orient.

Napoleon – as the self-proclaimed proponent of scientific optimism and rationality – brought with him a group of 167 scientists and technological experts, the Commission des Sciences et des Arts. From the start, he placed great emphasis on the expedition's scientific goals.[30] Days and evenings were spent with the scientists, discussing their work in Egypt. After the campaign was over and France had been defeated on the battlefield, the French published a monumental description of Egypt in thirty large volumes with more than 3,000 illustrations. Ancient, forgotten pharaonic memorials had been unearthed. Before the French arrived, for example, the Sphinx had stood up to its neck in sand. Vivant Denon, director of the Louvre in Paris, headed the scientific expedition and was the first to illustrate the Karnak and Luxor temples. Denon wrote his own travel narrative, *Voyages dans la Basse et la Haute Égypte*, in 1802. Almost immediately it was translated into English and German, and the book became a sensation. The Nile's cultural treasures were again introduced to the world. Napoleon's short stint as sovereign of the Nile Delta, though it ended in military defeat, lived on as a story of cultural and intellectual success – or so the campaign has typically been interpreted. In Europe, it made a new kind of journey attractive among intellectuals; the goal became to unravel the secrets of the hitherto uncharted ancient Egyptian world and of what was still seen as a quite closed and mysterious Arabic-Muslim world. Tales of Napoleon's army in Egypt spoke to the hearts of burgeoning explorers and to the fantasy of adventurers, and these further helped lay the groundwork for *Orientalism* as a European cultural movement; indeed, in their wake a kind of 'Egyptomania' took root. As Victor Hugo, in the preface to *Les Orientales* (1829), put it a few decades later: 'In the age of Louis XIV, we were all Hellenists, now we are Orientalists.'

Through Napoleon's campaign Egypt had been introduced to the world and the world to Egypt. Nonetheless, another and increasingly central perspective interprets it as a catastrophe, due precisely to the cultural influence it exerted. Islamic and postcolonial perspectives regard Napoleon's blend of military might and scientific secularism as an abuse of power when it comes to Egyptian culture, as well as a diabolical attack on Islam.

Critique of Orientalism

I am driving along the Agricultural Road through the Delta, past places I can barely distinguish in the close morning haze that erases all contours in the flat landscape. Last night was hot and uncomfortable, with an air-conditioning unit that did not work and a fan that kept me awake with a sound like a whimpering dog. I lay awake and thought about a novel published five years prior to Napoleon's arrival in the Delta: Xavier de Maistre's *Expédition nocturne autour de ma chambre*, published in English as *Night Voyage Around My Room* in 1825.

The novel begins with Maistre shutting his bedroom door. He has decided to take a trip – not away, into the world outside, but inside his own bedroom. His goal is to free his eyes from habit's torpor. He dresses for the journey by slipping into his pink and blue pyjamas. With no need for luggage, he sets off on tour, first to the sofa, the room's largest piece of furniture. By insisting on viewing the room as a fresh-eyed traveller, he succeeds in shaking off habit's torpor or blindness. He perceives his bedroom anew; that is, the room appears as if new because he looks at it with new eyes. He rediscovers a few of the sofa's qualities – its handsome legs, among other things. And he rediscovers his bed. Freed from routine's perspective, he appreciates his furniture in a new way, dwelling on the present and future uses to which the furniture has been and can be put.

The novel can be read as a parody of travel literature where mundane journeys become terrific voyages, but also as a contribution to the discussion regarding travel as a road to education. It rejects ideas surrounding the grand voyage's formative merits. The critical factor is not the destination nor the act of travelling to many places, but rather how people relate to their own experiences, particularly if capable of perceiving the surroundings unencumbered by the lethargy that habit and routine tend to create and reproduce. In the same way, in world literature, the Nile is like Maistre's bedroom: much is known, much has been described, simply because hardly any other phenomenon has been portrayed over so long a period and more systematically by travellers than has the Nile's history, and, along with it, the river's role in shaping civilization. Since the region has, for so long and in so many fields, provided raw data for dominant ideas regarding history's development, and for stereotypes of 'the other' and 'us' – and because conceptions are easily formed within this descriptive tradition's routine – it becomes necessary to constantly re-evaluate one's viewpoint in order to escape routine's torpor. As I travel the Egyptian Delta this morning, I do so not believing the journey will be intrinsically formative; Maistre's book reminds me that to observe and write is both difficult, demanding and only potentially rewarding.

Few have influenced the discussion regarding how the Middle East can and should be described more than Edward Said, a Palestinian who fled with his family to Egypt and who became an expert in European nineteenth-century literature. By the end of the twentieth century, Said was one of the world's leading intellectuals. Said particularly spent his life studying the way in which the European or Western intellectual tradition depicts the Middle East and Egypt. His book, *Orientalism*, was first published in English in 1978. Here Said launches a radical rejection of the entire European tradition of knowledge on Egypt, particularly criticizing Napoleon's scientific expedition and the interpretive method it legitimized.

Said depicts the French military invasion and its scientific project as being two sides of the same coin, a crowning example of the European pursuit of total knowledge of 'the other', the archetypal expression of the desire for control. For Said, Napoleon and his commission were no less than an original sin in the interweaving of Western power infringement and knowledge collection, the historical task of which was to repress the Orient. The European researcher or 'orientalist' mapped the Orient from above in order to gain oversight of the entire unfolding panorama – culture, religion, mentality and history. To attain this goal, every single detail must be viewed from oversimplified, schematic categories. Said's concern was the way in which frameworks that impact a society's knowledge production not only reflect but also produce inequality. His project led him to reject the thirty volumes published by Napoleon's scientific expedition and everything in their wake as an abuse of power regarding what the research described. As a result, this research was also by definition unscientific.

Said pinpoints an important general trait of any research that harbours an unarticulated, uncritical relationship to the day's dominant perspectives and power institutions, and he demonstrates how this fact influences what is discussed and how the discussion is conducted: such research does not grasp how power relationships impact upon what questions are posed, what concepts are used, what conclusions are acceptable, and so which are worth the researcher's time to draw. It is beyond doubt that many researchers who have worked with Africa, Asia and Latin America have remained little concerned with, or largely unreflective over, their relationship to and association with the power structure that influences their research – whether they are operating as troubleshooters for a colonial administration, the aid system, or for commanders and generals in wartime.

Said touches an obvious sore spot in Western scientific history. Nonetheless, he goes too far, for he presents a caricature of Western knowledge of the Orient. In his literature survey he highlights, on an arbitrary, methodical basis, only those examples that support his thesis. The most problematic component of his analysis, however, is that he explicitly negates the possibility of any Western scholarship on the Orient or on Egypt whatsoever, because this research will be biased. Orientalism is active, whether manifest or latent, to use Said's terms, and so the world cannot be described. Western research on the Orient creates its narratives or representations not according to fact but, rather, to a relationally formed aim of total control.

Said's critique of Western research on the Middle East in the 1800s uncovers and reveals how several authors detailed an Egypt that – aside from scenes onto which Europeans could project their cultural prejudices and at times their sexual fantasies – did not exist. Still, Said's analysis is too one-sided and arbitrary to be considered a valid empirical analysis of European ideas regarding 'the Orient'. Furthermore, it rejects an entire system of knowledge, and its totalizing ambitions expose the critic as much as what is criticized. Said's book is a two-way mirror; it reveals not only the linguistic pitfalls in Middle East interpretations, but also the consequences of Said's project. Instead of directly proposing that these depictions be scrubbed from history along with what is depicted, Said obtains the same effect with a more subtle approach: he asserts that orientalist analyses incorporate 'a sinful act' because they themselves repress 'the other'.

It is in this context and from such a perspective that rehabilitating Napoleon's Commission des Sciences et des Arts becomes necessary. Obviously, Said is correct that the Commission's work is coloured by the prejudices of its time, by French self-conceptions and world views at the start of the nineteenth century. At the same time, however, the Commission's work also provided fresh knowledge of an unknown region to a Europe that, for a variety of historical reasons, was then a technologically superior and emerging world power. The Commission, furthermore, provided an insight into Egypt and its history that the Egyptians themselves lacked, and which they themselves at that point had no tradition of exploring.

Ultimately, one of the reasons why it is possible to write a biography of the Nile is, not least, the existence of some of the research that Said rejected.

The Battle of the Nile: Paris versus London

In step with Europe's increasing political strength and military clout, leading European states began to eye the world's trade routes and hubs as a means to economic profit and expansion of power. One of the first countries to experience the consequences of this rivalry was Egypt. Initially, the country profited by it, because England, allied with the Ottoman Empire, forced France to surrender Egypt, something that increased Egypt's actual autonomy from Istanbul.

One of the most famous Nile Delta battles is the so-called Battle of the Nile, which was fought in August 1798. In addition to the battle's other baroque aspects, the event also exemplified early on the falsity of stereotypes that regard Western civilization as a unified force against the Orient – that is, that there exists a single, unified front whose goal is to crush the Arabic or Islamic world.

Admiral Nelson, the one-eyed, one-armed English war hero, who today stands and keeps watch over Trafalgar Square in London, wrote of the battle: 'Vanguard, off the

Nile, August 3, 1798. My Lord – Almighty God has blessed his Majesty's arms in the late battle by a great victory over the fleet of the enemy, whom I attacked at sunset on the 1st of August, off the Mouth of the Nile.'[31]

The way in which Nelson repeats the river's name, twice in this brief pathos-rich message, underscores the lustre that the river had already acquired in Europe in the late eighteenth century. Even as the French had just won the Battle of the Pyramids, so they were now crushed by London's fleet. London, which refused to accept an Egypt under Napoleon's sway, entered Abukir Bay under Nelson's leadership and attacked the French fleet that lay outside the Delta while Napoleon was encamped at Cairo. The battle lasted from 1 August to 3 August 1798.

While the ships made ready for battle, Nelson held a last dinner with his officers, where he declared: 'Before this time tomorrow, I shall have gained a peerage, or Westminster Abbey.'[32] The alternatives were clear: either a noble title, the traditional reward for such triumphs, or a military hero's traditional grave.

The French ship captains, wholly unprepared, were sitting together aboard the flagship *Orient* when the first cannon shots sounded. They jumped into small boats while shouting commands. *Orient*'s captain was knocked unconscious by flying objects in the chaos; his ten-year-old son's leg was shattered by a cannon ball as he stood by his father's side. By nine o'clock that evening, the flagship's lower decks were consumed by flame. The British directed all their cannon fire at the ship. Under the steady barrage, the French were unable to put out the fire. *Orient* became a burning inferno and the bay was filled with corpses and screaming, half-naked soldiers.

As Nelson remarked the following morning while surveying the bay: 'Victory is not a name strong enough for such a scene.'[33] Four days later, according to imperial British pomp and circumstance, Nelson became Baron Nelson of the Nile, even though he had never set foot on the river's banks or navigated its waters.

The sea battle was a major defeat for France and served to strengthen the imperial pathos of a Great Britain that would soon 'rule the waves'. Nonetheless, England's victory was as surprising to Europe as it was to Egypt.

Around the same time as Nelson's cannon were pounding away outside the Delta, Joseph Haydn, the usually optimistic and spirited Austrian classicist, sat down to compose his only mass, the Mass in D Minor. Heavy drumbeats, deep trumpet blasts and cold organ tones open the work, and on the score's cover Haydn titled the piece *Missa in Angustiis* (*Mass for Troubled Times*). That was in 1798, when Napoleon was still considered a threat by many, even far to the east in Austria's Eisenstadt where Haydn worked as an orchestra conductor. He had no idea that, even as he wrote his mass in dread of Napoleon and his army, that Nelson was crushing the French fleet in a surprise attack not far from where the Nile River emptied into the Mediterranean Sea.

The battle over the Rosetta Stone: thieves versus thieves

No longer does a mighty river pass Rosetta city. Rather, the river looks like a subdued, overexploited, modest canal impotently on its way to meet the sea where it slowly rolls in over the Delta. The Rosetta River, also known as the Rashid, flows through the city of the same name, carrying thousands upon thousands of plastic bottles that, for the time being, have progressed no further and so bob in the shadow of a walled promenade equipped with tall beautiful palm trees. On the river, fishing boats painted green cross up and down in pursuit of the fish that continue to thrive in the polluted river water, and the fishermen who accompany me on a boat upriver complain that the fish are steadily getting fewer and smaller. Still, the sky above the Nile's estuary this early morning is as it has always been – so transparent, so clear, you imagine you are gazing into a firmament beyond the one you can see. I am here for the sake of the stone that made the city famous.

Rosetta, or Rashid, named so under Abbasid caliphs who ordered a fort to be built on the site of the old Ptolemaic city, Bolbitine, in the ninth century CE, was for long periods of time, even as Alexandria suffered neglect, Egypt's most important harbour. Napoleon's campaign, however, made the city world famous – not as a trade centre or battlefield, but as the site where the French found a stone of world-historic significance, a stone that the Nile silt had kept hidden for generations.

In mid-July 1799, as Napoleon's soldiers were strengthening Fort Julien's defences a few kilometres north-east of the harbour city, they caught sight of a rock with numerous rows of characters in different lettering. The soldiers realized this could prove a valuable contribution to Napoleon's cultural expedition and sent a message to the French commander, General Menou. The discovery was also reported to the newly established L'Institut d'Égypte. Once again, Napoleon demonstrated his interest in Egyptian history: this warrior among warriors examined the stone himself before returning to France in August 1799.

His soldiers had found what would later acquire the name the Rosetta Stone. It measured 114.4 centimetres at its tallest point, 72.3 centimetres at its widest and 27.9 centimetres at its thickest, and it weighed 760 kilograms. What gave the stone a revolutionary significance in humankind's eternal quest to understand the past, however, was that the text was carved in three different scripts: ancient Egyptian hieroglyphs, Egyptian Demotic script and ancient Greek. For the first time, it was possible to crack the hieroglyphic code. Through this stone, modern humanity gained access to the ancient Egyptian world view, culture and economic system. Suddenly, the history of the Nile Delta was tangible for thousands of years further back in time.

The Rosetta Stone, meanwhile, is no longer in Egypt; it has been in London since 1802. That fact itself is a telling example of the rivalry for Egypt, where dominance over interpretations and narratives of Nile Delta history has proven the apple of discord.

After Napoleon travelled back to Paris, French land troops continued to defend themselves for another eighteen months against the combined British and Ottoman attack. In March 1801, however, new British troops arrived in Abukir Bay, outside Rashid. General Menou and his soldiers – and the scientific commission with them – marched towards the Mediterranean Coast to meet the enemy. Along with them went the spoils of war, including the stone and other antiquities. The French could not withstand the British and lost the battle. Menou and what was left of his army retreated to Alexandria, surrendering on 30 August 1801.

At that point, a struggle ensued over the ownership of the Rosetta Stone and other antiquities, a disagreement that is instructive if you are concerned with the power inherent in controlling interpretations of the past.

Menou refused to relinquish the antiquities, arguing that they belonged to the French institute. The British general, however, would not withdraw from the city until the French general surrendered the stone. Knowing the power to be gained in controlling such symbols of the past and in dominating history's interpretation, the British regime also sent its own researchers to the Nile Delta. Edward Daniel Clarke and William Richard Hamilton were charged with evaluating the French collection in Alexandria to determine whether the French were withholding anything. They were the victors, the British General John Hely-Hutchinson argued, and so all the antiquities were the property of the British Crown. To this, one of the French researchers replied that they would rather burn all their finds than see them in British hands. In a last, desperate, albeit futile attempt, Menou insisted that the stone should be considered his private property. The British, of course, dismissed this claim as ridiculous. Finally, the French were forced to yield this point as well, and the ceding of the antiquities became part of the 'Capitulation of Alexandria'.

Edward Daniel Clarke later explained that a French officer had, in all secrecy, conducted him and two others into the yard behind Menou's residence, revealing where the general had attempted to conceal the stone. After the French officer betrayed his boss, the stone was carried to the harbour and placed on board a ship that transported it to Portsmouth, where it arrived in February 1802. The instructions were to present it to King George III. The king then decreed that it should be placed in the British Museum, where it has been ever since. The stone became British but, to their great irritation, the text was cracked by a Frenchman. The young linguistic genius, Jean-François Champollion, obtained a copy of the scripts and broke the code but he succeeded only in giving notice of his discoveries before he succumbed to exhaustion and died following a gruelling research trip to Egypt at the end of the 1820s.

As such, the Battle of the Nile sealed, in addition to many other things, the fate of the Rosetta Stone, which for centuries had lain concealed by the natural workings of the Nile, but was now used to recapture a significant and key portion of both the Nile's and humankind's early histories.

The Albanian soldier who became the Nile's reformer

Not long after French troops withdrew, an Albanian soldier took power on behalf of the Ottoman Empire, which, along with the British, had forced Paris to retreat. Into the ensuing vacuum and onto the Nile scene stepped Muhammad Ali, a former tobacco dealer who did not learn to read and write before he turned forty. Coincidentally, he was born the same year as Napoleon, 1769, and, although he lacked the Frenchman's education, he had the same limitless ambition and will to power.

Where traditional warlords often limit themselves to palace intrigue and punitive expeditions, Muhammad Ali was a visionary. He knew how far the Middle East lagged behind Europe, both technologically and militarily, and realized it was from Europe that Egypt must retrieve its ideas and technology. As such, he would play an important role in Egyptian history, not least because he regarded development as being an integral process on many fronts. Muhammad Ali hired foreign experts and technicians to modernize Egypt's army, agriculture and education system and, most fundamentally of all, he was radically more ambitious than his predecessors when it came to utilizing the country's key resource. It was under this Albanian and his autocratic government that modern Nile history began.

The background events that allowed Muhammad Ali to become one of those individuals who most influenced the Nile Delta's development, are an example of the role of chance in history, clearly illuminated on a stage shaped by the Nile and highlighted by the river's regularity and permanence. In 1801 Muhammad Ali's army unit was sent as part of a larger Ottoman force to recapture Egypt after Napoleon's short interlude as 'Lord of the Pyramids'. This force ended up in Abukir Bay, which was strategically located at the river's mouth. The Mamluks had been weakened but not vanquished and the Ottoman troops clashed with them. Muhammad Ali fell into the sea but could not swim and, according to some accounts, he was rescued from drowning by a British boat. Muhammad Ali's forces would eventually seize control of Egypt, and the Ottoman sultan, Selim III, was in no position to oppose him becoming the country's de facto leader. In 1805 Ali declared himself ruler or *wali* (it was not until 1867 that his formal title became khedive – king). As it turned out, the dynasty that Muhammad Ali established would become a highly modernizing force in Egypt's history.

From the beginning of his rule, Muhammad Ali fought against British interference. Around 5,000 British soldiers disembarked in Egypt on 17 March 1807, to force Muhammad Ali into being more cooperative. They marched against Rashid and took the city without resistance. They were, however, met with a violent counter-attack once well inside and retreated only with great difficulty. The heads of the 185 British soldiers killed were sent to Cairo, and placed on stakes on either side of a road not far from where Napoleon did the same thing to the Mamluks a decade before. The British made a second, half-hearted attempt to take Rashid; it ended in catastrophe. The British prisoners were sent to Cairo where they were forced to walk between the stakes that held their fellow soldiers' rotting skulls.

It was four years later, however, in 1811, that Muhammad Ali forever entered the annals of the brutal side of world history. He had already secured his position to the outside world. Now it was time for him to fortify his position internally, and so he conducted one of the cleverest and most homicidal examples of statesmanship we know: he invited the remaining Mamluks to a great feast in the famous Cairo citadel. The banquet was in honour of one of Ali's sons, who was set to lead a military expedition to Arabia to crush the Wahhabis, the first sprouting of the religious movement that later won power in Saudi Arabia and that would inspire so many radical Sunni Islamists in subsequent years.

There are few, if any, parallels in any country's historical annals for what happened that night in Cairo's citadel. The conventional interpretation is that it was an act of statesmanship, an instance where abstract moral principles necessarily gave way to political expediency because such principles were beyond Muhammad Ali's world view. He certainly had not studied Machiavelli (though he did read parts of Machiavelli's work after he learned to read later in life). The Mamluks, in any case, arrived at the citadel without fear and suspicion. They were greeted in the warmest way by Muhammad Ali. Then, after dinner and during the evening, he had them brutally murdered – one by one – slaughtered in and around the citadel's narrow pathways.

Having disposed of all opposition, Muhammad Ali initiated several radical reforms, forcing Egypt into the modern world and becoming one of history's many modernizing autocrats. In order to stabilize Egypt's income, he annexed land by raising taxes on the so-called 'tax farmers'. The new fees were so high that the farmers could not pay them, giving Muhammad Ali the legal right to confiscate their land. He personally subjugated huge swathes of Egypt's territory and acquired personal monopoly of Egypt's trade. Muhammad Ali enriched himself and his family by exercising state power, though in contrast to many future state leaders in the Nile basin, who primarily used their power to increase their wealth, he was also a modernizer. All producers were required to sell their wares to the state. These were then resold, both domestically and abroad. Organizing state finances this way proved very profitable, especially when it came to Muhammad Ali's focus on cotton. He also tried to establish a textile industry to compete with Great Britain, but the attempt was not successful. In fact, it could not have succeeded in Egypt at all because the country lacked the prerequisite energy sources to enable such an industry to thrive.

Muhammad Ali's most important historical role, however, was as modernizer of the country's lifeline – the Nile. He wanted to exploit the Nile in ways never before attempted in Egypt's history, and in 1818 he launched the Mahmoudiyah Canal, which would run from the Nile to Alexandria, thus allowing boats to approach Alexandria without navigating the dangerous coastal way between Rashid and Alexandria. The edifice was already finished by 1820 and, of the many Europeans Muhammad Ali hired into his service, a French engineer, Pascal Coste, led the effort.

Even more significantly, Muhammad Ali started work on the enormous Delta dam structures crossing the two waterways into which the Nile splits directly north of Cairo. The goal was to raise the river level so that the water, aided by gravity, could flow more easily into the Delta's many canals. The engineer here was also French, Mougel Bey. His task was to convert significant portions of the ancient flood irrigation system, which had been dominant since pharaonic times, into year-round irrigation. The Delta barrier was poorly built, however, and when the project was finally finished after Muhammad Ali's death, it did not function properly. Nonetheless, almost a million acres were converted to farmland that could be harvested three times a year. Muhammad Ali's focus on developing all-year irrigation with French help was one of the most direct consequences of Napoleon's occupation of Egypt. As such, Edward Said's critique of the Western knowledge system conquering Egypt in the nineteenth century overlooked the significance of French depictions and understandings of the country's water system, which proved foundational for the country's subsequent modernization.

Muhammad Ali ushered in the historic era in which Egypt began to tame the river (and increasingly use more and more Nile water), such that it became possible to farm ever larger areas during the summer, a time when the natural Nile carried little water. Like all other profound changes rooted in the past, but which also signify fundamental changes in society's relationship to that which shapes and determines it, the causes of this process were undeniably deep and complex. Yet, any explanation that overlooks the individual's historical role, or Muhammad Ali's distinctive energy, will fall short.

In Egypt the corvée, or forced labour system, reached its high point in the nineteenth century, since it provided the labour force for Muhammad Ali's irrigation revolution.[34] New canals were dug in the Delta; old ones were repaired and expanded. And perhaps the most important of all: the canals were deepened in order to provide enough water for the profitable farming of cotton during the summer season. Massive work gangs dredged the canals and canal bottoms, and thousands were set to watch the banks when the river rose. The provincial governors, however, were responsible for the work and maintenance on the large canals. To build the Mahmoudiyah Canal through the north-west Delta all the way to Alexandria, local authorities had to ensure that one in ten regional inhabitants was on the job. Around 100,000 workers were gathered in 1817. Two years later, in 1819, the work tempo increased, and Lower Egypt alone supplied a corvée labour force of 313,000 workers. The new, ambitious Nile policy adopted by Muhammad Ali and his successors thereby led the detested forced labour system to be sharply expanded in the 1800s. As an Egyptian author of Syrian origin noted, this kind of forced labour had existed in Egypt for six thousand years and people had always regarded it as a burden placed on their shoulders by 'a divine providence' that was beyond debate.[35] However, now it had increased in scope, even as opportunities for cultivating the ground all year round had also radically increased. What was once subordinated to the annual rhythm of the Egyptian farmers' lives had now become an activity that could be carried on throughout the year. But faced with such an effective and merciless government authority, farmers were unable to muster any significant collective resistance. Instead of a mass movement, therefore, a form of individual protest arose that speaks volumes about life conditions along the Nile at the time: people mutilated themselves rather than be forcibly conscripted. Blinding an eye with rat poison or slicing a finger off the right hand were not uncommon courses of action.

Muhammad Ali was also successful as a regional colonialist and imperialist. The widespread idea that imperialism and the politics of conquest during recent centuries has been solely a Western project represents a narrow Eurocentric viewpoint. Muhammad Ali, who although he was not a classical nationalist has come to be regarded as the founder of modern Egyptian nationalism, had ambitious plans to modernize Egypt using European patterns and with French help. He conquered large swathes of Arabia, all the way to Aden in the south, and, most significant in a Nile context, he made Sudan a part of Egypt. Muhammad Ali and his successors followed a strategy that deliberately aimed at controlling the Nile basin upstream of Egypt proper as well. They subjugated portions of today's Uganda and attempted to take Ethiopia, but were met, by the end of nineteenth century, with growing opposition from another and more powerful imperial force – Great Britain.

The giraffe that sailed downriver and travelled to Paris

Muhammad Ali's regional ambitions had many consequences. One of them was that the Nile was rediscovered as a corridor between Africa and Europe, which meant that the river was more important now than it had been for millennia.

Toward the early 1820s, a remarkable transport took place down the Nile from Sennar in Eastern Sudan to Muhammad Ali's new palace in Alexandria. Thither went an uncommonly tall guest who resided in the palace gardens while awaiting an overseas journey to Europe.[36]

Not long after his troops occupied Sudan in 1821, Muhammad Ali sent a decree upriver to Sennar on the Blue Nile ordering that some giraffes be captured and sent to Europe. Two juvenile giraffes were taken after their mother was first killed. They were sent to Khartoum by boat. Afterwards, they continued past Shendi in northern Sudan and all the way to Alexandria. One giraffe spent the summer of 1826, its last three months in Africa, on the premises of Muhammad Ali's Mediterranean summer palace. By the end of September, the passage to and reception by Marseilles had been organized. The animal, ignorant of the fact that it would be the first giraffe in history to set hoof on this new continent, was then conveyed by boat across the Mediterranean to Europe. From there it made the further trip from Marseille to Paris, swaying along, metre after metre, along with its Sudanese handler.

The giraffe was one of the great celebrities of its time. On 5 June 1827 it entered Lyon. The route was packed by dense crowds; 30,000 people had flocked to see this curious, long-necked African beast that had hitherto been unknown.

The giraffe was a gift to France from Egypt's ruler. The man who had slaughtered the Mamluks in his citadel a few years earlier meant to win the European populace's favour with the aid of this long-legged animal. The travelling giraffe was supposed to not only soften up state leaders but also to gain public opinion. On the same day that people in Lyon stood gaping in awe at Muhammad Ali's gift, the Greeks were being forced to surrender to Ottoman troops under his control. Athens fell even as the giraffe majestically reached the centre of Lyon, the city of silk, in the war that Lord Byron described as Europe's great freedom struggle against the eastern Muslim-Ottoman Empire. Muhammad Ali was employing all means possible to garner European support; the poor giraffe simply had to accept its strategic diplomatic role.

And so it was that, at the beginning of the 1800s, a giraffe undertook the long journey from the banks of the Nile south of Khartoum to Paris, all because Egypt's leader expected that this highly exotic and thoroughly unknown animal from Africa would play its part in softening up European opinion. The long-necked creature's journey illuminates from a new angle how the Nile via the Mediterranean, throughout time, has functioned as a geographic and historic link between Africa south of the Sahara and Europe.

The long-distance runner who perished on his way to the source of the Nile

In January 1843, Egyptian farmers in the southern Delta could perhaps have seen, if they stopped for a moment and glanced up from the small fields they were cultivating, a man running at an even, swift tempo south along the blue corridor linking Egypt to Central Africa, while the sun stood at its zenith.

The runner was a white man, Mensen Ernst, one of the most famous long-distance runners of his time. His given name was Mons Monsen Øyri and he came from a small

Norwegian village, Fresvik, located on Sognefjord, directly on Scandinavia's rain coast. He was an international celebrity because the media had reported on his runs from Paris to Moscow and from Istanbul to Delhi. According to an 1879 article in the *New York Times*, Ernst consumed only biscuits and jam when running and, while he slept, he stood leaning against a tree, relaxed with a handkerchief spread across his face.

In 1842 the German author, nobleman and adventurer Hermann von Pückler-Muskau asked Mensen Ernst whether he would be interested in trying to solve the greatest geographical mystery of his time: to find the source of the Nile. Pückler-Muskau offered to cover all the expedition's costs and to richly reward the Norwegian if he succeeded. That same year Mensen Ernst began the run of his life. He ran from Moscow to Prussia across the Ottoman Empire to Jerusalem in thirty days. Afterwards, he continued to Cairo, determined to follow the Nile to its unknown source somewhere in the middle of Africa. The poor boy from a part of what back then was one of Western Europe's most impoverished outskirts had determined to solve the greatest of all geographical conundrums – that which had obsessed Alexander the Great, Caesar, Napoleon and generation upon generation of Egyptians. Would Mensen Ernst succeed in discovering how, inconceivably, water could flood the fields in Egypt, beneath a cloudless sky every autumn while the weather was still at its hottest? Would this lone runner triumph where the Roman Empire's legionaries had failed? Would this young man from the fjords of Norway solve the river mystery in Africa that Herodotus had spent so much time exploring?

Presumably, Mensen Ernst continued optimistically past Cairo, since January was a cool month this far north. He passed Luxor with the Karnak Temple on the east bank, but he ultimately made it no further than Aswan. It was there he died. Speculation has been that he succumbed to heat and thirst, but that is unlikely for that time of year. Probably it was some form of dysentery that stopped him for good that January day in 1843. Mensen Ernst was found dead in the sand by some European tourists a couple of days later. Probably, he lies buried somewhere beneath the Aswan Dam, hidden for all time beneath the water whose source he sought.

Mensen Ernst's run up the Nile is both a spectacular and pathetic example of hubris, or of negligence. Indeed, the runner succumbed before the true difficulties even began; just imagine a man running alone across the Nubian Desert, through the South Sudanese swamps, full of malaria and crocodiles, and over the savannah with lions and snakes. His expedition was probably the most ill-conceived of its time: a seaman from a small village in western Norway travelling to inner Africa armed only with biscuits and jam in a lunch pack, and without a rifle.

According to his German biography, Mensen Ernst's motto was: 'Movement is life, stasis is death'. An eloquent commentary on a life that ended in a run along the banks of the Nile on his way into the unknown.

The canal between the oceans

I am a little to the south of the port in Ismailia, standing in the shadows of palm trees, watered by Nile waters, transported all the way here in long canals, while I watch the supertankers as they slowly file through the narrow canal, majestic convoys of modernity against the brown, desolate desert mountains in the background. The sight is beautiful and surreal, and at the same time it symbolizes the power and the ability of global trade regimes to transform environments all over the world.

The house of Ferdinand de Lesseps, the French consul in Egypt and 'father' of the canal here, is also here. The house is closed to the public now, but I was given a tour by my Egyptian hosts when I attended a Nile conference in the early 1990s. The bedroom looks as if it has hardly been touched since he left it – old pictures and books scattered around the desk and by the bed, and de Lesseps' private couch, still in impeccable condition. The more than 26-kilometre-long canal that de Lesseps was so instrumental in devising opened on 17 November 1869. With that, an artificial waterway connecting the Mediterranean to the Indian Ocean, or Europe to Asia, was created, thereby altering the course of world history and Egypt's, and with it the Nile's, geopolitical role.

Canal building, of course, was nothing new in Egypt. Thousands of years earlier Egyptians had dug canals from the Nile to the Red Sea. The first person to build a canal along that entire stretch was Senusret III, almost 1,900 years BCE. The inscriptions beneath the statue of Ramses II (1279–1213 BCE) say that the pharaoh had either finished or repaired a canal from the Nile to the Red Sea via Wadi Tumilat and some lakes. At some point in the next 600 years the canal must have gotten clogged because Necho (Neko) II (who ruled 609–594 BCE) began excavating it again before ultimately giving up on the project. The Persians under Darius the Great constructed a canal that was presumably used for 200 years. Darius erected five monuments in Wadi Tumilat, named Darius the Great's Suez Inscriptions. The monuments contain the following text:

> King Darius says: I am a Persian; setting out from Persia. I conquered Egypt. I ordered to dig this canal from the river that is called Nile and flows in Egypt, to the sea that begins in Persia. Therefore, when this canal had been dug as I had ordered, ships went from Egypt through this canal to Persia, as I had intended.

It no longer functioned when Cleopatra reigned. The Romans, both under Trajan and Hadrian, began to repair it. When Amr ibn al-As and the Arabs conquered Egypt, this canal was, once again, no longer in use, but Amr restored it. A canal ran in the eighth century from the Nile south of the Delta to the Red Sea, known from the account of the monk Fidelis' journey from the Nile to the Red Sea (he was on a pilgrimage to the Holy Land). It appears that this canal was also used to send grain to Arabia. It was deliberately closed in 767 by Caliph al-Mansur, apparently to starve out rebels in Medina.[37]

During the few years that Napoleon ruled Egypt, he also had time to hire French engineers to evaluate the potential of building a canal to connect the Mediterranean with the Indian Ocean. The engineers concluded that it was not feasible with existing technology, though it later turned out that they had miscalculated by 10 metres the difference in height between the two sea levels. Such is history's development that no one knows how Nile history, and world history along with it, might have unfolded if not for that small mistake; we only know that it would have been very different. The mistake was discovered in the 1840s, and another Frenchman, Louis M.A. Linant de

Bellefonds, designed what would become the Suez Canal. The diplomat and engineer Ferdinand de Lesseps presented the plans to Egypt's new ruler, Said Pasha. Said implemented work at the Mediterranean, naming the site where the canal begins after himself, what today is called Port Said.

The British opposed the canal because they rightly feared it would weaken their trade dominance. Accordingly, London, among other political initiatives, supported a canal worker rebellion. The workers certainly had good reason to revolt, since they had been forcibly conscripted into very bad, even life-threatening working conditions. Nonetheless, British imperialists supporting a labour rebellion in Egypt, a movement that targeted better working conditions, ill fits the popular idea of imperialism, though for London the main goal was to weaken France's regional position. Support from France and Napoleon II, however, enabled the Egyptian government to see the project to its conclusion.

In 1869 the canal was finished. It was opened with all pomp and circumstance, as befit the royal Egyptian house. Along the canal's banks that day stood dignitaries and celebrities from near and far, among them the Prince of Wales, the Austro-Hungarian emperor and the Norwegian playwright Henrik Ibsen. The magnificent ball hosted 6,000 guests. The opening of the Cairo opera house was also a part of the festivities and the plan had originally been to stage the first showing of *Aida*, the opera Giuseppe Verdi had composed on commission from the Egyptian khedive (in the history of opera, this commissioned work is considered to be the highest-paid any composer has ever scored). However, *Aida*'s showing would have occurred immediately before Isma'il Pasha, the new khedive and Said Pasha's nephew, planned to launch in the name of progress his military expedition to conquer the Red Sea coast and Ethiopia. Verdi had captured this political atmosphere and delivered an opera that focused on Egypt's relationship with Ethiopia. *Aida* was finally performed for the first time in Cairo on 24 December 1871, two years after the opening celebrations of the canal.

The opera is also interesting from a perspective of the history of representation. The scene is set in ancient Egypt, and Verdi was advised on the libretto by the French Egyptologist, Auguste Mariette. The opera's central dilemma concerns how the victorious Egyptian general, Radamès, is torn by his love of two women, the Egyptian pharaoh's daughter and Aida, the daughter of the Ethiopian king with whom Egypt is at war and now made slave to the daughter of the king of Egypt. The Egyptian general finally takes the decision to betray his country, and so loses his life. For Verdi and other Europeans at the time, this operatic love triangle was experienced as a true predicament. In Egypt, on the other hand, it has been argued that it was a meaningless conflict at the time. There the solution for the man was simpler: take both women, even as wives.[38] Not long after the canal was opened, after *Aida*'s slave choir had premiered at Cairo's new opera house, and after the first boat had taken the shortcut between Asia and Europe, it became clear that Egypt was bankrupt. Isma'il and his predecessors had invested too much too quickly, and in too many projects. Egypt's leadership decided to sell Said Pasha's shares in the canal operation for £4,000,000. Britain now saw its chance. Even though France still owned most shares, the cards in the game about the canal, and about Egypt, could be dealt anew. The British prime minister, Benjamin Disraeli, was informed that the French were also negotiating to buy these shares. Swift action was called for. Disraeli immediately decided to purchase them; he could not wait on Parliament's blessing. Disraeli sent his secretary, Montagu Corry, to the wealthy Lord Rothschild. According to Corry, the following famous conversation took place as he explained that the prime minister required £4,000,000 by the following morning:

> Rothschild took a grape, ate it, and asked: 'What is your security?'
> 'The British Government', Corry replied.
> 'You shall have it'.[39]

The prime minister's resourcefulness helped to shift the strategic balance between France and Great Britain, something with consequences far into the future. The canal linking the Mediterranean Sea to the Indian Ocean altered power relations and trade routes: Egypt had been a backwater ever since the Portuguese discovered the sea route round Africa's southern tip around 1500, and now the country was suddenly key to one of the world's most important waterways. As such, Egypt's geopolitical location became radically more central and, for the British, Egypt was now a tremendously significant piece in their plans for what was eventually to become the world's largest and most successful empire.

Gustave Flaubert and Henrik Ibsen: 'From Cairo up the Nile'

As already mentioned, in 1829 Victor Hugo had written that 'now we are [all] Orientalists'. Hugo's orientalism should not simply be regarded as a comprehensive and repressive world view, however, as a new form of hypocrisy on behalf of the colonizing, powerful West, but also as a new hunger for knowledge. One component of this focus on, and enthusiasm for, learning about the Orient was that Egypt during the nineteenth century became an increasingly important travel destination for European authors. Two of the many to venture there were the French author Gustave Flaubert and his Norwegian colleague, Henrik Ibsen.

Flaubert reached Egypt in 1849, after a storm-filled journey from Marseille. At twenty-eight, he was one of many European intellectuals who visited Egypt in the 1800s. He saw the sphinxes, the Coptic churches in Old Cairo, as well as jugglers, acrobats and snake charmers; he met prostitutes and, of course, saw the Nile, which he described as being yellow and full of mud. He travelled to Luxor, Thebes and Karnak, and wrote to his mother that everywhere you looked, a temple seemed to be buried up to its shoulders in sand. Flaubert was moved by the chaos, inflamed by what he saw, since he had, after all, fled the dull, bourgeois, superficial, all too orderly France.

On the other hand, he needed to create conceptual order out of all these new, unfathomable things so he could hope to reflect on, and write about, what he was seeing. Flaubert thought from a purely philosophical and existential standpoint, that 'order' itself implied a condemnatory and self-righteous stance toward the human condition, counteracting, as it did, the openness, and lack of rigidity and rules, to which human beings should ascribe. By depicting the power of perspective as a process imposed upon him rather than simply subjecting himself to its dominating conventions, however, he could still maintain distance to what he observed. In a letter from Cairo dated 1850 he wrote:

So here we are in Egypt. [...] And yet I am scarcely over the initial bedazzlement ... [where] each detail reaches out to grip you; it pinches you; and the more you concentrate on it the less you grasp the whole. Then gradually all this becomes harmonious and the pieces fall into place of themselves, in accordance with the laws of perspective. But the first days, by God, it is such a bewildering chaos of colours.[40]

Flaubert's view of Egypt was influenced by what he considered to be Egyptian society's essential, urgent, ubiquitous dualism – death and life, and desert and river. He was particularly fascinated by what he believed to be the Egyptian ability to accept life's dualities, which he characterized as: filth/psyche, sexuality/purity, insanity/health. How splendid, he thought, that people openly belched in restaurants. Surrounded by the norms of daily life, no one seemed to find anything strange with 'a donkey that shit and a gentleman pissing in a hook'. A six- or seven-year-old boy greeted Flaubert on a Cairo street as he passed with: 'I wish you luck but most of all a big dick'.

In 1850 Flaubert travelled upriver by felucca – the traditional sailing boat that can still be seen in Upper Egypt – and he details how river life reflected the changing society around them. He writes that eleven of the fourteen crew members were missing their right index finger. Like so many others, they had severed their 'trigger finger' to avoid forced conscription into Muhammad Ali's army. He summarized the situation in the country thus: Egypt was a country where those who had clean clothes struck those with dirty ones.

Flaubert's writings evoke classic 'orientalist' texts in the sense that they depict things the author interpreted as foreign or alienating, often in an exoticizing and very paternalistic way. And it is doubtless that Flaubert's observations acquire some of their power precisely because they are based on a clearly expressed difference or distinction between France and Egypt, where Egypt becomes fascinating as France's antithesis. For Flaubert, however, France was not simply the model or idea against which he painted Egypt. He was intellectually isolated in his homeland, and very critical towards many of the day's dominant trends, not to mention the bourgeois lifestyle. Such dualism regarding France surfaces in Flaubert's descriptions of Egypt. Therefore, it is difficult, not to say unreasonable, to regard him as simply a kind of pawn for European expansionism or as an obvious illustration of an intellectual tradition that sought, if only latently, total control. Certainly, he exploited his position with respect to female and male prostitutes in Egypt, and he understood how privilege, when dealing with Egyptians, rested on power. He used words and arguments that, in retrospect, seem anachronistic, degrading and racist. However, Flaubert's enthusiasm for this Nile country appears genuine, fervent even, if it was also only a fantasy, drawn as an alternative to his detested homeland. Eventually, he wrote that Egyptian temples now bored him utterly.

Europe haunted Flaubert: he tried to escape what he regarded as the folly of the French bourgeoisie, but he failed. In Egypt he sought what he could not find – but what he desired – in France. The Egypt that obsessed him was, therefore, not so much Egypt itself but rather his idea of Egypt and the meaning he sought to give it in his life's project.

Around twenty years later, Henrik Ibsen embarked on an entirely different kind of journey. Ibsen, that razor-sharp analyst of bourgeois life in the modernizing, emerging Europe, travelled through Egypt with kings and empresses and other dignitaries. He was part of an officially sponsored trip to celebrate the opening of the Suez Canal on 17 November 1869. Ibsen had visited Sweden in the summer of that year, where he was being honoured as Scandinavia's foremost author. Once there, he became acquainted with King Carl XV. The king asked if Ibsen would serve as the Norwegian-Swedish representative at the canal's opening that same autumn. The poet said yes.

And here he was! The canal's opening was an all-out, month-long party. Thousands of foreign guests attended. They were given free trips, excursions and dinners financed by the Egyptian khedive. Most of Ibsen's biographers believe this trip made a deep impression on him, and it is an interesting facet of Norwegian literary history that *Peer Gynt*, perhaps the country's most famous national epic, retrieves its action for long stretches from – of all things – the land of the Nile!

Long before setting foot there, Ibsen had been fascinated by Egypt's place in history. In order to celebrate Norway's National Day in 1855, six years after Gustave Flaubert docked at Alexandria and the upper-class Englishwoman and nurse, Florence Nightingale, ventured on a boat up the Nile, and sent evocative and picturesque letters home to her mother, Ibsen wrote a poem based on freedom. In this poem, Egypt was depicted as a society mired in stasis and lack of liberty – Egypt was conceived as Norway's antithesis. The statue of Memnon, which still sits enthroned at Luxor in today's Egypt, 'a graven image, in an eastern land', was for Ibsen the precise metaphor, or representation, for the idea that freedom demanded action more than words. The frozen king stared with

soulless gaze toward the east's bright band.
So year on year he stood there, dully dreaming[41]

When four years later Ibsen wrote a satirical poem about an author who defended Danish as the appropriate stage language in Norway, Ibsen wielded Egyptian history against the man. Ibsen regarded his colleague's idea to use the language of the former master of Norway as the language in the new Norway as stone-dead, long rejected by what had happened between the countries. Ibsen sought extra ammunition for his attack by comparing his opponent's outdatedness with the most petrified conservative thing he could find, namely Egypt. As such, 'the balsamed corpse' lay proudly 'in its fossilised shroud', and had indeed 'quite forgotten how the sun caresses'. Therefore: ' "A bitter smile" played on its lips, emphatic / Scorn for the times – because they were not static'.

Ibsen, at that point, had never travelled along the Nile. It is, therefore, reasonable to interpret the poet's choice of metaphor as a testament to the fact that he was influenced by a general European viewpoint. Perhaps the German philosopher, Georg Wilhelm Friedrich Hegel, inspired him in this context as well, for the philosopher notoriously makes use of ancient Egyptian religious and artistic symbolism in his art and philosophy of history. As it turns out, however, the picture is more complex. In *Peer Gynt*, for example, Ibsen characterizes Peer's impression of the Sphinx thus: 'But this most curious mongrel here, this changeling, a lion and woman in one'.[42] Still, Peer also remembers 'the fellow! Why, of course it's the Boyg, that I smote on the skull'. In this case, the Sphinx does not stand for petrified Egypt but rather for Norwegian fairy tales; the Boyg and the Sphinx speak German – with a Berlin dialect! Instead of representing 'the stranger', or the diverse or 'the petrified', the image represents something European and Norwegian.

As the Swedish king's representative at the opening of the canal, Ibsen took part in an extended journey up the Nile, all the way to the Nubian Desert on the border of today's Sudan. He travelled with eighty-five other guests and the khedive, a twenty-four-day expedition. Ibsen had planned to publish a travel narrative, but nothing ever came of it. In 1870, however, he wrote a longer, kind of historical-philosophical poem about the journey with the veiled title: 'Balloon Letter to a Swedish Lady', where he described his Nile travels: 'On *Ferus* we shot up-stream / out of Cairo at full-steam'.[43] Here he saw the statue of Memnon, the 'stone colossus, – / he, you know, once sang a little'. And, like other tourists before and after him, he saw Luxor, Dendera, Saqqara, Edfu, Aswan and Philae.

In 'Balloon Letter to a Swedish Lady', Ibsen is concerned with the broad major outlines of world history and cultural development, interpreted within an idealistic conceptual framework where life opposes death, as stasis opposes growth. The value conflict between them is represented with the aid of Egyptian, Greek and Norse mythological imagery, where Egypt represents death and stasis:

Lo, then from the North a gust
[...]
Pharaoh and his house as well
lay forgotten, buried, scattered.
Where the throng once flocked as bidden,
now a lifeless, silent crowd; –
for a thousand long years hidden,
deep-entombed, all light forbidden,
[...]
What of Egypt's gods, though, solemn
lines of ciphers ranged by column?
What on earth was their life-mission?
Just to be, to stay the same,
painted, stiff with inanition,
stooled beside the altar-flame.

As Ibsen further writes:

[N]ot one felt life's urgent call,
felt the call to sin, to stumble,

raise himself despite the fall.
Hence must Egypt lie and crumble
like a crypted corpse that's nameless
after four millennia's sameness.

Ibsen's poem aimed to explain Egypt's development by pointing only to Egyptian culture or to pharaonic values. Egyptians did not have 'the call' or drive for innovation, so to speak; therefore, petrification set in. Ibsen's ideas were in line with dominant assumptions in the modernizing, nineteenth-century Europe about the Orient.

Such a perspective, which expressed the age's cultural self-confidence within the framework of an industrializing and triumphant Europe, overlooked – and was, therefore, naturally unconcerned with – Egypt's specific developmental barriers. The fact is, however, that aspects of the hydrological and topographical character of the Nile that had proven the basis for a flowering pharaonic civilization at a historical point when many Europeans were still living in caves and in primitive hunter-and-gatherer societies, were now the very same characteristics that made it extremely difficult, if not to say impossible, for Egypt to develop technologically in the early nineteenth century. Yet during those centuries when the more and more extensive use of the overshot waterwheel was revolutionizing first diet and agriculture, and then production technology in the iron and textile industries across many European countries, the slope or steam gradient of Nile and its irregular seasonal flow regime made it in general impossible to use it for driving such overshot wheels. In Egypt, agriculture and society's economic structure and activities remained fundamentally adapted to the Nile's natural way of flowing in the landscape. The reason for this conservatism was not simply Egyptian 'mentality', as Ibsen and many with him, including members of the Egyptian elite, assumed: it must be also sought in the fact that Egyptians did not, and could not, develop the technology required to harness the Nile as an energy source. In Egypt, moreover, there were simply no other rivers or streams available than the almost dead-flat Nile.

In his descriptions of Egypt, as in his overall authorship, Ibsen was concerned with mentalities, with ways of thinking and with conventions. His historical perspective did not give a central place to either geographical context or structures, despite the fact that he was born in Skien, a Norwegian city whose history demonstrates the limits of that very implicit theory on historical change and conditions for development that had influenced Ibsen. Skien became integrated into Europe's modern economy in the nineteenth century, because it was possible to exploit the River Skien running right through the city as a means to float logs down from the large Telemark forests, and as an energy source for frame saws, watermills and other water-powered industries. Over time this helped to develop an urban, entrepreneurial and modernizing mentality, which, of course, also had other reasons and backgrounds. But by overlooking – as was common during the era when modernity broke through – the different options or possibilities made available by different waterscapes in parts of Europe and in Egypt, Ibsen ended by blaming societal differences solely on people's differing mentalities.

Just as Victor Hugo, following Napoleon's failed Egyptian campaign, could declare that we are orientalists, and as European authors like Flaubert and Ibsen visited Egypt later in the 1800s, European knowledge of the region definitely increased, although the understanding of the country's history was framed and influenced by power relations between Europe and Egypt and by dominating modes of thinking among the travellers. As a result, even though Edward Said's analysis is too sweeping, as I have shown, he did identify an important aspect of European intellectual history.

Shares and occupation

In 1882, around ninety years after Napoleon's Egyptian campaign, the time had come for British soldiers to march up the Nile Delta. The British government had made its decision: Britain would take full control of the Suez Canal, and this made it logical also to seize power in Egypt. This occupation should ensure that European capitalists who had invested in the Egyptian economy in general and in the canal in particular, got their money back, though it quickly became evident that the British also intended to secure their empire's strategic interests in the long term by controlling the newest and most effective seaway to the empire's crown jewel, India; and the Indian Ocean, after all, was in the process of becoming a British sea. This latter motive was, however, downplayed for political and diplomatic reasons. Egypt, for its part, was once again conquered by foreign invaders, on this occasion, however, for just a few decades. Still, Britain's relatively short-lived Nile empire had fundamental and revolutionary long-term consequences, both for the Nile itself and for the relationship between people and the river.

The previous year, in 1881, Colonel Ahmed 'Urabi, an Egyptian-born officer, had led a rebellion against the Ottoman regime (Egypt was still formally governed from Istanbul), and, therefore, also against British and French economic interests there, which had been invited into the country by the government. The country was still ruled by the khedive and by Muhammad Ali's Albanian house. The immediate background for 'Urabi's nationalist rebellion was protests against the consequences of a money-saving campaign by the Ottoman army that resulted in a reduced number of Egyptian soldiers. 'Urabi, however, further broadened his political platform by allying with traditional nationalistic and religious forces that opposed Western influence in general.

When Egypt's new young khedive, Muhammed Tewfik, Isma'il's son, accepted many of 'Urabi's demands, the major European powers were no longer content to sit by and watch events unfold, and they intervened on the side of the weakened khedive. They feared losing control of the Suez Canal, and that significant investments in the canal venture, and in Egypt in general, might go down the drain. Muhammad Ali and his house had placed themselves at the forefront of a modernization drive, and they had many Europeans in their employment, something that required huge sums of money that they borrowed from European banks. The khedive and Egypt owed increasing amounts throughout the nineteenth century, and Isma'il's sale of his shares in the Suez Canal Company to Great Britain for next to nothing can only be understood in this context. European financial houses, with the Rothschild family at the head, grew increasingly anxious about the fate of their money. France and England had such substantial economic interests in Egypt that they established a European-led commission whose mandate was to oversee Egypt's finances and secure an economic policy that would place Egypt in a position to meet its obligations.

The two countries established what can be described as an early version of the World Bank's conditionality policy of the 1990s, only this was much more direct and much more humiliating. France and England agreed on one thing: Egypt must pay what it owed. Yet, beneath the surface of European unity there flourished an intense rivalry regarding power and influence in the region. In May 1882, after Tewfik Pasha requested foreign aid in defeating the rebel 'Urabi, a joint British and French fleet with warships was sent to Alexandria as a show of force.

In June, revolt erupted in Alexandria in protest at the warships anchored directly outside the city. Fifty Europeans were lynched by a mob, and in Britain anti-'Urabi sentiment increased, naturally enough. 'Urabi attempted to stop the riots because he feared the consequences of going too far. In July, Britain demanded that 'Urabi dismantle Alexandria's fortifications; if not, they would bomb the city. France, for its part, decided to withdraw its ships, thereby breaking the joint French and British military front. 'Urabi refused to stand down. The British bombardment set the city aflame, much the same way that Britain had set Denmark's capital, Copenhagen, afire almost a century earlier. On 15 July, British troops set foot on land. 'Urabi and his army retreated in order to organize military resistance.

British Prime Minister William Gladstone addressed the House of Commons. He lamented that they did not have wider European support in restoring law and order to Egypt. Nonetheless, he said, London was ready to proceed alone, with or without cooperation from other European powers. A stable Egypt under Great Britain's influence was necessary to operate the Suez Canal in a way that served the empire's overall interests. What Prime Minister Gladstone did not mention, but which historians uncovered later, was that he himself owned shares in the canal company and thus personally stood to gain money on the invasion he was giving the green light to.

London sent a force of more than 13,000 men under the leadership of British officers, but many of the soldiers were recruited in India. They went ashore at Alexandria, attacking an army of 20,000 Egyptians and winning easily due to superiority in weapons technology and organization. The British marched towards Cairo, but 'Urabi was determined to stop them – using the Nile as his weapon.

Where the Egyptians made the Nile a weapon of war

One aspect of travelling today is that every place seems to have been chronicled, and travel guides have defined what is important to see and think while you are there. Increasingly, the traveller is left trying to live up to a kind of authoritative enthusiasm and script, not least along the Nile in Egypt since the cultural landscape here, with its temples, pyramids, chambers and statues has been described for far longer, and perhaps appears in more travel books, than any other place on earth.

Tel el-Kebir in the Nile Delta, however, does not appear in any travel guide as far as I know, despite its significance in the history of the Nile. On 30 September 1882, a decisive battle took place here: Egyptian nationalists confronted invading British forces in what was intended to be a water battle, or an aquatic skirmish in the land of the Nile.

Colonel Ahmed 'Urabi had pinpointed Tel el-Kebir as a particularly suitable site in his defensive struggle against the British invaders. As a component of his military strategy, his soldiers had dammed the canal that flowed parallel to the railway. Their goal was to cut water supplies to the occupying army and to Ismailia on the Suez Canal. Using water as a weapon in this way would, it was hoped, strike the British where it hurt most.

Aquatic warfare, as it is known in technical terms, has a long tradition in some countries, and especially in China. Up through the centuries, volumes have been written on the art of waging battle using water against the enemy and a number of cases have been related about the way warlords have drowned their enemies or driven them to submission from thirst.[44] Egypt, by contrast, had no comparable tradition, only isolated instances. In 50 BCE, Julius Caesar faced such an attempt when he encamped and built up his defences around the great theatre on today's Hospital Hill near Ramleh Station in Alexandria. The locals attempted to strike at the Roman invaders by ruining the deep freshwater wells on which the army depended, and which received Nile water from subterranean canals – they introduced saltwater into the wells. In *The Alexandrian War* (a book attributed to Caesar, though that claim is doubtful), the army's freshwater problems are described. The water was polluted, and they were afraid it was poisoned.[45] The Roman solution was to dig the wells even deeper, all the way down to the water table.

Egyptian history does contain some instances of water warfare prior to 1882. As we have seen, Caliph al-Mansur attempted in 767 to starve out the rebels in Medina by closing the canal between the Nile and the Red Sea – an indirect sign of the Nile Delta's importance in consolidating the Islamic caliphate's power. In the war against the Crusaders, the Delta's waterways proved a strategic weapon against troops marching upstream. The Egyptians, for example, successfully opened the dykes in September 1163 near Bilbeis, as Christopher Tyerman writes in *God's War*. Water was also used as a weapon against Napoleon's troops at the end of the 1700s, though on a modest scale. The Emir of Damanhur had forged an agreement with Jean-Baptiste Kléber, then commander of the French troops in Alexandria, to deliver water to the city for the same price he had received from the previous officials. However, a rural village, Birkat Gittas, entered an alliance with other local leaders and closed the canal – to deliver a blow to the French. Kléber responded by sending 600 soldiers to the village. He ordered the head of every man killed to be staked so that passers-by could see them. Kléber then distributed pamphlets up and down the Nile that warned against following the village's example – and the threat of terror worked.

In 1882 'Urabi planned to use the water weapon in a way that was much more effective and on a larger scale, and as a component in the struggle against what was by far the world's strongest military power. According to 'Urabi's plan, the decisive confrontation between 'Urabi and Great Britain should take place at Tel el-Kebir. However, with multiple lightning-quick surprise attacks – the British travelled by night, navigating with the help of the stars – the British infantry and cavalry won every battle and, as day dawned, were already just under 140 metres from the Egyptian troops. The shooting immediately started. 'Urabi's rebellion was crushed before anyone could test the water weapon's effectiveness.

The way to Cairo was now open to British troops.

At the crossroads of history, river and sea

Misinterpreting the present is the unavoidable consequence of a lack of knowledge about the past. Conversely, spending time trying to understand the past without any interest in the present might be fun but, to me, is simply time wasted. The capacity to interpret in a historical context what is living and contemporaneous should, if anything, be the historian's true strength and contribution. Therefore, the historian in this sense does not dwell in the past, is not simply or only pursuing the 'primary movers', but *is* in the present, albeit with an historical awareness of the now. With such a perspective on what was and what is, it might become possible to free oneself from the 'blind power' of history, and it is only then that research, and the questions it poses, can hope to liberate itself from some of the present-day trends and influences.

The history of the Nile Delta emerges in a new light against the dark clouds that many claim will characterize its near future. Its present, furthermore, appears more clearly against the historical backdrop I have drawn. I am standing at Alexandria's greatest antique monument, Pompey's Pillar. It rises from the ruins of the ancient Serapis Temple – slightly south-west of the city centre. The pillar is made of red Aswan granite and is almost 27 metres tall, with a circumference of 9 metres. Disagreement exists regarding who built it, but most probably it was Diocletian, the Roman emperor who was responsible for the bloody oppression of the Christians. Near the pillar, I can see the remains of the ancient Nilometer, one of many examples of the kind of rationalism and engagement with nature's workings that was shared by the ancient Egyptians, by the Romans and, later, by Islamic Egypt. Now, this measuring stave for Nile water flow, and the magnificent pillar itself, are hidden among the ruins of the old city walls, a fact that symbolizes both the city's and the Delta's changing relationship to the river that was foundational for them both.

Alexandria has been left at the crossroads of history, river and sea – and, in significant ways, has been distinguished by its location at the fragile and varying intersection between sea levels that have risen since the last ice age; the periodic but lasting changes to the Nile's character; and state leaders' shifting water policy. And just so has the Delta also undergone diverse phases.

The Delta that Herodotus described was a place that had experienced dramatic ecological changes for thousands of years, both due to natural alterations in the Nile itself and to the pharaohs' attempts to control the river. The Delta through which Caesar and Cleopatra sailed, up which Napoleon's soldiers wandered, and which Ibsen and Flaubert saw, was not the same Delta that today is home to more than fifty million people. The situation today is disconcerting. The United Nations' Intergovernmental Panel on Climate Change has described the Delta as one of the world's most vulnerable regions. The Panel argues that a third of the region will be lost in just a few decades if the current trend continues. The most dramatic predictions claim that by 2050, the

Mediterranean will have risen by almost 1 metre, and, due to the Nile dams further upriver, large parts of the Delta will sink (however, some areas experience an east–west zone of geological uplift, which will counterbalance the overall trend), because a dammed river carries less silt to the sea. These prophesies might turn out to be alarmist exaggeration, but there can no doubt that the relationship between river and sea has been changed in ways that nobody knows the consequences of.

Once again, the Delta will be affected by its placement at the intersection between river and sea, and fundamentally impacted by humanity's attempts to tame the river. For 5,000 years nature dominated the river's constitution and function but, from the mid-nineteenth century until today, various Egyptian regimes have affected the Nile Delta more and more. Especially critical – as we shall see – has been the development following the British occupation of the Delta up until the Egyptians transformed the Nile in the 1970s to what, for all practical purposes, became an engineered canal.

Before the Nile in Egypt was completely tamed, the river had for millennia counteracted the tendency to erosion and subsidence in the Delta in relation to the sea. It carried with it close to 200 million tons of earth or sediment every year. Sea storms and waves have always eroded the coastline, but until recently they were met with a counterforce: the sediment-heavy Nile water. The Aswan Dam changed overnight this natural battle between silt and sea, and the effect of this historical shift has been felt only for a few decades.[46]

The relationship between Delta, river and sea finds itself in a new state of imbalance, and Egyptians living there might, it is argued, in the long run become victims of a slow-motion catastrophe also caused by water management on a truly grand scale.

Towards Karnak and the Nile Cataracts

The city the Arabs founded and the British took

There is no better introduction to Cairo and the city's historical geography than the view from atop Cairo Tower on Gezira Island. From here you see row upon row of tall grey buildings that seem to lean against each other, densely packed, having what look like black windows, like holes in the desert-coloured façade. The multiple bridges that stretch over the river connect the two banks, and traffic on them is often at a standstill. From the tower, you clearly see how the city huddles on both sides of the river, surrounded to the east and west by desert. When you realize how truly dense the houses are, standing shoulder to shoulder and back to back, and when you see the cars squeezed on the many bridges that arch across the Nile to the south and north of the tower, you can actually imagine that by day the city holds twenty million people.

From the south, flowing north from central Africa, the river enters the city, passing by the southern tip of Roda Island and the Nilometer there and running slowly towards you beneath the bridges. To the north, in the direction of the Mediterranean, the river exits the city, as if closing a chapter in both its geography and its biography, heading for the Mediterranean and the Delta. In the south-east, almost parallel to the river, stand the Mokattam Hills and the Citadel, which is not only a memorial from Salah al-Din's or Saladin's glory days but continues to dominate the city's skyline, as if it is the city's innate guardian. Only a few kilometres from the riverbank, the desert mountains are plainly visible against the horizon. To the west, Saqqara, Giza and, on a clear day, the pyramids.

Few things have inspired as many writers and been described more often in tourist letters home than the pyramids. Their construction began early in the Third Dynasty, c. 2650 BCE. It was the pharaoh Khufu (c. 2585–2560 BCE) who raised the greatest of all the pyramids, known in Europe as the Cheops Pyramid, while his son, Khafre (c. 2555–2532 BCE) built the second greatest (he could not erect one larger than his father's, after all). The Roman author Pliny the Elder is one of the few people who was not impressed: he dismissed the pyramids as world history's most substantial waste, as well as a sign of the rulers' megalomania. As he commented: 'We must make some mention, too, however cursorily, of the Pyramids of Egypt, so many idle and frivolous pieces of ostentation of their resources, on the part of the monarchs of that country.'[1]

When it comes to acclaimed wonders like the pyramids, it can be easier to experience them in art and as expectation, rather than as reality. The history teller's perception, and the artist's vision, can omit, condense and edit what is boring or irrelevant. Both gather attention or focus emotions on central aspects of the pyramids or critical moments in their history, thereby lending journeys to visit them a coherence and clarity, or a liveliness they may lack in reality: the present's endlessly distracting fog, when the traveller stands opposite his goal, but where it is also uncomfortably hot, one's socks are itchy and an unsolicited smiling guide abruptly appears from behind a rock or gaudily adorned camel, wanting to take you to some 'very special place' for an extra fee. Nonetheless, the pyramids have, despite all the distractions present when you are in front of them, produced throughout history descriptions that are surprisingly similar – as a rule dominated by observations of their exceptional size and emphatic durability. At a distance, their hyper-monumental aspect clearly reflects the leaders' ruthless capacity to erect monuments to themselves, thereby also trying to ensure themselves eternal life.

This city on the Nile was built because Arabic occupation force commanders settled at Fustat on the river's east side, on the outskirts of what would later become Cairo. One early explanation for this was that the chief military commander, Amr ibn al-As, at first wanted Alexandria as the capital, but Caliph Umar stopped him. Umar said that water should not separate any capital from Medina, and the Nile, of course, ran to the east of Alexandria. Amr, therefore, camped at Fustat following a battle against a Byzantine army in 642. A few centuries later, Fustat was burned as part of the scorched-earth tactics launched against the Crusaders. Thereafter, Cairo grew within the citadel that Saladin ordered built on the river's eastern side.

The citadel that today still marks the Mokattam Hills has proven the setting for many of the city's most crucial moments, but the structure also indicates the river's significance to the city, as well as interfaith relationships in Egypt. It was Saladin who raised the citadel, hiring two Coptic Christian architects to build both it and the city walls. Christian architects, working on behalf of the leader who had seized the Holy City from the Christians, were thus constructing a wall designed to protect the city against Crusaders. The wall ringing the citadel stretched in a half-circle from the Nile's banks and then back. Now, the Nile's eastern shores have shifted due to urban expansion, so imagining the scene requires the aid of historical drawings. Without protected access to the river, however, the citadel was obviously useless.

It was not only water that came to Cairo from the south: fertilizer in the form of silt from Ethiopia's mountains also arrived from that direction. Gold and ivory came that way and expeditions going south along the Nile to capture slaves to bring them to the north were, during some periods, very important. Especially after Muhammad Ali's occupation of Sudan, thousands of slaves were transported in huge caravans to Egypt. At that time, access to white slaves from the Caucasus had dried up after Russia expanded into the region, so there was an increasing need to obtain slaves from Africa. The slave market was a tourist destination for the first half of the 1800s, but it was closed mid-century, which meant that the trade thereafter took place more circumspectly. In 1831 Pastor Michael Russell wrote, regarding his encounter with the Cairo slave market: 'The Ethiopian women brought to Egypt for sale, though black, are exceedingly beautiful; their features being perfectly regular, and their eyes full of fire. Many of them had been purchased by the French during their stay in the country.'[2] The elite did not need slaves for agriculture, since no one could create more surplus than the hard-working Egyptian peasant farmers. Within the household, on the other hand, slaves were considered necessary, this partly due to polygamy and the harem. And state leaders required soldiers who would remain loyal to the current sitting ruler. Within this system, the Copts developed their own specialty: they were quite adept at turning slaves into eunuchs. There were two kinds of operations here: removing the penis or removing the testicles.[3] Because of the high mortality rate, eunuchs cost much more than other slaves.

Cairo's placement is strategic: the city controls the Delta's entrance both politically and militarily. At the same time, just like the ancient pharaonic capital Memphis, which was located right outside today's Cairo, it is an advantageous springboard for controlling Upper Egypt. Eventually, Cairo became the most important city in Africa and the Middle East.

In his 1326 accounts of Cairo, the great Arabian traveller, Ibn Battuta, described the city's coexistence with the river. He writes:

It is said that in Cairo there are twelve thousand water-carriers who transport water on camels, and thirty thousand hirers of mules and donkeys, and that on the Nile there are thirty-six thousand boats belonging to the Sultan and his subjects, which sail upstream to Upper Egypt and downstream to Alexandria and Damietta, laden with goods and profitable merchandise of all kinds.[4]

As Battuta continues: 'The traveller on the Nile need take no provision with him, because whenever he desires to descend on the bank he may do so, for ablutions, prayers, provisioning, or any other purpose. There is an uninterrupted chain of bazaars from Alexandria to Cairo, and from Cairo to Assuan in Upper Egypt.'[5]

At Ibn Khaldun Square in Cairo stands a statue of the Arab world's most famous historian. Ibn Khaldun visited Cairo in 1382, around sixty years after Ibn Battuta, and he gave the city its legendary description as 'the mother of all cities'. He wrote: 'I beheld the metropolis of the world, orchard of the universe, hive of nations, iwan of Islam, throne of royalty, bursting with palaces and iwans within, shining on the horizon with khanqahs and madrasas, illuminated by the moons and stars of its learned scholars.'[6] It is not so strange that Khaldun acquired a statue here.

From the Cairo Tower you can also clearly see, if you compare old maps and drawings of the city, how Cairo has gradually escaped the Nile's direct, despotic locational power. One of Cairo's most famous maps was made by Venetian cartographer and printer, Mateo Pagano, in the 1500s. After reading French orientalist Guillaume Postel's book, *Description*, published in 1549, Pagano drew an extraordinarily detailed and precise map of Cairo, the first of its kind – and without ever having set foot in the city himself.[7] Pagano sketched the map from an imaginary perspective, from above, and as I stand here snapping countless razor-sharp overview images with my Canon camera, I think that technological development has been a blessing to us lacking the genius of the Venetian cartographer.

Gezira Island, where the tower now stands as a self-consciously dominant landmark, was, before the mid-1800s, uninhabitable due to the Nile's annual flood. Isma'il, the khedive who opened the Suez Canal, brought engineers here, since he planned to transform Cairo into a Middle Eastern Paris of sorts. They reinforced the banks and, in 1869, the same year the canal was opened, his Cairo palace also stood complete. Around the palace were massive parks with exotic plants collected from across the globe. Here, the royal family could hunt, spend the afternoon on the trotting track, or playing polo, all designed by the French landscape architect, De la Chevalerie. Originally, the park spanned around 80 hectares, but today the many hotels and sports clubs make it difficult to discern that this green expanse was an early example of the ruling elite's desire to imitate Europe on the Nile.

Viewed from above, Cairo's river-dependence becomes brutally clear. Not only does it become obvious how this fact enabled the city's localization, but every single park has been wrested from the Nile; the more than five million vehicles that drive the city every day are washed with Nile water; every shower or bath that the twenty million or so people here take in a day happens with Nile water; and the soccer field directly beneath the tower, as well as the horses and riders galloping along the riding facility's outside perimeter to the north, also depend upon Nile water. Without the water that flows here from Africa, there would simply be no Cairo.

Today, pessimistic predictions about Cairo's future abound, but in history there is always comfort. It was here, in this region, that the myth of the Phoenix originated. For, it was to Heliopolis (called On in the Bible), around 8 kilometres north-east of Cairo, that the famous bird with the fantastic plumage returned every 500 years. The Phoenix landed on the sun temple's burning altar in order to rise again from its own ashes, a direct parallel to Egypt, which itself re-emerged from the desert – every year, after each inundation.

A Nilometer with nothing to measure

On Roda Island's southernmost tip (you can easily see it from Cairo Tower), and not too far a drive from the Giza pyramids, stands a structure with a brown conical roof; a must-see for anyone who wants to understand Egypt and Cairo. It is the House of Inundation. Each time I have visited, I have been alone: 'Custodian, hello, where are you?' He appears, bends, unlocks the door of the house – pitch black. He switches on the light and an unusually harmonious attractive room appears. Against the wall winds a wide marble stair. In the middle of the building is a large column. We are inside one of Egypt's many Nilometers, and the most beautiful. Having occupied a central place in Egyptian life for generation upon generation (the so-called Palermo Stone from the twenty-fifth century BCE has clear inscriptions regarding Nile floods), this one at Roda Island, like all other Nilometers, is completely meaningless now. Britain's Nile policy introduced technological developments that made the Nilometer irrelevant. And so, the Nilometer's current significance is precisely its insignificance, a shift in importance that highlights the fundamental revolution Egypt has undergone in its relationship with the river during the last century.

Roda's Nilometer was raised in 861 on orders from the Abbasid caliph, al-Mutawakkil. Yet, a Nilometer has presumably stood on this spot since pharaonic times. From early on, the Egyptian state had a special water administration: *per mu*. One of its tasks was measuring flood height and trying to estimate peak crest. This allowed predictions about the harvest's outcome to be made, as well as about which control initiatives to implement, but most important of all: it determined how much tax to demand from the farmers. Several 'Nilometers' were therefore established along the river, such as here in the House of Inundation. On the column is a series of carved marks. If the water reached too few marks, everyone knew food shortages and starvation would strike that year. If it reached more than twenty-five marks, the water would be too high and stand for too long, and it would destroy that year's crops.[8] Local rulers, therefore, hired people to travel around calling the number of marks the water had reached on the river's Nilometers.

In the sixteenth century, knowledge of the historical significance behind these measurements of the Nile's flow was so widespread in Europe that Shakespeare had Mark Antony, the Roman military commander who came to power in Egypt after Julius Caesar in the fourth decade BCE, say:

> Thus do they, sir: they take the
> flow o' the Nile
> By certain scales i' the pyramid; they know,
> By the height, the lowness, or the mean, if dearth
> Or foison follow: the higher Nilus swells,
> The more it promises: as it ebbs, the seedsman
> Upon the slime and ooze scatters his grain,
> And shortly comes to harvest.[9]

Because Egypt's economy and tax revenues were determined by a single factor, hardly any other economic and social activity has occurred so regularly, for such a length of time, and has assumed such weight as measuring the Nile's flow in Egypt. In the recent era of water and climate uncertainty, however, the Nilometers' data series have proven relevant in a new way. They are a source of global climate history.

The Egyptians, moreover, also developed one of the first calendars. That was around 5,000 years ago, and it was fundamentally based on the Nile's role in society and on the river's hydrology.[10] The calendar's most important task was to tell Egyptians when the flood was coming. For this same reason, they discarded the moon calendar and developed – as a first – a sun calendar (a precursor to the Julian calendar) with 365 days. They had discovered that the Dog Star, or Sirius, was visible right before sunrise for a few days preceding the annual flood. The Nile's significance for the work rhythm and state taxes, combined with the river's hydrological reliability, was a fundamental requirement for the sun calendar's conception and significance.

When the British took political control of the Nile basin and started to tame the river with dams and hydraulic structures, measuring the river's water flow became even more important and more scientific. The ancient Nilometers ceased to be used, however, because the relationship between society and river changed.

Conservative colonialists as a revolution's vanguard

When the British, after the bombing of Alexandria and the military campaign up the Delta in 1882, took control of an Egypt that was nominally still part of the Ottoman

Empire, they knew that they had become rulers in a country where control of the Nile meant everything.[11] As if to underscore that they had now become rulers of a hydraulic state, the British established headquarters at Zamalek, in the north of Gezira Island, not far from the parks landscaped by Khedive Isma'il a couple of decades earlier. It was here they met to drink tea and whisky, and to discuss and chat. At the centre of elite British social life was Gezira Sporting Club, where members played golf, polo, squash and tennis. Almost everywhere one went on this island, the Nile was visible, a perpetual reminder that Egypt was indeed a river state. The English poet, Percy Shelley, had a few decades earlier composed a sonnet to the Nile as the British perceived it:

> O'er Egypt's land of memory floods are level,
> And they are thine, O Nile! and well thou knowest
> The soul-sustaining airs and blasts of evil,
> And fruits and poisons spring where'er thou flowest.[12]

After the British took power in Egypt, mainly to secure London's control of the Suez Canal, they quickly realized that stability and development required control of the Nile. If the country was to be able to pay off its debt to European banks, and if the occupation was to serve British economic interests, Egypt's economy had to be improved. In Egypt that meant one thing: agricultural development. London decided to go for cotton, thus following in the footsteps of Muhammad Ali. As the most profitable export crop, its cultivation would at the same time not destroy the country's food production, because cotton was cultivated in the summer, whereas wheat and other types of grain were cultivated in the winter. And also, not least: Lancashire's cotton industry was on an aggressive hunt for cheap, high-quality raw materials. Especially after the American Civil War (1861–5), Egypt had become even more of interest in this regard. This fact created a compelling logic: because cotton was a plant that best grew during summer, when the Nile carried the least amount of water, the solution must lie in increased interference with the Nile's seasonal variations – and on a steadily larger scale. In the political arena, this meant the British became increasingly more involved in control of the Nile, eventually also on the military front and outside the country's borders.

In analyses and narratives of the past, it is necessary to understand the structures that help maintain old orders and status quo, as well as the mechanisms that prompt radical change, allowing new structures to emerge and unfold. At the same time, a subject-less history is every bit as fruitless as an historical approach solely concerned with the role of the individual. It is necessary, therefore, to also know how the actors of change, those who became history's true entrepreneurs, thought.

Lord Cromer, the Earl of Baring, was titled British Consul-General in Cairo, though in reality he was Egypt's uncrowned king – or its 'puppet-master', as he was also called – from 1883 until 1907. Although Egypt was never formally a British colony, few exhibit imperialism's arrogance and paternalism as well as Lord Cromer. He wrote, for example, that the British, and himself as an Englishman, look:

> towards the scene of other administrative triumphs of worldwide fame, which his progenitors have accomplished. He looks towards India, and he says to himself,

with all the confidence of an imperial race, – I can perform this task; I have done it before now; I have poured numberless blessings on the heads of the Ryots of Bengal and Madras, who are own cousins to the Egyptian fellaheen [small farmers]; these latter also shall have water for their fields, justice in their lawcourts, and immunity from the tyranny under which they have for so long groaned.[13]

And there were few with greater vigour than Lord Cromer. One of his first steps as Egypt's de facto ruler was to recall a few British water experts from India. Cromer had been chief of finance in India and had experienced first-hand how profitable artificial irrigation could prove in tropical regions. He was convinced that there was no true conflict between Great Britain's interests and those of the Egyptians. Seeing himself as a representative of a superior, rationally oriented civilization whose advantages were self-evident, he thought that Egyptians, due to their oriental psyche, were incapable of self-governance. In Egypt, he speculated, water control was the element required to convince what he called 'the Oriental Mind' of the pre-eminence of 'Western methods', and to give London legitimacy and authority in the country. Nile policy should produce stability, not to mention lasting British control of Suez.

As Lord Cromer further wrote on Egypt and 'the Oriental Mind':

Want of accuracy, which easily degenerates into untruthfulness, is, in fact, the main characteristic of the Oriental mind. [...] The mind of the Oriental, on the other hand, like his picturesque streets, is eminently wanting in symmetry. Although the ancient Arabs acquired in a somewhat high degree the science of dialectics, their descendants are singularly deficient in the logical faculty. They are often incapable of drawing the most obvious conclusions from any simple premises of which they may admit the truth. [...] Even highly educated Egyptians are prone to refer the common occurrences of life to the intervention of some supernatural agency.[14]

At the core of British rule in Egypt was control of the Nile; it was, in fact, in many aspects what can aptly be called a hydropolitical imperial regime. Its effectiveness during the first decades sprang, among other things, from the self-assurance and ethos of the bigoted arrogance to which Cromer gave voice. Lord Cromer was the indisputable ruler and all the reports and letters he sent to London bear witness to his solid grip on the Nile's hydrological and technical character and challenges. Water-planners were among his closest colleagues – people like Colin Scott-Moncrieff, William Willcocks and William Garstin. He gave the water engineers free rein, convinced that money invested in irrigation and Nile control would be always money well spent.

Over the period of a couple of decades, the water management system, still organized in most of the country as a basin irrigation system, was revolutionized, altered and replaced with a system that enabled all-year-round cultivation. Throughout the 1880s and early 1890s, increased demand for summer water was heard from all corners of Egyptian society and from influential European pressure groups, particularly Great Britain's own and very powerful cotton lobby. The Lancashire cotton industry was seeking to reduce its dependence on American cotton and wanted to import cheap and high-quality cotton from Egypt. In addition, British banks held a strong and growing interest in seeing a blooming Egyptian economy, mainly because Egypt's foreign debt was a staggering £100 million; the annual service fees amounted to £5 million, a large part of which went to Great Britain. And Egypt's ability to pay back its British bank loans was to great extent a function of cotton exports, as well as the value of agricultural land and production, which could be taxed. A highly evocative picture of the attention the Nile in Egypt attracted was the fact that the *Times* of London regularly reported on the river's water flow. In Egypt, furthermore, the elite was involved either in the production or the selling of cotton, with the khedive himself owning most of the land. Meanwhile, living conditions in Egypt improved and the population doubled over a couple of decades, reaching almost ten million by 1897. The process Muhammad Ali started took a mighty leap forward under Cromer's leadership.

Against such a background, it is enough to say that conservative, paternalistic and even racist Victorian colonial officials stood behind one of the most important revolutions in Egypt's history. The British transformed the country at a tempo, to an extent and in a way that Egypt had never experienced. Roads, railways, schools and, eventually, universities were built; women were enrolled in schools and the corvée system (mandatory forced labour) was abolished. But, first and foremost, and essential to all the other reforms, was that the British revolutionized the relationship between Egyptians and their life artery, symbolized above all by the first dam at Aswan, opened in 1902, which for the first time changed the way the river flowed in Egypt, by modifying its natural, seasonal patterns. It became possible to radically expand the cultivated area; three growing seasons became more and more common, and the annual rhythm that had permeated Egyptian village life for millennia was transformed.

The British officials who met for tea and polo at the Gezira Club, then, brimming with imperial self-confidence and paternalistic arrogance, but having also first-rate administrative support and technological and hydrological competence, astonishingly became leaders of one of the most fundamental upheavals in Egypt's many-thousands-of-years-old history. Their countless decisions and their deliberate initiatives were the basis for this revolution, although colonial expansion acted also as a blind force, when first let loose. The new imperialism swept over social life and existing power relations, it had the ability to uproot old traditions and production methods, and it organized new power relationships, economic muscle and technological competence, all of which exerted its strong influence 'behind the back', so to speak, of the British administrators who spent their afternoons playing polo on the Nile's banks, often engrossed in the day's trivialities.

The form that British imperialism took in Egypt in the first few decades of its rule proved, therefore, to be a revolutionary force, a powerful transformative agent that put traditional Egyptian institutions and the age-old seasonal rhythms of society under pressure. Thus, although formally Egypt never became a colony of London, in all matters concerning the Nile, the British occupied the master's seat. That meant they wielded power over the most important questions defining Egypt's fate. Because they ruled the Nile, they were also Egypt's de facto sovereigns, though officially they governed together with Egyptian administrators.

The river as carrot and stick

In 1916, during the First World War, Egypt became a British protectorate. While the Versailles negotiations after the war helped bring peace and short-term political stability to Europe, they produced in their wake revolution in the Nile Valley, as they also did in China. Both the Egyptian revolution of 1919, spurred on by the Versailles negotiation rhetoric of US President Woodrow Wilson regarding the right of nations to self-determination, and the collapse of the Ottoman Empire, happened with a violence that caught the British by surprise and started a process that in 1922 led London to accept Egypt's nominal independence. Meanwhile, Britain maintained its sway over the country's foreign policy, secured the right to build a large military base at Suez, and retained responsibility for canal operations – and, not least, the British were still to control everything having to do with the Nile.

From the close of the First World War and in the wake of the Egyptian revolution and its 'independence' in 1922, Britain's chief line was to develop Egypt's irrigation system on the one hand, and use their control of the Nile upstream of Egypt as a stick against Egyptian nationalism on the other hand. Britain publicized its plan to develop, with the backing of the English cotton industry, a gigantic cotton farm in Sudan with the aid of Nile water. This project was important both to the economy of Sudan and to British cotton businesses, but it also had a more covert diplomatic aspect. It served as a card in a Nile game whose purpose was to threaten Egypt into compliance in hopes that the peasant farmers would turn against the nationalist elite instead of against London. In other words, the British wanted the farmers to blame the nationalists instead of London when their small fields received less water. The tactic failed.

The Egyptian nationalists, as expected, condemned the project in the strongest possible terms and accused the British of wanting to 'turn off the tap', as they put it. They pressured for more independence from London, and in 1924 Sir Lee Stack, the British Governor-General of the Sudan, was murdered while driving through the streets of Cairo. After the murder of Stack, the British in Egypt and Sudan responded with what they considered one of their most effective weapons – the Nile. The logic behind this water diplomacy, or hydrodiplomacy, was that nothing would hurt more than using the river as a stick. The so-called Allenby ultimatum of 1924 did not deliver the expected jolt to the Egyptian masses. Then the British Governor-General of Egypt, Lord Allenby, and London, advocated breaking earlier agreements with Egypt regarding how much Nile water Sudan could use, as a punishment for the murder of Sir Lee Stack. The ultimatum instead fomented increasing and more extensive nationalist, anti-British rage. The nationalists exploited it for all it was worth, claiming it proved Britain's true intentions: while posing as Egypt's guarantors of Nile water, the British prepared to marshal the river as a weapon against Egyptians if British interests were threatened. By the end of the 1920s, the British decided to adopt a different hydrodiplomatic Nile strategy with regard to Egypt: the policy would now be that of carrot rather than stick when it came to Egyptian opinion, the country's elite, the Nile and London's control of it. In 1929, London, on behalf of its East African colonies, entered into a Nile Agreement with Egypt whose significance would be felt up to our day. The agreement, recognized on the one hand that the Sudan needed some more water for its development, and on the other hand, and more importantly, that Egypt had historic rights in the Nile waters and that the East African territories did not need Nile water for their development. The agreement took the shape of two letters: the first was addressed to Lord Lloyd, the British High Commissioner, by Muhammed Mahmoud Pasha, President of the Egyptian Council of Ministers; the second was the High Commissioner's reply. But most importantly: in practice, the agreement gave Egypt rights of veto over any water projects upstream. Egypt now had the right to deny all upstream projects if such projects reduced water flow into their country. And, as London assured Egypt, the upstream countries along the White Nile had, so to speak, no interest in Nile exploitation, because they had an abundance of rain. The 1929 Nile Agreement can be interpreted as a diplomatic move on London's part, where they attempted to convince the Egyptians that Cairo had a self-interest in maintaining a decent and friendly relationship to Great Britain – if they were going to be guaranteed water to live by.

It is no exaggeration to say that this water-use agreement proved a basic framework for economic development throughout the whole Nile basin for the rest of the British period. The 1929 Agreement has also defined, more decisively than any other diplomatic factor, the postcolonial era along the Nile's entire waterway. We will, therefore, return to it again and again.

The Muslim Brotherhood will 'secure the Nile's sources'

In March 1928, at a point when the British, self-consciously and with full colonial arrogance, displayed their values and lifestyle throughout Cairo in countless ways (not least in their famous evening balls at the grandest hotels), when steadily more Western tourists came to Egypt and placed their mark on society, and when large swathes of the Egyptian elite thought that only by following the Western way culturally and economically could their country progress, the Muslim Brotherhood arose in Egypt under Hassan al-Banna's leadership. The group was founded in the city of Ismailia; with Hassan al-Banna were six workers from the Suez Canal Company.

The Brotherhood immediately gained a substantial following and developed into a grassroots movement with hundreds of thousands of members. The group distanced itself from other anti-British resistance movements by fundamentally rejecting the entire Western project – its political ideas, its lifestyle and its values. The Brotherhood emerged in the Suez Canal area. It received support in part as a reaction against British conduct as the rulers of the area and against European morals in the ports along the canal. It took inspiration from similar movements in Islamic history that located all wisdom in the Qur'an and in the actions of the Prophet.

The Brotherhood was active in the struggle against British rule as they fought for *sharia* and the *Hadith* to be the single source of law. They pursued what they termed a modern Islam where religion, politics, economics and norms would all blend, guided by the true faith. For the Muslim Brotherhood, Islam represented a total system: it was necessary in order to create a beneficial and just social organization and – most importantly – it would allow for a society structured in accordance with what they interpreted to be Allah's will. The movement's long-term goal was to re-establish the Islamic caliphate so that this included Spain (Spain was partly under Islamic rule between 711 and 1492).

One of the group's most famous ideological leaders, Sayyid Qutb, most clearly illustrates the group's clear rejection of the West and all that it represented. Sayyid Qutb was educated at American universities, and it was there, at the very centre of Western politics and culture, that he thought he perceived and comprehended the manifest contrasts between Islam and what he interpreted as Western civilization's dominant values, issues such as secularism, ideas on gender equality, parliamentary democracy and so forth. From the very beginning, the Brotherhood held discussions regarding which, and how many, compromises were necessary, from a practical political standpoint, to attain their long-term goals; and to the present day this subject continues to be the one around which the Brotherhood's internal contradictions revolve, instead of whether such long-term goals are right or wrong.

In their programme, the Muslim Brotherhood identified not only *jihad* as an objective and ideal, but also the goal of 'securing the Nile's sources'. That idea still stands, but its concrete meaning is now unclear. When it was first formulated, back when the British controlled the Nile's sources, it had a military and politico-diplomatic overtone. It was, at the same time, a demand that contradicted passages in the Qur'an, where emphasis is placed on water being of Allah, as being Allah's blessing, a social good; in this context, great weight is also given to the fact that the Qur'an mentions water sixty-three times. As, after the ousting of President Hosni Mubarak in 2011, the Muslim Brotherhood got the majority of the votes in the elections in 2012, one of their major tasks in governing Egypt was to navigate and consolidate such religiously sanctioned ideas with a very complicated water diplomacy.

They failed, as we shall see.

A role awaiting a hero

Political developments in the Middle East after the Second World War, with a wing-clipped and bankrupt British Empire, the establishment of Israel as a state, and a strongly dawning pan-Arabic and anti-imperialistic movement, made it clear for many Egyptians that London's days as ruler of the Nile and Egypt were numbered. Resistance against the then current imperial world order grew strongly, from Asia's jungles to Latin America and in the Middle East, particularly in the densely populated Nile Delta where, in addition, the demand for more water became increasingly evident and politically potent.

At that point, Gamal Abdel Nasser entered the political arena with a lot of personal energy and popular support. Arabic and Egyptian resistance against London's control steadily strengthened. The Arabic world was on the lookout for a figure who could provide faith and leadership in the battle against European influence in the region. Nasser, who with great success managed to fill this role of hero in waiting, wrote: 'Today, in their new-found freedom, the Egyptian people have found self-respect. [. . .]

Already, our hope and faith in a regenerated Egypt are wiping out from our memory the humiliation and sufferings of an earlier time'.[15]

When Nasser, as leader of the 'Free Officers', seized power through a military coup in 1952, the foundation for a political revolution was laid, and, more fundamentally over the long-term, for a revolution in Egypt's relationship to its river. This was the first time in more than 2,500 years, since the Persians had occupied Egypt *c.* 500 BCE, that Egypt was governed by an Egyptian and that the country's lifeline was under Egyptian rule. The Nile was now dammed and controlled inside the country's borders.

Gamal Abdel Nasser was the son of a postal worker from a village in Upper Egypt and had been educated as a soldier in the British-led army. In 1952 he was thirty-four years old and well known as a hero from the war against Israel in 1948. For three years he had operated in secret to build cells within the army, ones that did not know of each other's existence, just groups of four or five people. From the beginning, Nasser's goal was to drive the British from Egypt, but eventually also to remove the corrupt and rich King Farouk, who had come to symbolize the imperial system and the colonial elite in the same way as representatives of Great Britain itself. Nasser had earlier been involved in an attempt to murder the army's chief commander Hussein Sirri Amer, but the sound of shots, women screaming, children crying and shouts for help pursued him throughout the night, he later recounted in *Egypt's Liberation: The Philosophy of the Revolution*. Nasser ended, therefore, by praying for the army chief to survive and renouncing terrorism as a strategy. Instead, a bloodless coup was waged by the rebels, set in motion by more than a hundred young officers under Nasser's leadership. After a lightning action, they took power on 23 July, and General Muhammed Naguib proclaimed Egypt a republic. The new regime's stated goals were ambitious and represented the coming together of anti-colonial nationalism and Arab socialism.

On 26 July, with the king's palace in Alexandria already surrounded by Nasser's soldiers, the king signed his abdication. Then, dressed in an admiral's uniform, he boarded his yacht *El Mahrousa* with his family members and sixty-six cases of gold, jewels and precious items – to go to Europe. The Ottoman-Albanian monarchy's time in Egypt was over; Muhammad Ali's and his family's governance was finished after 150 years. The erstwhile king was sent into exile, and the new regime did not have to punish him, it was argued, for history would sentence him to oblivion. The new regime did not need to waste its time on him.

Nasser was a charismatic, almost supernatural character; he was the man who could redeem past humiliations and restore Egypt's previous greatness, provide the country with growth and dignity, and allow it to take its natural place in the modern world. However, his greatest and most revolutionary idea, which more than anything else has come to survive him, was a new, high dam at Aswan, the Aswan High Dam, Sadd al-Ali, or the Nasser Dam as it would also be called. An unknown Greek agronomist, Adrian Daninos, living in Egypt had first come up with the dam proposal and had put it to Egypt's state leadership.

Nasser, on the other hand, had rejected a proposal from the British in Sudan to build dams along the entire river, and he did not buy the argument that it would cost less, reduce water loss through evaporation and, from a hydrological perspective, prove the most rational plan. The British idea was rejected as unrealistic because it required a political stability upstream that did not exist, and the new leadership also thoroughly understood Britain's strategic interest in this proposal.

Nasser also overlooked critical objections from many of his water engineers, who warned against the negative consequences of the Aswan Dam, especially that it would dam up the silt and prevent it from fertilizing the fields. These potential, exceedingly long-range consequences, were subordinate to Nasser's immediate and grand political and economic goal: a new and enormous dam on Egypt's own territory that could realize, express and market the new government's independent modernization policy. The dam's purpose, wrote Nasser, was to transform Egypt into Africa's Japan, at that time a non-Western ideal for political leaders aiming at developing their countries independent from Western powers.[16] Egypt, already one of the leading countries in the Non-Aligned Movement, would show the world that they could forge an autonomous path to modernization. One of the Nile experts in the Foreign Office described the idea of the dam suggested by Adrian Daninos, when he first heard about it, as 'fantastic and not worthy of serious consideration',[17] and a British development expert in the Middle East characterized Daninos as a man 'full of mad ideas for the Nile'.[18]

They remained particularly sceptical of the proposal on three grounds. Hydrologically, they believed it was smarter from a water economy standpoint to bet on their more comprehensive, integrated Nile Valley Plan. They were also doubtful about whether the dam could even be built, technically speaking, due to weaknesses in the geology of the area. First and foremost, however, they were against it because they knew what Nasser himself was also entirely convinced of: a new, gigantic dam within Egypt's own borders would undermine the political-diplomatic significance of London's control over the Nile upstream in Central Africa.

Nasser's dam would have world-historical consequences: the high political game surrounding it revealed that the British Empire, when it came to global power politics, had become almost impotent. It thrust the United States into the centre of Middle Eastern development, and it brought the Soviet Union fully into the global arena as an investor in developing former colonies to advance their own strategic aims. The dam also represented the first real show of relevance and power of the new international aid system that in the late 1940s had been established by the US government in this part of Africa, since it was, by far, the largest and most prestigious project the World Bank had supported.

The Suez Crisis and the dam

The summer of 1956 was a summer when the Cold War was at its hottest – the rebellion in Hungry and especially the Suez Crisis were in the headlines all over the world. Though the first was quickly reduced to an important memory, the second led to an immediate political earthquake.

The background to this conflict was tied directly to the Nile. Egypt and Nasser had sought international support for building the new giant dam planned at Aswan. The World Bank had decided to support what would be the largest project in the Bank's – at that time – short history; as such, one can say the project announced the aid epoch in the Nile Valley. Both Great Britain and the United States signalled that they would give Egypt loans for the dam, and both governments were focused on their own companies receiving the lucrative contracts. Prime Minister Anthony Eden in London officially confirmed Britain's support of the dam as late as December 1955. Yet, half a year later, both the United States and Great Britain withdrew their loan commitments.

In response, Nasser nationalized the Suez Canal. Fees on boat traffic would finance Egypt's dam he declared, to the British government's fury.

The history behind the various conflicts around financing the Aswan High Dam is complex and difficult to reconstruct. Because the question has proven so central when it comes to Africa's decolonization and to the Cold War's growth there, influential interpretations of what occurred are strongly coloured by the day's dominant politico-ideological movements and disputes. There are metres upon metres of archive boxes devoted to this history and I have been through much of what exists in London, at the Eisenhower Library in Kansas, at Princeton University and in the World Bank Archives in Washington, DC. The events and the diplomatic game were much more complex and intertwined than most influential studies have uncovered, and the conflicts of interests in particular between London and Washington were far more decisive for what happened during the Suez Crisis and the processes leading up to it, than what conventional ideas and illusions regarding a common Anglo-American front against the Soviet Union have left room for. Elsewhere, I have shown in great detail that in the mid-1950s it was more important for the United States to weaken British imperialism in the region than to fight the Cold War against the Soviet Union, despite what the official version emphasized and what later historical research has largely focused upon.[19]

Winston Churchill, who served as British prime minister from 1951 to 1955, was one of many who long and firmly believed that the United States and Great Britain had a special friendship after the Second World War, and that the United States would support London's interests in the Middle East and Egypt. The reality was, nonetheless, that President Dwight D. Eisenhower and Secretary of State John Foster Dulles consciously, and with great ingenuity, used the game for the Nile and Nasser's Aswan High Dam to undermine London's position as the Nile Valley's ruler and the chief power at Suez, even as they sought to preserve London as a close US ally. However, they also humiliated London before the entire world when the United Nations (henceforth UN) condemned the armed British attack on Egypt in 1956. Meanwhile, the United States continued to emphasize its friendship with London. What the United States mainly wanted was access to the region's markets and resources, and in that context Great Britain was in fact a greater problem, practically speaking, than the Soviet Union at the time, even if that was something the Americans obviously could not publicly say, allied with London as they were through NATO.

British policy up until 1956 was to offer Nasser loans for the dam that he prioritized much higher than all other development projects in the country. They authorized the loans long after they knew that Nasser had purchased weapons from Soviet allies, and after his anti-Western rhetoric at the Bandung Conference in 1955 had resounded around the globe. The reason for this was that the British government did not believe Cairo would be able to meet the loan conditions it had set, conditions that revolved particularly around Egypt's division of Nile water with Sudan. London had established as a requirement that, in order to receive the loan, Egypt and Sudan must agree on how much water the two countries would receive from the Nile. Given the wide gaps between Egypt's and Sudan's political positions in 1945 and 1955, this seemed an impossible goal. When Nasser, therefore, discovered that he must relent on this question, he would prove more biddable overall – or so the tactical evaluations went. As a result, when Cairo and Khartoum suddenly, and against all odds, forged an agreement on water distribution, and on the compensation Sudan would receive for the damming of land on their territory, the foundations for Britain's Nile diplomacy collapsed.

What should London and Washington do now? Neither was a proponent of the dam they had promised to support. They believed the dam was too large and that it would increase Egypt's autonomy and obstinacy at Suez. Nonetheless, the United States was even more concerned with weakening London's position and that of European imperialism in general. Washington understood the obvious: through loans and conditions, and particularly if British firms also built the dam, London would be able to maintain its position there and the Americans would have a more difficult time when it came to unseating Britain as a Nile power. The American government denied Nasser a loan because it understood that the move would end Great Britain's days as a power player in the region. The United States humiliated London in the very arena that was, and had been, London's chief display window and 'vote-getter' in Egypt and Sudan: Britain's ability to control the Nile and to develop the irrigation system. When the United States suddenly withdrew its loan commitment, Great Britain had no other choice but to follow suit. The country had neither the economic resources nor the political capital to provide the loan without US support.

But the Americans' unilateral decision surprised the British; it caught them unprepared and they were unsure which policy would best serve their interests. Publicly, both the United States and Great Britain created the impression of solidarity. When they withdrew their loan offers, both said that it was to punish Nasser for his weapons purchase from Czechoslovakia and his courting of Eastern Bloc countries. This explanation convinced contemporary observers and many subsequent historians, but it does not hold water. As mentioned, Nasser had had such contacts long before London and Washington issued their official loan commitments for the building of the dam. This Cold War rhetoric was employed because it provided cover for all parties and because the real explanation would not tolerate the light of day.

When Dulles, the US Secretary of State, summoned Egypt's envoy in Washington without first informing London, and informed him that the United States would not give his country the loan after all, Nasser responded a few days later by nationalizing the Suez Canal.

The Nile game, which had proven so important in establishing Great Britain as a colonial power in the region, would, as it turns out, now herald the British Empire's death throes in Africa; or as Nikita Khrushchev, the Soviet leader, triumphantly put it after the Suez Crisis in 1956, when the Cold War was at its zenith: Britain's attempt to stop Nasser militarily during the Suez Crisis was 'the last roar of the British Lion'.[20] London's role as Lord of the Nile was definitively over, and the new Aswan High Dam, which was finished (almost to the day) seventy years after the first dam, became a sure symbol that Egypt was finally master of the river and, therefore, of itself.

The British ambassador to Egypt, Sir Humphrey Trevelyan, received orders on 23 October 1956, to significantly reduce embassy personnel. Egypt broke diplomatic relations on 1 November and by noon that day Egyptians closed the door to the embassy. No one was allowed in or out and electricity and telephone lines were cut. The Swiss chargé d'affaires took over the handling of British interests in Egypt. Britain was forced to negotiate for days for its employees' safe passage out of the country. Eventually, it was decided that they would depart with a special train on 10 November. Sir Humphrey himself locked the ambassador's residence and that same evening boarded the train to Alexandria, and then proceeded further to Libya. The British Nile empire was finished, an empire that had left very clear marks on the region's history, and that represented the only period in the basin's long history where it had been under unified political control.

The Soviet Union as the modernizer of the Nile

The new Aswan High Dam became a symbol of Nasser's political power and prestige, but it also proved one of the most enduring testimonies to the technological capacity of that day's superpower.

The dam, for its part, freed Egypt from the despotic power of the river's seasonal and annual variations. The whole country received electricity, and millions of new acres could be cultivated. As mentioned, the Aswan High Dam was planned by Nasser and his regime to be the motor that would transform the country into Africa's Japan, and it was also meant to grant Egypt real national autonomy from the power of the upstream countries. It was the symbol of the Free Officers' revolution and their radical break with the past; it was the materialization of the New Age of modernizing Egypt.

As Nasser described the dam to his country in 1958: 'For thousands of years the Great Pyramids of Egypt were foremost among the engineering marvels of the world. They ensured life after death to the Pharaohs. Tomorrow, the gigantic High Dam, more significant and seventeen times greater than the Pyramids, will provide a higher standard of living for all Egyptians.'[21]

The dam *is* gigantic. It was, when it was completed in 1971, the world's largest artificial dam, and the power station there was the world's third largest. The dam was 111 metres tall and 3,830 metres long; material equal to seventeen Cheops Pyramids went into its construction. The new dam would prevent 32 billion cubic metres of water from running unused into the sea and have a capacity more than three times that of the Hoover dam, the world's most famous dam at the time. However, the impressive dam construction that we see is a dwarf compared to what lies beneath it. Russian experts injected the ground with a mixture of cement, bentonite and aluminosilicate at three times atmospheric pressure to create a kind of underground 'sealant screen', a hidden wall over a hundred metres deep that prevents subterranean filtration of the river water.

The dam's annual power output, furthermore, would be around 10 billion kilowatt hours. It would expand agricultural area by around 6 million acres, and around

2.8 million acres in Upper Egypt would now be harvested three times a year, as opposed to once, as had been the case previously. Egypt would be utterly protected from flood and drought. The dam would thus be both bank and insurance. When Ethiopians were struck by major famines in the 1980s, Egyptian farmers continued to cultivate as before. They could do this without reserve because the new Nile reservoir had collected and stored water for multiple years. When flooding struck Sudan in the 1990s, Egyptians could proceed without fear of the raging waters, because everything was halted by Nasser's High Dam. And finally, for the cruise industry the river would be improved for navigational purposes.

Today you can take an elevator to the top of the 70-metre high concrete lotus blossom erected in honour of Soviet–Egyptian friendship. Each of the five lotuses looks more like a sword than a flower stalk, and the carvings resemble a pharaonic version of social realism. The monument seems strangely anachronistic now, and for the Soviets it was an expensive project.

The Soviet Union's involvement in the Aswan Dam ended as the US Secretary of State John Foster Dulles had predicted, or foreseen, in 1957, when the Americans had just before given the Soviet Union an opening into the Middle East by allowing them, instead of the British, to finance and build the dam. This happened during the McCarthy era in the United States, and the US government and Dulles were sharply criticized for their inability to stop Moscow's entry into the Middle East, and for the perceived weakening of the West this entailed. However, Dulles, a man who was otherwise known as a Cold War hawk, dismissed the criticism. The United States, by luring the Soviet Union in, forced the country to assume commitments they would not be able to shoulder and keep. This would weaken the Soviet economy and after a time they would be tossed out of Egypt. Then it would again be the United States' turn, or so Dulles thought. Whether he was searching for an argument to cover up what he privately considered to be a defeat, or whether he was just exceptionally far-seeing, his predictions panned out.

The Soviet Union's activities in Egypt eventually became so visible and all-encompassing that they generated opposition. Just a few years after the dam was finished, Moscow proved the big loser. The new US-friendly president of Egypt, Anwar al-Sadat, who assumed power after Nasser died of illness, expelled the Soviet Union's experts not long after they had poured the dam's last few metres. Their expulsion from Egypt – the Middle East's most important country and, at the time, Africa's most populous – after the Russians had invested so much economic and technological prestige there, was a serious diplomatic defeat for the Soviet Union in the face of the Non-Aligned world. It was a harbinger of things to come, including how the Soviet Union would crumble just a few decades later.

'The Lady of the Nile'

Seldom has the gap between modern cultural history in Egypt and the Middle East on the one hand, and the West on the other, been more evident than when 'the Lady of the Nile' died in 1975. On 3 February of that year an enormous funeral procession wound through Cairo's streets. 'The Lady of the Nile', as she was known, was dead. The greatest singer in Egypt and the Arabic world, Egypt's cultural icon and soul, Umm Kulthum, was no more. In Europe and the United States, almost no one had heard of her. But the Middle East stood still.

Umm Kulthum not only sang her way into Middle Eastern history in general, but also into Nile history with the song 'Tahwil al-Nil' ('The Transformation of the Nile'). The song praised the building of the Aswan Dam and what this meant for Egypt. Its idealistic and pathos-rich lyrics underscore how Nasser's dam project gripped and mobilized an entire nation's enthusiasm.

Not only did Umm Kulthum sing about the dam but she encouraged women to sell their jewellery to help finance it. She became a living national icon, and she is the only woman ever to have been honoured with a statue in a public square in Cairo.

All cultures, so to speak, have their divas. The Arabic world has Umm Kulthum.[22] With a loyal audience stretching from North Africa to the Levant, and which encompasses the whole of Arabic society, she is considered to be one of the twentieth century's most gifted female singers. On Roda Island, just a few stone throws from the Nilometer, is a small museum dedicated to her memory. Several decades after her death, Umm Kulthum's popularity is still great, for as countless articles about her say: her voice strikes a chord in the Arabic soul. When she sang live on the radio the first Thursday of every month, Egypt listened.

'The Lady of the Nile' gave her last concert in the Palais du Nil on the riverbank in Cairo. It was there her voice cracked. Normally, she could sing for hours at a time. On a high note in the middle of the second song, it happened. The singer stiffened. The orchestra stopped playing. Total silence. The audience was shocked, for it was the first time in her long career this had happened. Then a spontaneous applause broke out, an applause that seemed to have no end. When she was finally able to continue, Umm Kulthum finished the song as quickly as she could. 'The Lady of the Nile' never performed again, but her song devoted to the dam demonstrates how the dam, at times more than anything else, brought the nation together.

Adrift on the Nile and a Nobel Prize winner

In the Mohandeseen area in Cairo stands the only statue in Egypt erected while its model was still alive. After Cairo author Naguib Mahfouz won the Nobel Prize, he became part of the branding of Egypt and of Cairo's tourist areas, and you can eat at Mahfouz Café and visit Midaq Alley, which gave its name to one of the author's most famous novels.

Mahfouz's books present a dense picture of life in Cairo, an overcrowded city where more than twenty million people go about their daily business, a dizzying array of human fates and histories. I enter Mahfouz's literary world, walking past one nameless passageway after the next, but where people seem somehow to live their secluded lives. It is as if every alleyway, every single street corner, has a particular atmosphere. Every time I have visited old Cairo I have thought: these combinations of boutiques and trades and shoppers belong to a vanishing world, surrounded by and gradually overtaken by a noisy, ever-chaotic urban space. But then you discover that they are still here, and when you walk from quarter to quarter, or sit at one of the countless tables standing rather askew in the street to have a cup of coffee or smoke a water pipe, it is easy to get the feeling that these alleyways are rooted together deep down and that, amidst this chaos and order, they shape the identity of the place that Ibn Khaldun called 'the mother of all cities'. The atmosphere of the entire area seems to exist according to its own force, separate from nature's might and divorced from the Nile world that has ultimately shaped it, and which itself changes at a rapid pace.

There are passages and side streets here running every which way, a metre or two wide, many under roofs – furniture makers, tailors, chess players, wagons, motorcycles, cars, donkeys, cyclists – and the air is full of a big city's smells. Islamic Cairo, the heart of medieval Cairo, is completely different from the modern downtown district and suburbs to the west. The area is neither more nor less Islamic than the rest of the city, but it is the part that harbours the most famous Islamic monuments, many of them raised by the Fatimids, such as the al-Azhar Mosque, begun in the tenth century, and the city gates, especially Bab al-Futuh, finished in 1087. In contrast to the Islamic quarters in other cities, the area continues to thrive as a large, busy centre for worship, trade, tourism and shopping – and all at once. It was of these street spaces and quarters that Florence Nightingale wrote in 1849 that Cairo was the rose of cities, the pearl of 'Moorish' architecture, lamenting that it was simply not possible to describe an Arab city, at least not with European words.[23]

Mahfouz has also written about the Nile. In literature in general, the river has become a metaphor for all the world's impulses and for developments in Egypt, not to mention an arena where human drama with its various forms and different content can play out. While George Bernard Shaw wrote in *Caesar and Cleopatra* of their being full of vigour and stamina in the country of the Nile, Mahfouz, the only literature Nobel Prize winner from the Nile Valley and the Middle East, wrote an entirely different book about life in Egypt, also with the Nile as a backdrop. The novel of Mahfouz concentrates specifically on people who *lack* energy, who simply allow themselves to be driven by history's flow, so to speak, even as they literally stand motionless, since the plot unfolds on a moored boat on Cairo's Nile. The title of the book is *Adrift on the Nile*.

Mahfouz wrote books about Egyptian nationalism and identity, about traditional values locked in struggle with modern ideas, but also about existential questions. In *Adrift on the Nile*, the river becomes a metaphor for a life beyond the individual's control, or more precisely, a life the individual cannot control. It deals with a group of people from different backgrounds who, during the 1950s and early 1960s, have turned their back on society. They take drugs and let society sail its course, while they themselves go with the flow of a subject-less history; they are passively 'adrift on the Nile'.

Nasser put a stop to whatever existed of such passive adaptation to 'the river's flow'. Around the same time as the book went to press, the Egyptians came together in a national vow: they would take charge of the Nile.

An artificial waterfall in the desert

We creep along at a snail's pace between cars whose drivers seem to think that traffic laws apply to everyone but themselves. Abruptly, traffic unsnarls; cars shoot forward and people cross the street as if putting their lives in Fate's hands. Thousands of noises crowd through the open car window (the yellow taxi is past its prime and I cannot get the window to roll up). We drive by the Papyrus Centre, where yesterday an attempt was made to trick me into buying overpriced papyrus paper I did not need, before we pass Giza and see the pyramids, rising on the left against a grey, polluted sky. I have always liked this chaos; it forms an element of Cairo's insistent charm, but it also feels good to get a break; to travel away from here.

A friend retrieves me from the hotel on the outskirts of the city; we are bound for his family's vacation home, located on the road between Cairo and Alexandria. He definitely belongs to the Egyptian elite, but his affluence is only such that, as we drive along what is suggestively called the Desert Road, the car's hood keeps popping open while he laughs in his charming manner at both himself and the car. The property sits in the middle of the desert, although, like other similar properties in the same area, it has been transformed into a small lush oasis: the high, thick grass on the green lawn protected by a thick hedge thumbs its nose at the surrounding desert.

West of the Cairo-Alexandria road, and 65 kilometres south-west of Faiyum city lies Wadi al-Rayan, a large depression in the middle of the desert. Here, of all places, is found Egypt's only waterfall. It is not exactly a Niagara or a Victoria, but it is more surprising for all that. After spending the night under the desert's starry sky and travelling for hours through a sandy sea, we spy a razor-thin strip of green vegetation running along the valley's bottom. It is the only green visible for kilometres around. We leave the road, and there, obscured by verdant growth, runs a small stream! I follow it and glimpse two quite large lakes downstream. And this is no desert trick; it is no Fata Morgana, but something real, a fact made abundantly clear to me by the eager offers I receive from Egyptians who have made a living organizing boat tours on the lakes. Just before entering the lake, the water cascades over several shelves in the landscape and forms a waterfall where Egyptians can stand in water up to their knees, where women lift their long skirts and hold their niqabs in place as they experience the universal pleasure of running water.

In 1974, the Egyptian government under President Sadat began constructing this artificial watercourse, which consists of a 9-kilometre open canal and an 8-kilometre tunnel. The Nile itself is more than 50 kilometres away and not visible here but nonetheless it is Nile water that creates this sparkling desert waterscape. The canal cuts between the sand dunes, carrying water from the Faiyum Oasis, water that is too saline to be used in artificial irrigation. The Nile water that flows through the desert here is no life-giver. It is dead water, drainage water that has been used to irrigate plants and trees, but which now has become so saline that it must be removed from the cultivated fields to prevent it from destroying the crop.

The waterfall is modest, but this fact provides precisely a spectacular example of how the Egyptians, generation after generation, have relocated and channelled Nile water – sending it criss-crossing the desert sand for every conceivable purpose; to build cities and vacation sites, farms and here also an artificial waterfall. But water control will – due to the many conflicting demands it must fulfil both in societies and nature and due to its infinite ability to ultimately escape humanity's attempts to tame it – always have a flipside.

This eternal and inherent dualism of Nile control is evident in Karnak, a place that at once symbolizes Egyptian civilization's persistence, as well as its intimate relationships with the river's way of running.

Thebes and Karnak in danger

Karnak! In the *Iliad*, Homer himself spoke in elevated and exalted tones of the riches of Thebes: 'Thebes of Egypt, where treasures in greatest store are laid up in men's houses, – Thebes which is a city of an hundred gates.'[24] And Florence Nightingale wrote that there are no words that celebrate death as this temple complex.[25] Yet perhaps the most iconic description is provided by her contemporary Flaubert, who captured a first impression common to many: Thebes as a 'land of giants'.[26] Today Thebes' magnificent temples near Luxor are one of many clear signs that Egypt has overestimated humankind's ability to take control of the Nile, or has underestimated the consequences of taming it.

On the south side of the Karnak complex is an artificial dam that holds what ancient Egyptians considered to be particularly sacred Nile water. It is not nearly so spectacular as the colonnades, and it is therefore easy to overlook. The dam is 200 metres long, 117 metres wide, and had been installed even before Hatshepsut's reign (1479–1458 BCE). However, the dam's significance within the temple complex as part of a ritual whole cannot be overstated. It was this dam that stood in direct contact with Nu, the primeval waters where life began. The water here was conducted from the Nile through subterranean canals. The stone walls enclosing the rectangular dam have a wave design, the hieroglyphic symbol for flowing or running water. The dam was used by priests for rituals and ceremonies and as a place to cleanse the soul. At the same time, it had a very practical function: it was also used as a Nilometer. When walking around it while the thermometer registers about 45°C, it comes as no surprise that the dam is one of the oldest and most obvious examples of how the sacred and the profane coexisted. How refreshing must it have been to cleanse the soul in this place?

In the last few years Karnak has also become interesting for a very different reason. This temple to which people have made pilgrimage for thousands of years, to marvel at, to be stunned by, and to come face to face with this incredible, almost superhuman but nonetheless human ambition, is threatened by the very Nile to which it pays homage. Slowly the water seeps along the base of the columns, beyond the reach of human eye and camera lens. Too much artificial irrigation and too poor drainage after the new Aswan Dam began operations in 1971 has resulted in the water table rising slowly and, it seems, inevitably. The porous sandstone absorbs the water. This process increases the air's moisture and salt content, something that threatens the monuments, including those parts above ground level.

At the beginning of the third millennium an international campaign was implemented with support from the United States, Sweden and other countries to keep the storm god Amun's feet dry and the ground beneath the columns stable. It appears that the campaign, at least for the time being, has been successful. The water level beneath Karnak has receded. And I can also clearly see that the water level has sunk in the sacred dam there. However, these targeted, technical interventions have not stopped the general trend, and the Nile, which in its day formed the basis for these remarkable civilizations, in the long run stands in danger of toppling what it once created.

In the early morning light, a flat blanket of fog rests over the plains around Luxor. To the east I can glimpse Karnak's columns, to the west the desert mountains that mark the entrance to the Valley of the Kings and, in between, the river winding northwards, a golden strip reflecting the rays of the sun. I observe all this from above, from the basket of a hot air balloon that glides soundlessly above the courtyard preceding Hatshepsut's temple and over the Colossi of Memnon, distracted only by the pilot who entertains us by repeatedly joking that he is going to jump out because he cannot tolerate heights. As he stops talking, as if he suddenly understands why we are here, a special atmosphere and stillness immediately grips those in the balloon's basket; the landscape's beauty and the grandeur and stillness of the ancient monuments are overwhelming; it silences us. As the sun shines on the green acres down by the riverbanks, I am tempted, however, to shout the question that playwright Ibsen posed when travelling here in 1869: 'Whereby have you deserved to see all this glory?'[27]

The Valley of the Kings and ideals of beauty

The ancient Egyptians were exceedingly focused on portraying their lives, and manifold detail-rich stories and colourful lifelike drawings and inscriptions have been preserved up to this day.

One of my favourites is not from Upper Egypt, but from the tomb of Ti at Saqqara, the first pyramid. Ti was a central administrator in the Fifth Dynasty and his title was 'overseer' of the pyramids. His tomb contains several unusually clear depictions of Egyptian life. One of them shows a shepherd driving cattle through a gap while carrying a calf across his shoulders. The small animal turns its head toward its anxious mother, who, with a body language full of tenderness, stretches her neck towards her calf. With such dynamic scenes it becomes possible to imagine how things looked and how people lived and worked along the Nile.

However, the paintings located not far from Luxor are the most impressive in the Valley of the Kings and Queens – the Great and Majestic Necropolis of the Millions of Years of the Pharaoh, Life, Strength, Health in the West of Thebes, as it was officially known in ancient Egypt. Many drawings in the many chambers and tombs are so exact and so well preserved that zoologists can recognize species living along the Nile thousands of years ago. The paintings on the walls are remarkably rich, but also strikingly stylized. The representation of humans is based on the idea that figures should appear perfect. But why did this notion of 'perfection' never change? The style and ideal remained the same apparently for three thousand years, thereby handing down antiquity's ideals of beauty to today – in frozen form, as if time had no effect or was irrelevant. This fact can be interpreted as yet another example of the immense power and conservatism of tradition, and it can also reflect the unique regularity in societal life that the Nile created and enabled. The especially stable weather conditions and the highly regular variations in the Nile's water flow, which for century after century supplied and determined society's rhythm, laid the foundation for a particular adaptation to the river. This shaped a distinctive, an almost logical form of rigidity and regularity in Egyptian social life that was not easy to alter as long as the Egyptians had no means to control the seasonality of the river. The Nile's constancy and structuring role and characteristics were thus able to form the basis for a remarkable continuity in type and character of societal activities, a continuity that, on a deeper level, cuts through and exceeds the rise and fall of dynasties and rulers.

Where travel literature arose

'If we were to try and collect all the works that in the last few years have been published about Egypt and Palestine, we could build monuments that were just as large, if not as durable, as those still situated on the banks of the Nile.' Thus wrote an anonymous book reviewer in the 1800s according to *Nile Notes of a Howadji* (1992), a book about literature on Egypt by the American librarian Martin R. Kalfatovic. He documented 1,150 titles narrating journeys up the Nile in Egypt. The flood of books about the Nile and its countries continues.

No country has been described by foreigners for as long as, and as often as, Egypt. Travel literature arose, as a literary phenomenon, many will argue, with Herodotus, in 400 BCE. The histories he wrote were followed by Strabo's travelogues from the Nile Valley a few hundred years later. Egypt was the world's first tourist country, for even in the first century BCE the Romans started travelling up the river. Their sightseeing programme has remained familiar throughout history: they travelled to the pyramids, to the Sphinx, took boats up the Nile, saw the monuments in Thebes and the Colossi of Memnon, as well as the temples at Dendera and Philae – that is, they followed the same travel route as taken by today's tourists.[28]

Modern tourism also arose along the Nile. Here, the world's first travel bureau saw the light of day – Thomas Cook & Sons, owned and operated by the man who is perhaps more notorious for having introduced traveller's cheques. By 1875, the company was running its first steamboat carrying tourists. Cook was so omnipresent in Egypt back then that it was said it was not the ruler in Istanbul, the khedive in Cairo, nor Queen Victoria in London who steered the country, but Thomas Cook. Since then millions of tourists have followed in the ancient Romans' wake. In 1877, Amelia Edwards wrote in a kind of travel guide for Egypt entitled *A Thousand Miles up the Nile*: 'The truth is, however, that the mere sightseeing of the Nile demands some little reading and organizing, if only to be enjoyed. [...] We can at least do our best to understand what we see – to get rid of the obstacles – to put the right thing in the right place.'[29]

Slowly the ship glides up the river from Luxor. On our way to Aswan, we pass one millennia-old temple complex after another, and the boat journey I am on is one of the most famous, most archetypal and most chronicled of all boat journeys in history. I break off a chat with an obese American; he is sitting bare-chested and in swimming trunks, his legs dangling into the pool to cool off, while he brazenly pats himself on the stomach and squints through one of the modern Nile cruise's must-read books, Agatha

Christie's *Death on the Nile*. He says that his father, grandfather and great-grandfather took the same tour up the river, and he cannot praise the waiters and the other boat personnel highly enough for their service orientation. Scattered on the small round tables around the pool are colourful fashion pages and women's magazines, as on any beach equipped with deck chairs and umbrellas. Still, people largely sit absorbed in travel literature about Egypt. A foreigner bowed over a travel account on the upper deck of a cruise ship is an evocative figure, an archetypal image in the country where tourism arose.

Yet, how does 'the traveller' or foreign observer form ideas about an unfamiliar country and culture? What influences their descriptions? Why does one see what one sees, and what characterizes the filters that organize all those impressions? These have always been important questions, but in a globalized world they are crucial. Few places offer greater opportunities to study these questions than Egypt in particular and the Nile basin in general, for here the source material is unusually rich.

Egypt has been described by countless conquerors who have wished to subjugate the Nile and the fertile Delta. Alexander, Julius Caesar and Nero all came here, as did the Arab conquerors in the seventh century, and the European Crusaders on the way to the Holy City around 400 years later, and Muhammad Ali and Napoleon, Churchill and Khrushchev, emperors and backpackers, American women artists and European authors, history professors and people with no education, all have come here, and have seen and described the same objects and attractions and landscapes for thousands of years. Egypt, which has so many years' worth of travellers describing the same monuments and phenomena, must accordingly prove an unusually fruitful starting point to study the relationship between power and representation, or how other societies are depicted by different people in different contexts over time.

The boat leaves Edfu; I sit on deck while the other passengers have gone to their cabins to prepare for the evening's pharaonic-Egyptian-Arabic costume contest. Since I do not have any costume, cannot stand the smell of the prerequisite perfume and cannot imagine myself in a turban, I choose instead to read Herodotus once again. His narratives are largely based on his own observations and on what was told to him. He has been criticized for being a shallow historian, since he relied on dominant accounts, often considered as being myths and legends. Precisely because they had survived and been repeated by generation after generation they must have coincided with societies' self-understanding and been in line with the world view of powerful societal groups, and therefore Herodotus' use of them have been met with a legitimate critique of method. Herodotus, however, was too wise not to attempt to distinguish between fact and fiction, and he recognized this as a problem of interpretation and understanding.

Egypt as the gift of the Nile formed the basis of the ideas and images Herodotus had of the country as a civilization or culture that demanded to be understood according to its own premises. For him, Egypt was the very opposite of his Greek world. The Nile itself behaved contrary to rivers in Greece or Turkey: it flooded in midsummer when normal Mediterranean rivers were at their lowest. This notion of the Egyptian Nile being the very opposite of what was normal and Greek, functioned as a kind of illustration and symbol for the rest of the country. In one famous passage, after travelling upriver to Aswan to discover more about the river's mystery, Herodotus wrote:

> The Egyptians in agreement with their climate, which is unlike any other, and with the river, which shows a nature different from all other rivers, established for themselves manners and customs in a way opposite to other men in almost all matters: for among them the women frequent the market and carry on trade, while the men remain at home and weave; [...] the men carry their burdens upon their heads and the women upon their shoulders: the women make water standing up and the men crouching down: [...] to support their parents the sons are in no way compelled, if they do not desire to do so, but the daughters are forced to do so, be they never so unwilling. [...] The priests of the gods in other lands wear long hair, but in Egypt they shave their heads: among other men the custom is that in mourning those whom the matter concerns most nearly have their hair cut short [...]: finally in the writing of characters and reckoning with pebbles, while the Hellenes carry the hand from the left to the right, the Egyptians do this from the right to the left.[30]

Herodotus described Egyptian culture as a kind of totality. He was focused on similarities and contrasts but was no chauvinist when it came to his own culture. He wrote convincingly that Greek culture had been deeply influenced by the Egyptian; that Egyptians had invented the altar, processions and ceremonial gatherings; and he considered the Greek gods to be products of Egyptian forebears. He had proof, among other things, that Heracles' forefathers came from Egypt, and that Heraclitus was an ancient Egyptian god. Herodotus' work is so enjoyable to read because it speaks in general of a wise man who sought knowledge for its own sake. And because understanding and describing the world had its own worth, he also largely succeeded in freeing himself from Greek short-sightedness or cultural narcissism.

As I hear the sounds from the other guests who excitedly prepare themselves for the competition for the best-dressed Egyptian/pharaoh/Arab, I begin, inspired by Herodotus, to draft an article regarding how theories about images and representations of 'the other' in general cannot be developed without analysing comprehensively historical material that includes descriptions of Egypt. I knew that I would never actually carry out such a study or write such an article, but I am a firm believer in the benefits of talking to oneself.

Ancient Aswan as a symbol of modernity

A few powerful lurches and the ship docks at Aswan beside all the other cruise ships. The city is located on the Nile's east side, with long promenades where lovers sit on green benches, talking quietly to each other while letting their gaze rest on the peaceful river. The traditional sailboats, or feluccas, glide soundlessly down the river, as they have always done, clearly visible with white sails against the desert mountains that plunge into the river on the west bank. I rent a small motorboat that takes me up the small rapids to the First Cataracts. We pass Elephantine Island and the settlements on the west bank, where colourful Nubian houses sit clustered, too high on the hill to be reflected in the Nile, and slowly all contours are erased by the seeping blue light before darkness takes over.

I climb onto one of the sluices constructed when the British, following the lead of their engineers, built the world's largest dam here at the very beginning of the twentieth century. They regarded the dam as crucial to Egypt's future and, therefore, to the future of the empire. Lord Cromer and his people thought they had accomplished much during their first decades of rule in Egypt, but the dam was regarded as their most important contribution; really showing the value of 'Western methods', as Cromer put it.

In 1894, the plan for the Aswan Dam was publicized. By 1902 it was already finished, a hydrotechnical masterpiece. Its maximum height was 54 metres, its length around 2 kilometres, and more than one million tons of rock was used in its construction. The dam had 111 arched openings, each with a sluice gate measuring 4.8 metres. The dam's capacity was 3.5 billion cubic metres and it increased the summer irrigation by around 980 million cubic metres of water. It satisfied perennial irrigation needs in Middle Egypt and Faiyum. It was the world's largest masonry dam and is generally recognized as being one of the finest water structures ever built.

Its size, however, was limited by two factors in particular. No one at that time had the technological capacity to build a large enough reservoir with walls strong enough to dam the entire Nile flood. The main problem was that such a reservoir would quickly fill with silt. Therefore, the chosen solution was to catch only 'the tail end', so to speak, of the Blue Nile's autumnal flooding. This water obviously brought with it much less silt and, as a result, could more easily be dammed for use during the next summer's cotton season.

In addition to everything else, the Nile proved quite early to be an arena for a type of conflict that has become increasingly important in recent times: that between preservation of historical monuments and modernization. In the 1890s, archaeological circles in France and Great Britain came together to condemn the Aswan Dam structure because it would place the Graeco-Roman Philae temple underwater. Cairo and Britain were surprised by the strength of the archaeologists' resistance. Despite the government's stubborn defence of their technological display window, and even though they could demonstrate that the dam would be a goldmine for Egypt, for political reasons London was forced to build a dam that had only half the planned capacity. Winston Churchill contemptuously wrote that archaeologists and tourists were willing to gamble with an entire people's livelihood because archaeologists dwelt on the past and tourists on their desire to 'scribble their names' on a few old ruins.[31]

Accordingly, the dam became smaller than planned and smaller than Cromer and London thought was necessary. Despite that fact, it was still so successful that it set Egypt's development on a track the country continues to follow to this day: a developmental strategy based on an increasingly comprehensive system for the control and use of Nile water. The immediate result was that Britain's role – and its elbow room – as an imperial power in the Nile basin was fundamentally widened. By staging themselves as a modern version of Isis, the ancient goddess whose tears decided the flow of the river, London and the British in Cairo wielded what they conceived as an extremely potent political and economic weapon: they could now, they knew, use their political and scientific control over the Nile as either a stick or a carrot, according to the British Empire's interests. Which course they would choose would depend upon the political situation, as we have seen, and as I will further show. 'On [...] the entire course of the Nile no works of any kind involving a control of its water – either direct or indirect – should be permitted to be constructed by any private Society or individual, and that all such works should be constructed by, and remain in the hands of, the Government of Egypt.'[32]

Through the darkness from where I am standing, I see Aswan's distant lights and the desert emptiness surrounding it. And as I stand at the structures of the old dam, the radical aspects of the city's history emerge. In the course of the twentieth century, Aswan became one of the most potent and clear symbols of human will and humanity's increasing capacity to transform itself into the master of nature and the river's ruler – and interestingly enough, it took place in Upper Egypt, where so many people during the 1800s had drawn such striking metaphors of a society at a standstill.

In the local military camp the next morning, following an obligatory cup of tea with the commander there, I climb on board an old Russian military helicopter with a crew of four and fly – with doors open – south along the Nile to the new Aswan dam: the High Dam, Sadd al-Ali. The noise of propellers, motor and wind exhilarates us all this morning and when, sitting as close to the door as possible, I let my gaze follow the dam's mighty curvature where it keeps in check a 500-kilometre-long artificial lake, I can well admit I must control my joy. After working for decades on the Nile's history and reading metre upon metre of old books and files on the river's hydrology and on the struggle to control it, the sight of this dam from above through the open door of a Russian military helicopter is a highlight of my life's involvement with the river.

Both dams had a revolutionary significance in their time, but the High Dam, or the Nasser Dam as it is also called, represented a turning point: in Egypt the timing of the annual flood was no longer critical but, instead, only how much water the Nile carried on an annual basis. At the same time, the dam has been one of the most contentious examples of how humankind can destroy what it took nature thousands of years to build. It displays human technological competence but also, and more cunningly, water's problematic dualism. Will the High Dam and the other dams being built upstream, in the long run destroy the Nile Delta? The dam represents a technological dilemma of a classic and grandiose character: it transformed the Delta and the rest of Egypt into a green, perennial garden and provided electricity to millions of houses throughout the country, but at the same time science is clear: it most likely forms the Delta's greatest threat.

The downstream complex

If you stand among the columns of the temple dedicated to the Goddess of Inundation on Elephantine Island, right in the middle of the Nile, directly across from the imperial Old Cataract Hotel built by the British in connection with the 1902 opening of the

Aswan Dam, and which is sited as if hailing the Graeco-Roman goddess, it is easy to understand the foundation of Egypt's downstream complex. Directing your gaze south of the temple, where the sun throughout the day burns perpetually in a cloudless sky, you can see how the desert plunges into the river's west bank and how the tall, arid granite cliffs on the east bank, where the stones for the pyramid originated, embank the river there. The water flows as if emerging from the desert itself into Egypt, unstoppable, as if from an immense hidden Sarepta's jar. Yet, the water is not unstoppable, and it does not stem from Sarepta's jar; it runs through ten water-thirsty countries before reaching Egypt's border. Because of this physical location, Egyptians have naturally enough developed a distinctive national psychology – a form of downstream complex. Isis, the flood's goddess, can no longer help them and this downstream complex rests fundamentally on a hydrological and geographical reality that is 'eternal'; it is independent of regime shifts, economic systems and national borders since it is caused by the very nature of the river.

It was also here that Herodotus came, well over 2,000 years ago. He wrote:

> I went myself as an eye-witness as far as the city of Elephantine and from that point
> onwards I gathered knowledge by report. From the city of Elephantine as one goes
> up the river there is a country which slopes steeply; so that here one must attach
> ropes to the vessel on both sides, as one fastens an ox, and so make one's way onward;
> and if the rope break, the vessel is gone at once, carried away by the violence of the
> stream. Through this country it is a voyage of about four days in length.[33]

For here is where Egypt ended in ancient times. The Nile cataracts upstream halted communication and formed a natural boundary.

Prehistory, though it may not be visible, is always present in Egypt. The country's position downstream on the Nile has, of course, been unchanged for thousands of years, but this location is more significant today and will be in the future, than it ever was in the past. No other country on earth is so dependent on a single resource that has shaped its entire history but which it does not control, and which comes from outside the country's own borders. It was this situation that President Anwar al-Sadat, not long after he returned home as winner of the Nobel Peace Prize, so clearly realized and emphasized when he declared that if anyone took a drop of water from the Nile, Egypt would not hesitate to launch a military attack.[34]

There are now different and profound historical movements all working in the same directions: the increased technological and economic capacity to control the Nile in upstream countries; a growing gap between demand and supply of water in the basin as a whole due to economic development and very rapid population growth; a new uncertainty about future precipitation patterns related to fear of climate change; and, not least, growing deterioration in the Nile ecology. These changes are in the process of becoming concurrent, and on a certain level this is a coincidence. This implies that Egypt's position downstream in the basin has never been more vulnerable, and therefore more important from a foreign policy perspective, than at present.

Egypt's water usage has dramatically increased in recent years. Despite this fact, annual reports show that the country's average per capita consumption is only 700 cubic metres of water. That is well below the 1,000 cubic metres that is internationally deemed necessary, and it is a dramatic decline compared to the beginning of the 1960s, when usage, due to a much smaller population, was nearly three times as high. The average is expected to fall to 500 cubic metres within just a few years. From more and more areas of the country, reports and complaints arrive of water shortages, and of conflicts between wealthy large landowners and small farmers over who should receive the water, and how much. In early summer 2012, for example, it was reported that 200 tourists were being held hostage not far from Abu Simbel because the farmers there wanted to force the authorities to give them a greater portion of the water that they insisted had gone to a large landowner.[35] The Mubarak government estimated that the minimum water requirement in 2020 would be around 86 billion cubic metres of Nile water, or 35 billion more than Egypt believes it has a right to use. No other question is seen as more critical to Egypt's development and stability by the Egyptian authorities than the Nile-sharing issue.

At the same time, the upstream countries have for the first time come up with clear national proposals and concrete plans for the use of the Nile's waters in industrial, agricultural and domestic settings. And, most importantly, they have joined in a common diplomatic effort to wrest from Egypt its historic right of having a veto over the exploitation of the Nile. Egypt meanwhile has argued that these efforts amount to a violation of internationally binding Nile treaties.

Egyptian state leaders are faced with demands they have never previously encountered to the same degree. For thousands of years Egypt controlled the river, but the Renaissance Dam in particular threatens that dominance. President Sisi repeated what leaders of Egypt has said again and again at the UN in September 2019: the Nile was 'a question of life, a matter of existence to Egypt'.[36] The country and the government of Abdel Fattah al-Sisi have a few conventional options, but none of them is very promising or easy to pursue.

What can the Egyptians do when they are no longer the unchallenged masters of the river? They can and they must try to reduce water consumption in Egypt by restricting cultivation of water-intensive crops like rice and bananas. During Friday prayers, clerics talk in line with government policies, about the need to conserve water. But in the short run at least this will not be enough to ease Egypt's dire water situation. They can, as Sadat suggested in the 1970s, declare war on countries that exploit the river in a way that Egypt will not accept. But that is becoming more and more difficult, especially given Ethiopia's and other upstream countries' growing strength and military might. They can bet on diplomacy and that the basin countries will focus on finding optimal solutions that will also seriously consider Egypt's interests. They can also try to develop different forms of economic cooperation with other basin states, in order to create an atmosphere that benefits and stimulate cooperation over water as well.

General Sisi and his government have primarily opted for another route – international diplomacy. The leadership of the military could not let the Muslim Brotherhood continue as political leaders of the country, partly because they thought that they mismanaged Nile diplomacy and rapidly weakened Egypt's position in the basin and in the world. The new leadership chose another route: by showing themselves a strong ally of the United States and their continued support for Israel, they received in turn support from the United States, Israel and the international monetary institutions in their negotiations with Ethiopia. This helped to strengthen Egypt's bargaining leverage in relation to Ethiopia and other upstream countries.

Whatever route is chosen, the leaders of Egypt must nonetheless convince the Egyptian population that the traditionally held idea of the Nile as being Egypt's own river belongs to the past and that the whole of society must adjust to this new water situation.[37]

Monumental monuments now and in ancient times

The helicopter has circled several times over what appears to be a gigantic factory on the banks of Lake Nasser but, in reality, it is a water pumping station named after President Hosni Mubarak, where Nile-produced hydropower is used to transport water from the artificial lake to the desert. The facility was completed in 2002 and is nothing less than a Nile Valley–oriented midwife. The plan was to lift 5 billion cubic metres of water into the desert each year.

The station operates its pump just a few kilometres from Abu Simbel, one of the most famous monuments in the world, cut from the Upper Egyptian cliffs three thousand years ago. UNESCO organized the relocation operation, and stone block after stone block was carefully sawn free, hoisted down and transported to a new location before being reassembled. Lake Nasser would have swamped everything, including Abu Simbel, but the international community financed and planned a rescue mission. Now the monument, in all its impressive grandeur and self-glorifying ostentation, has been rebuilt. Ramses II, who had six wives and a hundred children, raised what must be one of the most self-magnifying edifices in the world. Just outside the entrance are stationed four statues of the ruler, each more than 20 metres high, and within the halls are even more, while reliefs cut around the entryway itself depict the Nile gods who united Upper and Lower Egypt. These are shown in all their might, as with the utmost indifference and with the greatest possible casualness, they rest the soles of their feet on the bodies of slaves. Now, it is the Nile who is the servant.

The Russian military helicopter veers sharply over the desert, and beneath us a barren Sahara undulates to all sides as far as we can see, and beyond. The heat blurs contours and creates reflections. Then, like narrow, endless lifelines running between it all, I can see kilometre upon kilometre of arrow-straight waterways that disappear into the desert horizon. The main canal from Lake Nasser extends 50 kilometres into the desert. The plan is to build cities, launch industries and develop an export agriculture. Here in the Toshka region the desert shall bloom. Some 500,000 acres are set to be cultivated with lake water, and almost 200,000 acres more with water supplied from enormous subterranean aquifers beneath the Sahara. At its most ambitious, the Mubarak regime talked about settling 17 million people here, but gradually the number was reduced, and officially the plan promised that around three million people can live here.

'Well, you know, if we compare, and if we consider the pyramids as the projects of the Pharaohs, then this project is more than one hundred times bigger than the pyramids'.[38] Abu-Zeid, who was minister of water for many years, was clear about what the Egyptian government was doing when I spoke to him in his office in Cairo in 2005. We went out onto the roof of his ministry and from there we had a fantastic view of Cairo. He pointed, and then pronounced with certainty: 'We can't all live here.'

After the ousting of president, Hosni Mubarak, the policies of his government have been criticized in all arenas. The demonstrators at Tahrir Square in 2011 believed the government had entirely betrayed the country's Nile interests by both neglecting Africa and being too compliant regarding the upstream countries' demands. And many have also questioned the wisdom of the Toshka Project, seeing it as an example of the prior ruling elite's way of thinking. Politicians sympathetic to the Muslim Brotherhood strongly denounced the project in parliament from the very beginning. Other sites for agricultural expansion have been proposed – a few to the east and west of the modern Delta, or in the east/west-facing valleys that extend from the Red Sea Hills to the Nile – not least since these places are considered as being better and more comfortable places in which to live. Egyptians would rather move to these places, it has been argued, due to the more pleasant climate and the proximity to urban centres and larger cities. Furthermore, the argument runs, these places are located near areas that already have the infrastructure necessary for development. So, people ask: why throw away billions on Toshka? These alternative suggestions, however, overlook the greatest problem: where will they get the water? General Sisi's government has also tried to revive the Toshka Project, partly by enlarging it, but again progress has been slow, and the project has met with several problems.

But any government in Egypt, now and in the future, cannot avoid a key issue in its development; Egypt's economy and food prices continue to largely revolve around the use of the Nile, so how should it be used most efficiently? The governments' solution to the water issue, and thereby also the Toshka Project and population pressure within the Nile Valley, will remain crucial questions in Egyptian development. As always in Egypt's history, government success will to a large extent depend upon its ability to confront and solve the water question.

Egyptian gods and eternal life

The Aswan Dam is now a tourist destination, and understandably so. Here are tourists from Japan and China, Italy and France, the United States and the United Kingdom. I cannot know, of course, what they are thinking about, but when I am walking on top of the dam, I am reflecting on the fact that I am walking along an edifice whose significance far outstrips the pyramids and everything else ever built in Egypt. The power of ideas pales in comparison with the magnitude of such momentous, technological structures. This dam has already survived changes in Egypt's economy, politics and ideology, and while regimes have come and gone, it bears witness to perseverance; it radiates the authority and power of an eternal lifeline.

After following the colossal wall with my eyes, I find a shady place under some trees to read about Osiris and Isis. This concrete giant makes the old gods relevant in a new way, since the dam so clearly demonstrates that it is politicians and engineers who now determine the river's water flow instead of gods, as the Egyptians (whom Herodotus called the most religious of all peoples) believed for thousands of years.

Long before modern science triumphed, ancient Egyptians thought the tears of Isis controlled the magnitude and duration of the Nile flood. The Philae Temple, which was saved when the first Aswan Dam was built, houses a series of drawings on the stone walls in the room dedicated to Osiris. These show grain sprouting from Osiris's dead body while a priest waters the shoots. The inscription reads: 'This is the form of that which cannot be named, the Osiris of Mysteries, who grows forth from the water that returns.' The temple walls preserved that day's greatest truth, something revealed only to the deepest initiate. The grain god brought forth grain from his own body; he sacrificed himself so that people could eat; he died so that they might live.

Osiris, therefore, symbolized how life was able to maintain itself through death, and he further personified the river that created life after death. Osiris was murdered by his violent and jealous twin brother Seth. He arose afterwards blessed with eternal life. This story was interpreted and recounted as a promise of humanity's victory over death. The Osiris mysteries were honoured with ceremonies year after year, where participants returned to the temples to be reinitiated and to celebrate rebirth. To take part in the celebration was a sacred act.

The god-king Osiris and his sister-queen Isis ruled over the Nile's fertile Delta. His brother Seth and his sister-wife Nephthys, however, commanded the gold-red desert. Seth thought the situation was highly unfair. Osiris and Isis were revered and beloved in their country, for they had taught the people to work the earth and to live peacefully with each other. Seth's family, by contrast, was of a more warlike clan that had survived in the desert's difficult climate. Therefore, they desired all that Osiris and Isis possessed.

One time, when Isis was away, Osiris invited his brother Seth and all his followers to participate in an autumn festival to celebrate the fertility of the Nile, and there was food and drink in abundance. Seth came with a fine gift – a coffin decorated with jewels and gold. He said he would give the chest to the man or woman who fitted into it exactly. When Osiris tried the coffin, Seth and his seventy-two henchmen locked it and sealed the box with melted lead. Seth and his people hurried down to the Nile's banks and cast the coffin into the water to drown Osiris. The current carried it down river and finally into a foreign land. It was stranded near a tree, which grew around the coffin before finally encircling Osiris's body.

When Isis heard what had happened, she returned home to confirm whether Osiris was dead and that his younger brother was his murderer. In sorrow, she cut her long, beautiful hair and walked barelegged along the river to hunt for Osiris. She no longer resembled a handsome, Egyptian queen, according to the legend, but had a face more like that of a witch and she was ridiculed by her people. She discovered that the chest had sailed down the Nile, into the Mediterranean, and across the sea to Byblos (Lebanon). It was now entangled in the branches of a great tree.

In Byblos, rumours had spread of the great tree that had sprung up overnight by the coast. The king of that country was so taken with the beautiful tree and its quick growth that he ordered the tree cut down and brought to the capital, where it would form the pillars of his palace. Isis followed the tree to the palace gates and was able to slip inside. After a series of fantastic events, and after Isis had made life intolerable for the Queen of Byblos, the queen was prepared to give anything to be rid of Isis at the court. Isis said she would leave so long as they gave her the pillar that contained Osiris. The queen ordered the column felled and it was sent home to Egypt aboard one of the king's boats, with Isis also aboard.

Isis' misery was transformed into a festival of sorrow with a decided ritual. On the festival's third day, the priests went down to the riverbanks. Here they lifted a golden shrine set atop a chest. As they poured sacred water over it, they shouted: 'Osiris has been found!' Earth, spices, incense and water were combined to symbolize the reunion of Isis and Osiris. The Nile was the very scene of life's resurrection; the river was not only the image of fertility and eternal life, it *was* fertility.

While I am reading this story, I see new tourists pouring off the buses that brought them here to see the dam, this immense demonstration of human might and power, made in stone and cement. One does not need much imagination to see both the contrasts and links between the celebrations of Isis and the High Dam. The dam can be viewed as the antithesis of Isis, as the ultimate expression of a modern world view where engineers have completely assumed the goddess's power. After the mid-nineteenth century, when the Nile first began to be subjected to human will, the river could no longer provide raw material for this kind of religious myth-making. Now, with the building of mighty embankments and dams and large perennial canals filled with water many kilometres from the river, the river's development became the foundation for a new kind of world view, one based on stories of the triumph of modernity and technology and of humanity's victory over nature.

Nonetheless, despite the power the dam holds over the Nile, militarily the Aswan High Dam is Egypt's Achilles' heel. Israeli war hawks have repeatedly and publicly threatened to attack it. In 2011, Israel's foreign minister, Avigdor Lieberman, was one of them. Multiple news outlets reported him as saying that bombing the dam was a possible retaliation for Egyptian support of Yasser Arafat when he proclaimed in 1998 the establishment of the Palestinian state on the West Bank and in Gaza. In 2001, Lieberman apparently told a group of ambassadors that if Egypt and Israel should again have a military confrontation, Israel could attack the Aswan High Dam.

Egypt's neighbours to the south, moreover, have also threatened to bomb the Aswan Dam. The relationship between Egypt and Sudan became strained after the 1989 coup, when Islamists took power in Khartoum. Then came the Gulf War, where Sudan supported Iraq against the United States and Egypt. On 19 January 1991, large-scale demonstrations were organized in Khartoum in response to Egypt's position on the war. The demonstrators called for the Aswan High Dam and the pyramids to be destroyed.

For the rock-throwing demonstrators in Khartoum, this was easier said than done. But there can be no doubt: that the dam is vulnerable, and it is a strategic target whose significance Egyptian state leaders can never neglect. For in Egypt, there are no backup alternatives if the dam should be destroyed. Should that happen, the water would become a violent tidal wave that would sweep the country on its way to the sea.

In the real world of politics, bombing the dam in order to destroy it is a horror scenario. Such an action would create a catastrophe so enormous that it would most likely overshadow every other catastrophe in world history. If such a scenario were nonetheless to play out, it would require the world to already have sunk into a state of outright anarchy and barbarity.

'Revolt on the Nile' and water insecurity

'I'd bought the ticket, but the train wasn't running', Muhammed said. He was the man who in February 2011 was responsible for arranging a private boat tour for myself and some others up the Nile from Aswan through one of the many narrow branches that the various waterfalls and islands make of the Nile here. From the Aswan region, there were many people, too, who ardently desired to take the train to Cairo and Tahrir Square to join the revolt. The authorities, however, halted all trains. 'Instead,' Muhammed said in a high, intense voice, 'we demonstrated outside the Presidential Palace here in Aswan.'

While official news coverage in Egypt long tried to conceal what was happening, Western news coverage from the beginning took an activist approach and supported without reservation the rebels. It was as if Egypt's ruling elite, which had, in fact, been Western allies for decades and which represented a secular voice in a Middle East where Islamism was strongly on the advance, was somehow cut from the same cloth as the elite that James Bruce encountered in Egypt in the 1700s. As the Scottish discoverer of the Blue Nile's source wrote while travelling through the country: 'A more brutal, unjust, tyrannical, oppressive, avaricious set of infernal miscreants there was not on earth than the members of the Government of Cairo.'[39] That is to say, Western media coverage unanimously adopted the rebels' cause. Journalists and experts alike all spoke the same language: that of revolution. There was only a single truth about Mubarak: he was a dictator. He was corrupt. He was the world's richest man because he had stolen Egypt's national assets!

No one knows what lasting changes the revolution will bring to Egypt. But from a long Nile-historical perspective, the revolution represented a watershed occurrence. The uprising and the crippling it implied of the Egyptian government, both in the eyes of the world and to the country's own inhabitants, had immediate and far-reaching consequences for Egypt's ability to control or determine Nile exploitation. In 2011, six upstream countries finally signed a new Nile Agreement – against Egypt's explicit policy and expressed wishes. Images of protesters holding the regime in check, who were able to force the president to resign (and after only a few large demonstrations), as well as reports that Hosni Mubarak had been placed under house arrest by his own friends in the military, were viewed by the upstream countries as an indication of a new and unexpectedly weak Egypt. The government of the country that everyone had once perceived as the region's uncontested superpower could not even control unarmed protesters in Cairo.

The revolution occurred roughly and, from a long-term perspective, simultaneously with the upstream countries agreeing for the first time to build dams and embark on other projects without asking Egypt's approval beforehand. At the precise moment in history when Egypt's diplomatic situation in the Nile basin had become more uncertain and vulnerable than ever, demonstrators launched an attack on the regime. The upstream countries lost their fear of the Egyptian state leadership – perhaps even quicker and more generally than the demonstrators themselves.

For thirty years Mubarak and his closest advisers had steered Egypt's Nile policy. Mubarak himself was a seasoned fox in negotiations and had consequently defended Egypt's traditional position: the Nile is Egypt's lifeline, and the country cannot relinquish any of its acquired rights. The Nile was regarded as a national security question and, by the end of Mubarak's time as president, the main person responsible for all Nile policy was, therefore, Omar Suleiman, Egypt's chief intelligence officer. Egyptians did not view the agreement among the upstream countries as binding, and the hard line they adopted was solidly what it had been for decades: Egyptians would under no circumstance allow their Nile rights to be endangered, and they would take the necessary steps to protect those rights.

In 2011, Egyptian politicians had their hands full with domestic policy issues. In this situation, which was also characterized by impotence on the foreign policy front, Ethiopia's prime minister Meles Zenawi announced, only a month after Mubarak had fallen, that Ethiopia was going to build Africa's largest dam across the Blue Nile. Not long after that a large Egyptian delegation with the prime minister at its head travelled to Ethiopia. Cairo officially accepted Ethiopia's project – in exchange for being allowed to study it! So weak had Egypt become that, by the autumn of 2011, Egypt's new state leadership travelled to Addis Ababa and basically agreed to the new dam. Although the Ethiopian project would also offer advantages to Egypt, this policy was still the most palpable expression of the country's dramatically changed and weakened position in the Nile game.

Egypt's new Islamist regime was forced to lead the downstream country in an entirely new hydropolitical situation: the country no longer enjoyed the power to veto Nile projects upstream. Paradoxically enough, Egypt's most important friends continued to be the World Bank and the West, the powers in world politics which Egypt's Brotherhood-leaders were most against. The World Bank has written into its guidelines that it will not grant loans for projects upon which not all basin countries have agreed, thus allowing Egypt to put its foot down regarding many possible projects upstream. The United States continued to be Egypt's most crucial ally, and Washington's influence in Addis Ababa, Kampala, Nairobi and Kigali was the only power that could place pressure upon the upstream countries in Egypt's favour. The Muslim Brotherhood was ideologically bent on taking a hard-line against Israel and the West, but it proved difficult to implement such policies, not least on account of Egypt's weakened position along the Nile.

From this perspective, it was significant that the second country visited by the Egyptian president from the Muslim Brotherhood, Mohamed Morsi, was Ethiopia – the Nile's water tower, where almost all the water in Egypt originates, and that he was there for three days.[40] And the first prime minister the president appointed was a man previously responsible for the Nile's use within Egypt. But no matter how much the government of the Muslim Brotherhood gave priority to the Nile question, it was clear to everybody that Egypt's position on the Nile was weaker than at any other time in history.

Nubia and the Country Where the Rivers Meet

Eighty kilometres of artificial desert lake

When I first travelled across the enormous – and artificial – Lake Nasser in 1983, I was heading from Egypt to Sudan aboard an old ship that, just a couple of trips later, would sink in a flaming inferno with several hundred people on board. The crew had hardly any tools. People sat smoking right next to the gas containers, which were stacked in chaotic disarray on the deck. And the navigation controls were hardly top-notch since the boat kept running aground. When the captain dropped anchor for the night, near to land, we were told it was a strategy to make it easier to escape the crocodiles – should the boat sink. But that was only one problem, one crew member said with a smile: the area was full of deadly scorpions, and both banks offered a dry, inhospitable moon-like mountainous landscape.

I camped out on the boat roof, which consisted of sheets of thick cardboard, suspended across iron mounts. There, I reclined on top of my sleeping bag to catch what little breeze the hot air offered, as close to the edge as possible without risking a fall into the lake. Through the night I watched the stars shine with singular, relentless intensity, insistent on their role as navigation signs in a sky that seemed to arch over the fabricated lake in order to keep it and the mountains in place. And whereas the sky in Europe tends to grow lighter around the moon and more blue-black toward the horizon, here it was deep blue around a moon perched on the ridge. It was an astonishing tropical night whose beauty only increased until it reached its climax – exactly at the moment that it came to an end.

The journey across the lake lasted one-and-a-half days. Like other trips, it would have been a fleeting adventure – an exotic and exciting event, but no lasting experience – had it not been so fraught. The boat trip started in Egypt but continued to Lake Nubia, the Sudanese portion of the Aswan Dam, after we had crossed the invisible border into Sudan. The lake testifies to the forces of nature, societies' ability to control water and humanity's hubris all at once; and, perhaps, in ways one must experience to understand. Crossing this lake, constructed by human hands in the Sahara with natural water coming from Africa has, in the perspective of societal development, a schizophrenic aspect about it, since the lake is both a monument to nature and to technology. The trip acquires an added dimension when you know that the artificial lake played a crucial role in the collapse of British colonialism, that it was central both as an object of and a scene of superpower rivalry during the Cold War, that its construction reflected shifting power relations in the basin during the postcolonial age, and that it inundated parts of ancient and modern Nubia.

In the 1960s, after Russian and Egyptian engineers had dammed the river, the tamed water forced its way, profoundly, relentlessly, between the bone-dry cliffs, placing all the Nubian towns next to the river here under water for all time.

Nubia: gold and cataracts

For many, the name Nubia stirs to life the mythical bandit stories they have read about the hunt for gold in Africa. Indeed, the region's name supposedly originates from the ancient Egyptian word for gold. But ivory, ostrich feathers, mahogany and spices were for millennia also transported to Egypt and Europe through Nubia.

For others, Nubia brings associations of old Christian Nubia, remembering the time when Christianity was the dominant religion in this part of the Nile Valley. And for others still, Nubia is the homeland of the African Pharaoh, a many-thousand-years-old blooming African civilization that, in historical narratives, has long lived in the shadows of the Egyptian pharaohs and their pyramids. Distant Nubia – 'distant' because it was located upstream of the Nile cataracts – also captured the romantic imaginations of the ancient Greeks and Romans.

Nubia is situated between the Nile's Second Cataract and the large, distinctive S-swing the river makes in the middle of Sudan. Nubians are an African people who live between what has become Arab Egypt and Arab Sudan. Their cultural self-awareness has varied in strength, but archaeological findings in recent decades have ensured that Nubian prehistory and the 'Black Pharaohs' have definitively stepped out of history's shadows. Nubia encompasses what is typical for the Nile Valley – a cultural and ethnic cacophony. Nubians are, to use what in the postcolonial period has been the basin countries' own categorization, one of about a thousand ethnic groups who inhabit the countries sharing the river.

Wadi Halfa is located near the banks of the Aswan High Dam, here also called Lake Nubia. For thousands of years, the site was the meeting place between two worlds – Africa to the south and Egypt and Europe to the north. It possesses one of the most extreme desert climates in the world, with just 3 millimetres of annual rainfall on average. Not a single drop of rain falls in most years. Animal life is scarce, but scorpions claim children's lives every year, and the Egyptian vulture flies slowly over the landscape looking for carrion.

South of Wadi Halfa, the river runs like a blue silk ribbon drawn across an enormous brown carpet of sand. On the narrow banks, vegetation grows, beautiful and lush compared with the desert wasteland; nature here is largely coloured burnt sienna. Chalk-white houses, but some painted yellow or blue, built from clay – the kind of houses the famous Sudanese author Tayeb Salih compared to a ship that has cast anchor in mid-ocean – stand in the protective shadow of palm trees and give the cultural landscape a distinctive identity and atmosphere, at once a protest against and an acceptance of the great desert as a neighbour. From the riverbanks, the houses are accessible via paths of sand, pathways that twist between verdigris fields before vanishing into the horizon, into an overwhelming impression of nothingness, of hot air trembling over a seemingly endless desert.

It was the Nile cataracts of Nubia that created Egypt's natural border. Upstream of the First and Second Cataracts in today's Sudan, a society characterized by African tradition and local ecology emerged thousands of years ago. When Nubia blossomed, rainfall was much richer than it is today and, with the help of simple irrigation methods, people could farm at least two crops per year in what was very fertile ground.[1] In many places it was also possible to use the Nile as a transport route. Since only limited areas were habitable, this encouraged city formation and social stratification that was unknown in other parts of Africa. Three kingdoms developed: the first lasted around a thousand years with Kerma as its capital (2600–1520 BCE), the second, the Kingdom of Kush, had Napata as its capital, and then Meroë as its capital under about 350 CE.

Kerma was able to become the centre of a Nile civilization because it was situated on a huge floodplain, somewhere between 15 and 40 kilometres wide and about 200 kilometres long. This allowed for basin irrigation, the only site along the Nile's Nubian corridor where this was to any extent possible.[2] Even in Neolithic times (from the sixth to the fourth millennium BCE), people lived in Kerma, and they domesticated animals and practised agriculture. The position of the rulers there also steadily strengthened, and this fact must have contributed to their ability to control trade on the Nile. By the mid-seventeenth century BCE, the kingdom stretched as far north as Elephantine Island by today's Aswan. After Egypt was reunited around 1550 BCE, the pharaohs relaunched plans to conquer Kerma and not long after that the kingdom fell.

A little to the south-east of Kerma, not far from where the river takes it large swing through the desert, lies Meroë on the Nile's east bank. The city was the capital of the Kingdom of Meroë and the area is typified by more than two hundred pyramids, identified as Nubian on account of their distinctive proportions. Recently, evidence has been found of many small rivers or streams that, when Meroë was at its zenith, flowed richly with water and ran out into the Nile.

It was from this region that the Greek historian Diodorus of Sicily in the first century BCE told of a special dynastic tradition: the king was always murdered at the end of his reign. Up until the time of King Ergamenes (also known as King Arkamani I, ruling 295–275 BCE) who was a contemporary of Ptolemy II of Egypt (285–246 BCE), it was customary for the priests to send a message to the king, apparently as if it were from the very god Amun himself, informing the king that his earthly reign was over. He must die. Traditionally, the kings obeyed the god's orders and took their own lives. But Ergamenes, who had been educated in Greek philosophy, opposed the order. Instead of taking his own life, he ordered all the high priests to be slaughtered. Whether the story is a myth, or an interesting account of dynastic practices is of course discussed by later historians. It was also here that archaeologists in 1910 found a bronze statue of the Roman emperor Augustus. According to the Greek geographer Strabo, the Cushites attacked Egypt and took the statue of Augustus as a spoil of war. The Romans sent expeditions up the Nile to claim it back, but they could not find the head. This had been symbolically buried in the sand before the entrance to the Cushite temple, and there it was found – almost 2,000 years later.

Meroë's position and wealth was due to a thriving iron industry coupled with expansive trade operations that extended to India and China. The city, due to its production and trade of iron, has been called Africa's Birmingham. Meroë was situated at the crossroads of two large trade routes: the Nile north to south and caravan routes east to west. The city connected Central Africa, via the Blue and the White Niles, to Egypt, the Red Sea, and the Ethiopian highlands. The contemporary information we have on Meroë is sparse but relatively detailed, again thanks to Strabo. He had access to the reports Emperor Nero's expedition produced when it travelled here *c.* 60 CE to discover the Nile's source. According to Strabo, the population traded in salt, copper, iron, gold and various precious stones, as well as in forest and animal products such as ivory, and lion and leopard skins. The reason it was possible to establish so extensive and permanent a settlement here was the waterscape and the topography. Meroë was inside the rain belt, so it received a little rain every year. In addition, the area was well suited to the use of the *sakia* – a type of water-lifting apparatus imported from Egypt that made it possible to haul water up to the fields. And, for the most part, the Meroitic rulers controlled the Nile from north to south, a stretch more than 1,000 kilometres as the crow flies – that is to say, large swathes of Sudan north of where Khartoum now lies. Meroë's collapse was probably due to a combination of military attack from Aksum – the centre of the mighty kingdom on the Ethiopian highlands – and changes in the water system caused by less rainfall, which meant that the region's small rivers could not be exploited as before. No one has yet been able to decipher the Meroitic script, so historians have not been able to explain with certainty how it could grow to become the wondrous city that Herodotus wrote about *c.* 430 BCE.

The Nubian kings converted to Christianity in the sixth century. According to tradition, it was a missionary sent by the Byzantine empress Theodora who started preaching the gospel around the year 540 CE. Perhaps conversions were spurred by the Coptic missionaries arriving from Egypt. Because all these missionaries represented the Monophysitism belief, it is natural that the Christian Nubians joined them. The Nubian kings recognized the Coptic Patriarch of Alexandria as their spiritual head, and the kingdom reached the height of its prosperity and military power in the ninth and tenth centuries.

Gradually, this Christian kingdom was weakened because Muslim dominance in Egypt made it difficult to maintain contact with the Coptic Patriarch and to recruit Egyptian-educated clergy. Saladin, the victorious Kurdish soldier who defended Islam against the Crusaders and took power over Egypt, also launched a military attack on the Nubian Christians. Nubia received no help from the patriarchs in Alexandria; they were too fully engaged with their own matters and so neglected their fellow believers to the south. In 1372, presumably the last bishop for Nubia was ordained, and Nubia ceased being a Christian region following a rather non-violent cultural diffusion process. Nubians broke with Christianity around 600 years ago and actively contributed later to the Islamization of other parts of the Sudan and parts of northern Uganda.

Meanwhile, one of the most influential historians in the early post-war years, Hugh Trevor-Roper, wrote in his book, *The Rise of Christian Europe*: 'Perhaps in the future, there will be some African history to teach. But, at present there is none: there is only the history of the Europeans in Africa. The rest is darkness ... and darkness is not a subject of history.'[3]

If you travel around Nubia or wander among Kerma's millennia-old grave sites and pyramids, it is not difficult to understand why many people are disturbed by what, during some periods, have been dominant Western descriptions of Africa, and to understand why postcolonial criticism, therefore, has many examples it can condemn or deconstruct. Nonetheless, the critique of Western scholarship as an abuse of power overlooks the flipside of that same scholarship's effect: Western archaeologists and historians have, in many places, made a significant effort to map and document Africa's history, and Nubia's past has been rescued from oblivion thanks to German, American, English and Scandinavian archaeologists and historians.

Muhammad Ali's river war

Shendi is an ancient trade hub on the Nile, but even if today it is a place you can bypass without much regret, it conceals a dramatic history regarding the river and the relationship between Sudan and Egypt. To this place came huge trade caravans that had crossed the desert from Libya and Egypt, and to this place came Muslims from West and North Africa on hajj to Mecca. The reason for this was simple and geographical: it was easier to cross the river at Shendi than at other places in northern Sudan. This allowed the site to become a trading centre, one that offered an unusually rich variety of wares, supplying objects from both India and Venice. Here, the huge caravans transporting slaves, gold and other wares through the desert did not need to be afraid of the highway robbers that had trailed them like vultures. On the riverbank in Shendi, those accompanying the caravans could finally relax.

Because of Shendi's strategic significance, Muhammad Ali's military force arrived here in 1821, with the aim of conquering what is today called the Sudan, or 'The land of the blacks'. It was a motley troupe that had left Egypt, one led by his third son, Isma'il. Historical sources differ, but apparently this force consisted of around 4,000 soldiers, half of them Albanians and Turks, each accompanied by his slave and a donkey. There was also a group of Kurdish riders, a contingent of Bedouins dressed in mail, and some half-naked paupers with spears who had come along in the hope of sharing the spoils of war, not to mention the 50 piastre reward for every ear sliced from an enemy's head.[4] Including servants, prostitutes and parasites, there were altogether 10,000 souls who made camp every evening. There were also a few Europeans along – for example, the Frenchman Frédéric Cailliaud, who published the first magnificently illustrated books on the ancient Nile civilizations in Sudan. These books were almost a metre tall and contained superbly detailed drawings and plans of hitherto unknown pyramids and classical edifices – books it is impossible to remain unmoved by when you see them today, especially in light of the bloody and violent campaign in which the author and adventurer, on a hunt for Sudan's gold, took part.

Egypt's campaign to the south in the first half of the nineteenth century against Shendi and Sennar was, like other campaigns in the history of this region, fundamentally effected by the Nile's water flow. It determined the timetable of their advance: the river could not be in full flood because then it became impassable, but neither could it contain too little water because then it would be impossible to get the boats over those cataracts that characterize the Nile in the area. On 12 June 1821, Muhammad Ali's annexation of Sudan was proclaimed in Sennar, capital of the Funj Dynasty, which lay on the Blue Nile's west bank just south of where that tributary meets the White Nile.

Early in November, Isma'il made a tour of inspection down the Nile. He left his escort and travelled to Shendi on the main Nile, where what would be a fateful meeting with the local leader, Mek Nimr, took place. Isma'il ordered Mek Nimr to collect a large sum of money, plus 6,000 slaves and equipment for the entire campaign, within forty-eight hours. The background for this impossible demand was that Muhammad Ali had expressed dissatisfaction with the Sudan campaign. The gold mines in Fazogli yielded less than expected and Egypt had only received 15,000 slaves rather than their goal of 40,000. Mek Nimr reacted immediately and said it was impossible to fulfil Isma'il's demand. Isma'il then struck him across the face with the end of his long Turkish pipe. Mek Nimr stood and drew his sword. He was restrained by Isma'il's guards and forced to beg forgiveness. A banquet was then arranged for Isma'il and his company but, while the belly dancers performed, Mek Nimr and his men encircled the tent and set it on fire. Isma'il burned to death. The soldiers who escaped the flames were massacred.

Mek Nimr's actions in Shendi unleashed a revolt. Egypt's representative in Sudan swore that he would send 20,000 skulls to Cairo as revenge. A man who attempted to assassinate him was captured and condemned to be staked alive, but before the punishment was carried out it was altered: instead he was sliced to ribbons by a sword expert until dead. Other men were castrated, women had their breasts cut off, people were buried alive. Using terror to crush all resistance, the Ottoman, or the Turco-Egyptian subjugation of northern Sudan, was completed in 1824.

Muhammad Ali's goal was to make the entire Nile Valley part of Egypt, not because the Egyptian leaders at that time viewed the Nile hydrologically as a single Egyptian territory, but because the river was, quite simply, the corridor between Egypt and eastern and central Africa.

The most important reason for Muhammad Ali's march south, however, was the need to recruit slaves for the army. He wanted to build a new army, loyal to himself and trained by European specialists. He had begun to mistrust his Albanian and Turkish soldiers because they were inclined to mutiny. Using slaves as soldiers had a long history in the Islamic Middle East and in parts of north-east Africa, but the practice was gradually becoming a thing of the past. The campaign into Sudan and South Sudan revived this tradition. Muhammad Ali himself succeeded in his regional imperialism only in part, but by 1870 the khedives controlled Sudan and large swathes of Uganda – formally on behalf of the Ottoman sultan. Egypt had got an empire as large as Western Europe, and its occupation of this great area was a major military feat.

Mek Nimr, who murdered Muhammad Ali's son, became, however, a national hero in the Sudan. When President Omar Hassan al-Bashir held his commemorative address in 2011 on behalf of the nation's fifty-fifth anniversary celebration as an independent state, he traced the nation's birth to Mek Nimr's revolt against Isma'il and the Turco-Egyptian occupation force, and the only bridge connecting Khartoum to Omdurman and crossing the Nile is called Mek Nimr Bridge. The events in Shendi in 1821, therefore, pinpoint a key issue in Sudan's history – their relationship to their northern neighbour.

A key axis around which this relationship has revolved for the last 150 years is the Nile's economic and cultural role, and how Egypt and Sudan should approach the use of the river on which both so fundamentally depend.

The politics of geography

Outside the car window, desert stretches in all directions. I am heading to Khartoum, the capital of Sudan. I am travelling from Dongola, about midway from Wadi Halfa, and the quickest route is straight through the desert. The monotonous landscape, the deadly repetitiveness of view, flat, grey and never-ending, and the sounds of the Land Cruiser are soporific, so I take a drink from a water bottle and pick up an article I brought along that fits the landscape; the article is written by Sulayman Huzayyin, one of Egypt's most famous historical geographers.[5] His scientific project took the form of formulating what he thought were useful concepts regarding geographic regions in the Nile Valley, making no effort to conceal the political goal that drove his conceptual innovations: an Egypt that also included Sudan. Achieving a form of alliance, be it in a form of union or merger between Egypt and Sudan, has been a main aim of Egyptian diplomacy since the beginning of the nineteenth century – indeed, Egypt's modern political history long considered a full union to be an obvious goal. Huzayyin's article was meant as a scientific and historical-geographical justification for this policy.

The discussion surrounding how historians have contributed to 'inventing' a nation's national traditions is well known in a European context, and the classic work is *The Invention of Tradition* by Eric Hobsbawm. Huzayyin did what many historians and historical geographers have done during critical periods or moments in the history of the countries they lived in: he took on the role of an expansionist nation-builder and placed his research at the service of a political project larger than himself.

Huzayyin introduced concepts or distinctions between *wadi al-Nil* (the Nile Valley), *hawd al-Nil* (the Nile basin), and *hadbat al-Nil* (the Nile highlands). From a geographic standpoint, it was only the parts of the Nile Valley formed by Egypt and the central areas of Sudan that represented what he called a specific *al-bia'h-al-niliyya*, or Nile environment, and it is only here that homogenous geographical and ecological relationships are found which create an integrated geographical unity where the Nile signifies everything, or where the Nile is the all-eclipsing and decisive geographical factor. On these grounds, Huzayyin sought to establish what he called a 'national space' based on 'geographical fact', whereas he dismissed former Egyptian demands of an Egyptian territorial *Lebensraum* as mystical and invalid.

For, in this part of the Nile basin, he argued, people had been shaped into a kind of common organic unity that over time tended to develop the same ideologies, religions and institutions. Culture reflected and served, one could almost say, the ecological and social structures in society, explained them and ensured their integrity, stability and endurance. From this perspective, Egypt not only becomes the civilization-producing unity, but an actor that does nothing but what nature demands. Or, put more directly:

Egypt was the route or road that culture and civilization took in order to reach Sudan; Egypt brought Sudan 'the light of culture', so to speak.

In this context, Muhammad Ali's occupation of Sudan was a reunification of those parts of the Nile basin that belonged together as an organic unity, based profoundly on the social and cultural conditions that the specific Nile environment tended to create. The Nile Valley's unity is, therefore, a natural given, it is as straightforward as that. As a historical geographer, Huzayyin wrote, it was his duty to present the scientific truth regarding 'the unity of the Nile valley', and as an Egyptian nationalist he was called to fight for the concept's usefulness and for the notion that it captured reality as it actually was. The Nile created a natural corridor between Africa and Egypt for culture, trade and contact, and it was the Nile's particular natural aspect in Egypt that formed the basis for the country to create an entirely distinct Egyptian civilization, an integrated, leading and unique civilization, which from its start was exceptionally clear on its uniqueness, and whose 'task' it was to assemble the Nile Valley. This geographic analysis matched the Egyptian nationalists' slogan of 'Unity in the Nile valley', as well as the fact that the Egyptian king styled himself, as recently as 1948 in a talk at the UN in New York, as 'King of the Nile', or the king of Sudan and Egypt.

After travelling along the main Nile from Alexandria to Khartoum, it is easy to understand and have sympathy for the Egyptian geographer's Nile Valley perspective, and the logic of his argument is, from a downstream point of view, enticing. Therefore, it is paradoxical that the Nile, from the 1990s on, emerged as perhaps the most critical dividing factor between Egypt and Sudan since the time of the British Nile empire, when London used their Nile policies to encourage an independent Sudan from Egypt. Huzayyin could not have known that the Nile will, probably, remain a divisive issue in the relationship between the two neighbours. And what will happen within an even longer time perspective? Perhaps the passage of time will prove more friendly to his project, thus illustrating how the long term in many cases tends to solve history's provisional judgements and responses. With a new Sudan that after 2011 consists only of the northern portions of a country that up to that year was the biggest in Africa, and with an increasingly overpopulated Egypt, there is reason to believe that political and religious groups both in Egypt and Sudan will be entertaining new thoughts and ideas regarding how the relationship between the two countries should develop in the truly long term, the extent to which modern national state borders ought to be lifted, and if these state-societies should instead be organized as an *umma*, as a collective community of Muslims.

I put the article back in the brown bag next to my seat and say to the driver – rather abruptly, judging by his reaction, because he glances at me as if he thinks I am suffering from heatstroke – that Huzayyin's theories have gained renewed actuality.

Explorers who vanished

In the desert south of Egypt, two young British men disappeared without a trace at the beginning of the nineteenth century while on the hunt for the source of the Nile. This is how it happened.

In 1822, the Association for Promoting the Discovery of the Inner Parts of Africa, known as the African Association of London, hired a certain James Gordon to discover the Nile's source. He departed London a year after Muhammad Ali's forces entered Sudan, probably at the beginning of the year, and reached Cairo in early summer. From Cairo, news of him arrived in London. In 1823, one could read in the *Quarterly Review* that: 'Captain Robert James Gordon of the Royal Navy left Cairo in May last [1822] for the purpose of ascertaining the source of the Bahr el Abiad (the White Nile in Arabic). He is alone and sets out with a full determination never to return without making some important discoveries.' Apparently, he had said: 'If, I should find it advisable for my purpose to travel as the slave of some black merchant, I will most gladly do so, for I feel there is no retreating from what I have undertaken to perform – en avant is my motto, and trust to fortune!'[6]

James Gordon disappeared somewhere in the deserts of Sudan, dressed as an Arab and without an interpreter, and no one has ever found his remains.

Another explorer who literally vanished from history on his way to find the source of the Nile was Henry P. Welford, who also had been hired by the African Association to travel to Egypt, then to Sennar, and as far up the White Nile as he could go. The Association, as usual, informed the Foreign Office, and the Foreign Secretary, as was customary in such matters, sent a letter requesting that the British ambassador in Alexandria provide Welford assistance via Muhammad Ali's administration. Yet, it was also the case with Welford that darkness shrouded his movements once he entered Sudan. The last that we know of him alive is that he was in Nubia and had reached the Second Cataract.

A little later, on 20 June 1831, a notice appeared in the *Times*, presumably regarding Welford: 'We regret to announce the death of another African traveller. Captain Woodfall [*sic*], sent out by the African Society to penetrate into the interior by way of Abyssinia (Ethiopia), only reached Kourdefan, where he fell sick and perished.'

The past, we well know, is largely a victor's narrative. None of Mensen Ernst, James Gordon and Henry P. Welford succeeded in the quest to find the source of the Nile, and they have been forgotten as explorers. But their defeat – their willingness to risk their lives in the struggle to solve the Nile's geographical mystery – underscores perhaps more clearly than any success just how much so many were willing to risk in order to resolve what was considered to be the most important geographical puzzle of their time.

Wanderings and castles in the sand

'My fatherland is where it rains. My fatherland is where it rains.' When I was awakened by a slight touch, I clearly recalled the song that the camel drivers had sung around the fire the previous evening. Leaning over me stood a man with a dark face and a white turban against a stark morning sun. They had stopped a car with which they told me I could travel to Khartoum. They were also already fully packed, ready to continue their journey into the Sahara, westward away from the river and towards Darfur, where people may greet each other with the expression: 'Has it rained for you?' – by which they mean: 'How are you doing? How are things going with you?' For these camel nomads, the Nile's banks were only a temporary halt.

A few years later I am in Nubia again. I am standing among some craggy, black stone formations in the desert and witnessing how the wind has incessantly built, and is still building, sand dunes in the form of small pyramids that often vanish as quickly as they appear. Here, it is not so difficult to understand why poets have proclaimed that the desert with its emptiness, the colour of the sand, the apparent loneliness of the stones, and the wind as it blows, are an invitation to the lyrical mode – to the excessively lyrical, I would say. For to the extent that these enormous flats, where nothing grows aside from isolated thorny bushes insistent on a meagre existence, tells us anything, it must be about the value of silence or moderation, or both.

It is the middle of Ramadan. The two Sudanese with whom I am travelling are both Muslims and are strictly fasting. When Hassan prepares the fire as the sun sinks over the stony desert landscape, tinting the whole sky in different shades of red, as he pours water into pots, readies the sausages and chicken in a pan, and retrieves the field beds from the top of the car, he has not eaten or drunk a drop since sunrise. It has been around 50°C in the shade all day and we have been working. I, for my part, have consumed litres, continually, so to speak, supplying my body with water. I cannot help but admire his perseverance and self-control, not least for the fact that, right before the fast breaks, he insists upon taking charge of dinner preparations and organizing the night's resting place. Or, is what I am witnessing the psychology of submission, the blind obedience to Allah that does more good the more painful it is? Is it instead an example of the desert religion's harshness? When I ask him if he is, in fact, ready to drop, he simply proceeds as if he has not heard me. He only says, optimistically, after everything is prepared and he has even whipped up some hot vegetables: 'Dinner is served'.

Laying on my field bed while gazing up at the sparkling night sky without even a thin sheet pulled over me, for it is much too hot, I reflect on what a camel nomad told me and what I later had read somewhere: 'Things with kinship seek each other out. Water flows towards what is wet. Fire turns towards what is dry. Rain follows clouds. And wind follows heat.'

Where the great rivers meet

Khartoum lies where the Blue and the While Niles meet. Here, it is as if the two rivers come running at each other, attempting to eclipse, or perhaps escape, their separate identities, and becoming The River. An Arab poet has famously called this meeting of the two Niles 'the longest kiss in history'. At its widest point, small waves appear on the river, like the wrinkles on an old, experienced face that has seen what there is to be seen.

The city is surrounded by desert; sandstorms emerge suddenly to darken it. Then it can turn so black that if you hold your hands before your face, you cannot see them. But just as quickly as the sandstorm comes, perhaps after only a quarter of an hour, the sand clouds depart and the sun shines once more from a clear sky, as is usually the case in Khartoum.

Khartoum is a classic river city, though its architecture has historically mostly directed it away from the water – as a move to defend it against the annual flood and the danger this always has represented. When Muhammad Ali's military force moved their headquarters from Shendi to Khartoum in the 1820s, they transformed what was then a humble fishing village. Because of the site's strategic location, they established a military post and thus planted the seeds of a permanent and large settlement. After the Turco-Egyptian administration in Sudan succeeded in opening the swamps in southern Sudan to river traffic in the mid-nineteenth century, the city's strategic and economic importance as a trade centre increased. It became the springboard for countless expeditions upstream, for ivory, slaves and gold, and eventually also for mapping the Nile. As such, Khartoum very quickly became the regional centre for the slave trade, as Zanzibar was on Africa's east coast. Following substantial pressure from Europe, the Turco-Egyptian government prohibited public slave trading in 1854, but the trade continued, albeit in more clandestine forms.

The British adventurer and explorer, Samuel Baker, was not impressed of the capital when he arrived there in the 1860s, and wrote:

A more miserable, filthy, and unhealthy spot can hardly be imagined [...] The town, chiefly composed of huts of unburnt brick, extends over a flat hardly above the level of the river at high water, and is occasionally flooded. Although containing about 30,000 inhabitants and densely crowded, there are neither drains nor cesspools; the streets are redolent with inconceivable nuisances; should animals die, they remain where they fall, to create pestilence and disgust.[7]

Khartoum and its twin city Omdurman, became, however, important sites in the history of the country. If one crosses the Mek Nimr Bridge over the Nile and swings right, one will be heading in the direction of Omdurman, the stronghold of the first Islamic revolution in modern world history. The Mahdi – 'the Chosen One' – who led the revolution, has abruptly become a contemporary figure due to the growing support for political Islam or Islamism, and his function as an inspiration and role model for some of today's radical Islamists. His mausoleum lies on the Nile's western bank, a couple of kilometres from the bridge.

The Mahdi, Muhammad Ahmad, best known in the West from Lawrence Olivier's character in the film *Khartoum* from 1966, is one of the most influential Sudanese politicians in history. He was born in 1844 on an island in the Nile, close to Dongola. His family moved south and Muhammad, like all his brothers, followed in his father's footsteps as a boatbuilder on the Nile. He also began to study the Qur'an and other Islamic texts and eventually earned renown as an exceptional speaker. He travelled extensively around the country and became an increasingly strong opponent of the Turco-Egyptian regime. When he returned in 1881 to his base, Aba Island – an island in the White Nile south of Khartoum – Muhammad Ahmad declared that he was al-Mahdi, 'the Chosen One', or Muḥammad Aḥmad ibn ʿAbd Allāh al-Mahdī. His mission, he thought, was to reform Islam and return it to the pristine form practised by the Prophet. His ambition was to cleanse Islam of everything that had ruined the religion after the Prophet Muhammad's death. It was necessary to return to the form of Islam that was practised during the Prophet's time. Tobacco, alcohol and dance would be forbidden – indeed, in one of his first proclamations, he warned that handclapping and playful looks were to be prohibited. Departure from the Mahdi's understanding of the Qur'an and the Hadiths was defined as heresy. Quickly, he began to build a group of followers, or *anṣār* ('helpers', a term referring to one group of Muhammad's early followers), and an army of jihadists.

The Mahdi proclaimed Holy War against the Ottoman-Egyptian Islamic rule in the Sudan. For a long time, he was simply overlooked and considered to be yet another of the many religious fanatics to turn up in Sudan at that time. But, after several successful military actions, the Mahdi was capable of mustering and leading an army of 30,000 men. He had attained a religious and political position and a military following that made it very difficult to crush him. Just a couple of years before this Islamic rebellion triumphed and took control in Sudan, the British had seized power in Egypt. In Sudan, only the port city of Suakin, reinforced by Indian soldiers, and Wadi Halfa remained in Anglo-Egyptian hands. For a short time, they also retained power in Khartoum, but the Holy War's soldiers soon had the city surrounded.

The 'light-bearer' in Khartoum

The date is 13 March 1884, and one of the most famous sieges in history is beginning. The Mahdist troops have surrounded the city of Khartoum for ten months and, when they are finally able to enter the city, the entire garrison of Egyptian soldiers is killed along with 4,000 Sudanese civilians. But the reason for the siege becoming so famous is the role played by Charles Gordon.

Gordon (also known as 'Chinese Gordon' for his role in helping the Manchu-led Qing Dynasty to suppress the Taiping rebellion in China some decades before) has through his life story – and perhaps more than any other individual – spoken to, and been exploited by, European conceptions and myths regarding what was conceived as a battle for Christian civilization and values on the outermost edges of Western civilization. To anti-imperialists, his final days in the Sudan served, on the other hand, as proof that European imperialism could be beaten. The Nile became his fate in a double sense.

Gordon returned to the Nile many times. First, in 1873 he was appointed governor of Equatoria province in southern Sudan by the occupying Egyptian-Ottoman rulers. In this position, he worked to map in detail the Upper Nile and he established a set of administrative centres in southern Sudan and northern Uganda. In 1877, he became governor-general, that is to say, the chief representative in Sudan of the Turco-Egyptian government. In 1880, ill and exhausted after many years of labour, he returned to Great Britain. His reputation, however, ensured he remained in demand. King Leopold II of Belgium asked him to shoulder responsibility for the Congo Free State. Gordon rejected this offer. In 1880 he was appointed private secretary to the Viceroy of India. He served in this post for a short time. Then he was ordered to China, where he helped arbitrate a conflict with Russia, and in crushing the Taiping rebellion.

In February 1884, this early administrative globetrotter returned to Sudan and Khartoum. The situation there was completely different from the one he had left four years earlier. The Mahdi threatened to overrun and take the city, but it had not yet fallen. In England, Prime Minister William Gladstone was unwilling to intervene. London's decision not to send troops to assist Gordon has been interpreted as proof of what influential historians have termed the 'defensive imperialism' of the Victorian era.[8] According to this theory, the British were not actually interested in colonial possessions in this part of Africa. They were instead grudgingly forced to march up the Nile from a fear that European rivals would seize control of the river upstream from Egypt. They would then be able to use their power over Egypt's lifeline to force Great Britain away from Suez.

A close reading of contemporary sources, however, shows that this explanation, which has completely dominated historical interpretations regarding the partition of Africa and London's policy concerning the Nile countries and Sudan, can be falsified. Lord Cromer in Egypt and the government in London, had a clear strategy, one that concluded that it was not in London's interests to occupy Sudan in 1884. The British had just conquered Egypt and their priority was to get their 'Egyptian house' in order. Cromer was not worried about an Islamic regime in Khartoum, since that government was not focused on controlling the Nile, nor did it possess the technological competence or capacity to do anything with the river. The British rulers in Egypt, therefore, accepted the Mahdi's position with crushing calm. Indeed, an independent Sudan meant a weakening of the Ottoman Empire's interests in the Nile basin and was therefore advantageous to London's long-term strategic goals. Cromer planned to retake Sudan later, but not before the military campaign could be funded by a financially stronger Egypt and diplomatically justified to a sceptical outside world. The British would also need enough resources to take actual control of the country, and to do soon the pretence that it was a joint occupation with Egypt. No one viewed more clearly than Cromer the necessary long-term goal of Sudan's occupation, but he was against doing it in the 1880s. Cromer was no colonial dreamer but a true imperialist – that is to say a practical imperialist with a policy based on cost-benefit analyses of what was in the interest of Britain, their banks and the cotton industry.

Pressured by growing public opinion, London had accordingly sent Charles Gordon, who in the Sudan was associated with the detested old regime more than with Great Britain since he had previously served the Egyptian khedive there. His instructions from London and Cairo were to secure the evacuation of loyal soldiers and civilians and to depart with them. But, as soon as Gordon was back on familiar ground, he began to go his own way. After fighting his way to Khartoum, he refused to leave the city. He thought the city had enough provisions and secure communication lines north to British-controlled Egypt via the Nile. He also apparently began to see himself as a Christian warrior for civilization and light, battling against Islamic hordes and Muslim barbarity.

Eventually, as the situation became increasingly precarious and the Mahdi's forces ringed the city, Gordon asked London for military support. He did not receive it, or rather, when he at last received it, it was too late. Cromer and London, however, could not disclose the true reason behind their actions, because that would have revealed their long-term strategy amid what was an important but very complicated diplomatic situation. European and English newspapers published large spreads devoted to

Gordon and his plight, depicted as a light-bearer of civilization amid a sea of Islamic fanaticism. Gladstone was criticized for denying Gordon adequate military support. Demonstrators hurled rocks through the windows of 10 Downing Street and the prime minister was accused of being 'Gordon's murderer'. Newspapers sported large war-font headlines of the Khartoum siege. 'It is alarming', Queen Victoria wrote to Lord Hartington, the Secretary of State for War. 'General Gordon is in danger; you are bound to try to save him'. Pressure from the growing public movement under the slogan 'Save Gordon' prompted, albeit in haste and mostly to relieve public opinion, a rescue force being assembled, but they arrived in Khartoum two days too late.

The Mahdi's troops had simply waited for the flood to occur before they attacked Gordon's poorly defended garrison. Since they knew the river would then be difficult to use for the transport of troops and military equipment, they were quite sure that he would not be receiving sufficient reinforcements. It turned out that Gordon's communication lines rested upon political and hydrological illusions. The Mahdi's troops stormed the city during the night. Gordon was murdered in his palace just before dawn on 26 January 1885, and his head was delivered to the Mahdi's tent as a trophy. Ernest A. Wallis-Budge described the scene in this way:

> His head was cut off at once and sent to the Mahdi, and his body was dragged down the stairs into the garden, and stripped, and it lay there naked for some time; many Arabs came and plunged their spears into it. [...I]t was afterwards fixed between the branches of a tree and all who passed by cursed it and threw stones at it.[9]

The *New York Times* published its own myth-producing version: Gordon was murdered while he read the Bible.

Yet, there is another story that has endured and that is largely due to an iconic painting by George William Joy entitled: *Gordon's Last Stand*. The painting, which hangs in the Leeds City Art Gallery, has been reproduced in countless books and is one of the foremost examples of Victorian imperial myth-making. The image has been described as depicting a frozen moment of imperial valour; it shows General Charles Gordon, majestic, defiant while facing sure death and, thus, a true heroic figure. His white face is expressionless. What is most striking with the painting as a source to the long history of cultural representation is that the Islamic insurgents in the painting are paralysed, as if in awe at the sight of this Christian warrior-diplomat who stands at the top of the stairs, apparently not afraid of anything, not even death. It served to reassure the world views of the Victorian mind, it represented both a convincing and conventional image of the ongoing confrontation between order and Western civilization on the one hand and anarchy on the other hand.

'Gordon in Khartoum' became a living, effective Victorian myth. Political and religious forces in Great Britain exploited the 'Fall of Khartoum' and Gordon's murder for all it was worth. This narrative about the fate of this 'Christian martyr' and the need to revenge him became, later, an argument for colonial expansion in the Upper Nile that many British politicians exploited and which public opinion accepted as the basis for the campaign to occupy Sudan between 1896 and 1898. No one cared that Gordon did not match the hero he had been described as; among other things, it later came out that he drank heavily. The Mahdi, on the other side, at the time was described as a barbarian, religious fanatic, utterly lacking the humanity that was ascribed to him in the 1966 movie *Khartoum*, where Laurence Olivier, who played the Mahdi, exclaimed when he received Gordon's decapitated head: 'Take it away! Where is Abdullah? I forbade it, I forbade it!'

A few years after the 'Fall of Khartoum' government spokesmen in London talked about 'revenge for Gordon' as a motive behind the military campaign upriver, but the occupation of the Sudan was not primarily motivated by religion or vague notions regarding the struggle for civilization. Britain's conquest of the Upper Nile resulted from a cold, calculated water imperialism. The campaign upstream did not revolve around Bible versus the Qur'an, or Christianity versus Islam, but rather around something much more prosaic, something that would not so easily inflame Victorian opinion: Nilometers and dams. 'Revenge for Gordon' – the slogan was exploited as a public relations argument to sway any opposition or indifference in a British populace not always equally thrilled by military adventures in Africa, and to persuade the missionary milieu over to the government's side. The successful propaganda that called for occupying Sudan as payback for Gordon's murder was an early example of successful rumour-mongering, or *spinning* as it would be called today, with a political goal in mind.

The Christian missionaries who believed that 'Revenge for Gordon' reflected official policy on religion were in for a surprise. One of Lord Cromer's first decisions after becoming the real ruler of Sudan was: no missionaries would be sent to North Sudan. Indeed, he prohibited outright Christian evangelism in Egypt and North Sudan. In 1899, on his travels to the newly conquered Khartoum, he assembled Islamic leaders in Omdurman and assured them that the new government would respect Islam and completely refrain from meddling in religious questions.

When the occupation of southern Sudan had become a fact in the autumn of 1898, Cromer, however, granted the missionaries permission to travel there. That was, in the first instance, a problem for the missionaries because they had learned Arabic and believed that they, with the government's support, would bring the Gospel to the Muslims in the north. In the south, by contrast, British colonial strategists divided the non-Islamic parts of the country between the various competing missionary organizations and gave them responsibility for education and schools within each of their enclaves. It was a clever design that was said to protect the Africans against the former Arab slave raiders in the north, and at the same time it fitted well with Britain's overall Nile strategy. If the British were to have a hope of succeeding with this plan, it was imperative that they cultivate loyalties in southern Sudan (as in Uganda) that would produce stronger lines of separation between these areas and Egypt and North Sudan, and to this end religion has throughout history often proven a useful tool.

The dance in the sand

Not far from Sheikh Hamad al-Nil's tomb in Omdurman, a memorial in honour of an Islamic scholar from the Funj Dynasty (1505–1820) and one of Khartoum's few historical attractions, a group of men gather each Friday and seek to attain a state of trance by dancing fervently around and around on the desert sands. Every week on the same day members of Qadiriyya, a Sufi sect, gather outside the tomb. For hours these legendary dervishes dance to the urging of drums, tramping barefoot on the sand, pirouetting with one foot, again and again, and then turning around by moving both feet lightning quick, again and again, until they achieve the trance state and, according to their belief, reach a point where their soul communes with Allah and is cleansed of all sin. The dance has for decades become a spectacle for sightseeing foreign tourists and Sudanese; but it also points back to the Mahdi Uprising in the 1880s and Islam's role in the Sudan.

After Gordon was killed and the Turco-Egyptian government was crushed, the Mahdi was the uncontested ruler of all Sudan. He introduced strict and traditional Islamic laws, reorganized the country's administration and declared himself to be the Prophet's representative. The Mahdi justified these reforms of Islam by proclaiming that they were answers to instructions given to him by God in the visions he had received. Unfortunately for the uprising, the Mahdi died of typhus six months after conquering Khartoum.

By establishing the first Islamic state in modern times, Muhammad Ahmad exerted an unusually strong influence on Sudanese history and politics. He established a relatively well-developed government administration in parts of the country and his personal governance was carried out via bureaucracy. The uprising can also tell us much concerning assumptions about modern Islamic fundamentalism. The interesting point is that this was not a revolt against the West or against European imperialism. Rather, it was primarily a reaction against Sudan's Islamic leaders and the Ottoman regime, which still governed the Islamic caliphate (abolished in 1924 by Kemal Atatürk). These Muslim leaders were perceived as simultaneously tyrannical, corrupt and modernizing. It was against the Turco-Egyptian administration, which had governed Sudan for around sixty years, that the revolution turned. Opponents were therefore branded as being al-Turk: 'Turks'. Mahdists described them in a thoroughly negative fashion, as a'da Allah – Allah's enemies. The revolution in 1885 refutes, therefore, those interpretations that view modern Islamism as a response to Western and US policies alone.

The story of the Mahdi revolt and how it has been understood can also show that leading Western politicians have again and again underestimated Islamism's ability to renew itself and to mobilize people. Winston Churchill utterly disliked the Mahdi's political project and participated in the war against the regime that the Mahdi established. The future British prime minister wrote in his introduction to Richard Bermann's *The Mahdi of Allah* (published in 1931), while referring to the Mahdi's sudden death after just a few years: 'It is always interesting to know what kind of book the devil would have written – but the theologians never gave him a chance.' Churchill, however, compared the Mahdi not only to the devil but also to William Booth of the Salvation Army. He wrote that the Mahdi's project was founded on a religious enthusiasm that was just as serious and philanthropic as that which inspired St Dominic and General Booth. But then Churchill adds that Bermann's book is probably the first and last word on 'Mahdism'.

In keeping with his era's strong faith in the ideological power and transforming influence of European civilization, Churchill underestimated Islamism's force and mobilizing capacity. Winston Churchill was, of course, also the man who, after the UN had adopted the Declaration of Human Rights in 1948, proclaimed that the West had finally succeeded in 'enthroning Western values' in the global arena. As it turned out, neither developments in the Nile Valley, nor in the world in general, would confirm such optimism on behalf of Western values or that religious fanaticism would fade away.

'Come here. See, the Islamists are dancing!' a Dutch tourist shouts at me while standing on his toes and trying to take pictures, since the expression on the dancers' faces resembles what he imagines a trance looks like. A Sudanese standing next to me smiles indulgently and mildly informs him that: 'They are not Islamists. They are Sufis. We are not the same.' The men in green and white jalabiyas, who swing around on a single leg in trance outside the tomb of Sheikh Hamad al-Nil in Omdurman, are therefore Sufis and not Islamists. But because their attempts to commune with Allah through dance were the only form of dancing publicly allowed in the Sudan for almost three decades after the coup of Islamists in 1989, it is definitely yet another expression of Islamism's strength and influence, and it illustrates how in the religious arena, the present is a stage for the past on its way towards the future – also with consequences for how the Nile will be exploited, controlled and shared.

Time and the river folk's daughter

From the Mek Nimr Bridge over the White Nile in Khartoum, you can see the Blue Nile coming in from the east and watch how these two world-famous rivers flow together near Omdurman and disappear over the horizon to the north. Standing here, I realize I have no idea how to describe what I am seeing. These two rivers that have shaped and interacted with societies since civilization emerged: is it an eternal lifeline in motion, a kind of timeless, yet also varying and at the same time utterly stable order? And, can the river, precisely because of its characteristic dualism, since it is at once timeless and mutable, prove an object for true knowledge?

Yet for a historian, for whom nothing can be timeless, and everything is mutable, what is a timeless order when confronted with this type of river? The philosopher Plato believed that behind all changes in knowledge and morality lay such timeless order. For him the immutable and everlasting were all that ultimately was real and, therefore, those were the only things that could truly prove objects for genuine knowledge. Everything that is given in space and time, the so-called phenomenal world that is communicated to us through our senses, is mutable and transitory. True reality must accordingly be found outside of space and time and must be known by virtue of something besides the senses.

However, is it not possible to imagine that such distinctions between the transitory and the timeless are drawn because of an all-too-short time horizon? Is it not expedient to regard the river, from a societal perspective, as a timeless order, compared to the ordinary, variable world of phenomena, things like state formation, technologies, kingdoms, the outbreak of the Suez Crisis, or the fall of Hosni Mubarak and Omar al-Bashir, or the death of Meles Zenawi? Is the river not a timeless order and, simultaneously, an order that shifts, though within its own eternal time frame? I believe it is fruitful to think in this way, for while conceptions of the river are always changing throughout different countries and cultural regions and contexts, the river itself remains timeless, even though it is radically marked by time. And it is only by regarding it as both timeless and time-marked that it can become an object for genuine knowledge in a societal sense. It is also for such reasons that great rivers can stimulate discussions from new perspectives, such as historian Fernand Braudel's sense of time and place and his famous classification of history's three types of temporalities: the long-term, the conjunctural, and that of events. This story about the Nile presents empirical analyses that seek to contribute to thinking about the usefulness of this threefold division of historical time spans and their relation to different levels of human activity. In addition to the concrete stories of the past that rivers carry with them, and of which they themselves are a part, the rivers' roles in society and nature may challenge, as both historical agents in their own right and as arenas or passive scenes for all types of human activity, dominant periodizations of regional and global history. For example, the coming British occupation of the Sudan created an often overlooked but still fundamentally transformative shift in its history: it became a hydraulic state.

From the Mek Nimr Bridge, I can also see the place where a ten-year-old girl was tossed into the river. It happened right at the point where the White and Blue Niles meet, and it was because people thought she was an angel. In an article in *Sudan Notes and Records*, one of the best journals the British administration published while London governed the country, a British colonial administrator told one of many similar tales that have been circulated along the Nile.[10]

It was during the time that Abdullah governed – that is, right after the Mahdi's death and before the British seized power. A fisherman cast his net into the river, as fishermen have always done, and caught a girl who was around ten years old. He asked whose daughter she was. She replied that she was the River Folk's daughter. The fisherman had no choice but to take her to the caliph, who asked her the same question. She answered: 'Oh Khalifa, I am a daughter of the River Folk and I had just gone out of my house to chop up a little firewood when the net swept me up.' When the caliph heard that she belonged to the River Folk, he became afraid to receive her and, after consulting his advisers, they placed her back in the fisherman's boat and she was thrown back into the river at the point where the White Nile meets the Blue Nile.

Similar stories about people who appear small and white, and who shrivel when they are taken out of the water, have been told up and down the river for generations. Such river stories now seem to belong to an age of the past, thereby providing yet another example that conceptions of the river and its role and potentials change, whereas the river remains the same, if different.

Queen Victoria's river war

The riverbanks here and the plains around Omdurman were also the scene for perhaps the most brutal battle the advancing British Empire waged. A conquering Anglo-

Egyptian army with modern weapons slaughtered a Sudanese force largely equipped with swords and spears and weapons of inferior quality. It was an important step in a development that would make Queen Victoria the ruler of a British Nile empire.

From the very beginning of the 1890s, the London government, and Cromer and his men in Cairo, had been convinced that occupying Egypt would mean securing British interests in the whole Nile basin. In 1890, they had already secured acceptance from their European rivals that the river would be recognized as London's 'sphere of interest'. As such, political leaders in Cairo and London did not debate *whether* these regions ought to be occupied but *when* it would be most expedient to do so. In 1894, London seized control of the White Nile's natural reservoirs – the big lakes in the interlacustrine region, i.e. Lake Victoria and Lake Albert. In 1895, it was decided that it was Sudan's turn, even though the campaign was not launched until the following year. As already argued, for the British in Cairo the Mahdi's rule represented no danger, nor was London concerned about the Islamic revolution's possible wider effects in Egypt. The British also knew that Sudan had suffered terrible crop failures in 1889 and 1890, a harvest situation only aggravated by the leadership's military disposition. Stories were told of 'silent villages whose people starved quietly to death'.[11]

What chiefly concerned Britain's strategists and water engineers in Cairo was the fact that the Mahdi's government in Sudan made it more difficult to rationally exploit the Nile in Egypt. They no longer received information about discharge variations of the river before it entered Egypt. In the 1870s Egypt had established measuring stations along the river in Sudan in order to secure such hydrological data. In the early 1880s the British Nile experts in Cairo had been telegraphed daily information regarding the water flow upstream. They also knew, of course, that any rational or optimal use of the planned and revolutionary Aswan Dam, to be completed in 1902, required regular access to hydrological information about the river flow before it entered the reservoir. This required some form of political control over the upstream regions through which the river ran.

Exactly ten years after the 'Fall of Khartoum', the British government finally awarded full authority to General Herbert H. Kitchener and gave him the order: plan the conquering of Sudan! With the aid of clever diplomatic manoeuvres and use of the media, which not least involved the spreading of stories that exaggerated the threat France posed upstream to Egyptian interests, London managed to convince the Egyptian government, still nominally under the Ottoman sultan, to finance the campaign and to provide most of the 25,800 soldiers for what, significantly, was called the Nile Expeditionary Force. The British, meanwhile, exercised full military and political control over the army of occupation, while at the same time selling British-produced weapons to the campaign, another expense bankrolled by Egyptian taxes.

By the mid-1890s, London had succeeded in putting Egypt's finances into order, something that had been a prerequisite for Cromer and London to give the occupation of Sudan the green light. They had accomplished this task by focusing on the Nile and water management. First, they repaired and rebuilt the irrigation system. That gave agriculture and cotton exports an enormous boost, and state finances improved with surprising alacrity, so that the bankers and private speculators in Europe got their money back. British leaders, at whose head was a member of the wealthy Baring family

(Lord Cromer was the Earl of Baring), understood that an even more comprehensive irrigation system would bolster this positive economic trend while also fortifying the position of Britain's occupation force. The basis for such an expansive water policy in Egypt is what I have termed 'water imperialism' outside of Egypt's borders; the development of irrigation and cotton exports made it simply a rational imperial policy to take control of the Nile upstream.

The river war began in 1896. Under Kitchener's leadership, the Anglo-Egyptian army marched south. A major war – whose goal was to achieve hydropolitical control over an international watercourse – was under way. Winston Churchill, then a war correspondent and soldier, published his famous two-volume work on this campaign, *The River War*, in 1899. Churchill wrote:

> [The Nile was] the great melody that recurs throughout the whole opera. The general purposing military operations, the statesman who would decide upon grave policies, and the reader desirous of studying the course and results of either, must think of the Nile. [. . .] It is the cause of the war: the means by which we fight; the end at which we aim.[12]

The Nile, meanwhile, only allowed for the transport of troops and heavy weapons over certain stretches. The British therefore concocted what many at the time considered to be a wildly ambitious idea. So intent were they upon conquering Sudan that they built a railway straight through the North Sudanese desert. The railway would make it possible to avoid the Nile's cataracts, which were a general's logistical nightmare. The caliph's capital, Omdurman, and his army there, were now within easy reach for Britain. With the aid of the railway, troops could be sent into the heart of Sudan no matter the season or the river's level. The railway made it possible to send food, ammunition and gunboats not just to Khartoum but even to the Upper Nile.

Eventually, as tracks were laid, the first trains began to roll through the desert's suffocating heat carrying the necessary wares – the first with tracks and supplies, the second, according to Churchill, with 'the letters, newspapers, sausages, jam, whisky, soda-water, and cigarettes which enable the Briton to conquer the world without discomfort'.[13]

Around a century later, I also took this train through the desert. We perched hour after hour on hard wooden benches placed next to windows that could not be closed, and for more than a day sand became our world – in our hair, beneath our shirts, in our mouths, in our rolled-up sleeping bags, in our ears – while Sudanese with even cheaper tickets clutched tight to the flat roofs of the train's carriages. From the window, I saw only desert and mirages, and if I really looked, I caught glimpses of water almost everywhere in the distance. While I trembled from lack of sleep and the morning-chilled desert wind, I thought of Samuel Baker's famous description from *In the Heart of Africa*, of soldiers and their mirages here in Sudan. Baker writes of an Egyptian regiment that vanished in the desert. The soldiers were permitted to carry only a little water and they suffered from extreme thirst. Abruptly, they caught sight of a beautiful lake. They insisted a local guide take them there. The guide, however, told them it was pointless because the lake did not exist. He did not want to waste precious time chasing a mirage. They shot him. As Baker writes:

The whole regiment turned from the track and rushed toward the welcome waters. Thirsty and faint, over the burning sands they hurried; heavier and heavier their footsteps became; hotter and hotter their breath, as deeper they pushed into the desert, farther and farther from the lost track where the pilot lay in his blood; and still the mocking spirits of the desert, the afreets of the mirage, led them on, and the lake glistening in the sunshine tempted them to bathe in its cool waters, close to their eyes, but never at their lips. At length the delusion vanished – the fatal lake had turned to burning sand! Raging thirst and horrible despair! the pathless desert and the murdered guide! lost! lost! all lost! Not a man ever left the desert . . .[14]

With the help of the narrow-gauge railway that Kitchener's troops had built, the British pressed relentlessly on. The town of Abu Hamed was taken on 7 August 1897. On 8 April 1898, they won the Battle of Atbara. Winston Churchill writes: 'On the day that the first troop train steamed into the fortified camp at the confluence of the Nile and the Atbara rivers the doom of the Dervishes was sealed.'[15] During August 1898, the British advanced on towards Omdurman: the stronghold of the Mahdists.

The British massacre on the banks of the Nile

On 1 September 1898, British gunboats appeared on the Nile outside Omdurman. Caliph Abdullah, the Mahdi's successor, bravely tried to stand against this superior force, superior not in men but in weapons.

At dawn on 2 September 1898, 15,000 men launched a frontal attack against the Anglo-Egyptian force, but the result of the battle was a forgone conclusion. Armed with spears and antique weapons, the Sudanese army had no chance. Kitchener's men, on other hand, with their new European rifles, Maxim machine guns and artillery, mowed down the opposition, who unflinchingly billowed toward them. In the course of five hours, around 11,000 Sudanese died, while Anglo-Egyptian losses stood at less than fifty soldiers. Winston Churchill, who took part in the slaughter, described in gruesome detail the actions of the Anglo-Egyptian force during these autumn hours. He depicted them as being half-barbaric, as unnecessarily violent acts committed by men from a civilized country, but perhaps most astounding to readers today: he defended the victorious soldiers' actions of moving among their wounded enemies and systematically murdering them. While the Mahdi himself had died when his regime was at its height, before its weaknesses had become clear, his successor lived long enough to see his army defeated and his capital seized. He died in flight, during a last desperate attempt to preserve the Islamic government.

Can this battle between a British-led Anglo-Egyptian army and Islamic warriors on 2 September 1898, be compared to the war between the West and the Taliban after 11 September 2001? Does this battle play into the long and bloody history where Islam and the West fight it out in a struggle for ideas and value systems? The British historian Niall Ferguson is one of countless authors who has focused on this battle, and who is occupied with such comparisons. In his book *Empire: How Britain Made the Modern World*, from 2003, Ferguson writes that, in many ways, the Mahdi was a Victorian

Osama bin Laden, that he was an Islamic fundamentalist who murdered General Gordon, and that for this reason the British decided that his regime must be crushed.[16] On this basis, Ferguson compares the Battle of Omdurman at the end of the 1890s to 'the kinds of war the US has fought [...] against the Taliban' a hundred years later.

Drawing historical parallels is always problematic, for what characterizes history is precisely the fact that it never repeats itself. To compare the Battle of Omdurman with the war against the Taliban is to juxtapose two phenomena that do not have any significant points of contact, aside from the fact that the West's opponents were Muslim on both occasions. The goal in 1898 was not to vanquish Islamic fundamentalism, and the Mahdi was not – nor was he perceived to be – a threat to British interests. In order to understand this campaign and its background, it is thus necessary to widen the perspective and locate the war within a Nile context, that is as a chapter in the Nile's brutal biography.

Today, one can visit the Mahdi's restored grave not far from the historic battle scene. The British rebuilt the mausoleum in 1947. They erected a copy of the more than fifty-year-old original that they, in their conqueror's arrogance, had destroyed in 1898. The Mahdi's grave monument had been raised by the caliph in honour of his predecessor. It was a whitewashed stone structure, about 30 metres tall, and topped with a white dome that rested upon a 15-metre-high hexagonal base. Four small domes also decorated the corners of the building. Within, the mausoleum was painted green and chocolate brown, and all the woodwork was done in green, the colours of Islam. Surrounded by a worked iron railing taken from the Austrian Mission Church in Khartoum, there stood a green-painted wooden sarcophagus containing the Mahdi's remains. Kitchener knew that the mausoleum was a pilgrimage site. He determined, therefore, that it would be politically astute to destroy it, and Cromer agreed. The task of destroying the mausoleum was awarded to 'Monkey Gordon' as he was called, that is Charles Gordon's nephew, who willingly stepped into the role as a kind of nemesis on behalf of a righteous history. After the monument had been reduced to rubble, he concluded his task by casting the Mahdi's ashes into the Nile.

On 4 September 1898, representatives of the different regiments paraded along the Blue Nile's western bank in front of the ruins of General Gordon's palace. The upper level of the building was gone and the famous stairs where Gordon was killed had been razed. Two boats transported troops from Omdurman, one of them commanded by Gordon's nephew. These were moored directly beneath the remains of Gordon's palace. On the roof, not far from where Gordon had been killed, two flagstaffs had been raised. Beside one stood two British officers, beside the other a British and an Egyptian officer. The British leaders had carefully planned the whole ceremony; it was a diplomatic scene and game, and they wanted from the very start to make it clear that what had been portrayed as a joint military campaign between Egypt and Great Britain, in reality was a British-controlled enterprise. It was therefore Kitchener who was the master of ceremonies. When he lifted his hand, the Union Jack and the Egyptian flag were raised. Twenty-one cannon were fired from the gunboat *Melik* on the order of Charles Gordon's nephew. Kitchener called for three cheers for Her Majesty and for the Khedive. Then a short service was held. After that, the commanding general, with all the pathos invoked by the occasion, ordered that the whole ceremony be concluded with General Gordon's favourite hymn, 'Abide with Me'.

Not long afterwards, the British began constructing the governor-general's palace on the very site where Gordon had been murdered and where the Mahdists triumphed. With the self-consciousness typical of the Empire's first decades, they called the structure Gordon's Palace. From this building, set back enough from the river so it would not be caught by the autumn flood, but oriented towards it, the British governor-general would determine Sudan's development during London's period as ruler of the Nile.

Omdurman, which was visible from the palace's windows, had become a city controlled by Britain, and over the brown walls and whitewashed houses the Union Jack now flew.

The unknown engineer and a historical report

The British administration in Sudan quickly established control over the central parts of the country. This effort was organized by London's Foreign Office rather than the Colonial Office, due mainly to Sudan's political significance to the whole Suez strategy. The administration the British built here was distinctive because it was composed almost exclusively of people who had read Humanities subjects at university with doctoral degrees from Oxford or Cambridge, and who were required to learn Arabic before they could join what was called the Sudan Civil Service.

Although the country was reoccupied in Egypt's name, and London formally governed it together with Egypt through the so-called Anglo–Egyptian Condominium Agreement of 1899, the British from the very beginning developed a policy that would ensure them increasing influence and leave Egypt with an increasingly weaker foothold. This policy line was noticeable in all areas, and particularly when it applied to Nile policy. Britain's chief geopolitical strategy was based on the idea that whichever power controlled Sudan 'had Egypt at its mercy'. A memo from 1923 summarized this strategic vision: 'The power which holds the Soudan has Egypt at its mercy, and through Egypt can dominate the Suez Canal'.[17]

Bureaucrats in London's Foreign Office prepared one top-secret strategic document after another. It was underscored that since Sudan was located above Egypt on the Nile, controlling Sudan was a way of controlling Egypt. Because Suez and Egypt were so important to the British Empire's overall strategy, moreover, the British determined that parts of northern Sudan should be modernized, and since that process must occur with Nile water, they knew that it would lead to conflicts between Egypt and Sudan. By building a Sudanese economy that produced cotton for export to Great Britain, and by helping to establish an elite with economic interests in irrigation agriculture, they would kill two flies with one swat: Sudan would be capable of financing Britain's administration of the country, and Lancashire would receive greater and more secure access to cotton than it would if the industry was dependent solely on Egypt, and parts of the Sudanese political elite would develop economic and political interests that would place them on a collision course with Egypt, thereby indirectly strengthening Britain's position at Suez.

The Sudan campaign, therefore, revolved foremost around power over the Nile. Indicative of the weight that London and Cromer placed on the Nile question, as well as the study of what could be done with the river, was the fact that no sooner had they ordered the army up the river and raised the British flag along its banks at Khartoum, than they sent their principal Nile expert in Egypt on long exploratory journeys upriver all the way to Uganda and the Congo. It was this man who came to describe Sudan's position, both economically and politically, in the overarching British strategy for Nile exploitation in a number of seminal Nile reports.

This almost unknown man was William Garstin. There are no statues of him, hardly any descriptions and almost no photographs. He was a Scotsman who had served in the colonial service in India, and he became one of the many talented water-planners Britain employed. Not only was he the chief person responsible for control of the Nile in Egypt, but he was also responsible for agriculture, ancient monuments and public works. He had an enormous arena of responsibility, therefore, and he was forced to adopt what in modern parlance would be called a 'multipurpose approach' to the water question since the water would have to fulfil so many needs within 'his' sectors. He also had Cromer's ear, something documented in Cromer's numerous water reports. One British writer, after meeting Garstin twice by chance on his travels along the Nile upstream of Khartoum, and having each time been similarly impressed by his knowledge and practical approach to colonial development commented: 'This then is the type of man who makes England what she is, the leader of the world, in all great civilising enterprises as well as in the commercial projects of our own land and her dependencies.'[18]

It was this Scotsman who travelled up the Nile in the wake of the Sudan campaign, studying for months and years the river's topography, vegetation, geology and hydrology. He evaluated where dams could be built, canals dug and huge cotton farms established. He wrote his first report on the main Nile from Dongola as early as 1897, almost before the gunpowder there had settled. Then he carried out one survey after another on the Nile tributaries in the Sudan. The most influential report by far that he wrote was finished in 1903 and published in 1904 and was based on observations made and data collected during extensive travels to survey the Upper White Nile region.

Report upon the Basin of the Upper Nile from 1904 is one of the most important documents from the British period in the Nile basin, and the one that has had the most far-reaching and fundamental significance for the region's development. The report summarized and formulated Britain's basic Nile strategy at the beginning of the century and established policy guidelines for the whole period when the Union Jack flew there. The way this report conceptualized the Nile as a single river basin system was uniquely modern in its approach. It represented a conceptual conquest of the premodern Nile, by conceiving it as one planning unit, as one hydraulic entity – from source to outlet. It was not only impressive in its grasp of the Nile issues, but was government report writing at its best.

Garstin's report can be regarded as a monument to a particular time – more illustrative or revealing than novels and sculptures, more adequate to the spirit of the times than even the best fictional narrative – because it provided an authoritative account of how the *entire* Nile river system was conceived at the turn of the century. The report reflects and summarizes the colonial power's attitudes towards people and nature along the watercourse, even as it voices Britain's crystal-clear self-assurance when it came to taking the very Nile itself in hand. To Sudan it was important, because it confirmed a British Nile strategy that defined Sudan's development as being second to Egypt's Nile requirements.

Moreover, Garstin described southern Sudan with its swamps as a pure aqueduct with the potential of delivering more water to the irrigation economies in the north. He also identified the Gezira region as a key area where Sudan could undertake large projects without directly affecting Egypt, something critical to British strategy at the time. He described potential dams along the cataracts in northern Sudan that the government in Khartoum is now building, if on a larger scale and for other purposes, and the report outlined concrete projects for taming the river in Ethiopia and Uganda. The foundation for Garstin's self-assured descriptions and analyses was the strength and entrepreneurial power of the British Nile empire during these early years of London's rule.

This man and his plans were, for the next hundred years, overlooked in the literature devoted to London's power in the region. Garstin's travels did not make headlines, and his calculations, maps, diagrams, plans and hydrology could not become public reading material. It is an interesting expression of the trends and conventionalism within the historical discipline that Garstin's work for a long time was hardly ever mentioned. Historical research harbours a general water blindness which, paradoxically, also at times has dominated the research concerning the conquest and rule of the Nile basin. It has resulted in dominant interpretations of this history not only dismissing the river's political and structuring economic significance, but also overlooking those individuals who changed it or the engineers who sought to tame it.

The Blue Nile and the explorer from Norway

At Bumbodi, not far from the border between Sudan and Ethiopia, a steamboat was moored for the first time in 1903; several decades would pass before this happened again. On board was Burchart Heinrich Jessen, the Norwegian captain of the boat and head of the expedition.

Who was this Jessen from the small city of Larvik in Norway and who wrote himself into late Nile explorer history? How did he end up here as a steamboat captain on the Nile? Jessen writes about the expedition in an article entitled 'South-Western Abyssinia' (1905) and also in a book published in 1906 where he tells his story about McMillan's African expedition: *W.N. McMillan's Expeditions and Big Game Hunting in the Sudan.* Jessen betrays nothing about himself, aside from the fact that he was hired by McMillan, a wealthy American big-game hunter.[19]

At the beginning of the 1890s, Jessen moved to the Norwegian town of Horten to pursue his education. There he met Amalie Berg, fell in love, and got married on 23 July 1892. After a time, Burchart Jessen left for America, like so many other of Horten's young men educated in engineering. Amalie went with him to America. Burchart, meanwhile, continued to write letters. Among them is one posted on letterhead from the 'European Offices for American Car and Foundry Company' in London, and dated Glasgow, 4 May 1902. It was the twelfth anniversary of their first meeting in Horten. The letter begins: 'To my beautiful wild flower', and it is signed 'Your Babit'. It is, you might say, a relatively lyrical, high-flown love letter from a man whom, as he writes, fate has 'relocated to foreign ground'. In farewell, he begs her: 'Forgive me, my own beautiful flower'. Why he is begging forgiveness we do not know.[20]

The next time we hear of Jessen, he is on his way up the Blue Nile in 1903, financially backed by American big game hunter, W.N. McMillan and given the political green light by the British Governor-General in Sudan, the powerful Sir Reginald Wingate. Wingate met Jessen and promised him all possible support for the expedition. The goal, among other things, was to discover if the river was navigable enough to be used as a trade route between Ethiopia and Sudan.

'An undertaking of this kind would naturally be very expensive, but fortunately this was only a matter of detail to Mr. McMillan, and no expense was consequently spared in order to ensure success', Jessen wrote. He then continued dryly: 'Unfortunately, however, the best equipped expeditions do come to grief sometimes, no matter how well fitted out they may be.'

And indeed, despite being well-financed, most things did go wrong. Among other things, Jessen's men were utterly inexperienced when it came to river-boating:

> The men I engaged consisted of a headman or Rais, a sailor, a fireman, and a boy whom I called Sambo, all green, and none of them had been on a steamer before. The Rais who was to steer had no knowledge of a steering wheel, while the fireman had not fired a cookstove even, so I prepared for squalls and hard work.

At one point, Jessen's team attempted to force the boat over the Roseires Falls, where around fifty years later Sudan built its first power plant, but they failed on their first attempt, and the boat sat with 'her nose right under, leaned over to one side, and looked as if she was going straight to the bottom' – until the undercurrent caught the boat and cast it back to where it started.

But Jessen's determination was unwavering and the book he wrote is full of irony and splendid descriptions of the landscape through which he journeyed. His motto was: Succeed or Sink. No compromise was accepted. After they had crashed into some large boulders, for example, and water was pouring over the bow, the steersman cried: 'Stop the engine!' Jessen, however, had a different idea:

> On the contrary I called to the men to pull like fury and put full speed on. Ahead she went slowly inch by inch, grating along the boulder, and at last we shot ahead and were in smooth water. It was an exciting moment and we were all glad to take a little rest up above on a sandbank. For the rest of the day we had some minor excitements, such as running onto blind rocks, and getting the propeller blades badly bent. By the way, we had put on the old brass propeller before starting after straightening it. At last we tied up for the night [...] and] so we had a delightful supper, with whisky and soda and cigarettes after, then a much needed rest.

Jessen's tale is one of an expedition where difficulties stood waiting in line. The French newspaper *Le Figaro* sent a journalist, Monsieur de Bois, to write about the adventure. He was supposed to cover McMillan's part in the expedition but, alas, was instead castrated by local people before he was murdered in the Danakil region. And the Blue Nile was, as Jessen wrote, surrounded by nothing but rocks, high peaks and cliffs.

McMillan and Jessen set out on another expedition two years later. This time Jessen started at the border between Sudan and Ethiopia. After an onerous journey upriver with Sudanese bearers, where almost all the camels and donkeys died of exhaustion, he was again forced to conclude that the Blue Nile could not be used for transport. One of the Sudanese who formed part of Jessen's group was captured and murdered by locals, perhaps because they thought he was a slave driver. Jessen described the murder, writing that they stuck two spears into him, slit his throat, cut off his testicles as a trophy, and used part of the meat of his upper arms as fish bait. Jessen was in no position to stop it. Finally, he was forced to give up. The river could not be navigated, and Wingate and the British received confirmation of what they already knew: the river was not a viable transportation route. Instead, it would be used to irrigate Sudan and Egypt.

Jessen himself vanished into the vast, dark space that is history's oblivion.

Sudan's possibilities and the birth of a hydraulic state

Whenever British administrators met in Gordon's old palace, now the British governor-general's headquarters, or at Hotel Gordon on the banks of the Blue Nile, opened by Governor-General Wingate in 1902, for afternoon tea, we know that for years they were worried about the danger of a new Islamic uprising. As their power was eventually consolidated, however, the discussions increasingly turned toward Sudan's possibilities as an agricultural country. It was not Islam that London was chiefly concerned about combating: to the contrary, they had not only prohibited Christian missionary activity in northern Sudan but allowed many of the country's Muslim institutions to remain intact, also tying themselves firmly to two different and competing Islamic sects and families.

It is clear from reports and from the minutes of the Governor-General's meetings in Khartoum that both the government in London and the British in Sudan increasingly understood that the country's development, as well as its capacity to finance the British administration there, hinged on the Nile. The country had enormous areas of flat, fertile land that only lacked water. Together with the textile interests in Lancashire and the very important 'Nile bureaucrats' in the Foreign Office in London, British envoys in Sudan were more and more concerned with exploiting the country's potential as an alternative producer of long-staple cotton for Britain's textile industry. For quite some time, Sudan's Nile policy, in keeping with the guidelines London had established, was under the control and daily leadership of the British in Cairo. After the Egyptian Revolution of 1919, however, the plan to establish in Sudan a separate ministry of irrigation was already overdue, and it did not become a reality until 1925.

Due to increasing anti-British sentiment in Egypt, London wanted to secure alternative sources of raw cotton for its textile industry, and from cotton-producing regions they would not have to sacrifice on the altar of a necessary 'political game', as the British expressed it based on their recent experience from Egypt. They had already identified the Gezira Peninsula as the place where they should locate their gigantic cotton farm on the Blue Nile. Garstin had described the peninsula in his 1904 report as being very well suited to large-scale irrigation agriculture, assuming a dam over the Blue Nile upstream was built. The British government had already approved financial support for such a project in Gezira in 1914, and during a secret meeting in 1917 in Whitehall Gardens, London, the man in charge of Nile control in Egypt, Murdoch MacDonald, described the fantastic potential for cotton production in the Gezira region. The participants at the meeting agreed to create a continuous farm as large as the Egyptian Delta, and that they would also build the Nile dam that would make such a farm a reality.

From the first moment, this massive water project became a part of world politics. When, during the First World War, it became public in Egypt that the British were proposing to build a dam in Sudan straight across the country's lifeline, national fury erupted: the Sennar Dam on the Blue Nile would give Britain the power to 'turn off the tap' as it was put in coffee houses across the Delta and shouted in Cairo's streets.

But the Egyptian perspective was not the only one. In contrast, the Sudan's Anglican bishop prayed during the Sennar Dam's opening ceremony:

> Almighty God, Eternal, Unchangeable; the only wise God, the great Father of mankind: we pray Thee to bless this Dam, the Reservoir and the Irrigation Scheme, not only that thereby the people may get wealth and prosperity, but that rightly using these Thy gifts they may increase in wisdom, in learning, in religion and true righteousness. [...] We praise Thee for the wisdom and foresight of those who conceived the idea of harnessing the waters of this river for the use of man: and herein do we especially remember William Garstin and Herbert Horatio Kitchener.[21]

Afterward, the Mufti, the supreme Islamic leader, spoke – and he was no less subtle on behalf of the Nile and Allah: 'We stand here to-day to raise our hands in supplication to thank the Almighty, the Highest, the most Exalted of the Greatest of Kings for the great favors he has shown to us by the completion of this lofty building, and of the great Gezira irrigation scheme.'[22]

The Bishop and the Mufti presided over what, in a long historical perspective, amounts to what can be seen as an ecumenical baptism of Sudan as a modern Nile state. The new dam was hailed as a gift from God and Allah, and as a triumph for humankind – and for the British colonial administration. No longer was the Nile being worshipped as a divine entity but, rather, was being revered as a human-made, impressive structure of concrete and cement.

A dam 3,025 metres long and with a maximum height of 40 metres had now been raised across the river. It functioned both as regulator and reservoir. As regulator, it would increase the river's water level, thereby allowing more water into the Gezira

Canal during the time the Nile was at its height. As reservoir, it enabled water from the water-rich season to be stored against the poor season. How much could be stored was established through an agreement with Egypt. Both dam and river water were the essentials for the world's largest cotton plantation.

The project also became part and parcel of Britain's long-term, and quite subtle strategy: after Sudan had jointly been occupied by London and Egypt, London had systematically worked to weaken Egypt's position there. The British had succeeded in 1913 in making Sudan financially independent of Egypt, more or less at the same time as the government could receive its first loan for the massive irrigation project planned on the Blue Nile.[23] The Declaration of 1922, which ended the British protectorate over Egypt, also established Sudan as one of four policy areas, in addition to the Nile, over which the British reserved supremacy. The Nile and the Gezira project were employed as a very effective wedge to make the conflict between Egyptian and Sudanese nationalists greater. Since the economic interests of both national elites were tied to usage of the river, disagreements regarding how much water Sudan could use would inevitably produce feuds again and again. The idea was that this would undermine the Egyptian visions and plans to create a single Nile state under Cairo's dominance and leadership.

A white-spotted gecko and the Prophet

Any narration of a river's history must revolve around people's attempt to control it, to bend it to their will. This fact will inevitably put the spotlight on societies' key institutions and structures, since dams and canals normally significantly alter the living conditions and power structures in those societies that benefit from them or are affected by them.

I am standing next to the Gezira project's main canal, one of those water projects that changed the course of a country's history, and which still runs more or less as it did when the British first laid it. Here, the water flows at such speed and in such quantities that the canal looks like a powerful, natural river. But its arrow-straight course, which extends as far as the eye can see, reveals it to be humankind's work. From the banks, only an immense sky and green fields are visible in all directions, and yet, when I flew over this area earlier the canal system's human geography was readily apparent: thousands upon thousands of rectangular green fields, all watered via small canals dug from larger canals, which themselves carry water from the river. The whole construct can be described as an unusually clear expression of modernity's disciplining and conquering of nature, as a grand effort to make water the servant of society.

From one of Gezira's many arrow-straight irrigation canals, dug by the British, you can rest your gaze on endless fields and the equally endless sky above. As I wait for the farm's general secretary, who will be giving me a tour of what has been described as the world's largest farm under a single administration, I allow myself to be entertained by a white-spotted gecko clambering up the canal's walled side. It is difficult to travel in Sudan without stumbling upon these animals, which are traditionally disliked and viewed with distrust.

As with all other important things in the world, reality here is blended with myth and tales. I had just heard the story of the gecko who betrayed the Prophet, when Muhammad was fleeing his enemies in Mecca on the way to Medina. Those pursuing the Prophet saw a spider's web at the entrance to the cave in which he had taken refuge. Naturally, they assumed he could not be there. Then a gecko, a large gecko, appeared and it began to cry: 'El Rab fik Shak!' ('The Master is in the cave!') A gecko, therefore, betrayed the Prophet to his enemies!

According to tradition, the gecko's bite is venomous and decidedly harmful to humans. Science, meanwhile, has demonstrated that the gecko's bite is, in fact, harmless.

I glance again at the white-spotted gecko. It is particularly exciting when it climbs or dashes across vertical surfaces with the help of a sort of suction cup beneath its feet combined with claws on its fingers and toes, while moving its elliptical pupils in characteristic fashion. I have ample time to study it – not much is happening on the farm today, it is Ramadan, and since the sun is at its zenith and my shirt is sticking to my body in the heat, I am sitting in the shade of some trees. As I see in the distance the general secretary approaching in his white pick-up truck, between the enormous fields with their low, green cotton plants, I let myself be amused. I do not believe anything can appear more undisciplined, or more optimistically bewildered, than a gecko unsure about which way to take up a brick wall.

Winston Churchill: 'Munich is situated on the Nile'

London's strategy from the start of the 1900s up until 1956, the year Sudan became independent, was to exploit disagreements between the political-economic elites in Egypt and Sudan over the use of the Nile, in order to increase opposition between the two countries. Britain obviously had several goals in Sudan. They wanted to retain the country as a potential political-strategic weapon against an anti-British Egypt, and they wanted to preserve it as a production site for cheap raw materials for the textile factories in Lancashire. In addition, Sudan was also a market for British goods; the country served as a reservoir of soldiers in case of war; and naturally – in a time when imperialism was still the order of the day – to rule the biggest country in Africa was in line with both Britain's colonial paternalistic instincts and its altruistic dispositions.

An imperial Nile policy in relation to Sudan and Egypt had great potentials as a power play, because the chances for success was great if it was implemented with cleverness and restraint. This potential success factor was due to a combination of Sudan's modernizing economic structure, which completely depended upon artificial irrigation, and the Nile's physical character, for the amount of water Sudan took out of the river to cultivate their lands had a negative effect on the river's water flow into Egypt. This geopolitical reality generated a Sudanese economic and political elite whose interests, when it came to Egypt's lifeline, were at odds with those of the Egyptians.

A typical and revealing example can be found in statements made by Mekki Abbas, one of Sudan's most influential politicians, in May 1944 during the opening session of the newly established Advisory Council for the Northern Sudan. Abbas protested and condemned the Nile Waters Agreement of 1929 because it gave Egypt all the benefits and awarded too little water to Sudan. The people of Gezira, he said, compared themselves with 'a camel laden with skins of water dying of thirst in the desert'.[24] Sudan required significantly more water, and they had what they needed behind the modern-day waterskin – the dam across the Nile. The problem, as Abbas saw it, was that Egypt denied them the opportunity to use that water. At the same time, he said, there were also enormous opportunities at other places along the Nile northwards in Sudan. But the Sudanese did not even receive water for their pumps because the Gezira project consumed the limited quantities of water allotted to Sudan (at the time the country had rights to 4 billion cubic metres of water). The Sudanese (and their British supporters and spokesmen) could therefore with some justification blame Egypt's monopoly of the Nile for posing a critical hindrance to Sudan's development.

In their secret diplomatic correspondence, the British repeatedly described control of the Nile in Sudan as a weapon against Egypt and Egyptian nationalism. The Egyptians, for their part, did not conceal the fact that they regarded Sudan as a natural part of Egypt, especially because of the Nile. The clearer it became that London's days as 'the King of the Nile' were numbered, the more important it was for the British to secure Sudan's independence from Egypt; this also because they presumed – correctly, as it turned out – that British water policy could still play a key role in applying political pressure to Cairo. Without its own large water projects and a strong water ministry, however, Sudan would quickly fall under Egypt's hydropolitical influence. The protracted negotiations on water division throughout the 1950s, where British advisers in Khartoum relentlessly underscored Sudan's development potential, if only the country could obtain more Nile water, were an important reason why, in 1956, the Sudanese went to the polls and chose independence rather than unity with Egypt.

In 1954, however, the outcome was still unclear. The situation stood in the balance. Winston Churchill, at that time was prime minister of Great Britain, was as determined as ever not to preside over a collapsing empire. Churchill had participated in the river war of 1896–8 as a common soldier and author, he had biked to Uganda's large lakes, and had visionary plans for East Africa's energy development. As Secretary of State for the Colonies, he had travelled down the length of the Nile in 1907 and had written a book about his journey. As Minister of Trade in the 1920s, he had been instrumental in finding white settlers whose productive work in Kenya could help finance the upkeep of the Nile railway there. As Prime Minister during the Second World War, he had been very active at meetings in Cairo, planning how British troops could stop Rommel in the Desert War west of the Nile. But even Churchill, with his enormous experience, was in 1954 at a complete loss about what to do to prevent Sudan from choosing unification with Egypt.

Frustrated with the increasing anti-British and pro-Egyptian sentiment in Sudan at the beginning of the 1950s, Churchill suggested bombing Khartoum. 'Munich is situated on the Nile', he said, clearly referring to his criticism of Neville Chamberlain's meeting with Adolf Hitler in Munich in 1938. Churchill had claimed that, as prime minister, he would never preside over the Empire's defeat, but now he sat in 10 Downing Street – and was about to do exactly that. The logic behind his Munich rhetoric was based on his understanding of the importance of Sudan's upstream position.

If Sudan were to fall to the British, Egypt would also fall. It would prove the end of Britain's imperial position in the Middle East and Africa. In Egypt, there were ongoing demonstrations against Britain, and Britain had no more to offer there. Nasser and the Free Officers drove them from one trench to another. Their best card then was Sudan – a Sudan they thought Egypt was entirely dependent upon, particularly because of the Nile. For the British, Sudan was still a key to their strategy, because the basic idea continued to be: whoever holds power in Sudan has Egypt in the palm of their hand. But now control over Sudan was in danger of slipping away.

Churchill's private secretary recorded the Prime Minister's bellicose suggestion in the diary he kept about life with Churchill, and he also relates that Anthony Eden, then Foreign Secretary, was one of those who talked Churchill out of the idea.[25] As we shall see, Eden, when he became prime minister, later discussed an entirely different policy for securing London's interests in Suez: diverting the Nile in Uganda as a way to desiccate Nasser into surrender.

Sudan and Egypt share the Nile

It is 1959 – three years after Sudan declared independence and three years after Britain's humiliating defeat at Suez. Representatives from the independent Egyptian and Sudanese governments have met to sign a historic accord: the Agreement for the Full Utilization of the River Nile. It was an agreement that, from its inception, was considered critical for Sudan's and Egypt's development. The Agreement was internationally praised as an example of 'the new age', of the possibilities opened up by the postcolonial era, of the Non-Aligned countries' strength, and as a demonstration that former colonies could solve those problems created during the colonial era and which had stumped the colonial powers themselves. The Agreement, therefore, was promulgated as an accord from which countries located in other international basins should learn.

Egypt agreed that Sudan would receive 18.5 billion cubic metres of water a year. In Egypt, many nationalists believed that Cairo had surrendered too much authority over the river, but the Nasser government understood that compromise was necessary (the Sudanese government had first insisted the country required 26 billion cubic metres). Partly, it was seen as a necessary compensation for Khartoum allowing Egypt to build the Aswan Dam, which placed large portions of Sudanese territory underwater, and partly it was because Nasser knew that such an agreement would weaken Britain's ability to use its upstream control of the Nile to fish around in troubled waters (Britain was, after all, still the colonial power in East Africa).

In Sudan, the Agreement, entered into by the new military coup government, was celebrated as an important national victory, even though protesting voices claimed that the country had sold itself too cheaply. The country, in any case, had by this agreement strongly defined itself as a Nile state with which Cairo had to reckon, and the fact was made clear that Sudan's future development would largely depend upon how the Nile was used. The Agreement signalled that Sudan had now become Egypt's partner in the exploitation of the river. The two Arabic-led downstream states stood unified. No other country was party to the Agreement, even though its official name underscored that it dealt with dividing the entire water supply of the Nile.

Sudan had now ensured itself enough water to undertake modernization and development. By the 1970s, Sudan had already proclaimed, under President Gaafar el-Nimeiri's leadership, that the country would become the Middle East's food basket and granary. The 1959 Agreement provided the Sudanese for decades to come with all the water they needed. In addition, rainfall-based agriculture was possible in parts of the country. What was lacking, however, was an effective administration and money to divert water to the fields; Sudan was short on both. Governmental bureaucracy, lack of political vigour, increasing political opposition and weak state finances eventually ensured that this objective came to be viewed as an unrealistic dream, as empty rhetoric – that is to say, as one of the many broken hopes that many people began to think characterized the Nimeiri regime's period.

Dump the whisky in the river!

President Gaafar el-Nimeiri stands on the Nile's banks at Khartoum one particular day in 1983. He is not opening a new dam or celebrating an irrigation project. So, what exactly is he doing on the riverbank this 23 September?

Standing by the river this day, the president is, in fact, dumping alcohol into the Nile. It is the opening shot in an operation whose purpose is to eliminate every drop of alcohol in Khartoum. Crowds are gathered along the riverbank. Sudanese television broadcasts the celebration as the president arrives with a motorcade to commence mass destruction of cases, bottles and boxes of alcohol. This alcohol was seized from Khartoum's bars and boutiques a day earlier, according to a new Islamic law, by soldiers and police. President Nimeiri dances around an enormous heap of confiscated drink, and bulldozers arrive to bury the rest.

The Sudanese I knew viewed the spectacle at first as an unfortunate joke. As it turned out, they underestimated the resolve with which the new legislation was introduced. Sudanese liberal Muslims, and there were many of them, had a relaxed attitude towards alcohol. Some drank, some did not, but no one I met would prohibit someone else from enjoying a glass of beer. Those who were concerned with Sudan's unity also glimpsed the potential consequences, since alcohol was widespread in southern Sudan, not to mention among the southern Sudanese living in the north. Nor did this policy win over 'the hearts and minds' of Islamic hardliners; they did not trust Nimeiri, this former communist, and his Islamic conversion, in the slightest. On TV everything looked well-rehearsed: the audience wept with delight when the sin vanished into the depths. At the same time, it was announced that the law prescribed forty lashes for anyone caught with alcohol. Nimeiri's PR campaign on the river signified that he was introducing his version of *sharia* into Sudan, and on Christmas Eve in 1983 it was proclaimed that women and men could no longer dance together.

On 23 September 1983, Nimeiri thereby conducted one of the most memorable actions of his presidency. By dumping alcohol into the Nile, he tried to make one thing clear: the self-described communist, socialist and Arabic nationalist, who apparently had single-handedly shot an opponent from his desk in connection with the coup he conducted in 1969, had become an ardent Muslim and, accordingly, the state's policy would be Islamized. The introduction of *sharia* law on 9 September 1983 established Islam as the new basis of Nimeiri's political philosophy, as if it had also become his personal anchor. The Nile was in this case exploited – not for irrigation or for agricultural development, but as a metaphor: it would symbolically expunge the 'old society's' non-Islamic values, more or less like other great rivers the world over, since the dawn of time, have performed purification tasks in countless religious rituals. Nimeiri's action not only held great symbolic worth; it was also conducted in a religious language that acquired an increasingly greater significance in Sudan throughout the 1980s. The whisky bottles emptied into the Nile that September day in 1983 served both to express and bolster a profound historical transformation process whose outcome President Nimeiri neither foresaw nor could imagine.

Two years later, having drunk polluted water, I lay incapacitated on my bed in Juba, the regional capital of southern Sudan. Dozing and feverish, I had just managed to turn on the radio when, in my delirium, I realized that the BBC World Service – the radio station that was the sole tie expats had to the outside world at that time – was reporting that Nimeiri had been toppled. When my Arabic instructor was able to return after a few days of security problems in Juba and its surroundings, it was unavoidable that we would discuss his country's political situation. I had not previously noticed any religious zeal on his part, but now it seemed that not only was he a firm believer, but he was also a proponent of a radical version of Islam. Nimeiri's problem, he felt, was that the president had not gone far enough. My teacher sought a comprehensive, totalizing view on the world, he told me, and he hoped that the society could be shaped into harmonious unity with the Qur'an's teaching. As I understood him, he believed that what threatened to keep this social circle from closing, so to speak, was what he perceived to be Western values. I listened to his argument, but thought he was being naïve because he was using Western influence to explain society's characteristic as the disjunction between the individual and society itself. We had previously discussed my work on the Nile's history and on Britain's significance for the modernization and development of Egypt and North Sudan. I thought he had understood me, as he was sitting there, politely listening, smiling amicably, posing some questions. Now, however, I realized he *could* not understand me; the totalizing view he sought of the world could only be attained, and the disjunction he perceived could only be annulled, by neglecting or defining away that which in society did not fit his viewpoint. My teacher's understanding of the world's past, or of Sudan's history, must necessarily be one lacking in its factual complexity and dilemmas. The way that British water policy had transformed parts of the Sudan and ensured the country's water interests with respect to Egypt and to other countries in the region must, from this perspective, be elided from history because it would either be considered meaningless, or as something his view on history could not at all accommodate. If Britain's role is systematically overlooked or neglected in this way, however, and with this kind of justification, a picture emerges of the country's history that is not only false and revised but is simply unintelligible.

An Islamic coup

The main opponents in the Sudanese civil war that began in May 1983 were what, in the literature on Sudan's contemporary history, has been termed 'the central riverain elite' in the north and the Sudan People's Liberation Army (SPLA), established in the spring of 1983 and led by a southern Sudanese army officer of Dinka origin, John Garang. As the movement's name suggests, his goal was not an independent South Sudan but a reformed, secularized and democratic Sudan. The SPLA made such inroads in the war against the government in Khartoum that the military leadership ousted President Nimeiri in 1985 while he was on a private trip and health visit to the United States. The head of this military coup, General Abd al-Rahman Muhammad Hasan Siwar al-Dhahab, who was Nimeiri's minister of defence and chief of staff, promised to implement a democratic general election within a year. And the general did what he said. He declared that he wanted to be a farmer rather than a president, and by consistently reminding politicians that he meant what he said about retiring to the farm, he sought to pressure them into taking responsibility. Elections took place as promised, and a new government under Sadiq al-Mahdi was established. The government's position, however, was weak: the economy was poor, the civil war only grew more irreconcilable and increasingly cost more human lives – even as the SPLA guerrilla forces only further strengthened.

The elected president, Sadiq al-Mahdi, was toppled in 1989. When, on 30 June 1989, Omar Hassan al-Bashir moved into the presidential palace in Khartoum with its Nile view, it was after this as-yet-unknown army brigadier general had carried out a short, effective coup. He headed what the coup-makers described as an Islamic revolution. Al-Bashir, who on TV evening after evening discussed the fact that he had been a member of the Muslim Brotherhood since he was eighteen, thereby, moved into the building once known as Gordon's Palace – an ironic historical twist.

The officers who seized power in 1989 did so in alliance with the National Islamic Front party, and its leader, Hassan al-Turabi. This Sorbonne-educated academic had established the party in 1985 and was long regarded as the new regime's strongman (until he fell into disgrace and was jailed for plotting a coup in 2004). Al-Turabi was a man with a mission, and his aim was to promote a political agenda based on Islamic teachings. A strict Islamic government was introduced in Sudan, inspired, among other things, by the Mahdi at the end of the 1800s. The coup, for its part, was remarkably bloodless. The leading politicians went into exile; none were killed – and most returned to Khartoum after a few years. The military force behind the coup consisted of about 300 men. They were an elite unit responsible for stability in Khartoum, and, as part of US aid to the city, had received American support, equipment and training over several years. Al-Bashir himself had a long military career behind him: in 1973 he fought for Egypt in the October War; he was a military attaché in the United Arab Emirates from 1975 to 1979; and he had also attended courses in the United States.

The coup turned out to be an important event in Nile history because it increased the disagreements between Egypt and Sudan, the two Nile allies from 1959, thereby by implication threatening to weaken the position of both downstream states. The coup also definitively helped create the basis for the process that concluded in 2011 with

Sudan being split into two separate countries, because parallel with Islamization, the contentions between Sudan's northern and southern regions increased. When it came to the Nile, however, this split did not change the rules of the game but only how it was played.

The new authorities lacked the political elite's traditional close ties to state leaders in Cairo, where Mubarak was now rather regarded as an enemy and bridgehead for Western and anti-Islamic forces in the region. Hassan al-Turabi had stronger ties to the Muslim Brotherhood in Egypt, that is to say, to the organization that Egyptian state leadership was occupied fighting tooth and nail. By openly supporting Egyptian opposition against Mubarak, Khartoum could no longer appear to be, or act like, Cairo's close ally, certainly not when it came to the Nile issue. The first Iraq war increased divisions between the two countries when Mubarak backed the United States while Sudan backed Saddam Hussein. So poor was the relationship between the two neighbouring countries that a short border war broke out, and pro-government demonstrators in Khartoum chanted: 'Bomb the Aswan Dam!' while marching through the city streets.

Osama bin Laden as Nile contractor

Around a decade before he became one of world history's most well-known men, Osama bin Laden was invited to settle in Khartoum, the city on the two Niles, as a major investor, after being forced to leave what was essentially house arrest in Saudi Arabia. This invitation was one of many signs of Sudan's increasing independence from Egypt. In Sudan, bin Laden developed connections to some of the most active Egyptian Islamists, those whom Egypt's leaders regarded as the nation's mortal enemies. In 1992, bin Laden was visited in Khartoum by the Egyptian Ayman al-Zawahiri. It turned out to be a fateful meeting, one that led to al-Qaida and the Egyptian Islamic Jihad joining with Zawahiri, who later became bin Laden's doctor and adviser in Afghanistan, and who took over as head of al-Qaida after bin Laden's death.

Osama bin Laden went to Sudan for two reasons. In the first place, they allowed him into the country; many other Arabic states barred him from entering their country. Furthermore, he had sympathy with the country's policies and he appreciated the role of the religious leader Hassan al-Turabi, that shrewd player in Sudanese politics who, in typical fashion for the country's modern turbulent history, had been in and out of prison cells and top political positions since the 1970s.

At the beginning of the 1990s, al-Turabi was the real power holder in Sudan. His goal was to shape a pure Islamist state and he welcomed bin Laden, but foremost as an investor. Sudan needed bin Laden's money and his entrepreneurial competence. The Sudanese obviously knew that bin Laden's family had built much of Saudi Arabia's infrastructure. At a reception given shortly after bin Laden's arrival in the country, al-Turabi hailed him as 'the Great Islamic Investor'. And bin Laden was indeed, from that point on, one of Sudan's richest men. Little did al-Turabi suspect, and probably nor did bin Laden either (back then he had not yet decided whether to become businessman or warrior) how this invitation to Sudan would affect the country's, the Nile Valley's and the entire world's history.

Osama bin Laden established offices on McNimr Street and in the Riyadh quarter, and he set up multiple companies. His contracting company built several major roads, including to Port Sudan, but it was agriculture that really interested him. Since the authorities could not pay money for his services, he instead received land, and soon he became one of the country's largest landowners. Bin Laden publicly declared that he was in complete agreement with the goal that Sudan's leaders had had since the 1970s: that the country could and should become the granary of the Middle East.

On the four farms that he worked near the Nile, bin Laden also indulged his one hobby, aside from reading Islamic thinkers and studying contemporary knowledge: riding. He was a member of the racetrack, but he apparently did not enjoy the music or the crowds and so stopped going. He picnicked now and again with his sons on the Nile and taught them to drive cars in the sand along the riverbank. In his house in Khartoum, he held receptions every day at 5.00 pm. Along with his business activities, bin Laden developed the seed for what later became the feared al-Qaida. It was at this point that the organization opened bank accounts the world over, and the few thousand al-Qaida members were employed on building and agricultural projects.

Sudan eventually faced growing pressure to extradite bin Laden. In the early 1990s, the regime was re-evaluating its Islamism in several important areas, adapting it to fit the need for economic growth and adjusting it according to the country's foreign policy ambitions. Sudan's leaders were desperate for investment, especially when it came to the oil industry, and so Sudan implemented an economic policy recommended to it by the World Bank. At the same time, the country attempted to brush up its international profile by adopting some surprising measures to make it seem like an enemy of terrorism. Suddenly, in 1994, they extradited 'Carlos the Jackal' to France. Ilich Ramírez Sánchez had long been the world's most wanted terrorist after he kidnapped eleven OPEC representatives in Vienna in 1975 and flew them to Algeria to demand their ransom. Later, he settled in Khartoum, where he posed as a French arms dealer. Even though Sánchez was wanted throughout the world, he was easy to find – he liked to breakfast at Hotel le Meridien in the centre of the city, thereby revealing for God knows how many times that Western intelligence cannot always be trusted. And then one day, like something out of a Ken Follett novel, he was extradited to France after being anaesthetized at the hospital where he was to undergo an operation. After this, bin Laden felt that his own position in Sudan had become more uncertain.

The United States was pressuring for his expulsion. This was due, they said, to his campaign against the leadership of Saudi Arabia for, among other things, giving in to the Americans. According to Gutbi al-Mahdi, the chief of Sudan's secret police force, Mukhabarat, Sudan had no objections of principle. They only hesitated, according to al-Mahdi, for practical reasons: in Sudan, bin Laden was under control. They knew where he was and what he was doing. If he was expelled, he could become a full-time radical Islamist.

Sudan wanted its name crossed off the list of countries that supported terror and so asked the United States for an outline of what was required. The United States wanted information on the foreign radical Islamists residing in the country and wanted bin Laden ejected. Saudi Arabia would accept him, but Sudan refused to send him there without guarantees that he would not be imprisoned or tried. Osama bin Laden thought it was unreasonable for Sudan to cast him out after all he had done for the country. Conversations were held with al-Turabi, who said that bin Laden must either stop expressing himself publicly or depart. Ultimately, the head of al-Qaida decided to leave. Hassan al-Turabi apparently called Sudan's ambassador in Afghanistan and asked them to prepare for bin Laden's arrival. The Sudanese state then largely confiscated all his assets in the country.

Osama bin Laden left Sudan on 18 May 1996, and his wives then settled in various countries. According to Egyptian intelligence, around 300 Afghan fighters went with him. His presence in Sudan had done important damage to the relationship with Egypt, significantly affecting the two countries' ability to stand together against the upstream countries' Nile revisionism.

A new city in the middle of the world's longest kiss

Even though the United States had tried to isolate Sudan, under Islamist rule Khartoum was significantly modernized. It is important to stress this fact. Occasionally, the idea gets aired that Islamists are incapable of developing their society, or that the society will become Westernized because it uses Western technology or modern social media. The perception, however, that technology is a package – that if excavators or jeans or TVs are imported from the United States, then, in the long run, US values will also be imported – has been proven false. The Islamist regime in Sudan has modernized the country, albeit under Islam's stern gaze, with many of its core personnel being educated in information technology at American universities.

In the 1980s, Khartoum was still a dusty city with a minuscule centre. I stayed there for three months, the first time in 1983, when I was gathering archive material for a study of the very ambitious British project for the canalization of the Nile in southern Sudan, one for which the British had already prepared plans in the 1890s. I immediately liked the city. The atmosphere. The congeniality. The conversations with Sudanese and other European researchers over café tables in the golden afternoon hours beneath the palm shade. The cold beers I occasionally afforded myself on the terrace of the Hotel Gordon, with it its sandstone façade, garden and airy halls, reminiscent of British imperial grandeur. British influence could still be observed, and not just in the layout of the streets. Perhaps the most fantastic thing of all, however, for a poor student: I lived on one dollar a day. Forty cents went on a hotel room whose door did not lock, and that I shared with a refugee from Uganda. Since my roommate had been in the war together with Idi Amin and had been shot in the leg, I could always hear his approach by the way he dragged his leg over the rough asphalt outside the room. The shower was shared by all the hotel residents, a feeble stream of cold water set behind a brick wall in the courtyard. The trick was to get up at the right time, and since I am not one of those who think it a sin against nature to rise before dawn, when I turned off the tap I could hear the singing from some of the countless birds that pause in Khartoum's gardens on their way to Europe, as well as the camels snorting behind the wall. Breakfast I ate standing outside a kind of kiosk not far away. Every day I bought eggs on a roll (which the owner every day, with the same welcoming smile, fried on both sides), and a small bottle of cola for ten cents altogether. For lunch I drank red hibiscus tea with a healthy amount of sugar while sitting on the balcony of the archive, looking out over the garden of palms, listening to the birds and discussing Sudan's history with the other students who had come there, a girl from the United States and a guy from the Netherlands. The tea kept me going until evening, when it was time for a new roll with eggs (fried on both sides). I was having a fantastic time, and it was during these days spent at the archive, when, always with the same eagerness, I would open one dusty archive folder after another, with their handwritten notes by British district officers and generals, that I realized I wanted to become a researcher and that the Nile would never lose its grip on me.

Compared to the Khartoum of 1983, the capital under the Islamic regime had modernized at a quickening pace. New city suburbs appeared with well-equipped supermarkets and expansive golf courses. Muammar al-Gaddafi's gift from the beginning of the new millennium – the five-star Corinthia Hotel Khartoum, aptly called 'Gaddafi's Egg' due to its appearance – dominated the city's skyline along the Blue Nile's banks.

It was also under the Islamist government that plans were gathered to develop and transform the overgrown banks of the White Nile before it meets the Blue Nile in Khartoum. An entirely new city section called the Mogran City, meaning the city 'where the two rivers meet' began to appear. The capital, which for generations had practically turned its back to the river here as if refusing to acknowledge the nature that shaped its foundation, should now get set to acquire a new skyline at the very joining of two of the world's most legendary rivers. As experience since these plans were first published at the beginning of the new millennium has shown, it will take time, but Khartoum has taken definite steps towards becoming a more modern-looking city; 'the longest kiss in history' is supposed to give the capital its soul.

Sudan rattles its Nile weapon

On Saturday, 1 July 1995, Sudan's president, Omar Hassan al-Bashir, delivered a speech in Wadi Halfa, on the edge of Egypt's water bank, the High Dam. He said that the country had to prepare for a military attack from Egypt and called for mobilization to protect Sudan against what he termed an Egyptian conspiracy to topple the government.

The president's bellicose rhetoric against its neighbour to the north came after steadily more Egyptian reporters were accusing Sudan of having tried to assassinate Hosni Mubarak the previous week in Addis Ababa. For, on 26 June 1995, President Mubarak of Egypt had suffered an attempt on his life while on a state visit to Ethiopia. Mubarak was travelling from the airport to the centre of Addis Ababa to attend an Organization of African Unity session and to discuss the Nile question with Ethiopia's leaders. On the highway between the airport and the city centre, his motorcade was set upon by armed men. Shots were fired at the cars: Mubarak's vehicle was struck multiple times, but the bullets could not penetrate the armoured Mercedes Benz. The assassins used AK-47s and grenade launchers, but several sources report that the grenade launchers failed. Mubarak's car turned around and headed back to the airport. This was a fortunate decision: if the motorcade had continued into the city, they would have encountered a new attack planned further along their route.

Suspicion was quickly directed at Sudan's government; they were accused of cooperating with Egyptian Islamists. At the press conference Mubarak gave at Cairo's airport after returning home unscathed, he was asked if their neighbouring country could be involved, and he answered that that was possible. Ethiopia also believed that Sudan's government was involved in the assassination attempt. Mubarak described the Khartoum government as criminal gangsters and said that the Egyptians could easily wipe them from the face of the earth – if they so desired. Mubarak spoke openly of a military attack on their southern neighbour. Sudan's foreign minister, for his part, denied that Sudan had anything to do with the assassination attempt.

Sudan's religious leader, Hassan al-Turabi, was also careful to tell journalists that Egypt's accusations had no basis in fact. Their purpose was merely to distract attention from Egypt's internal problems, he said. And he went further still – quite significantly so: he rattled the Nile weapon amid this crisis. When asked how Sudan would react to a possible Egyptian attack, al-Turabi responded in a way reminiscent of Britain's strategic Nile thinking. As he told *Reuters*:

> We don't want to aggravate nationalist tension [. . . but] Egyptian society is totally dependent on the Sudan, the water supplies come from this country. They [Egypt] have no [. . .] underground supply of water. And if the Sudan reacts and is provoked to react and interferes with the water going to Egypt, this is going to be deadly for the Egyptian society.[26]

Sudan's religious leader was aware of his country's ability to wield the Nile as a weapon against their Muslim neighbour to the north. At that point, meanwhile, his threats were meant as diplomatic sabre-rattling in a heated situation. To what extent this ploy succeeded is unclear, but Egypt, in any case, quickly put all war rhetoric behind it.

From the end of the 1950s up until the 1970s, the Nile had been central to cooperation between the two independent neighbouring countries. Not only did they enter a political union, which admittedly lasted only a few years, but they also started to implement a huge and joint project for canalizing the river in southern Sudan. By the 1990s and into the 2000s, however, this alliance between the two downstream states came under pressure, certainly due to internal, political-ideological reasons, but also due to general changes and technological and economic development in other parts of the Nile basin, affecting the established Nile regime.

Sudanese state leadership had been clear on the Nile's political-strategic significance. Particularly after the country started earning money by selling the oil it was pumping from southern Sudan, Khartoum began developing more ambitious plans for realizing its old dream of transforming Sudan into the granary of the Middle East. As restaurants and bars where people could buy alcohol and go to dance were being closed on the one hand, the authorities were on the other hand busy commissioning reports detailing how the Nile could be tamed and the country changed – and without first asking Egypt. Altogether, this caused a schism to develop between Egypt and Sudan throughout the 1990s, making it easier for the upstream countries to wrangle initiative and power in the diplomatic battle over the Nile.

The Islamic regime's policy in Sudan helped weaken Egypt's strategic position not only when it came to the upstream countries, but in the entire basin as well. It taught them a lesson: if Egypt's partner could engage in such activities, surely the other upstream countries could show Egypt the same resolve?

'A project of the century' (and let them eat that arrest order)

'The dam is a project of the century [...] it is a pride of Sudan, the Arabs as well as the world [...] a great milestone of our development, and we will continue building more similar projects for the welfare of the Sudanese people in the future'.[27] On Thursday, 3 March 2009, around 40 kilometres north-east of Merowe, Sudan's President Omar Hassan al-Bashir ceremonially declared the Merowe Dam open. Standing next to the dam, he stressed his rhetorical points by gesturing with his cane – a cane he had managed to transform into a personal trademark throughout the years. The opening ceremony took place amid a rare carnival atmosphere in the Islamist Sudan, complete with confetti and music. Chinese workers had, in just a few years, built the German-designed Merowe Dam, or Hamdab Dam, as it was also called, financed by China, Arabian investors and the Sudanese government. Not only does the dam produce a powerful impression as its concrete wall rises up dramatically from the desert sand, but it is also without a doubt one of the clearest monuments to the Islamist government's modernizing will and ability. The dam is, for the time being, the end result of the process started by the British almost a century earlier, when it shaped Sudan as a hydraulic state by erecting the Sennar Dam straight across the Blue Nile.

President al-Bashir spoke grandiosely that March day in 2009, but his words were fitting. The dam will have extraordinary significance for Sudan's development. No other single project in the country's postcolonial history can, if it succeeds in its goals, compete with the dam's societal importance. It was also meant, of course, to play its role in elite consolidation and nation-building, aiming at rekindling the identity of both the regime and the country – more or less in the same way as huge dam-building projects have functioned in other countries.

President al-Bashir also used this moment of triumph – this celebration of his government's vigour – to criticize the International Criminal Court (ICC) in The Hague. He ridiculed the ICC and dismissed it as an outright political tool for Sudan's and Africa's enemies. For what were the realities here, he asked? While he was here building the country, lawyers in The Hague were focused on producing papers that supposedly proved he was behind the genocide in Darfur! As he had stated just a few days ago: the ICC should rip apart, indeed, it should eat, the arrest order against him. As he stood on the platform with the dam wall rising behind him, al-Bashir also used the occasion to announce a cut in electricity prices for households, somewhere between 25 and 30 per cent.

The Merowe Dam was meant to be the manifestation of a radical turning point in Sudan's energy situation and to herald a future with more artificial irrigation in that part of the country. It exemplified the fact that internal developments in all the Nile states have a particular international dimension, since what happens with the river in one country affects water use in all the others. From a long historical and geopolitical perspective, the building of the dam demonstrated that Sudan was ready to compete with Egypt when it came to Nile control. Eventually, and if Sudan succeeds, this will impact power relations and alliances in the entire basin, with the most dramatic consequences for Egypt.

Nubia and Nile control

Nubia's situation at the beginning of the third millennium has been clearly defined by the fact that the Nile River is cutting through the region, and by the fact that government authorities have had the firm conviction that trapping Nile water behind giant dams here can create more revenue than all of Nubia's gold mines combined.

Nubian history and fate both illustrate in an unusually direct way how time can endow the same physical geography with societal ambiguity. For thousands of years, the Nubian people and their kingdoms were protected by the many waterfalls along the river, which made it difficult for Egyptian rulers to conquer the centres of the old Nubian civilizations. That same river ecology also made it problematic eight hundred years ago for the Nubian Church to maintain contact with Church leaders in Alexandria. Today, these waterfalls, or cataracts, are the reason Nubian culture is under more cultural and political pressure than ever before.

No other people along the Nile have been more affected by the modern 'Nile control era'. Over just a couple of generations, Nubia has been completely transformed by artificial changes to the river's course through the landscape. First, thousands of people were forcibly evacuated in the 1960s when Lake Nasser was established at the Second Cataract, drowning hundreds of villages for all time. Then, a few years back, the traditional Nubian heartland was threatened by two colossal new dam projects, one at the Third Cataract next to rural Kajbar and one at Dal.

When it became public that Khartoum was planning to construct hydropower plants that would mean thousands of displaced families and countless archaeological sites being put under water, a storm of protest erupted from Nubia itself and from the international archaeological community. The Sudanese government re-evaluated its plans, although, as it turned out, Khartoum did not shelve these projects: they simply postponed them until the Merowe Dam was complete.

The government of al-Bashir in Khartoum held its cards close to its chest. However, when Sinohydro, the largest hydropower company in China and in the world, announced on 28 October 2010, that they had won a $705 million contract to build the Kajbar Dam over a period of five years, Khartoum's plans were also made public. According to press reports, at the end of December 2010, some fifty-nine Sinohydro employees travelled from China to Sudan. At the same time as China advertised for extra workers in Pakistan, I travelled to Kajbar. If the dam were to be built, I wanted to see these Nubian stretches along the Nile before they disappeared from human gaze for all time. I also wanted to see the ruins of the old Christian fortress strategically located at the waterfalls, just where the foot of the dams were planned. The other proposed dam, the Dal Dam, will have a height of between 25 and 45 metres and a production capacity of between 340 and 450 megawatts. At the same time, around 2.5 billion cubic metres of water – some 3 per cent of the Nile's annual flood – will evaporate here due to the reservoir's size. According to the Anti-Dal-Kajbar Committee, two alternative plans for the Dal Dam have been suggested: the 'Low Dal' and the 'High Dal'. In the first case, all villages below 201 metres above sea level will be flooded upstream of the Dal. In the second case, the artificial lake will drown everything below 219 metres, including famous monuments such as the Sai and Kerma cemeteries.

The Nubians I met in the proposed dam area were very sceptical of these dam schemes, and all of them wanted more information from the authorities. As they said: 'The Nile is life. It is everything here. The dam will change all this and bury it.' Many protested the dam's construction. On YouTube there were uploaded films of of Nubian demonstrators in the villages along the Nile. They established committees that called the plans 'a human catastrophe'. Some promised that, if necessary, they would take up weapons to stop the dam plans. According to the pamphlets circulated, these people refused to sacrifice themselves yet again for an Arabian country's water interests. The plans were criticized not only because they would affect Nubia but also because they were described as hydrologically and hydropolitically irrational. After all, the evaporation alone will consume what remains of Sudan's allotted portion of Nile water. Therefore, according to Nubian oppositional forces, the project should not be regarded simply as a dam project but rather as the key element in a diabolical plan whereby the governments of Sudan and Egypt are coming together to solve two issues: Egypt's overpopulation and the goal of Nubia's complete Arabization.

Nubian activists have produced reports claiming that Khartoum and Cairo have launched a secret war against Nubia and the Nubian culture; they have deliberate plans to remove Nubians from ancient Nubian land areas. The strategy is said to be twofold: they will forcibly relocate Nubians with the help of this dam structure over the Nile, and the region will not be developed economically, socially or culturally. Instead, the region will be kept in poverty and, with Egyptian aid, Nubian culture in Sudan will be stifled because the people there will remain forcibly isolated from Nubians in Egypt. Nubian spokespersons claimed that both governments will sell Nubian areas to foreign companies. Rumours have abounded about a secret agreement that has been struck between Sudan and Egypt and that would relocate millions of Egyptian farmers to the Nubian Triangle, which lies on the Nile between Wadi Halfa, Dongola and Owainat Mountain.

The conflict and disagreements about these dam plans in northern Sudan have been so deep that opponents of the dam projects have threatened that the planned dam will unleash a civil war whose result would not be a consolidated Arabic-Islamic Sudan tightly integrated with Egypt but, rather, a Nubian nation that unites the millions of Nubians living in southern Egypt and northern Sudan into a single Nubian state.

The lion's share

One Nubian told me a story, perhaps meaning it as a comparison so I could understand how he judged his people's situation. It went something like this.

One fine day the lion, the hyena and the jackal set out to hunt together. The hyena, who is a skilled runner, caught a hare. The lion, meanwhile, took a gazelle by leaping from the bushes as the animal drank from a spring. The jackal, for its part, has its own way of catching dinner. In the middle of the day, when the heat was at its worst, he saw a zebra napping in the shade of a tree. Concealing himself at a cliff edge, he began to make the sound of running water. The zebra rushed over to investigate the sound, and, since he was moving so quickly, he rushed over the edge and broke his neck. The three hunters brought the three dead animals together.

The lion said to the hyena: 'I trust you to divide the food fairly between us. Remember that I am bigger than you, so I require more food.'

The hyena, who was always eager to please others, said: 'I think it would be best, sir, for you to have the zebra, a large, plump animal.'

Because the jackal had caught the zebra, the hyena thought he was being clever by giving the zebra to the lion. He thought the lion would agree with him, since he was the biggest animal and required the most food. The hyena said: 'Maybe I can keep the gazelle as a reward for my services.'

'And now you, like the gazelle, are going to die!' roared the lion, unexpectedly furious. 'I caught the gazelle and I will eat it.'

With these words, he lifted his paw and smashed the hyena's skull so that it instantly fell dead.

'Mr Jackal,' continued the lion in a calm voice, as if nothing had happened. 'Will you now divide the food to our mutual satisfaction?'

'Of course, sir,' said the jackal. 'Might I suggest that you have the gazelle for lunch, the zebra for dinner, and the hare for breakfast?'

Surprised but pleased, the lion asked: 'When did you get so smart, Mr Jackal?'

'The moment I heard the hyena's skull crack,' the jackal replied and quickly disappeared into the brush, leaving all the food to the lion.

'The lesson for the Nubians is,' the Nubian remarked as he showed me the data over historic changes to the Nile flood that he had assembled, 'cut your losses when facing an absolutely unscrupulous opponent.' Only later did I learn that the story he had told me was a well-known fairy tale in Nubia, but it served his purposes.

The Middle East's granary and a sugar company

Sudan's leadership – be it the toppled Islamists in 2019 or the toppled Nimeiri-government in 1985 – have been convinced that the key to the country's development lies in developing its agriculture with the aid of huge, mechanized farms. Calculations vary, but the official estimates are that Sudan has 200 million acres of arable land. The

Islamic government, as governments before them, set forth Sudan's goal of becoming the Middle East's granary. But the government failed, although it leased 1,000,000 acres to Saudi Arabia and 100,000 acres to Qatar, and other countries also joined in. Nearby countries are in dire need of more food. Egypt is the largest wheat importer in the world. And the food-poor Arabic oil countries are not far behind. As under President Nimeiri, however, it is a question of investment, of political will and unity, and of administrative effectiveness, and most people will say that very little has in fact happened with agricultural productivity.

Sudan's state finances have continued to suffer, due not least to almost fifty years of permanent civil war at one place or another in the country. The country has not had the economy to self-finance the required projects. It has instead needed loans to undertake the heavy investment in the necessary infrastructure. Yet, due partly to political isolation and partly to an inability to pay them back, such loans have been difficult to acquire. The World Bank also has political guidelines that prevent it from issuing loans for dam projects upon which not all Nile countries agree. China's entrance into the African arena, however, changed the rules of the game. China did not impose the same requirements for agreement between the countries, and the relationship between loan, investment and project implementation was different from the policy conducted by Western countries. China's pragmatic approach governed by self-interest challenged the established legal regime of water division and water administration, and thereby also traditional financial institutions' power and possibility of controlling development.

Although Sudan's government increasingly had its eye upon oil rather than agriculture, the regime modernized the irrigation economy more radically than previous governments. The Roseires Dam over the Blue Nile was being expanded with the stated aim of increasing the area that potentially can be irrigated by 400,000 hectares. A new dam over the Atbara should increase it by a further 200,000 hectares over five years.

Sudan has also – and this is a critical fact when it comes to future power struggles in the region – profited from Ethiopia's dam-building. Sudanese farmers now receive more water during the dry season because the Tekeze Dam over the Atbara in Ethiopia (the river there is called the Tekeze) has evened out the differences between the flood season and the dry season. That has already meant that farmers can cultivate larger areas and can harvest in the same region multiple times, all without costing the Sudanese state any significant investment. Therefore, Sudan's political leaders have stated that they welcome the Renaissance Dam, Ethiopia's and Africa's largest dam. Construction was launched in 2012.

To whatever extent Sudan succeeds in its ambitions, the demand for more water than the country has will only increase. Sudan's landscape is flat and easy to artificially irrigate. And the ground can be harvested multiple times a year.

Driving south from Khartoum, you cross enormous, desert-like plain land and you pass Britain's massive dam on the White Nile, Jebel Aulia from the 1930s, built for the sake of Egypt, and then the city of Kosti, far to the south and close to what, in 2011, became the new country of South Sudan. The city lies on the Nile's west bank. Not too distant is one of Africa's largest sugar plantations, the Kenana Sugar Company. I stopped by there when I was travelling the area as a student. The plantation's management gave me a tour of the irrigation works and offered me lunch, where eleven Sudanese and I ate with our fingers from the same large pot deliciously filled with chicken, sauce and rice.

The Kenana Sugar Company, with a farm of about 200,000 acres, was once the world's largest integrated sugar concern and, judging by the atmosphere at lunch, those who worked there were happy and proud to do so. The company was, indeed, nothing less than a landmark within the global sugar industry's geography, as it lies 1,200 kilometres from the nearest seaport, more or less in the middle of what was then Africa's largest country. The company marketed itself as a monument to what President Nimeiri could, at his most effective, accomplish, and when it was inaugurated officially in 1981, the president stated that Kenana was 'a testimony to our country's future prosperity'. The project was set in motion by Nimeiri, being a brainchild of the English investor, 'Tiny' Rowland, a notoriously ruthless capitalist, and supported by Edward Heath, the British Conservative prime minister. It was also supported by Arabic capital. The requirement for any such undertaking was, of course, Nile water. Earth and sunshine were delivered by nature; water must be delivered by humans. And this water had to be brought all the way from the White Nile; at maximum capacity, 1.9 million litres of water were pumped every minute. Every single drop had to be retrieved from the river, transported through 29 kilometres of greater canals and 300 kilometres of lesser canals, and then out onto the fields. The entire construction took eighteen months to build.

The sugar company's configuration required iron discipline from all involved. They related how the twenty-ton trucks carrying the newly cut sugar cane must reach the company day and night, around the clock, seven days a week throughout the long harvest season, which lasted between 150 and 160 days. Furthermore, each crop was closely tied to the next because sowing must occur at exactly the right time.[28] Gradually, the company was taken over by Sudan, Saudi Arabia and Kuwait, and even though the company has had its ups and downs, it is still a very important production facility in the Sudan.

One of the managers drove me to Kosti late that evening, following my introduction into how such an operation could take place in sub-Saharan Africa. As we drove, I rolled down the car window, leaned out to feel the hot air coming off the desert not too far away, and turned around: there, behind me, was the sugar company and it looked like a gigantic, modern space-monster, an impression only strengthened by the endless darkness surrounding it.

The following day, I sought out the rest area in Kosti, where all the trucks that conducted trade between north and south were parked, and where the drivers in the middle of the day dozed in the shadow of their trucks. I did not have to ask many for a lift before a tall and burly driver made me an offer. He was an Arab, he said, but his skin was as black as the blackest African, thereby clarifying the nature of the Arabization process in a country whose name, after all, means 'Land of the blacks'. For five Sudanese pounds, I could ride on his truck bed. Unfortunately, he said, he did not have any room in the cab, since his assistant sat there, and also the mechanic he always had with him, due to the lack of shops along the way.

I accepted immediately.

The Nile Wetlands and the New State

The land of distances

'It was further from Nagichot the most easterly of the district headquarters, to Raga, in the extreme west, than it is from London to Moscow.'[1] When Sir James Robertson, one of the British leaders in Sudan between 1945 and 1953, and later state head in Nigeria, writing in his memoirs reflected upon what was so particular and so difficult about administering what back then was the region of Southern Sudan, he identified *distance* as being an overarching political problem. Today's South Sudan is about the size of France but has an estimated population of around 10 million (the last census in 2008, amid controversy, concluded that the population was 8.2 million), something which corresponds to a population density of about fifteen people per square kilometre. The central regions consist of enormous open plains, and, almost everywhere you travel outside the few populated areas, the impression is of distance and a characteristic stillness. Conditions here persist in many places like they were under the British – usually no cars, no trains, and the boats are chiefly the canoes that move almost silently along the rivers and narrow waterways. For most of the people, the most typical and often the only means of transportation here is still one's own two feet.

The British colonial administrator's heartfelt sigh over geography's influence on policy is certainly understandable and indicates a characteristic feature of this new country that lies almost completely within the Nile basin. And it is easy to understand his frustration, for everyone who comes to South Sudan will be struck by how the absence of modern infrastructure and a very scattered populace create an overwhelming feeling of space and isolation.

Having arranged a lift with a lorry in Kosti, I spent the next few days on a cluttered, open truck bed together with twenty or so *southerners*, as they were called in Sudan's political discourse at the time. None of my fellow travellers spoke English and I only had a little pidgin Arabic, the local variant of Arabic. Each time we halted, the driver invited me, as the only white person in the party, exclusively to tea. He became my friendly and benevolent guide over the savannah and the endless plains.

The lorry journey continued south, and with the sun at its zenith we drove through landscape that at times resembled a park, almost picturesque, an impression that was constantly challenged by the immense space. We passed waterholes where animals came to drink in the afternoon, and where there lay carcasses of dead animals, caught and eaten by lions, I was told. Hours could pass between the sighting of one group of clay huts and another. Evening falls quickly on the African savannah, and the wind across the truck bed became abruptly cool, sometimes even cold. The disc of the sun sank quickly, in an explosion of red, seeming to saw down into the earth. Then the darkness rolled in. The sky was suddenly unfathomably star-studded, as if the stars had been switched on. Along the way, thorn bushes scratched at us, so we pressed closer together on the open lorry.

Just as we were creeping along a pockmarked and bumpy road, the truck stopped. The cab doors opened. I saw the three people riding up front hop out and climb under the lorry. They spoke calmly. There was, I understood, a problem: something with the axle. Was it broken? Rumours flew across the lorry bed.

We saw no one, but in the distance, we heard drums and someone singing as a campfire flared in a landscape shrouded in absolute darkness. Above us a crescent moon, lying on its back, as was typical here. With the help of mimicry and body language, an almost 2-metre-tall, slim Nuer youth asked me if we had the same moon where I came from. Another came up to me and asked in a low voice: 'Do you know my hero?' No, I did not know who his hero was. 'Moshe Dayan', he whispered, perhaps so the driver would not hear him. Then he showed me what he meant – by drawing his hand across his throat. 'Kill Arabs!' Israel's role as undercover arms supplier to southern guerrillas during Sudan's first civil war, which ended in 1972, had obviously borne political fruit, I thought.

Using a flashlight, the driver and mechanic managed to fix the problem – with steel wire, it looked to me. After driving on a short distance, the driver pulled into a flat clearing where some other vehicles stood. The message was given: this was our stop for the night. We would sleep here, with the trucks as protection against wild animals. Water was set on the campfire, and after a small cup of warm sweet tea, I found a place on the ground, wound my arm through my backpack straps, and waited for morning.

The next day, the same thing: bumpy roads, motor stops, small collections of huts, now and then large cattle herds, giraffes stretching their necks to graze from acacia trees, a group of elephants crossing the road in sovereign disdain for a mere truck, and ostriches that raced the vehicle – and won by a clear margin. Some Nuer women appeared from nowhere as we stopped for lunch and offered to sell me the distinctive pipe that they smoke. During the evening, enormous armadas of fireflies and frogs – probably only a few, but their deafening performance made it difficult to hear what people were saying. The next day the landscape was also much the same but, slowly, it assumed a stronger element of green. We had reached Equatoria province, and rain there had been better. In the middle of the day, we reached Juba, which at that time was capital of the autonomous Southern region. I hopped off the lorry bed, thanked the driver and the other passengers for the journey, and sat down at a local bar; I wanted to sit still and observe people, as many people as possible.

I knew no one and was nearly broke. I stood up and began to walk on, interminably it seemed to me, because I had a heavy backpack and had forgotten to buy water. My goal was Juba's radio station. I was going there to ask if it was possible to copy some recordings of local music that they had used in their programmes. When I returned to Norway, I planned to use them to present another image of Southern Sudan than the dominant one that only focused on poverty and the role of development aid. I had brought with me empty tapes, and with a helpful technician from Radio Juba, I managed to record on my tapes music made by local Madi, Acholi and Azande musicians. On the way back, I sat down at a café. A man took a chair at my side, and apparently he noticed my concerned look when something appearing to be a snake moved on the roadside: 'Snakes have their own university, or high school,' he said, 'where they learn to trick humans.' I nodded at him, saw that he was convinced of what he was saying, and left. The city gave an overwhelming impression of being more a large village than the country's second most important city.

I spent some days in the Juba University Library, which prior to the last civil war was a beautiful and well-kept library under an English woman librarian's mild, but firm, leadership. There, I found the early colonial reports for which I had long been searching – but which the archives in London and Khartoum did not contain. I could now return to Khartoum – through the huge swamps of Southern Sudan.

One must travel by boat if one wants to truly see and grasp the extent to which central South Sudan is an enormous wetland ecosystem and swampy lowland region. I had read many descriptions of journeys through the swamps, and they all tend to agree on one thing: monotony characterizes the landscape. For hour after hour, there was nothing but water, sky, papyrus, the odd bird and, if lucky, you might get a glimpse of a crocodile gliding slowly and fearlessly through the water. We cross a dead-flat plain with innumerable swamps, lagoons and side channels, and several lakes. The river was so narrow in some places that the papyrus pressed against the boat, as if trying to prevent us from pushing farther into the swamp or from getting out of it. At one place the boat did get stuck. Since there were no telephones here, no radios for many kilometres distant, and no roads to take us to centres that did not exist anyway, I found myself thinking for an instant of stories from the 1800s about people who got trapped on the river by plant remains and ended up eating each other. But that was back in the day before boats had good solid motors, so we wrenched loose after several attempts and backed into another and more navigable route. Sometimes we saw huge 'islands' of papyrus ripped loose by the water they grew in. They drifted like miniature green ships, driven by the wind more than the current, and made it even more difficult for the captain to find the correct route to the north. In the distance, I saw smoke from grass fires against a hazy grey sky.

Fires in the distance showed that there were people here, despite everything. At night I lay out on the roughly three-by-two metre foredeck, because the air there was slightly less uncomfortable and suffocating than in the cramped, light green cabins where the temperature, even during the night, was, I was told, above 35°C. I was well protected against the swarms of malaria mosquitoes, where I lay without a sleeping bag, completely happy, feeling a strange sense of harmony while looking up at the stars through a fine net I had bought at the Khartoum market before travelling south.

A dictatorial river

Both nature and society in South Sudan have plainly been formed by the water landscape. One of the world's largest swamps is created by the Nile's annual flood and by the torrential rainy season. The swamp at its largest has been estimated at 80,000 square kilometres, but it can radically retreat in the dry season. Enormous pastures, called *toich* or 'mother' by the local population, owe their existence to the river's natural overflow and by the heavy precipitation during the short rainy season. On the grasslands – some pastures can stretch continuously for more than 300 kilometres – the flood lasts long enough to prevent trees from growing but not long enough to produce papyrus, which would have destroyed the grass. This very particular landscape, coupled with this distinctive physical water system, has created the conditions for a semi-nomadic cattle economy that in turn has formed the basis for the way in which the Nilotic peoples have organized their society.

In the northern parts of this swamp area, the average annual rainfall does not exceed 400 millimetres, and all of this rain arrives over the course of only a few days or weeks, often in the form of violent downpours. During the dry season, people live on the riverbanks, where there is water and the grass continues to grow. When the flood comes and the river rises, they must retreat with their cattle herds and all their possessions to the ridges on the swamp's edge, often hundreds of kilometres from the river. By the time the river recedes, it has managed to water enormous areas of pasture. The activities and pulse of society follow the water's rhythmic, though flowing, movement throughout the landscape in an unusual but still distinct fashion. This forced mobility for generation after generation, this merciless need to decamp from one's abode when the water comes and when it disappears, has made it difficult for the Nilotes to establish permanent administrative centres and forms of state power.

The water landscape has also functioned as a hindrance in their contacts with the outside world. The swamp has made it extremely difficult, if not impossible, to build railways or permanent asphalt roads. And the river itself has blocked travel, in contrast to many other large rivers that have been described as highways into a country's or continent's interior. Transport on the White Nile – or on the Bahr al-Jabal and the Bahr al-Zaraf, which are the Arabic names for the White Nile's two main tributaries in this region – has for long periods been impossible due to the barriers formed by plants driven by the current. These could form natural bridges across the river, bridges so solid that elephants could walk across them. The Arabs, therefore, had good reason when they simply gave the whole area the name *sudd* or 'barrier', even though it is more precise to apply the term to the accumulated plant remains flowing with the river.[2]

It was this that halted the Roman Empire's expeditions 2,000 years ago, and stories abound of tradesmen stuck on the river, trapped among these naturally formed obstacles. The swamps made communication both north/south and west/east very difficult for large stretches of the year. The region was almost locked in, with little or no communication and in long periods was almost cut off or shielded from influence from both Western and Islamic civilization, as well as from contact with broader regional and global markets.

Why didn't the population do anything with this water landscape, which certainly formed the basis for a viable cattle economy, but which simultaneously contributed to keeping the people in poverty and underdevelopment while the rest of the world was taming rivers, digging canals and building hydropower-based factories? Why didn't they simply seize control of the rivers creating the swamps like the Egyptians millennia before had done, building dams on it and canalizing it? Why did they not try to overcome or reduce these fluctuations in water flow that always and eternally had forced them into seasonal migrations? The answer is simple: it was not possible. The landscape was too flat for dam-building; the water would simply run around it. And there were also no rocks for many kilometres, so there was no building or repair material; much less was there a foundation to which these dams could be affixed. Even today the technology does not exist that could dam the Nile tributaries on this huge plain, or that could effectively distribute the water during the dry season. The reality has been that, if people were going to live here, and maintain their semi-nomadic cattle economy, they had no other choice than to adapt to the Nile's natural fluctuations: they had to submit to its dictatorial whims.

The Nilotic water world and a river chieftain

In Nilotic stories about themselves and their history, water and rivers naturally play an important role, since these have fundamentally shaped the region's economy and its social institutions while also posing an extreme factor of uncertainty. Creation myths are based on the fact that Nilotes live both in the forest and along the river, and the existence of the female gender is directly tied to this river which the Nilotes learned later was called the Nile in the outside world:

'In the beginning' men were creatures of the forest who hunted buffalo while women lived in cattle camps close to rivers, tending cattle, cultivating durra and fishing. Women went to the riverside and opened their thighs, pushing the foam of waves into their vaginas, giving birth to only females. At one point men emerged from the forest, whence developed the institutions of marriage and bride wealth.[3]

In terms of Dinka (the main Nilotic ethnic group) mythology, all human beings were originally 'in the river'.[4] As one central narrative has it: 'In the old days, a very old woman, after bathing in a river, suddenly felt she became pregnant from the river spirit.'[5]

There are many examples of stories and myths that connect women, the river and life-giving gods. A myth among the Shilluk, one of the Nilotic peoples living here, describes how Okwa, the father of the holy spirit incorporated by every divine Shilluk king or *reth*, married Nyakae, the river's mother: Nyakae never died nor will she die.[6] The western regions of the Sobat basin, one of the Nile tributaries, and parts of the White Nile basin are her favourite dwelling places. She sometimes reveals herself to people, but only in the form of a crocodile, and always on the riverbank or in the river. In his article on Nuer religion, the famous anthropologist E.E. Evans-Pritchard writes of another female spirit who revealed herself as being part of the Nile system:

A spirit of great interest is *buk* [. . .]. This female spirit, known throughout Nuerland is associated with rivers and streams. [. . .] Nuer sometimes offer first-fruits of their millet and make libations to it in streams and in times of sickness they may sacrifice animals to it on the banks. They also throw beer and tobacco, and maybe a bound goat as well, into the water as offerings when they take their herds across rivers or engage in large-scale fishing.[7]

When the Dinka moved to the summer pastures along the river, they traditionally made an offering before they drank or used the water. This ritual could be performed by any man and it was practised within small groups. Everyone present, including the children, stood on the riverbanks, and the person conducting the ceremony, called Beny Wir or the river chief, took a sheep or goat and a skull with fat from a holy cow. The adults then bound one or multiple decorative items around the animal's neck and all lifted their arms toward the sky. The small children were lifted onto the adults' shoulders and the river chief drowned the animal or made it vanish beneath the water. Typically, the river chief bound the animal to an anchor secured beforehand. After that he tossed the fat into the water and then everyone waded in up to their waist and drank. Before this ceremony with its religious significance had been carried out, the river was taboo.

A thread that winds everywhere

The Sudd region in South Sudan is so peculiar that anthropologists who travel here from abroad for extended fieldwork must also be a little unusual and weird. In Shambe, where the boat I was travelling with stopped a few hours, I stumbled upon just such an anthropologist, an American with a bushy red beard, sitting alone on a chair by the riverbank.

We exchanged a few words concerning the weather and the boat, but since there was neither a telephone nor any mail connections home, he had little time for small talk; he would rather speak about his research, and he did, thoroughly and almost without pausing. I rather quickly grasped the nature of his project. Of premodern man it has been said that he dwells in his culture like a fish lives in water. Therefore, he had no need of the culture concept. It was anthropologists who instead gave us the modern understanding of this concept. Anthropologists argued that culture did not originate from nothing; genes mean something, nature contributes something, but culture is still an invention, something created, something that cannot be reduced to a single factor outside itself. Humans are probably the only biological creatures that not only inherit biology but also culture. However, the American anthropologist said, the concept of culture, as it is typically used in the wake of his discipline's conceptual triumph, is also problematic: it reduces our ability to explain human actions, especially the fact that people break out of the patterns of action expected of them. As a historian, concerned with both geographical structures and the role of the individual actor in shaping developments, I nodded my head; I agreed with the anthropologist.

Few ethnic groups have fascinated Western anthropologists like the Nilotes. A series of very well-known and influential studies has been produced about them – on their religion, rituals, system of kinship, economy, on the Nuer and their prophets, on the Shilluk and their strong faith in 'the evil eye', and on the Dinka and their world of cattle, or their 'cattle complex' as some have termed it.[8] Whether because of the climate, the malarial mosquito swarms or the wrenching poverty, or whether it was because the tone-setting archaeologists were employed by the British administration in Sudan, Nilotic cultures – in contrast to a number of other 'exotic cultures' (the term that anthropology originally used to categorize them) – were never described by researchers as being an alternative to, and more authentic than, cultures of modern, Western societies. They have not been depicted as role models of Modern Man, as, for example, Margaret Mead did with her idealistic narratives of free adolescent sexuality among Pacific Islanders.

Nilotic societies have instead been described as almost an ideal type; illustrating in reality the abstract, hypothetical concept of what the literature terms a 'stateless society'. The largest groups, the Dinka and Nuer, have traditionally employed a political organization that, for simplicity's sake, has been called 'anarchic'. Even the institution of chieftain did not exist. As such, the Shilluk kingdom with its seat and traditional base in Kodok on the White Nile was one of the few exceptions among the Nilotes. But even then, the Shilluk's 'divine kingdom' with the *reth* or king at the top, had no power like states in most societies. They had limited influence even over the selection of chieftains and could only interfere in conflicts when both rival parties agreed to bring the matter before the king's tribunal. Distinctions and complicated lines of conflict between lineage, kinship and clans have helped counter the development of more centralized institutions and of loyalty to a single state. The absence of a state or a centralizing agency, however, has in no way meant that these societies have been egalitarian or without internal power hierarchies.

The background to the fact that we now regard culture as a category, as a veritable package of ideas, beliefs and traditions that can explain people's actions, the American anthropologist continued, is that the concept, understood in this way, has been developed through studies that particularly focus on ethnic groups with no history of writing and, therefore, without a written history. The individuality that texts make evident has not, therefore, counteracted the tendency to depict culture and cultural codes and systems as being more fixed and unified than they are.

And culture interpreted in this way, I interjected, has become a concept winding like a thread through public debate on all sorts of issues. Often it embraces everything and thus nothing. Culture explains what one thinks and what one does, how society is organized, and which rituals survive, and whether one likes to play soccer or not. It becomes a problem for understanding what is going on when the concept is used as if it were in itself an established reality or fact of life, when it gives the impression that there are general, and to some extent immutable and determined values and traditions, that are themselves sufficient to explain why people act as they do.

The American anthropologist and I found ourselves in surprisingly quick agreement as we stood there – inept and fundamentally outsiders – in a country and a region that was one of the least developed and modernized in the world. On the one hand, as Evans-Pritchard's book on the Nuer had taught us, the significance of dominant models of thought and ideas regarding people's behaviour can hardly be overestimated. On the other hand, all experience, including historical scientific accounts, suggests that individuals and groups consistently break with their 'culturally prescribed' behaviour. If not, historical development simply would not exist. Therefore, analytically it is more useful to talk about the different kinds of behaviour-governing values rather than culture, values that are strengthened or challenged by reflection over societal experience. This makes it easier to avoid stereotypical descriptions of peoples or ethnic groups based on ideas regarding their 'culture', and it makes it easier to avoid the compelling power inherent in a near deterministic concept of culture and instead replace it with concrete analyses of actions and how and to what extent and in what contexts they are repeated. The ideas that anthropologists documented during colonial times and afterwards have also later influenced the Nilotes' conceptual world and societal life. They have become an even stronger part of their behaviour-governing values. The anthropologists have both explained and legitimized the conservatism of a lifestyle that basically presupposes that a kind of symbiosis exists with their cattle, hence the idea about the Nilotes' 'cattle complex'. But this interesting focus has marginalized another non-cultural factor, the hydrology of the Nile. The fundamental symbiosis that can explain the existence of semi-nomadic cattle economies is its relation to the regional waterscape. Therefore, it is only through radical transformations of the Nile's hydrology that the Nilotic societies and their conceptual worlds can be altered. It is not 'the culture' or 'the cattle complex' that is the primary immutable factor here, the main barrier to change which individuals cannot break. It is *the place* that persists unchanged, and the characteristics of this reality require specific and repeated courses of action if adaptation is to succeed and the established order maintained.

The boat blew its whistle and, since I had no plan at all to remain, I hurried aboard. I waved to the American anthropologist, sitting there on his chair by the riverbank, whom, I believe, never finished his PhD thesis.

Arabic invaders from the north

'Then came the government. First it came through the Egyptians. They came together with a people called the Turks. When they came, they used to quarrel with our people. Our forefathers fought with them using spears [...] Then came the people of the Mahdi. They also captured our people and treated them like slaves.'[9] What happened when the Arabs opened the Nile in the mid-1800s to boat transport? The man quoted here is Stephen Thongkol Anyijong, told to Francis Deng, who quotes it in his book, *Africans of Two Worlds*. Mr Anyijong was a British-appointed chief, but his account was shared by most people in the south. Historical research has in general confirmed the invasion's violent nature.

Anyone sailing by boat on an almost placid, peaceful Nile in central South Sudan, whether it is over the large and shallow Lake No or on the narrow, winding river stretches with papyrus to either side, where there is nothing in view except papyrus, flatlands and sky, will easily imagine the shock that people here must have experienced when foreign intruders with modern weapons and organization broke into their isolated world around the middle of the nineteenth century.

After Muhammad Ali's soldiers had crossed the Sudanese border and consolidated power in central, northern Sudan, expansion continued further up the White Nile. When his successors from the 1840s onwards succeeded in clearing the river of papyrus and plants that at the time blocked it as a waterway, boats were suddenly able to reach even very remote villages in southern Sudan. What quickly followed was more slave raids and an increase in the slave trade with Egypt and the Arabian Peninsula. This nineteenth-century, Turkish-Egyptian imperialism – which gave Egypt and, formally speaking, the Ottoman Empire control right up to the Nile lakes in today's Uganda – was an example of the kind of imperialism that steals rather than builds. If the British Empire in Asia, as George Orwell wrote in *Burmese Days*, was 'despotism with theft as its final object', this was tyranny with slavery as the immediate object. No matter how sympathetically disposed one might be to the first Turkish-Egyptian administrators who sought to establish government outposts in the mid-1800s, the conclusion must still be: their administrative centres and military forces contributed to opening up the river to trade, to Arabic and European traders, to Muslim expansion and Christian missionaries, but for the local people the most important and immediate effect was that it became easier to hunt for them, as well as for gold and ivory.

The way in which this expansion up the Nile took place came to play a decisive role in the relationship between the predominantly African southern Sudan and the predominantly Arabic northern Sudan and does so even to this day. Cairo had problems in conquering the entire southern Sudan due to the region's size and isolation, and limited its administrative establishment, especially during certain periods, to isolated outposts on the riverbanks. The Turco-Egyptians were unable to establish anything resembling a state administration in the region as a whole. They succeeded only in building up a few bases that largely functioned, especially initially, as departure points for raids directed against the local populace.

Even so, the politically compelling stereotype of the 'Arabic slave trader' who captures and chains his African victims and then transports them north is too one-dimensional. Some ethnic groups were practically decimated by this activity and it had, of course, a devastating effect on the victimized societies. But slavery was not unknown in the region prior to the coming of the Arabs. Local rulers, such as the Azande kings, themselves kept slaves for different purposes, and distributed slave wives as a way to acquire more followers.[10] Eventually, as the anti-slavery movement in Europe grew stronger, European politicians started also to object to the Arabic slave trade in East Africa and along the Nile. Charles Gordon and Samuel Baker, and the Italian Romolo Gessi, all in the Sudan service of the Turkish-Ottoman Empire, attempted to stop the slave trade in the south, and, with some backing from the central authorities conditions improved somewhat. It has been argued, however, that the slave trade was still the dominant occupation of the northern Sudanese at the end of the 1870s.

During the period of Mahdi rule the slave trade was resurrected. The Islamist government actions regarding slavery became part of a bloody history that left deep traces in the southerners' interpretation of their past. Whatever the role it played in encouraging the revolt of the Islamists (some, like P.M. Holt argue that the government's suppression of the slave trade was the main grievance leading to the Mahdi's success, while others, like Kim Searcy,[11] argue that it was opposition to the imposition of poll taxes), one southern leader, Chief Makuei Bilkuei, saw the Mahdi rule as being synonymous with slave raids:

Destruction came with the Mahdi. Mahdi was the man who brought destruction[...]. It was Mahdi who destroyed the people. His people called Ansar were the people who came with destruction. That is what is called the spoiling of the world [...] The Ansar were the people who turned the country upside down, together with the Mahdi and the Egyptians. If you want the real truth, those were the people who destroyed us. That was the disaster which reached us. They said, 'La Illah, ila Allah, Mohammed Rasul Allah'. That was the way they chanted while they slaughtered and slaughtered and slaughtered. Those were the people who destroyed the country.[12]

Historical research has somewhat moderated this viewpoint but, even so, it cannot be denied that Chief Bilkuei both pinpointed and summarized a crucial experience that people in the southern parts of the Sudan, had with the new, religiously based government in Khartoum.

European adventurers in the swamps

After the river had become navigable south of the twelfth parallel, there were opportunities for European explorers and tradesmen. And there were more and more of these throughout the 1800s. In Europe, there was a fast-growing demand for ivory – for piano keys, billiard balls, knife handles and decorative items. J.P. d'Arnaud, one of those to first describe the Nile in South Sudan, had documented a load of 900 tusks brought back to Khartoum from a Turkish-Egyptian government expedition led by Selim Qapudan in March 1842.[13] European adventurers wanted to share in this profitable trade.

According to Edward Evans-Pritchard, any observations and ethnographic interest exhibited by the first explorers was only 'incidental to their purpose, and it was in any case difficult to reconcile with their plundering of the natives whenever they were able to do so without risk to themselves'.[14] These people were largely adventurers and businessmen rather than explorers with a geographic mission.

Evans-Pritchard, who was himself appointed by the British colonial administration to advise the government on how to most effectively govern their new African subjects, was merciless in his criticism: 'Few of the earlier travellers seem to have understood how their depredations appeared to the natives, or cared how they appeared to them'.[15] In the same essay, he launched a frontal attack against several prominent European explorers. Regarding Ferdinand Werne, who published *Expedition to Discover the Sources of the White Nile* in 1848, Evans-Pritchard wrote: 'He was a vain and vituperative person with a great hatred for the French; and it must be said also that he had a very superficial understanding of what he saw among the native peoples with whom he came into contact [...] and even less of what he was told'.[16]

Another famous explorer who received assessment was the Welsh engineer John Petherick, who published *Egypt, the Soudan and Central Africa* in 1861. He was characterized as 'a not very reliable authority or estimable person'.[17] Evans-Pritchard also argued that the majority of what the French explorer Antoine Brun-Rollet wrote was 'rubbish'.[18] Regarding the Italian explorer Gaetano Casati's *Ten Years in Equatorial Africa* from 1891, he said: 'if the translation was faithful, [the descriptions are] not only nonsense but would appear to be invention'.[19]

One discoverer about whom Evans-Pritchard did not write was Alexandrine Tinne, a lone woman among the men. She was ridiculed in the British publication *Punch* with derisive advice concerning how women ought to stick to the kitchen, but David Livingstone was taken with her and wrote that he respected no one higher. She had even travelled further up the river than Caesar's centurions.[20] Tinne was one of the Netherlands' wealthiest heiresses. She lost her mother and her aunt while she was journeying up the Nile on the search for the river's source but did not give up. When Livingstone praised her, he did not know that she had already been hacked to death by a group of Tuaregs. The event occurred as she was attempting to reach the Nile's sources by following an alternative route to the swamp – namely, straight across the Sahara. John G. Millais mentioned her in his book *Far Away Up the Nile*: 'Miss Tinne is a romantic figure in Nile exploration. She was beautiful, a daring rider, a good linguist, but too kind and trusting to venture among the savage marauders of the desert, who acknowledge only one thing – the power of the sword and the rifle.'[21]

The Egyptologist and philologist E.A. Wallis-Budge also admired her:

From Prince Halim she obtained a steamboat, and in May she began to ascend the White Nile. She was received with kindness by all except the slave-dealers, who feared and hated her, but who proposed to her to join them on their slave hunts! The fame of her wealth, and youth, and beauty was carried by the caravans to all parts of Africa, and the natives called her the daughter of the Sultan of Constantinople. The infamous slave-raider, Muhammad Kher, even offered to marry her, and make her the Queen of the Sudan![22]

The opening of the Nile for river communication also created opportunities for Christian missionaries. The Austrians had already in 1851 established a mission post as far south as Gondokoro, not far from today's Juba. Fifteen of the twenty missionaries sent there died after just a few years, mostly due to different tropical diseases, and there were no converts during the first decades.

Only long after the death of these first pioneers would other Christian missionaries reap the fruit of what they had sown; they had helped open the Nile basin in the Upper Nile area to evangelization.

Europe on the brink of a water war in South Sudan

'Long live Fashoda!' 'Vive la Fashoda!'

By the end of the 1890s, southern Sudan and the village of Fashoda were abruptly at the centre of world politics. Paris and London were, according to the war-font headlines in English and French newspapers, on the brink of battle over a tiny Shilluk village on the banks of the White Nile. Union Jack and *Le drapeau tricolore* were facing off in the middle of Africa. In the streets of Paris people demonstrated for a more active French policy against what they perceived to be British arrogance on the Nile; in Victorian London, French expansion towards the Nile was strongly condemned.

The boat on which I travelled almost hundred years later did not dock at Kodok, today's name for Fashoda. We took on supplies from some Shilluk who had rowed out to us, and they also ferried to shore passengers who had reached their destination. Kodok is the Shilluk people's holy centre, where ceremonies connected with royal rites have occurred for centuries. *Juok*, or God comes here, an omnipresent spirit closely tied to the river spirit or river god who created Nyikang, the founder of the Shilluk dynasty. And Nyikang also comes here, so that his spirit can be transferred to every new king. As I consider this modest village on the river's western bank, it seems unbelievable, indeed, almost surreal, that in 1898 Europe should have been on the brink of war here; that the English government sent a gunboat up the Nile one autumn day as Europe held its breath, to plant with great fanfare the Egyptian flag, here at Fashoda!

So, what happened here, just before the turn of the twentieth century?

The Fashoda Crisis, on what was called 'the Upper Nile', and the partition of Africa belong to the most studied questions in the history of European colonization. Interpretations regarding what occurred here have functioned as crowning examples in support of two different, competing, but almost equally influential, explanations of the race for Africa. The Marxist school argued that this rivalry was proof of their theory that colonialism and imperialism necessarily arose as a result of the deadly fight for power and profit between capitalistic states in Europe. The liberal school, by contrast, argued that imperialism or colonialism was not in fact necessary; it happened instead by 'mistake' or accident, so to speak, and pointed to the fact that London had shown no imperial interest in controlling these remote African huts. The problem is that neither of these models can explain what occurred here in 1898, when Europe's newspapers were full of stories of a potential European war centred around Nile control in southern Sudan!

As press reports circulated that a French expedition of adventurers and imperialists under the leadership of Brigadier Jean-Baptiste Marchand had reached the Upper Nile in South Sudan, the story in Great Britain was presented as if France were challenging London's control of the Nile basin. Diplomatically speaking, this would have been a particularly serious affair, since the region belonged to that part of Africa which other European powers had acknowledged as Britain's 'sphere of interest' back in 1890. Furthermore, what angered the British imperialists was that Paris seemed to threaten London in the very Sudan the British had just conquered by crushing the caliph's army at the Battle of Omdurman a few days before.

The British acted resolutely and with superior military force and diplomatic cover. They sent their fleet up the river from Khartoum under Kitchener's command to prevent the French from planting their flag on the Upper Nile. Would there be skirmishes? Would the British shoot French soldiers on the banks of the Nile, right there, in what was perceived as the interior of Black Africa? The problem with this familiar and thrilling narrative of European rivalry on the Upper Nile, of French adventurism and English distractions, of Christian torchbearers in Khartoum and Islamic fanatics in Sudan, of explorers and a British political leadership that unwillingly found itself the head of an African empire, is that the narrative simply does not correspond with what the sources can tell us. These interpretations have been formulated without considering the importance of the Nile's ecology, and the British strategists' understanding of it.

The explanation that long has served as the chief interpretation of the Fashoda Conflict completely ignores the fact that the British, since the beginning of the 1890s, had concrete plans to occupy the entire Upper Nile and the headwaters of the Nile. They occupied Uganda in the great lakes region in 1894 and mapped out occupation of the Sudan and its swamps in 1895, long before Marchand's expedition was even conceived. The dominant interpretation also overlooks the fact that, also since the beginning of the 1890s, plans had been drawn in Cairo for ways to exploit the Nile south of Egypt's borders. The explanation completely neglects, furthermore, the large, hydrological projects on which British water-planners in Egypt worked together with Cromer and London. The liberal theory of the 'reluctant' or 'hesitant' imperialist is based on the argument that southern Sudan lacked resources, that the country was 'the bottom of a barrel' as the most influential historians characterized it.[23] Southern Sudan was, however, no 'bottom of a barrel', but rather – on account of the Nile's character there – a bucket filled with a lot of water. It was this hydrological (and political) relationship between the water wealth of Southern Sudan and Egypt's prosperity that in particular determined the region's fate, since the people in charge of Egypt's cotton economy thought that it could be expanded almost endlessly, provided they could supply it with what they considered to be the 'wasted' water evaporating into the sky in the southern wetlands.

The reality is that London was waging a methodical, expansive water imperialism whose shape was not determined by any fear of France but by demand for water in Egypt – and which cleverly exploited the 'French threat' as a diplomatic card or weapon. London and Cromer did not fear Marchand and his gang of shabby exhausted soldiers. The Frenchmen obviously would have no chance against Kitchener's army in Sudan. But France's presence gave London the perfect diplomatic alibi: by presenting the French position as better than it was, the British could more easily legitimize their conquering the whole of Sudan. And by painting a picture of the French threat to Egypt, it was easier to convince the Egyptians to both bankroll and muster soldiers for a campaign designed officially to protect Egypt's interests in the Upper Nile.

The attention surrounding the 'French threat' or 'French ambitions' in the Upper Nile enabled London to present itself as Egypt's protector, both inside Egypt and to the international community. The conflict at Fashoda provided the perfect smoke screen for their true plans, which they began immediately to implement. Even as the British General Kitchener, with a shrewd diplomatic strategy, stood theatrically, dressed in Egyptian garb at the gunboat's railing while sailing up the White Nile in the autumn of 1898, on a course to raise the Egyptian flag at Fashoda on 18 September, Cromer and Kitchener were already, and with all secrecy, busy formulating how London, under pretence of governing Sudan together with Egypt, might seize power in Sudan and gradually squeeze Egypt out. And Marchand? As mentioned, he had no chance at all against the British. There would be no life-and-death struggle; on the contrary, in the end the British hoisted the French, British and Egyptian flags at Fashoda, and rescued Marchand and his officers from probable death, and sent him safely home on a boat over the Mediterranean.

And Fashoda, like the rest of the Sudan, slowly but surely came under British control.

A sacred pool

In March 1921, a pool, which more accurately resembled a small lake, appeared near Khor Lait in the region where the Agar Dinka lived. Such an event was naturally enough interpreted in a religious, as well as a political, light, and pilgrims gathered in the area.

The small lake was considered to be a miracle, one that boded well for the Dinka and ill for foreigners, or so thought those who were sceptical of the new intruders. The locals believed that Kejok would reveal himself to the Dinka, bringing fortune and well-being. Kejok was a mystical hero born of the woman Quay, who was impregnated not by a man but when she waded into a lake some time during the eighteenth century. The hero was especially revered for being able to bring forth water simply by tapping the earth with a finger, and when this body of standing water suddenly appeared it was interpreted as Kejok's work. In order to strengthen the ill feeling against the colonial masters, the most anti-British of the Dinka aimed to transform their version of events into the dominant interpretation of divine will. As the miracle itself attested, they said, God's will be that the foreigners should leave, and the Dinka should refuse to cooperate with any new government the foreigners tried to establish over them. This mandate had been made clear through conversations with the spirits at the pool's bottom. The spirits also said that the enemy's weapons would be powerless near the lake.

The British District Commissioner, Vere Ferguson, who would be murdered by rebellious Nilotes not too long after, travelled to the new water body to demonstrate that the lake's god was as ready to accept British offerings as those of the Dinka and, therefore, it was not the god's will that the British should leave. There were 800 Dinka at the pool on the morning Ferguson arrived. All knelt with faces and eyes turned toward the water. Ferguson went into the lake to offer a sheep. The animal did not sink, but Fergusson did not disappear either, as had been prophesied. The fact that the lake rejected his offering showed that the Briton did not belong among the local populace but, since he had not drowned either, there must be something about him that was acceptable. A Dinka who was positively inclined towards the British government said that the offering had taken place at the wrong time, in the morning rather than the afternoon. Ferguson, therefore, returned in the afternoon, and this time he did not go out into the open water but stayed along the shore where some scrub grew. There were many people following him and one of them took the sheep and dunked it into the water so that it could not emerge again due to all the scrub. The offering was accepted, and Ferguson could conclude that the rebels had interpreted the deity's will falsely.[24]

Ferguson's approach was the one the British typically preferred in pacifying and conquering the peoples in Southern Sudan: the district commissioners governed with 'an ear to the ground', acquiring knowledge of local traditions and values, and employing locals as their assistants. Given that Britain's strategic goal was to maintain peace and order at the least expense possible, all in expectation of the great Nile canalization project to drain the swamps, this policy was both effective and rational.

In terms of the local populace, no common resistance against the new European rulers was ever organized. Many viewed them as liberators from the Egyptians and the Mahdists and thought that was the reason they had come. Influential Southern

Sudanese intellectuals, such as Francis Deng, later wrote that the local population regarded the British as the very source of peace, security and dignity.[25] And he quoted one chieftain arguing that the British came to Southern Sudan because they had heard what the 'Egyptians' and the Mahdists had done to them, and therefore they 'came to help'.[26]

At the same time, the region's poverty and the lack of modern weapons among the ethnic groups made them a very easy conquest should they offer resistance. One British district commissioner described how the Nuer selected its warriors, every five or seven years. The cattle chieftain, the *wut ghok*, presided. On the appointed day, the young boys lay in a row with their forehead on the ground aside a small hole that had been dug. The medicine man then walked along the row, opening a slash in the forehead of all the boys with a knife and letting blood drip into the hole. Afterwards, the boys were kept in isolation for a month while the wounds healed. Finally, assuming they had not succumbed to infection, they were met by their fathers, who gave their sons a spear and an ox. With that ceremony the boys became warriors. Not exactly a terrifying military force compared to the British, but London still sent RAF bombers at the end of the 1920s to crush a rebellion that was fomenting among the Nuer, a people who again and again showed their opposition to any form of state power.

On travelling the swamp and theories of Africa's development

The experience of travelling does make it easier to understand that where one person believes they are building a house on a solid foundation, another sees only clay and bog. Where one person sees a paradise, others see only a dreary swamp. Where one person sees a beautiful mountain, others see a burdensome road. For no one has only ears and eyes to their name; we inherit more than our facial features and physique. Thoughts, beliefs, conceptions and prejudices often seem to flow together with blood, and it is easy to forget that most things can also be turned on their heads.

During my journey through the swamps, I recalled one of the classics that discusses travel as a project. Joris-Karl Huysmans's novel, *Against Nature*, is centred around the decadent and misanthropic aristocrat, Duc des Esseintes. It is a handbook in decadence, but he is also concerned with the idea of travel. He ultimately concludes that it is better to pretend to travel than to actually travel, also because he chose solitary life to the pleasures of normal existence.

Des Esseintes, therefore, copies the travel routes of the largest shipping companies onto maps and frames them. He then uses them to cover the walls of his bedroom. After that he fills an aquarium with seaweed and other necessary things. Now he can enjoy the pleasures of sea travel with the help of fantasy and avoid its uncomfortable aspects. Unlike Xavier de Maistre, Huysmans was not concerned with the habituated gaze's power and tedium. Fantasy, he thought, could prove more than substitute enough for – in Huysmans's words – the 'vulgar reality' of actual experience. The traveller, after all, becomes distracted and distanced from the present moment due to all kinds of worries, and he will end bewildered by all the conventional things to which he will be exposed; he will always be subordinated to the demands of the situation.

Compared to a monotone journey surrounded by papyrus and malaria in Southern Sudan, des Esseintes's remarks seem intensely uninteresting and narrow-minded more than decadent. His journey could only go to places he could imagine; that is, places he knew already, and which were thus accessible to this type of imagination and where the conventional could be re-enacted by himself. Heat, humidity and insects make it uncomfortable to travel in the swamps, and the reality here is thus vulgar in Huysmans's sense, but the journey is at the same time unconventional and not easy to imagine or experience if you have not been here. Anxiety for what lies behind the next river bend, or for whether the captain will find his way through the sea of papyrus, as well as the incessant work of keeping the malaria mosquitoes at bay, especially during the afternoon and as the sun is sinking, do not impose a distraction between yourself and what you are there to observe. It is the journey itself, that offers the experience only actual travel can give, in contrast to movements in a fantasy world. The central swamp region is a world unto itself, a sight worth seeing, and it especially becomes a unique experience the moment one understands that this same area is viewed and described as a paradise by those who live here.

'The culture is what keeps Africa from being more developed!' The discussion was loudly under way among the riverboat's passengers, since there was ample time to talk here. A local man with hollows cut into his forehead, and who has just introduced himself as a Shilluk, dismissed this with a forthright: 'No, it is corruption that destroys everything! Corruption is the scourge.' I stood on the edge of the group of people leaning over the railing. It was beginning to approach midday and the heat was becoming increasingly paralysing as we passed the villages along the riverbank – cattle enclosures, some isolated earthen huts, children running around and shouting at us, men standing at rest on one leg in keeping with the Nuer stereotype, utterly naked as they tended their cattle, and leaning upon their wooden spears. A German PhD student suggested it was the British colonial government that was the problem, while a Dinka in an elegant, freshly ironed khaki shirt argued that it was all the fault of the Arabs. For myself, I kept silent. I was in partial agreement with all of them, after all, and I thought of all the theories I had read that tried to explain Africa's history and development. As such, I did not have anything to say until the boat abruptly stuck fast in some papyrus and I said what I had been thinking, but almost did not have the energy to start discussing in the heat: 'What about role of the water system here?'

Any book that seeks to reconstruct the biography and history of the Nile must try to show how the river, as a complicated system in itself, and the experiences of the people living within its basin, are interacting and influencing each other, and thus are made relevant to general discussions and theories on society and development. There can be no doubt that a river and the spatial dimension of it as a geographical system – housing such diametrically diverse societies: world history's most stable state formation in the lowest and driest part of it; the most typical examples of stateless societies right here in the swamp region; the African kingdoms around the great lakes further up the river; and an ancient empire on the Ethiopian mountain plateau where the Blue Nile comes from – has much to tell that theories of society and development with universal ambitions cannot overlook. What, then, about the theory that Africa's development cannot be understood without also grasping and integrating into the analyses of the continent's distinctive water landscapes?

There is a long, albeit extremely problematic tradition that has sought to use natural conditions to explain social conditions. A classic natural or ecological determinism claim is that what is called a people's culture is largely decided by its environment. Aristotle claimed that inhabitants of colder European countries were undoubtedly brave but were also backwards because of the climate. The French Enlightenment thinker Montesquieu, a key forerunner of the modern social sciences, emphasized nature's direct influence on people's mentality: hot climates produce indolence, a strong pain sensitivity and an exaggerated indulgence of the sexual drive. The German philosopher Georg Wilhelm Friedrich Hegel is not particularly associated with giving material explanations for society's development, so for that reason his underscoring of geography's definitive role in history's course is more interesting, as it shows how widespread this climate-deterministic way of thinking was in European, pre-industrial times. In extreme zones, Hegel said, cold and heat are too dominant, and the spirit will be unable to build a world for itself. As such, the theatre of world history is the temperate zone. Herbert Spencer believed that history's course was a displacement from warmer and more productive environments that demanded lower levels of social development to colder and less productive but more challenging regions farther from the equator.

While we stood at the rail in the almost unbearable humidity and heat, until forced to seek shelter from the sun in the wheelhouse's short shadow, I said that I did not buy either of these explanations or the many more- or less-well-based theories that Africa's lack of development is due to the heat, the soil or the general climate. In a long time perspective and compared to other continents it is impossible to understand Africa without grasping the significance of the constant and uncertain shift between rainy season and dry season and how this has affected settlement patterns and economies. Nor will one understand the continent if one does not include in the analysis the Sahara desert's role as a barrier between Africa and the outside world, as well as the character of the continent's major rivers, which almost without exception have large waterfalls not far from their outlet (the Nile is an exception, since its closest waterfalls to the sea begin at the Sudanese border), and so have not been suitable as transport routes between the continent and the outside world. It is impossible to understand the Nilotic societies without considering elements of the swamps' ecology and the rivers' seasonal fluctuations. In other words, it is both possible and expedient to talk about a structuring causal relationship in a very specific sense: this river system has set the framework for what societal development was possible, even if the river has not determined what actually happened.

From the boat's railing we saw plains in all directions and as the discussion faded away we entered that mood where the monotony had become so monotonous that it becomes fascinating. The flat plateaus were completely treeless, obscured just here and there by some brush along the riverbank. Small brown islands of dead papyrus and dry grass floated in the water, to be replaced by newly dislodged water hyacinths. The sky was heavy and grey. The colours of the landscape of the Sudd was largely tones of silver and bronze now, as if the rest of the spectrum had been burned out of nature. On the banks, one kraal followed another kraal (a kraal is temporary settlement with a cattle enclosure at the centre). From fires fed with cow dung, smoke floated over the plains as it had for generations. Everyone was preparing to strike camp one more time. As they had done last year. And the year before that. And for hundreds of years previously. No one can stay here when the rain and floods arrive.

Yet for more than a century a Sword of Damocles has hung over this entire gigantic plain, like an enduring moment of uncertainty – the plan to change the whole region's pulsating geographical heart by excavating a new Nile that would alter the water's course, the appearance of the pastureland, and the way people might live and animals migrate.

Jonglei: a new aqueduct to the north

Hardly any other water project of the same order of magnitude has a longer and more tangled history than the Jonglei Canal.

The idea for the canal was first proposed by William Garstin in a British government report in the last year of the nineteenth century.[27] Two years later Garstin wrote a new and longer report in which the canal was also central,[28] but it was only in 1904 that the seminal *Report upon the Basin of the Upper Nile with Proposals for the Improvement of that River* was published, in which the canal project was fully described and situated as a key element in Britain's overall plan for the whole basin. Garstin himself had spent months in the Sudd area, and after his studies he drew a new line on the map representing the river he wanted to create, a line eventually called the 'Garstin Cut'. The aim was to reduce what they conceived as being the 'loss' of Nile waters in the swamps due to evaporation. This was to be achieved by digging a canal 360 kilometres long that would hasten the river current and thus increase the amount of 'white gold' reaching the cotton fields of Egypt.

Cromer supported the plan, and the government in London did the same. The first modern excavators were sent all the way down to the swamps only a few years after, in order to test the project's feasibility. Visions about a region full of water which, if tamed, could then be sent north, was one of the reasons the British found it necessary to seize control of Southern Sudan in the first place. Britain was, as always, concerned with securing control at Suez, and to achieve that they needed to control the Nile.

Because cotton was cultivated during the summer – the White Nile was by far the most important river during this season – Cairo and the cotton interests there considered it an incomprehensible waste that half the river's water 'disappeared' in the Sudd region. Even more, as long as the river courses through Southern Sudan were so poor, there was no point in building the prodigious Nile reservoirs in Uganda, such as London had fantasized doing since the beginning of the 1890s, because the 'extra' water they could store there would vanish on its way through the enormous South Sudanese plains and wetlands before it ever reached Egypt. The Nile's geography, the river's appearance, must simply be transformed, and so the most prodigious water project of its time was elevated and given top priority in Cromer's plan to take 'the Nile in hand'. As it turned out, however, a combination of technical, economic and political problems resulted in Britain failing to excavate the canal, though they continued to work on plans for doing so. Comprehensive plans, therefore, were drawn up and published in 1919, 1920, 1925, 1929, 1934, 1936, 1938, 1948 and 1954.

Throughout the 1920s and 1930s, British leadership in Sudan became increasingly concerned with the planned canal's national, regional and local consequences, and so they became more sceptical of the plan in its current forms. Local district commissioners and governors of Southern regions wrote notes and letters to the government in Khartoum, informing the government that local economies would be destroyed and the Nilotes' way of life threatened or utterly transformed. They also pointed out that this could increase the danger for unrest and create significant problems when it came to pacifying and calming the whole region.

The British in Khartoum gradually understood that this scepticism surrounding the Jonglei Project ultimately corresponded with London's overall Nile diplomacy, which aimed at keeping Egypt on its toes when it came to Britain's ability and will to solve the country's water problems. When it was starting to become obvious that the days of the British Nile empire were numbered, the Governor-General of Sudan wrote of the Jonglei Canal, or the 'Jonglei Cut', as it then, in a less pro-imperial time, was called: 'The Jonglei Cut would involve the importation of hundreds of Europeans, plus far larger numbers of saidis etc., and its completion would completely dislocate the lives of the Nilotic living in that area. Only a Government endowed with immense patience and with strong humanitarian views combined with complete power could carry out this scheme with fairness to the local inhabitants.'[29]

In the period that Britain ruled the Upper Nile, therefore, this most planned of all projects never left the drawing board. The conflicts of interest within the imperial system combined with Egypt's scepticism of British intentions and the regional opposition from people and British district commissioners in Southern Sudan, stopped the canal project from being executed, and transformed it into a hydropolitical card in the diplomatic play against Egyptian nationalism and in support of London's position at Suez.

The struggle for a new, more efficient Nile aqueduct through what is today South Sudan has dominated the region's history for 130 years and will continue to do so in the future. The plans for the project contributed to Sudan's uneven development and to the fact that Southern Sudan remained undeveloped and devoid of investment, simply because no other large infrastructure projects could be implemented. The whole Sudd region would be radically altered by any eventual canal, so to the extent that there was talk about external investment, the policy was to postpone it until after the consequences of such a transformation were clear.[30] Nor could the British, in terms of their policy of positioning themselves as the guarantor of Egypt's water, overtly enter into large irrigation projects in Southern Sudan – even had they desired to so. Within the context of the great British imperial project, water should not be withdrawn from the river in Southern Sudan; rather, the regional Nile was regarded primarily as an aqueduct to the north; and as an aqueduct that must be improved with respect to increasing water needs downstream.

Razzias and peace

The British had one overarching political-strategic goal in Southern Sudan: to 'pacify' the area. That meant establishing sufficient security for the least possible cost. At the beginning the administration was chiefly a military administration with limited influence on local life and with few ordinary state functionaries. Up until the 1920s, the British governors in Southern Sudan were largely military officers. As soldiers in the Anglo-Egyptian army, they had been sent to the region in order to secure peace and order. They had little knowledge of the local language, history and culture, and the British themselves characterized their policy as 'administration by razzia'. When it came to Sudan, the noted observer of British imperial policy, C.S. Jarvis, described the difference between the administrations in the North and the South at that point in time: standards, he noted, gradually fell as one moved south up the Nile, and if the government summoned administrators from the more remote districts for consultation in Khartoum, these 'wilder members of humanity', as he termed them, destroyed the atmosphere.[31]

From the 1920s on, 'indirect rule' became the hallmark of British colonial administration in general, including in Southern Sudan. This was a policy born of necessity here. London expected the colonies to be financially self-supporting and, in Southern Sudan, the local economy yielded no surplus that could be efficiently taxed, in contrast to other parts of the Nile basin such as Egypt, Northern Sudan, Uganda or Kenya. Tax collection occurred 'with an ear to the ground' so as not to provoke local discontent. State finances made it thereby impossible, and the local economy made it inexpedient, to finance the build-up of a large colonial bureaucracy. There was also little money to invest in development, if that had been the plan. Capital exports to, or huge investments in, Southern Sudan were definitely not London's objective either, because external economic actors could create problems for any implementation of their canal plans and for their overarching 'Southern strategy'. In the entire Southern Sudan, there were typically no more than thirty to forty British administrators.

And then, in the Upper Nile province, writing about different aspects of politics and administration, sat Governor Willis, supported by a handful of British officials at isolated administrative outposts within a huge region predominantly peopled by the Nuer. Paternalistic and wielding a language full of stereotypes, something common to several colonial administrators, he described 'his people': 'intellectually incapable of doing semi-skilled work and physically and temperamentally incapable of unskilled work'.[32]

Yet, even though the British for a number of reasons did not focus on a plan for economic development, they succeeded, even with an exceptionally modest administration, in establishing peace through large swathes of the region, especially during the 1930s. Hunting parties no longer wandered the region in search of human slaves, and interethnic fighting was substantially reduced. It contributed to stability that some of the colonial administrators remained in the same place for ten or twenty years. These individuals became near-legendary figures, not just in British colonial history but also locally. Administrators who stayed in place for short periods, that is, for about two years or less, were rather contemptuously called 'passing birds'. In the Azande District, the extreme case was a single change in district commissioner in the period from 1911 to 1951. But the large Bahr al-Ghazal province also saw only four different British governors between 1910 and 1934. It was typical for district commissioners to know a lot about 'their people', so that they could 'evaluate all persons with respect to how much tax they should pay', as it was stated in the Native Administration guidelines in the Juba District.

The myth of the solitary British administrator who wandered around, weaponless and on foot (there were almost no roads or airstrips, so they were in general without cars and planes), who dwelt with the 'natives' over whom he governed, is not false when it comes to Southern Sudan. The ability to solve local conflicts due to their knowledge of local cultures enabled the British, as already mentioned, to bring a kind of peace between the different peoples in the region. British administrators wrote home that it was as safe to journey along the Upper Nile as it was to cross Hyde Park in London after dark.

But the 'Man on the Spot', as the district commissioner has been termed in the literature on British colonial government, nonetheless had limited influence on the formulation and effect of Britain's overarching policy, and this was especially the case in Southern Sudan, although the literature has tended to give him a highly influential role. The reason for this is that London and the British in Cairo had a relatively clear strategy when it came to the region's place in the greater imperial Nile game. Southern Sudan was primarily considered an aqueduct for the irrigation economies in North Sudan and Egypt. The very ambitious plans for altering the Nile's natural course in Southern Sudan would have radically changed the ecological and economic basis for the semi-nomadic population's way of life. The less that development of modern economic businesses and institutions happened in the region, the easier it would be for London to use the region and the Nile projects there as a diplomatic card in the future. This overall Nile strategy helped to create a political situation where the colonial power could not become a force for modernization, in contrast to what was the case in the irrigation economies to the north – unless, as some suggested, the swamps were drained.

As one of the district commissioners wrote in 1938 – after citing a travel report from 1899 where Southern Sudan was described as being without water in the dry season and overflowing with water in the rainy season – after thirty years of British administration the situation is unchanged.[33]

'A human zoo for anthropologists to study'

It is March 1931: the Governor of the Upper Nile in South Sudan is bent over his *Handing Over Notes*, a type of written report that provides fresh and telling insights into the British administrative way of thinking. After the British had established a Pax Britannica at the end of the 1920s, one expressed principle aim was a 'regeneration of the tribal soul'. The administrators were urged to hunt for the 'true organization' that the tribes had 'lost'. In this way, Britain wanted to strengthen traditional cultures and build up the chieftain structure where it did not exit. The governor summarized his task here with a one-liner: the goal was to 'interfere as little as possible'. The British supported the Chiefs' Courts and gave some judicial powers to cooperating tribal leaders. The aim was to facilitate administration as well as to awaken and strengthen tribal consciousness. As has been stated; these courts came to be 'bastions of local loyalties, not the citadel of nationhood'.[34]

The British feared that modernization would undermine the region's stability and simultaneously make the population more susceptible to Western political ideas like nationalism and self-determination. The so-called 'Southern policy' took aim at blocking Arabic influence in the south of the country. The point was not to stop Islam, a question that little concerned the British, but to hinder the diffusion of modern nationalism and anti-British sentiments that were being spread by Arab nationalists. In the 1920s and 1930s, Egyptian and North Sudanese junior administrators were accordingly dismissed from Southern Sudan, and people with Arabic names were forcibly baptized. So nervous were the British that a Sudanese soldier who, in 1924 in Malakal, shouted: 'Long live Fouad, King of Egypt and the Sudan!' received eighteen months imprisonment and dismissal from the army. Following the 1919 anti-British revolution in Egypt and the nationalist demonstrations in Khartoum in 1924, which was led by a soldier from the Dinka people, the British, by now almost panic-struck, drastically reduced the number of Egyptian and North Sudanese administrators in Southern Sudan, and English was adopted as the school language. The British also helped to keep alive memories of the Arabic slave trade and hoped to strengthen them.

The goal was not to cultivate an elite group of southern Sudanese administrators to replace the administrators from the north, since the British feared that such groups would be 'poisoned' by modern ideas, that is to say, by nationalism and anti-British attitudes. What the British strategy wanted to avoid creating was a detribalized and dissatisfied intelligentsia in South Sudan. The British encouraged southern Sudan as a bastion of tribalism, as a counter to the emerging nationalism in the north.

Up until the 1940s and the Juba Conference in 1947, a conference organized by Great Britain to combine northern and southern Sudan into one political entity, the British colonialists had debated whether Southern Sudan should remain part of Sudan or whether the region rather should become part of other East African countries further south. This was, however, more a debate in Sudan than in London. In Whitehall, the view of Southern Sudan was coloured by how the region could be used in a diplomatic strategy aimed at maintaining influence and control where it mattered most, in Egypt and at Suez. The British in Sudan had a more narrow perspective and, influenced by the fact that some of them had developed a real affection for the country and its people, discussed the issue partly in terms of what they thought was best for the country's population and for Southern Sudan.

London and the British in Khartoum ultimately agreed on a unified Sudan, and subsequently also decided to bury the 'southern policy'. Many of the southern district commissioners thought this was a betrayal of the people in the south and argued that Southern Sudan ought to be made independent, or part of East Africa. Some of the district commissioners strongly criticized the British strategy. One of them complained that the British had done nothing but create a 'human zoo for anthropologists to study', and that the population in the south would be too weak and would be repressed anew, both culturally and economically, by the country's northern elites. The Governor of Equatoria wrote in a confidential memo to Khartoum in 1954 that the area was backward; that it was their responsibility to develop it, but that they had achieved nothing in this regard, They should rather start doing something useful, something they could be 'proud of', and give the people what they wanted more than anything else; water for themselves and their animals.[35]

In retrospect there can be no doubt that Britain's 'southern policy' strongly contributed to what many district commissioners thought was the only solution in the long run, but which London was against: an independent South Sudan. The Nile strategy that dominated until the end of the Second World War bolstered the regional stalemate, cemented the unequal development trajectories between north and south, and stimulated historical processes that ultimately led to the Sudan becoming two separate states.

World-class colonial research in the swamps

The stereotypical British colonial official – a blend of Cecil Rhodes with his lust for profit and Lord Cromer with his paternalism – is not without its roots in reality. However, there are too many examples that show that this description cannot be applied to the colonial administration as a whole, in any case not for the British who governed in southern Sudan from the 1930s onward.

One research report prepared in Southern Sudan during the 1950s illustrates the way in which the British Empire and its administrators could execute excellent research based on a thoroughly detailed knowledge of the areas over which they were set to govern. When the Jonglei Investigation Team in 1954 and 1955 published five volumes on the Jonglei Canal and its consequences for the local ecology and economy, they submitted one of the best research reports on a development project that has ever been produced on Africa. The man in charge was the Oxford-educated anthropologist, P.P. Howell, who was also district commissioner in the Nuer region.

London and Khartoum had engaged this research team in order to evaluate the consequences of the Jonglei Project, which the British in Cairo supported and which the Egyptian government had suggested in 1948. London's backing of the team's research was, among other things, a tactical move to exert pressure on an Egypt grown increasingly critical of the British presence at Suez. Egypt strongly desired, then as now, to excavate the Jonglei Canal but, by implementing the study, London made it clear to the Egyptians that the British still held sway upstream. The colonial administrators who conducted the research (and who were educated at the best British universities), meanwhile, viewed the question from a different perspective. They were as doubtful of the project as they were of Southern Sudan's continuing administration from Khartoum, and they reported that, based on the project's current proposed shape, it would serve Egypt and to some extent North Sudan, but not the people living in the southern parts of the country. However, even though their conclusions were clear, the report was balanced and presented a wealth of new information concerning a region about which very little was known beforehand.

Behind the Jonglei Investigation Team's five volumes lay a total of fifty years' work, and the report radically increased our knowledge of Southern Sudan's central regions. And, despite all later research on the same project, no study has been published that can compete with this work in terms of originality, quality and breadth. The report concluded that the project the Egyptian government desired could not be implemented in its current form because it would be detrimental to the needs and interests of the local population. Extensive adjustments to the plan were required, they argued, and the team also presented arguments outlining why the local population had to be properly compensated for the disruptions it would cause. In this way, the report formed the basis for the many other studies that were written on the same topic in the 1970s, and that will probably be written in the decades to come when the canal project again hits the drawing board.[36]

A 'Nile Republic'?

During the summer of 1955, rumours flourished among the Southern Sudanese soldiers stationed at Torit on the Nile's east bank. All knew that Sudan would get its independence on 1 January 1956, but in Southern Sudan many were uneasy about what this would mean for them. At the beginning of July, the contents of what later turned out to be a false telegram were being circulated, apparently signed by Ismail al-Azhari, the prime minister of Sudan. In the telegram, he encouraged the northern Arabs to repress and abuse the peoples of the south. Many of my friends in Sudan stubbornly claim that Israeli intelligence stood behind the telegram, and the spread of its content. Their line of argument is as follows: Israel sought at the time to weaken the governments in Khartoum and especially in Cairo. Israel knew that nothing would be more effective than a rebellion in Southern Sudan because it would not only decrease Egypt's downstream control of the Nile, but Cairo and Khartoum would get serious problems in their own backyard. Disregarding here who wrote the false telegram, its effects were as could be expected: soldiers of the Equatorial Corps, which had been established by the British as an independent military unit, composed exclusively of soldiers from the south, rebelled, and the armed battle for the 'Nile Republic' began. It happened like this.

On 22 January 1955, a southern member of the National Assembly had been jailed after a dubious trial. The imprisonment triggered riots in which eight demonstrators were killed. The atmosphere became increasingly tense. The government in Khartoum decided to transfer the Equatorial Corps north and to send new soldiers from the north to the south. The division stationed at Torit, however, refused and instead attacked the officers and broke into the weapon stores. That same day other soldiers rebelled in other barracks. Khartoum declared a state of emergency and immediately flew 8,000 soldiers to Juba, which boasted the region's only airstrip.

The rebels expected British support, but it did not arrive. Governor-General Knox Helm hurriedly returned to Sudan from his holiday in England and persuaded the rebels to surrender, while promising them a fair trial. The rebels, who had hidden throughout the jungle, met and decided to follow Helm's advice. They would surrender their weapons at Torit on 30 August 1955. But when the day came, no rebels were present; suspicious and fearful of what Khartoum would do, they had changed their mind at the last minute. Khartoum dissolved the entire military unit, and Helm left Sudan for good on 15 December 1955. The British period as rulers of Southern Sudan was now definitely over. The rebel leader, Reynaldo Loyela, was executed early in 1956. It has been claimed that 300 others suffered the same fate.

Few nations have been born with greater suffering and with more national disagreements than Sudan. When on 1 January 1956, the country celebrated its newly won independence with all pomp and circumstance, Southern Sudan's rebellion against the new state, of which it was a part, was already under way.

This new state had fundamental structural problems. It lacked the unifying institutions and ideas that other states typically possess. Religion was not a consolidating factor but rather a divisive one. On one side stood an expanding Islam with many followers who thought the state's legal system must be based on the *sharia*. On the other side there was evangelic Christianity whose followers could not accept an Islamic state. Caught between these two world religions, and regarded as a mission field by both, were millions of animists. Nor did the state have any unifying personalities, like for example a Garibaldi, Nyerere, Mao or Gandhi – only leaders whose primary power base was in one of two large sectarian, religious brotherhoods in North Sudan, Khatmiyya and Umma. Much less did Sudan have a national liberation movement, such as existed in many other African countries. The Mahdi, who in the north was considered to be the nation's spiritual forerunner, was associated in the south with terror and slavery. The British, who in the north were termed imperialistic exploiters, were in the south viewed as protectors and benefactors. The flag that was raised in Khartoum on 1 January 1956, was green, blue and white, but it had no resonance in Southern Sudan's history.

In Southern Sudan, the population's central political representatives demanded that the British should stay on, and not depart quickly. Next, they sought solutions that entailed various forms of connection to East Africa rather than to Khartoum, while for the population what mattered most was the fate of their ethnic group or clan.

The leadership in Khartoum attempted to implement an Arabization or Islamization policy in the south in order to enforce unity and to expand its power base. This policy was met with resistance and a stronger identification with what they called Black Africa and Christianity, not least after Khartoum expelled all Christian missionaries in 1964. The rebels received support from Israel, which clearly understood that a pro-Israeli South Sudan would act as a threat to Egypt's and North Sudan's water resources, something that could be used as a negotiation card when the need arose.

The guerrilla movement Anya-Nya (meaning 'snake venom' in Madi, one of the local languages) emerged against such a background of distrust between north and south. The civil war in Sudan paralysed development initiatives and processes until the beginning of the 1970s. The peace treaty signed in Addis Ababa in 1972 was a result of solid diplomatic hard work and political shrewdness, represented by President Nimeiri in Khartoum and General Joseph Lagu, the leader of Anya-Nya. The fight for a separate 'Republic of the Nile', as some Southern Sudanese leaders had wanted to call their new, independent country, was replaced by a scheme for national unity. As it would turn out, however, this period of peace and reconciliation was very short-lived, and one factor that contributed to renewed war in the 1980s was Garstin's canal idea from 1899, which never seems to disappear from its central place in the region's development.

Stop the canal!

'There are occasions in the recent history of developing nations when a development project captures the interest and attention of a wide international audience. The Jonglei Canal is such a project.'[37] Thus said Gamal Hassan, one of the Sudanese leaders of the

Jonglei Project. And he continued: 'Far from an insular fear of the Jonglei Canal Project, there is every indication that the people await it with anticipation. It has become, in fact, a manifestation of their desire for change – which is why development must be implemented at an early stage in the wake of the canal.'[38]

Gamal Hassan was correct in that description. The statement was issued in 1982, three years after independent Sudan and Egypt had again taken up the project that was first proposed around the turn of the century by the British colonial rulers. Now the main focus was to drain the swamps only, whereas the British 'Equatorial Nile Project' of the 1940s had also included damming up the Central African lakes in order to hurry much more water through what would then have become a near-drained swamp area. The project was now limited to a modified canal project. The swamps were, relatively speaking, even more important now because, following the High Dam in Egypt, they were the only place along the entire Nile where it was possible to increase the river's water flow.

Gamal Hassan, the Sudanese in charge of what was now called the Jonglei Development Project, emphasized that the project itself represented the deepest interests of the southern Sudanese population; it had become 'a manifestation of their desire for change'.[39] He insisted that this desire corresponded to the local population's highest hopes for the future. Gamal Hassan was not alone in thinking that the canal was in Southern Sudan's interests, but others were less optimistic when it came to the local population's ability or willingness to accept that it was, in fact, in their best interests. In 1974, the Vice President of Sudan and President of the High Executive Council of the Southern Sudan Autonomous Region, the Dinka Abel Alier had said that Southern Sudan must be developed, even if it took the whip. The Jonglei Project was this whip, he argued. The project was also described as a key factor in strengthening communication between north and south, since it would bring with it an improved waterway and a new road that was being constructed along the canal.

I was there in March 1983 when the work was in full swing and so could watch the Bucket Wheel, the largest canal excavator in the world in the 1980s, a giant of a machine, moving forwards like a monster alien through the African savannah. It dug out 120 metres a day – powerfully and systematically – through hard cotton clay. Simultaneously, with the help of a conveyer belt, the machine deposited masses of material at the canal's edge. There, a new and much quicker and straighter road between the north and the south in Sudan would be built, and it was even envisaged to connect Cairo with Cape Town, thus realizing a version of the old railway dream from early in the British imperial era. This excavator was a very potent symbol of modern technology's might as it ate its way forwards, juxtaposed against the earthen huts that surrounded it and the people who walked the footpaths barefoot and with spears in hand. The machine that would alter so much, however, was not a component in a gradual process of change, effected through thousands of earlier small and larger signs and hints, such as changes often have been heralded in many other societies, but appeared abruptly, without warning, as a shock. It thus challenged not only the local population's traditional way of living but also many theories of societal change itself. On the way down to Jonglei and the construction site, I stopped and talked with the Frenchman in charge of the project headquarters in Malakal. I asked him his opinion of the canal. He replied enthusiastically: 'What do you think? We're building a new Seine in the middle of Africa!'

Not long after, the Frenchman in charge died from malaria and the project collapsed. The guerrillas of the Sudan's People Liberation Army stopped the Jonglei Canal in 1983 after kidnapping and killing some of the Pakistani workers employed by the French company, Compagnie de Construction Internationale. It was not that the rebel leaders were against the canal per se, but by stopping the work on it they hoped to hit Khartoum where it hurt most.

Roughly midway between Malakal and Bor stand the remains of the Bucket Wheel today – a machine that first had been dismantled into parts, freighted by boat over the Indian Ocean from Pakistan, where it was used to excavate some of the country's 60,000 kilometres of canals, and then brought by train and truck from Port Sudan and down to Southern Sudan, before being reassembled screw by screw. Now it stands alone, rusty and abandoned, next to a broad overgrown trench, a resonant memorial to the most extensive cooperative development project between Cairo and Khartoum. That is all that is left of one of the world's most ambitious, but also contentious and planned water projects, and, at the time, a symbol of Sudanese–Egyptian friendship and collaboration. In the future, Cairo and Khartoum will have to negotiate with the leadership of the new South Sudan, a leadership that represents the same political movement that used its weapons to stop the Jonglei Project in the 1980s.

Even though the canal excavator stands rusting in the middle of the southern savannah, the Jonglei Project as an idea and vision is far from dead. The political context, however, has changed completely: now the region where the planned canal is located is in the new, independent country of South Sudan. A chief goal of Egyptian Nile diplomacy during the last century has been to secure political influence in Southern Sudan to get support for canalization projects. For Sudan's leadership, the water resources of South Sudan have been an important component in the country's stated plan of becoming the granary of the Middle East.

The politicians have come and gone, and countries have come and gone, but the Nile ecology and Nile hydrology remain the same: the governments in Cairo and Khartoum thus still hope and believe that the Nile's water flow in South Sudan can be increased by up to 30 billion cubic metres. It is entirely natural and rational that they will do whatever they consider necessary to realize this dream. Negotiations about the resumption of the Jonglei Project and its implementation will be even more complex now, and in the future, than they have been in the more than a hundred years that the project has lingered on the drawing board.

In the shadows of the rainforest

On the first leg of my trip from Juba to the Acholi Mountains in Sudan, I had flown in a light aircraft. Since it was just after the second civil war had broken out and no one knew for certain where the front lines were, the pilot flew as low as he could over the treetops to avoid being shot at. He said that the guerrilla soldiers might think we were with the government and, if they heard us coming, they would try to gun down the plane. By flying so low, they would not hear us until we had already passed overhead. Before landing, the plane made a sweep of the runway, the usual procedure to check for too large potholes and to chase away the goats. After we had landed, bouncing on the uneven clay and gravel airstrip, we drove by pick-up truck into the hills and, on a ridge overlooking the blue mountains towards the Kenya border, we rented space from a Scottish gold-digger who had settled here to spend his final days with a couple of young local women.

A few shafts of sunlight filter through the foliage in the cool forest on one of the hill ranges in Equatoria province where the Kinyeti River runs towards the Nile. The combination of tall trees, the powdery blue sky over the ridges, the pale grey rocks with no fleck of green, the brown of the fallen leaves, the pockets of darkness where rays from the tropical sun never reach, the verdant surface of the water puddles, the cascade of strange sounds, especially the sound of birds I do not know – all this shapes a world where imagination takes free rein. Everything is hazy, and I understand what the locals say when they argue that thoughts spring about without any fixed point, like a hyena following a hawk's shadow. Standing alone in the rainforest in the early morning hours, so early in the morning, creates an intense, receptive mood that you otherwise experience only in dreams perhaps, where anything seems possible – you can kill a lion by ripping its head off or you can fly like a bird.

It is just after the end of the rainy season and the hillsides are lush with many shades of green. When nature looks like this, it is difficult to grasp the rainmaker's significance in this part of the Nile basin. The entire region, however, is a victim of the rain's unpredictability. In central South Sudan, nine months can pass between rainstorms, and even further to the south, towards the border with Uganda and Kenya, the rainy season may be treacherous. Sometimes the rain arrives as expected, but often it fails to materialize, or it emerges in the wrong way or at the wrong time. Thus, the rainmaker's power is part of the region's religio-cultural history, and therefore also part of its political history.

I sit and gaze at an endlessly green and beautiful landscape, recalling that it was only a few years ago that a female rainmaker was killed in the area. She was blamed for the fact the rains did not come, when needed. After all, people reasoned, if she had power over the rain, she was the one who should suffer punishment when it did not manifest. I also well remember the first times I travelled from Juba to the Madi and Acholi districts, meeting local leaders who suggested I had a good standing with the rain gods since it always arrived when I did. Then the rain for a period suffered an irregular pause. Suddenly, I understood it had not been mere politeness with which I had been met, and I avoided the villages for a time so that I would not be associated with drought. But here in the beautiful Acholi mountains, in the wake of the rainy season, the ridges are sheathed in green – green trees, green peaks, green grass – and the earth seethes with life, abundance and fertility.

The new Nile state and George W. Bush

No single Western politician was more significant to Sudan's peace agreement in 2005 than President George W. Bush, and few had greater impact on South Sudan's ultimate choice of complete independence from Khartoum. From the very first day of his presidency, Sudan and South Sudan were at the top of the president's agenda. Bush was determined to achieve an important foreign policy triumph, and it would happen in this Nile country.

There were many reasons for Bush being especially interested in Sudan. The country had gradually become a greater domestic policy concern, especially among some of Bush's most important supporters. Directly after Omar Hassan al-Bashir's coup in 1989, American missionaries in Sudan sent home reports about forced Islamization and even mass murder of Christians in what was then Southern Sudan. From the beginning, conservative Christians in the United States characterized the civil war in Sudan as purely a religious conflict, and missionaries and organizations used the term 'genocide' to describe what was happening to Sudanese Christians. This was an exaggeration without any basis in fact but, in America, and to some extent in Western opinion in general, it eventually solidified to a truth that strengthened the engagement and advocacy of Christian conservatives.

What truly put wind in the sails of their Sudan activism, however, was when these groups first began to focus on the war against slavery in the country. The campaign was initiated by the US Director of Christian Solidarity International (CSI), John Eibner. Quickly, thousands of Christians raised money to purchase individuals, described as African Sudanese Christians, from Arab slave traders. Together with the evangelist Charles Jacobs, who founded the American Anti-Slavery Group in 1994, Eibner claims to have bought at least 80,000 slaves from slave traders operating in the Nile region in South Sudan.[40] Millions of dollars were donated by evangelical Christians in the United States, and slavery in Sudan became a worldwide media topic. But was this practice of slave redemption in Sudan a 'corrupt racket', as was charged by some? The *Washington Post* and a *CBS News* report questioned the effectiveness and authenticity of slave redemptions.

The TV programme *60 Minutes* aired a segment with John Eibner as he was purchasing the slaves' freedom. During the interview, Eibner is asked if he believes he has freed 60,000 (or 80,000) people. He answers yes. Then Jim Jacobs, who worked for Eibner, is interviewed. Jacobs says on camera that scenes are staged beforehand: the group had to cooperate with the Sudan People's Liberation Army (SPLA) to find 'slaves' and to buy their freedom. SPLA procured transport, negotiators, protection and interpreters. Jim Jacobs talks about a time they arrived unannounced – something was wrong with the radio connection – at a village to buy the freedom of some children apparently being held as slaves. There were no children when they arrived, but Jacobs said the SPLA representatives assembled some village children beneath a tree and then said: 'OK, here are the slaves. Buy their freedom.' At that, Jacobs quit his job and decided to tell the story to *60 Minutes*.

The programme had also found a Catholic missionary who had lived in Sudan for twenty years and who spoke Dinka. The missionary said that interpreters working for Eibner translated incorrectly, that individuals introduced as slave traders were hired for money, and that it was the SPLA that controlled the whole operation. And Eibner knew he was being tricked! But irrespective of who was tricking whom: it worked for both parties. The SPLA got their money, their opponents received poor PR, the Christians became heroes to their donors at home and to the SPLA, while the world

– was fooled. A coalition of civil rights groups calling for an end to slavery in Sudan attacked, on their side, the report on *60 Minutes*. 'It was disappointing that whoever wrote the story never even cared to indicate whether CBS acknowledges the very existence of slavery', said Abdon Agaw Nhial, vice president of the Sudanese Human Rights Organization, in a letter to the show's producer, and the Director of the Center for Religious Freedom at Freedom House, said the media were practising a 'herd instinct' when it came to reporting on Sudan.

The evangelical organizations became, from the 1990s on, steadily more important actors in American foreign policy when it came to Sudan.[41] Their goal was more ambitious than just creating peace: it was to form a new state in the Nile basin with a Christian leadership and base. Christian conservatives in the United States considered this to be a highly worthwhile objective and believed that it would at the same time set the region on a path of peace and more prosperity.

There is, however, reason to believe that groups within the US foreign policy establishment also had a more traditional geopolitical goal, and that they definitely acknowledged the strategic significance of a new, eleventh Nile state located upstream from Egypt and Sudan, just as Egypt, the Arabic world and Israel had long done. The United States' relationship to Khartoum steadily worsened throughout the 1990s, partly due to the growing influence of anti-American Islamism there. Following the assassination attempt on Hosni Mubarak in Addis Ababa in 1995, the United States was very active in the UN pushing through resolutions on sanctions against Sudan, and in 1997 the American Congress enacted extensive economic sanctions, based on the argument that Sudan represented a threat to the United States. These sanctions were broadened in the summer of 1998, when all Sudanese interests and accounts in the United States were frozen; President Clinton bombed Khartoum, and it became almost impossible for Americans to maintain any relationship to Sudan except through aid programmes. In Southern Sudan, however, they were very active throughout the 1990s and up until the peace accord. The US government, for example, gave hundreds of millions of dollars to Norwegian People's Aid, the biggest NGO that officially sided with the guerrilla movement, to support their work in SPLA-controlled areas. For many years, Norwegian People's Aid was the largest recipient of support from the American government; tenacious rumours abounded that the organization was smuggling weapons to the guerrilla army, with the trucks and planes crossing the border from Kenya with food and other deliveries. The organization at the time denied all these charges, but it did not help: Norwegian People's Aid, now became known, in parts of the NGO-milieu as the 'Norwegian People's Army'. What was documented beyond doubt some years later, was that the United States was involved in secret weapons deliveries. This was exposed through the episode of the Ukrainian cargo boat, which, after it had been hijacked by Somali pirates off the coast of Somalia, was found full of tanks bound for Southern Sudan. The British newspaper *The Daily Telegraph* remarked that the story resembled a John le Carré novel, and WikiLeaks revealed the way American diplomats became firefighters after the awkward revelation of this trafficking of illegal arms.

The United States pressed for a peace settlement and backed Southern Sudan's right to choose independence at the forthcoming election. Washington subsequently played an important role in training South Sudan's army and in supporting the organization of elections and celebrations of independence. The United States has done its part to establish an independent South Sudan with close ties to the United States and Israel, and in 2012, South Sudan was the first country in Africa to locate its embassy in Jerusalem.

However, the original goal of John Garang and the SPLA was not an independent state in the south. In contrast, those who advocated such a position were removed from SPLA leadership posts and quite a few were executed for treason. Garang's goal was a secular, democratic and more just Sudan, what he called a 'new Sudan'. Just after the 2005 peace accord, however, Garang was killed when the army helicopter that had brought him back from a meeting with the Ugandan president crashed not far from the SPLA's headquarters. Then the outcome was decided: the new SPLA leadership opted for independence and, not long after, there was a new state in the Nile basin, and it would define itself as a Christian, Western-oriented country.

The clash between Islam and Christianity that Kitchener back in the 1870s predicted would come to pass in the Upper Nile area, a struggle that due to its location on the continent would have great significance for the whole of Africa, was, at least temporarily, won by Christianity; a new Christian state had emerged, allied with Israel and the world's most powerful country.

Another Nile granary?

'The Nile is everything for South Sudan. It is life itself.' Independent South Sudan's first minister of agriculture, Ann Itto Leonardo, also then acting secretary-general of the Sudan People's Liberation Movement (SPLM), the liberation movement's political party, was very clear on how she saw the Nile when I met with her to find out about the new government's vision for the country's future. I wanted to talk to her when the euphoria of independence was still having an impact on the political leadership; the new state had not even formally been born.

'Do you want to hear the new national anthem? I have to practise.' She was preparing for the big celebration of the nation's birth, she said, and wanted to show me how beautiful she thought the melody and words of the national anthem were. The song begins with 'O Lord' repeated twice, as if to make the new country's religious foundation crystal clear. According to rumours that I was told, the anthem originally had 'O Lord' four times, but after a trial chorus led by the then vice president, Riek Machar, it was decided to reduce the number to two. One argument that was used was related to worries about how the text would appear when it was translated to Arabic and the word Lord replaced with the word Allah.

When I spoke with Leonardo, she underscored the Nile's mystical and cultural significance in her people's lives, but also emphasized that economically the river meant everything to South Sudan. It very soon became clear that South Sudan would join the group of upstream states, demanding negotiations around a new agreement on Nile water use and how exploitation of the river should be organized. Leonardo stated that the country has great potential as an agricultural nation. 'It can become the world's granary,' she optimistically declared '– if investments come and we can use more water,' she added. I have heard such visions before.

This is what appeared in *Scientific American* in September 1976:

> The Southern half of the Sudan is potentially one of the richest farming regions in the world, with the soil, sunlight and water resources to produce enormous quantities of food as much perhaps, as the entire world now produces! [...] To unlock the promise of the Southern Sudan those swamps would have to be drained, a rural infrastructure put in place, and the nomadic cattle raisers of the region somehow turned into sedentary farmers.[42]

Every new state needs ambitious goals as part of the state-building process, and this is particularly true of South Sudan, since it lacks the national, unifying myths and heroes that have been so important in state formation processes elsewhere. Unrealistic ambitions can, however, act like a boomerang, and readily formulated policy goals can, in the long run, turn into accusing fingers pointed at a leadership that fails to deliver on its own promises. One part of me wanted to warn Leonardo; I should be frank, tell her that reality would soon overtake her. Although, technologically and theoretically, it is possible to cultivate enormous quantities of food in South Sudan, it will meet with many practical and political hurdles. It will, probably, remain unfeasible because the government is too weak and the infrastructure too poorly developed. But what purpose would such an intervention from me serve? Perhaps they would succeed this time.

It is easy to understand the minister's impatience and ambitions. The longer that South Sudan remains undeveloped, the starker the contrasts become between what modern technology does in other parts of the world and what it could have accomplished in South Sudan. There are many ways to experience the potential of South Sudan and its enormous agricultural acreage, as I did it when, by chance, I was present on a fire hunt. While travelling in the Equatoria province with the chief of the Luo people, he suddenly and loudly gave an order: 'Stop the car!' We hurried out and ran to a field that stretched, so it seemed to me, kilometre upon kilometre to the horizon. In the far distance, I saw flames and smoke, and the flames grew and grew and came closer and closer. There were loud shouts in a language I did not understand, and through the smoke rolling across the plain, I could now and then get a glimpse of small groups of spear hunters. And then they came – hurtling antelopes. One after another. Blinded by smoke and crazed by the fire. They were now easy prey, not protected by the distances and emptiness of the plains.

After independence, what some people term 'land-grabbers', but what the South Sudan government called private 'investors', began to express interest in agricultural investments. According to reports, areas spanning tens, even hundreds, of thousands of hectares were leased. Some people argued that this was the way ahead for developing the country, while others argued that what they called rampant land-grabbing was fuelling ethnic strife and was unlawful because the land belonged to the local communities. Whatever the case; if these investments are ever to be profitable, political stability and better infrastructure must be in place, and the water must be better controlled, to produce hydroelectricity also.

The major issue for the future of the country is still, however, what happens to the largest wetland area in the world. It lies at the heart of the new South Sudan's relation to the other Nile countries. Plans have been circulated that not only talk about taking up a new version of the Jonglei Canal project, but to canalize much larger parts of swamp areas, thereby making it possible to send northwards billions of cubic metres more water per year, in exchange for investments in infrastructure and development plans for South Sudan. Egypt in particular has laboured and lobbied for such plans. The goals are ambitious, and the supporters of the idea argue that the plans are realistic and rational, pointing to how other countries like China and the United States have transformed their water and river systems. So why not South Sudan, which in addition is caught in a developmental trap forged by the existing ecological system of the swamp? But what will the local peoples do? Will the cattle-keeping semi-nomads renounce their way of life, which has been based so closely on their relationship to this same swamp ecology? Or will they willingly join this push for modernity, or will they simply be forced to accept it, as the well-respected president of South Sudan's regional government, Abel Alier, thought opponents of the canal ought to do when demonstrations against it were being held in the 1970s?

What will happen to the region's ecology if the swamp is drained? How will it affect evaporation locally, and then also perhaps rainfall and precipitation patterns in Ethiopia, where the Blue Nile comes from? And will draining the swamps lead to less seepage to the aquifer beneath the deserts of Sudan and Egypt? No one knows the answers to these questions about the behaviour of such complex ecological systems.

Minister of Agriculture Leonardo was very clear: she stated she understood Egypt's wishes when it came to building the Jonglei Canal, and said it was positive that Egypt wanted to help South Sudan improve some of the Nile tributaries' transport capacity, although she, of course, knew that what concerned Egypt the most was to increase the Nile's discharge northwards. Nonetheless, in response to Egypt's eager desire to implement the canal works as soon as possible, she reiterated the government's position: if this huge plan is to be implemented, it must be done carefully and therefore slowly. Leonardo indicated that the project and its regional and local consequences must be studied anew. If experience is any guide, this will take many years, even with a stable government in Juba. And even if the government ends up supporting the project, it is not certain that the local inhabitants will accept the plans, and this creates its own challenges in a region where it has been demonstrated again and again that the state cannot successfully claim that it has a monopoly over the legitimate use of violence. Egypt and Sudan must, therefore, most likely continue to wait for the water they both so desperately want to receive from South Sudan.

State formation and hydrodiplomacy

The date is 9 July 2011, the day on which South Sudan's new national anthem was being played and its new flag raised over Juba for the first time – and a day that not only saw the birth of a new African state but also the entrance of an eleventh state-player into the diplomatic struggle about the partition and use of the waters of the Nile. Some would say that an Egyptian nightmare had come to pass, others that a weakened Sudan was a benefit to Egypt, and more important in the long run. In the previous century, Egypt's Nile diplomacy had sought to avoid just this: the establishment of an autonomous state in the Nile's most water-rich region, especially a state independent of Egyptian influence. In 2011, however, such a state was indeed founded – a state born in a war against what they described as Arabic and Islamic countries in the north, and with the United States, the West and its African neighbours further south in the basin as its closest allies.

South Sudan faces many challenges, not least because the state resembles no other. The influential idea originally formulated by Karl Marx, that the state is nothing more than the ruling class's 'executive committee', does not fit South Sudan. Many leading politicians both before and after independence have largely sought to serve their own interests, or they have acted on behalf of their ethnic group or clan or close associates, rather than being agents of a ruling class, because such a class is non-existent. As such, the government can neither be described as an executive committee for a ruling class, nor as representatives of the population, being answerable to them, but rather as a kind of social forum, financed by oil money and development-aid funds, where competing groups and individual careerists have battled it out for access to state resources.

Nothing was established that resembled a normal, bureaucratic and independent civil service or an army or police force with enough legitimacy and authority to secure peace and stability. The state did not enjoy a legitimate form of monopoly of violence. Instead, it became increasingly clear that different armed groups had weapons enough both to challenge each other and to undermine the country's unity.

In addition to establishing themselves as the leaders of a functioning nation, some of the new leadership's most pressing issues were how to handle the Nile question. What will be the consequences for South Sudan if the government in Khartoum changes alliances when it comes to the Nile question? And what should South Sudan demand of Sudan's share of Nile water, given to them in the 1959 Nile agreement, when they were one, much bigger, country? And how will South Sudan approach Uganda's ever more ambitious plans for damming the Nile, before it reaches South Sudan, with hydroelectric plants, a type of control that might even out seasonal variations in water flow and thus, in the long run, affect cattle-keeping in the wetland areas? And will Ethiopia's future export of hydroelectric power make it possible to modernize the agricultural sector in South Sudan, thus also increasing the demand for Nile water? Many of these questions have not been addressed to any great extent, and the political leadership in Juba has, in comparison with the governments of other Nile countries, only limited experience and knowledge, both when it comes to addressing the technological issues of Nile control and the strategic issues of Nile policies.

After the civil war within South Sudan broke out in December 2013, just four years after independence, it has been estimated that millions of people fled their homes, with more than two million taking refuge in neighbouring countries, and as many as 200,000 people fleeing to six UN 'protection of civilians' sites across the country. Numerous peace agreements were signed and thereafter violated by government and opposition leaders. All parties to the conflict, moreover, carried out indiscriminate attacks against civilians, and were responsible for arbitrary detentions and torture, sexual violence and the use of child soldiers. The vision of South Sudan's first minister of agriculture in the weeks before they would celebrate their independence day for the first time, did not materialize. South Sudan has, some people argue, been hijacked by a kleptocratic elite, but seen in a broad and long historical perspective the state's problems are even more fundamental. The new state has been at war with itself for most of the time it has been independent. While civil war and uncertainty prevail, not very much is happening – not with the Nile, either.

I ask myself, as I read one story after the other about renewed fighting between pastoral groups and interests in the Jonglei states: what would South Sudan have been today if William Garstin and the British had managed to drain the swamps and to build the Jonglei Canal at the beginning of the twentieth century?

6

The Country with the Great Lakes

The race to the source

A caravan set out in June 1857 from the Zanzibar coast toward the centre of the African continent to find the sources of the Nile. It announced fifty years of successful and purposeful British surveying of the Upper White Nile and the river system's hydrology and it ended up providing London with strategic arguments for a British Nile empire.

The expedition consisted of 130 men and thirty draught animals and was headed by John Hanning Speke and Richard Burton. They took with them beds, folding tables, tools, chairs, tents, bed sheets, ammunition, weapons, mosquito nets, knives, shields, fishing equipment, a dozen brandy bottles and, for gifts, clothing, brass wire and pearls. The two men were moving in an area where no European had previously set foot, following the routes taken by the Arabic traders who searched for slaves and ivory near what locals described as 'the great lakes'. On the way Burton became so sick that he could not continue, and he could hardly eat; he lay in a delirium and fantasized about strange beasts and men with heads growing out of their chests. The two Europeans were tormented by mosquitoes and bees, and by scorpions and small, bitey creatures that were venomous enough to kill a rat. Speke, meanwhile, lost his hearing after using his knife to try and remove a beetle that had crept into his ear. Burton and Speke disliked each other, the region through which they travelled and the people they encountered. Speke viewed the Africans with racial contempt – they were lazy and could not to be trusted; they were 'hideously black and ugly' – and, in contrast to Burton, Speke was not, according to himself, able to overcome his shyness in regard to African feminine nudity. After a fatiguing journey, the expedition reached Lake Tanganyika, but they quickly decided it could not be the Nile's source.

Speke returned to London and for his next expedition to the Nile acquired a new companion, James Augustus Grant, 32-year-old son of a Scottish minister and who had been a soldier in British service in India. This caravan started from the East African coast as well, though a little further north. Speke and Grant were well received by many of the leaders of the African kingdoms that could emerge in this area of benevolent rainfall due to the existence of 'the great lakes'. When they reached the Karagwe people, the southernmost and weakest of these kingdoms, King Romanika welcomed them to his harem, which, according to Speke, consisted of unbelievably obese women. The explanation he was given for this was that the young girls were raised on milk, and they were beaten if they did not drink enough. The ideal was the bigger, the better. Speke asked if he could measure one of them. He concluded that her bosom measured fifty inches, or 132 centimetres.

From Isamilo Hill above Mwanza in today's Tanzania they saw for the first time that lake Speke would name Lake Victoria after the Queen of England. Grant later wrote in his book, *A Walk Across Africa*: 'The now famous Victoria Nyanza, when seen for the first time, expanding in all its majesty, excited wonder and admiration.'[1] After this, Speke continued alone; Grant had become too sick to travel further. On 21 July 1862, he caught sight of the river where it ran out of the lake. Speke wrote in his *Journal of the Discovery of the Source of the Nile* that the scene was beautiful – 'nothing could surpass it.'[2]

On 28 July Speke walked down to the outlet. He had now accomplished his life's great aim, what he for years had fixed his gaze on and what many people thought was impossible. In his diary he congratulated himself on having proven his theory. He had finally found what he described as the very source of a holy river; the Christian civilization's very cradle: 'I saw that old Father Nile without any doubt rises in the Victoria N'yanza, and, as I had foretold, that lake is the great source of the holy river which cradled the first expounder of our religious belief.'[3] He told the men who accompanied him that they should shave their heads and bathe in the holy river, likened by him with Moses's crib.[4]

When John Hanning Speke returned to Europe, he became one of his generation's great celebrities. The President of the Royal Geographical Society, Sir Roderick Murchison, credited him for making the discovery of his time. Not everybody agreed, however. On 16 September a debate about the source of the Nile was to be held in Bath at the Royal Mineral Water Hospital, as part of the British Association for the Advancement of Science's annual meeting. It was one of the most anticipated encounters of the time, and Speke would debate his discovery with his rival and former companion, Richard Burton, who did not accept the proofs Speke had presented. The hyped duel on the Nile could not take place, however, because Speke died the day before. Speke had gone partridge hunting at his cousin's farm. There he shot himself by accident. Speke had made his way through Africa, battling lions and elephants, yet a hunt for birds in Wiltshire took his life.

Few are more associated with the European mapping of the Nile than the Welshman Henry Morton Stanley. After having located the missing David Livingstone some years before at the shores of Lake Tanganyika, Stanley found himself again in Africa in 1874. His objective now was to explore all of Lake Victoria to determine if it had other outlets than the one Speke had discovered. On 27 February 1875, the expedition arrived at the lake's shores. One of his European companions came running through the woods to Stanley, who was too sick to walk, and shouted at him: 'I have seen the lake, sir, and it is grand!'[5] On the journey from the coast, Stanley had lost sixty of around 220 men, to desertion or disease, or because they were killed by the local people.

On 8 March 1875, Stanley set out in his boat *Lady Alice*, named after a woman he had fallen in love with during a short trip back to Europe. After rowing and sailing along the lake's shores for fifty-seven days, he could with certainty confirm that the lake's only outlet was Ripon Falls, which Speke had named in honour of the first President of the Royal Geographical Society, the Earl of Ripon.

Egypt's lifeline in the nineteenth century – the White Nile tributary with its water that made the land inhabitable in the summer and formed the basis for the lucrative cotton farming – was fed and controlled by this easily manipulable lake in the centre of Africa. This observation made Lake Victoria and the land that surrounded it central to the future British Nile empire.

The adventurer and his slave wife

On 14 March 1864, Samuel Baker and his wife Florence, who was younger than him by fourteen years, stood on the banks of the lake Baker would name Lake Albert after Queen Victoria's consort. Baker had led an adventurous life; thanks to a rich father, he had been able to travel the world hunting big game. On one of his hunting trips to Turkey, he travelled through Widden (Vidin), a village in today's Bulgaria, where a seventeen-year-old female slave from Transylvania, the only member of her family to survive a massacre following the Revolution of 1848, was being offered for sale. Baker bid on her and bought her for a few Turkish lira, they fell in love, and later married. He knew that it would not be acceptable to take her back to England, so he determined instead to do what he had long desired: hunting big game in Africa and searching for the Nile's sources. Together with Florence, whom he described as a woman who feared nothing, he travelled up the Nile past Khartoum, meeting Speke, who was heading downriver, at Gondokoro in South Sudan. After a two-year journey, the Bakers finally reached Lake Albert in March 1864. As Baker wrote in his bestseller, *The Albert N'yanza: Great Basin of the Nile*: 'There, like a sea of quicksilver, lay far beneath the grand expanse of water, – a boundless sea horizon on the south and south-west, glittering in the noonday sun; and on the west, at fifty or sixty miles' distance, blue mountains rose from the bosom of the lake to a height of about 7,000 feet above its level.'[6]

Now, at long last, he saw the lake. This *was* the very moment, this *would be* his moment in the Nile's long history – oh, how he had fantasized about it for years while toiling through swamp, savannah and rainforest, overcoming illness and defending himself from Africa's wild beasts. It was here that Baker, in his own words, had planned to raise a cheer three times over the lake. Yet, when he finally reached the place, he was unable to speak a world. He was so overcome, he later wrote, that he could not make a sound. Instead, he and his wife dismounted in feverish excitement from the oxen upon which they rode. Severely weakened by sickness and hunger, they descended the steep slope to the lake's edge. Baker writes:

> I led the way, grasping a stout bamboo. My wife in extreme weakness tottered down the pass. [...] After a toilsome descent of about two hours, weak with years of fever, but for the moment strengthened by success, we gained the level plain below the cliff. [...] The waves were rolling upon a white pebbly beach: I rushed into the lake, and thirsty with heat and fatigue, with a heart full of gratitude, I drank deeply from the Sources of the Nile.[7]

He continues with the triumphant self-consciousness of history-making that was so widespread among the Victorian explorers who succeeded in reaching their aims:

No European foot had ever trod upon its sand, nor had the eyes of a white man ever scanned its vast expanse of water. [...] Here was the great basin of the Nile that received *every drop of water*, even from the passing shower to the roaring mountain torrent that drained from Central Africa towards the north. This was the great reservoir of the Nile![8]

The finding of the enormous lakes from where the White Nile came, would have immense consequences for the scramble of Africa. When the British took power in Egypt in 1882, they already knew that the downstream country's prosperity depended on the waters of these lakes. They knew also very well that Lake Victoria could be controlled for the benefit of Egypt as well as for the purpose of controlling Egypt. The British discoveries therefore implied that this area would become central in the European partition of Africa. As long as Egypt was dependent upon the Nile's waterflow in summer, the lakes, as British water-planners in Cairo pointed out time and again in the 1890s, were 'as valuable as gold'. Indeed, it was this insight that was the basic reason behind London's diplomatic strategy, urging the other European powers to accept London's claim that the Nile basin was their 'sphere of interest'. The Nile's character and the distinctive political logic of its geography meant that, when it came to the Empire's strategy, it was not a question of *whether* the British should occupy the regions of the Upper Nile, but *when* and *in what way* they should do it.

The lakes form the axis around which Uganda's modern history has revolved. Uganda as a state is not a product of the Nile's hydrology, but was foremost a result of Britain's strategic grasp of the Nile as one hydrological system and as an important geopolitical weapon.

'Discoverers' or discoverers?

In our time it is easy to rent a small propeller plane in Entebbe and fly low over the place where the Nile leaves Lake Albert, to peer out over the long and narrow lake that today holds the border between Uganda and the Democratic Republic of the Congo, crossing eastward up the Victoria Nile, gliding slowly over the Murchison Falls and the swamps of Lake Kyoga, then further past Ripon Falls, the Nile's only outlet, and on to Lake Victoria. All this can be seen in an hour or two, through the window of the aircraft, effortless, while drinking your bottled water. It is easy, therefore, to forget the dangers and difficulties the explorers in the 1860s and 1870s overcame, and to ridicule, render banal or underestimate the fascination that the mapping of these Nile lakes exercised in Europe 150 years ago.

Postcolonial criticism has raised the question of whether it is meaningful even to describe these Europeans as discoverers, and that one rather should speak of 'discoverers'. These types of quotation marks may have fallen into discredit following postmodernism's hyperboles, but they may still be warranted here. For is it possible to say that the White Nile's main source was discovered by Speke and the Lake Albert's outlet by Baker, and that Stanley in the 1870s really discovered that multiple rivers were not flowing out of Lake Victoria?

A historical outline of European exploration history as it unfolded in Africa and in the Nile basin, should reflect ambivalence and duplicity. Europeans' fascination with the quest for finding the sources of the Nile puzzled the locals, and they called the white men travelling through their regions *mzungu* (literally translated as 'someone who roams around aimlessly'), still being the synonym for white people in Swahili. The explorers not only uncovered geographical secrets; they became simultaneously symbols of a familiar cultural relationship. These self-assertive fellows with their tropical helmets came to embody dominant perceptions of Europe's encounter with Africa in the West, but they also have represented African views of what Europe is and stands for – not just during the era of geographical exploration, but up until today. Their legacy is and will be characterized by the fact that their explorations heralded the European scramble for Africa, and that they themselves were active driving forces for European conquest and the declared aim of civilizing the continent. In the very first section of the book about his journey to what he termed the source of the Nile, Speke described Africa and Africans in such a stereotyping way that colonialism along the Nile could be seen as justified, even as being a historical necessity.

The explorers had no doubt that it was Europe's mission in Africa to 'civilize the primitives'. Nonetheless, should not Stanley's role in establishing the terrible colonial venture that became Belgian Congo be separated from his painstaking descriptions of the Ituri Forest in the eastern parts of the Nile basin, or of the Ruwenzori Mountains, or of Lake Victoria's banks? Cannot Baker's racist depictions of the 'natives' be considered distinct from his relatively detailed descriptions of Lake Albert's outlet and the Nile system in northern Uganda? Speke's and Burton's habit of taking measurements of Africans wherever they went – skulls, breasts, genitalia – makes for appalling reading today and was degrading when it occurred, but, in spite of that, cannot their accounts of Lake Victoria as a lake in the 1850s be read independent of their views on African society? It cannot be the case that an individual must oppose the colonial system to warrant the title discoverer, or that an individual must be dismissed as a 'discoverer' of geographical phenomena on account of his social and political attitudes.

It has also become common to assert that the explorers did not discover anything because they only chronicled what people already knew but had not written down. One of them, Henry Morton Stanley, who has often been a target for an almost collective postmodern or postcolonial-inspired condemnation of 'discoverers' in general, was one of the first to offer justification for this critique. As he wrote in the book, *In Darkest Africa*: 'They will observe with pleasure that we have not much to boast of; that the ancient travellers, geographers, and authors had a very fair idea whence the Nile issued, that they had heard [...] of the springs which gave birth to the famous river of Egypt.'[9]

Certainly, this lake was known before the two British adventurers came there in the mid-nineteenth century. In the second century BCE the Greek astronomer, mathematician and armchair geographer Claudius Ptolemy sat in the Library of Alexandria and collected all known travel accounts, and he wrote about the Greek traveller Diogenes who had journeyed into the African continent from the Indian Ocean and who had reported that two lakes and the Mountains of the Moon were the river's sources. In his *Geography* from the middle of the second century, Ptolemy described the Nile as a holy river that began around 12° south of the equator, originating from a large number of tributaries that formed lakes, and from which two rivers further ran, eventually joining to form the Nile. Ptolemy also mentioned 'Selenes Oros' or 'the Mountains of the Moon' in Central Africa as the Nile's source, but his map was never more than a thesis, a contention, a drawing made on the basis of unclear information, which moreover was not confirmed by people who had been there.[10] Later, an Arabic map from the twelfth century, the so-called Tabula Rogeriana, drawn for the Norman King Roger II of Sicily in 1154 by Muhammed al-Idrisi, showed a large lake in Africa's centre from which the Nile flowed. It is also obvious that those living in its proximity knew that they lived by an enormous lake from which a river ran out. They saw this river every day. The local population called the lake Nalubaale, which means something like 'God Mother' (*Lubaale* is the generic word for 'deity' and the prefix *na* gives it a feminine association). In 1850, however, none of these maps and stories had been confirmed; they were only a few of the many myths that flourished regarding the origins of Egypt's lifeline, and no one had yet written or documented that they had seen the source.

So when the Royal Geographical Society in London launched their expeditions in the latter part of the nineteenth century, they initiated a process that with surprising accuracy charted and mapped complex geographical contexts and hydrological systems that extended from the heart of Africa to the Mediterranean – systems that no one had previously documented with sound evidence. Observing what is directly observable cannot be compared to scientific discoveries, and if these two types of observation are equated, the differences between science and mere observation or local knowledge vanish. As such, it is legitimate and not necessarily Eurocentric to describe Speke and Grant and Stanley as great discoverers and pioneers in their own right.

Naked resolution and scientific evangelism

Ignorance and the prevailing uncertainty regarding the Nile's origin, and the conception of the river as being sacred and divine, were connected to and nourished by the same inexplicable phenomenon: how could a river that ran hundreds of kilometres through the desert under a cloudless sky and a scorching sun arrive every single year as a benevolent flood over Egypt, transforming an extremely barren landscape into the most fertile region in the known world? As long as this mystery remained unsolved, the Nile was an ideal object for geographical and religious speculation.

Herodotus discussed different theories of where the Nile came from in *The History*, and he also proposed his own. He dismissed those Greeks who wanted to showcase their insights, as he wrote, and claimed that it was trade winds that caused the river to swell in the autumn because they slowed the river on its way to the ocean. Even more illogical, he noted, was the theory that the Nile came from Okeanos, a kind of river or ocean that encircled the earth. Herodotus instead proposed the theory that it was the sun that drew water from the Nile in winter.[11]

Plate 1 The Nile mosaic of Palestrina (photo by Leemage/Corbis via Getty Images).

Plate 2 A frieze depicting Egyptians using the water from the Nile for irrigation, *c.* 2000 BCE (photo by Hulton Archive/Getty Images).

Plate 3 The Pyramid of Cheops stands reflected in the Nile River, at the time when it still flooded at Giza, Egypt (photo by Felix Bonfils/Library of Congress/Corbis/VCG via Getty Images).

Plate 4 One of the salt lakes in the northern Egyptian Nile Delta. Before the new High Dam was built, opened in 1971, large parts of the Delta looked like this every autumn as the flood arrived (photo by Terje Tvedt).

Plate 5 Cairo, 'the mother of all cities'. More than 20 million live or commute every day to this busy metropole, surrounded by deserts and kept alive by the Nile (photo by Terje Tvedt).

Plate 6 The area around Luxor and the Valley of the Kings, Upper Egypt, seen from an air balloon. One can clearly observe the sharp line between desert and irrigated areas (photo by Terje Tvedt).

Plate 7 Feluccas on the Nile near Aswan, Egypt. . On the other bank one can see the Egyptian desert, without the greening effect of the Nile (photo by Terje Tvedt).

Plate 8 In Nubia, northern Sudan, the river winds its way through a brown-coloured landscape, with a very thin strip of green on its banks where it is possible for humans to dwell and cultivate (photo by Terje Tvedt).

Plate 9 In Khartoum, the Blue and the White Niles meet in 'history's longest kiss', as an Arab poet lyrically described it. This geographical fact has made the Sudan a key country in the quest and struggle for the control of the Nile (photo by Terje Tvedt).

Plate 10 The narrow outlet of Lake Victoria, Uganda, where the White Nile begins its long journey northwards to Egypt (photo by Terje Tvedt).

Plate 11 The enormous and flat plain that the White Nile crosses before it enters Lake Albert in northern Uganda (photo by Terje Tvedt).

Plate 12 Reed boat on Lake Tana, the main water source of the Blue Nile in Ethiopia (photo by Terje Tvedt).

Plate 13 Orthodox Christians on the shores of Lake Tana as the sun rises and just before they are rebaptized in holy Nile water during the annual Timkat festival (photo by Terje Tvedt).

Plate 14 The famous Blue Nile Falls before the river was tamed for hydroelectric purposes. In the local language it is called the Tissisat Falls or Tis Abay; 'the smoking water falls' or 'the smoking river' (photo by Terje Tvedt).

Plate 15 Lake Victoria as seen from the Speke Resort, Kampala, in the 'Blue Hour'. The lake is about as big as Scotland and often gives the impression of being an ocean rather than an inland water body (photo by Terje Tvedt).

Plate 16 This small replica pyramid at the source of the Nile in Burundi was built in the 1930s, and its symbolic meaning was to emphasize the geographical bond and community of destiny that exist among the countries in this gigantic river basin (photo by Terje Tvedt).

Plate 17 Bernini's fountain 'The Four Rivers' on Piazza Navona in Rome, unveiled in 1651, is one of the clearest expressions of the Nile's very special place in the world's mythical and religious history. The Nile god's head is covered by draping fabric, meant to illustrate that no one at that time knew exactly where the Nile came from (photo by Terje Tvedt).

Plate 18 The Nile Barrage that the khedive of Egypt, Muhammed Ali, took the initiative to construct, was finished in the mid-nineteenth century. It should heighten the water level of the river in the Nile Delta, thus making it possible to cultivate bigger areas more times every year (photo of postcard by Terje Tvedt).

Plate 19 The Aswan Dam was completed in 1902. It was the foremost symbol of the British quest to tame the Nile and to develop irrigated agriculture and cotton production in Egypt (photo by D.S. George/Hulton Archive/Getty Images).

Plate 20 Hardly any human project has been carried out so regularly over such a long period of time and has had such great economic and political significance as the measurement of the Nile's water flow. This pillar of the Nilometer on the Rhoda island in Cairo, was erected in 861 on the orders of the Abbasid Caliph al-Mutawakkil (photo by Terje Tvedt).

Plate 21 The world's largest excavator – brought from Pakistan, dismantled down to the smallest screw, transported by boat across the Indian Ocean to Port Sudan on the Red Sea and moved by large trucks down to the swamp area of southern Sudan. The picture shows the bucket wheel as it looked in operation when the author was there in March 1983. When the civil war started the same year, it was abandoned by everyone, and finally destroyed by rust (photo by Terje Tvedt).

Plate 22 The Toshka Project was one of the big projects pushed by President Hosni Mubarak and it aimed at channelling about 10 per cent of Egypt's share of the Nile water into the Sahara to build a new Nile valley, with cities, factories and millions of people. This picture was taken in 2006, when the project had just started to change what was clearly a desert landscape (photo by Terje Tvedt).

Plate 23 The pumping station, proudly called the Mubarak Pumping Station when it was built, should pump water up from the Aswan Dam and thus make the desert green (photo by Terje Tvedt).

Plate 24 The Tekeze Dam under construction in 2006 on the Tekeze river in Ethiopia (called the Atbara in the Sudan). It was finished four years later and was the first dam upstream that indicated that the power relationship between Egypt and Ethiopia on the Nile was about to change (photo by Terje Tvedt).

Alexander the Great was also very much interested in the origins of the Nile, at the time when he founded Alexandria more than 300 years BCE and was the ruler of Nile Delta. According to Father Balthazar Telles (who wrote about his travels in the country of the eastern Niles, Ethiopia, in 1710), the first question Alexander supposedly asked the famous Oracle of Amun at the Siwa Oasis, in the desert west of Alexandria, was where the Nile began.[12] Presumably, Alexander later believed for a short time that he had found the sources of the Nile when he encountered the rivers Hydaspes and Akesines, even though these ran into the Indus in today's Pakistan. Greek geographers knew that Hydaspes could not be the original source of the Nile, but they still linked these rivers to the Nile system because they also arrived by flood in the summer, and the geographers thought that the amount of silt in these two rivers indicated that there must be some connection to the Nile.

Julius Caesar desired so ardently to know where the Nile's source was that 'discoursing in Egypt with the grave old man Achoreus, and enquiring where the Nile had its origin, he went so far as to tell him it was the thing he most coveted to know in the world ... adding that he would quit his country Rome for the satisfaction of discovering that source.'[13] Emperor Nero also sent soldiers and officers to find the river's source, but this expedition failed. The soldiers did not get further than the swamps in today's South Sudan, according to Seneca the Younger, the Roman author, philosopher, and Nero's adviser – until he was forced to commit suicide.

In the European Middle Ages speculations continued. The Spanish traveller Pedro Tafur (1410–87) wrote, for example, about the legend, Prester John. His idea was that, for a Nile expedition to succeed, everyone who participated must be able to live exclusively on fish. Therefore, it was necessary to create that kind of man. The African monarch assembled a group of children, denied them milk and reared them solely on raw fish. When they were finally grown, they were sent upriver. According to the story, they reached the Mountains of the Moon, saw that the Nile streamed from high in the mountains, through a hole in a rock, and came no further.

In tandem with this mythological Nile tradition, significant strides were made in understanding the geography of the Nile, even as confusion persisted. Ansel Adorno, for example, who travelled in Asia in 1470–1, wrote that the Nile originated in India and ran to Egypt through Ethiopia. The Franciscan monk Suriano, whose travel accounts were published in 1524, noted that the Nile's sources were located directly in earthly Paradise, and he added, thinking within a conceptual universe that today is difficult to fathom, that the river in Ethiopia flowed over a bed of pure gold.

As Speke, Grant, Baker and Stanley solved the puzzle about the sources of the Nile, this accomplishment must be analysed based on this previous history of myth and speculations. After countless explorers throughout the centuries had failed to wrest from the Nile its geographical secrets, this breakthrough happened in just a few decades. Indeed, Margery Perham has remarked of these explorers that 'these discoverers ... illustrate human purposefulness in such extreme and naked fashion as to take on a symbolic meaning'.[14] Africa's interior was at that time largely unknown to the outside world, and the continent was far from charted by the geographical and cartographical disciplines. The reason for this was a combination of the facts that navigating all the river upstream from the Mediterranean was very difficult and risky, and that Europeans could not easily tolerate the climate. The malaria mosquitoes have been described as Africa's best defence. Stanley alluded to these ideas:

> Fatal Africa! One after another, travellers drop away. It is such a huge continent, and each of its secrets is environed by so many difficulties, – the torrid head, the miasma exhaled from the soil, the noisome vapours enveloping every path, the giant cane-grass suffocating the wayfarer, the rabid fury of the native guarding every entry and exit, the unspeakable misery of the life within the wild continent, the utter absence of every comfort, the bitterness which each day heaps upon the poor white man's head, in that land of blackness, the sombrous solemnity pervading every feature of it, and the little – too little – promise of success which one feels on entering it.[15]

The explorers overcame their fear and repressed doubts and ambiguities – if they were persons prone to those things, and to this their biographies give no definite answer. They proudly represented European expansionism, to be sure, but they also regarded themselves as a kind of spearheads for a militant, scientific evangelism, as firm believers in the ideals of rationality and science. In the mid-nineteenth century, this way of thinking coincided with a powerful historical-ideological trend where faith in a natural law-like progress of humankind – that the meaning of history itself was for societies to progress from a primitive stage to a developed stage and hence also from mythology to science – dominated the world of ideas. These world views and ideas about the directions of history allowed and encouraged the explorers to develop a self-image where, on behalf of the White Man, they brought the torch of progress to an Africa still in a state of deep darkness. Geography was, at that time and in this sense, a militant discipline, directed at conquering or seeking mastery over wild nature and other continents. Most scholars today agree that African explorations, therefore, on a deeper cultural level revolved around control, and that the explorers' books, maps and illustrations should accordingly be analysed as weapons of conquest as well as works of contemplation or science. The current tentativeness and scepticism regarding the role of the explorers reflects the historical duality of their roles and functions. They continue to be in some connections regarded as heroes, as people without doubt, indecision and fear, overwhelmed by their personal ambitions to observe something new and to write about it. At the same time, they are conceived as being almost caricatures of themselves, figures in tropical helmets leading their troop of bearers in their struggle against sickness, lions, elephants and natives; so full of themselves that the bearers and guides on whom they were utterly dependent might vanish from their narratives. Some of these explorers, of course, were unsympathetic racists, but even so, or perhaps because of this self-image of being special, they were encouraged to search for and finally uncover the Nile's secrets, whatever the cost.

They created more interest in and fascination for Africa's and the Nile's geography and made invaluable contributions to the continent's exploration. Simultaneously, they helped enshroud the peoples and cultures living in the Nile basin in a veil of prejudices and 'negative reporting'; that is to say, their sensational bestsellers helped to create and popularize the perspectives and stereotypes that have to such large degree influenced the rest of the world's understanding of Africa even up to our day.

The African kingdom at the Nile's source

'An African kingdom at the Nile's sources in the heart of Africa!' This was bombshell news in the mid-nineteenth century Europe.

When Speke and Grant reached Lake Victoria and told the world that they had discovered the source for which Julius Caesar and Nero themselves had searched, their accounts of the previously unknown Africa kingdoms around the lake also stirred great interest.

Buganda, which was a relatively well-developed kingdom with a history of several centuries, did not fit the day's dominant narratives of Africa. Social anthropologists and historians have worked to reconstruct the history of the Baganda. The Baganda people's own story is that they arrived from the Mount Elgon region north-east of Lake Victoria at the end of the fifteenth or in the early sixteenth century. At first the kingdom was chiefly structured through marriage alliances between the king's family and other big men's families. By the early eighteenth century, however, the king, or *kabaka*, began conquering regions outside of the Buganda heartland and this led both to a firmer centralization of power and to the development of a layer of royal officials. Royal succession was a perpetual problem, however, and conflicts around the kingship regularly broke out. As a rule, whichever aspiring heir lost suffered his family's extermination.[16]

The first meeting between a European and the king of Buganda occurred on 20 February 1862, on a hill next to Lake Victoria in today's Kampala. The scene received a lively description in Speke's journal, told from the viewpoint of this nineteenth-century European. First, Speke and King Mutesa I sat for a long while, simply staring at each other, neither saying a word. Speke sat beneath his parasol, a fact the king's court found strange and amusing. Speke had, he writes, ample time to study the king. He saw an attractive, tall, athletic man around twenty-five years old who wore a fine, multicolour-patterned necklace and many other jewels. Everything he had on was tasteful and elegant, according to Speke. The king sat surrounded by his spear, his shield, his white dog and his women. After having studied each other for an hour, the king retired to dine, without offering anything to Speke. Speke waited until he was again given an audience. First the king showed him a hundred of his wives, then they began to talk about the Englishmen who came up the Nile, and when Speke wanted to tell of his discoveries, the king was more interested in the weapons Speke had brought. The meeting signalled what would become the Nile's history over the next centuries and the axis around which it would revolve: Britain's interest in the river coupled with a regional play for power and influence in what had become a British Nile empire.

The kingdom was based on agriculture, particularly on growing plantains. In Buganda the rainy season lasted more or less all year due to the amount of evaporation, especially due to the presence of Lake Victoria. Buganda's king had also established a military fleet – with boats constructed from hollowed-out tree trunks – that patrolled the 'God-mother' lake. In the seventeenth and the eighteenth centuries, Buganda was, according to some Ugandan historians, the 'fear of their neighbours'.[17] The first Europeans who arrived there were impressed by the fact that the Baganda, unlike other peoples in the region, were clothed. The cloth, called *olubugo*, was made from the soft bark of the fig tree. In order to make the bark both pliable and durable, the outer layer was carefully removed, and the bark was then alternately water-soaked and beaten with a grooved wooden hammer. Cotton garments, for their part, arrived with the Arabic traders who travelled inward from the East African Swahili coast and who had given that area its name.

Mutesa I ruled over a rather well-developed kingdom, though his form of power was that of a despot. Those admitted to his presence, Speke wrote, thanked and praised their master and ruler according to local custom:

> [They knelt] on the ground – for no one can stand in the presence of his majesty – in an attitude of prayer, and throwing out the hands as they repeated the words n'yanzig, N'yanzig, ai N'yanzig Mkahma wangi, etc., etc., for a considerable time; when, thinking they had done enough of this, and heated with the exertion, they threw themselves flat upon their stomachs, and, floundering about like fish on land, repeated the same words over again and again, and rose doing the same, with their faces covered with earth; for majesty in Uganda is never satisfied till subjects have grovelled before it like the most abject worms.[18]

Speke also related that, while staying with the king, he one day gave him a rifle. After having admired it, the king handed the rifle to a young servant for testing. The servant left, shot the first person he saw, and triumphantly returned. The man was dead, he reported, and the weapon had functioned well. On a near daily basis, a few of the king's concubines were killed. Speke saw them, he wrote, shrieking, with a rope around their necks, being dragged to certain death. The harem, meanwhile, was regularly bursting with women. Those working in the palace, according to Speke, led an uncertain life. One day, when the king was dissatisfied with his meal, he put a hundred to death before Speke was able to stop it. One of Speke's merciless critics, the geographer James M'Queen, reviewing Speke's book in the English magazine *Morning Advertiser*, wrote that Speke was a pathetic, immoral man, particularly because he regularly accepted gifts from Mutesa and his queen in the form of young girls, if only the ones he found most appealing. In fact, M'Queen claimed, sometimes Speke was so busy with these that he never quite found the time to study the lake.[19]

The missionaries arrive

On 3 April 1876, King Mutesa wrote a letter to Queen Victoria in which he titled himself the 'greatest king of Africa'. He tells the queen that previously the 'Muhammedans' had attempted to win him to their side, but now he wished to subject himself to her. He closes thus: 'May God be with the Queen, may God be with your Majesty, and I beg you to send me paper, ink and pens, because all my paper is finished.'[20] This letter would usher in a process where religion and Nile ambitions blended into an imperial policy that is difficult to get an overview of and to reconstruct, also because these two political and rhetorical arenas were so different and almost worlds apart.

King Mutesa's letter to Queen Victoria caused quite a stir in its day. A Christian greeting from 'Black Africa' to the ruler of the greatest empire in world history, in a letter in which the king begged to become her son! It was written after Stanley had visited the royal seat and had spoken with the king about Christianity – and about British weapons technology. Significant changes had taken place since Speke's sojourn there. The kingdom now had around one million inhabitants and stretched 200 kilometres along the north-western shores of Lake Victoria. The *kabaka*, who had meanwhile converted to Islam, and who now ruled over an army of tens of thousands of soldiers in addition to the fleet of canoes, desired for political and tactical grounds to establish a religious competitor to Islam and a European counterweight to the increasing Arabic and Egyptian influence. When the first missionaries arrived from Europe in 1877, Mutesa decided to send two emissaries from Buganda to London. They were received by Queen Victoria in May 1879. After a journey that lasted a year and a half, they returned and wrote an interesting account that gives a good impression of how Europe, from an African point of view, was perceived.[21]

The letter from Mutesa and the visit to London also signalled that the region around the great Nile lakes would become a central arena for a new type of missionary – martyrs of the evangelical expansionism, they were people willing to sacrifice themselves, not for profit or for a particular ideology, but for God. They followed in the footsteps of the legendary German missionary to East Africa, Johann Ludwig Krapf, who, as he was learning Swahili and Nyika, the local language, lost both his wife and daughter to malaria, but continued his mission work undaunted. This brand of missionary furnished British and modern European colonialism and imperialism with certain traits that turned out to be important to the Nile basin's history. The solitary missionary who, on his own or together with a few like-minded Christians, journeyed into the Africa continent and to the Nile lakes, animated by evangelistic energy, provided missionary history with its early type hero.

From the east came Alexander Mackay, a Scottish Anglican sent by the Church Missionary Society. He reached Kampala in 1878 and immediately made an impression, particularly because, in contrast to many later individuals, he had mechanical aptitude. From the north the following year came the Catholic White Fathers. It was not long before both groups had their supporters. Mutesa pitted the different religious groups against each other and against the traditional priests, seeking to thereby strengthen the kingship's independence and position. Because he also feared the young Baganda at the royal court becoming too positively inclined toward Christianity, he ordered all missionaries to reside in the area around the *kabaka*'s seat, so that he could control their doings.

King Mutesa died in 1884, after reportedly having fathered ninety-eight children, and was succeeded by one of his sons, Mwanga II. Mwanga took a harder line toward the Christians, and in Europe it was particularly broadcast when he burned three Christians alive during his first year in power. An even more infamous act – indeed, almost iconic for the mission perception of its own history during these years – was the murder of the missionary James Hannington. Hannington was born in Hurstpierpoint in Sussex and had left school at fifteen to work for his father. At age twenty-one he opted for a church career. In 1874 he was ordained as a deacon, but when he heard in 1882 about the murder of missionaries on the shores of Lake Victoria, he decided to enter the Church Missionary Society and left England on 17 May. Severely weakened by fever and dysentery, however, he was forced to return after only one year. In January 1885, he again left for the Upper Nile area. He found a new way that missionaries could take from the coast to the lakes, and he arrived on Lake Victoria's shores on 21 October. King Mwanga immediately imprisoned him.

Hannington wrote in his diary the same day: 'to my joy, [I] saw a splendid view of the Nile, only about half an hour's distance, country being beautiful'. Not long after he and his companions were attacked by around twenty men. 'Twice I nearly broke away from them, and then grew faint with struggling, and was dragged by the legs over the ground. I said, "Lord, I put myself in Thy hands, I look to Thee alone". [...] I sang "Safe in the arms of Jesus" [...] and for a whole hour expect[ed] instant death.'[22]

A few days later – on 29 October 1885 – Hannington was stabbed to death on the king's direct orders. He was among the first Christian martyrs in Uganda, and as an expression of the significance of this event, his death day is a Memorial Day in the Church of England. Within church and mission history, the first African converts also occupy a heroic chapter. In one case, thirty-two converted Ugandans were burned to death. The missionary Robert Pickering Ashe writes:

> When Munyaga (a newly converted Christian) was captured he was in his house [...] The executioners came cautiously up. They saw a gun leaning against the reed lintel of the door and stopped, hesitating, believing it was the possession of a loaded gun that gave Munyaga such confidence. He, seeing their evident fear, told them they need not be afraid of the gun, for he did not mean to use it. He begged to be allowed to put on his 'kansu' (white gown), which they agreed to, and then they led him away. His trial was a cruel mockery, and he was ordered to be hacked in pieces and burned. His torturers cut off one of his arms and flung it into the fire before him, then they cut off a leg, and that, too, was flung into the flame, and lastly, the poor mutilated body was laid on the framework to be consumed. Ashes to ashes, dust to dust, in sure and certain hope of the resurrection of the dead.[23]

Mutesa's chief objective had been to channel European influence in such a way that it strengthened the kingdom. He and Mwanga both welcomed a small European settlement, one that would be kept under the kingdom's control and used to protect Buganda against possible attack, especially from their traditional enemies, the Bunyoro, another quite strong kingdom to the north, in the vicinity of Lake Albert. However, this tactic failed because the kings had underestimated London's determination and expansionist plans for the Upper Nile following Britain taking control of Egypt. King Mwanga became quickly convinced how the situation would end: Uganda would be controlled by Europeans. As he said: 'I am the last King of Buganda. The whites will take over the country after my death. While alive I will be able to prevent it, but I will be the last of the black kings of Buganda.'[24]

The king was foresighted, but he was also wrong. The British toppled the too powerful and headstrong Mwanga and after a brief war, which he lost, sent him into exile to the Seychelles in 1897. He thus experienced the defeat he saw coming while still living. Britain's colonial strategy, meanwhile, aimed to preserve the kingdom as such, albeit in another form, their intent being to secure their strategic objective with the least possible expense. They fortified their political control over Uganda by working with the new *kabaka*, who was four years old when a formal agreement with London was signed in 1900. The Baganda leaders hoped that, as a reward, their people would find a privileged place in the new British order.

Volumes have been written regarding the violent religious conflicts that took place in Uganda between Muslims and Christians, and not least between Catholics, Anglicans and Protestants, in the 1890s. Interpretation of their role has run the gamut from admiration to criticism. In 1916 the following analysis regarding the missionaries in Hannington's organization, the Church Missionary Society, was published in England: They were 'anti-intellectual, fundamentalist, Bible-believing, strongly anti-Catholic and belonged to a world of moral absolutes and few neutral arenas'.[25]

A widespread interpretation of Britain's occupation of the country at the beginning of the 1890s has assumed that London intervened to solve these conflicts. The missionaries tried to mobilize support in their homelands against what they described as African barbarism, Islamic fanaticism, Catholic perversity and so on. Religious arguments blended with a strong consciousness of European civilization were wielded in public debates concerning the reason Central Africa should come under British influence.

Nonetheless, the religious question was not of overriding or decisive importance to those who shaped British imperial Nile strategy and policy. Prime Minister Salisbury and Lord Cromer were certainly not as concerned with civilizational conflicts and the spread of Christianity in this part of Africa as they were with economics and geopolitics. The deciding factor was their firm belief that Egypt could be controlled from Uganda, and it was therefore important that these Upper Nile regions, including South Sudan, developed religious and cultural identities distinct from those dominating in Egypt and North Sudan.

Decisive for Egypt's future

The British in Cairo had long been eager to occupy the region. In 1892 Lord Lugard travelled around Buganda as a representative for the private Imperial British East Africa Company.[26] When he returned to London in October of that same year, he launched the campaign for British occupation with a speech to the Royal Geographical Society. Lugard wrote about the subject in his two-volume work on Uganda and in articles he published at the time. He provided many different arguments for British occupation, both religious and economic, but he also emphasized the importance of the Nile question. Well aware of the debate that occupied the elite in Cairo and the central strategists in London, for example, he said in his 1892 speech that London must conquer the region militarily and politically because it would, among other things, make it possible to telegraph information concerning unusual waterflow in Uganda to the British in Egypt, so that those who directed irrigation agriculture there could take their precautions.[27]

The British leaders in Egypt were discussing at that time extensive plans for the regulation of the Nile that presupposed military control of the lakes. In 1893 one of the leading water politicians in Egypt, J.C. Ross, spoke on the subject at a meeting in Great Britain. He indicated that Egypt could receive thirty times more water than the country would ever need, just by raising the water level of Lake Victoria by one metre. This was music to the ears of those who had invested in Egypt's agriculture, to the capitalists Egypt owed money to, and to the Lancashire cotton industry. In Cairo one of Britain's foremost water experts, William Willcocks, published plans for the lakes that same year; the year before, he had written a secret government report describing the water in these African lakes as being critical to Egypt's future.

London and its central strategists had also, however, another motive for seizing control of the lakes. With that move, they hoped, they would gain command over the source of the White Nile and hence also over Egypt's political will in the long run. In this context, it is therefore both significant and symptomatic that Samuel Baker – the adventurer and explorer who was regarded by his contemporaries as one of the foremost Nile experts, had said in an 1884 interview with *Pall Mall Gazette* a decade earlier, just two years after the British occupied Egypt: 'The Arabs have drunk at these wells for five thousand years. Erect a fort to command the wells, and the Arabs are at your mercy.'[28]

If London's position at Suez should be threatened at some point in the future, the British would have this weapon in reserve, they thought. In articles written during the 1880s arguing that Britain should take control over Sudan and the Upper Nile, and that Egypt, on account of the Nile, should include Sudan in its territory, Samuel Baker was clear on the necessity of such a plan:

> Regardless of the difference between Egyptians and ourselves, we have attempted to thrust down their throats the blessings of a British administration [...]. We found Egypt at that period as helpless as a baby in arms; we took it as a child of our own, and the Khedive represented our adoption [...] that we should quickly exhibit the invigorating effect of Liberal institutions grafted from the British oak upon the Egyptian date-palm. Such a graft was a botanical impossibility.[29]

Baker believed that the attempt to make the Egyptians more like the British would act like a boomerang. This arch-imperialist gave an ironclad critique of imperialistic arrogance and callousness, and he saw where it would lead: 'We compelled him [the Khedive] to administer Egypt according to our dictation, leaving him no choice, and destroying all liberty of action, at the same time that we attempted to Anglicize all Egyptian institutions, which would evoke the hatred of the governing classes against their passive ruler who had submitted to our usurpation.'[30]

With such an analysis of the way the British and Egyptian relationship would play out; it was natural that Baker believed London should assume control of the Nile's sources to acquire a potential future political weapon. Among the Victorian politicians in London, who formulated themselves more diplomatically, the way of thinking was just as simple and direct: if their ability to control Suez and Egypt and the sea route to India became uncertain, they would push the panic button. On this button stood written: Seize the entire Nile! As a first step: gain acceptance from rival European colonial powers that the Nile is Britain's sphere of interest. They accomplished this in

1890. Next: seize political and hydrological control over the entire river basin. The main White Nile reservoirs were the most important at the time, since it was from there that almost all the summer water for the cotton plants came.

London seizes control of the Nile lakes

By the 1890s, the British had already established a permanent colonial administration in Entebbe, located in a bay of Lake Victoria not far from Kampala. It was only in 1893, however, that London formally assumed the power that the Imperial British East Africa Company had until then exercised in the region. In December of that same year, the British launched a military campaign against the Bunyoro king, supported by an army of 10,000 Buganda armed with spears and 420 Nubian Sudanese under the leadership of British officers. The affair, according to a British traveller in the area, did not deserve the term war, since they won the brutal onslaught easily. London now took control of the regions along the Nile north of Lake Victoria.

Then, in 1894 the government in London designated Uganda as a British protectorate, an area largely corresponding to today's Uganda; and on 28 May 1895, London decided to bring all the territory from the lakes down to the Indian Ocean under the British throne (what is Kenya today). This was colonialism at its most classic, with one important exception: it was dominance over physical space, and it aimed at what was described as reformations and gradual transformations of 'native' ways of thinking and world views through Westernization that occurred in many regions, but it was, however, only a measured and partial integration of the local economy into a larger colonial system. In contrast, what was integrated, thoroughly and completely, was its defining natural characteristic; the Nile lakes were subordinated to a comprehensive colonial structure, and with a very clear purpose. Uganda's conquest, therefore, is yet another example of the fact that colonialism and imperialism must be studied concretely to be understood, and that superfluous and popular notions of imperialism in general will make such concrete power relations incomprehensible.

In the years that followed, several British water-planners and engineers travelled to Uganda to study its water resources and to evaluate what could be done with them relative to Egypt. Plans for damming up both Lake Albert and Lake Victoria were drawn up and discussed. One of the first things the British did after they seized the region was to implement Lord Lugard's idea from 1893: they erected a Nile waterflow measuring station at the lake's outlet and sent the down data to Egypt. More plans for exploiting the lakes were debated and prepared. Nile entrepreneurs in Egypt – they might be called modernity's avant-garde in the basin – insisted that the entire Nile must be regarded as a hydrological unit and as one planning unit. Archival documents from the time provide solid evidence that this vision was shared by Britain's political leadership, even if there was disagreement on how quickly to proceed, how the development should be financed and how the balancing act with Egypt should be handled.

In a speech given in London in 1895, the year after London took control over the great lakes, the previous head of the Egyptian Public Works Department, Sir Colin Scott-Moncrieff, summarized Britain's 'Nile Vision'. For him, as for all others concerned with the Nile, it was not a question of *whether* the British should subordinate the entire river. Scott-Moncrieff complained that he, like his audience, had had to go to 'the works of Speke, Baker, Stanley and our other great explorers' for information regarding anything higher up than Philae and said that 'if a foreigner were to lecture to his countrymen about the river Thames, and were to begin by informing them that he had never been above Greenwich, he might be looked upon as an imposter'.[31] Other senior water-planners described these years when it came to hydrological studies as if 'the thick veil had settled down on the Upper Nile'.[32] Since Scott-Moncrieff was no military strategist, however, he was not focused on the when and how of the occupation of the entire basin. For him, as the man responsible so to speak for what was now the lifeline of British Egypt, it was simply evident *that* the river should fall under single control: 'Is it not evident, then, that the Nile from the Victoria Nyanza to the Mediterranean should be under one rule?'[33]

Based on an increasingly solid understanding of the Nile as a natural phenomenon and increasingly better data on the Nile's hydrology, the British knew that hydraulic works on the great lakes in Central Africa could have enormous significance for Egypt. They were also aware that it did not help to build reservoirs and dams in their newly acquired territory if they failed to improve the river's transport capacity downstream, through the swamps of Southern Sudan. A plan for the Upper Nile that only looked for a dam in Uganda was to be rejected if it did not simultaneously implement a project to modify the river through Southern Sudan in order to improve the area's function as an effective aqueduct to the north. The British in the 1890s were already well aware that the Blue Nile represented 80 per cent or more of the Nile's total waterflow in Egypt, but for London, Lord Cromer in Egypt and his water engineers, it was much more important that almost all the summer water was supplied by the White Nile. It was for that reason that this tributary at the time was viewed as the most critical Nile river. The engineers also knew that due to the very different, but partly complementary hydrological characteristics of the two main tributaries, the Nile should be tamed and exploited according to an overall basin plan in order to be utilized rationally. In this perspective, they became forerunners or pioneers when it came to the increasingly stronger spotlight that posterity has placed on the contemporary approach that river basins in general should be seen as a hydrological unity and as one planning unit in order to use the water most efficiently and in the most sustainable way.

Britain's hydrological vision and hydropolitical plans for the Nile represented a new, original form of water imperialism, and the aims and requirements of this imperialism were what chiefly shaped the way London expanded its empire in the Nile basin. The agreement into which Britain entered with the weakened Buganda kingdom in 1900 reflected the goals of this Nile strategy. The British extended their control from the Buganda kingdom to the surrounding tribes or ethnic groups, and, by using the name Uganda for the entire region, they helped to make the kingdom an ally in the struggle for imperial peace and order. The alliance with the Baganda, on the other hand, made it difficult to advance any agriculture by colonial settlers. This was no paradox, however, for London was not especially interested in exploiting the region's resources in that way. The Baganda alliance became the basis for an effective and relatively inexpensive administrative system in a region where the British strategy was primarily focused on the natural Nile reservoirs and their geopolitical and economic potential.

London's overall policy aim until after the Second World War was that the use and control of the Nile in Uganda should serve their Nile policy in Egypt, while what happened to the development of Uganda was of less significance. Through the Nile Waters Agreement of 1929, the London government, as we have seen, established that Uganda, like the rest of their East African territories, had no real need for any Nile waters. Potential projects that these countries should nonetheless come to consider required, moreover, according to that same agreement, Cairo's approval. There were many reasons why the Nile in Uganda was not utilized until the 1950s, but this agreement and British Nile policies and the whole thinking about Ugandan development it fostered among the colonial officers, obviously played its role. In Uganda the Nile remained untamed.

Where the animals rule (by the grace of humankind)

The boat glides slowly up the White Nile between Lake Albert and Lake Victoria in North Uganda, and in the afternoon sun, as I look out across the river, the water is white, like a mackerel sky. There is nothing elevated or monarchical about the craft in which I am sitting, even though the skipper calls it *The African Queen* (as I suppose all skippers tell foreigners taking boat rides here) after the boat Humphrey Bogart and Katharine Hepburn took in the same-named film that was shot here in the 1950s. The boat is about as large as one of the hundreds of hippos that float in the water, very close, while twitching their ears. It would not take more than one of these hefty creatures to tip the boat, which sits disturbingly low – so low that the crocodiles we see can easily snap up a wandering arm. The boat driver assures us that this has never happened; the crocodiles have plenty of fish here, but nonetheless we sit with our arms held tight against our bodies as the boat glides from shore. After ten minutes on the river we have already seen large hippo families, a herd of water buffaloes in full tilt along the banks, and the isolated old bull who, according to the skipper, has been banished from the herd and now lives alone, near the water, so he can save his skin if lions attack.

The hippos act as if they rule the river. In every riverbend I can see them; they snort as if in superiority, in sovereign contempt of beings such as us. So, it is natural that Murchison Falls National Park is also called Paraa National Park or 'Home of the Hippos'. On the sand banks, in the shadow of thick trees whose branches reflect in the river, enormous crocodiles doze. Now and then I see parts of their heads break the surface, just a couple of metres from the boat. The river here is host to Africa's most teeming hippo and crocodile populations. Next to the river, which makes it way north, incessantly and with a pace of inevitability typical of great floods, wander elephants, giraffes and buffaloes. The bird life here is unparalleled – heron species, the little kingfisher, an African osprey, various kinds of storks, and small bright birds of every conceivable colour.

All this gives the impression that here it is the animals' arena and home turf. We humans are the exotic creatures here; it is we who sail along in cages. Nowhere else on earth is it possible to approach wild, dangerous animal life more closely than here on the Nile, east of Lake Albert – without being killed, in any case. It is one of the many places along this manifold river that seems completely untouched by humans. The animals seem to continually insist on their dominion; they ignore us, as if they have not yet awoken to the reality that has emerged in the last tens of thousands of years, and realized which creature is sovereign.

The river becomes increasing full of white-gold foam caps, which at a distance seem misplaced since they resemble small icebergs. The current grows stronger, and the old man who steers the boat grows steadily more alert. And then, after a slight swing of the river, the White Nile's most dramatic waterfall comes into sight. In no other place on its almost 7,000-kilometre journey towards the sea does the river explode like it does here.

Stairs from the riverbank lead to the lookout spot, baptized Baker's Point. It is here that Samuel Baker supposedly stood around 150 years ago. The sight is spectacular – frothing water, foaming spray, tropical forest in the background, all of it accompanied by a perpetual, deafening sound. It as if the waterfall drains the last of the river's energy, before it becomes the peaceful river upon which I was just sailing, farther down entering Lake Albert before flowing toward Fola Rapids at Nimule in South Sudan.

Waterfalls and images of 'the other' and 'us'

The waterfall marks where the Bunyoro plateau meets Acholiland's stretching plains. It is called Murchison Falls. If you climb the stairs winding through the jungle from the base of the falls, you also occasionally get a glimpse of Uhuru Falls, or Freedom Falls, as the Ugandans call them. These emerge when the river bursts through the mountains after unusually heavy rain. The name refers to the fact that these falls, which today are usually considered a part of Murchison Falls (even though they did not exist in Baker's day, when he gave the falls their name), were symbolically enough 'born' in 1962 – the same year that Uganda got its freedom from British colonialism and saw daylight as an independent state.

Each time the name Murchison Falls is evoked, it confirms the success and lasting influence of the nineteenth-century explorers, not to mention how the conquest of Africa in their wake made them central actors in the continent's history. The name, however, also reveals a cultural hubris and the way in which power can appear self-glorifying and, therefore, banal. For there is something very childish here, the way in which the empire-builders were so obsessed with naming the world after their countrymen and supporters. When I stand and look over the narrow cliff through which the water rushes, with its din drowning out everything around me so that the rest of the African, tropical landscape seems to exist as if behind a kind of looking glass, there is no escaping the fact it is strange, even rather unfitting to be forced to think about a British gentleman who never set foot here.

Sir Roderick Impey Murchison was born in Scotland in 1792 and first earned renown as a skilled fox hunter before taking up science and geology. He served as the Director General of the Geological Survey of Great Britain for fifteen years, up until 1871, and his studies of the Silurian and Devonian systems were very influential on stratigraphy's development. Murchison found, among other things, that the Oslo field's sediments in Norway were folded, and that they belonged to the Silurian system, a discovery that heralded this kind of scientific, geographical exploration in that part of the world. Yet, despite his importance in the country across the North Sea, in Norway he does not even have a memorial plaque. In Murchison's home tracts, name-giving was also different from that in Africa; he named the geological periods after Devonshire in England and Silurian for the pre-Celtic Silures who lived in the area of Great Britain where Murchison made his discoveries.

I am standing on the edge of a plunging waterfall surrounded by dense jungle forest – you get wet here, as if you experience a downpour in the sunshine – thinking of Murchison, who never set foot in Africa. Because he was the leader of the Geological Society of London, however, the White Nile's largest waterfall was named after him.

The way the outside world, and especially the West, have staged themselves, producing stories and perceptions of the Nile region, is not only part of Africa's history but also a definitive part of the West's conceptual and cultural history. The way 'Africans' and 'Africa' have been depicted and described has always reflected and influenced contemporary relationships between Europe and Africa. The early travel literature from the Upper Nile was formative, shaping to some extent a way of thinking and a way of seeing because the authors were famous, and their books became bestsellers and classics. This literature and the narrative it presents about History's own development, so to speak, and the West's role therein, thereby assumed significance not only when it comes to conceptions of Africa but also those of the West.

The great Nile lakes and Murchison Falls can thus be used as springboards for a comparison of different images of Africa created in three different periods of the Western world's relationship to the continent, images that have influenced perceptions of the West in Africa and Africa in the West.

'Baker of the Nile'

Samuel Baker's narratives of Africa, the Nile and the people living along the river were an immediate success. His dramatic prose and romantic tale of his and his wife's travels moved Europeans of the day. He told how they journeyed around in the region for several years and resided for a long time in North Uganda as the Bunyoro king's guests. Baker's books exude inquisitiveness and the joy of seeing new things at the same time as it reflects his prejudices. Yet, his accounts mirror and promote a type of curiosity towards the unknown that belong to a time when the world was still considered young and inexperienced.

Meanwhile, the world-famous British anthropologist Evans-Pritchard, whom we have already met, was very critical of Baker and his books. A few decades after the books became bestsellers, Evans-Pritchard wrote full of contempt about 'the sententious Sir Samuel W. Baker', describing him as 'the most disagreeable and stupid of them', that is to say, of all the many explorers who travelled up the Nile.[34] There is obvious disagreement regarding whether this character portrait of Baker is completely accurate, but all agree that Baker openly embraces a 'we must civilize them' perspective. In his book on Lake Alberta, he refers to England as 'the great chief of the commercial world' that possessed 'the force to civilize' – indeed, England was 'the natural colonizer of the world'.[35]

Baker's books can be described as thoroughly racist, but since they were written before race theory had established a rigid system of thought, with a developmental theory and world view that was based on race, the racism here is more immediate, almost careless in a way. Baker simply asserts that in the Upper Nile region 'there are no ancient histories to charm the present with memories of the past; all is wild and brutal, hard and unfeeling'. He further wrote: 'Charming people are these poor blacks! as they are termed by English sympathizers'. At another point he continued: 'There is no such thing as *love* in these countries [. . .]. Everything is practical, without a particle of romance. Women are so far appreciated as they are valuable animals'. And finally: 'However severely we may condemn the horrible system of slavery, the results of emancipation have proved that the negro does not appreciate the blessings of freedom, nor does he show the slightest feeling of gratitude to the hand that broke the rivets of his fetters'.[36]

Baker's Africans were a people that differed immensely from the British, not only in mentality and culture but also in spiritual apparatus. There was no doubt that the Africans must be civilized, and that the British could accomplish it. Baker, however, was unsure whether this project would ever be successful due to what he perceived as the chasm – cultural, mental and spiritual – between the British and the Africans.

Winston Churchill in the jungle

Around fifty years after the Bakers were cast ashore by an angry hippo that attacked the boat carrying them toward Murchison Falls, Winston Churchill was cycling towards that same destination. He was then, early in the twentieth century, Under-Secretary of State for the Colonial Office, already well-known not least due to the book he had written on the British campaign up the Nile in 1898.

When Churchill, following in the wake of Florence and Samuel Baker, travelled to the falls as the Colonial Office's representative, Uganda had already become an English colony and Britain had taken control of the White Nile's sources. Churchill wrote *My African Journey* as a narrative account of his travels down the Nile from Uganda to Egypt. Here he described Uganda and the kingdom there as something like a 'fairy tale'. Furthermore: 'You climb up a railway instead of a beanstalk, and at the end there is a wonderful new world'.[37] Nature was different, people were different. Pondering what message to send home, he answers: 'Concentrate upon Uganda!'[38] He then wrote famously: 'Uganda is the pearl'.[39]

After cycling north from Kampala through a forest that he described as more fantastic than any forest he had ever crossed in Cuba and India, he arrived at the falls.[40] There he climbed the narrow stair alongside the waterfall, equipped with mosquito net and gloves against tsetse flies, which at the time represented a mortal danger; just a few years previously, several hundred thousand Ugandans had died of sleeping sickness after having been bitten.

It is easy to imagine Winston Churchill standing on the waterfall's edge as a young politician, on Baker's Point – his cheeks undoubtedly flushed after having covered part of the road on bike and on foot beneath the tropical sun's roasting heat – letting himself be impressed by the river throwing itself violently down the cliffs. Or, as he summarized it after travelling whole Nile: 'These Falls are certainly the most remarkable in the whole course of the Nile.'[41]

But Churchill saw Uganda through a colony-builder's eyes, as a genuine imperialist with a civilizing, developmental mission. He was concerned with what could be done in this new colony. It was here the (temporarily) Liberal politician stood and became enthused by what he described as state socialism: it would be 'hard to find a country where the conditions were more favourable than Uganda to a practical experiment in State Socialism'.[42] The country was wealthy, the people industrious and peaceful, capitalist individuals would only think on their own profits and not on the welfare of the Ugandans, and there were no European special interests to hinder development or 'block the way', as he formulated it.[43]

The rational precondition for this almost exalted, state-socialist rhetoric was in the physical and potential economic characteristics of the Nile in Uganda, as Churchill saw them. 'All this water-power belongs to the State', he wrote.[44] This was the resource base for his entire theory. Churchill saw a future in Uganda where the whole Nile river valley would be dotted with factories and warehouses; he thought that perhaps no other place in the world existed where it would be possible to exploit so much water at so little cost and with so little construction. It was thus in favour of state socialism in Uganda that Churchill wrote, later twice a Conservative Prime Minister, just after he had been appointed to the first of a long line of ministerial posts and went down the Nile river.

Churchill was obviously a remarkable person in many fields and played important historical roles in many areas and, where the Nile is concerned, he appears on the scene at decisive moments, again and again, as journalist, author or government minister. And here, as in other places, he demonstrated a striking ability to condense complicated situations to memorable one-liners. It is against such a background that Churchill's account of his African journey (which the eventual Nobel Prize winner in Literature in 1953, with typical self-critique, viewed with dissatisfaction on a literary scale) can be read as an evocative reflection on how spokesmen for a well-established empire, at the height of their power, regarded their subject peoples.

The book also reveals how influential statesmen and powerful politicians like Churchill cannot avoid being children of their age, or rather – they rather become great *because* they are children of their age. His perspective is insistently paternalistic but not racist, it seethes with inquisitiveness, yet his interpretive framework is the imperial drive's normative and political self-assurance. For Churchill, it was beyond doubt, indeed, it was a self-evident truth that the British best knew how to develop Africa – not due to any racial superiority but rather to a historically produced superiority in culture and knowledge. Churchill's travel accounts, viewed in this way, provide a condensed image of the Victorian gospel of improvement and development, simultaneously expressing both paternalism and optimism.

Bogart, Hepburn and Hemingway at the Nile Falls

Fifty years later, in the 1950s, several Americans turned up in the Nile region, in keeping with the United States' increasing political influence in Africa after the Second World War.

Murchison Falls formed the background for Humphrey Bogart and Katharine Hepburn in John Huston's film *The African Queen* from 1951, the film for which Bogart won an Oscar for his role as riverboat captain. Instead of relying upon the African sets that had been built in London, Huston transported the film team to Africa, due in part to the fact, it has been suggested, that the director wanted an opportunity, and an excuse, for hunting big game. One of the movie's most famous scenes is shot directly on the White Nile. The church and village of Kungdu were built on the shores of Lake Albert at Butiaba (the Butiaba Port has hardly been used since the film was made but has been rebuilt due to oil discoveries in the lake). The film also showcases Murchison Falls, and the rushing river below it is the scene of Hepburn and Bogart's famous clash, with crocodiles and hippos sporting in the background in the surrounding water.

Hepburn relates her experiences in the book *The Making of The African Queen or How I Went to Africa with Bogart, Bacall and Huston and Almost Lost My Mind*. Her descriptions are light and lively, also about her becoming ill and how Bogart did not bother or notice it. He drank too much to be able to observe such things, she indicates, not without envy. The book also treats of Africa's 'wildness', of the sense of difference, of finding a black mamba, just like that, in the toilet, and so on – and also that she loves the extraordinary life. Hepburn's notes, of course, are written by a person outside the colonial administration's tasks and responsibilities, with no pretence to any paternalistic leader role. People easily emerge as equal but exotic; they are like members of the film crew, though they live on civilization's perimeters. The jungle, so to speak, represents to her 'what is foreign'; Hepburn speaks about the joy of living and surviving at civilization's outpost, and where it is so beautiful that she would gladly return.

In a *New York Times* article from February 1952, Huston, for his part, and no doubt as parcel of the film's media promotion, said that he hired local natives to assist the movie crew, but that many refused to show up for fear that the movie-makers were cannibals. The picture he painted corresponded to still widespread conceptions of Africa as the incarnation of the 'wild', a continent as yet untamed by civilization; that is to say, an Africa representing civilization's fascinating margin, at the same time both a new frontier and one of the final frontiers remaining.

Another person who also described Africa as on the fringe of civilization was Ernest Hemingway. He too made a visit to Murchison Falls, although it was an unwilling one. In January 1954 he and his wife crashed there in a small aircraft, not once but twice, only a day apart! On 21 January, the couple had been on the way from Nairobi to see and experience the Belgian Congo. Hemingway called it his Christmas gift to his wife, writing about the trip in 'The Christmas Gift', which was published in the magazine *Look*. One morning, as the fog was lifting, they were in the air on their way over Lake George and Lake Albert and then up the river to Murchison Falls. Mary photographed the waterfall – which I can confirm is really beautiful when seen from a small plane through a morning sky still clear following the night's chill, and you see how the river casts itself fearlessly over the high plateau's edge as the sun glints on the water and elephants move along the river.

But the Hemingways that day are unlucky: as their pilot tries to avoid an ibis, the plane hits a telegraph line that slices through the tiller and radio antenna. The plane crashes into the bushes not far from the falls. Unbelievably, all three walk away unscathed. They have landed at least 50 kilometres from the nearest village. The heat is intense as they drag themselves uphill, away from the crocodiles and hippos. There they make camp. Early the next morning, they discover a boat going upriver toward the falls. The boat is the *Murchison*, bound on a private cruise with a British doctor who takes them on board. In Butiaba they happened to meet a pilot who already was there searching for them. They can continue their journey, using a provisional runway created by Huston's film crew. As the plane is taking off, however, the pilot loses control. A new crash. The plane is in on fire. Mary manages to squeeze through a window, but Ernest is too heavy. He has to use his head to squeeze through the door, while his arms are still black and blue from the crash the day before. He succeeds in escaping the plane, but some claim it was here that his physical and psychological deterioration started. Ernest Hemingway had a serious leg wound, a broken nose, reduced hearing capacity, and a crack in his skull that oozed a clear liquid.

The article in *Look*, meanwhile, sketches an Africa that is different in a very special sense; it primarily functions as the author's place of adventure – it is the continent of adventure. It is useful to read the article together with *Green Hills of Africa*, one of Hemingway's few non-fictions. The author wrote this book after two journeys he undertook to Kenya and Tanganyika (now Tanzania), and it is especially based on his experiences from the Lake Manyara region in Tanzania. Hemingway noted in the foreword that he had attempted 'to write an absolutely true book to see whether the shape of a country [. . .] can, if truly presented, compete with [the depictions in] a work of the imagination'. Hemingway's true-in-my-own-eyes observations are characterized by both condescension and contempt, but also by devotion and at times even yearning. He loves Africa: 'But I would come back to where it pleased me to live; to really live. Not just let my life pass. [. . .] I knew a good country when I saw one.'[45] Still, for the majority of the time, Hemingway is fundamentally uninterested in Africa as a place with societies with their own histories and futures, thereby distinguishing himself from Baker, Stanley and Churchill. He is most happy and content in Africa when blissfully ignorant; that is, he prefers Africa to be a backdrop for his own experiences for the short time he is there, but nonetheless, he writes, as if he is convinced of it, that the local hunters regard him as 'a brother'.

At the beginning of the book, Hemingway meets Kadinsky, an Australian ethnologist who despises hunting. What draws him to Africa is instead the opportunity to live like a 'king':

> Then too, in reality, I am a king here. It is very pleasant. Waking in the morning I extend one foot and the boy places the sock on it. When I am ready, I extend the other foot and he adjusts the other sock. I step from under the mosquito bar into my drawers which are held for me. Don't you think that is very marvelous?[46]

Hemingway writes sympathetically of Kadinsky; indeed, he is in complete agreement. 'It's marvelous', he replies.

Nonetheless, the most interesting aspect of this non-fiction book on Africa is not Hemingway's portrayals of hunting and animal life, but rather that the book is not actually about Africa, or about a precise presentation of the 'shape of the country', which the author promised in the foreword. The 'natives' we meet are simple people, almost types, and to the extent Hemingway is interested in them or their personal characteristics, it is largely about whether they admire him. The key to understanding the book's depiction of Africa is found in Hemingway's idea of the continent as a 'borderland', and via this conceptualization of the place he is in, he himself becomes a sort of parallel to the brave, independent American homesteader whom he so strongly admires, and whom he now has the chance of becoming.

Hemingway's view of Africa as being on civilization's periphery was also the energetic perspective shared by the American settler. And like Hepburn, Hemingway completely lacked the imperial sense of responsibility and paternalism so common among the British, and he was further devoid of the subsequent development-aid epoch's focus on development and developmental possibilities. Africa was simply a sanctuary where he could crash through the jungle and gun down big game. His Africa was not a place to be remade in the image of the West, rather Africa was the antithesis of home. He was freed from the boundaries of civilization. The adventures of the safari were the restless soul's haven.

A Nile empire full of inner contradictions

Even as the United States in particular and, later, the Soviet Union became more active in Africa, the British colonial administrators came under steadily increasing pressure from the newly established United Nations, from anti-colonial movements and from the rivalry among the new superpowers, both of which denounced imperialism as a system. In Entebbe's government corridors, the British noticed the rising demand for colonial development.[47]

The British in Uganda also grew more and more frustrated with London's policy on the Nile question. The colonial administration had long pressured London to support the building of hydropower plants in Uganda, in line with what Winston Churchill had suggested fifty years earlier. They were also certain that this was the key to Uganda's development. The colonial administrators in Uganda, who often gathered on the Victoria Hotel's veranda, located next to the enormous lake, drinking their afternoon whisky as they cast (perhaps wistful) gazes toward the deep-blue inland sea which blended seamlessly with the distant sky, had never been enthused about the 1929 Nile Agreement and the limitations it placed on Uganda's water utilization. Furthermore, they believed that Egypt's and London's resistance to the proposed power stations was both ignorant and irrational, since these dams would not reduce the Nile's waterflow.

For anyone concerned with colonialism as a phenomenon, or with imperialism as organizer of a distinctive politico-economic relation between countries, the British Nile empire's inner contradictions, and how these played out, are interesting. Since

Britain's overarching strategy, which in its time established this empire, revolved around the Nile, the disagreements that evolved on how to exploit the river can demonstrate the gradual dissolution of that same colonial system.

Increasingly, the contradictions became evident among the colonial power's regional centres in Africa, and between them and London. The way the colonial system had been constructed, with British legations or administrations located in the different countries, functioned in an effective and self-regulating fashion as long as Britain's imperial objectives were coherent and the individual administrations were subjected, and allowed themselves to be subjected, to a common and clear strategy directed from London. Eventually, as the Nile basin's different regions experienced uneven development, and the British administrators who controlled these regions generated different ideas and plans regarding how the river should be utilized in their country, the need for a powerful imperial centre with a clear and coherent strategy grew stronger than ever. Yet London was being forced to take increasing account of several overriding strategical considerations and tactical circumstances that were in conflict, and thus its policy became less and less resolute and more and more indefinite.

It now turned out that the colonial system that had been built around goals of unity and drive under the leadership of the government in London was instead a system that produced and fortified internal policy conflicts. The different ideas regarding Nile exploitation held by the British in Entebbe, Juba, Khartoum, Cairo and Addis Ababa reflected contradictions based on actual conflicts of interest between varying regions and countries relative to utilizing the river. Nor were these conflicts' viewpoints easy to manage or overcome. In the moment the contradictions arose, they could not simply be swept aside or wished away because they were sustained and generated by the river itself. Conversations in the British clubs, which could solve many other disagreements, could not help here, since there was no talking away the disputes that appeared and were reproduced based on varying geographical localization in this huge, extremely varying river basin.

Viewed from Zamalek Island in the middle of the Nile in Cairo, the main political goal was still to preserve control at Suez and the British military base there. Nile governance continued to be regarded as a very central key to Egyptian stability and Britain's legitimacy in Egypt. The country's need for more water had become increasingly obvious as the population rose, and with general economic development. All the assessments provided by British water experts and their Egyptian partners in the ministry dealing with Nile control concluded that Egypt could absorb much more water, and that the country's development consistently depended upon increased Nile control. Everyone understood that any plans for industrialization in Egypt would require the Nile as a power source. The catastrophic flood of 1947 underscored, moreover, that the Nile was far from tamed.

The British Nile experts, who continued to be highly influential in the Egyptian ministry that worked to control the river and advance irrigation agriculture, believed that the best way to tame the Nile in the interest of Egypt was through what they called the 'Century Storage Scheme'. One element of this grandiose plan was to dam Lake Victoria and Lake Albert and to dig the Jonglei Canal to tackle the problems of the evaporating water in the swamps in South Sudan. Even a one metre increase in Lake

Albert's water level would yield approximately as much new water during summertime as that which was at that time stored in the old Aswan Dam. A similar water level increase in Lake Victoria would provide 12.5 times as much. Since evaporation and precipitation in the great lakes equalize each other, an increase in the lakes' surface, furthermore, would not lead to increased evaporation, so no water would be lost. The foreign policy strategists in London saw that such a dam in Uganda could also be used to apply pressure against Egyptian nationalism, if the need arose, as Baker had suggested in 1884. Even though, for these reasons precisely, Egyptians in the ministry were sceptical of a dam on the Nile in a country thousands of kilometres to the south, the Egyptian government decided to test Uganda's reaction.

Uganda dismissed the proposal outright. The British governor there, Sir John Hall, emphasized that the planned project would be directly contrary to Ugandan interests. It would place Ugandan territory under water, it would negatively impact the Victoria Nile, and it would reduce Murchison Falls' energy potential by 50 per cent (at that point, the government in Uganda were proceeding with vague plans to build a power plant there). To strengthen their negotiating position, the Ugandan government subsequently engaged a water adviser, Mr Hawes.

Almost seventy-five years after Cromer brought the first British water-planner to Cairo, and more than twenty-five years after Sudan established its own water administration, Ugandan colonial authorities hired their first water expert. Mr Hawes and his team conducted several investigations of lakes Albert and Victoria, also including areas in Kenya and Tanganyika. Based on these investigations, Uganda's first national plan concerning the country's water resources was presented.

Governor Hall and the British in Uganda now came up with a concrete alternative for how the Nile lakes could be used. They wanted to develop hydropower, and their language was as an echo of Winston Churchill's visions from the beginning of the century. Churchill was invoked and quoted. 'So much power running to waste, such a coign of vantage unoccupied, such a level to control, the natural force of Africa ungripped?'[48] The administrators wrote that Uganda, with the help of hydropower, could attempt to produce 'not copper ore but electrolytic copper, not bauxite but aluminium, not lime but cement, not raw cotton but piece goods, not oil seeds but soap, not grass or pulp but finished paper'.[49] And the best site for the construction, they determined, was Owen Falls, just downstream from Lake Victoria. By damming the lake and lowering the falls here, they could secure a drop of about 18 metres. With a constant output of 632 cubic metres of water a second, the country would immediately receive an installed capacity of 150,000 kilowatts. This idea was the origin of what would later, following many years of diplomatic tug of wars and disputes, become the Owen Falls Dam.

At the Thames in London, the government and its Foreign Office tried to solve the contradictions between competing British visions and plans for the Nile. The establishment of the UN and its focus development and getting rid of colonialism, the growth of anti-Colonial sentiments in their main ally, the United States, and the growing anti-colonial struggle in the wake of India's independence in 1947 and the Chinese revolution in 1949 created a political atmosphere that forced London to undertake more development initiatives in their colonial regions. The colonial system was looking to acquire more legitimacy in a time when it was being condemned from all sides. The British could not overlook the fact, for example, that Richard M. Nixon, who was then vice president of the United States, was travelling around Asia, making public speeches where he denounced the European colonial system: it oppressed human will and free trade, and he would like to see it relegated to history's scrap heap. As such, the British were obliged, on the one hand, to ensure more development of their colonies, including Uganda, even as the game for the Suez and their position there became more critical within global geopolitics.

The British in the Nile basin were forced to bite off more than they could chew, and they did it with damaging consequences for the empire.

Owen Falls: 'Uganda's beginning'

If you stand at the railing of the path built along the top of the Owen Falls Dam in Uganda, or the Nalubaale Dam, as the Ugandans now call it, then you find yourself at one of the country's truly historical sites. The struggle about the dam is an instructive example of high politics and hydropolitics, of diplomatic labyrinths and diplomatic patience, but it also reflects the issue of deep mistrust between the basin countries. The dam's history also torpedoes widespread conceptions regarding 'the interests of imperialism', or ideas resting on perceptions of imperialism or colonialism as a unified phenomenon with a single and common interest.

In the Nile basin, the colonial system faced an insoluble dilemma, one particular patterns distinctively attired, where there was no good solution, and where what was decided on satisfied no one. The contradictions between the British stationed in the different countries, and their policy considerations, were developed around and structured by the river's physical character: if London leaned too much towards Egyptian interests regarding a dam in Uganda, then Uganda would be negatively impacted, and Britain could be criticized for hindering the country's development. If London supported the Ugandan government's project on the lakes, then it would reduce the river's potential benefits for Egypt and rouse Egyptian fury that the Nile had been dammed in 'enemy territory'. Such a move could destroy the British relationship with Egypt, and it could negatively impact Britain's position in Sudan, as well. If London supported Egypt's demands for the dam, they could justly be criticized of failing to help Uganda in the service of their own imperial interests. These were contradictions of principle and they did not go away, nourished as they were by the Nile's physical character and reflecting the colonial administration's geographical locations relative to the river. The in-between solution London ultimately adopted produced irritation and criticism in Egypt, and neither was it enough for Uganda's needs.

During the 1940s and 1950s, project proposals and plans for the lakes in the British-governed country trickled into Entebbe, accompanied by policy guidelines from London. Governor Hall knew that, for Egyptian nationalists, it was almost unthinkable to accept dams built across the Nile in what was regarded as enemy territory. Egyptians had been forced to acquiesce in the 1920s when it came to the Gezira project in Sudan. Now they would not concede on Uganda, Hall thought, especially because the construction site lay so far beyond Egypt's borders. Therefore, Entebbe was surprised when the Egyptian government abruptly accepted their construction plans with few amendments, just that the dam would take more account of Egypt's interests. Cairo also demanded that Egypt be allowed to place four technicians at the dam site, so they could always ensure that the hydro plant did not take out more water from the river than the coming Agreement on the dam allowed. Kampala was against this and London was hesitant to open the door to a lasting Egyptian administrative presence in Uganda, in a region where Egypt had previously made territorial demands by alluding to the fact that the area had been under Egyptian control in the last decades of the nineteenth century. Such administrative bridgeheads could also be used as bases for anti-British propaganda when Anglo–Egyptian relationships became particularly strained. London, however, swallowed these diplomatic camels, so to speak, so the dam could finally be built.

Foreign Secretary Ernest Bevin announced in the House of Commons on 19 May 1949 that Britain and Egypt had reached consensus on the dam. The Egyptian nationalists immediately protested. The entire Owen Falls accord was based on invalid documents and discussions, they argued, because it was based on the 1929 Agreement and placed a European country, Great Britain, in a position in Africa that neither international law nor Egypt, with regard to its national interests, could accept. The newspaper *The Egyptian Gazette* of 25 May quotes *Al Balagh*, which criticized the Owen Falls Agreement vehemently, and wrote: 'The British were certainly right when they applauded their Foreign Minister after his Commons speech announcing the conclusion of the agreement, but as far as the Egyptians are concerned, well, God help them!'

Diplomatic labyrinths can sometimes highlight the complexity of hydropolitics, and Owens Falls is an example of this. The question of who should lay the dam's ground stone and who should be present at the ceremony was, for London, a hard diplomatic nut to crack. If the Duke of Edinburgh opened the ceremony, the dam would not be viewed as a common Anglo-Egyptian project, and Egyptian scepticism would be further justified. If both he and King Faruk participated, the King would have to place the stone. And yet, that would give the impression of Egyptian ownership of the project, and it would seem that London had suddenly accepted the old Egyptian demands for control of the lake regions. This would be like waving a red flag in front of Uganda. The government, therefore, wanted to tone down the entire ceremony; better that than to send the wrong political signals. The Foreign Secretary might miss a chance at the spotlight, but it was more expedient to have the management at Uganda Electricity simply issue an invitation to a few selected 'technical' representatives. As a politician, however, Bevin desired more blast; he wanted the ceremony to be broadcast on TV and followed by several educational radio programmes concerning the Owen Falls project and the Nile policy. The Foreign Office re-evaluated their whole approach and concluded anew that there was no need for any extra fuss.

When the dam was finally opened in 1954, the political situation had shifted; Nasser and the Free Officers had taken power in Egypt, and Britain's relationship with the country was worse than ever. The new British government, led by the ageing prime minister Winston Churchill, could now send the young Queen Elizabeth to Uganda to open the dam. Fifty years after Churchill, as Colonial Secretary, had proposed building several dams in Uganda, he could finally back the inauguration of Uganda's first dam at Owen Falls and simultaneously demonstrate, vis-à-vis the rebellious, anti-British officers in Egypt, London's clout upstream.

On Saturday, 23 January 1954, commercial energy production at the dam began. From Uganda's perspective, it was as if the country had received new life. Not only had they received almost £1,000,000 in compensation from Egypt for the loss in generated hydropower they would suffer due to Egypt's water requirements, but the project transformed Lake Victoria into what became known as the world's greatest reservoir. Fifty years almost to the day after Garstin had published his Nile vision, it was, as one African journalist put it, 'Uganda's beginning'. It would be another sixty years before this process was continued under President Yoweri Museveni.

A British prime minister as 'water warrior'

It is the summer of 1956, Prime Minister Anthony Eden, who had finally assumed the position of prime minister after Winston Churchill, his father-in-law, was sitting in 10 Downing Street, desperately searching for possibilities to stop Nasser. The Egyptian officer and leader had just nationalized the Suez Canal. On 26 July, in an anti-British speech given in in Alexandria to the Egyptian people, Nasser mentioned the name Lesseps twice. That name, which belonged to the European engineer behind the proposal to build the Suez Canal in the mid-nineteenth century, was the secret code word upon which Nasser's trusted soldiers waited: when they heard Lesseps mentioned in a speech, they would spring into action. The next day Egyptians resolutely seized power over the canal's administration from the British company that hitherto had managed it. The Suez military base, which was around the size of Wales and which, in 1954, still had around 7,000 soldiers stationed there, was already history and the last British unit to leave departed Port Said on 24 March 1956. And now in July, Nasser threatened Europe's economic lifeline, the canal through which all the continent's oil was shipped. It was past time now for Nasser – the Arabic Mussolini, as Eden termed him – to be crushed.

Nasser nationalized the canal with the justification that Washington and London had withdrawn their promised support to finance the High Dam, the new dam at Aswan, his great Nile development project. In order to fund the project, which the government had promised would transform Egypt into Africa's Japan, Egypt needed all the money it could find. And nothing was more lucrative as a potential source of income than shipping fees charged to use the canal cutting through the Egyptian desert between the Mediterranean and the Red Seas.

London raged. Paris raged. Tel Aviv raged. Washington, however, continued to request that they show restraint. The United States, as we have seen, did not back London in the struggle against Nasser. The American goal was to weaken and undermine the European colonial system in the region because it reduced US economic opportunities and weakened the West's general reputation, they thought. To Britain's great annoyance, the US Secretary of State, John Foster Dulles, had just three years earlier, in 1953, presented one of the leaders of the Egyptian revolution, General Muhammed Naguib, with a pistol as a gift, just as Egyptian state leadership was encouraging a revolt against British control of the canal zone. Churchill perceived the gesture as a direct encouragement of Egypt's anti-British campaign, but understood only gradually, and too late, what the United States' actual goal was in the region. So, what could a frustrated Eden, who had waited so long for Churchill to leave Downing Street, do that summer in 1956?

As a final alternative to war, he wondered if it was possible to use the Nile as a weapon; was it possible to redirect the Nile in Uganda, thereby forcing Nasser to surrender? In deepest secrecy, he prompted an investigation of Uganda's water system, and London requested the British water experts in Uganda to assess the possibility of striking at Egypt with the Nile's help. Could this force Nasser into submission? If it had not been done before, the British conjectured, perhaps such a weapon could be used now, as a pistol to the head of an independent Egypt. The geopolitical idea was clear and simple: it revolved around implementing what Samuel Baker had already suggested in 1884. And it meant carrying out a Plan B such as Lord Lugard had speculated about in 1892. The idea in 1956 was straightforward and despotic: without Nile water, no Nasser. And the logic was: Nasser had stolen the canal from Britain. Now they would take the river from him.

But was it possible? By late September 1956, London's Board of Trade issued a 'Note on Egyptian Crops and Water Requirements'. This note rejected what they described as the simplistic scenario suggested by Hawes, the water expert of the Uganda colonial government. It stated that it was:

> difficult to forecast which crops would be affected by a reduction in White Nile water, because the Egyptians might choose to release water from the Aswan reservoir earlier than usual, in order to cover the shortfall from Jebel Aulia. The critical period would then be deferred until June/July, and an important factor would be the timing of the Blue Nile flood – its onset varies appreciably from year to year.[50]

On 9 October, the Colonial Office debated the pros and cons of such a project. They concluded that it was no simple affair to simply turn the Nile tap off and on. A waterflow reduction at Owen Falls would only produce a noticeable effect in Egypt after several months, since it takes a long time for water to run from Uganda to Egypt, due to distance and to the swamp's hydrological role and the Blue Nile's natural damming effect at Khartoum. Towards the end of October, a new note was produced by the Foreign Office: 'The Effect on the Sudan and Egypt of Restriction of the Discharge at Owen Falls'.

Eden ultimately rejected the idea. The project could potentially jeopardize Britain's relationship to their allies in Sudan. It was they who would first be impacted by reduced waterflow, since Sudan and the elite with which the British cooperated had had economic interests tied to irrigation agriculture along the White Nile. Furthermore, it would take far too long between the moment the weapon was prepared and used and the moment it would be felt. And in the meantime, Britain would be fiercely criticized the world over for using such a despotic weapon against a country that formerly had been part of the European colonial world.

At dusk, on 31 October 1956, French and British planes began to bomb Egyptian positions at Suez, while Israel attacked Sinai.

British Nile policy during the autumn of 1956 had been based on several false assumptions. They overestimated the Nile weapon's potential as a geopolitical instrument by overlooking central characteristics of the river's hydrology. They underestimated the demand for Nile waters in the other Nile countries, which also had to be taken into political account, given the fact that the Nile ran through these countries on its way to Egypt. And they did not adequately grasp that the British political administrative environments that had developed in the various Nile countries had conflicting ideas on how the river should be used and exploited both economically and politically – because everyone tended to view such questions in the perspective of the place they were stationed. As it turned out, hydropolitics was in practice far more complicated than Eden and many of his colleagues hoped and believed during the summer and autumn of 1956. They realized, however, that the Nile could not so easily be subjected to human hubris.

That same year, in 1956, even as Egypt nationalized the Suez Canal, Sudan gained its independence. The British Nile empire was fundamentally weakened, and the upstream country of Uganda also became less important to London's global strategy. The winds of change blew through Africa, and in 1963 Uganda declared its independence. Colonialism as a system collapsed, though the legacy left by British Nile policy has, up until the beginning of the third millennium, fundamentally affected Uganda's developmental policy. The river has, however, also in many other arenas played an important role in the domestic policy of numerous other counties, often in bizarre ways – including, as we shall see, in Uganda.

Idi Amin claps for well-fed crocodiles on the Nile

An extended scene from Barbet Schroeder's famous documentary, *General Idi Amin Dada: A Self-Portrait*, from 1974 takes place on a Nile boat just downstream from Murchison Falls. We can see hippos, elephants and crocodiles – and President Amin seems especially enthused about the crocodiles. Smiling, he claps his hands to try to get them to move. The director tells us in an interview for Criterion Collections DVD that the crocodiles in question were well-fed on Amin's executed opponents (the interview was not recorded as part of the documentary, neither has the documentary images of Amin clapping his hands for this reason). Henry Kyemba, Amin's cabinet secretary and minister, later wrote from exile that all those corpses created a real problem. Therefore, truckloads of bodies were dumped in the Nile at three places – at Owen Falls in Jinja, at Bujagali and here, at the hippo park. They ended up as crocodile fodder, he writes. But it turned out that there were too few crocodiles to consume the dead bodies. Kyemba describes corpses floating around the lake by Owen Falls Station. At one point, as he travelled across the dam at Jinja, he writes that he saw 'six bodies, revoltingly puffed up and decomposed, floating in the waters'.[51] Even though there was a boat tasked with removing the bodies from the dam, the workers at nearby industrial companies had said to him that almost every day they saw dozens of corpses in the lake.[52]

Under Amin's leadership Uganda's economy was generally weak, nor were any new significant initiatives taken when it came to Nile control. Instead, Amin used the river as a dumping ground, not just for his enemies but also, according to reports, for people with physical disabilities. He was notorious for liking to appear as a man of the people. One day he took his car, drove to one of Kampala's car parks, entered a nearby boutique, and joined those playing *Ajua*, a popular board game. There were many people who came to watch, among those a well-known disabled man in Kampala, Wandera Maskini. He approached the board, stared at Amin, and began to berate him: 'There are no goods in the stores and it's because you have expelled the Asians.' And he continued: 'Son of a bitch. Kill me if you want.'[53] Amin said nothing and after a while he left. That same evening Radio Uganda announced that anyone who was blind, deaf, lacked hands, or felt so weak that he or she needed government assistance should report to the nearest police station. The next morning thousands of disabled individuals sat in military trucks and were driven to Jinja, where they were dumped in the river. Those who tried to grab hold of something were shot. When Amin in the film was shown clapping his hands, this should tell two stories: the dictator was not only startling the dangerous beasts dozing at the water's edge or resting in the shadows of a tree; he was greeting and applauding his executioners.

Schroeder's idea was original; he wanted to capture a self-portrait, he said, by filming an individual who portrayed himself through the film. But the documentary also provides some background for the conditions in Uganda under Amin – that he expelled the Asians from the country (he also expelled 500 Israelis), who had owned around 80 per cent of all the shops, and how this contributed to throwing the country into economic chaos, which again unleashed enormous inflation and severe difficulty acquiring even the most basic supplies of key food products. The film does not document but refers to reports of mass killings and hundreds of missing persons, and it underscores this with fleeting images of military executions. Yet, Amin does not stage himself as a classic dictator or as a power-happy individual with tyrannical leanings. The impression is rather that Amin perceives himself as a jovial, country guy. He tells stories of his past, and we see him dancing to an African band. Amin talks about his friendships, as he claims, with the Israeli leaders, Moshe Dayan and Golda Meir, but also says that Israel, in order to initiate the ultimate mayhem, plans to poison the Nile.

Another, far more famous film, *The Last King of Scotland* from 2006, also professes to be a film about President Amin, though the movie largely is, and has also been promoted as such, a thriller about a white, gullible aid worker that becomes entangled in the charming dictator's net. The feature film also draws upon Nile scenes, but in the movie the river, like Africa itself, is a backdrop against which to tell what is primarily a Scottish do-gooder's drama.

Director Kevin Macdonald's goal was to create a 'true film' about Amin, because, according to Macdonald, he is the most well-known African in history besides Nelson Mandela. His declared ambition, therefore, was to fill something of a void: the film would show who Amin really was, and by so doing being able to finally explain the outside world's preoccupation with him.

One of the film's paradoxes, however, is that Amin is not at the story's narrative centre. The Scottish aid worker is the true axis around which the film revolves: Doctor Nicholas Garrigan, who comes to Uganda to work in a rural hospital but ends up as Amin's personal physician and closest adviser, is the movie's protagonist. He, the doctor, is the Africa's Samaritan or helper, proves the emotional focus; the doctor represents hope, good intentions and conscience, and so the film delivers a representative and classic thought-figure from the aid epoch. The film illuminates this epoch's world views and self-images, revealing their character in a new context. *The Last King of Scotland*, which according to the director is a movie about Amin, indirectly discloses the aid system's self-centred world view, that is to say, its foundational archetype. For how else are we to understand why a movie that is supposedly about Amin is not capable of conveying Uganda without the helper or benefactor at the story's centre?

The director emphasized that the film was not meant to create a new 'Heart of Darkness' (patterned of Joseph Conrad's novel) in its depiction of Africa. He wanted to avoid reproducing the stereotypes to which the continent had fallen victim. Instead of *repeating* these obsolete clichés, however, the film strengthened what were originally and the most powerful contemporary clichés by scripting them into a historical event that essentially unfolded outside the universe of aid relations. The young Doctor Nicholas distinguishes himself from earlier epochs' types or heroes; unlike the classic European adventurer, he does not seek excitement on the 'wild' continent. Instead, he embodies the aid epoch's type hero: the Western Samaritan who seeks 'meaning' on 'the dark continent'. This becomes doubly problematic when the film, even as it places the aid worker at the centre, relativizes the policies with which Amin is associated.

The legacy of Amin as we know it, was a soldier who cleverly played his cards, seized power and instituted a dictatorship. Because stories of Amin's cannibalism and sorcery are familiar to many, and because he, more than any other individual, symbolizes what many Africans consider to be the worst of Africa, it is startling that the movie places Amin in a rather eccentric, humorous light – representing him, indeed, as a childish figure with a psychopathic streak. Forest Whitaker's interpretation of the role makes Amin seem almost fatherly, as if he could have been one of 'us'. If more Ugandans, as dynamic, individual actors, had also been included in the story of the movie, the limits of the film's perspective might have been more clearly revealed.

The woman and the water meant to bulletproof warriors

In May 1986, a woman of around thirty was sitting at Wang Jok, or the 'Devil's Eye', as Murchison Falls is known in the Acholi language. Since the Nile gushes over the cliff edge here, straight and fierce and with a deafening roar, the site has become, like many other similar watery places, a setting for local magic rituals. In 1986 it was the birthplace of one of Africa's strangest ideological-military movements in recent times, and it was this woman who started it.

If one did not know any better, it might seem that Alice Auma, a childless local woman, was sitting there and talking to herself, for her mouth was clearly moving. But Alice could barely speak or hear. Her father had taken her to various local healers, but they could not cure her. It was instead the local spirit Lakwena who had seized her and talked through her.

The spirit had ordered her to visit the Nile falls and had led her here, to Wang Jok. And here she sat for forty days, and it was not with herself she was communing but with the river spirits.

According to the story, Lakwena had held court with the animals in Paraa National Park concerning the ongoing war in Uganda between the army belonging to then rebel leader Yoweri Museveni and the army belonging to the Okello brothers. The brothers belonged to the Acholi tribe, as did Alice, and during a short period in 1985-6 they held power in Kampala.[54]

The spirit said to the animals: 'You animals, God sent me to ask you whether you bear responsibility for the bloodshed in Uganda.' The animals denied they were to blame; the buffalo displayed a wound on its foreleg and the hippo displayed a wound on its hind leg. Lakwena then said to the waterfall: 'Water, I am coming to ask you about the sins and the bloodshed in the world.'[55] The water replied: 'The people with two legs kill their brothers and throw the bodies in the water.' When the spirit asked the water what it did with sinners, the water said: 'I fight against the sinners, for they are the ones to blame for the bloodshed. Go and fight against the sinners, because they throw their brothers in the water.'

After a short return to her village, Alice was led by Lakwena to Mount Kilak, which welcomed her arrival with great explosions. The spirit said to the mountain: 'God has sent me to find out why there is theft in the world.' The mountain replied: 'I have gone nowhere and have stolen no one's children. But people come here to me and name the names of those whom I should kill [by casting spells]. Some ask me for medicine [to bewitch]. [...] I want to give you water to heal diseases. But you must fight against the sinners.'

In August 1986, Lakwena ordered Alice to stop working as a local healer. It was pointless to continue such work while the war was raging. Instead she came to start the Holy Spirit Movement. She would spearhead the battle against evil – she would put an end to the bloodbath. Alice regarded this task as a message and instruction from the gods. It required the capital in Kampala to be retaken. With that, the Acholi would be free from all the violence that had assembled in the Luwero Triangle, and they could establish a paradise on earth.

The Holy Spirit Movement and its soldiers viewed military defeat as resulting from moral decay and not from an enemy with superior military force. Their rebellion, therefore, was regarded not only as a rebellion on the part of morality but also as a rebellion of nature against the current state of affairs. Nature was on their side – if they treated it right. Besides the soldiers, there were 14,000 spirits, bees, snakes, stones and rivers that supported them. Water was of great significance to warriors. Not only was it central to the purification process necessary to make them into warriors, but it would also protect them against bullets. The spirit, after all, had declared that: 'Whatever it is, it will be washed away by water!' and 'There is nothing greater than water' for 'God had created water before anything else'. It was God's 'first-born child'.[56]

Alice inspired the Acholi during a historical period marked by military defeat and moral and cultural confusion and dissolution. Even so, the ethnic group's religious traditions and beliefs meant that her visions were given the power of faith. An uneducated woman with no military experience whatsoever quickly mobilized thousands of soldiers. She led them into war without any modern weapons, only sticks and stones and the Nile water that would make them invincible.

The first attack took place near Lira in North Uganda, by an arm of the shallow Lake Kyoga through which the Nile slowly runs. Armed with bags full of rocks and carrying sticks – as they sang songs, splashed water, and were coated with sesame oil – the Holy Spirit Movement marched to war. Astonishingly enough, they inflicted severe losses on the governmental troops, even though their rocks did not explode like grenades and the enemy bullets were not stopped, as Alice had promised.

But eventually, as Alice's army suffered greater and greater losses, she was accused of being a witch, one possessed by evil, destructive spirits. When the Movement experienced its final defeat without ever reaching Kampala, Alice fled to a refugee camp in Kenya – she claimed that Lakwena had deserted her – and disappeared from Uganda's history.

The woman who sought advice at Wang Jok, or the 'Devil's eye', was gone, but the concept of the power inherent in Nile water also has a much longer history in this part of the basin.

Stories about the sacred water

Alice Auma's faith in the effectiveness of sacred water is part of a long-standing and extensive African water cult tradition, which also has been significant in many Nile countries. One of the most famous African uprisings against Europe's conquering armies during the scramble for Africa was the Maji Maji Rebellion against the Germans in Tanganyika at the beginning of the twentieth century – *maji maji* means 'water water'. Armed with an arsenal of shoddy weaponry, spears and arrows for the most part, the rebels launched a fearless attack on the German garrisons, apparently utterly convinced that this special water made them invincible. With millet wreaths on their foreheads, they marched against the heavily armed German soldiers and were mown down. On 21 October 1905, the Germans began a counter-attack and the rebel army was forced into chaotic retreat while many cried: 'The maji is a lie!' The German army won a crushing victory, but the revolt is nonetheless considered the first relatively well-organized and comprehensive rebellion against Europe's colonization in this part of East Africa, and it led to Germany adapting its policy in the country, fearing the repercussions of similar rebellions in the future.

The idea of the water's distinctive power survived the Maji Maji Rebellion. Around the time that the First World War broke out in Europe, another water prophet emerged, this time in Uganda. His name was Rembe and he came, according to the propaganda of his movement, to give the Lugbara people, the Acholi's neighbours in North Uganda, divine power. This special power could be acquired by drinking the water from a spring in the Lugbara area of the Nile basin, where a snake with a human head also lived – one who could give oracles. Rembe promised his followers that drinking this 'Yakan water' would protect them against the rifles of the British-led occupation troops, and followers of this water mythology believed magic could affect the enemy's weapons, transforming bullets to water. The British understood the potential for revolt these ideas contained, and so in 1917 they arrested Rembe and executed him. Nonetheless, the Yakan cult, or water cult, persisted in a region where people had also long believed it was possible to determine innocence or guilt by tying the accused to a tree at night in the bush and waiting to see if they would be eaten by hyenas.

After the First World War ended, unrest broke out anew in North Uganda and it was also encouraged by faith in the magic water, and the protection it would give them. The Yakan Rebellion in 1919 resulted in the death of a dozen policemen. Again, the colonial authorities acted resolutely: they imprisoned the leaders, and when several of them died in prison, the cult also died.

During recent centuries, water cults have emerged again and again, often with significant political-military consequences. Given a higher education level in the country and the growing strength of monotheistic religions, Alice Auma might have been the last representative for water cults as central elements in religious-political movements. Yet, a perverted shadow of this lived on.

The Wizard of the Nile and the Lord's Resistance Army

It is the end of the 1990s. Around Gulu, one of the larger cities in Acholiland, you can see children streaming in every evening from the neighbouring villages – long lines winding toward the city's centre. The children are heading to bed – in schools, hospitals or pavements. They are seeking safety and protection against random kidnappings perpetuated by the Lord's Resistance Army (LRA).

Earlier, the LRA had attacked nearby schools and kidnapped children and young girls. I had been in Gulu a few years before these dramatic events and had slept in one of the city's best hotels, with cockroaches dominating the bedroom walls with peeling paint, and the only thing available for dinner being goat, rice or yucca. Bullet holes and houses torn apart by bombs bore witness to the brutal conflicts in the 1970s between the local arch-nemeses, the Madis and the Acholis, which had left tens of thousands of people dead. Joseph Kony had not yet stepped onto the bloody scene that for decades was the hallmark of this part of Uganda.

In the wake of defeats and Alice Auma's flight, Joseph Kony had taken over the Holy Spirit Movement in 1987 and rebaptized it the LRA. In Acholi *kony* means 'to help', and Joseph Kony's programme was, he said, to build a society founded on the Ten Commandments and on freedom, not just for the Acholis but for all Uganda, from the new Museveni government that took power in Kampala in 1986.

The many reports that came out of Uganda were clear: Kony would shape one of the most brutal military movements of our time. Children were kidnapped and turned into killer robots who acted on their leader's commands. Under threat of being killed themselves, these LRA child soldiers attacked villages where they cut off people's lips, ears, hands, feet or breasts; sometimes they are also said to have force-fed victims' families the severed body parts. To punish those who reported their activities to the Ugandan authorities, they drilled holes in informants' lips and padlocked them. Victims were burned alive or beaten to death with machetes and clubs. For his part, Joseph Kony claimed he was only following the Holy Spirit's commands.

But why did this movement appear? And what was its role in the power struggle taking place in this part of the Nile basin? Attempting to understand the movement's historical background and the context in which it operated does not imply an excusing of Kony or a relativization of the values he promoted. The twenty-eight-minute documentary video about Kony, released in the spring of 2012, called *Kony 2012*,[57] was made by an organization called Invisible Children in the US. Suddenly and unexpectedly it became one of YouTube's greatest sensations ever, viewed by millions of people the world over in the course of a few weeks. This clearly shows that one thing we are also dealing with here is a media phenomenon, and that the history and image of the LRA must also be viewed in this context.

When the LRA took up weapons against Museveni, it was a normal expression of what had long been the country's political culture: the power struggle for the capital, Kampala, had many times led whoever lost to form a guerrilla army. The relative strength of Kony's group reflected the absence of other leaders among the Acholi at the time, and the movement's religious convictions and rhetoric functioned because it apparently solved practical political dilemmas to which no realistic solutions existed. The LRA succeeded apparently, in the same way as Islamic terrorist organizations, in legitimizing extreme forms of violence among its followers. Even as the LRA developed into a caricature of a liberating army, recruiting soldiers by kidnapping children, the rebellion was also caught in a set of inner contradictions that over time weakened the movement internally and particularly in relation to the outside world.

One of the few books written about Kony is *The Wizard of the Nile* by the British journalist Matthew Green. The cover of the book features a warlord and an AK-47. And indeed, as the Kenyan author Binyavanga Wainaina suggests in his famous essay from 2005, 'How to Write about Africa',[58] if you want to write about the continent, then the absolute rule is this: 'Never have a picture of a well-adjusted man on the cover of your book.' Instead: 'An AK-47, prominent ribs, naked breasts: use these.' Book with such covers will sell in the West because they correspond to widely held stereotypes. *The Wizard of the Nile* follows both sets of advice, but in this case, the picture of a warlord and an AK-47 is illustrative, indeed fitting. What is interesting with Green's book is that it does not limit itself to an analysis of Kony but also tries to locate the movement in a larger regional game for political power and influence. He argues that Sudan's Islamist government financed Kony's resistance army so it would help in the war Khartoum was waging against the Sudan People's Liberation Army (SPLA) in Southern Sudan. According to multiple reports, although not confirmed by independent sources, this alliance resulted in the LRA, which claimed to be based on the Ten Commandments, having 'Allahu Akbar' as their war cry. The government in Kampala also has had interests in keeping this war going, and in portraying Kony partly as insane and partly as an instrument of Khartoum's Islamist government. If it was possible to claim that Kony waged his lunatic, murderous war against Museveni and the Ugandan government, Kampala could receive the West's support for building up its own army.

Green's book is at the same time thoroughly conventional, since it is one of many books on Africa that is written as an allegory of Joseph Conrad's novel *Heart of Darkness*.

Green describes his journey 'into one of the wildest corners of the African continent', as the publicity put it, into barbarity, away from civilization. His goal is to track Kony, a kind of black Kurtz (a central figure in Conrad's novel), and to interview him. The book, however, lacks the eeriness required for this idea to function, for while he waits on Kony, Green passes the time as whites often do in Africa: he makes the obligatory visit to a witch doctor, talks to a Catholic priest risking his life to convert Africans, and meets sex-glad female aid workers. *The Wizard of the Nile* is another of these books written for a reader who is not African, or whose knowledge of Africa or of Uganda is merely superficial. The book represents a classical reportage tradition that revolves around the outsider, the Western observer; the journalistic calling, but what saves it and makes it worth reading is that it does all this with self-irony. The way in which Green describes what should be the climax of the book – his meeting with Kony – is telling. He narrates it as an anticlimax – it was a press conference in the jungle, and it was so easy to go there that dozens of other journalists also were present, and Kony, the very symbol of despotism and primitive savagery, looked like any other ordinary middle-aged man in a suit.

Peace negotiations between LRA and the government in Kampala collapsed in April 2008 when Kony did not appear to sign the agreement. Instead, he demanded that the International Criminal Court in The Hague withdraw its arrest warrant, which it issued in 2005 for Kony, his deputies and three other rebel commanders. Naturally, this action prompted Kony to flee; he decamped with some of his soldiers to the Democratic Republic of the Congo and the Ituri Forest, around the same region that Henry Stanley travelled in the 1870s, and which he depicted as the most terrible place in Africa.

Joseph Kony and his army, moreover, were not forgotten by the outside world, as the famous YouTube video from spring 2012 claims. On the contrary: Kony was the stated objective for George W. Bush's final great initiative within African military affairs. According to the press reports, Kony was also the objective for the first military operations in the United States' new Africa Command, or AFRICOM. Washington provided military support for what was termed 'Operation Lightning Thunder', and which was carried out by soldiers from Uganda, DR Congo and South Sudan. In November 2008, on one of his last days in the White House, President Bush authorized financial and logistical support for a coordinated attack on LRA in the north-eastern DR Congo. AFRICOM contributed a team of seventeen advisers and analysts, intelligence, satellite telephones and a million dollars in fuel. The operation would destroy LRA's main command centre and eliminate Joseph Kony. Despite three months' military activity and Ugandan troops on Congolese soil, however, they failed in capturing Kony. As a censorious Ugandan press wrote: they apprehended cookware and weapons and food, but no Kony. This development lent increased support to all those who have claimed that Kony is not actually supposed to be caught. Instead, he serves powerful interests by remaining the 'dangerous enemy' in the jungle. The war against Kony continued under President Obama. Late in 2011, the United States entered a defence cooperation with Uganda that meant new American troops were sent after Kony. In early summer 2012, it was confirmed that 100 American soldiers were on the ground gathering information and providing advice to troops from four countries, all of whom were involved in 'the hunt for Kony'.[59] Foreign Secretary John Kerry promised a ransom of $5 million to those who helped capturing Kony. He was never found, however. In 2017, however, the United States declared mission accomplished on its six-year, $800 million hunt for Kony. The official justification, given by General Thomas D. Waldhauser, commander of AFRICOM, was that the Lord Resistance Army did not anymore threaten US or Western interests in the region.[60]

For outsiders it is almost impossible to find out what occurred in this region over recent decades. Any larger or smaller enterprise looking for very valuable resources in the border region between Uganda, Sudan and DR Congo, and that wants to beat others to the punch, have been and are served by the wider world viewing the region as dangerous, barbaric and unpredictable. And, not least, the United States has had interests in Kony as a living justification for having involved itself militarily in this very resource-rich region over many years, without any questions asked about what they might be doing there. Unconfirmed regional rumours hold, among other things, that the Americans and their local collaborators have closed off large areas to outsiders. What is certain, on the other hand, is that American military technology is completely dependent on the metals found in the region, and that Obama, while still a congressman, got one law approved, and that concerned the resources in this part of Africa and their significance to the United States. Into such a perspective enters that sensational YouTube video from 2012: it led to new and strengthened rumours that Kony has been required to serve as a kind of 'barbaric outpost' in Africa, for, in the shadow of the 'war for good' being waged against this crazy child kidnapper and warlord, rare metals could be retrieved from the DR Congo in the border areas with Uganda.

In the meantime the International Court of Justice in the Hague opened its trial, not against Kony, but against Dominic Ongwen. He is alleged former Commander in the Sinia Brigade of the LRA, but also himself a child soldier and indoctrinated by the rebel leaders at the time. On 6 December 2016 the trial opened, and he was accused of seventy counts of war crimes and crimes against humanity related to attacks against the civilian population: murder and attempted murder; rape; sexual slavery; forced marriage; torture; enslavement; outrage upon personal dignity; conscription and use of children under the age of fifteen to participate actively in hostilities; pillaging; destruction of property and persecution. Ongwen denied all the charges. Closing statements were made in March 2020 and, at the time of writing, the verdict was still awaited, after the prosecution has presented testimonies of 116 witnesses, and the defence, 69. Much of the public discussion has been about the role of local magical beliefs and whether it is these spirits that are on trial.

Nonetheless, with Kony situated 'someplace' in the Democratic Republic of Congo, peace came to the Nile basin for the first time in half a century.

New discoveries: oil in the Nile!

The Western parts of the Nile basin in Uganda, as it turns out, contain many types of resources. Around 150 years after Mr and Mrs Baker ran down the slope toward the lake, another Briton, Tony Buckingham, wrote himself into Uganda's and Lake Albert's history of discovery. Buckingham was behind a company that discovered huge oil deposits in the Nile lake. It is a historical coincidence that Prince Albert, after whom the lake was named, lived in London's Buckingham Palace and that Tony Buckingham bears the palace's name, but it is no coincidence that it was also a Briton who discovered oil in the lake mapped by his countryman.

Buckingham is one of many British who continued to conduct rather shady business in Africa after the empire dissolved. This group of entrepreneurs often consisted of people who previously had lived in South Africa or Rhodesia (since 1980 called Zimbabwe), and who exploited the networks established during colonial times or in the wake of the empire's collapse. Buckingham was long one of the central people involved in the controversial South African company, Executive Outcomes, that delivered mercenaries for the many small wars ravaging Africa in the 1990s – wars which Western media, almost without exception, portrayed as mere local ethnic disputes, all the while overlooking the roles of the weapon dealers and the interests they promoted and represented. Buckingham was also one of the leading figures in Sandline International, the company that obtained mercenaries, training and weapons for the regime in Guinea when they needed help crushing a revolt. This activity garnered international attention when a plane fully loaded with mercenaries and weapons bound for Guinea was stopped on the airfield in Zimbabwe's capital. Some of Buckingham's erstwhile companions, like Margaret Thatcher's son, Mark, received a four-year sentence and a $500,000 fine after having pleaded guilty to coup-planning in Equatorial Guinea. Buckingham and his oil-drilling company subsequently focused their energy on emphasizing that he had not had any contact with the mercenary business since spring of 1998.

As *The Observer* noted in 1997, however, Executive Outcomes had larger goals than simply acquiring weapons and mercenaries. The wars they supported served as deliberately created smoke screens to hide what they were actually after: 'The Executive Outcomes mercenaries are not simply "guns for hire". They are the advance guard for major business interests engaged in a latter-day scramble for the mineral wealth of Africa,'[61] which includes oil, gold and diamonds. If this truly was the company's strategy, it functioned in this case perfectly: Buckingham's enterprise could drill for oil year after year without fearing an attack in a region that was otherwise characterized by conflict and war, not just between DR Congo, Uganda and Rwanda, but also between the government and guerrilla groups in both North Uganda and East Congo. Whereas the rest of the world was exclusively focused on war and brutality in North Uganda, Buckingham and his people transported heavy drilling rigs, exploration equipment, geologists and workers to Lake Albert to search for oil. When Britain had ruled the country, multiple reports, such as that by E.J. Wayland in 1927, confirmed that oil could be found in Lake Albert and the Rift Valley. Since then, no one had searched for it and no one else had read the reports sent to the colonial authorities. Buckingham found what he sought, and what the reports had indicated.

In Uganda, where conspiracy theories flourish because many people simply do not trust the official versions of things, it is entirely common to hear explanations regarding particular wars as being conducted and perpetuated by outside interests and investments in order to conceal the extraction of diamonds, gold and other valuable metals from the area, and the hunt for oil resources. Such wars, of course, always have an internal foundation as well, but there can be no doubt that states and external, private actors have interests served by, and have also backed, regional unrest in many places in the Nile basin.

Buckingham's investments in Heritage Oil have been described as unusually lucrative. He and his partners ventured, it is claimed, somewhere between $135 million and $150 million in the company. Buckingham alone could, in 2010, pocket $84 million after having sold half of his shares to some of the world's leading oil companies.[62] In 2016, the leaked Panama Papers indicated that his company 'urgently even moved its corporate registration from one tax haven to another', in order to avoid paying hundreds of millions of pounds in tax to Uganda.[63] In 2018 it became clear, however, that Uganda's first oil production was again postponed, this time to 2022. This time delay was explained by the joint venture partners Total, China National Offshore Oil Company and Tullow reconsidering final investment decisions. There were plans to start oil production, first in 2013, then in 2015/16, then in 2018 and then in 2020. The amount of oil so far discovered has in the meantime been reduced from 6.5 billion barrels to 6 billion barrels. Some twenty-one oil fields have been discovered, but no oil yet produced. This also has affected investment decisions both concerning the refinery and the crude oil pipeline.

The company's oil discoveries are, however, thought to be of major significance to Uganda's economy. Uganda's Bureau of Statistics has predicted that the country will produce between 100,000 and 150,000 barrels of oil a day. Oil will flood the region, the most optimistic say. And it is the Nile lakes on which exploration ventures are concentrated. As such, their economic and political role will change and become even more complex. Increasingly more international actors will come onto the stage and acquire interests in how these Nile reservoirs are exploited. South Africa, with an oil company directed by Jacob Zuma's nephew, is involved, as are Russia, China and Italy, and if conditions in the region grow even calmer, the large Western companies will get involved as well. Oil can also become a strengthening factor in Uganda's economy, and the country's president has repeatedly said that the income will be used to produce more hydropower. In Uganda, whose borders are entirely within the Nile basin, this will signify more exploitation of and control over the Nile and its tributaries.

Central Africa's inland lake

Anyone arriving by plane over Lake Victoria and landing at Entebbe after hours of flying over the thin, blue strip flowing through Sudan's and Egypt's endless deserts will be struck by the lake's overwhelming size. And scattered around in this inland lake are several islands that are the very image of tropical holiday getaways, complete with palms, lapping waves and bungalows along the beach.

The air feels infinitely clear and pure because there are hardly any polluting industries in the region. Sundown over the lake has its own distinctive beauty – bursting with colour, but nonetheless measured, like East Africa's magnificent and famous transitions from day to night. And yet it is still different – for here the sundown has both the horizon and the water's surface to play upon, one moment enhanced by the surface, the next diminished.

The lake in many places is ideal for water sports. The wind is reliable from morning to late afternoon throughout the year. Although the waves can at times be rough – from this perspective, the inland lake is more akin to an ocean – the wind never blows stronger than six or seven on the Beaufort scale. Typically, the lake is calm in the morning and late in the afternoon, so it can alternatively be used to water ski and to sail. If you take a motorboat out to the islands from Kampala or Entebbe, you will usually see white sails in every direction towards the horizon. Observed from a deckchair beneath island palm trees or from the deck of a boat, this inland ocean's size and the sound of waves lapping against the sandy beach provides a definite impression of permanence, of 'eternity'.

Newer research, however, indicates that this lake, which appears both endless and eternal, might have been dry as recently as about 14,000 years ago, when it was refilled with water. The Nile's source has not always been the Nile's sources of today; the river in Egypt was dry for large swathes of the year in prehistoric times, making it impossible for people to live there on a permanent basis. Many of the tributary rivers upstream from Lake Victoria today run eastwards into it, including the Kagera River, though for millions of years, right up to the Pleistocene, the Kagera ran westwards, out of today's Nile basin.

Lake Victoria, which is now ranked as the world's second largest lake, with an area of between 60,000 and 68,000 square kilometres and an adjacent watershed of 184,000 square kilometres, is, accordingly, a young lake, one that has varied radically in volume and size. The lake is shallow; it has a maximum depth of only around 80 metres and an average depth of about 40 metres. The lake's coastline is 3,500 kilometres long, with countless small, shallow bays and coves. In volume, however, the lake is quite humble; it holds about 2,500 square kilometres of water, or only 15 per cent of the volume in Lake Tanganyika.

Because the lake is so shallow, climate change has had, and will continue to have, an immediate effect. A reduction in size means reduced precipitation, and reduced precipitation again leads to reduced size. If the balance between input and output, between evaporation and precipitation, is radically disturbed, the lake itself will radically change, with significant consequences for local utilization of the lake, but obviously also for agreements on water distribution and exploitation, since the Nile river's waterflow will also change.

In 2007 the alarm was sounded throughout East Africa: Lake Victoria's water level had sunk three metres below normal. What caused these changes? Humans? Weather? Natural fluctuations? Accusations rained down. Some blamed the Ugandan government: 'They pumped too much of the lake to produce electricity', the argument ran. Others said, 'What did I tell you?' before pointing out they warned that the new dams would destroy the lake. Still others blamed the West, global warming and climate change, whereas some claimed it was an expression of the lake's natural fluctuations, thereby indicating an irrefutable hydrological and historical fact: the British took lake measurements showing the water level in 1913 was lower than it was at the beginning of the 2000s.[64]

'Do you remember the Laputans in *Gulliver's Travels*?' The Ugandan researcher regarded me as we discussed historical variations in the Nile's waterflow in 2011. In his descriptions of Laputa, Jonathan Swift poked fun at those who consistently walk around feeling and believing the world is going under or that everything will collapse. The Laputans were eternal doomsday prophets and they coined every possible theory regarding how the sun would someday stop warming the earth. Every morning they greeted each other with anxieties of possible destruction. 'When it comes to the Nile and the great lakes, there is no shortage of people who are like the Laputans', the researcher continued. Nonetheless, we agreed, as we drank our tea and placed the cups on the table located on the beach near the water's edge, that we were not capable of determining if the current fears are as groundless as those doomsday prophets Swift lampooned.

And this is the precisely Nile's Janus face. When it comes to climate change and large-sized basins, the future is not easy to predict because the mechanisms that determine development are so complex. In the case of the Nile basin, there are no hydrological and meteorological data covering an extensive enough time series for the basin, nor proficient enough models capable of capturing its diversity in an exact way.

In the years after 2007, the lake has gradually risen again, until today it nears its average from 1900. Some years later, in 2019, measurements were published that showed that the water level was higher than normal. The amount of rainfall received in the Lake Victoria Basin in the March to June season was more than normal long-term average. The water levels in the major Ugandan lakes – Victoria, Kyoga, Albert, Edward – all rose due to rise in the amount of precipitation, the rainfall pattern being attributed to the persisting presence of the rainfall belt over the East Africa. Undoubtedly, the lake's water level for many reasons will also vary in the future. And studies, analyses, and discussions of the lake's health will continue as long as there are people in the Nile basin. Changes will be interpreted politically and exploited politically. The almost 500 million people living in the basin countries, however, cannot wait on scientific results as a basis for action, especially because these will be disputed in any case. Therefore, the river and its exploitation must be planned as if dramatic scenarios will occur. Nature's eternal, hydrological variations strengthen for this reason the river's lasting significance for society's development and as an object of high politics.

Darwin's Pond, evolution's teaching and mass extinction

Even though the Nile basin is most famous for great cats and flocks of wildebeests, for the zebras and giraffes that roam the savannahs the region's most extensive wildlife ecosystem can be found underwater, right in Lake Victoria, not far from where Mutesa I's antelopes wandered and grazed.

The small white motorboat glides slowly through Murchison Bay, just outside of Kampala. I am under way with some researchers from the Universities of Makerere and Bergen who are searching for cichlids. Cichlids themselves are small, unattractive fish, anything but spectacular. What is astonishing about them is that 400 species of these fish emerged here, and all developed from five different ancestors in this lake.

What makes this ecosystem so fascinating to evolutionary ecologists is that experts believe this species diversity occurred over an exceptionally short time period – perhaps just over 14,000 years. Despite its youth, Lake Victoria managed to become one of the most species-rich lakes in the world. For this reason, the lake has been termed Darwin's Pond.

But then, in the course of a couple of decades at the end of the twentieth century, dramatic changes occurred. The once crystal-clear lake became filled with sludgy, stinking water, and parts of the lake were for periods almost suffocated by algae and water hyacinths. In an Africa where appalling accounts of famine and revolt has been so common, a 'dead' Lake Victoria would have proven catastrophic for the tens of millions of people living on its shores. Reports were produced showing the lake's ecological health was being negatively impacted by a fast-growing population, the clearing of natural vegetation along the lakeshore, a blooming fish export industry, very productive algae growth and the dumping of untreated waste from operations located in coastal regions. Rain also washed agricultural chemicals from regional plantations into the many Nile tributaries and so into the lake.

Even more dramatic: up until the late 1970s, the lake's biomass composition was relatively constant, but in 1980 an investigation showed that conditions had flipped. The cichlid count had fallen dramatically and now composed only 1 per cent of the lake's total fish weight, whereas Nile perch now formed 80 per cent. The number of cichlid species had plunged to 200, and it was suggested the Nile perch was responsible. The loss of half the cichlid species was, as one chief researcher at Boston University remarked, the largest known mass vertebrate extinction in history.

The main villain of this story became the Nile perch (though other people believed pollution was more the cause) and blame for this hardship was placed on the man who had introduced the perch into the lake. This was a British colonial officer who had secretly released the fish into the Ugandan part of the lake in the 1950s. Thereafter, the fish spread throughout the whole lake, and in the early 1980s there were huge stock in Tanzania, Kenya and Uganda. With no readily available food source, the Nile perch turned to cannibalism – larger fish consumed smaller fish. Hundreds of endemic species that had developed according to the conditions specific to Lake Victoria were lost – according to this account of decline.

There is, however, an alternative narrative: the Nile perch's introduction was the start of an economic adventure. Ton after ton of this popular fish is taken from the lake by large commercial boats. The fish are sold to foreign-owned processing plants where they are quickly cleaned, filleted, packaged and frozen to be shipped to expensive restaurants in Nairobi and to delicatessens in the Middle East and Europe. Nile perch has become a moneymaker. The skin is used to make belts and purses, the bladder becomes a filter for English alcohol manufacturers, and it goes into Asian soups. In response to increased international demand for Nile perch in particular, commercial fishing fleets have replaced local fishermen. Around 200,000 tons of perch are shipped from the country every year, and at the beginning of the 2000s, fish sales surpassed coffee and cotton as the country's most important lucrative export.

Critics emphasize that, while the fish export business has brought money into the countries around the lake, it has not made the local communities any richer. Instead of proving a decent local source of protein, the fish have become too expensive for the local population to afford. The profitable fishing opportunities, moreover, led to the Nile perch being radically overexploited; the number of fishermen doubled in the course of only five years. Average fish size also shrank dramatically. Meanwhile, several years of a protection policy enforced by the three countries that share the lake yielded positive results. And the cichlid population, it turns out, has also increased. Fish species that researchers long believed to have been exterminated in all-out mass murder never disappeared after all, and since the Nile perch are now less numerous, new ecological niches have emerged.

The Speke Resort, Museveni and the Nile

Not far from Kampala's centre, on the banks of Lake Victoria (you can see the lake between the palms of the park located right next to the outdoor restaurant), is Speke Resort, an unusually large conference centre built by President Museveni in connection with the Commonwealth Summit at the beginning of the 2000s. He called the resort Munyonyo after the district where it is located, but the name people typically use is Speke, one of many examples that the explorer, probably to attract European tourists to the country, is enjoying a renaissance. Right over the check-in desk, which is curved like a large bow, is a gallery. There, right in the middle, Museveni holds sway, complete with his hallmark: the broad-brimmed hat. The statue is large and impressive, and hardly commensurate with his original attacks on 'the personality cult' under President Obote, the independent Uganda's first leader.

Museveni is a contentious leader in Uganda – a position impossible to avoid in Nile countries, chiefly due to ethnic differences and pronounced social inequality. It is not, however, Museveni's way of handling ethnic relationships, the influence of the different kings and their ethnic followers, or the multiparty system that is most interesting from a Nile perspective. Obviously, Museveni has been criticized for being authoritarian, dictatorial and for favouring his own people. And there is something to all that: the military's top positions were for long periods of time largely reserved for individuals from his own ethnic group, the Ankole from south-western Uganda. Museveni has pushed through constitutional changes ratified by parliament extending his presidential term beyond what the previous constitution allowed. Meanwhile, under his leadership the country has generally enjoyed peace, except for the war against the LRA in the north and the war in the Congo. The economy has blossomed, the middle class has substantially increased, Asians have been welcomed back, and a kind of multiparty system has been introduced. Since assuming power after a very brief guerrilla war in 1986, he has governed the country in a way that has put Uganda on the path to become a Nile power, both in the diplomatic arena and concretely through river dams.

Seen in a wider time perspective, where the Nile and humankind's relationship to the river is central, one can say that Museveni and his government have implemented a revolution in Uganda and that the Nile river system has defined the country's modern history. And it is now, following the necessary reconstruction period in the wake of the country's many wars that, according to Museveni, the country will truly be developed, and the river tamed.

Here, at Speke Resort, President Museveni gave a long speech on water and the Nile during the African water conference I attended in 2010. He spoke about the Nile's length, about its significance to all the countries in the region, about how important it was to safeguard the basin, to protect it against erosion and other destruction, and – not least – that the 1929 Agreement belonged to history. He described the idea that Uganda could manage with natural rainfall as being hostile to development, and he spoke about Africa as a 'dark continent' from an electrical viewpoint, though harbouring enormous hydropower potential.

A couple of years earlier I had had a long meeting with the respected, long-term water minister, Maria Mutagamba. Like the rest of the government, she was focused on the necessity for Uganda to now stimulate its own industrial revolution and that this must largely be based on power from the Nile. In addition, Museveni and several other ministers have discussed Uganda's need for artificial irrigation. Some regions of the country are regularly struck by drought, for example, Karamanjong in the north, and many other places lack water during the dry season. Museveni returns steadily to Uganda's plans to conduct Nile water to Karamanjong, even though the Egyptians, for their part, have vetoed the project which, according to them, would drain water from the Nile system.

Central sources have informed me that Museveni has privately remarked that Uganda must increase its population, in the event of a war with Egypt over Nile water. And when Uganda's government bought new fighter planes in 2011, the claim emerged from several different wings that the reason was that the country must be ready to protect its Nile interests against future Egyptian attack. The reliability of such information is difficult to determine, and it is also beyond doubt that the 'struggle for the Nile' can function as a popular smokescreen to arm the country for reasons having nothing to do with the Nile. Even as such sabre-rattling war rhetoric occurs, however, Uganda's government emphasizes that they wish to cooperate with all basin countries, particularly with Egypt. As Uganda's water minister told me: 'It is God's will that the river flows as it does. Ugandans, too, must change their mindset and both admit and understand that Egypt truly depends on the river.'[65] And there is no reason to doubt this desire is genuine. The Ugandan government knows that such cooperation will grant the country access to international financial aid, and they also perceive the benefit of Egyptian technical expertise.

Meanwhile, it awoke consternation in Uganda when in 2010 it was reported that the Egyptian minister of agriculture had told the Egyptian press that Egypt had leased enormous amounts of land from Uganda's government. I spoke with the Egyptian ambassador about it when I saw him shortly after that at Speke Resort. He insisted that it was false that such an agreement had been made. In the long run, however, it is probable that such investments will take place. These could make exploitation of the river more optimal, though simultaneously the Nile struggle will become more complex. Should this happen, wealthy Egyptians will have interests in Nile water being used in Uganda, but that will also mean water for the millions of poor farmers in rural Egyptian villages.

The Industrial Revolution comes to Uganda

It is 19 August 2007. At Bujagali Falls just north of Lake Victoria, a traditional Busoga healer, Nfuudu, inserts a spear packed in bark into a powerful waterfall. This is the climax of an animistic ritual meant to transfer the spirit of the falls to another site the Ugandan government has provided for the local population. The spirit needed a new home because the government was set to build a 250-megawatt power station where the spirit had dwelt since time immemorial. After a moment, Nfuudu withdrew his spear from the falls and took the spirit with him to the new site. The transfer was successful, the healers confirmed. This ritual signalled that the local population's opposition to the dam belonged now to the past. They had, the government stated, finally and astutely resigned themselves to the changes required of them by Uganda's modernization.

The Bujagali Falls lie 10 kilometres from where the Nile runs out of Lake Victoria. Historically, the region has functioned as a ritual centre for the Busoga, Uganda's second largest ethnic group, which comprises around 7–8 per cent of the country's population. The area around the fossils, therefore, has long been a sacred place. The Bujagali spirit has protected the Busoga community, provided the right rituals were conducted there. Based on this premodern benefit evaluation, traditional leaders were long against any change to the Bujagali Falls' nature, and some of them accordingly fought the dam. Here, as with so many other third-world locations, such groups have become the most important allies to the international NGOs in their opposition to large dams.

The Bujagali Falls, however, were also East Africa's most important rafting locale. Thousands of rafters from across the globe have paddled the frothing rapids, especially drawn to the unusually large amount of water that forces itself down several smaller rapids. The aesthetics were distinctive: around a million litres of water per second cast itself over the rapids, surrounded by an extreme fertility – a verdant tropical vegetation that covers the riverbanks and islands in the river, and an unparalleled bird life. I was standing there knowing that the place would soon become history, and the rafters were aware that they would be among the last to conquer these rapids.

A couple of days after the Busoga healers had relocated the water spirit, 21 August 2007 was a historical day in Uganda's and the Nile's life. On this day, Yoweri Museveni and the Aga Khan, Prince Karim al-Husseini, the leader of the Ismaili Muslims, laid the Bujagali Dam ground stone. The power plant was co-financed with the World Bank. The goal is that this dam, along with other planned power stations, will end the perpetual power cuts and provide more of a predictable power supply so that industry can operate systematically, and households achieve a better life. The plant consists of a power station whose five turbines will be able to produce 50 megawatts each. The dam is 52 metres high and stretches 30 metres below ground. More than 2,000 of the workers who built the plant were Ugandan and all were outfitted with safety equipment like helmets, boots, high-visibility vests and ropes, so there were almost no accidents during the project period.

Friday, 1 April 2011, was another of these watershed days in the Nile's history. Engineers began directing water away from the river's natural bed because the Nile itself had to be drained of water before the plant could be finished. By mid-May, the riverbed here was dry for the first time in 15,000 years. Then, after the dam was complete, the water returned to its natural course. Meanwhile, engineers had changed the Nile for good.

In 2012 the dam was finally officially opened. Too little too late, many said. Winter 2012 saw steady strikes and demonstrations in Kampala. Energy shortages forced factories to halt operations and people dared not venture out in the evening to shop because the darkness brought thieves. Shop owner slit tyres in the streets. If Bujagali is exploited to capacity, it can produce 250 megawatts. However, the government estimates that in a decade the country's daily requirement will be 1,350 megawatts.

The Nile will electrify Uganda, and electrification will modernize the entire country. Even larger projects are planned, among others the 650-megawatt Karuma Dam that, without comparison, will become Uganda's most significant investment ever, and a dam at Murchison Falls where Winston Churchill, at the beginning of the 1900s, stood and fantasized about Uganda's future.

Uganda is in the process of realizing something of its natural potential as East Africa's powerhouse, as well as its political potential as an important mid-basin enactor of Nile policy – with big plans for the river.

The world's largest insect swarms and Nile time

Bulago Island in Lake Victoria is located about an hour's boat ride from the mainland. I am standing at the top of the island as the sun is sinking into the inland ocean. There, right there, there arise from the water – as if in protest – enormous, billowing columns; there, to my left, right behind me, over my head, and also in my mouth if I forget myself and succumb to the temptation talking to the owner of the bungalow where I am staying. She drove me up to the island's lookout point on her motorcycle.

Lake Victoria is home to some of the world's largest insect swarms. Enormous columns with millions upon millions of individuals move over the water's surface. They eclipse the sun as they are swallowed by the lake. They progress sideways in vertical formations, like an army of soldiers marching atop each other, without rhythm but with a dancing motion. There are too many of them to shoo away. But they are harmless and do not bite.

The adult flies' avid movements are natural; they only live for a day. The females die after their eggs are laid; the males peter out after mating. The resulting mayflies hatch in a lake that, viewed from a socio-historical perspective, approaches the eternal. Fourteen thousand years, however, is just an eye blink from an evolutionary-historical perspective, and it can perhaps, when it comes to geological time, be compared to day-old flies versus a human lifetime. There are different time variants, and historical narratives should maintain a conscious relationship to these, particularly when it comes to accounting for the Nile's societal role. Nile time is obviously not the same as mayfly time, and it is certainly not human time.

The French historian Fernand Braudel has influenced how historians are thinking about time in general, and his suggestion of operating with three different kinds of time: 'the long timespan', 'cyclical time' and 'episodic time'. These are useful concepts, but the existence of physical entities like the Nile, as parts of history, makes it necessary to adjust this understanding of historical time as well.

Societal development can usefully be interpreted against the backdrop of an almost changeless history that repeats itself in regular cycles over thousands of years. The water system in the different Nile basin regions has enjoyed a relatively stable character. The rainy season has sometimes failed to emerge with catastrophic consequences, and the river has sometimes overrun its banks with equally fatal results, but rainfall has, over diverse, extended climactic periods, still varied within clear bounds. And whereas the river's size and direction has certainly changed, the river as a physical entity has been relatively the same for the last five thousand years. Together, both the river and rainfall patterns have fundamentally impacted how societies could develop, which different forms of economic activity were possible or advantageous and also, therefore, which social organizations proved suitable and so survived. This idea does not imply, meanwhile, that the Nile's character, or some water ecology, has necessarily given rise to particular economies, state systems or governmental forms, or that increased control has signified less dependence on the river's natural fluctuations. Rainfall and the river have been determinative in the long run, also for the way they have affected society's range of choices.

This particular form of geographical determinism, which is connected with a historical analysis of the very long term, has nothing to do with Montesquieu's and Aristotle's form of geographical determinism, which argues that there is a direct link between climate and nature on the one hand and mentality on the other. I am also not advocating here for a comprehensive historical theory or a developmental theory where natural conditions are regarded as overarching causal explanations. When I show that the Nile has indeed played such a formative role in some cases, it is not the same thing as accepting that it is possible to establish a general, logical structure of cause and effect that, broadly speaking, can be translated into a scientific discourse regarding necessary and sufficient conditions. The determinism to which I am referring here also has nothing to do with ecologist George Evelyn Hutchinson's widely influential thesis that ecological relationships should be interpreted and analysed as systems governed or controlled by causal interactions. Talking about the long run yields a clearer picture of profound connections between the Nile system's variations and Nile societies' various developmental possibilities.

One can, however, also focus on another kind of historical time – a history of slow rhythms, groups and groupings, as Braudel expressed it.[66] Within such a time perspective, it is important to understand the significance of changes (both temporary and systematic) in climate, river course and waterflow, in order to grasp hydroecological and societal consequences and to focus on significant new technologies in water harnessing. New forms of water control have, in revolutionary ways, burst, and continue to burst, established frameworks for societal development and intergovernmental relations. Lake Nasser in Egypt, the Renaissance Dam in Ethiopia and pump projects withdrawing water from Lake Victoria in Tanzania are all examples of measures that have shifted the frameworks for Nile exploitation. Such changes can be interpreted using a variety of explanatory models. General postulates of 'society's needs' and widespread theories of 'adaptive processes' have a tendency, however, to overlook the individual's role, as well as humankind's ability to redefine society's developmental possibilities relative to the geographical surroundings in which they emerge.

Revolutionary plans for water exploitation or technological new formations for water control are continually being developed. Their success has also been influenced by the waterplanners' understanding of the river's physics and hydrology, and the possibilities these open. Rivers like the Nile sanction human behaviour because the water's form of movement cannot be subjugated to any plan whatsoever, but only to plans that take enough account of the river's physical nature.

During the last century in particular, human control over the Nile's water radically altered its character. Nonetheless, society and humankind are far from escaping the river's direct power. Increased human control of the water does not produce any less dependence on it, as conventional wisdom and traditional evolutionary thinking imply. The relationship between 'control' and 'dependence' is much more subtle, for the more control countries exercise over the river, the more dependent they become, both on the river and on the presupposition that it will continue to flow as it did when they first determined to tame it.

In a short term, event history as well, it can be interesting to place water at the centre – to allow the water, that is, to function as the axis for interpretations of events. Braudel made the Mediterranean to his protagonist, in his study of the region's history under Philip II, the king of Spain from 1556 to 1598. Rivers can, in certain areas and under particular conditions, with even better arguments become protagonists in reconstructions of the history of immense regions. But – and this is important, for it allows this book to avoid some of the problems Braudel encountered in his analysis – in contrast to the Mediterranean, the Nile is constantly changing, not just from year to year and season to season but from minute to minute. Its role is, therefore, at once both structural and varying, permanent and temporary, rigid and shifting. The Nile makes it possible for space and different concepts of historical time to co-exist within a single subject of analysis.

The Nile is a resource that can be placed, and that has been placed, directly under human intervention and control, where people not only have changed the river's character and local function, but often also the society's relationship to it. As such, you cannot reduce the Nile to a backdrop and stow it away in an introductory chapter, as history and social scientific literature often treats nature: the river flows continually, the life-giving water arrives regularly, plants sprout, electricity is produced year-round. All these processes have a normal 'present'; and it has consequences for the farmer's harvest, and so for bride-price and marriage; for companies' power supply, and so for the production of goods; for the king's taxes, and so for the ruler's plans. Abnormal years, or acutely abnormal years, which are often the case when it comes to running water, make studies of politics and ecology on related to both the long term, the mid-term and the short term both natural and possible. This approach by the fact that facilities at one place along the Nile will have immediate consequences for other locations in the basin, either because they effect the river's flow or they effect how the people who share the resource will perceive it.

We climb back onto the motorcycle, wearing thick sunglasses even though it is completely dark outside, while we squint our eyes and keep our mouths shut. On the way down to the bungalow, in the motorcycle's light, we seem to be surrounded by insects; they stand like a grey wall between us and the silent darkness. Before I wake up to a new day over the lake, to relax on a deck chair and let my eyes rest on the inland ocean glinting in the morning sun, they will be dead.

East of the Inland Ocean

The train through the country at the source of the White Nile

The train trip from Mombasa to Kisumu, from the Indian Ocean through the Rift Valley and up to Lake Victoria, is one of the classic train journeys. I took the Port Florence Express, as the route from Nairobi to Lake Victoria was called until it was replaced in 2017 by a fast daytime standard-gauge railway built with Chinese help. It still carried the hallmarks of former colonial style and elegance, with white napkins on the tables in the dining car and a waiter who, clad in a white shirt and freshly ironed black trousers, politely and attentively set the table for the three-course dinner that is included in the ticket price. All great train journeys have their own poetry, but here it is reinforced because few things equal the atmosphere in the half-empty coaches as they move through this beautiful African scenery while the wheels strike rhythmically against the rails. At intervals I lean out of a half-open window (as I always do if the train allows it), thus strengthening the dream-like aspect of moving, enclosed by landscapes hitherto unknown to me. I absorb the heat and the smells, hear the sounds from the villages past which the train quickly rolls, see zebras, antelope, maybe elephants and giraffes more clearly, and have the urge to shout: Wait! Stop! Can the scenes not be frozen? Yet, the train steams tirelessly on, its rhythm transmitted throughout one's body, with an impatience that merges with my own.

I am at the front of the locomotive; I have been invited there by the train driver, I can see more precisely the narrow, single-track railway stretching across the empty Kenyan highlands before it curves down the hills toward Lake Victoria, at times running over attractively constructed viaducts. From this vantage point, it is not difficult to grasp the critique launched against the railway as it was being built at the beginning of the 1900s: that it ran from nowhere to nowhere.

Nonetheless, I know as I stand here and feel the hot air against my forehead, leaning out of the window and with the enormous Rift Valley grasslands filing past, that I am riding a railway that, in fact, created a country. I also know as I stand here and observe the tracks winding down towards Lake Victoria, that influential descriptions of Africa's modern history which emphasize that the effect of colonial policy only became first apparent after the Second World War, must empirically be false.

Sleeping sickness and colonialism

My destination, Kisumu (formerly Port Florence), which is now the largest city on the Kenyan coast of Lake Victoria, offered no draw for foreign capital or domestic trade interests at the beginning of the 1900s. It was hardly any place at all at the time, neither did it possess the resources that adventurers sought. There was no gold, silver, rubber or cotton here. But it was on the Nile lake, and that framed its future.

At that time, a deadly epidemic of sleeping sickness was raging across the entire lake region and was spreading up along the Nile basin. Hundreds of thousands of people died in just a few years. In 1903 there were reportedly 90,000 deaths in Uganda alone. In September 1904, the Royal African Society in London estimated that during that year 40,000 people had already perished. Death was unavoidable if you were bitten by the tsetse fly and did not receive treatment. And so, the British colonial administration acted.

Everyone agreed that changes in the local water system had led to the resurgence of the disease. During the years 1898–1900, East Africa was plagued by severe drought. This resulted in significant crop failures and starvation. Meanwhile, in 1900 it rained violently, which resulted in a quick revival of the bush vegetation along the lake. The British documented that only a few hundred of the many hundreds of thousands of deaths happened in regions *not* along the lake. As such, it quickly became clear that the tsetse fly was the source of infection, and that the scrub by the lake was what enabled the fly to breed so quickly. Since there were so many insects, and they transmitted the disease from person to person through their bite, a deadly epidemic ensued.

The British pushed through a variety of measures. They built a quarantine hospital in Kisumu, which, as the railway's terminus, had become an important site. Everybody suffering from sleeping sickness was removed from the lake shore areas and forcibly transported to the quarantine camps built in multiple locations. Once there, they would either die or be healed. Every chieftain who owned land received orders to evacuate for the following six months all who lived within 2 kilometres of the lake. This relocation effort took place without any serious resistance; every family received a small sum as an incentive and taxes were waived for a couple of years.

Between 1900 and 1904, 200,000 of the 300,000 people living along the shores of the lake died. Britain's programme was the main reason that the total death count from 1905 to 1909 proved less than 25,000. The progress was clear: in 1905, 8,003 died; in 1906, 6,522; in 1907, 4,175; in 1908, 3,622; and in 1909, 1,782. The relocation policy reflects the typical imperial ideology of the day, and the campaign was a chance to demonstrate London's mastery of its colonies, both to itself and to an often sceptical opinion, back home in Great Britain not least.

Like so many other battles in the history of development, the war against the tsetse fly was not won once and for all. The shores of Lake Victoria yield first-hand experience of the distinct variation or permanence of ecological phenomena. The tsetse fly, against which Winston Churchill had to cover himself (as if he were a beekeeper) when he visited Uganda at the beginning of the 1900s, is still found in the area. Today they are just unpleasant and irritating – so irritating that a driver I had hired to show me around in the area, became so nettled by them that he started aiming to kill them while he was driving. Instead, he lost control of the vehicle and drove off the road. The vehicle rolled several times, and while I was held in place by the only seat belt, I heard my travelling companion being thrown around behind me. Since he was large, the racket was loud. We were able, however, to force open the heavy door of the vehicle, almost without getting scratched, and, as we scrambled out, we had to wave our arms around to keep from being bitten by flies. Three men thrashing their arms frenetically in the air on an empty, silent highway was undoubtedly a strange sight, but not so disturbing as to prevent the first vehicle that passed by from stopping and giving us a lift.

The railway that created a country

There was little about the old steam train gliding slowly into the station in Kisumu, a station obviously deemed as low priority for years by those in charge of the Port Florence Express, that called to mind high politics, Europe and the London financial metropolis. It is, after all, typical for a country to build a railway. What is atypical, however, is for a railway to create a country. Kenya is presumably the only country in the world that exists because of a railway, and in this case, a Nile railway.

The background is this. The British government had already decided to build a railway to Kisumu in 1895. Opponents dubbed it the 'Lunatic Railway'. A radical member of parliament, Henry Labouchère, who occasionally wrote lampoons (George Curzon was Under-Secretary of State for Foreign Affairs at that time), put it like this:

What is the use of it, none can conjecture,
What it will carry, there's none can define,
And in spite of George Curzon's superior lecture,
It is clearly naught but a lunatic line.

British strategists, however, refused to be influenced by what they considered to be narrow-minded, ignorant critique. The railway was a key element in the general imperial strategy because it would help make the British masters of the Nile. Indicative of the railway's political significance, the rail-laying work and operations had a special committee in London's Foreign Office. The railway made it clear to everyone that London in practice regarded and treated the sources of the Nile as their territory. The British built the 930-kilometre line, which undulates across the many hill ranges between the Indian Ocean and Lake Victoria, in record time.

The British also negotiated an agreement with the Maasai, the Nilotic ethnic group that several centuries previously had migrated from Southern Sudan and now controlled large swathes of the Kenyan highlands and was a group that many feared. Olomana, their spiritual leader, accepted that the railway could be built straight across their land, thereby destroying grazing routes. This event thus corresponded to an apocalypse narrative among the Maasai; coincidentally, their doomsday myth contained an 'iron snake' that would slither through their land.

On 19 December 1901, the tracks reached Lake Victoria, almost 1,000 kilometres from Mombasa. The terminal station was called Port Florence, named after Florence

Preston, wife of chief engineer Ronald O. Preston. Mrs Preston had accompanied her husband on the maiden trip and was given the honour of driving the first train over the last few metres towards the great Nile lake. Port Florence was later renamed Kisumu, though the train from Nairobi to Kisumu was still for more than a hundred years called the Port Florence Express.

Both the single-track railway and the port where the train ended had an air of belonging to the past, but when I left the train after two days, sleeping overnight in a couchette, it was easy to understand the early nineteenth-century descriptions, euphoric and somewhat hyperbolic, of the railway, winding its way from sea level to 2,300 metres:

> The Uganda railway, which is now practically completed, is a magnificent monument to the skill, perseverance, and energy of the engineers who have designed and constructed it. The railway rises from the level of the sea at Mombasa, with a maximum gradient of 2 feet in 100, to a height of 8,320 feet above the sea, and then it drops again to 3,770 feet at the shores of Lake Victoria Nyanza. Throughout its length of 584 miles from the sea to the lake the railway is rarely on the flat, and its course is rarely in a straight line. It is almost always twisting and winding among the hills, and, at the same time, either raising itself on gradients, often as steep as 1:50, over some eminence, or dropping into a valley at the same rate of descent.[1]

In books written about colonialism, this railway is usually described as a classic example of how Britain siphoned out raw materials from the continent's interior: they built the railway in order to ship cotton out of Uganda. However, in the first place, there was nowhere near enough cotton in Uganda to justify the investment. In the second place, it was obvious from the start that this was a 'political' railway – as Winston Churchill also termed it in *My African Journey* – more than an enterprise motivated by this type of conventional colonial resource extraction. Finally, the actual course of its construction underscores the point: the railway only reached Uganda and Kampala in 1931. That is, it took thirty years to extend the railway from Eldoret to Kampala, but only a few years to lay it all the way from the Indian Ocean to the lake. The goal, therefore, was not to transport Uganda's cotton out of the continent to Lancashire but, instead, to make Lake Victoria a part of the empire.

Kenya was occupied by Great Britain not because the British were primarily interested in acquiring the territory as such. The region was poor in raw material, and trade there was very limited, indeed. Economically, the area was described as a 'dead country', just bare wilderness. Obviously, there were economic groups in Great Britain that earned money by financing this government project, but the region was occupied only because it was on the way to Uganda and Lake Victoria.

The construction of this railway has also fascinated Hollywood, mostly due, I would suggest, to the role played by man-eating lions. Both *Bwana Devil* from 1952 and *The Ghost and the Darkness* from 1996 achieve dramatic high points with railway workers being eaten by lions. Tracks were laid over a bridge that would span the Tsavo River. The workers lived in camps along the riverbank. Night after night lions appeared in the camps and broke into the tents, seizing one worker after another. Panic spread, and the movies centre on Hollywood's undying obsession with the battle between humans and wild nature. Only after the lions had claimed twenty-eight lives were they shot and nature conquered.

To follow the Nile railway is to follow the axis around which Kenya's modern history has revolved. Later, it would also prove significant to the country's development. Both the 'settler question' and the 'Asian question' in contemporary Kenya are direct consequences of this railway. In addition, British attempts to provide the Jews with a national home here are also connected to the railway.

The Asian and the Jewish questions

'The Asian is the eternal "other"', wrote author and Nobel Prize winner Shiva Naipaul after visiting East Africa in the 1970s.[2] He pointed to the position of the Asians in the societies there and attributed this, in his typical melancholy fashion, largely to what one might call the Asian self-image and world view, and to the ways in which the individual Asian relates to Africa. Naipaul's novel, *A Bend in the River*, also portrays Salim, an Asian man caught in a susceptible ambivalence: he is neither European nor African. Salim cannot become African or an African nationalist; nor is he an apologist for the West, although he recognizes the West's historical significance. This historical position as an 'outsider' in East Africa is primarily a result of Asian immigration history. Asians were summoned to exercise Western technological superiority on a continent that was foreign to them.

The British did not use African labour to work on the railway. Rather, they used Indian railway builders, of whom they already had experience on the Indian subcontinent. The Indians arrived by dhows, the generic name for the traditional Arabic sailing vessels that are still used in trade between the Persian Gulf and East Africa. By the end of the nineteenth century, these sailing vessels had transported, with the help of monsoon winds, 34,000 Indians to Kenya.

When the railway stood finished, thousands of Indians were already employed as farmers or gardeners, or they conducted small business ventures. Kenya had acquired an Asian minority. Conflicts steadily emerged between the Asians and the British rulers, not least over position and number of places in the country's legislative assembly. The Indians considered it a victory when, in the wake of hard political battles, they acquired five places in 1929 against eleven held by the whites – despite the fact many times more Indian than white settlers were in the country. Africans, for their part, had no legislative representation. At the time, they were not even considered when it came to debates about governing the country.

Today, Indians live across Kenya, and also in Uganda, where they have returned after Idi Amin expelled them, and they play an important role in the region's economic and technological development.

As the train slowly travels the high plains towards Lake Victoria, I gaze north out of the window and ask myself: what if these Upper Nile basin plains had indeed become the Jewish national homeland? How would world history have looked then, and what would have happened in the Nile region?

It is 23 August 1903, in Basel, Switzerland. Theodor Herzl, leader of the Zionist movement, which he founded and organized a few years before, strides towards the rostrum and looks out upon the assembly of 600 delegates from different Jewish communities. Like a shock wave, it runs through the gathering that Herzl, their leader, supports the British government's proposal for a Jewish national homeland in East Africa! This proposal threatens to splinter the entire Zionist movement.

Since 1895 London had been concerned with how the railway to the Upper Nile could produce enough revenue to support its maintenance and operation – preferably without calling on the British taxpayer. Therefore, the British dreamed up various ideas for transforming Kenya into a more profitable colony and for securing the railway's running and upkeep. The government wished to solve two problems at once, and, as leaders of world history's greatest empire, they naturally thought big. In August 1903 the British government issued a public statement: Joseph Chamberlain, Secretary of State for the Colonies, had offered the Zionist leader, Dr Herzl, a Jewish national homeland in East Africa!

The new Jewish homeland would be built on the Kenyan high plains. London offered Herzl and the Jews swathes of the Mau Plateau, the area south-east of Mount Elgon. The southern border would be drawn approximately along the railway, and the western border almost down to Lake Victoria. In the literature there are now and then references to a Jewish homeland in Uganda, but this is false. The actual proposal concerned a large region within today's Kenya, and the misunderstanding regarding Uganda could be because this area was part of the Ugandan protectorate up until the turn of the century. As such, it was along the White Nile's tributaries north of the railway line and in the western part of the country that the Jews could settle, but without, however, being given territorial rights over the railway or over Lake Victoria's shores.

The offer was proposed directly after the violent pogroms against the Jews in Russia. When the idea was taken up by the Zionist Congress in Basel in 1903, Herzl recommended the Kenyan high plains as a temporary site of protection. Yet, the matter was so divisive that the Uganda Plan, as it is termed in the Zionist historical literature, almost destroyed the new Zionist movement. With a vote of 295 to 177, it was decided to send an 'investigatory commission' to the region around the Nile railway. The next year the delegation was dispatched. The commission's report was critical, both due to the Maasai and to the lions in the area. The next Zionist Congress in 1905 rejected London's proposal. In Israel, the label Latter-Day Ugandists is sometimes used by the most active Zionists as a contemptuous label for peace movements in the country, as a characteristic of those willing to surrender the 'promised land'.

Still, how would the Nile Valley appear today if the Zionist Congress had followed Herzl's advice in 1903? Given the ability of the Jews to make the desert bloom in arid Israel, it is obvious they would have focused greatly on agriculture and irrigation in the regions down toward Lake Victoria. Today, rumours in Egypt have it that Israel is plotting war over Nile water to weaken the Arab world and Egypt. Had the Israeli 'promised land' become a twelfth Nile basin state, not only the Nile's but all of world history would have turned out very differently.

The Jews, therefore, did not become the solution to Britain's railway dilemma, so London had to look elsewhere. The answer was to import white settlers.

The white tribe on the high plains

Here we have a territory (now that the Uganda Railway is built) admirably suited for a white man's country and I can say this with no thought of injustice to any native race, for the country in question is either utterly uninhabited for miles and miles or at most its inhabitants are wandering hunters who have no settled home, or whose fixed habitation is the lands outside the healthy area.[3]

Thus, wrote botanist, author, colonialist and British Special Commissioner to Uganda, Sir Harry Johnston, in 1901 regarding the Uasin Gishu Plateau, directly after he, as London's negotiator, signed an agreement with the four-year-old *kabaka* of Buganda in 1900. Uasin Gishu is a Maasai name, since the Maasai had long lived there. At the beginning of the twentieth century, however, they had been largely driven away by rival ethnic groups. For many explorers and administrators, it was clear early on that the Kenyan highlands, with their cooler climate and the relative absence of any African population over large regions, held enormous possibilities for European settlement. Johnston and others regarded the site as no less than perfect for white settlers. For this reason, Johnston was also strongly critical of the proposal to send Jews there: the country ought to be reserved for subjects of the British Empire, ideally from Great Britain itself. After all, were they not the ones who paid taxes and had financed the railway?

Johnston is also interesting as an example of the way colonialists created their own historical narratives and ensured their propagation. In 1899 Johnston wrote *The Colonization of Africa by Alien Races*, a book that until the early 1960s was used by many African universities in the countries the British governed as the best and most scientifically weighted text on Africa's history.

For those in the British colonial administration at the height of the empire's power, the issue was simple and crystal clear. Here there were enormous open land areas with a good climate, and both the state and the British-built railway needed more income. Only white emigrants had the competence to make the land sufficiently profitable, 'so let us import them'. Of course, this would affect the natives but, in the grand scheme of things, it would benefit the region. Thus, ran the main line of thought. The segregation, furthermore, of Europeans, Indians and Africans was considered an entirely acceptable policy well into the 1920s, and was justified by culture, languages, interests, cleanliness and so forth. This policy, it was emphasized again and again, especially by people within the Church, should not be regarded as discrimination. Instead, it was simply a practical solution, an organization the British believed to be in everyone's best interests, a vivid example, in retrospect, of how self-interest has the perpetual tendency to be represented as being in the interests of all.

Historically, it is an indisputable fact that, prior to British arrival, these regions were incapable of supporting large numbers of people within the existing frameworks of dominant and traditional African modes of production. When the Europeans arrived, large areas were also uninhabited due to local wars. The Europeans could increase productivity by introducing ox-drawn ploughs and by digging deep wells that would solve what was a permanent problem – water. The imported white farmers were also better equipped to manage and cope with bad harvests since they had technology that enabled them to store supplies over longer periods of time. The British, therefore, posed the question: why not cultivate these immense areas, since the world needed food? It was ridiculous – indeed, a sign of indolence approaching iniquity – to let them lie fallow. British missionaries and political radicals, by contrast, were against importing white settlers to conduct agriculture, and they insisted that the country belonged to Africans: given time the Africans themselves would develop the country and the agriculture. The victors of this tug of war were ultimately the people who believed the region was both a No Man's Land and a White Man's Land.

The need for tax-producing economic activity and thus for white settlers after the railway was built required the region through which it ran to be distinguished as a country separate from the much larger Protectorate of Uganda. The reason for this was simple: one article of the agreement from 1900 that the British had entered with the Buganda kingdom stated that they could not rent land to European immigrants. In order to open the door to such land areas, in 1902 parts of the Protectorate of Uganda (which until then stretched all the way to the Indian Ocean) were renamed the East African Protectorate – later called Kenya – with a single stroke of the pen. Now the land could be leased to outsiders and the king of Buganda could not protest the action on legal grounds. It was, however, in the fertile highlands up towards Mt. Kenya that most of the immigrants eventually moved and confiscated the land of the kikuyu farmers living there.

Since Kenya was now directly and formally annexed by London, the attitude toward Asian land rights in Kenya became a hot political topic in India. The obvious discrimination in Kenya put wind in the sails of nationalists in India. They waved the policy as proof that the British were not truthful when they talked about 'equality' in the Commonwealth. The Kenyan policy established 'the dangerous, non-acceptable principle of white dominance', as the Indian nationalist party put it.

It was the British overall Nile strategy, therefore, that was the foundation for the distinctive relationship between Europeans, Asians and Africans in Kenya. The railway's history can serve as an example of the many benefits that lie in studying a question with the help of comparisons over long time spans. As a rule, it tends to turn out that, within a long-term perspective, things are more intricate and complex than the conventional perspective would have us believe. To discuss colonialism as a 'calamity' or a 'one-armed bandit' is as mistaken as discussing it as overall civilizational progress. This is the Janus face of colonialism, and the same is true of the railway that winds so materially and concretely through Kenya and the country's history.

Kenya's segregation policy cannot simply be explained as a general result of the nature of colonialism: rather, it is an unusual consequence of an unorthodox railway. The settler regions formed a unique society, probably one of the most aristocratic in modern European colonial history. The settlers shaped their own world. The highlands' enormous wheat fields, coffee plantations and wide sheep pastures alternated with cricket pitches, polo grounds and tennis courts, and the enormous swathes devoted to big-game hunting, eventually giving the landscape an exceedingly fashionable air. In her novel, *Out of Africa*, a story about white settlers on the Kenyan highlands, Karen

Blixen wrote that 'perhaps the white men of the past, indeed of any past, would have been in a better understanding and sympathy with the coloured races than we, of our Industrial Age, shall ever be. When the first steam engine was constructed, the roads of the races of the world parted, and we have never found each other since'.[4] Yet, even for the white settlers, life was uncertain, and Blixen was forced to surrender the farm she loved because the government failed her.

The British colonial authorities bet on 'the white man' to increase the railway's revenue and thereby to secure support and legitimacy for the imperial system in Britain. They simply had to create economic activity to finance the railway's operation and maintenance. Recruiting agents were sent to England and South Africa to search for settlers. The land areas these people received were mainly located in regions connected to the railway. The presence of the white population in Kenya is one of the many reasons it is impossible to understand Kenya's history without understanding both the Nile and Britain's Nile strategy, and it is therefore striking how marginal the Nile question has been in the country's own historical narrative of itself. Even the city that became the capital, Nairobi, is a result of Nile policy: the city was built at its precise location because it was approximately midway on the railway line to the Nile lake.

A Nile state with no nation

'We Kenyans never learn. We have to stop blaming the colonial past every time something goes wrong.' I am talking to one of Kenya's history professors. We are standing and looking out at the University of Nairobi's lawn where groups of stylishly dressed students sit and chat. She talks about the murders in Eldoret on Uasin Gishu Plateau. On New Year's Day in 2008, a local church was set on fire and thirty unarmed people were burned alive because they belonged to the wrong ethnic group. Twelve hundred were killed and almost 500,000 fled from their homes before a truce between the parties, negotiated by former UN General Secretary, Kofi Annan, once again established peace and order in the country.

My friend, the professor, had a valid point: colonialism has long shouldered too much blame for Africa's lack of development, its corruption, political chaos and ethnic struggles. Such traditional critique is, as some influential African intellectuals insist today, often unjust and non-reflective. It introduces an unfruitful historicization of Africa's own contemporary problems, which might also be created by the country and its population.

At the same time, there can be no doubt that the state the British created between the Indian Ocean and the Nile's main reservoir was uncommonly artificial and lacked both an organic and an historical basis. Kenya essentially exists today because leading British strategists regarded the Nile as a geopolitical factor in the 1890s, something that once again reflects the Nile's hydrological character, and which resulted in the Protectorate of Uganda being divided. What is the significance of the way that Kenya was established and developed to theories of state formation in general?

One of the most contentious questions within the fields of history and social science is the way in which states emerge. What I mean by 'state' here is an autonomous political unity that encompasses and includes many smaller communities within its territory, and where there exists a centralized administration with sufficient power to impose and collect taxes, implement laws, and institute and establish armies and other forms of power. In the Nile basin, it is evident that state formations are not necessary products of a natural, generic historical development. For hundreds of thousands of years people lived in small groups, as hunters and gatherers. Eventually, they established fixed dwellings and agriculture emerged. Only around 5000 BCE did small groups of people begin to gradually merge into greater political unities. In the Nile basin this process occurred in what today is Egypt around 3000 BCE, when the country – Upper and Lower Egypt – was united under one pharaoh. In Nubia a similar development took place around 4,500 years ago; in Ethiopia almost 2,000 years ago; in Uganda 400 years ago; and in South Sudan only in our own day.

In order to understand the Nile basin's history and the present situation of the Nile, it is imperative to realize that states do not develop naturally but instead are created, often under exceedingly diverse conditions. After all, how did this region look in 1890, when the British won acceptance from other European countries to declare the Nile its sphere of interest? Egypt was definitely a state formation, strong as always. Sudan was a state under the Mahdi's theocratic rule, though its legitimacy was unclear in parts of the country. There were kingdoms in parts of what became Uganda, and in what was Rwanda and Burundi, some of them with strong positions also legitimized on religious grounds. And in the Ethiopian highlands the emperor governed together with the Orthodox Church. Otherwise, there were no nation states. No empires. No caliphates. Large regions were ruled by clans and tribes without any state interference. Borders existed but not in the European sense. They were cultural and linguistic and at times military, but they were also porous, entirely lacking the sharp divisions that became the European tradition after the Peace of Westphalia. The colonial nation-state logic that originated in the spirit and mentality of the Peace of Westphalia process conflicted with traditions and relationships in an Africa with an entirely different political-ideological background. New borders were drawn, not necessarily in place of the old more expedient borders, but relative to an external logic, to the empire's logic. It was the imperial rationale that mattered, and in Kenya this rationale was – viewed from the position of the people who inhabited the region from which the state was established – fundamentally connected to an artificial, irrational, foreign and imposed state formation.

In order to understand today's Kenya, it is of course imperative to acknowledge that there were no conditions in the region's history prior to 1890 that would dispose the people living within the future country's borders to develop a plan for a greater nation-building or state-building process. Economic activity, population size and the natural environment were such that a voluntary surrender of autonomy for the sake of state formation was irrational, nor was there anyone with sufficient economic interest, or who was strong enough economically or militarily, to subjugate all the other ethnic groups, illustrated by the fact that local conflicts over grazing land and cattle formed part of the region's daily life. The Africanist, Basil Davidson, has characterized Africa as if it were a continent of strong kingdoms, with autonomous actors who apparently were, and desired to be, midwives to their own state's birth: Africa's current states did not emerge from 'the void of a motionless past'.[5] There can be no doubt that Davidson is correct in pointing out previous state formations such as Egypt, Nubia and Ethiopia. The moment, however, that these descriptions are generalized to cover the entire Nile basin they become erroneous, and interesting and differing histories of state formation disappear.

In order to illustrate just how unusual Kenya's state history is, we can compare it to some other widespread theories regarding why states emerge. Kenya as a state formation certainly cannot be characterized as the unavoidable product of a general form of cultural globalization, which itself produces a new framework for identity politics in the wake of modernity's triumph, and which, on that basis, creates nation states and national feelings. Nor can it be regarded (as the national state is in many other places) as a remnant from, or a rediscovery of, an earlier era of nationalist mobilization and conflicts. The Kenyan state is not the remains or product of historical precursors, nor the residue of another epoch. And it is also not the consequence of modernity. Kenya exists; it is a state represented in the United Nations, it has its own flag, its own parliament, its own national symbols and national heroes, but the presence of these attributes or borders cannot be interpreted as an expression of the way in which modern society organizes its encounter with globalization. The Kenyan state also does not serve as an example of a third explanatory model – that nations are a constant, that is to say, that they are neither remnants of, nor a functional answer to, the challenges of the modern or premodern world.

The borders of modern Kenya were drawn as a solution to no other societal need than Britain's strategic interests and the plans to secure its control over Lake Victoria. This state formation lacked any roots in the societies it brought under its domain: it was created exclusively by an external power, and that external power's dominant minority, which entered the scene and built a state that would benefit their interests.

The British colonies in the Nile basin were not self-governing entities. The role of the governors-general or the district commissioners was to implement imperial policy. Whitehall and the Colonial Office held the power. The governors in Nairobi were their instruments and received their orders. The local government was, therefore, primarily a machine designed to execute London's overarching strategy. This did not mean, however, that the centre was always all-powerful. For example, Churchill criticized the unnecessary brutality in the establishment of British authority over isolated ethnic groups at the beginning of the twentieth century, and disagreements often surfaced, and sometimes persisted – as, for example, regarding how to handle the so-called Mau Mau Rebellion in the 1950s. Even if the white settlers felt themselves to be the chosen elite in Kenya, they did not have the power or opportunity to consider developmental projects related to the use of Nile waters. On the Nile question they had no influence whatsoever. When it came to the distribution and use of its waters, London determined all.

During the colonial era, Kenya's white rulers must have felt a strong need for the order and context that rituals create, and must further have had a certain understanding of their ability to legitimize an externally formed state: the archives in Nairobi contain five hundred files on just such rituals.[6] Uncertainty regarding the legitimacy of power is a general phenomenon in many state-societies, and this could be one of the reasons that so many states at times appear like stages in theatrical power plays. Rituals tend, of course, to re-enact and reconfirm a society's values, and elevate forms of social organization as being especially attractive or valid. A basic aspect of the rituals practised by the elite in power might be to give those in control faith in their ability to exercise power through the state, and in Kenya this might have been particularly important as compensation for the absence of other preconditions.

It is common to distinguish between nation and state: the first is an organism, the second a territorial organization. The modern notion of nation states assumes that it produces the best aspects of both: power becomes accountable and society can defend itself against that power. What contributed to creating an African and Kenyan nationalism was, paradoxically, the segregation of Africans vis-à-vis whites and Asians. After all, the British state-bearing ideology was a distinctive brew – not based on any form of nationalism but on rhetoric about civilizational values and ethnic separation. This organization, however, eventually shaped a kind of 'Africanness' among the country's original ethnic groups, for it was through this very segregation policy that they developed a sense of common community; they all found themselves in the same subordinate relationship to the same state authority. Within this cultural atmosphere, the tale of one of the leading Kenyan nationalists, Tom Mboya, can serve as a telling expression of a collective feeling of segregation and discrimination. He writes in his book, *Freedom and After*, that many years ago, when the English still ruled Kenya, a European woman walked into the office where he sat working. She looked around and said, more to herself than to anyone else: 'Is there anybody here?'

The state that the Kenyans took over and inherited in 1963 has steadily become stronger under the leadership of presidents like Jomo Kenyatta, Daniel arap Moi, Mwai Kibaki and Uhuru Kenyatta. There has, of course, been legitimate criticism of authoritarianism, ethnic favouritism, elite corruption and the like but, seen in long perspective, the political leadership has aimed at shaping a nation based on the state they were handed by mobilizing the new middle class elite and trying to incite faith in Kenya's future. Nonetheless, they have not yet entirely succeeded in taking what has been described as 'the bread out of the chief's mouth'.[7] But even the dreadful clashes and ethnic violence in 2007–8, and the extensive political debate following the adoption of a new constitution in the conflict's wake seem to have had a nation-building effect.

Amid the ashes of the Eldoret church bonfire was, however, an uncomfortable truth: the Nile strategy that framed and channelled London's thinking in specific directions throughout the region had profound consequences in many other areas of society besides simply those concerned with water use. It is a historical irony that this country, which was built because it happened to be located on the British route to the sources of the Nile, can now more easily realize itself as an independent state by fighting for its rights to exploit the rivers running down to the very lake that the British came in order to conquer.

Olympic masters from the 'stony river'

Eldoret, the capital of Uasin Gishu, is situated in the heart of the African continent, not far from the railway line running between the Indian Ocean and Lake Victoria. It was one of the many cities to emerge in the railway's wake, and which, over the course of a few years, brought central portions of Kenya into contact with the global market and with global trade.

The name Eldoret comes from a Maasai word meaning the 'stony river' – a river that runs through what would later become a city and which finally empties into Lake Victoria. The city was founded right after the turn of the nineteenth century and originally it was just a post office called '64', because it was located sixty-four miles (103 kilometres) from what was the centre of the world, namely, the railway. The first inhabitants came from South Africa, 280 of them arriving in Mombasa in 1909. Equipped with prefabricated houses, ploughs, wagons, cattle and sheep, they slowly made their way toward the highlands, forty-two wagons heading for '64' to establish the city.

Eldoret is not world famous today due to its origin, and certainly not because of its size, even though it is currently one of Kenya's fastest growing cities. Instead, Eldoret and the Kenyan highlands achieved international renown with the 1968 Olympic Games in Mexico City. Kenya's great hope, Kip Keino, had first collapsed during the 10,000 metres race. After that he took silver in the 5,000 metres. In his third race, the 1,500 metres, he was racing against the favourite, the American Jim Ryan, notorious for his merciless sprints. In order to beat Ryan on the final lap, the Kenyans used team tactics. Keino's teammate, Ben Jipcho, adopted a murderous tempo during the first two laps. Then Keino shot ahead at just under 800 metres. His lead on Ryan was too great for a sprint to save the American. To wild applause, for the first time a Kenyan had won a gold medal in the Olympic 1,500 metres. His time was an Olympic record: 3 minutes 34.9 seconds. This victory was the start of a Kenyan racing adventure, in which runners became the country's foremost ambassadors.

Keino came from Eldoret, and the Upper Nile basin city has since become a Mecca for long-distance runners; international companies exploit the city's fame and invest in training equipment and studios. The reason is obvious: From this area, the Nandi Hills, the world's best long-distance runners come. The Kalenjin people, who make up approximately 10 per cent of Kenya's population with around three million individuals, have earned more medals in long-distance running in the Olympics and World Championships since the early 1990s than the United States, Russia and Europe combined. Kip Keino, Mike Boit, Wilson Kipketer (who became a Danish citizen), Moses Tanui, Tegla Loroupe, Paul Tergat, Moses Kiptanui – all Kalenjin and coming from the same area.

The reasons for this are debated. The local climate is essential. At around 2,000 metres above sea level, the region is assured a comfortable climate and the height increases oxygen intake. The region, furthermore, has little in common with classic images of African poverty. Malnourishment is, so to speak, non-existent, and almost everyone attends school. When Keino was a boy, he cared for his family's animals and darted around a landscape dominated by hills. Born to modest circumstances, he became responsible for feeding and watering the family's livestock. He then began school at twelve years of age. Together with his friends, he ran well over 10 kilometres every Monday, carrying enough food and milk on his back for a whole week, and then he ran back every Friday evening to help his family with the cattle. Keino has said that they ran in groups to protect themselves against leopards.

Others have suggested that the development of special genes might be the root cause of the runners' success. Over time the Kalenjin people evolved bodies that could endure high speed and long distances, and the best runners prevailed. Since they did not have horses, camels or cars, they simply had to use their legs. But no matter what the true and most fundamental cause is, it is also important in this context that the British exported their sports culture, including track sports and racecourses, to Kenya. This meant that the country was ready to launch their own national team the very same year that the colonialists' flag – a British Blue Ensign with a red lion – was lowered as the national flag for the last time. And since then practically all the top runners have come from this Upper Nile basin region.

Masai Mara

'Ready?' The pilot turns to look at us and smiles. After that, she provides no more information but gives the engine plenty of gas. The small plane takes off from Wilson Airport, Nairobi; we are on our way to Masai Mara. We are looking down on enormous swathes of forest, a village here and there, large farms in between, with cloudlets lovingly brushing the light brown and green landscape. We land at the Masai Mara reservation, located in south Kenya in the eastern part of the Nile basin.

Driving from the airport to the camp where we will spend the night, we pass giraffes, lions, hyenas and ostriches. This is the land of the Maasai, of whom it is said they know the grass's song and the snake's speech, and who move like slender shadows across the savannah. There is scarcely a more iconized people along the entire Nile river system, and here they conform to their touristic stereotype, standing with red blankets thrown across their shoulders and wandering the plains with spear in hand, silhouetted against the sun.

A few mornings later and the sun is not yet up. I am standing with a small group of people, shivering in the cool morning, as a weak light flickers a few hundred metres away. The sound from that direction grows louder and louder. A large, yellow-and-green striped balloon opens as the sky is just taking on a red sheen in the east. The balloon pilot summons me and explains how to crawl up into the basket and sit hunched over and calm as the balloon takes off. There is hardly any wind. As the flames extend up into the balloon, filling it with the hot air we need in order to leave the ground, the sun brightens the Mara Plains, though the mountains in the distance are still partially obscured in mist. Mornings come quickly on the equator and soon the entire plains are bathed in sunshine.

Beneath me is Masai Mara – the nature reserve where wildebeest arrive in their millions every year in search of grass and water (their numbers increased particularly after the 1970s due to the successful control of rinderpest). Across the plains flow rivers, large and small, and there are streams and waterholes; it is a true Eldorado for thirsty animals trekking from the dry Serengeti that lies to the south of us. It is here that the world's largest, and by far most spectacular, animal migration takes place.

I can hear the long grass bending against the basket as the balloon lands. I stand, climb out and receive a glass of champagne while the pilot talks about his fears regarding changes to the Mara River's water flow, which could cause the wildebeest population to collapse, bringing it down to a level from which it could not recover. If that happens – so say the most pessimistic – thousands of jobs will be lost, significant local income will vanish and tourism will be destroyed. The Mara River could thus set in motion a chain reaction that will lead to an ecological and economic disaster.

The Mara River originates in the Napuiyapi swamp on the Kenyan highlands, 2,392 metres above sea level, and it meanders in a great arc about 395 kilometres long and down to Lake Victoria. After the Mau Escarpment, a 3,000-metre-high cliff formation on the Great Rift Valley's western side, it runs – having now absorbed numerous smaller rivers – through open savannah and over the enormous grass plains where the Maasai and their cattle rule. After crossing the Masai Mara Reserve, the river then becomes the Kenyan–Tanzanian border, where it passes into the even more famous Serengeti National Park. The Mara River forms the main artery within the Masai Mara and Serengeti national parks. The river itself is no impressive, foaming flood, but even though it appears humble, it plays a fundamental role in the local ecology and economy. In the dry season the river is shallow, but its discharge may double during the rainy season. The quantity of water varies significantly over a period of years, and during a single year. At the start of the 2000s, however, it was suggested that climate change and deforestation had also reduced the river's flow over time.

Within the debate in Kenya, two causes are typically blamed for such changes to the ecosystem: climate and upstream land use. Since vegetation has increasingly been cleared to make way for large farms and indigent settlements, rainwater flows more quickly into the river. That produces more flooding and results in large portions of the Tanzanian Mara wetlands becoming more permanent. If this trend continues, the wildebeest will no longer need to undertake their seasonal migration to Masai Mara and the spectacular animal migration will be history, along with parts of Kenya's tourism industry.

After he was elected in 2008, Prime Minister Raila Odinga said that few things were more critical to Kenya's future than saving the largest indigenous montane forest in East Africa, the Mau Forest. The government introduced stricter laws, evicting (against heavy protests), the poor who had settled there illegally, and initiating an afforestation campaign. By focusing on afforestation, the government not only implemented a local solution but also presented itself as a high-profile, good example of how, in the age of globalization, new types of global movements can emerge which give legitimation and justification for local political initiatives. Afforestation, in addition to its local benefits, has become a global rite meant to express community spirit and belief in the future: it is meant to solve ecological problems but it will also, due to the ritualization of expectations of growth and life, engender a useful community attitude through the reminder or idea of a common experience.

There are few countries where the global afforestation movement figures so prominently as in Kenya. In part, that is due to Kenya's Nobel Prize winner, Wangari Maathai, who was awarded the prize specifically because she focused on afforestation as a tool against conflict. However, this movement can also be interpreted as symptomatic of a new political-ecological consciousness spreading throughout the basin. The Nile river system is a treasure, people say more and more often, a treasure more valuable than anything else, but it can be destroyed if the water and river and basin, along with all the trees that grow within its precipitation area, are not properly cared for.

The Luo and Barack Obama's journey

The Luo people, who live along the east coast of Lake Victoria in Kenya, were until recently an ethnic group unknown outside the country. That all changed in 2008, at least for a while, for Barack Obama, the former president of the United States, is half Luo.

Within the Nile basin, it is not only water that has been in constant motion for millennia. There has also been a steady stream of people and ethnic groups who have defied the rainforest's darkness and impenetrability, who have awaited the dry season along the riverbanks in order to ford the water after the rain has stopped and the flooding receded, and who have clashed violently with other ethnic groups, in a constant search and battle for water and grazing grounds. The Luo arrived on the shores of Lake Victoria around 500 years ago.

The Luo are called River Lake Nilotes and this name underscores how their entire society is woven into and affected by the hydroecological conditions in which their social institutions and traditions have developed. The group migrated from today's South Sudan, presumably from the area where the tributary rivers, the Meride and Sue, meet before ending in the Bahr al-Ghazal, another tributary of the White Nile. The Luo are linguistically related to, among others, the Nuer and Dinka in South Sudan; to the Anuak in Ethiopia and Sudan, who are still cattle-owning people; and to the Acholi in Uganda, who, like themselves, have established permanent settlements. It is uncertain why the Luo left South Sudan but, according to oral tradition, it was the warrior chieftain Ramogi Ajwang who some 500 years ago led them into today's Kenya.

When Lord Lugard, as a representative for the British Imperial East Africa Company, approached Lake Victoria's east bank in the early 1890s, he came across this large group of people who engaged in agriculture, fishing and a little cattle-herding, and who always went about naked, men as well as women. No one attended school because there were no schools; no one lived in cities because there were no cities; no one wore clothes because there were no clothes; and so forth. Another Briton, John Wallace Pringle, the Nairobi–Kisumu railway's chief engineer, wrote about the Luo in step with the paternalistic ideology of conquest that characterized European public opinion at the time, and, not least, the first colonists:

> They have the negro type of face, with large mouth, thick, protruding lips, and prognathous jaws. They are not a warlike race. Their spears have very long shafts and small, badly-fastened iron heads, which are nearly always rusty and dirty; their shields are also ill-shaped and ill-made. As a rule, they carry no weapons of any sort, but a pointed stick; and when once they have ascertained that a caravan has no ill intentions, they swarm into the camp entirely unarmed and unclothed, and show most friendly feeling. [...] They have fine herds of cattle, sheep, and goats, but

have no encouragement to increase their flocks, which are always a great attraction to their more warlike neighbours of Nandi and Lumbwa.[8]

Today, the Luo are among Kenya's largest ethnic groups, though their spokespersons have long criticized the government in Nairobi for neglecting the group's needs and interests. The Luo also never allied themselves with the British, as the Kikuyu did for long periods, and have historically regarded themselves as having been dominated by the Kikuyu. Like most ethnic groups in Africa, they have been extensively studied by European and other foreign anthropologists, but in recent years also by Luo anthropologists. One of the most conspicuous characteristics of the traditional culture was the connection the group had to their land and that of their ancestors. The Luo, especially children and pregnant women, were known as 'dirt eaters'. It has been debated whether this compensated for a living oral history about being a wandering folk, and whether this attachment to ancestors and earth helped shape a general conservatism, a kind of lack of willingness to change. Whatever the reason, you can today walk into supermarkets in Kisumu and buy dirt collected from different places, and which is meant to be eaten.

Kit Mikayi is a stone formation about 20 metres tall that stands some 29 kilometres north of Kisumu on the west side of the road leading to the Obama family's village. The name means 'the stone of the first wife' or 'the first wife stone' in the Luo language. The fact that all things have a story to tell is a recurring theme in African animism or nature religion, conveying an anti-modern conception of how the present perpetually turns towards the past. The story concerning the stone goes like this. Long ago an old man lived here whose name was Ngeso and he loved the stone dearly. Every morning when he awoke, he made his way to a cave in the stone and remained there all day, and so every day his wife was forced to bring him his breakfast and lunch there. The old man became so violently enamoured of this stone, so obsessed by it, that one day people asked his wife what had happened. She answered that he had returned to his first wife, Mikayi. After that the rock was called 'stone of the first wife' (Kit Mikayi). The stone and the story therefore also represent the Luo tradition of polygamy.

For a long time, this stone has been a holy site for Luo celebrations and offerings. Seldom has the celebration been so great as on 1 November 2008, though there was no need for offerings then: Barack Obama's victory in the presidential election was regarded as a groundbreaking collective triumph; it was seen as a triumph over dominant stereotypes regarding Luo culture.

Nyangoma Kogelo was no longer the sleepy village it was before Obama's victory. At a restaurant in the local, newly built hotel that is appropriately called 'The White House', I some years later had freshly grilled, spicy fish. The road leading to the village had been freshly paved and power lines had been strung out here in record time. After all, was the message: this is where Obama's grandmother lives, it is where Sarah Obama lives, the old woman Obama has called 'Granny Sarah'!

I am driving down a red dirt road, passing women carrying corn to market and children in school uniform on their way home. At the end of the road, I reach the Obama farm, where calves lope and avocado trees grow, and where the locked gate is guarded by a policeman. Granny Sarah points me to one corner of the yard, which holds the grave of Obama's father. The words are simple: Barack Hussein Obama, born 1936, died 1982.

When talking to a smiling and very friendly Sarah Obama in the garden outside her house about life in Kenya, it strikes me what a fantastic journey the Obama family has undertaken, from here to the White House in Washington DC, from the Nile basin's periphery to the world's centre. Other things no doubt occupy Barack Obama's mind when he goes to bed at night, but such an abrupt and steep rise is something that no theory on the way societies function can explain. In this context, ideas like class mobility, class travelling, 'breaking with role expectations' or 'social mobility' appear like antiquated trivialities. Barack Obama's story makes our concepts about societies and roles seem archaic, for if anything is possible – and this example testifies to this – the usefulness of such concepts must be reconsidered.

Barack Obama himself, meanwhile, explained that this fairy tale was made possible by a foreign policy initiative launched by President John F. Kennedy. During a campaign rally in Selma, Alabama on March 2008, Obama said: 'So, the Kennedys decided "we're going to do an airlift [...]. We're going to go to Africa and start bringing young Africans over to this country and give them scholarships to study so they can learn what a wonderful country America is". This young man named Barack Obama [senior] got one of those tickets and came over to this country.'[9]

That story, however, was not entirely accurate since Obama's father was one of eighty-one students who went to the United States and began studying at the University of Hawaii a year before the Kennedy's idea was implemented. Still, it was the Kennedy family's private foundation that funded air travel for 243 students in 1960. Senator John F. Kennedy was the driving force, and Harry Belafonte and Sidney Poitier were among those who mustered support for the campaign. The Kenyan nationalist leader, Tom Mboya, also a Luo, lobbied for the initiative as well. Meanwhile, CIA documents that have later been made public show that the whole thing was also a cover-up to hide the heavy American foreign policy interests that lay behind the project, which was geared toward shaping a pro-American East African elite while the country was still under British control and the Cold War prevailed. Whatever the motives behind it, on 14 September 1960, two planeloads of African students landed in New York, thanks to the Joseph P. Kennedy Jr. Foundation.

Between 1959 and 1963, these operations brought almost 800 East African students – mainly Kenyans, but also a few from Tanganyika (now Tanzania) and Uganda – to the United States. The 'air transport generation' achieved remarkable success. When the students returned home, they became key politicians and researchers in their own countries. In Kenya they quickly occupied half the parliament and many of country's ministerial posts and highest offices. One of them was Wangari Maathai, winner of the 2004 Nobel Peace Prize.

The most important point here is not that the CIA or the Kennedys were behind the initiative. Instead, it is that the air travel was one of many examples of how the United States intentionally sought to win over the new elite in what everybody knew would soon be independent African states, and there can be no doubt that this was also the case with Kennedy's policy. The idea was not only to halt the spread of communism, as the Cold War rhetoric insisted, but to weaken Great Britain's privileged position in what would quickly become former colonies. I have read enough classified notes written by British envoys in the various Nile basin capitals to know that the British early on grasped the American threat to their Nile empire. One can almost picture their representatives in Africa, sitting and tearing their hair out. With an almost limitless sense of colonial paternalism, they viewed themselves as Africa's 'guardians', the ones who *knew* the continent, the ones who knew the language, the ones who had built the national institutions, and the ones who had the contacts and influence among the elite. And then came these young, ignorant Yankees, as they wrote, to squeeze them out. And they could do it, since Washington had the dollars, whereas London was bankrupt after the Second World War. As such, there is a clear connection between Secretary of State John Foster Dulles's gift of a pistol to the Egyptian anti-British coup-maker, Naguib, in 1953 and the airlift of East African students to New York in 1960: the United States wanted to end what they called the archaic European colonial system, which is to say, they wanted free trade. And they won; in the early 1960s the former British colonies in the Nile basin gained independence, and most of them turned to the United States as an ally.

The Luo's transformation from an ethnic group that a century ago walked naked along Lake Victoria's shores, in one of the world's least developed societies, to being able to claim the US president in 2008 as one of their own – and also to be able to celebrate that, for the first time, a Luo was prime minister in Kenya – took place against the backdrop of a practically unaltered Nile ecology. Until recently, all the rivers running through the Luo regions in western Kenya have flowed as they did when Lugard travelled the landscape in the 1890s.

Now that is also in the process of changing.

Kenya and the Nile question

'Flood, Death, and Destruction Across the Entire Country.' The front pages of Kenyan newspapers during December 2011 were full of dramatic stories about the way enormous quantities of rain over several weeks had 'left a trail of destruction'.[10]

I was in Kisumu when I heard about the catastrophic local flooding, so early in the morning we drove to the Nzoia River in western Kenya, the country's largest Nile tributary, to observe the damage and to talk to people. Tens of thousands were forced to flee to higher ground when the river overran its banks, decimating the dykes that had been built, and costing dozens of people their lives. Boutiques were half under water, schools and hospitals were closed, and the river had become a mighty and violent flood, surging through a village that typically stood dry-shod on its banks.

In western Kenya there are no significant dams to restrain water or to store it from the rainy season to the dry. There are a couple of power stations in the hills leading down towards Lake Victoria, and these have changed the region's social and economic life, since there is now electricity day and night and in many villages that previously were without. As one of the men with whom I spoke remarked when talking about these benefits: 'Now young people can get onto Facebook in the villages instead of having to travel all the way to Kisumu.' I also spoke with an American entrepreneur who owned and worked Kenya's largest rice farm, which is in the same region, and who became the country's most important rice producer in a matter of just a few years. Their goal is expansion. Now, the American told me, they largely use drainage water from the local swamp, but it is clear that in the long run the farm will need Nile water.

After 2010 the Kenyan government adopted a new Nile policy, a policy that has had, and will have, important consequences, both within the country and in the basin as a whole. This Kenyan Nile experience can be likened with a long and bumpy road. Independent Kenya viewed the colonial Nile agreements radically differently from the British in Kenya and had freedom to express their opinion about matters. Already in the early 1960s, the Kenyan parliament was considering asking Egypt for compensation for all the water the country was sending north, and which they were thus not able to use themselves. In the wake of the 1973–4 oil crisis, this Nile rhetoric gathered new wind in its sails. As Kenyan politicians said: since the Arabs take so much for the oil we buy, they will pay for the water we give them. Yet, every time politicians aired such initiatives, the government made them shut up. Kenya, meanwhile, has long made it clear that it does not accept the 1929 Agreement. The country's first president, the legendary Jomo Kenyatta, declared as early as 1963, the year in which Kenya gained its independence, that whomever had entered into any agreements on Kenya's behalf, prior to the country's independence, must step up and register themselves in the United Nations. He gave them a two-year deadline. Since no one accepted responsibility for these Nile agreements, Kenyatta declared them invalid.

The Nile rhetoric steadily became more explicit, including from top political quarters. In 2003, Minister of Foreign Affairs Moses Wetangula – coming from Kenya's western regions, which are located in the Nile basin – remarked, to applause from members of parliament: 'The government will not accept, under any circumstances, any further restrictions on the use of Lake Victoria waters as it was not party to, and was not consulted, before the treaty was signed.'[11]

Raila Odinga, former minister of energy and later prime minister, was also clear that the Nile Agreement from 1929 must be reviewed. As a representative of West Kenya and the Luo, he considered the matter urgent. Shifts in the geographical and ethnic centres of gravity in Kenyan politics toward West Kenya and the Nile basin are bad news for anyone in the downstream countries wanting to maintain the status quo in Nile-sharing arrangements. Kenyans have introduced more proactive water policies. They have plans for hydropower plants, but they especially want to use more water to irrigate the regions down towards Lake Victoria's shores. They will follow in Tanzania's footsteps, and intend to pump more lake water to cities and settlements with water shortages.

As quickly as it could, Kenya joined the agreement that Tanzania, Uganda, Rwanda and Ethiopia had entered and signed in Entebbe, Uganda, on 14 May 2010. When Kenya's water minister signed on Kenya's behalf, she said: 'Nothing now stops us from using the waters as we wish. It is now up to Egypt and Sudan to come on board in the spirit of cooperation based on One Nile, One Basin and One Vision. [...] Two states out of nine cannot stop us from implementing this framework.'[12]

In Kenya, people have long and publicly asked: is it fair that a country located thousands of kilometres downstream rules the lives of millions of people upstream? How long will the East Africa region entirely depend on erratic and undependable rainfall to feed itself? What kind of hypocrisy allowed Great Britain to bestow special status on Egypt at the expense of countries that have permanent problems with producing enough food to feed their populaces – because they have not been awarded the right to use their own water?

In 2010 President Mwai Kibaki and Prime Minister Raila Odinga launched an initiative that they claimed would solve the country's food crisis. The key to this new strategy was like that in other places: to transition from precipitation-based agriculture to irrigation agriculture. Old projects that had not functioned would be rehabilitated and new ones would be established. This focus on artificial irrigation should secure Kenya 14 million more bags of corn per harvest. Kenya's plan for self-sufficiency required, they claimed, that the country begin using Nile water, which until now had run almost unexploited and uncontrolled down to the world's second largest lake. This artificial irrigation strategy is part of the plan to achieve the goals of Kenya Vision 2030, which seeks to 'transform Kenya to a middle-income country by 2030 and provide a high-quality life to all citizens'.[13]

When I travelled along the Nzoia, I met people who were impatient, even as many were sceptical of any large, government-proposed dams that would force many to move. In 2012, in the wake of the flood catastrophe, the local and central authorities reached an agreement: the entire basin had to be subject to a comprehensive developmental plan. As a first step a large dam should be built, serving more than a million people in the basin, protecting them from flooding and providing them with energy and water for irrigation. The dam was viewed – as are all similar structures across all of Kenya's watercourses – as the very basis for regional development.

Kenya plans to put its straws into the Nile tributaries that run through the country's western regions down to Lake Victoria. This can seem threatening for Egypt, but the Egyptians should not worry too much or be too concerned. The Nile's physical nature will come to Egypt's rescue. Additionally, lack of political decisiveness in Kenya might postpone and reduce stated Nile ambitions.

Humanity's cradle

Tanzania is known throughout the world as a probable site of the beginning of history. To the west: the wide Serengeti plains; to the east, the Ngorongoro Crater. Around 500,000 years ago, volcanic activity located here, on the outermost edge of the Nile basin, forced the river to change direction. Over tens and hundreds of thousands of years it then cut its way across the savannah, exposing layer upon layer of fossils. A far distant past was revealed, and it was discovered by pure chance.

The story behind the discovery of the Olduvai Gorge is legendary in archaeological circles. A German entomologist, Wilhelm Kattwinkel, chased a beautiful butterfly here in the early 1900s. Abruptly, he tumbled over the gorge's edge, nearly killing himself in the process. When he regained his senses, he discovered, almost in a daze, that he had fallen into an archaeological dream world.

A few decades later, in the 1950s, palaeontology's 'first family', the Leakey family from Britain, laid the groundwork for their fantastic career when they began to dig here. In 1948 Mary Leakey had already discovered on Rusinga Island in Lake Victoria the skeletal remains of ancestors belonging to both humans and apes, named *Proconsul africanus*. In the Olduvai Gorge she excavated an early hominid skeleton fragment in 1959. Her husband, Louis Leakey, baptized the individual *Zinjanthropus boisei*, though he was nicknamed 'the Nutcracker Man' because it was believed his enormous canines came from nut-eating. Whether this was truly 'humanity's cradle', as Louis Leakey, with his famous sense for PR and one-liners, suggested, is obviously up for debate. Pinpointing humanity's cradle for good will always remain impossible because there is no certainty that a still older fossil will not be discovered at some future date. Nonetheless, the discovery was significant for an understanding of evolutionary history.

Mary Leakey's fragment of skeleton was estimated to be around 1,750,000 years old – and Nutcracker Man was a sensation. In 1960 Mary Leakey and her son, Jonathan, uncovered even more skeletons. They believed these to be different from, and more developed than, older hominids and termed them *Homo habilis* or 'Handy Man', a more human-like creature. In this region the footprints of erect creatures have also been discovered that are around 3.5 million years old (exact dating here is difficult because there are three individuals who used the same track, which follows a riverbank, at different times).

Homo habilis weighed around 40 kilograms and was only about a metre tall. He was not an ape but not a man. His teeth are more like a man's than an ape's, but since he apparently had longer arms than the modern human, he probably climbed more in the trees. He had a larger brain but smaller muscles than anthropoid apes. The creature that lived here in the Tanzanian portion of the Nile basin was, therefore, somewhere in the middle of the transition between ape and human.

Nutcracker Man and 'Handy Man' are early examples of how the Nile Valley has been a region central to humankind's evolution and history; they pose a clear connection to some of the oldest instances of tool use that are found on the Nile, north in Sudan, and to the mighty ancient civilization that arose on the riverbanks in Egypt. And, somewhere in between, people wandered down the Nile and populated the world.

Bismarck and the rock at the water's edge

In the harbour at Mwanza, Tanzania's second largest city, a peculiar geological rock formation can be seen sticking out of Lake Victoria. The formation is named 'Bismarck' after the German chancellor and foreign minister, Otto von Bismarck, the Prussian who brought parts of East Africa under Berlin's sway in 1885. When the Germans ruled in this part of Africa, they raised a statue to their 'Iron Chancellor' on top of the rock. After the First World War, the British, who received Tanzania as a mandate from the League of Nations, tore down this symbol of German imperialism and defeated ambitions. The stone formation, in contrast, continues to stand rock solid at the water's edge, polished by wind and the Nile lake's waves and has become Mwanza's landmark.

Tanzania's Nile history revolves around Mwanza. Due to its location on Lake Victoria, the city became a natural hub for the slave trade between what today is known as the 'Great Lakes Region' and Zanzibar. For thousands of years different ethnic groups have come and gone in this region, as a rule a mix of hunters and gatherers. Agricultural societies based on subsistence farming and fishing also existed here.

Written history emerged with the Arab trade interest in the region. Throughout the nineteenth century, Africans were chained together here to be driven like animals down to the coast. Many of them were sold by the local chief in Mwanza to Arab tradesmen in exchange for small gifts, but most of them, after being captured by local leaders on the far side of the lake, were herded by tradesmen on the route to Zanzibar. The place was the hell along 'Hell's Highway', as Stanley called the slave routes from the Lake Victoria regions to the Indian Ocean. It was here, also, that John Hanning Speke, as he stood atop Isamilo Hill, saw the great Central African lake from which the Nile came, the first European to do so. However, it was with the Germans at the end of the nineteenth century that modernity came to Mwanza, if in a rather perverted fashion.

The history of Germany's conquests in the Nile basin is bizarre, and it represents the colonial spirit of conquest at its most unsavoury.

Dr Carl Peters (1856–1918), the man who, for a period, came to symbolize German nationalism and expansionism, and whose works were later published in three volumes during the Hitler era, travelled in late 1884 together with two companions inland towards the Usambara Mountains in the area that today comprises north-east Tanzania. Later that same year, on 17 December, an odd caravan moved in the direction of the coastal city of Bagamoyo. Dr Peters, who was a historian by trade and a Schopenhauer scholar, was travelling back from a brief inland foray. He was sick, and as he was carried along in his hammock, he gestured with his revolver for his bearers to move faster. Peters was only twenty-eight years old when he arrived at the coast. He was carrying with him signed, pre-written treaties. One local chieftain after another had signed a paper they could not read, but in which it stood written that they conceded their territory with all its rights and privileges to Dr Carl Peters, representative of the 'Society for German Colonization'. This feverish and failed academic, who had previously written on metaphysics, was now the conqueror of an African empire for Germany.

When Peters returned to Berlin, the Berlin Conference (1884–5) was going on, trying to formalize the division of large parts of the African continent among European colonial powers (a representative of the Ottoman Empire was also present). Peters could now inform Bismarck that a German East African colony already existed – they had only to seize it. In February 1885, Bismarck first gave his nod to German colonialism and then provided financial backing for Peters's idea of establishing an East African protectorate. Meanwhile, Peters recruited multiple agents in Africa to continue the work of securing treaties. Their instructions were: *schnell, kühn, rücksichtslos* (quick, daring, ruthless).

When the Sultan of Zanzibar heard about the proposed protectorate – which included what he viewed as his own territory – he sent a note of protest to the German emperor. It reached Berlin in May and Bismarck asked Peters how he should respond. Peters's answer was gunboat diplomacy at its most direct: there is a lagoon across from the Sultan's palace in Zanzibar and it is deep enough for warships to anchor there. Not too long after, on 7 August 1885, five German warships entered the lagoon near Zanzibar and directed their weapons at the Sultan's palace. Bismarck's demand was that

Sultan Barghash must cede his mainland territories to the German emperor or face the consequences. When London learned of this ultimatum – and since it was now the age of the telegram, this happened straightaway – Britain pushed for a compromise: the two countries needed to agree on the borders of the East African regions. This plan was accepted before August was over. The next year the Anglo-German Agreement of 1886 was signed. The British consul, who did not agree with London's Nile strategy and how this affected his country's attitude to Bismarck's activities in Zanzibar, was reluctantly forced to carry out London's diplomatic order and convince the sultan to sign an agreement that meant surrendering the lion's share of his mainland territory. In September the German gunboats returned to Europe; Bismarck had got his colony.

In 1890 Carl Peters travelled inland again, and this time he reached the Kingdom of Buganda. His goal was to sign a treaty whereby the king accepted a German protectorate over the region. This was obviously out of the question for Britain, and, through diplomatic agreements, Bismarck confirmed that the Germans recognized the Nile as Britain's sphere of interest. At that point, Peters's ambitions were halted by Berlin. Carl Peters was appointed imperial commissar and participated in the Anglo-German border commission that in 1892 drew up what is still the border between Kenya and Tanzania.

Meanwhile, Peters's brutal treatment of the local inhabitants around Kilimanjaro resulted in a rebellion among the Chagga – the people who had developed sub-Sahara's only irrigation civilization based on the control and exploitation of the glacial water that perennially flows down the cliffside from the snow-covered peak. Today they still use this water source to conduct irrigation farming around the foot of Kilimanjaro. In 1897 Peters was convicted in Germany for crimes he had committed in Africa. Apparently, he had grown suspicious that a servant was sleeping with one of his African lovers. The young girl was first whipped and then hanged. (It was the famous German Social Democrat, August Bebel, who published the letters that revealed Peters had acted as executioner.) This scandal, and a steadily strengthening German anti-colonial movement, led to a reformation of Germany's East African policy.

During the years that followed, German authorities made considerable efforts to develop their East Africa colonies. The introduction of new and more profitable agricultural products, like coffee, sisal and cotton, however, was met with deep animosity by large sections of the local population, particularly when forced labour was employed to recruit workers. In 1905 the Maji Maji Rebellion broke out, notorious because it was the first large-scale, violent revolt against European colonization in East Africa. For anyone interested in nature mythologies and in water's cultural significance, this rebellion is fascinating because it was one of the precursors to Alice Auma's Holy Spirit Movement in Uganda eighty years later and her conversations with the river spirits at the Nile waterfall, Wang Jok.

The Maji Maji Rebellion was fuelled by the belief that a mixture of water, castor oil and millet seeds could make people invincible to bullets. The spirit of revolt spread like fire through dry grass. Equipped with millet stalk wreaths, the population launched a murderous attack on the Germans. When German reinforcements arrived and the rebels realized that water could not protect them after all, defeat was inevitable. The German commander, Count Gustav Adolf von Götzen, was merciless in his punishment of the local people: he decided only hunger could make them obedient. The troops, therefore, went throughout the country destroying crops and granaries and setting whole villages afire. More than 100,000 Africans are thought to have perished in what one can safely call a man-made famine.

German East Africa was composed of today's Tanzania (not including Zanzibar), Rwanda and Burundi. Germany, as we have seen, became a colonial power overnight, an entirely different case from England and France, which had built their empires over many decades. In less than a year, between April 1884 and February 1885, Bismarck procured colonies in Africa and the Pacific that were many times larger than the motherland. From the viewpoint of Great Britain, German occupation of these areas did not present any strategic problems, and the historical literature thus exaggerates the contradictions between Berlin and London at the time, not least because history has a tendency to be studied backwards – typically, in this context, it became influenced by the conflicts between Germany and Great Britain during the First World War. Germany offered no opposition, however, but rather supported the British when, at the end of the nineteenth century, London defined the Nile basin and also Egypt as their sphere of interest. Furthermore, the regions that lay south, east and west from Lake Victoria did not interest London, so the fact the British gave Germany an African colony here was not indicative of growing conflict between European states. The Upper Nile region was rather an example of a moment in colonialism's history when two European powers agreed upon how the colonies should be divided.

A good story, which often gets trotted out in order to document the randomness inherent in the way the colonists drew borders, is also inaccurate. The story goes as follows. The boundary between Tanzania and Kenya was drawn on the map as a straight line, except for Mount Kilimanjaro. The break in this straight line has been attributed to Queen Victoria who, after reflecting upon the issue, said that her grandson, Kaiser Wilhelm, so thoroughly enjoyed tall mountains that Kilimanjaro would be her gift to him. The problem with this story is that the border was established in 1886, two years before Wilhelm became Kaiser. Furthermore, it overlooks the fact that both parties knew that the glacial water flowing down the cliffs proved the basis for the only irrigation civilization in Africa south of the Sahara – the Chagga civilization – located at the mountain's foot in Tanzania. Carl Peters's personal, unrestrained imperialism was thus replaced by the rationality of state diplomatic imperialism.

An unknown European naval battle on a Nile lake

On 5 August 1914, just months after the shots fired in Sarajevo, and one day after Britain had declared war on Germany in Europe, troops from British Uganda attacked the German river posts along Lake Victoria. London had decided that German stations that lacked a telegraph connection would be eliminated and the navy deprived of its bases. The First World War had arrived in the Upper Nile. The modest clashes here were not so much a result of the Nile question, even though Berlin obviously was aware of London's obsession with Lake Victoria, and the significance that control of the lake represented for Britain's overall imperial strategy. Instead, the lake battle in 1914 demonstrated that the Upper Nile had become an arena for power struggles in Europe.[14]

As it turned out, the Germans had attempted to build up a navy on Lake Victoria. This consisted of a large steamer, the 90-ton *Muansa*, built in Hamburg in 1910, the 12-ton *Heinrich Otto*, built in 1907, a smaller steamer, *Albert Schwarz*, and the motorboat *Schwaben*. Small dhows (the local sailing vessels), which were often drawn by steamer, were used to transport troops.

The Germans sought to finance the increased expenditure for campaigns in East Africa with gold discovered in Tanganyikan mines. Consternation stirred in London, meanwhile, when rumours began to circulate that the Germans wanted to pump Lake Victoria's water for use in gold-mining operations south of the lake. This threatened British monopoly over Nile exploitation, and if the German plan became known, it would also weaken Britain's position in Egypt. The British navy on the lake consisted of six steamers, in reality the transportation boats of the Uganda railway, but upon which they had mounted weapons.

Captain Wilhelm Bock von Wülfingen, the German commander in Mwanza, was told to proceed against Kisumu in order to destroy railway bridges the British had constructed as part of their Indian Ocean to Lake Victoria route. During September 1914, 52 Germans, 266 askaris, the name given to local Africans serving as soldiers in European armies, and 101 helpers from the Wagaya, a people who inhabited the south-eastern shores of the lake, bringing with them three machine guns and a 3.7-centimetre field cannon, marched against the railway's terminal station in what is today Kenya. The British garrison in Kisumu consisted of 90 askaris, 100 policemen and 130 volunteers from the city guard. The German commander crossed the border and took the port at Karungu on 9 September. On Lake Victoria, the armed German steamboat *Muansa* followed as a support. The Germans then proceeded towards Kisii, at that time a tiny village with only a few inhabitants. The British responded by sending as many soldiers as possible across the lake from Uganda. They were protected by the armed steamboat *Kavirondo*. While German troops had swarmed into Belgium in August 1914, the British pushed forward at Lake Victoria with its small force. On 13 September they retook Kisii and discovered five wounded Germans and sixteen wounded askaris still on the ground. British control was re-established over Kisii and over the areas in the vicinity of the lake.

On 6 March 1915, the *Muansa*, which had been anchored at Nafuba Island, was the victim of a surprise cannon attack from the British boat *Winfred*. The Germans abandoned their wounded ship. A German *Schutztruppe* (protection force) on the beach, meanwhile, fought back a British attempt to board the boat and seize it. Later, the Germans towed the badly damaged boat *Muansa* to Mwanza, where it was docked on 15 March. The repair took three months. On 12 September 1915, the Germans had received a 10.5-centimetre cannon from Königsberg. It was mounted on a hill above Mwanza to protect the settlement from British raids from the lake. As part of the 1916 British offensive, Mwanza was indeed attacked and the Germans retreated south. The British blew up the cannon and the telegraph connection and sank the *Muansa*. London was master once again of all of Lake Victoria.

These encounters on the Nile lake have an operetta-like quality to them. Yet, the war between Germany and Great Britain in East Africa was deadly enough. Together, the allied forces consisted of around a million men, including 600,000 African bearers.

Tens of thousands died, mainly Africans, due to sickness, malnourishment and exhaustion.

Colonial agreements and the Nile's present

The outside world typically views Tanganyika – or, from April 1964, the United Republic of Tanzania (Tanganyika was united with Zanzibar) – as a country oriented towards the Indian Ocean and the Swahili coast. The reality, however, is that large parts of the country are in the Nile basin, and the authorities have at different times also discussed plans to use the river tributaries before they run into the inland ocean in the upper basin. The north-western parts of the country receive just a little, very unpredictable, rainfall. During the First World War, the Germans, as I have mentioned, debated plans to pump lake water for use in local gold-mining operations. They also evaluated taking water from the lake for use in irrigation, transportation and the production of electricity. London put a stop to all such initiatives.

When the British took control of Tanganyika after the First World War, all such plans and ideas were shelved. In the context of Great Power rivalry and imperial strategy, the most important issue was always to take account of Britain's interest in Egypt and of their position at Suez. Furthermore, the 1929 Nile Agreement blocked any development of the Nile basin in Tanzania as long as the British governed there; London, after all, had sworn that nothing would happen in their East Africa basin regions that infringed on Egypt's water interests. It was only in the mid-1950s that this policy changed, and when relations with Egypt had worsened to such an extent that it was high time for Britain to use their control of the Nile upstream as a coercive policy weapon against Cairo. But at that time the empire was weakened. Even as the colonial authorities in Uganda discussed (futilely as it turned out) secret plans to change the Nile's course in their country, the British seized the opportunity to pump water from Smith Sound bay in Lake Victoria for irrigation in Tanganyika. They argued in reports on the country's development that the most important limiting factor in agricultural growth was rainfall.[15] The sporadic rainfall was unevenly distributed within the country and often arrived in torrential downpours, which meant the water quickly ran off, so the plants received little benefit. But nothing concrete happened regarding Nile control before London was forced to surrender its colony.

On 30 November 1961, just days before the country was set to become independent, it became clear that Tanganyika was planning to do more with the Nile than the British rulers had done during the previous decades. Britain's overarching Nile strategy no longer placed a damper on exploiting the lake and the rivers that flowed into it. Accordingly, the National Assembly in Dar es Salaam adopted what international juridical literature would later call the Nyerere Doctrine of State Succession: the country argued that there was no legal reason for the country to comply with the 1929 Agreement, entered into by the British on their behalf, wherein London had waived all of Tanganyika's rights to exploit the Nile without Egypt's approval.

The Nile question quickly become one of many significant issues that would determine the new state's place in world politics. Julius Nyerere, the first prime minister, quickly distinguished himself in the international arena as an opponent of the Nile Agreement. Nyerere was born in 1922 in Butiama, which is in Tanganyika's Mara region, far to the south-east of the Upper Nile basin. One of twenty-six children, his father was a Zanaki chief. He was the first Tanganyikan to study at the University of Edinburgh, where he took a master's degree in economics and history at the beginning of the 1950s. After that, Nyerere returned to Tanganyika to lead the resistance struggle against the British. He also became interested in the exploitation of the rivers flowing from his home region down to Lake Victoria and the uses to which they could be put. He especially considered the Kagera basin, which the country shared with its two neighbours to the west, Burundi and Rwanda.

For the new state leadership in what was now Tanzania, it was natural to pose the question: could they do whatever they wanted with the Nile rivers, or must they first seek approval from Egypt as the 1929 Agreement between London and Cairo stipulated? Was independent Tanzania bound by treaties signed by their European rulers? And, more generally, were newly independent states on the whole bound by international agreements signed by their colonial masters?[16]

A new state can formally emerge in several ways, something that will pose different juridical consequences for the legality of previous agreements to which the state is a party. A state, for example, can achieve independence from a colonial power, thus entering a community of nations as an equal. A new state can also be created after the original state, of which it was a part, dissolves. That was the case for the Soviet Union, Yugoslavia and Czechoslovakia, which saw new state formations spawned from other and larger states. New states can also be established by previously independent states that, by international agreement, enter into a larger polity. The question of the legitimacy and status of signed diplomatic agreements is, therefore, important, and how these issues are handled will have global consequences.

Generally, new states inherit the international commitments ratified by their predecessors. Throughout the 1950s and 1960s, however, many African colonies achieved independence. The Nyerere Doctrine holds that such new states must adopt a selective stance towards agreements signed by the colonial powers. Nyerere believed that colonial era international agreements must be renegotiated when a state achieves independence because a state or nation cannot be bound by agreements adopted when the nation was not itself in a sovereign position to ratify them. According to Nyerere, a newly independent state could review those international agreements signed on its behalf and decide which of these to accept and which to reject. Even though such an eclectic approach was not new, being already a recognized part of conventional international law, Nyerere is considered to be the person behind the modern formulation of this doctrine regarding the law of state succession.

The Nyerere Doctrine neither excludes nor rejects the possibility of a renewal and extension of agreements. Nyerere tried to establish a measure for the practical application of the doctrine: the parties should be given a certain period for reflection, where earlier agreements attain temporary status as the successors assess which to renew, which to renegotiate and which to set aside.

Nyerere took the 1929 Agreement to the International Court in The Hague in the 1960s. Tanzania lost, but the court supported Egypt's interpretation of the Agreement as being binding also for former colonies. Since then, however, the Nyerere Doctrine has gained increasing support. First it was backed by other countries with a colonial past and gradually it received support more generally. It has also become an important inspirational source for the two Vienna Conventions on State Succession. The ruling in The Hague in the early 1960s, therefore, has, it seems, less standing and legitimacy today than it had then. The Nyerere Doctrine eventually also played an important juridical role in the upstream countries' growing opposition to the 1929 Agreement as being still binding. One of the countries that has remained most outspoken on this matter is Tanzania, and the country's minister of water was also elected spokesperson for the countries that signed the Entebbe Agreement in 2010, when for the first time the upstream countries formally, and in conjunction, challenged Egypt's supremacy in relation to Nile issues and the position and content of the 1929 Agreement.

A country with gift economy

'Did you know that our main opposition leader entered the election with the promise to say no to all development aid to Tanzania?' The Tanzanian researcher with whom I was working aimed at surprising me – and he succeeded. I did not know the issue was important in the 2010 election. Such news seldom makes it into the Western media, where the dominant image of Africa is still that of a continent dependent on Western NGOs, aid and Angelina Jolie.

Few countries have experienced a more mixed bag with this kind of gift economy than Tanzania. The short book, *The Gift*, written by the French sociologist Marcel Mauss and published in 1925 by the French sociological journal, *L'Année Sociologique*, is a classic. Even though it uses data taken from Native Americans living on the northeastern coast of the United States, and additionally bases its anthropological studies on people from the Western Pacific, still it is used to understand internal relationships characterized by clientelism and family obligations in many African societies. *The Gift* can also be fruitful for analysing one side of the relationship between 'donors' and 'recipients' within the international development-aid system. Few regions have been more defined by the aid era's gift economy than the Nile countries in general and Tanzania in particular.

Mauss writes about exchanges of gifts in societies he terms archaic. The system of mutual exchange of gifts and its reciprocities are 'total', and thus can provide general insight into these societies. The gift swap represents an interaction that at once involves every institution in society. Through his gift, the giver obtains power over the receiver, a power that is equalized only with difficulty. The exchange of gifts further ensures that the society is enshrouded in a fog of obligations, a fine-meshed net of all-encompassing and circulating liability. Everyone is indebted to everyone else, and Mauss thereby emphasizes the gift economy's potentially integrative force.

Mauss describes the circumstances that accompany gift giving and receiving. In giving, an individual represents himself as generous, and as someone who accordingly deserves respect. In receiving, an individual shows respect for the giver, and thereby also demonstrates generosity. In reciprocating, an individual proves that his personal honour is as high – at least – as that of the person who did the giving first. Gift giving is, therefore, permeated by morality, in the sense that, by giving, receiving and reciprocating, moral bonds are established between the actors in the exchange. At the same time, Mauss underscores the competitive and strategic aspects of the giving act. By giving more than one's rivals or, I would add, by showing more gratitude than others who have received gifts, a person demands greater respect. Mauss demonstrates that a gift in traditional societies plays an extremely complex role, for it is economic, political, kinship-oriented, legal, mythological, religious, magical, practical, personal and social. The fact that a gift is woven into the social landscape in such multifaceted ways forms the basis for its power.

Within the international development-aid system, the gift relationship is typically expressive of a more cynical game. The giver gives with the expectation that the recipient will do as asked – whether that is introducing another economic policy, another human rights policy or another policy in the environmental arena. The gift is rhetorically described as the binding factor in an equal partnership of development, but it always contains an element of coercion. On the other side, the gift recipient does not feel the same form of mutual obligation as in Mauss's model. Recipients know that givers are more concerned with being *shown* gratitude than whether recipients actually *are* grateful, because people and NGOs or state representatives who give depend upon being viewed as successful givers in their homeland, in the donor countries. Therefore, all the ceremonies where village folk come together in dance and salvos of applause in honour of the givers, and which the givers never tire of displaying and basking in, may be socially degrading for those who are dancing, but they are also a clever and cynical investment, with an eye towards receiving new gifts – that is to say, they are calculated actions.

A wealth of material has been written about the colonial era's significance for the development of the Nile basin countries. The aid epoch has already lasted as long as the British Nile empire in the basin. Despite this fact, hardly any overall analyses have been written on the gift economy's effect on this region, so our knowledge is superfluous and scanty about the consequences of the billions upon billions of dollars, defined as gifts, which in the course of a few decades have been invested in the development of these countries.

The modern history of Nile control, however, cannot be understood without also understanding the gift's power and its role. For example, one of the international aid system's most central institutions, the World Bank, has – due to the Bank's interpretation of the Nile Agreement's legitimacy – been against supporting investments in Nile projects upstream in the Nile basin if one of the countries in the basin has voiced opposition to these Nile projects. In the context of basin-wide hydropolitics, the understanding of the gift must thus be freed from Mauss's perceptions of it. It is possible to use the gift, or its denial, as a conscious diplomatic tool, more effective than practically everything else due explicitly to the gift's character. One can accordingly up-end the French philosopher, Jacques Derrida, who argued that the gift is an impossibility, and assert instead that, in such a context, the gift is the only possibility.

The international community and its gifts could have a certain role to play in reducing the threat of war and conflict surrounding Nile use. Its gifts can, due to their potential usefulness for the recipient, represent an important form of power and can help attract parties to the negotiating table and to stimulate economic cooperation in other arenas, as a reward for showing positive attitudes to diplomatic or cooperative behaviour over the Nile.

The wildebeest crossing

A billowing sea of muscles, of strength, but also an insistent illustration of the timidity and power of herd mentality, approaches the Mara River: wildebeest, fearing they-know-not-what, hesitant and snuffling on the Mara River's southern bank, compelled to reach the other side of the river, for the smell of rain and fresh grass drifts on the wind from that direction. A herd stands by the river on the edge of Serengeti National Park, with its seemingly boundless plains; the park is so wide, open and flat that one can see clouds between an ostrich's legs. The least sign of danger – a shift in the direction of the wind, a log of a suspicious shape floating down the river, the lazy flap of a vulture's wings as it takes off from the far riverbank – can cause the whole herd to turn. And is there any sound that can rival the hollow galloping thud of those thousands upon thousands of hooves against the earth? The herd is so large that it can take the wildebeest an hour or two to change direction. But they return, every single time. Every single time they return. The force of instinct is relentless: they just must reach the promised land of grass they feel is there, on the other side.

There is no way around it: the wildebeests *must* cross the river – sooner or later. Something in the animals' constitution drives them forward. The need for freshly watered green grass outweighs the dangers of the river crossing. Those at the front of the herd will finally bow to pressure from those behind, and suddenly the whole herd springs forward, as if by command and without hesitation.

The wildebeest must enter the water to reach the other bank. It is necessary, determined; they have no choice. There is no other path than this to the rain and green plains. The wildebeest, could they have formed the thought, have a single hope: to be among the fortunate to escape the crocodile's jaws, not to be forced to offer themselves for the collective good, so to speak. It is a brutal game in which they are both pawns and victims. Hyenas, lions, leopards and even panthers also benefit from the way the Nile system creates this surplus of fresh meat.

The wildebeest and zebra and antelope on their eternal migrations across these Upper Nile Basin plains can be described as leading lives utterly determined by the need to adapt to the shifting character of this water landscape. In this sense, the wildebeest share traits with migratory birds. In the dry season, smaller herds band together to form an army of around a million animals, plus half again as many zebras and gazelles. Then they follow the pattern and movement of the rains, in a spectacular thundering herd north from the Serengeti in Tanzania to Mara in Kenya, and back again in October.

The wildebeests' trek across the Masai Mara plains provides an ultimate illustration of water's importance. The wildebeest are doing what every living creature must, but they do it in a way that dramatizes and underscores an irrefutable fact: everybody, animals and human beings, must have the water they require, no matter the cost, for otherwise they will only last a few days. The migration also shows how the Nile system's ecology highlights the artifice of national borders. For, every year, after a short hiatus where several hundred thousand wildebeest calves are born far south on the Serengeti plain in the Olduvai Gorge region in Tanzania, the wildebeest resume their eternal pursuit. The migration does not actually have a beginning or end; it structures the wildebeests' existence, as together with them wander 300,000 gazelles and 200,000 zebras, not to mention hyenas, lions and other scavengers, from Tanzania to Kenya and back again, as has been the case since time immemorial.

What is the Nile?

Tanzania has long argued that a tributary the Egyptians insist is part of the Nile basin does not belong to the basin at all. If the Tanzanians are correct, then it is simply a national river and the country can do with it what it will. The Egyptian take, on the other hand, has long been that all tributaries are part of the Nile system and, therefore, fall under the 1929 Agreement.

Such disputes can serve as examples of how values, ideas and perceptions creep between humans and nature, and influence what we perceive. When I stand here and look at the Mara River, it is obvious I am unable to see the river as it is; I perceive it according to my perspective. That does not mean, of course, that the Nile does not exist independently of myself or of the way I see it. It exists, it runs, it has consequences and creates opportunities, although urban elites in Dar es Salaam, Entebbe, Nairobi or Cairo would never think of it or mention it. Central to an understanding of the river's structuring role in societies, even as it is not thought of or talked about, is that the way the river is flowing and has been used in different parts of the basin has had an impact on social life – whether people have realized it or not. Indeed, at times it has achieved a purely mechanical, blind and lethal significance in those regions where the populace has not discussed it or viewed the Nile as relevant or important.

In the last century the Nile's average annual water flow was established at about 84 billion cubic metres of water. The river, however, has never had the flow 'everyone' asserts it has had. Stated annual water flow is obviously only an average. For example, the Nile carried with it 150 billion cubic metres of water in 1878–9 and 42 billion in 1984–5. In the period from 1871 to 1953, the average was 92.4 billion cubic metres, whereas from 1871 to 1901 it was on average 107 billion. In the latter part of the 1960s and the early part of the 1970s, the average was almost 90 billion cubic metres, whereas in the period from 1977 to 1987, it was only 72 billion. From 1899 to 1959, the average was 84 billion – and that became the official figure for the Nile's water flow in the agreement that Egypt and Sudan ratified that same year. Eventually, this figure became synonymous with the river's general water flow, and countless reference works state this as a fact.

Since the place at which water flow is measured will decide the water quantity a river is said to have, and it is impossible to determine the 'correct' measuring site, either objectively or based purely on natural scientific criteria, the place selected for measuring a river's water flow is of great political importance. At the end of the nineteenth century, the British decided that Aswan should be the main measuring site, and since that time this site has been maintained. From a purely hydrological point of view, they could just as well have chosen the measuring stations the British established upstream after the occupation of Sudan in 1898. The Aswan site reflected, however, the imperial Nile strategy and hydropolitical decisions. (If the chosen site had instead been where the Atbara enters the main Nile, for example, the Nile would presumably have 'had' around a 10 per cent greater water flow.)

When water must be divided between numerous water-thirsty states, the central question becomes: how much water is available? Since there is no way objectively to determine this, the officially declared water flow in such large international rivers is the result of power relations and political wrangling. Even the choices made when it comes to establishing the years on which to base average water discharge will reflect political power relationships. Hydrological data, accordingly, do not represent objective information concerning a river, but reflect the influence of politics and diplomacy. Therefore, the way such hydrological data are described will also have political consequences that are easily overlooked if one believes that hydrological science is simply presenting objective facts.

The river's nature cannot be described objectively, no matter how much natural scientists, water-planners or politicians insist to the contrary. Disagreements on what the Nile is and how it should be exploited also reflect the place along the river from which it is conceived and characterized. If you view the river from the perspective of the cattle nomads in South Sudan who follow the Nile's seasonal rhythms across the *toich*, or from that of the farmers in the Egyptian Delta in dire need of more water, or from the perspective of people living in a clay hut overlooking the river but with no electricity in Ethiopia, portrayals of the river will vary when it comes to how the water is seen, what characterizes it and how it can best be exploited.

An outsider like myself must therefore break with the widespread notion that all social dissent can be explained with reference to social relations alone. Disagreements between actors in the different Nile countries also have a physical basis. Even so, one cannot accept the idea that the Nile can be described as 'objective' nature, because the river, as a physical phenomenon, will always be viewed through particular social and cultural lenses. Yet I, as an outsider, have one advantage; I might be able to distance myself from all the geographically determined perspectives, whether they are marked by an upstream or a downstream position. Although even I, in this sense, can cultivate a disinterested viewpoint and can describe the river from a variety of positions and perspectives, I cannot describe the river how it really is, because that is impossible.

Pumping the lake and defying Egypt

In the early 2000s, the Tanzanian government made a dramatic decision: they proclaimed they were going to pump water from Lake Victoria without first asking Egypt. Indeed, even if Egypt opposed the action and pointed to the 1929 Agreement, still the state would take lake water for use in dry areas south of the lake. From a Nile-historical perspective, this decision to undertake a relatively modest project in Tanzania was a watershed, because the country was behaving as if the 1929 Agreement was no longer binding. In the 1950s and in the years before independence, the Tanganyikan press, then under British control, hammered at the Nile Agreement, and reported on the existence of a 'secret' proposal for watering the whole Lake Province in Northern Tanganyika with the waters of Lake Victoria. The whole scheme 'hinged on the water agreement', and it could be interpreted as an aspect of British Nile diplomacy against Nasser in Egypt. This survey in northern Tanganyika was hoped, it was said, to 'eventually lead to one of the largest irrigation schemes ever to be drawn up in the world'. Another article appeared on 1 August, expressing sympathy with those members of the Tanganyika Legislative Council from the Lake Province who pointed their complaints with phrases like 'all that water at our doorsteps in the lake, but we cannot get any for our houses'. Lake Victoria and the Nile were two of the biggest things in Africa, the article continued, and highly important to East Africa but vital to Egypt and the Sudan – 'matters in fact of life and death'.[17]

A few decades earlier the Tanzanian government had launched a study to find out whether it was possible and expedient to take water from the lake at Smith Sound bay and transport it to Shinyanga and some cities in the Mwanza region. A new study was conducted in 1999 and 2000. This concluded that the project was technically feasible. The next step was to fund the project and in 2001 the president issued a directive asking that the possibility of funding the project internally, within Tanzania, be explored. In 2004–5 funds for the project were set aside from the budget and the work could start.

The government had decided to pump water from the lake and use it to improve the water situation in the relatively dry and water-poor parts of Tanzania, where most rivers are seasonal, and where the strong, traditional power of rainmakers is a clear expression of the rain's irregularity and capriciousness. In the lake – of which 49 per cent is in Tanzania – there is plenty of water to be had, the Tanzanians argue. The government's project is called the Kahama Water Project, as well as the Lake Victoria Project or the Shinyanga Project.

The project was implemented in February 2004, and the government emphasized that it would be self-financed. The Tanzanians would take water from the Smith Sound bay and transport it to the cities of Kahama and Shinyanga, also benefiting the large gold industry in the region, and, via a 170-kilometre pipeline, to fifty-four villages located along the main pipeline. The water is pumped from the lake to Mabale Hill, where a tank collects it before it is carried to Kahama and Shinyanga. The goal is first to provide 450,000 people with enough good water. The next phase is to increase the water supply to about 120,000 cubic metres per day and to serve around a million people by 2025.

In September 2010 President Jakaya Kikwete of Tanzania visited the area to address the regional population. He described the project as a triumph for the country, and, according to press reports, there were women who spoke up at the meeting, to thank the government for saving their marriages! They said that previously they had to walk hours to fetch water for the household, and that this had negatively affected themselves, their families and their marriages.

Egypt argued against the project from the standpoint of its own interests and insisted it could impact negatively on the Nile's water flow downstream. Therefore, Tanzania – and Egypt pointed to what they regarded as valid and binding international jurisdictions and agreements – had no right to implement the project without Egypt's prior acceptance. Within the region, Tanzania's decision to proceed with the project despite Cairo's resistance was regarded as evidence that the country had lost patience both with Egypt and with the other countries taking part in the persistent ongoing negotiations surrounding Nile water use – and which never seemed to reach any definite solutions. Meanwhile, Tanzania emphasized that in launching the project the water would mainly be used for households rather than for irrigation. As such, the project would not affect the water levels in the lake or in the Nile, and so fell outside the 1929 Agreement's jurisdiction, they argued.

The media reported threats of war and announced that Egypt would oppose the project at any price. At the end of the day, however, Egypt limited itself to expressing a strong verbal disagreement. The country certainly protested, but only using traditional diplomatic measures, even as its spokesmen underscored that, while Egypt was opting for dialogue, that did not mean that other methods were not under consideration, including the use of force.

Tanzania's actions were historic: for the first time an upstream state broke directly and openly with Egypt's right of veto for controlling the Nile, as laid down as a principle in the 1929 Agreement. And it turned out that Tanzania had even more ambitious plans. One of them involved sending water to the Vembere Plateau to irrigate around 200,000 hectares. The project was first suggested by German settlers during the First World War, but Britain and the 1929 Agreement put an effective stop to the plan – back then.

Gradually, Tanzania's leadership formulated development ambitions that made the Nile waters more relevant in the country's future. They plan to improve their agriculture and thus increase artificial irrigation. President Kikwete was entirely clear in 2011: under the existing ten-year plan, the government is planning to invest more than US$5 billion, and the goal is irrigation (because dependence on uncertain rainfall poses a principal challenge).[18]

Although a country at the periphery of the Nile basin, Tanzania has played a significant role in unleashing foundational changes within the Nile system. It happened in a way that Egypt had always feared: a rather insignificant Nile country with a rather insignificant water outtake started a process that undermined the legitimacy of the old colonial agreement apparatus.

Towards the Nile's Sources in Central Africa

Where the river splits and collects

In 1994 the Ugandan government declared parts of Lake Victoria an area of catastrophe. Thousands of corpses were floating in the lake where people collected drinking water and where the fish they ate swam. In Kisumu on the Kenyan lakeshore, the government declared the fish off limits because they were feeding off human remains. From being an economic and legendary source of life for thousands of years far down in the basin, here it had become a physical artery of death and mutilation. The corpses in the lake were a manifestation of the Rwandan genocide – a country where a local priest apparently said hell no longer had any devils, they had all come here – made the world concretely aware that the small but very densely populated country of Rwanda was also a part of the Nile basin.

As much as 80 per cent of the territory of Rwanda lies in the Nile basin, the most important rivers being the Nyabarongo, the Akanyaru and the Kagera, all which flow into Lake Victoria. The Nyabarongo rolls slowly across the country, winding in a great arc. The Kagera's or Akagera's catchment area is in east Rwanda and collects water from the Ruvubu River, which runs from Burundi, and from the Nyabarongo. The Nile rivers in Rwanda, however, have scarcely been exploited and controlled for irrigation purposes, and not at all for energy production.

These Nile tributaries have, however, served as important ritual symbols and political weapons, as well as cultural metaphors and mystical boundaries. When the most violent Hutus threw the Tutsis into the river, often beheaded or with their hands bound, this action was given a code phrase – 'to rent them a bus to Ethiopia', the country they believed the Tutsis originated from. It was an action rooted in a deep tradition of mythology about water. Extremist Hutu ideologies described the river as a means of deportation, not just from the Tutsis' home but from this world, something that, according to traditional mythological ideas, barred the Tutsis from entering the life-giving circle.

In the wake of 1994, Rwanda itself has undergone a spectacular transformation. The country has, throughout the 2000s, been marketed and to some extent recognized as one of the primary symbols for what has been called an African renaissance. Rwanda's declared goal is to become Africa's Switzerland. These ambitions also impact the country's role in the struggle surrounding the exploitation and division of the Nile waters. In precolonial Rwanda it was the Nyabarongo River that, according to dominant religious conceptions, split the country into two sacred parts. Now this river will instead be exploited in a national project whose goal is to modernize and unify the country.

Plastic bags and fire extinguishers

Before reaching the border crossing between Uganda and Rwanda, I had taken a car from Kampala along Lake Victoria. On one stretch of the road we passed a sign that informed us that we were passing the equator line. It was the start of the rainy season, so rivers and streams raced down toward the inland ocean. When we stopped, it was to listen to the optimistic sound of running water, or to film a verdant steaming Nile landscape – the ultimate contrast to the desolate deserts crossed by the Nile in Egypt and Nubia. I had an appointment to meet President Paul Kagame in Kigali, Rwanda's capital, and was also heading towards another newly discovered Nile source in Rwanda, close to the border with the troubled DR Congo.

'Fire extinguisher', the driver said, though in indistinct Ugandan English. Rather, I gathered he had said fire extinguisher; but surely, I thought, that could not be right. I glanced uneasily at the backseat and looked around, but nothing was burning here! The driver repeated the same word several times and insisted there was nothing to do but wait. He had to acquire both this apparatus and a sign, he said. I was certain I had misunderstood. 'Did we really need a fire extinguisher? And a warning triangle?' I asked him again, doubtfully. Yes, he must borrow these things from an acquaintance, he said. So, I sat down, bought a cold cola at the local café and waited patiently for the driver to complete his errand. After several hours of forced pursuit, he returned, happy with himself, carrying a triangular sign and a fire extinguisher under his arm. I had, most definitely, been stuck in this Uganda border town – for a fire extinguisher. The driver did what he had to do, because no one was allowed to drive on Rwanda's roads without carrying a fire extinguisher and a triangular warning sign in the car. I really looked forward to visiting this country for the first time. And as the Ugandan driver put it: there you cannot buy your way out of problems by bribing a policeman.

The border crossing on the Ugandan side was like other border crossings I had been accustomed to in Africa. Crowds of people, shouting, chaos, filthy and reeking toilets. At one point, I had to extract myself from three men, all offering energetically to escort me to a certain cola kiosk, for a small percentage of the sale, I assume. They took hold of me Wizard of Oz-style until I stopped, sat down and glared at them like the village idiot I was in this crowd, and as I undoubtedly also appeared. Meanwhile, what concerned me, was that no one, for whatever inexplicable reason, should direct me to the wrong line of people.

When we finally crossed the border into Rwanda, it was like entering another world. The atmosphere was completely different. Relaxed. Orderly. At the window, a polite toll employee: 'Welcome to Rwanda. Do you have any plastic bags? If so, I'll have to confiscate them.' The way the Rwandans had organized their border control had, I believe, an immediate psychological effect on all who had travelled a bit in Africa and who crossed the border that day. In this country where people once slaughtered each other with machetes, they were simply asking us to give them our plastic bags! I felt the urge to applaud, and at the same time disconcerted: how, in such an atmosphere of purposefulness and eagerness to transform, could I maintain the observer's distance? Many people have criticized the country under Kagame for being a police state, terrorized by the government army's murder of tens of thousands of people. We climbed into the car, drove no faster than 60 kilometres per hour (which was the new speed limit), with our fire extinguisher and a warning triangle, and I felt safer than I ever had in a car on the road. Along the streets, and outside the houses and mud huts that we passed, there was not a slip of paper litter to be seen, and the Nile, which looks like a repository for plastic bottles at many places along the river, had a tributary here that was quite clean. Nothing corresponded to the stereotypes of Africa or to my previous experiences as a traveller. This made me uncertain. Was all this organization merely a surface gesture, an absurd sign of enforced public spirit and the result of an authoritarian leader's iron fist? Was it a perverse expression of 'image management', staged by a dictatorial regime that violated human rights, as many Western journalists reported? Or was it an expression of a large-scale state-building project, or a civilizing project for this sorely tried Nile country with enormous challenges? Rwanda is, after all, one of the most densely populated countries in the world. Its territory is around 26,338 square kilometres. In 2002 the country had 326 inhabitants per square kilometre (compared with 191 in 1978), in 2018 an estimated 12.3 million people lived here whereas in 2030 it is calculated that 25 million people will live in Rwanda, i.e. close to 1,000 people per square kilometre. The large majority of the population are aged under twenty, and more than 80 per cent live in rural villages.

Kigali – a city and name that, more than any other place in the world, has come to represent post–world war civilization collapse. As the city appeared on the hillsides in the afternoon sun, I flipped through a couple of the books on Rwanda I had brought in preparation for the meeting with Kagame, even as I evaluated different travel routes to the Nile's source through the tropical rainforest from which it flowed.

Hotel Rwanda and the river road

'Take the river road back. It's clear.' One of the Hutu militia leaders gives this advice to Paul Rusesabagina, manager of the Hôtel des Mille Collines, in the world-famous movie *Hotel Rwanda*. We see Paul driving down the road in Kigali towards the Nile river. It is foggy. The drive is difficult: so many bumps. The viewer suspects exactly what it is that Paul is driving over and watches how unrest gradually grips Rusesabagina, with a fear his eyes cannot conceal. The sense that something terrible has happened overwhelms both the viewer and the hotel manager, but no one knows for sure what the wheels are hitting. They stop the car, and when Paul gets out, he stumbles. And what he stumbles across are dismembered corpses. He sees bodies everywhere. The Nile river, running slowly away in the background, is full of dead people. The river flowing there is the Nyabarongo, heading toward Lake Victoria, unhurriedly carrying with it evidence of the darkest chapter in Rwanda's bloody history. On the radio we hear a newscaster say that 40,000 bodies have been retrieved from the lake.

Hotel Rwanda is a shocking film. It tells the story of Paul Rusesabagina, cast as a Rwandan parallel to Oscar Schindler and his list, a Hutu who desperately tries to help his family, but also the Tutsis and the moderate Hutus that the Hutu militia wants to exterminate. Where everyone else fails, including the United Nations, Rusesabagina is not only the saviour but represents what is still civilized in what otherwise is a total breakdown of civilization. Don Cheadle stars in the role as the hotel manager who bribes, inveigles and manipulates – but always with his eyes on a humanitarian goal. The movie is also about General Roméo Dallaire, who discovered he had made promises to protect the population that he could not keep. The UN general later suffered a mental breakdown, reportedly living for a time on a park bench in Canada and trying to commit suicide.

The film helped to give Kigali a new aura; it is no longer only a shadow of bestiality that hangs over the city, but also a kind of merciful light. If one sees the film today, its ambiguity will be further reinforced by the fact the hotel owner and protagonist, Paul Rusesabagina, has become one of President Paul Kagame's most profiled opponents: from exile, Rusesabagina has issued a steady stream of damning proscriptions against Kagame and his regime, for human rights abuses. For a period, they became public enemies of each other. Rusesabagina alleged that Rwanda had become a state governed by and for the benefit of a small group of elite Tutsis, while Kagame supporters on the other hand struck back, criticizing Rusesabagina, now a refugee in Canada, for hijacking heroism and trading with the genocide, and for supporting Hutu guerrillas against the regime.

Hôtel des Mille Collines is only a five-minute walk from Kigali's modern centre. It is surrounded by huge trees and ardent bird life. A swimming pool dominates the area, and if you sit there today, as children play and adults engage in mild and friendly chat during one of the comfortable afternoons that Kigali, due to its climate and height above sea level (900 metres), richly boasts, it is difficult, not to say impossible, to understand what happened when organized evil ravaged the country, exporting its physical manifestations to the downstream basin countries.

Letter from Ground Zero

'But daddy, but daddy?' the boy asks patiently and with childish innocence. His father is obviously trying to find the right words, for how can he explain to a child the act of neighbours hacking neighbours to death?

I am at the Kigali Genocide Memorial. It is in the Gisozi region, a large white building with an extensive view, built on the site where, according to the museum, 250,000 people are buried. Here, the year 1994 is documented in gruesome detail, but at the same time with restraint and without dramatizing effects. The report-like sobriety makes the museum contents even more forceful. Records of hate, betrayal and barbarity in room after room.

Next to me is a small Rwandan family – mother, father and son. The father slowly reads the wall plaques to his son. I can hear that he is struggling to find adequate words to explain what happened. The combination of the darkness, silence and even tranquillity, and the father, mother and son in front of these wall plaques that document collective insanity, conveys an outrageous reality. The attempt to transmit experience over generations is touching, just as the gap between goodwill and the fact of falling short can be. I think, as I feel tears gathering: 'No one can see me now. I am pathetic. Uncomprehending and an outsider.' I take out my yellow notebook, regain my self-control, and continue quoting the text on the plaques. A central line of dialogue in *Hotel Rwanda* is when Paul Rusesabagina says: 'I have no history. I have no memory. I am a fool.' And yet here, surrounded by all these photos and documents that testify to the human will and capacity to exterminate one other, I think: would it not be better to forget all this, wipe it from the collective memory, just go forward and focus on the future? But Rwandans and the Kagame government have made their choice. They will not, and they say they cannot, forget.

The government is obviously aware that its version of the events in 1994 is critical in legitimizing its position of authority in the new Rwanda. The stories regarding the genocide and the international community's passive response engender feelings of guilt in the outside world, thereby making it easier for Rwanda's current government to act reproachably without fear of reproach. And the government, given its vision for a modern Rwanda where ethnic groups no longer exist or are no longer discussed, will have a need to demonstrate the consequences of ethnic hate and to ensure Hutu extremists shoulder the blame for the genocide.

The Nile countries share a history full of exciting social experiments that challenge conventional conceptions of how things should be done. In Rwanda, where the White Nile's tributaries were viewed as central weapons in the Hutu extremists' ultimate historical solution to the Tutsi question, ethnic groups must reconcile with each other, without reconciling with their past.

What is ethnicity?

'We are all Rwandans now.' She bends her stout body forward and raps her index finger emphatically on the table. Around fifteen years after the genocide, I am sitting with a few Rwandans around a café table, drinking coffee and discussing Rwandan politics. The woman is very forthright: there are no ethnic groups in Rwanda. There is no true difference between Hutus and Tutsis. The distinction is a colonial era relic. 'We are all Rwandans now', she repeats. Another person argues, even as he glances around, knowing he is saying what should no longer be said in Rwanda: 'It is obvious there are still Tutsis and Hutus. The Belgians didn't create these categories, even if they strengthened them. But I can't see any differences between us either.'

The enormous field of study devoted to what ethnicity is, and how ethnic consciousness arises and justifies itself, has retrieved many of its examples from the countries of the Nile. That is only natural, since it is estimated that hundreds of ethnic groups, with highly varied languages and cultural traditions, live in the basin countries. Many of these ethnic groups have occupied different niches within the Nile basin's varied ecology, whereas others have been fighting for the same resources and territories. This broad and influential research tradition devoted to ethnicity was supported and financed by European colonial powers. The colonial administrations in all the Nile countries hired several outstanding anthropologists to study local societies and their cultural traditions, and it was during this period that foundational concepts about tribalism and ethnicity were formulated and groundbreaking data gathered. Ethnicity studies have also generally focused on the countries of the Nile because conflict levels among some ethnic groups have been intense and, not seldom, bloody. Thousands of books and tens of thousands of articles have been written on the Nuer and the Azande, the Maasai and the Kikuyu, the Amhara and the Oromo, the Baganda and the Lango, and – not least – the Hutus and the Tutsis.

Few political issues will, in the long run, prove more significant to the Nile's future than how these countries choose to manage their challenges relating to ethnicity, cultural pluralism and national unity. Each state has followed different policies, and in all of them the 'tackling of the ethnic problem' has changed radically over time. In the 1990s the entire country of Ethiopia was administratively reorganized: from a situation in which the central state government combated ethnic organization, the government of Meles Zenawi decided that the various ethnic groups should govern 'their' regions. Linguistic and cultural self-consciousness were encouraged, but within the framework of a unified Ethiopian state. In Rwanda around the same time, discussing different ethnic groups like the Tutsi and Hutu was forbidden; there, everyone was declared to be Rwandans. This was necessary, the government argued, for only such a policy can root out the conflicts that have repeatedly cast the country into civil war.

General theories and statements regarding ethnicity, therefore, must also consider the enormous variation in how ethnicity has been articulated and approached in the Nile basin. After the bloody ethnic conflicts in Kenya, Uganda, Sudan, Rwanda and Burundi between 1990 and 2010, it has become nearly impossible to talk about these regions without viewing them through an 'ethnic filter'. Indeed, the concept of ethnicity, after being completely absent from the public debate for decades (as late as the mid-1980s it was not acceptable to employ the concept within Western, official developmental discourse about Africa's challenges) has now become a dominant, if not to say overly dominant, filter through which to interpret Africa's development, even among Africans themselves.

When you travel along the Nile, you constantly encounter new ethnic groups with their different languages, and you are often exposed to their mutual hatred and prejudices, and after you realize how many of the region's conflicts have been interwoven with ethnic disputes, few questions become more pressing than what exactly creates feelings of 'shared ethnicity'. What forms the basis for describing people as part of an ethnic group?

For what precisely are Hutus or Tutsis? The Rwandans around the café table can hardly observe or hear the difference between a Hutu or a Tutsi, and the Hutu extremists themselves had to demand passes in order to determine who were to be their murder victims. After all, the aspect shared by Rwanda and Burundi is the coexistence of peoples with minimal observable differences and a bloody history filled with perpetual clashes along ethnic lines. Historians and researchers point out that the two groups speak the same language, have a history of intermarriage (during some periods at least), and share many cultural traits. Traditionally, the distinctions between the two groups were based to a certain extent more on what they did than who they were. The conception, however, that Hutus were farmers and Tutsis cattle folk has been proven by recent research to be too simple. According to colonial theory, Tutsis were tall and thin, whereas Hutus were shorter and more thickset, but it is very often impossible to tell which group an individual belongs.

One theory suggests that ethnicity is an identity selected by actors in transactions between benefit-maximizing individuals, or to put it in a simpler but less precise way: in interactions between individuals who are focused on their own interests, emphasis is placed on the question of whether ethnic association in specific situations pays off. There can hardly be any doubt that ethnicity becomes more or less relevant in different situations, but the question is this: can this theory also explain the intense emotions that ethnic conflicts mobilize and unleash, very often with deadly consequences, in the history of the Nile countries? At issue here are conflicts that endanger the state's very legitimacy, and that consciously seek to undermine the unity upon which the state is founded. In other words, can the Tutsi and Hutu massacres be reduced to a struggle between identities created or made relevant in transactional situations?

To explain the history of the Nile countries and the problem of ethnicity here, I think one must consider the hatred that has repeatedly unfolded in various situations as a real emotion, as a value the killers possessed – even if an entirely perverse one – that is nourished on stories that concern collective experiences, on specific historical narratives. Hatred attempts to eradicate the other. The goal can be to achieve revenge, not to find happiness. Hatred is indifferent to whether a person's actions impact upon themselves; it is concerned with something much more basic than a calculated gain in a transaction process. It is concerned with values, convictions and certainties that exist independent of the specific transactions in which people participate, but that is obviously strengthened or weakened by them. The bloodbath in Rwanda concerned something much more critical, something thoroughly material but also cultural, than the idea of 'establishing difference' or strengthening personal identity.

Reducing the ethnicity problem in this way, you make it easy for yourself; it is an anti-intellectual approach to the study of the ethnicity problem, at the same time as it intellectualizes ethnicity as a problem. But ethnicity theories based around the concept that belonging is established as a bargaining chip, so to speak, will have problems explaining the events in Rwanda. This ahistorical approach to ethnicity, however, can be understood in a historical context; it reflects dominating ideas about development in the 1950s and 1960s – when ethnicity, as religion, was regarded as a transitory, short-term mood, an emotion or attribute, one that the process of development or modernity would place on history's scrapheap. Ethnicity and ethnic mobilization were viewed as marginal phenomena, something development itself would increasingly sideline, but that could also re-emerge within certain social situations.

Meanwhile, it has been shown time and again that ethnicity has substantial content, relatively (but not absolutely) independent of the context it is articulated in. It has a historical background, though it cannot for that reason be viewed as being something basic and invariable, as static or unchanging. Within a society, ideas and notions about a certain group's ethnic background or characteristics will continually be reinterpreted in the light of new experiences; that is to say, ethnicity is dynamic. Ethnic identity, therefore, is also a narrative of a life's course – it is a history that is perpetually unfolding, that is growing and branching, but that still retains a special continuity with a collectively defined past. Ethnic identity, as such, is a fusion of essential differences, historically defined through the weaving of countless stories about the background for, and value of, these differences – differences and stories, moreover, that are often strengthened in particular social transactions between individuals and groups.

But the matter is even more complicated. What is the basis, for example, for the different relationships between the two ethnic groups in the twin countries of Rwanda and Burundi? The differences clearly indicate that the extent of the massacres cannot and should not be traced back to a degree of ethnic self-consciousness or to transactional processes. The societal organization must also be analysed. The extent of ethnic violence can reflect social structures as much as the degree of cultural differences experienced.

Historical differences between the two countries during the time of the Tutsi immigration affected the geographical distribution of where the ethnic groups settled and remained, and thereby also impacted the relationship between the groups and how this was discussed and handled. In Burundi most of the Tutsis lived in a specific area, called Bututsi. There, they have formed between 80 and 85 per cent of the population. Most other regions in Burundi have only a few Tutsis. In Rwanda, by contrast, the pattern of Tutsi settlement was more dispersed across the entire country. The only exception was the northern region, where Tutsis never composed more than a fraction of the population. In practice that meant that Rwanda's rigid caste system – where a Tutsi minority dominated a Hutu majority – existed throughout the country, while local variation in Burundi's settlement pattern created greater flexibility within the caste system. Such differences in external, non-ethnic relations have proven significant for how ethnicity has been tackled in the two countries.

Political scientist Samuel Huntington has convincingly shown that the more stratified a society is, and the more complicated its social structure, the more gradually political mobilization will occur. Differences between classes, between occupational groups, between city and countryside, create a series of arenas that split the society and, as a rule, allow the mobilization of only one group at a time. On the other hand, thoroughly homogeneous societies, or societies that have very simple horizontal distinctions – perhaps between an oligarchy that owns everything and a peasantry that owns nothing – or societies that are divided vertically into clear ethnic or localized groups, have greater problems when it comes to moderating or halting the capacity for swift mobilization.[1]

The Rwandan genocide is considered the most brutally 'effective' in world history – up to one million people were reportedly killed in the course of three months. There are aspects of how the murder was carried out that point to a cosmological understanding of the world, one tied to a traditional and powerful rainmaker ideology.[2] Many of the victims were subject to extreme violence that included castration and genital mutilation.

Within traditional Rwandan kingship ideology, the king was a rainmaker who controlled the flow of vital forces. Within this ideology, the king can lose his office or be killed if he cannot control and distribute vital forces like rain and fertility to and on behalf of his people. In Hutu propaganda, the Tutsis shouldered the blame for blocking the cosmic and vital forces within the country. Given the logic that the king can be killed in such cases, the destructive role ascribed to the Tutsis, where they apparently halted the flow of life-giving water and forces, posed an obvious threat to the whole of society. It was a cosmology that was apparently more historically foundational than the question of ethnicity, and several such different ideologies and convictions fused together and produced a civilizational collapse.

It requires an unusually strong will, mission and sense for statesmanship to lead such a society onto a course that leads to development, democracy and stability and, further, to nurture these elements in a world that continually seeks to exploit their weaknesses and internal contradictions, which have themselves often been formulated precisely in ethnic terms. Descriptions of statesmanship or the state leader's role in Nile countries that ignore this context will easily end as arrogant moralizations. For nothing is simpler, or more self-reinforcing, than to condemn others' infringement of values that you yourself hold to be universal or God-given. There is a large analytical gap between cultural relativism and ahistorical universalism in the understanding of historical development – particularly in the Nile basin. A theoretical goal of this book is to show that it is by moving around from place to place within the space defined by the unifying element of the Nile basin, that history best can be reconstructed and the present apprehended.

A metamorphosis

In 2010 – fifteen years after the genocide – there was fee-free primary school in Rwanda. National health insurance was accessible to all. One in four Rwandans had a mobile phone, and the state had completed the laying of 2,300 kilometres of fibre optic cable that connected the country to the global web. In Kigali you could bank from a smartphone, farmers could receive updates on market prices through a messaging service called eSoko (e-market), you could take the bus with a smartcard ticket system called *twende*, read about debates in parliament where the majority of representatives are women and, according to those I met and talked to, take it for granted that bureaucrats arrived at their job precisely when the workday began. No matter if Rwanda's supporters exaggerate the country's achievements, there can be no doubt that a transformation has occurred. Rwanda is among the countries that in recent decades have seen the highest annual economic growth in the world; some even reference the 'Rwandan model' as a parallel to the 'Asian Tiger' in Asia. For Rwanda is a resource-poor country that has, with astonishing rapidity, in arena after arena, entered the modern era. Gross domestic product per capita has doubled many times over. No one will deny that huge changes have occurred, and most will also agree that this is largely due to one man's vision and will: the former soldier and general turned president, Paul Kagame.

Despite the progress made during his presidency, Kagame has also remained a controversial statesman. Sweden and the Netherlands, for example, decided around 2010 to halt all aid to Rwanda due to what they characterized as the government's anti-democratic policy. The international journalism organization, Reporters Without

Borders, demanded that the EU cut financing for Rwanda's presidential election; they asserted that Kagame had closed newspapers, imprisoned journalists and silenced the opposition under the pretence that they encouraged ethnic hatred and denied the genocide. Ten years later, both Sweden and the Netherlands give the country aid and a kind of independent media commission in Rwanda has produced assessment reports of the media situation in Rwanda almost praising its liberalization,[3] while Reporters Without Borders continues to call Kagame a 'predator of press freedom' and claims that 'freedom of information has been declining steadily for years'.[4]

On the other hand, Kagame has received several awards based on the idea that he is Rwanda's saviour, a model for Africa; the United States and Great Britain supported him even before he took power. From the beginning, Kagame and his government have argued that it takes time to educate Rwandans, that everyone is served by the government's crackdown on attempts to ethnicize politics, and that freedom of the press must therefore be limited, and only gradually liberalized.

After a short walk through a well-tended, park-like garden and, after politely being escorted through the few security controls, I am standing in the simply furnished room where I am to meet the president. I already know that the man I will soon meet is not the saint his supporters proclaim. He served as a head of security for Museveni's guerrilla army in Uganda. The military movement he led killed innocents during the war in Rwanda. He has shown himself merciless against his opponents, and he has never been entirely cleared of the accusations that he ordered the plane carrying Burundi's and Rwanda's former presidents shot down, an action many will argue unleashed genocide.

The president enters – a tall, thin man who attentively exchanges greetings with a firm but modest handshake. Without wasting time on pleasantries, he seats himself in a simple wooden chair and remains sitting, slightly leaned back, in the same uncomfortable position throughout the short hour I converse with him. Kagame's words are precise and straightforward. He tells me about the goals for Rwanda 2020, the very ambitious plans being discussed at public meetings all over the country and in the newspapers; he says that it concerns removing the basis for new genocide, and that small things, like the plastic bag ban, are small steps in a much broader developmental strategy that hinges on strengthening self-reliance and self-trust, and the conviction that you can create positive change without waiting for outside support. The president is also crystal clear on the fact that Rwanda needs to exploit the Nile for both irrigation and power if the country is to develop any further. He rejects the Nile Agreement from 1929, describing it simply as antiquated, though emphasizes at the same time that all countries must cooperate in order to exploit the river in the best possible way.

When the conversation is over, I am left impressed, I would say, and with the indelible impression that Paul Kagame is a man with visions for his country that far exceed self-interest or chauvinism, but simultaneously I am aware that nothing can be more misleading than such an impression.

History does not give him much support and encouragement; in order to succeed, therefore, he must take the country on to a new path. When Rwanda achieved its independence in 1962, the Hutu elite took power in the country since the Hutus were in a large majority. This government was both corrupt and entirely inept but proved a useful ally for the Belgian companies that, in the wake of independence, continued operations there as part of the Africa order that the Western powers established after the colonial system's collapse. Eventually, France took – as it was described at the time – responsibility for the prior Belgian colonies of Rwanda and Burundi. The Hutu elite in Rwanda retained power with military and political support from Paris and with the help of anti-Tutsi demagogy. Shortly after independence, this resulted in an attack on the Tutsi population, and many fled across the borders to neighbouring countries, especially to Uganda.

In 1987 the Tutsi-dominated guerrilla organization, the Rwandan Patriotic Front (FPR), was established with its base in Uganda. In 1990 the FPR entered Rwanda and attacked governmental forces in a bid to seize power. FPR was backed by Uganda's president, and many people who were active in the organization had also helped to bring Museveni to power in Kampala in 1986, among them Kagame. US political leaders, international businesses and Kagame himself were obviously well aware of the absolutely crucial natural riches that were hidden in Central Africa's rainforests, but it was only after the Cold War ended that American authorities mapped out a strategy to increase US influence in the region, particularly at the expense of France's position. As the Tutsi guerrilla FPR attacked Rwanda from bases in the US-friendly Uganda, the United States used that as an opportunity to strengthen its own position. The first attack in 1990 was thwarted by Rwandan governmental troops, and so Kagame immediately returned home from the United States, where he had received military training, to lead the FPR forces. He reorganized FPR and, armed with Ugandan military weapons, he launched a new attack in 1993.

Naturally, France ended up a defender of the status quo. The country supported the Hutu-dominated government and its allies in the Hutu elite. FPR was considered a serious threat not only to Rwanda's government but also to continued French influence in the region. Paris flew in paratroopers to fight beside the Rwandan army. Not only the ruling Hutu elite, moreover, but many ordinary Hutu citizens feared FPR's advance. The horror scenario was a return to the old state of Tutsi rule. And many remembered the Tutsi's brutal attacks on the Hutus in Burundi and also earlier in Rwanda's history. Hutu mobilization occurred parallel with Kagame's troops as they clashed with governmental soldiers and increasingly threatened the government's power. A ceasefire was declared between the government and FPR. FPR, however, which had grown stronger and had support from Uganda, the United States and Great Britain, was not interested in stopping halfway when the chance to seize power in the country seemed within reach.

What sparked the chain of events that led to the bloodbath was the downing of the plane carrying President Juvénal Habyarimana of Rwanda and President Cyprien Ntaryamira of Burundi, on 6 April 1994. Both presidents were Hutus, and both were killed. It has never been established what exactly happened or who was behind it. The opposition in Rwanda claims that Kagame's troops were responsible and that they thus bear much of the responsibility for the bloodbath that followed. Kagame refutes these claims as empty, unsubstantiated accusations. After the two Hutu presidents were killed, war broke out anew between FPR and the governmental forces and, almost simultaneously, Hutu extremists began massacring Tutsis all over Rwanda. Massive anti-Tutsi agitation was spread through the media, and Hutu chauvinists across the land armed themselves. Plans were reportedly made for eliminating 'the enemy', that is to say, the entire Tutsi population and all those Hutus who refused to join the Hutu chauvinists' programme. Mass murder was under way. After hundreds of thousands had been killed, FPR marched into Kigali and Paul Kagame became president.

Over a very short time, the country was transformed. And, more importantly for an understanding of the complex Great Power politics in the region, the country was anglicized. France was condemned for its support of those responsible for the genocide, and diplomatic relations were for a short time suspended after a French judge announced he wanted to drag Kagame before the court for his alleged role in the downing of the plane carrying the two presidents. Kagame turned to the United States, and got their economic, political and moral support. After Tony Blair stepped down as prime minister of Great Britain, he was officially named Kagame's adviser. In 2008 English became the only instructional language heard in Rwandan schools from primary level to university, where just a few years earlier it had been French.

France had again become a marginal, rather insignificant player in the Great Power politics of the Nile basin.

But in the same way as London's vociferous campaign against Jean-Baptiste Marchand and French influence at Fashoda in 1989 was primarily a smokescreen to promote British imperial interests in the region, it is not which language they speak in Rwanda that is most interesting to the major powers, but rather which of Central Africa's resources and natural riches the various actors can access through an alliance with Kigali. It is well known that diamonds and coltan (the latter used in smartphones, consumer electronics and military technologies) from DR Congo pass through Rwanda.

Rwanda's relative success can become Rwanda's greatest problem, for the more the country develops and the more stable it seems, the stronger will become the demands that the country behave as if it were an established, well-proven democracy. The question is whether Kagame and his government will succeed in developing the state, as well as a new form of Rwandan nationalism and identity, in a bid, so to speak, to liberate the country from its history. Handling the Nile issue in a reasonable way can spur development, create a national feeling that transcends ethnicity and become a driving force in other ways for the regional cooperation that is critical for this little country, without a coastline, uppermost on the Nile.

An American pastor at the source of the Nile

The United States and Great Britain have achieved steadily stronger positions in this upstream country, and via diverse channels.

When Barack Obama was inaugurated president, he chose the controversial evangelist, Rick Warren, to lead the religious part of the ceremony, a pastor described as Obama's prayer partner and friend, and who told Larry King on CNN that his agenda consisted of two things: the United States' spiritual climate in an era of decline, and Rwanda.

So, who was this Rick Warren, who made Rwanda a matter of great personal importance, who was Obama's prayer partner to boot, and who participated in two presidential inaugurations – Obama's and Kagame's? In 1980 Warren founded Saddleback Church, which would become the eighth largest church in the United States, and he later wrote the book, *The Purpose Driven Life* (2002), which reportedly sold between 20 million and 30 million copies. Obama spoke in his church in 2006 and Hillary Clinton in 2007. Warren was invited to speak at the United Nations, at the World Economic Forum in Davos, and at Harvard University. He was designated a member of the Council on Foreign Relations between 2005 and 2006 and was named one of 'America's Top 25 Leaders' in 2005 by *US News and World Report. Time Magazine* declared him one of the '15 World Leaders Who Mattered Most in 2004' and one of the '100 Most Influential People in the World' in 2005. In 2006 *Newsweek* called him one of '15 People Who Make America Great'.

The official story of how Warren ended up in Rwanda is as follows. President Kagame was visiting a man named Joe Ritchie in Chicago. There, he saw Warren's book on the shelf and asked if he could have it. Shortly thereafter, Warren received a letter from Kagame, in which the president asked the pastor to come and help rebuild his country. Kagame explained that he thought Warren operated practically and was future-oriented, and that was what Rwanda needed. Whether or not this story is true, there can be no doubt that Warren's close relationship with Kagame fitted the United States' overarching strategy in the region, perhaps too neatly for this to be entirely coincidence.

By the time Kagame sent his letter, Rick Warren was already a famous and powerful man. It was, therefore, by no means an insignificant pastor who decided to concentrate his efforts on Rwanda. Warren's stated plan was, over a period of fifty years, to build up an extensive international network of Christian volunteers who should be able to help those in need wherever they were. Rwanda was a model and a test case for the network's global strategy. Apparently, the pastor encouraged more than 2,000 Saddleback Church members to travel to Rwanda in small groups in order to implement a national strategy in cooperation with 600 Rwandan churches. Businesspeople and members of Rwanda's parliament were also involved.

Warren began his work in Rwanda in 2005. By July 2008, he had already made around ten trips to the country. He said he had plans for long-term engagement there, and he was training pastors to provide healthcare also. By July 2008, 200 participants had completed a three-year programme designed by Warren and his associates.[5] The graduation ceremony was held at a stadium with 20,000 people and Warren preached a sermon. The theme: God has not created people who have no purpose – who are not 'purpose driven'. Warren's mentor, Peter Wagner, wrote in his book, *Dominion*, that Warren's project went hand in hand with the greater strategy of giving Christianity power in society.[6] In March 2012 Warren, now a member of Kagame's advisory board, gave a speech in which he praised the president as a man full of integrity, saying that Rwanda was already Africa's model but that in ten years it would become the world's model![7]

Kagame, who, as mentioned, has also had Tony Blair as his personal adviser, has received strong support from the American foreign policy leadership to both build and protect his own and Rwanda's good reputation. This relationship came to light in connection with a UN report regarding the war in Rwanda. The *New York Times* wrote on 27 August 2010, that a 545-page UN report existed accusing Rwandan governmental troops of killing tens of thousands of Hutus in Congo during the years after 1994.[8] Rwanda has never denied that it attacked militias hiding among the civilian population in the neighbouring country, but the UN report claims that civilians were also deliberately targeted. The report is entitled 'Democratic Republic of Congo, 1993–2003'.[9] Rwanda reacted negatively when it became known that such a report existed.

The *New York Times* followed up with another article on 30 September 2010. This article stated that a team of UN investigators had already concluded in the autumn of 1994 that Rwandan rebels under Kagame's leadership had killed tens of thousands of people. After heavy pressure from both Rwanda and Washington, and an internal UN debate, the report was, however, never published. Sixteen years later a fourteen-page official summary was released. There it was stated that the rebels methodically and systematically collected unarmed civilians in order to exterminate them. Those who participated in the 1994 investigation say that the Americans in the UN were very active in preventing the UN from publishing its findings – presumably because they feared that news of violations against Hutus could make civil war flare up again – and Rwanda's government has dismissed both reports as false.

A new era as the border shifts

Rusumo Falls on the Kagera River, on the boundary between Rwanda and Tanzania, does not compare in size and splendour with the Blue Nile Falls – as they were before the Ethiopians built a power plant there at the beginning of the 2000s, thereby reducing them to a shadow of their former self – or with Murchison Falls. But the falls are strategically placed, right at the point where the river in this part of Africa is most easily crossed, and that has guaranteed the site a place in the country's history. It was here that Count Gustav Adolf von Götzen, who later became governor of German East Africa, entered Rwanda for the first time at the beginning of the 1900s, and it was here that the Belgians, planning to conquer the territory, dug trenches during the First World War in preparation for a battle against the Germans, who occupied the other side of the river. The falls also got their 'fifteen minutes of fame' in 1994 when journalists reported directly on the chaotic exodus from Rwanda, as thousands tried to cross the bridge in desperation. They described the scene while standing on the bridge and counting the corpses that were washed over the rapids by flowing water.

Now, the three neighbouring governments of Burundi, Rwanda and Tanzania have come together to build a power plant at these same falls. According to the plan, it will produce 90 megawatts that will be divided equally between the three countries. It will not be a gigantic project, but it is a significant historical step in the region, partly because it is the first time the Nile is set to be controlled in this part of Africa, and not least because it is a cooperative project between three countries that follow very different developmental strategies. In 2013 the World Bank and the African Development Bank approved loans towards completion of the project. In 2016 contracts were signed in Kigali for construction of the power station. The groundbreaking ceremony was held at Ngara, in Tanzania, on 30 March 2017. As of

2019, completion and commercial commissioning are expected in 2020 or 2021. The project is, therefore, an example of how water control can overcome contrasts and different traditions, because this resource's multinational character does not make it possible for anyone to 'walk alone'. In January 2010 the government signed a loan agreement with an Indian bank and an Indian company to build another power plant along the Nyabarongo. Nyabarongo Power Station was completed in October 2014, across the small river Mwogo, a tributary of the Nyabarongo. It is the largest hydropower installation in the country to date and was officially inaugurated by President Kagame on 5 March 2015.

Even so, the Nile system also represents a potential source of conflict between Rwanda and Burundi, because the Akanyaru/Kanyaru and the Kagera/Nyabarongo rivers that form the border between the two states have shifted course since 1960 when those same borders were established.

Gorillas in the mist

In the heart of Africa, so high up in the mountains that you shiver more than you sweat, one finds enormous ancient volcanoes up to 3,500 metres in height; and there are the Virunga Mountains, almost entirely covered by a rich, verdant rainforest. This was the land of Dian Fossey, the world-famous expert on the mountain gorillas that live here. Here the warm equatorial air, blown inland by winds from the Indian Ocean, rises due to the volcanic mountains and creates an unusually humid but quite chilly climate.

In the morning, when I leave the bungalow I have rented on the plateau and look up at the mountains where the gorillas are living, the area is shrouded in mist. That is exactly as it should be, for the primates I am about to see close-up are called the gorillas in the mist. Thanks to the battle against illegal hunting, the Nile basin's mountain gorilla has been saved. The largest groups are now found here in the Volcanoes National Park. Rwanda, with a sure sense for public relations, has transformed these gorillas into the country's symbol, and the group I will visit here, almost on the border with Congo, is called Amahoro, or peace.

After travelling for a couple of hours in a four-wheel drive – the last stretch on an unusually bumpy road where we are forced to drive so slowly that children can run along beside the car and beg for 'dollars' – and after having passed the cultivated fields at the foot of the mountains, we arrive at a place to park. The experienced guide, Paul, leads us towards the mountains. The sounds of the rainforest, and its humidity – yes, particularly its humidity – and the way the light falls on the lianas and old tree trunks, create a distinctively mystical atmosphere, an uncommon intimacy with one's surroundings. Colourful birds flutter between the trees and make unexpected noises, while Paul, with the stick he pulled from a tree, shows us elephant and buffalo tracks that we are crossing.

We force our way through the plant growth and the dense forest of young trees, the guide with his machete in front. All at once we are there: just a few metres away is a family of large black mountain gorillas. On Paul's orders, we stand completely still and in utter silence. Suddenly, he claps his hands and shouts; he shouts at the gorillas, talks to them, raps with his walking stick. He demands action, and soon there is movement in the trees and branches on all sides: some gorillas dash up the trees, others climb down, while still more swing from one tree to the next as if asking us to relive a Tarzan film. The mountain gorillas behave just as they should when tourists come. And the big boss himself, a silverback, so-called for the characteristic stripe down his back, a huge, manlike male gorilla around one-and-a-half metres tall, without any hair on his breast and with enormous hands and feet, watches me fearlessly, and with much less curiosity than I watch him.

We continue into the forest and meet more gorilla families. In contrast to other large animals and to humans, mountain gorillas have never depended on the rivers or lakes that attract other animals, and humans. The gorillas get enough water from the plants they consume in the rainforest, which nearly always lies in fog, shrouded in cold, moist clouds. As a result, they do not need to wander away or migrate over large areas. They truly are the gorillas in the mist.

On the way back down, Paul talks about the mountain gorillas and their lives and repeatedly mentions the name Dian Fossey, since she deserves, he says, part of the praise for the fact that the Nile basin still houses these examples of our close relatives. She wrote the book *Gorillas in the Mist* in 1983 and became world famous, particularly when the book was filmed five years later with Sigourney Weaver in the lead role. In her diary, Fossey wrote that it was neither fate nor coincidence that brought her to Africa but rather a deep wish to live with wild animals that were not yet completely altered through human contact. She found an ideal base for her work, and from where she could see the Virunga Mountains. The camp became known as Campi ya Moshi – or Smoky Camp. Fossey's life here is also shrouded in mist. Not only because of her somewhat strange diary entries and because she fell out with practically everyone she possibly could – shooting at her enemies, throwing ape scat at intruders, and having people sent to jail as soon as they threatened her gorillas – but because she was murdered while together with the gorillas she had spent her life protecting and studying. No one knows who did it, but everyone knows she had many enemies.[10] She was buried in the camp she founded, next to the graves of her gorilla friends. Her gravestone reads:

Dian Fossey
1932–1985
No One Loved Gorillas More

Her last journal entry before she was murdered, famously reads: 'When you realize the value of all life, you dwell less on what is past and concentrate more on the preservation of the future.'[11]

The Nile source in the rainforest

I was picked up by the local police chief at the hotel in Gisenyi, situated by the astonishingly beautiful Lake Kivu, right on the Congo border, as daylight arrived to give the water's surface a peculiar milk-white hue. There was not a ripple to be seen aside from the rings made by the oars of two fishermen. I had been sitting on the hotel's balcony with a fresh fried egg and hot, fresh coffee, and was really anticipating our 'expedition' to the furthermost source of the Nile, as measured from its outlet in the Mediterranean. Even so, the atmosphere was surreal, since it was here, right in this location, that according to reports one of the largest, most desperate, exoduses in human history had taken place: more than 850,000 people – men, women and children – had, over the course of five days, from 14–18 July 1994, fled from Rwanda and into Congo after the regime change in Kigali. They feared that the Tutsis under Kagame, who was now in power in Kigali, would exact revenge on all Hutus. Here I was sitting in the beautiful morning light and what I thought was: finally, I will get to see the White Nile's source.

After several hours driving south-west through this country known as 'the Land of a Thousand Hills', we arrive at Nyungwe Forest National Park, which is host to 280 bird species and much of Africa's fauna. At the time I was there, few Rwandans had ever been to the source of the White Nile, since the modern national road network had so far avoided it. We are met on the park's edge by a small division of the Rwandan Army that the president's office has ordered to protect us in what at the time was still a complex and potentially troubled region; or they were there to ensure that we have no plans other than those we stated.

While we silently penetrate deeper and deeper into the rainforest, I picture in my mind's eye the Mediterranean and Greek coasts far to the north, more than 7,000 kilometres away, and think that what comes from here is a component in the Nile waters that washes up onto the south European beaches where tourists flock to enjoy the heat. As I hop over tree trunks fallen across our path, I am thinking of Cairo, Karnak, Nubia, Khartoum, Bor and Lake Victoria – all so completely different, and then this.

We neither see nor hear the source before we are right upon it. The White Nile's source or birthplace is in no way remarkable or sensational. A narrow, very thin strip of brown water trickles from a small overhang. That is all. That is the Nile's rather ludicrous, humble beginning. But it is the very diffidence of the source that makes the site a perfect illustration for the Nile's significance to the eleven countries from which it collects water and through which it runs. The whole basin's character is summarized in this humble source: what the river does is collect water drops that fall over about a tenth of the entire vast African continent. This tiny source thereby underscores the basin's geographical breadth and the water's singularly connective role. It is the hundreds of thousands of such small streams that transform the Nile into a historic river, and into an object for intense political tugs-of-war among countries that soon will have more than half a billion people.

The discovery of this birthplace of the Nile, which is the most distant point on the river from the Mediterranean, also has its history. Richard Kandt, the German physician and explorer who founded Kigali in 1907, first suggested in his book on the sources of the Nile that the 'true source' had to be where the Kagera River began, and he said he had found a source in the Nyungwe Forest.[12] In 1961 a German priest living in Rwanda, Stephan Bettentrup, set out to find what Kandt was convinced had to be the source. He supported his countryman's theory and identified a swamp located further up along the river basin simply by following the Nyabarongo.

Then, in the 1960s, a group of local researchers, called the Waseda Group, published a hand-drawn map of the swamp region that Bettentrup had visited a few years before. They discovered a small tributary to the east: the Rukarara River. After closer investigation, they concluded that this must be the source farthest from the Mediterranean, and they affixed a wooden plaque to a tree trunk inscribed with the words: 'SOURCE DU NIL 1969 27 APR'.

In 2006 the source was again 'discovered' by the significantly better known 'Ascend the Nile' expedition. A group of three people from Great Britain and New Zealand staged their adventure into innermost Africa as a modern expedition in the spirit of Speke and Stanley. They travelled 6,700 kilometres upriver in three boats. In North Uganda, one of the expedition members was killed. The other two continued on and, aided by GPS and an inflatable rubber raft, they continued up the Rukarara. They concluded that the Nile was 107 kilometres longer than was previously assumed. When the expedition leader reached the source, where it trickles from the overhang, he declared to the media: 'History has been rewritten'.

It is no understatement to say he exaggerated somewhat, since he basically confirmed the Waseda Group's sketches from four decades earlier. In 1969 Rwanda was still a Francophone country, as the first plaque proclaiming the Nile's source would confirm if it still hung here. When I visited the source in 2009, there was a new notice: 'Source of the Nile'. A simple, but evocative symbol of France's historical setback in this region during the last decades, a setback that is also significant for the Great Power politics about the Nile.

I cast a last look at the source. I know I will never set foot here again. But I also know that this tiny stream, these first droplets of the long and famous river, will forever bind Rwanda to political developments in Egypt and to all the other Nile countries, and it is precisely all these small trickles that ultimately bind the countries together in a political and economic relationship that none of them can escape.

Heart of Darkness, Joseph Conrad and a Nile biography

A book conceived as a journey up the Nile from the Mediterranean to innermost Africa cannot be written as if Joseph Conrad's *Heart of Darkness* and the famous tale about the journey up the Congo River did not exist. The short novel was published in 1902 and has retained stature as the incarnate story of civilization and Africa.[13] At little more than a hundred prose pages, the work is a strikingly telling example of the potential power of literature and ideas, and in this case, when it comes to creating perceptions and images of the 'other' and 'us' and of relationships between barbarism and civilization.

Conrad's novel is one of those canonical books that are impossible to read unprejudiced; it has become not only part of the literary consciousness but also a part of modern society's self-reflection. Francis Ford Coppola's film, *Apocalypse Now* from 1979, helped to make the book a popular cultural icon. Among literary critics the novel has often been interpreted as a deep and devastating critique of European imperialism in general and Belgian colonialism in particular, and as an exposure of prominent ideas about a civilizing Europe; a self-glorifying notion that conceals a barbaric truth. The book can, of course, also be read as a journey into inner space; a metaphorical investigation into the turbid waters of the human soul. The book is ambiguous – one of the reasons for its success.

I am reading *Heart of Darkness* again as I sit on a balcony overlooking the Nile in North Uganda. The only thing that disturbs the silence before the frogs begin their evening chorus are the hotel employees, as they attempt to chase a few wild elephants out of the hotel yard by roaring like lions and clapping their hands loudly. Conrad's text draws me in to the disturbing tale of Marlow's journey up the great river to the mysterious inner heart of Africa, which is also the heart of evil, and while I sit here, in the very same region that for decades was terrorized by the Lord's Resistance Army, it occurs to me that the book is about something other than I first thought, and something other than the dominant interpretations claim.

The author sets the mood with an ingenious and ambivalent title that is loaded with significance. The 'heart of darkness' is a bleak, disturbing metaphor that contains the paradoxes that carry the story – an internal, merciless contradiction, a struggle between creation and destruction, between heroism and treachery, between truth and falsehood, but also between reality and the possibility of describing what is inherently taking place in the meeting of cultures.

In Conrad's novel the first-person narrator is the sailor Marlow. He tells his story sitting on a boat at the mouth of the Thames, and over a day he relates what happened after he signed on as riverboat captain for a Belgian company that conducted trade along a major river in Africa. Marlow's riverboat journey has become one of literary history's most famous educational journeys. The trip up the great river changed him for life.

After Marlow repaired the boat he was to travel with, he gathered a crew of cannibals and began the trip upriver. The farther he travels into the continent, the coarser his descriptions of life there become, and with these also the plot of the novel.

The mood is ominous and grim: 'We were cut off from the comprehensions of our surroundings; we glided past like phantoms, wondering and secretly appalled, as sane men would be before an enthusiastic outbreak in a madhouse.'[14] Conrad sketches the violence and bloodshed with restraint, but it works as a literary device to reinforce the overall feeling of pessimism and darkness: '[I]n and out of rivers, streams of death in life, whose banks were rotting into mud, whose waters, thickened into slime, invaded the contorted mangroves that seemed to writhe at us in the extremity of an impotent despair. Nowhere did we stop long enough to get a particularized impression. It was like a weary pilgrimage amongst hints for nightmares.'[15]

The text gives the reader a vague sense that it is now, after Marlow has penetrated so far into the continent, that he can finally recognize the truth about it. He has entered the 'heart of darkness' – synonymous with the darkness of life itself.

Far into the jungle he finally finds the German trader, Kurtz, who is widely known as a tough ivory trader, but also as an accomplished musician, journalist, indeed, as a universal genius, and as an altruist and a torchbearer for civilization's values. Marlow gets Kurtz with him downriver to the trade station, and along the way Kurtz's roughness, cynicism and brutality become steadily clearer. Then Kurtz falls gravely ill and entrusts to Marlow his personal records as well as a photograph of a woman. He asks Marlow to return with this to civilization. Then, as Kurtz dies: 'He cried in a whisper at some image, at some vision – he cried out twice, a cry that was no more than a breath: *"The horror! The horror!"'* Kurtz summarizes here what, for Marlow, amounts to his life's wisdom and experiences in the jungle.

Marlow ends up defending Kurtz, despite witnessing what he describes as Kurtz's boundless greed and barbaric behaviour. Rather than criticizing him, Marlow goes in to bat for him; his actions are relativized. As Marlow sees it, Kurtz might have become mad, but he had nonetheless deciphered lies and deceits; he had, therefore, something to say and he said it. Marlow travels through what was an actual, physical nightmare, but he escapes the emotional consequences of it by merely observing. And, when he later meets Kurtz's 'fiancée' and is forced to account for Kurtz's last words, Marlow answers untruthfully, and thereby fails himself. He tells the fiancée that, with his last breath, Kurtz said '[y]our name'.

Geographically, the novel's action is moving up a large river, from place to place, but – and this is important, for it seems to underscore that the story's theme is a general one – to indefinite places more expressive of a mental state than of concrete points on a map. Conrad does not portray Africa, or the Congo, as Europe's contrast or antithesis, as has been suggested. His book is not a book about the Congo River and its development, or about its actual histories. Instead, the river serves the role as an exotic scene, or as a dream-like arena in which to unfold a complex civilization drama and onto which Marlow projects his own dilemmas and fears. The Africa described here, in other words, is an Africa that says more about Marlow's and Conrad's perspective than it does about Africa itself.

Even the name Congo is never used in the book. The journey up the nameless river acts as both metaphor and stage for a recognition process, an educational process in which Marlow, among other things, realizes, or draws the conclusion (unclearly, it is true), that European education is only a mask of humanism, one concealing an evil worse than 'primitive' bestiality. The beginning of the 1900s was the political-ideological zenith of the self-promoting idea of the civilizing Europe, and the novel is critical of the way in which this was understood and expressed at the time. However, the book functions even more precisely as a commentary on Europe's naïve conceptions and self-images.

What Kurtz had deciphered was nothing less than the dominating culture's deceptive self-understanding. And that is why Marlow respects Kurtz and consciously lies about him – in order to preserve not just his memory but his existential project, that is, the refusal to be overpowered by convention. Kurtz must be respected, even if jungle life had made him coarse and cynical, not because he wished to live in truth, like some German version of the heroes of some of Henrik Ibsen's plays, but because he had succeeded in breaking out of the dominant perspectives of his time.

Thus, in this context, the novel is interesting by proving to be an example of the very thing it sets out to critique. It provides a source to the history of Western ideas and perspectives of Africa. The book appears today to be clearly coloured by time in its depictions of Africans as human beings lacking personal identity, as being culturally primitive; they were in a way seen as a kind of metaphysical extension of the dark and dangerous jungle that the Europeans traversed. The novel thus characterized the world views and self-images of the late European explorations of Africa.

To read this novel as a conventional critique of humankind's eternally warlike nature, or as a protest against imperialism, is to rob it of some of its originality and power. To cast Marlow as a spokesperson of traditional anti-imperial views results in a simplification and a banalization of the book and erases its double nature. To place the book within such a schematic is to obscure its truly disquieting elements, and to make the opposition it offers against the conventions of its day appear almost pedestrian.

The book's political and moral ambiguity, furthermore, reflects the fact that in the Congo the author himself was an active participant in the colonial project, and it is precisely this ambiguity that African intellectuals, such as the Nigerian author and critic, Chinua Achebe, for example, pinpoint when they critique the novel for being racist as opposed to anti-imperialistic. Conrad describes a reality that is grotesquely brutal, though it is a reality one cannot help but relate to; indeed, it is something one must reflect upon if civilization is to be preserved. Conrad unveiled European falsehoods about Africa, but what he did not unveil was the falsehood about Europe existing in Africa. Dominating, conventional interpretations of the book have, therefore, created new conceptions about Europe and Africa – both stereotypes – of Africa as the 'dark' barbaric continent, and of Europe and its colonialism as being synonymous with the collapse of civilization.

And it is this aspect of the novel that has enabled it to become a kind of model, indeed, a cliché for other authors in their meeting with Africa. Countless descriptions of travelling through Africa in general, and on rivers in particular, have availed themselves of Conrad's metaphors and images, or have referenced his book as a literary source of inspiration. It is almost impossible to say *the Congo* without thinking of Marlow.

Conrad's book should instead be read as an historical document of a zeitgeist, where it was still possible to describe Africa as faceless, unfixed, as existing in a projected dream, and where European influence was formulated in a language that today seems unacceptable and archaic. Conrad allows Marlow to free himself from the catastrophe, from the terror and the heart of darkness by allowing him to fail the truth, thereby ultimately allowing Kurtz's grim, almost prophetic-like view of the relationship between civilization and barbarity to pass without comment. Because the novel's epic framework is Marlow's first-person narration, the book also becomes a story about himself. The novel is a journey into Marlow's own twisted mind and his 'dark heart'. Yet, more than becoming a psychological study, this literary method underscores an interpretative problem: in order to narrate or describe or comprehend the 'other', you must, in addition to seeking the truth behind conventional images and stereotypes, understand yourself.

Because of the very influence of *Heart of Darkness*, it has been important to write *The Nile: History's Greatest River* without a single parallel to Kurtz's, or Marlow's, or Conrad's river expeditions into 'the heart of darkness'. Even if my book depicts a journey up a huge river extending from the ocean to innermost Africa, as Conrad's also does, I have made it a point to distance myself from the associations of darkness, exoticization and the courageous traveller. Here I sit on a balcony with a view overlooking the river not long before it flows into Lake Albert, at the border with

Congo, under a peaceful afternoon sun, with a mobile phone and internet and television in my room. After hearing that a tourist was killed by an elephant outside the hotel (the tranquillity here probably lured her into thinking the animal was tame), it is perhaps unnecessary to emphasize that it is exceptionally ahistorical and pathetic to draw parallels between Marlow's journey up the Congo at the beginning of the 1900s and journeys along the Nile about hundred years later.

A snow-covered Moon Mountain on the Equator

From the Mountains of the Moon [...] the Egyptian Nile takes its rise. It cuts horizontally the equator on its course north. Many rivers come from this mountain and unite in a great lake. From this lake comes the Nile, the greatest and most beautiful of the rivers of all the earth.[16]

Since the Greek astronomer and mathematician, Claudius Ptolemy, almost 2,000 years ago produced his map proposing that the Nile originated in the Mountains of the Moon and two lakes in the centre of the African continent, myths regarding these mountains spread. But it was Henry Morton Stanley who finally was able to assess their role in the Nile hydrological system. In his famous book *In Darkest Africa*, he put himself within this history of discovery and minimized his own significance at a time when pro-imperial contemporaries insisted on elevating him to the clouds. Stanley travelled up the Congo River in 1887 and followed the Semliki River (which flows into Lake Albert) upstream toward Lake Edward.

It was there, on 25 May 1888, following a two-hour trip, that Stanley became the first European to view Ptolemy's and what he referred to as the Arabic geographer Scheabeddin's Mountain of the Moon, as 'a vast mountain covered with snow' emerged.[17] Stanley chose to give the mountain another name, Ruwenzori (now spelt Rwenzori), one of the many names that the locals used. It was a good choice, for in the language of the Mtsora people it means 'rainmaker', and that is precisely what the mountain is. Clouds develop continually around the mountainsides, and therefore the peak is hidden for months every year. And yet suddenly, if only seldom, the whole mountain can, as it were, spring forth out of the heavy clouds. Even in the short intervals between the rainy season and the dry, it is only during the earliest morning hours that the peak is visible; in the dry season it is shrouded in a seemingly everlasting haze.

The Italian mountaineer and explorer, Luigi Amedeo, Duke of the Abruzzi, was the first European to reach the mountain's peak. Even though it was almost twenty years after Stanley first saw and described it, the duke was in a great mood – indeed, he was in an exalted and poetic state of mind, if one is to believe his own narrative:

Having unfolded the little flag which had been given me at Rome by Her Majesty Queen Margherita before my departure, I fastened it to a staff planted on the highest point of the snowy dome to the triple cry of 'Viva Margherita!' 'Viva Alexandra!' and 'Viva l'Italia!' The winds blew out the tricolour above the snows, which up to that time had known nothing but the breath of the tempest . . .[18]

The duke's expedition also demonstrates in a paradoxical, self-glorifying way the European habit of naming Africa after themselves. In this context, the duke's suggestion at a Royal Geographical Society meeting in London, where the British king was also present, is highly suggestive:

> I propose, therefore, to call Mount Stanley the mountain or massif that carries the five highest peaks – Margherita (16,816 feet), Alexandra (16,750 feet) Elena (16,388 feet), Savoia (16,340 feet), and Moebius (16,214 feet). To the second group in order of height, the Duwoi seen from Ibanda, I give the name of Speke, in memory of the discoverer of the Ripon Falls, the origin of the Nile; and the highest peak of this massif I call after the King of Italy, Vittorio Emanuele (16,080 feet); and the lower and more southern seen from the lower Mobuko valley I name after Sir H. Johnston (15,906 feet). To the third massif (Semper, Kiyanja, or Ngemwimbi) I give the name of Mount Baker, in memory of the traveller who discovered Lake Albert, and was the first to see these mountains, calling its highest point (15,988 feet) after the King of England.

And so on and so forth, until he had named every mountain after Italians and Britons.

King Leopold, a robber state and Nile diplomacy

It was a person from a European country other than Italy that came for all time to be associated with Congo, and it is one of the ironies of history that he came from Brussels, capital of the new post-war Europe. In the late nineteenth century this city became the capital for what most historians agree was European colonialism at its most barbaric. King Leopold II has remained a 'prince of evil' of sorts, an arch-imperialist who in his Congo Free State created his personal brand of colonialism.

It was the king's cooperation with Henry Morton Stanley that started what would end up as an enormous private colony and a terror regime. At the time he was approached, Stanley had not yet been recognized as the 'Napoleon of African travel', and it was long before anybody would suggest that 'The map of Africa is a monument to Stanley'.[19] He had, though, just returned to Europe as David Livingstone's very famous saviour.

On 12 August 1877, the Welsh-born Stanley had concluded a three-year expedition straight across the African continent. On his journey, he had established for good that Lake Victoria had no more outlets than the Victoria Nile, and he had also confirmed Baker's description of Lake Albert thirteen years earlier. In addition to these accomplishments, he had followed, despite the difficulties and dangers he met with, the course of the Congo, a river he attempted to rebaptize the Livingstone River by consistently referring to it thus in his Royal Geographical Society lectures in 1878, and by using it in the title of one of his books on Africa. Stanley returned to Europe with ivory and a wealth of personal impressions. With an unparalleled sense for what the British termed self-publicity, he allowed his image to be used to sell everything from soap to the meat extract Bovril. He did not, however, succeed in changing the river's name from Congo to Livingstone after the famous Edinburgh missionary.[20] Nonetheless, in Congo the country, he left powerful traces.

Stanley attempted to convince London to support his next Congo expedition, but the British were not particularly interested in that part of Africa. King Leopold, on the other hand, had already sent two representatives who had met Stanley on his way home from Congo. Leopold had formed an organization whose name emphasizes a continuing theme in the outside world's relationship to Congo: African International Association for Development in Central Africa. A blatant example, it would turn out, of self-interest cloaked as altruism, of resource-plundering under the banner of the Good and of atavism packaged as modernity. Two years after his return from Africa, Stanley headed the Belgian king's Congo expedition.

This time the expedition was quite different. It consisted of several hundred men, dragging with them two heavy steamboats. Stanley brought with him a silver service from which he enjoyed his tea every morning, and they brought weapons – lots of weapons. It was the excesses and violence of this Africa expedition that eventually would be associated with Stanley's legacy. One of the stories to emerge went like this. James Jameson, the heir of an Irish whiskey producer, in exchange for six pocket handkerchiefs bought a ten-year-old girl as a slave so he could turn her over to cannibals. He did this in order to document and sketch the way she was dismembered, cooked and then consumed. Stanley himself was not a witness to the event and he was furious when he heard what had happened, even though there were contradictory accounts about what really occurred. As leader, however, he was responsible. Jameson himself died of fever in the jungle.

King Leopold continued to tenaciously implement his project and, thanks to London's tacit support, he succeeded. With a morbid sense for the propaganda potential inherent in the written word, he called the state he created the Congo Free State, though historians have compared the Belgian's treatment of the Congolese to the Holocaust and have estimated that as many as ten million people were exterminated.[21] Leopold became the largest landowner in the world, probably in world history. Historians agree that the King of Belgium in the mid-1880s would not have succeeded in acquiring a colony of around a million square kilometres if he had not had support from the major powers. And an important reason he received London's support during the first decades of his colonial adventure was Britain's Nile strategy, a policy consideration largely overlooked in the large literature on Congo and European colonialism.

In 1894, and only four years after the British had the Nile confirmed as their sphere of interest, London entered into an agreement with the Belgian king whereby he was given the status of private empire-builder. It was, therefore, as a private person that King Leopold II was given dominion over this enormous portion of Africa, and not as the King of Belgium. In explicit exchange, however, Leopold formally accepted, via agreement, that the British sphere of interest was the Nile Valley. So tight was this relationship that London offered Leopold the chance to 'rent' the Nile's west bank in South Sudan, all the way up to Fashoda, for as long as he lived. The king's troops in Congo also accomplished a job that London itself could not – namely, fighting to reduce the influence of the 'Dervishes', the nickname for the remaining troops belonging to the Turkish-Egyptian empire in the region, as well as for a large number of Nubian soldiers from northern Sudan, and against whom the British themselves could not wage war due to their allies in Cairo. The British relied on Leopold because they knew he was weak and depended on them. As a result, the British government long turned a deaf ear to reports critical of Leopold's rule. They were more concerned about a potential power vacuum in this Nile basin border area.

This manoeuvre from 1894 – the same year that London occupied Uganda and the year before General Kitchener was ordered to plan the occupation of Sudan – gave the British a guarantee that this part of the Nile basin would not come under another power's sway, even as they ensured that King Leopold could not undertake anything of significance regarding the river. London supported Leopold if Leopold supported Britain's Nile strategy. And the king was by and large Britain's willing instrument: if he desired more land, said Foreign Secretary Lord Lansdowne later, a person who repeatedly proved his grasp of the Nile's geopolitical role, Britain should give him that as long as he did not interfere with their interests on the Nile.

William Garstin's hydrological assessment missions on the Upper Nile and in Congo at the very beginning of the twentieth century,[22] made it necessary to reformulate and expand the agreement with Leopold from 1894. Leopold had suggested around the same time as Garstin surveyed the Upper White Nile that the Semliki River be used as a transport route and that it could also be improved as a communication route. Garstin informed Cromer that this idea would require heavy investment. It would lead to changes in the river, and everyone knew that it would create demand for more permanent ports on Lake Albert.[23] That might harm potential future British plans for Lake Albert as a regulating reservoir. Leopold's proposals were, therefore, rejected by the British in Cairo and London. These new ambitions for the Congo Nile basin may, furthermore, have driven the British to help expose the colonialism of the Belgian king, thereby undermining the old agreement they had with him and instead get a more predictable, long-term cooperation with a Belgian government.

Around the same time that Garstin was reporting on Leopold's Nile plans, the British government appointed the commission that would eventually expose King Leopold's style of rule to the world. In 1903 Roger Casement, then the British consul at Boma in Congo, was asked by London to investigate the work conditions in the country. Casement produced a long, detailed account: the so-called Casement Report was delivered in 1904.[24] The report expanded the political foundation for the process that ended with Leopold being forced to surrender Congo as his private colony.

Another of these dates with great diplomatic significance in the Nile's history, for the entire region's development and for world policy: 9 May 1906. On that day, London signed a new agreement with Belgium and King Leopold, which also underscored the continuity and steadfastness of Britain's Nile strategy at the time. Article III concerned the Nile and was crystal clear. It stated that 'The Government of the Independent State of the Congo undertake not to construct, or allow to be constructed, any work on or near the Semliki or Isango River, which would diminish the volume of water entering Lake Albert, except in agreement with the Soudanese Government'.[25] The Anglo-Belgian Agreement of 1894, slightly modified in 1906, therefore ended up prohibiting any structure to be built in Congo that could affect Nile water flow.

The Congo Nile

I am driving over the Yei River, a Nile tributary in South Sudan, and then further south towards the Congo border. At the crossing, I am brusquely stopped by a border guard, who in a rough French-English asks: 'What the hell are you doing here?' He eyes me as if he takes me for one of these white European adventurers who smuggle diamonds from the Democratic Republic of the Congo. 'I'm here to see the Nile', I say. The answer must have surprised him; in any case, he suddenly smiles, stamps my passport and waves us on.

For the pure joy of having entered DR Congo so easily, my Sudanese companion and myself stopped in the closest village for tea. The café owner, or maybe some visitors, must have read the Kenyan Ngũgĩ wa Thiong'o 's novel, *A Grain of Wheat*, from 1967. Within the novel, the protagonist heads to the African quarter and finds a café named Your Friend Unto Death, or Friend for short. That café had numerous customers, and flies, flies everywhere, just like here. The café's motto was painted in large letters across the wall: COME UNTO ME ALL THAT ARE HUNGRY AND THIRSTY AND I WILL GIVE YOU REST.[26] This particular café lacked the Bible verse, but not far from where the woman running the cash register was standing there hung a piece of paper in the same way and with the same poem as in the novel:

Since man to man has been unjust,
Show me the man that I can trust.
I have trusted many to my sorrow,
So for credit, my friend, come tomorrow.

We travelled further into the country, but abruptly the dark, threatening clouds we had seen earlier in the day broke into a frenetic artillery of crashes and lightning – few things are comparable to thunder on the Nile plains. The lightning struck with a terrible sound, again and again, and I knew what was coming next. There was nothing else to do: we simply stopped the car. And indeed, after a minute or two, the rain arrived. It rained like it never does in Europe, and we were almost deafened by the incessant drumming on the car roof. We sat idle and did not move another metre. Nothing to do but light a cigarette and wait. And the magnificent downpour stopped as quickly as it had begun. Then, as if out of nowhere, men and children and women arrived, smiling and hollering, and pushed us onto solid ground after the rain had turned the road into a quagmire.

Hydrologically speaking, the Congolese portion of the Nile basin is still relatively little researched. What occurs along DR Congo's largest tributary, the Semliki, is of comparatively marginal significance for the Nile's water flow downstream. Once British water-planners in Egypt and Sudan had secured agreements with King Leopold that he would not tamper with the tributaries without prior British approval, they were relatively uninterested in the river.

The Semliki flows out of the northern end of Lake Edward and is generally between 20 and 30 metres wide. It falls about 290 metres along its 150-kilometre journey from Lake Edward to Lake Albert. In its upper portion, the water flows quickly; the river is rocky and surrounded by dense forest. At some places it is only 10 metres wide and flows between sheer mountain cliffs. No detailed studies exist of the river's hydropower possibilities, but the river holds significant potential: it has been suggested around 100 megawatts. On the savannah lower down, it flows slowly along before meandering lazily toward Lake Albert. A chain of oxbow lakes west of the watercourse indicates that the riverbed has long been making its way eastward across the plains.

The Rwenzori mountain range consists of six massifs separated by deep chasms. Meltwater and rainfall from different parts drain north – towards the Nile. The Nile in DR Congo is a complex hydrological system whose key elements are Lake Edward and Lake Albert, and the Semliki with its tributaries. So enormous is this country that the Congo Nile only covers around 1 per cent of its area.

For people living in the north-east of East Congo, however, the river is still very important, and both parts of North Kivu and Orientale Province lie in the Nile basin, along with the Ituri Forest, the area which Stanley so ardently feared and described in such detail. In Ituri, the organization Démocratie et Civisme pour le Développement Intégral de l'Ituri backed, in 2004, a concrete development project that, for the first time in this region's planning history, included use of the Nile. Plans have also been discussed for building hydropower plants on the Semliki and for rebuilding port facilities in Kasenyi and Mahagi on Lake Albert. Furthermore, it has been suggested that around 10,000 hectares can be artificially irrigated from the Nile's tributaries, but again these numbers and scheme plans are based on as yet limited research and studies. The government in Kinshasa views the support and implementation of these projects as a way to advance its authority in the region, affirm the state's sovereignty and gain the local population's trust.

As a water resource, the Nile will never prove an issue of great national economic significance to DR Congo. Yet the basin itself could prove in the future to be an important national political issue. Kinshasa has limited instruments at its disposal, as it attempts to establish the state's authority in the eastern, mineral-rich regions of the country. By backing the Ituri people's projects, the government in Kinshasa could perhaps manifest itself as a state authority in a region where lawlessness and resource bandits, not seldom cloaked as guerrilla soldiers, have dominated, and where the whole world has strong economic interests due to all the minerals there, and where a few make enormous profits.

It is only the central government and the state that can promote the local population's interests in the local exploitation and use of the Nile, since these actions necessitate diplomatic activity on the state arena, both vis-à-vis the other countries in the region and in terms of the international donor community or international investors. The government in Kinshasa, however, has had – and still has – an uphill struggle. There are too many powerful international interests working against stability and state control in this part of the world. The Nile basin in DR Congo is an area too rich in minerals and resources – especially those of crucial importance to the modern weapons and data industries – for Congo's government to be allowed to establish control and enforce stability. To the outside world, or to the 'international community', the image of eastern Congo has thus become one that proves that everything remains unchanged in Africa;

it represents, so to speak, a preconceived African paradigm – it serves as the ultimate proof that Africa must be developed by someone other than Africans, even while the chaos there is to a large extent, perhaps even primarily, due to actors within that same 'international community'.

Lake Albert or Lake Mobutu

If you fly over Lake Albert, you see a large deep-blue Nile lake stretching far to the south, and on the DR Congo side the mountains plunge steeply down to meet their reflection in a body of water that could have been called Mobutu Sese Seko Lake, had the country's herostratically famous leader got his desire.

Joseph-Désiré Mobutu had, like so many others from the Belgian Congo, studied in Brussels before he returned to his homeland at the beginning of the 1960s. Congo became independent in 1960. Not long after, the liberation hero and the first president in the then Republic of Congo, Patrice Lumumba, was killed – poisoned by the CIA according to a book later written by an American agent.[27] In the meantime, it has come to light that the Belgians, the UN and the Americans were all involved, and American president Dwight D. Eisenhower supposedly told the British Foreign Secretary that he imagined Lumumba tumbling into a river full of crocodiles.[28] That was immediately before Che Guevara renounced all his titles in Cuba and jumped a plane bound for Congo – disguised in a large grey hat, beard shaved off and wearing large sunglasses with thick black lenses – in an attempt to mobilize a revolutionary people's war.[29] Yet, with a CIA-backed coup in 1965, Mobutu took over as president. As part of his political programme, and with the official aim of forwarding a stronger Congolese national consciousness and identity, he wanted to develop something that was called a Zairian 'national authenticity'.

Mobutu, who was long supported by the United States in part at least due to his opposition to Angola and the Soviet and Cuban presence there, will long be remembered for one of the greatest public relations scoops of the time. He invited Cassius Clay, the reigning world heavyweight champion, and George Foreman, to a title fight in Kinshasa. Cassius Clay had converted to Islam and assumed the name Muhammad Ali. The match would become history's most famous ring fight, taking place on 30 October 1974, in Congo's capital, with 60,000 attending and the biggest worldwide TV audience ever. Muhammad Ali won by knock-out in the eighth round after a match that had it all. The events before and during the match quickly became iconic; they proved the theme of the American author Norman Mailer's book, *The Fight*, from 1975 and of the Oscar-winning documentary *When We Were Kings*. In *Ali*, the biographical movie about the boxing legend, from 2001, this fight serves as the film's climax. The title 'The Rumble in the Jungle' and the descriptions of this brutal fight played also on those associations that Conrad and Kurtz had created about the country, as something dark, wild and beyond the borders of true civilization.

As part of the programme to create a new national authenticity, Mobutu renamed the country Zaire, derived from the Portuguese *zaire*, which is again derived from the Congolese word *nzere* or *nzadi*, 'the river that swallows all rivers', a fitting description for the majestic river that flows through the land, and which is now called the Democratic Republic of the Congo. It was, therefore, natural that Mobutu would not accept or be pleased with the idea that the country's largest lake should bear the name of a British royal consort, because Samuel Baker had dubbed it so in 1864. Mobuto rebaptized Lake Albert and named it instead after himself. Now the lake *should* be known as Lake Mobutu Sese Seko.

The Ugandans, who, after all, shared this natural Nile reservoir with Congo, did not think that this attempt by Mobutu to conquer the lake conceptually and make it his own was a particularly good idea. Eventually, as Mobutu's rule progressed from bad to worse, proving ultimately to become the very symbol of kleptocracy as a form of government (it has been estimated that almost 90 per cent of the state's income went straight into Mobutu's pocket, and although this figure might be an exaggeration, the regime was utterly corrupt). It also became clear that the United States could no longer shield him, and fewer and fewer of his countryman found it a brilliant idea to call the Nile lake after their increasingly reviled leader. Mobutu was toppled in 1997 by Laurent-Désiré Kabila, backed, among others, by Rwanda, Uganda and the United States, and the queen's consort Albert was, for the time being, left in peace. The lake in Central Africa, where Albert never set foot, still bears his name.

Kabila was assassinated in 2001 and his son Joseph took over. His government has long been concerned with establishing the state's legitimacy in the part of the country where the Semliki flows. This goal is set to be accomplished with development projects along the river. Gradually, the Democratic Republic of the Congo's government has unfolded a policy for how the Nile basin's resources might be exploited. This will prove a central element in any plan for establishing Kinshasa's power in this region, where unrest has been an almost permanent factor, where different guerrilla groups have waged various types of war, prompted more by the quest for the area's natural resources and minerals than by political principles. The need for a secure and permanent water supply, and for industry and energy development along the Nile basin within the country, means that DR Congo also does not accept the colonial Agreements of 1894 and 1906 as binding. More important for Kinshasa, however, is regional stability. The government's Nile diplomacy is part of a strategy based on what, for DR Congo, is much more pressing than the country's need for Nile water: to secure a guarantee from neighbouring countries that they will not interfere in DR Congo's internal affairs, something that other countries and their neighbours have consistently done for a long time. Here, Kinshasa has sought Egypt's support, and that is one of the reasons they refrained from signing the Nile Agreement of 2010, unlike the other upstream countries, which did sign.

'Are you the only person who can write about the Nile in DR Congo?' We had searched high and low for a Congolese who could write a chapter in a book I was editing about the Nile in the postcolonial era. 'Yes, I think so,' Raphael said, 'but it's not something I can really do either, it's not my field.' Nonetheless, in a very short time he produced a fine chapter.[30] As this story well illustrates, even though the country's past is so tightly woven with the Nile's history, independent Congo is still a marginal player in the Nile basin, and the country's national research tradition is limited.

A shifting border

'The river is shifting here, so therefore the border is shifting also.' As if the Congolese did not have enough problems in this border region, they also share a border with Uganda that shifts due to natural causes. The Semliki River, which William Garstin studied at the beginning of the 1900s, and which King Leopold planned to develop for boat transport, is changing its course. Semliki runs north from Lake Edward into DR Congo before debouching into Lake Albert, and for long stretches it forms the border between DR Congo and Uganda. The Belgian-Ugandan border commission at the beginning of the twentieth century simply determined that the river should act as the boundary between the two countries, but did not know, or have knowledge about its behaviour over enough years, to realize that it was a shifting border they had fixed, and left behind them.

On 7 December 2010, the British newspaper *The Guardian* carried an interview with a local Ugandan farmer: 'The land where our grandparents used to cultivate – it is now in Congo. It is now being controlled by [the Congo government] ... I have to go and kneel before them: Congo's leadership.'[31] It was dramatically established that Uganda was shrinking – to Congo's benefit. A serious accusation, if it had been true, but the reality is rather the reverse. In some places DR Congo has lost territory, in other places Uganda has. Since 1960, however, it is Uganda's territory that has increased; the river has changed course and Congo has shrunk.

The Guardian also directly established why they thought the river was shifting. It was due to global climate change:

> The snowy peaks have changed rapidly in the last 100 years or so, almost certainly as a result of the increase in global temperatures caused by human greenhouse gas emissions. It is the changes to the climate on the mountains – and the heavy rainfall that comes with it – that is partly to blame for the shifts in the river on the vast plain below.[32]

The Rwenzori mountains have fewer glaciers and, therefore, Uganda is getting smaller, the paper claimed. Yet, it proved a snap judgement. In the first place, no one has precise information about local glacier development over time. The snow that the Duke of Abruzzi described in such an exalted style in 1906 could have been entirely atypical, due to a year especially rich in rainfall. It is not enough to compare one observation from a single past year in order to determine developmental trends of such proportions. Furthermore, melting ice comprises only a fraction of the river's water flow: it is local rainfall that primarily influences its water flow, and that is what determines the river's meandering. In the years prior to 2010, it rained quite a bit, although not more than in the mid-1960s, when glaciers also, according to the same researchers the newspaper cites, were reportedly numerous. In the years after *The Guardian*'s article, many studies and articles have been published that forecast that all the Rwenzori glaciers could melt completely by 2025. This would have dramatic local consequences, but since our knowledge of the behaviour of these glaciers in the past is so scant, there are good reasons for questioning the validity and accuracy of this alarmism.

On the Ugandan side, the local population has been mobilized in several places to conduct afforestation on the riverbanks, and to keep the cattle away, in order to protect the riverbanks and to prevent the river from eating up even more land and shifting into Uganda's territory. However, the Nile tributaries also follow their own laws, reflecting their hydrology and topography.

'Dr Livingstone, I presume'

In Burundi's then capital, Bujumbura (in 2018 they moved the capital to Gitega), I check into the city's upper-class hotel, which is called Source du Nil. My assigned suite must be around 50 square metres, divided into two rooms. The Source du Nil has served as the expats' or aid workers' hotel – used, one can almost imagine, to underscore the distinction between those who give aid and those who receive it. Both rooms offer views onto a large swimming pool where one of the guests, a UN employee from Kenya, swims length after length for hours on end, and whom I later, being thoroughly impressed by his stamina, greet at lunch.

On the table in front of me in my room are some dusty brochures and books on the country, which I have brought from home. Their stories about the stone honouring Livingstone and Stanley, the Nile's source, and the city's soccer stadium, produce only a mixture of indifference and self-loathing; apathy suddenly overshadows eagerness and curiosity. I am worn out, tired of travelling. My greatest wish right now is ridiculous: stay in bed and then take the first flight home.

I open my suitcase, toss some clothes onto a chair, find Herodotus and begin reading the Greek historian's dry, dispassionate prose. Here and there the book is packed with tedious details. Yet, it is precisely such tedious details that appear so trustworthy and confidential, and that, in a strange way, make portions of the book so timeless, and thus still readable. I enjoy in particular those parts where he speculates on the Nile's source, and his straightforward statement that he has no chance of discovering the truth about that question. I try to picture to myself – as I sit here in the deep, rather frayed armchair in a 50-square-metre suite at Source du Nil – how Herodotus stopped at Elephantine Island in Egypt more than 2,500 years ago because it was impossible to travel any further, and, as I do so, I start pulling myself together, I get dressed, tie my shoes, boil a cup of water, stir in a little instant coffee, and head down shortly thereafter to drive to the Nile's source in Burundi.

South, out of Bujumbura, I take the highway and go into Mugere, a small village on the Burundian side of Lake Tanganyika. On a plain with a wide, open view of the deep-blue lake stands a large, lonely stone. The grass is as sharp green as it gets in the light from the sun before it sets, making the grey stone seem even more out of place in this flat, stone-poor landscape. On the other side of the lake, DR Congo is easily visible.

On the rock is carved:

Livingstone
Stanley
25–XI–1871

The missionary David Livingstone and the journalist-turned-explorer Henry Morton Stanley were together here for two days and nights in November 1871. Livingstone was sent to these areas south of Lake Victoria in 1865 by the Royal Geographical Society, for many believed the Nile's true source must be here somewhere. His wanderings did not produce any breakthroughs, however, and in 1871 the European and US media became very much engaged in what had become of him. Stanley was hired by an American newspaper to find the European hero, the famous missionary and explorer, who had disappeared in Africa.

The meeting between the two on this plain at the lake shore took place two weeks after one of the more iconic moments in world history. In Ujiji, a place a little further south along Lake Tanganyika, whose Swahili name means 'sail in the wilderness', two white men approach each other. Stanley holds out his hand, greeting the bearded man coming towards him, and apparently, according to his own account, simply said: 'Dr Livingstone, I presume.' After he had risked his life to find the man whom all Europe and the United States were speculating might have vanished in Africa, I believe it must have been this odd mixture of boundless pomposity and reserve that has fascinated posterity. The rationale behind the greeting is interesting. Stanley wrote:

> I would have run to him, only I was a coward in the presence of such a mob – would have embraced him, but that I did not know how he would receive me; so I did what moral cowardice and false pride suggested was the next best thing – walked deliberately to him, took off my hat, and said: 'Dr Livingstone, I presume?'[33]

After this meeting, the two continued north on the lake in a canoe rowed by locals, sitting beneath a covering in the shade at the back of the boat, to judge from the sketches. They wanted to investigate whether any rivers ran out of the lake to the north-east. The trip took twenty-eight days. They arrived at Mugere on 25 November 1871, in order to determine whether the case was, as Livingstone believed, that the Nile ran out of Lake Tanganyika. As such, it was not in this spot that Livingstone and Stanley first met, as countless articles on Burundi and Livingstone suggest. Instead, they went here together to find the Nile's sources. Livingstone was convinced that Lake Tanganyika was the source. However, as it turned out, he was completely wrong about the river systems.

Nonetheless, he was closer to finding the source at the time of his death than the world realized. One of the Nile's tributaries indeed starts just a few kilometres from the large stone at Mugere. The mountains the two admired from Lake Tanganyika to the north lay between the Mugere stone and the source – it was simply the watershed, and on the other side of it, the water ran toward the Mediterranean.

Kingdom and colony

He explains everything from the ground up. A Nile conference is under way at the university in Bujumbura. I am there to give a talk, and another of the speakers, one of Burundi's few water experts and a former minister of water resources, Pascal

Nkurunziza, has to explain the basics about the Nile's role in and for Burundi: what the tributaries are called, where they flow from, their relative significance and so forth. It is 2009, when the regional, diplomatic 'battle of the Nile' is at its most intense, but the Nile question is obviously far beneath the radar of most academics in Burundi, even among those gathered for this seminar on Burundi and the Nile basin.

Burundi is a country that has only very recently come to regard itself as a Nile country. They have had a lot of internal conflicts and issues, and the Congo basin was more important to it than the Nile river. Burundi was originally Twa land, peopled by one of best known of the many Pygmy groups that lived scattered across equatorial Africa. Then, the Hutus arrived, and in the 1500s Tutsi immigration began, with the Tutsis establishing a kingdom with themselves as the ruling caste. The Burundi kingdom was founded in the second half of the seventeenth century by Ntare Rushatsi (Ntare I) and had roughly the same borders that Burundi has today. The society was starkly stratified, organized according to ethnic distinctions and largely dependent on cattle-herding and on rainfall-based agriculture.

European imperialism has been blamed for Africa's many ethnic conflicts. The argument is that Europeans drew borders straight through ethnic groups, which then suffered from a divide-and-conquer policy. Burundi and Rwanda, however, defy this general theory. Both countries have precolonial borders, but they have also definitely seen their share of Africa's ethnic conflict and mass murder. Burundi became a part of German East Africa in 1890. The Germans were relatively uninterested in the colony and, although the country experienced some economic development, Berlin did not bother very much with modernization or centralization. This strategy naturally favoured the ruling class, simply because it made it simpler and cheaper to govern the colony. Hans Meyer, the German authority on Burundi, speculated that the secret of Tutsi dominance lay in their inherent superiority – in 'their superior intelligence, calmness, smartness, racial pride, solidarity and political talent'.[34] A more generally accepted explanation is that the Tutsis used cattle as leverage, as a form of economic power, to suppress the Hutus. They implemented a special form of cattle contract, where the Tutsi oligarchy inherited sovereign political rights over the Hutus.

There can be no doubt that the colonial powers exploited and magnified existing distinctions. Belgium occupied the area in 1916 during the First World War – about the same time as London and Berlin were shooting at each other on Lake Victoria – and was given responsibility for it by the League of Nations in 1923. In 1925 the Belgians formed an administrative region that covered what they then called Ruanda-Urandi as well as the Belgian Congo. They established a loose 'union' between these most peripheral Nile countries, governed from Brussels. Throughout, their overall Nile policy remained unchanged: the Belgians had promised London to keep their hands off the river in the territory they ruled.

The Belgians, however, sought to implement economic activity that would help finance the colonial administration. The solution became the forced cultivation of coffee. They used the Tutsis to pressure Hutu farmers into obeying their will. Obviously, this alliance between the Tutsis and the colonial power bolstered opposition between Hutus and Tutsis, and eventually the policy acquired a racial justification. Researchers who were focused on racial hygiene began to produce suggestions that Tutsis were of

Caucasian origin and were therefore racially superior to Hutus. Every inhabitant was given an identity card that defined them as Hutu or Tutsi.

In 1946 Ruanda-Urundi became a Trust Territory under the United Nations, but still under Belgian administration. As the 'winds of change', to paraphrase British premier Harold Macmillan, swept over Africa, Belgium also understood that their administration of these countries must undergo reform. It seems clear that the Belgians feared that a Hutu unrest would destabilize the region, since the Hutu majority had been excluded from political power by Brussels's alliance with the Tutsi minority. In practice, however, the Belgians themselves contributed to the unrest when in 1959 they took the Hutu side. A large Hutu rebellion encouraged by Belgian military personnel took place in November 1959. The die was cast in what would become a series of massacres that reached their climax in Rwanda and Burundi in 1994. The 1959 rebellion led to the murder of tens of thousands of Tutsis, and it was claimed that the massacres were organized in cooperation with local Belgian authorities. The 1959 rebellion, however, changed the political and social structure in Ruanda-Urundi. More than 150,000 Tutsis fled into exile, and those who remained were excluded from positions of political power. In 1962 the Belgians withdrew, and Rwanda and Burundi became independent countries with Hutu majorities. As it turned out, this would be the start of unrest and bloody ethnic strife and civil wars.

Self-reflection and masks

'Can this be right?' I wonder, as I sit at an outdoor restaurant in Bujumbura, where the atmosphere is exceptionally nice, friendly and hospitable. A few lamps are all that keeps the pitch dark at bay. People converse in mild tones around the tables, someone laughs, but everything seems, first and foremost, to be peaceful, so completely peaceful, and I almost want to say – maybe it is the heat that influences my mind here – intimate.

I am definitely not observing what one could expect to see in a country that is the only place where the UN has declared two genocides. I am sitting in a peaceful outdoor restaurant in the capital of a country whose people have killed each other repeatedly, where thousands have been slaughtered as if they were worth less than animals, and I only see mildness, amiability and restraint around me. Whatever the brain does, it does not always collect confirmation over discoveries. The reality I observe is definitely not the reality I expected to see, but then, on the other hand, what I see is not the entire reality, either. I have been here a few days now, but the senses lie. In order to understand Burundi, it is not enough to use just your eyes and ears, or to talk to a waiter or a taxi driver or a president – it takes work, pure and simple.

If one hopes to understand Africa, or 'the other', or Europe, or oneself, for that matter, thought must be given to how the power of dominant perspectives influences what is seen and understood. Whether one is a European or an African, one should not interpret East Africa's history without reflecting on one's own history and position relative to what is being described, as someone writing about Europe must also reflect on the potential filters created by his or her own position relative to that continents, and the constraints and limitations of different interpretive traditions.

One must further clarify to oneself how one's own background, and the totality of one's life, influences what is seen and how one interprets what is observed. Any observer must try to explain to themself the potential implications of one's own mental states, opinions, theories and viewpoints, because the act of interpreting in a serious way a social phenomenon presupposes the need for some aspect of self-reflection. Being familiar with one's own history when it comes to ideas, convictions and political-ideological attitudes, as an individual and a socially situated subject, is a precondition for being able to try to view oneself from the outside (which is not entirely possible, of course) but can be especially fruitful within contexts dominated by stereotypes and image-producing activities. It is an important component of every project attempting to understand the surrounding world (and for realizing oneself as one's self). When seeking to interpret non-European traditions, a European should be aware of the European tradition, how it has been affected by the history of its relationships to other countries and be conscious of its interpretive traditions. Also, of course, when European areas are to be understood, an Arab or an African ought to be conscious of the relationship to their own traditions of interpretation when European history, or indeed their own history, is to be analysed.

It is impossible to escape Eurocentrism or Arab-centrism, defined in this way, because it is not possible to free oneself from one's position, either as a white or black person from Norway nor as a white or black person from Uganda, when writing the Nile's history. That is to say, no one has access to a perspective-free 'truth' on the Nile's biography or on the development of the Nile countries. But to be a non-African or a European observer is also not a flaw, no comparative disadvantage or barrier, as many have insisted, influenced by Edward Said's orientalism critique. To be European is not 'worse' than being Arab or African when it comes to analysing the Nile, because everyone has their own blind spots. The moment that such intrinsically judgemental lines of distinction and hierarchies are accepted as being defining and excluding, the basis is removed not only for communication among equals, but for social science and history as both idea and project.

An awareness of the history and power of ideas and world views allows one some measure of freedom in choosing one's own analytical position. Such awareness, through the adoption of a critical attitude to past ideas, makes possible choices that need not be systematically illusory, and allows for alternatives and viewpoints that would not otherwise have been. It enables the individual to engage in a self-dialogue; indeed, it renders it impossible to escape conversations with oneself and one's own history, at the same time as encouraging one to be more open regarding 'the other's' perspectives and projects.

As observer and outsider, I thus cast myself into the discussion about Burundi with my friend Pascal, a former minister who decided to become a researcher, and who has been kind enough to show me his country.

Rivalry on all fronts

The battle for power and influence in the Nile has been one of the central conflicts between France and England for the last two centuries, with the balance of power shifting back and forth up and down the Nile basin. It began with Napoleon's march through the flat Nile Delta in Egypt in 1799 and, geographically, has moved up the basin over time. After the Cold War ended, Anglo-American cultural and economic interests swept the French aside, from place after place and region after region. As we have seen, Rwanda even broke diplomatic relations with Paris for a short time and in 2008 the government there instituted English as the language of instruction. Tony Blair became President Kagame's adviser and the United States became Kagame's closest ally, whereas French officers could no longer be seen in the capital's streets. After this it was only Burundi in the Nile basin that could still be termed Francophone. The trend, however, seems irreversible; Burundi might also switch to English in the not-so-distant future due to increased cooperation with its economically stronger, English-speaking neighbours.

From the time that Burundi became independent in 1962, France has had military and political advisers in the country. There has been a lot of unrest and smaller and larger civil wars, especially between the Hutu majority and the Tutsis, who have largely possessed government power and military control. In 1970–1, civil war broke out between the Hutus and Tutsis. Hundreds of thousands were killed, an event largely unnoticed in a world much more taken at the time with the Vietnam War, with ping-pong diplomacy between China and the United States and with the wars against the Portuguese colonial powers in Angola and Mozambique. When Hutus attempted to seize power in April 1972 the government, aided by the military, took a terrible revenge. Around 200,000 Hutus (and some Tutsis) were reportedly massacred, and more than 300,000 fled, most to Tanzania. It was Hutu leaders and intellectuals who were targeted most.

The country's first presidential election, held on 2 June 1993, was won by the Burundi Democracy Front candidate, Melchior Ndadaye. However, President Ndadaye, the first Hutu to hold power in Burundi, was assassinated after only a few months. The second Hutu president, Cyprien Ntaryamira, was killed on 6 April 1994, when the plane carrying both him and the Rwandan president was shot down. As a result, Hutu youth gangs began killing Tutsis, while the Tutsi-controlled army killed Hutus.

The frequency of ethnic clashes increased and developed into a low-intensity civil war. A six-nation regional proposal to send troops into Burundi to maintain peace and order was put together in July 1996. Mistrusting of this process, the Tutsi-dominated army launched a coup to replace the Hutu president and hand power to the Tutsi, Pierre Buyoya. With a short hiatus, he maintained power until 2003, and, in the meantime, he established a transitional government, agreeing that he would govern the first eighteen months and then step down. He did as he promised, and in April 2003 the Hutu, Domitien Ndayizeye, became president.

Throughout this period of internal conflict, Burundi had more than enough to handle, and 'developed' into one of the poorest countries in the world, where illiteracy, infant mortality and the lack of modern economic activity were striking. France's 'allied partner' in the region did not, therefore, exactly serve as a display window for Paris in Africa.

The guerrilla leader redeemed by a Norwegian preacher

It is Saturday, 23 August 2003. On a hill behind the football stadium in Bujumbura lies the renowned rebel leader, Pierre Nkurunziza, fully armed, together with his elite troops. His father, who was a member of parliament and governor, had been killed in one of the country's many ethnic conflicts, when Pierre was nine years old. Five of Pierre's siblings lost their lives in similar conflicts. He himself was wounded when the army stormed the university in Bujumbura in 1995, and he fled thereafter to the bush, where he later became a guerrilla leader. This Saturday, Nkurunziza and his soldiers are listening to the Norwegian evangelist, Aril Edvardsen, who, via powerful loudspeakers, conducts an evangelical campaign in the city.

Burundi's people must choose! Either let Jesus into Burundi, so the country can become a shining star for all of Africa, or Barabbas controls the foundation, and you all know what he can do, preached Edvardsen. Peace negotiations in South Africa between Burundi's government and the opposition movement CNDD-FDD (Conseil National Pour la Défense de la Démocratie–Forces pour la Défense de la Démocratie) had just broken down. Instead of immediately retreating to the rebel headquarters on Tanzania's border, the guerrilla leader had hidden himself in the bushes on a hillside behind the Bujumbura stadium to listen to Aril Edvardsen's words.

Pierre Nkurunziza had a Catholic background and did not become a 'born again' Christian that very day. The rebel leader returned to the front and was participating in a battle against government troops, even while continuing to maintain contact with Burundi's president. But Nkurunziza apparently could not make peace with himself. According to one of his officers, he said that he had heard God's voice. Three months later, according to that same officer, Nkurunziza accepted Jesus Christ as 'his personal saviour by the faith in his heart', as Edvardsen's Norwegian missionary organization Troens Bevis wrote.[35] Then, on 16 November 2003, he entered a peace treaty with President Domitien Ndayizeye, which hinged on sharing governmental responsibilities. The rebel movement would be converted into a political party. On 23 November the president reorganized the government to make room for Nkurunziza as the Minister of Good Governance. On Saturday, 6 December 2003, he arrived in Bujumbura together with many rebel soldiers and laid down his weapons. The country was in shock because the war so suddenly came to an end, and many people celebrated for joy.

Nkurunziza appeared a short time after in the national media, where he said that he had been redeemed and wanted to work for peace in his country. Publicly, he acknowledged that he was now a Christian. He asked the entire nation for forgiveness for the evil he had perpetrated on the people.

On 19 August 2005 Nkurunziza was elected president, taking up the post less than a week later. He received 92 per cent of the vote, with voter participation officially at 70 per cent. Burundi adopted a new constitution to replace the one from 1962. It introduced the regulation that the president and vice president would have different ethnic origins. The government and parliament would moreover be composed of 60 per cent Hutus and 40 per cent Tutsis, and 30 per cent of those popularly elected would be women. Three seats in parliament would be reserved for representatives from the country's Twa population. According to the new constitution, no ethnic group would occupy more than 50 per cent of the military.

Nkurunziza's leadership style turned out to be unusual. He and his wife instituted prayer and Bible study groups in their home. Guests who had attended told me that meetings could suddenly be interrupted because the president had to pray, or because his private choir entered the room to sing a religious song. The president has been criticized by the opposition for being authoritarian, despite his informal, populist style. Nkurunziza launched a campaign called a 'prayer crusade', and he also arranged soccer matches. For example, his Hallelujah FC played a match in August 2010 against Rwandan officials at the Bujumbura stadium (Kagame sat in the audience, while Nkurunziza served up soccer tricks and dribble series to great jubilation from the crowd). In the same place and the same month, almost to the day seven years after the president heard Edvardsen speak, thousands of people participated in one of the president's huge public meetings, which were also religious events. Nkurunziza washed the feet of the poor and handed out shoes. His reason is clear: a president must be humble in the face of those who elected him. In a black suit and T-shirt, armed with a microphone, he sang and danced with his choir, Komeza Gusenga, which means 'keep on praying'.

There is no doubt that the president managed to create a more stable and peaceful Burundi. In 2010 he was elected with over 90 per cent of the votes in an election that international EU observers declared free and fair, but which the opposition boycotted because they claimed there had been significant election fraud in local elections that same year. Analysts continued to discuss the danger of new civil wars, and in June 2011 Western envoys in Bujumbura took the step of writing a memo, where they expressed concern for instances of murder and torture committed by security officers following the 2010 election. In April 2015, Nkurunziza announced that he would seek a third term in office. The opposition said that this would violate the constitution, as it bars a president from running for a third term, while those who supported Nkurunziza, said his first term did not count as he was appointed by parliament and not directly by the people. The result was demonstrations and unrest. Radio stations were shut down. In mid-May, Godefroid Niyombare, a general and former head of Burundian intelligence, declared a coup while the president attended a summit in neighbouring Tanzania. One of the coup leaders called for armed rebellion against Nkurunziza. The Burundian government, after some fighting, declared that they had killed rebels who had crossed into northern Burundi through the Nyungwe Forest from Rwanda, but the government in Kigali denied this. Elections were held in July, partly boycotted by the opposition, and Nkurunziza won the election with almost 70 per cent of the vote. Whatever disagreements there are about the rule of Nkurunziza; in the decades after he came to power, Burundi has experienced a long period of relative stability and significant economic growth, and the country has succeeded in breaking its isolation, among other things, by becoming for shorter periods of time a central player in the struggle for the Nile.

Courtship, carpets and water

'Burundi supports Egypt's quest to defend its rightful share of Nile water', announced Burundi's deputy president, Gervais Rovkiri, to Egyptian media at the beginning of December 2010 at a joint press conference with the Egyptian prime minister, Ahmed

Nazif. It looked like Egypt's strategy of courting Burundi to prevent that country from following other upstream countries and signing the Nile Basin Cooperative Framework Agreement from 14 May 2010, had succeeded. The media emphasized that Rovkiri was focused on dialogue and cooperation, and Egypt's prime minister thanked Burundi for its support.

In January 2011 Ethiopian newspapers mentioned rumours insisting that Egypt had mobilized Burundi's Muslims to support Egypt's stance on the Nile question. Muslims make up 10 per cent of Burundi's population, and the annual Eid festivals had not long ago been declared national holidays, the newspapers wrote. In the autumn of 2010, there had also been unverified rumours about Egypt attempting to bribe Burundian politicians and officials with gifts, and that planeloads of oriental carpets had been sent to ministers in Bujumbura.

All the Nile basin countries were now looking to Burundi: would the country sign the agreement initiated by the other upstream states? Burundi suddenly weighed heavy on the hydropolitical battlefield. The country's decision would be of decisive significance for the handling of the entire Nile question.

Burundi's part of the Nile basin consists of the Kanyaru/Nyabarongo, the Kagera and the Ruvubu rivers. The country is relatively rich in water. Rainfall is good, and for the country as a whole the Congo basin is more important, especially due to the Ruzizi River, and the three hydroelectric plants that have been developed along its course from Lake Kivu to Lake Tanganyika. The Ruvubu River is 480 kilometres long, has a precipitation area of 12,300 square kilometres, and flows into the Kagera right above the Rusumo Falls where Tanzania, Rwanda and Burundi are building the region's largest power plant. Burundi sends around 2.6 billion cubic metres of water to the Nile but has itself never partaken of it. Since the country is south of Lake Victoria, it fell outside Britain's sphere of interest in the 1880s and was thus never formally bound by the 1929 Agreement. Instead, the Belgians entered into a separate agreement with London on Burundi's behalf whereby they swore not to undertake anything with the Nile basin rivers without the prior approval of London or the British Nile empire. This agreement was never interpreted as binding by independent Burundi, so the country has always been a thorn in the side of Egypt's Nile politicians.

At various points Burundi's government has been explicit. Environment and Water Minister Degratias N'Duimana proclaimed openly that Egypt must stop dictating how much Nile water Burundi could use. And both N'Duimana and President Nkurunziza told me when I interviewed them that they could not accept a Nile policy that hindered them or other upstream countries from using Nile water. They did not make these statements aggressively, but in a 'matter of fact' manner. Without a hint of critique of Egypt or other downstream countries, the president diplomatically stated: 'No agreement is perfect. All agreements reflect the time period they are signed in. An agreement can therefore always be improved.'[36]

On 28 February 2011, Burundi finally made its viewpoint clear – just when the flag of rebellion in Tahrir Square was waving most fiercely in Egypt. The country signed the Nile Comprehensive Framework Agreement, which was now ratified by six states.

The pyramid at the source

The source of the Ruvyironza, the local name for the upper Kagera River, lies in Rutovu, in southern Burundi. We are heading there along the RN7. The road winds along the hillside above Bujumbura, and the view steadily widens and becomes more panoramic over the city and the lake. There are few houses along the road here, and we pass long lines of women walking along it in the heat, colourfully dressed, carrying a bucket, the laundry, groceries or whatever else on their head – providing an image of Burundi's impoverishment, but also of the country's perpetual struggle to overcome it. In the background I see the gentle outline of city and landscape, wrapped in a haze that seems to creep between the hilltops down to an emerald-blue lake.

In 1910 the German Duke of Mecklenburg gave his impressions of Rwanda and Burundi, as places 'where the breeding of cattle and bee-culture flourish, and the cultivated soil bears rich crops', and where there was '[a] hilly country, thickly populated, full of beautiful scenery, and possessing a climate incomparably fresh and healthy; a land of great fertility, with watercourses that might be termed perennial streams'.[37] A century later, the scenery is largely the same, though it is not possible to view it without a certain sadness, a kind of melancholy, due to the country's history. Once cannot help contrasting the optimism from 1910 with later images of bloody ethnic conflict and poverty.

As we drive through this hospitable green landscape with its small hills and photogenic tea plantations, which give the hilltops a characteristic round but finished form, passing tiny villages located close together, as if they are seeking each other's company, we turn up the car radio. We are listening to Burundi's drummers. The heavy beat of the country's world-famous royal percussion ensemble speaks to us from the radio as we cruise through the distinctive rolling landscape.

Burundi's drummers are part of a long tradition. There is a legend about a king who, many centuries ago, arrived in Burundi from a foreign land. With him came an ox. He killed the ox and stretched the skin over a hole to dry it. Then the king lay down to sleep. Suddenly, he was awoken by the sound of a snake slithering out of the hole. The creature stopped with its head right beside the skin. At that, the king ordered his subordinates to fashion a hollow drum out of a tree trunk and to stretch the ox skin over it. This became the sacred drum *Inkiranya*. The drum symbolized the royal family's power and legitimacy and the kingdom's prosperity.

I had heard the fascinating rhythm of the drums before; the dancing drummers are included in Joni Mitchell's *The Hissing of Summer Lawns*, and represent 'bushmen drumming' in Werner Herzog's *Fitzcarraldo*, an unforgettable and extraordinary film about a fantastic entrepreneur and his determination to transport a steamship up the Amazon.

After a few hours' drive, we reach Bururi, the province where the source of the Ruvyironza lies. Along the road are a few signs that show we are headed in the right direction, but when we reach the site where the source is supposed to be, we cannot find it. No café or tourist kiosk either. No people. An old man finally walks towards us. I do not understand anything he says but, by his gestures, I realize he is indicating that the source is attractive and the Nile basin huge. He leads us to a small depression, where the source spurts from a wellspring protected by a stone-and-cement wall. As prosaic and workaday as possible, and indicative of water's status here in this precipitation-rich country – entirely without the aura of religiosity and respect that surrounds water in many other societies where it is a precious, unreliable factor in shortage, and thus a dire need.

On the other side of the road, meanwhile, atop a hill overlooking the Congo and the river plain to the north, is a pyramid. Here, on a small Burundi hilltop, stands a mini replica of the Egyptian pyramids. In 1937 the German explorer Burkhart Waldecker determined that this place was the Nile's source. There was no site further south in Africa from which the water ran down to Lake Victoria and then into Egypt. Accordingly, the pyramid was subsequently built to place Waldecker's and Burundi's stamp on the Nile basin.

The pyramid embodies the geographical basis for Burundi to emerge abruptly as an actor in the geopolitical game for control over the Nile. No longer is it merely an architectural curiosity and a monument to an explorer's vanity. Instead, the pyramid expresses a new, incontrovertible realpolitik truth that will persist into the conceivable future. As Burundi's water minister told me in his office in Bujumbura, this city located not far from the heart of the enormous African continent: the Nile is like an umbilical cord that connects Burundi to the Mediterranean.

9

The Water Tower in the East

A train trip and an art deco capital on the Horn of Africa

The steam train crawls slowly up the arid mountainside. The narrow-gauge railway has been chiselled from the mountain, and sometimes the shelf it occupies is only a few metres wide. When I lean out the window, I see sometimes hundreds of metres straight down. The train driver casts an energetic glance at me through the open window; a smile lights his sooty face and he gives me a thumbs-up, while his crew shovels coal. One of the workers is standing on an outdoor platform at the back of the train car. His job is to brake the train manually on the descent, and to prevent it from running riot if the locomotive has problems. We are served strong coffee brewed from freshly roasted beans, entirely appropriate considering we are in an area where coffee plants grow wild, and where people first discovered the drink's invigorating properties. A gang of boorish monkeys perch on the mountain shelf above one of the tunnel openings and entertain themselves by throwing rocks onto the tracks.

This railway line was finished in 2011, stretching from Massawa on the Indian Ocean to Asmara, located at an elevation of 2,325 metres, making it one of the highest capitals in the world. Finally, the Roman Empire's self-proclaimed heirs had returned to the Nile basin, 2,000 years after Caesar. Now Rome could place its personal stamp on Eritrea. Twenty years earlier the Italians had taken control of the country. The railway was an engineering feat: twenty tunnels and sixty-five bridges dot the short stretch from the plains up to Asmara. The ascent, for the most part, was one metre for every 30 metres.

Italians began laying the railway line from Massawa to Asmara as they gradually claimed large inland swathes of territory, for the local coffee they could acquire and export, and in order to be able to brand themselves as a colonial power that had come to stay. The railway was designed and built as an investment to help Italy realize the grand plans they had for economic activity and for Italian settlers in Eritrea, and also as a potent symbol of modern civilization and of Italy's technological competence. The line would contribute to legitimizing an expanding European imperial power – technology's posturing attributes were exploited for all they were worth – and the result, quite literally, was memorable traces of Italian influence.

I said thanks for the coffee and the nice company and, full of impressions, I hop off the train after it has slowly rolled into Asmara's old ochre-coloured station. I was quickly struck by how the train trip had heralded two key characteristics of today's Eritrea: the influence of Italian colonialism certainly, but even more particularly, Eritrea's political independence and the country's self-reliance ideology. The colonial railway was destroyed during the extended Eritrean war of independence from Ethiopia between 1961 and 1991. Just a few years after Eritrea formally achieved independence in 1993, however, the Eritreans repaired the railway. The UN had concluded that the restoration would be too expensive, but the Eritreans went ahead and fixed it themselves, and the government succeeded in mobilizing the people. The railway is only used by tourists now, and due to the long uneasy relationship with Ethiopia and the international boycott of the country there are few visitors to this mountain country with kilometre upon kilometre of beaches and coral reefs. We few who took the train, therefore, rented the locomotive with its single carriage. It was worth it, however, because I think this must be one of the most spectacular train journeys in the world.

'I won't go with you to the post office. Sometimes I do stop by there just to take in the atmosphere, though, that feeling of order, meaning and aesthetics that the frescoes and postboxes create.' The Sudanese refugee whom I met, the friend of a friend, looked exhausted, but he continued: 'We should meet at an Italian restaurant instead this evening.'

In the centre of Asmara is one of the world's most attractive post offices, built in 1916. I had determined to visit it as soon as I had heard about it. The post office itself is neither overwhelming nor grand. If it appears unusually harmonic and measured, that is due to the relationship between space and frescoes and counters and postboxes. Since it was meant to be (and still is) a functional and functioning post office, the decoration is unpretentious. Nonetheless, it emerges as a workaday cornucopia, something underscored by the fact that the atrium's frescoes feature agriculture and forestry motifs from various places in the country. The post office was built so that the Italians arriving here in steadily larger numbers at the beginning of the 1900s could maintain contact with the homeland. It was meant as an architectural, material expression of the progressive nature of Italian colonialism – and it also pointed towards Rome's even greater ambitions in the region.

Asmara was named the capital of the Italian colony in 1900. The colonial powers divided the city into four clearly distinct zones. One district was preserved exclusively for Europeans. Then there was a mixed district for Europeans, Jews, Arabs and a few Eritreans. The third was the 'native' district, and the fourth was devoted to industrial activities. Italy had occupied the Eritrean coast ten years earlier, on 1 January 1890. It was under Benito Mussolini, however, and especially during the years following 1936, that Asmara became a focus and was built up as a kind of fascist, urbane utopia in East Africa.[1] The city was meant to provide home for the thousands of Italians who would surely flock here. Eventually, more than 300,000 Italian soldiers arrived in Eritrea in the 1930s. In addition, 50,000 Italians, who were working on the various infrastructure projects, lived here. Italians composed about 12 per cent of the population.

As such, the city was developed during a time of great imperial visions, nourished by a strong Italian nationalism. For Mussolini and his architects, this highland city was a laboratory to experiment with architectural styles such as rationalism, futurism and monumentalism, all blended in a way which, it has been claimed, would never have worked in Italy. The architecture, nonetheless, does not advertise the omnipotence of fascist megalomania that one might expect. Instead it signals moderation and aesthetic balance.

Asmara consists of an architectural blend drawn from different epochs. Not far from Liberation Avenue are the upbeat restaurants with cappuccino machines and delicious food, and Italian villas with Romeo and Juliet balconies; there are houses built by North Korea, mosques, churches and an opera house, and cafés with wood-burning ovens – the pizza we ate that evening had thin crust! The Italian segregation policy is definitely history now, and in the district where the post office stands you can have the feeling of walking around in an Italian-African city, peaceful and friendly, an art deco city that has become a part of Eritrean culture.

Italy as a Nile power

When Italy conquered this portion of the Horn of Africa at the end of the 1800s, it was only after a secret agreement with Great Britain and was allowed as part of Britain's Nile strategy. The Italians won London's support because London needed an ally and a counterweight to the Turkish-Egyptian zeal for regional expansion. The Ottoman Empire had occupied Massawa and conquered parts of Eritrea in the 1500s, and Muhammad Ali's house sought to seize Ethiopia in the 1870s. The Italian occupation helped undermine that empire's continued regional ambitions, rather like King Leopold who, in cooperation with London, erased the last remnants of the Turkish-Ottoman Empire's influence on the British Nile basin's other flank, the Congo. With London's support, Rome also acted as a counterweight against a too powerful Ethiopian emperor, Menelik II. British strategists evaluated the situation thus: the Italian presence in Eritrea would prevent the emperor from implementing what the British suspected was his project, namely, to establish an excessively robust and, therefore, excessively wilful Ethiopian empire. The British banked on the threat that Italy presented to the emperor enabling them, the British, simultaneously to play the role of friend to the Ethiopian emperor, thereby giving them the regional influence they sought. Much of the literature devoted to the division of Africa has emphasized that it was the rivalry between Italy and Great Britain, together with Britain's fear of Italian ambitions and plans, that in part prompted Britain to occupy the rest of the Nile basin.[2] That is simply not the case. The British accepted through a secret agreement that Rome could take control of Eritrea at the beginning of the 1890s because they needed Rome as an opponent to the Ethiopian emperor in order to succeed in their long-term Nile strategy.

From the very beginning London also established a clear boundary to Rome's expansion: the Italians had to stop at the banks of the Nile. Italy tried to acquire a border with Sudan that would include Kassala, and one with Ethiopia that would include control of the Tekeze or Atbara river, as it is called in Sudan and Egypt. The British government rejected these plans. In London on 7 February 1891, the prime minister, Lord Salisbury, sanctioned Lord Cromer's proposal of giving Rome a few regions in Sudan (Suakin and Tokar) as a countermove. On 15 April 1891, the Anglo-Italian Protocol was signed (although exactly where the border between Ethiopia and

Eritrea was drawn proved to become a highly contentious issue), with disagreements about it being the main cause of border conflicts, which during the period 1998–2000 led to bloody clashes between the two countries' armies. In Article III of the Protocol, the Italian government gave what for the British was the most important commitment: that the Italians would 'not [. . .] construct on the Atbara river, in view of irrigation, any work which might sensibly modify its flow into the Nile'.

In 1899 the Italians also entered into an agreement with Ethiopia and Emperor Menelik II – the so-called Treaty of Wuchale – which has been thoroughly discussed in the historical literature, and which is a particularly important national issue to both Ethiopia and Eritrea. In the treaty, the emperor recognized Eritrea as an Italian colony. The Italians, however, claimed that the treaty also made Ethiopia an Italian protectorate. In 1893 the emperor rejected the treaty on the grounds that the Italians had interpreted it falsely. The British shared the emperor's interpretation, for they had no desire to see Italy become the ruler of Ethiopia – the Nile's water tower – just a few years after they had seized power in Egypt. Since the emperor had rejected the treaty, the Italians declared war on Ethiopia two years later. After one of the bloodiest battles of the entire colonial era – the Battle of Adwa – Ethiopia emerged victorious on 1 March 1896, having had, among other things, Russian military support. In a settlement afterwards, the Treaty of Wuchale was cancelled, Italy recognized Ethiopia as completely sovereign and independent, and was allowed to retain Eritrea. Things unfolded largely as the British had calculated and hoped.

A few decades later a new wave of imperial activism gripped Italy. Mussolini had taken power in Rome in 1922, and it became increasingly clear that Italy was not satisfied with its limited African conquests and territories. The Italian fascists fomented a strong nationalist desire for revenge against the Ethiopians; the humiliating defeat of 1896 was not forgotten. In the short term, the government was concerned particularly with the railway connection between Eritrea and those parts of Somalia under their control, so-called Italian Somaliland. Ethiopian emperors from Menelik to Haile Selassie (the latter crowned as emperor in the late 1920s, but in reality Ethiopia's leader from the end of the First World War up until he was executed in the 1970s) continued, for their part, to regard Eritrea as a natural extension of the Ethiopian empire. For Addis Ababa, it was not only a question of territory: Eritrea was of critical strategic significance since it would ensure the empire access to the ocean.

The geopolitical game for Eritrea from the 1890s on must, therefore, be examined in the context of Ethiopia's location in the Nile basin. British plans for a dam on Lake Tana, the Blue Nile's main reservoir in Ethiopia, was the axis around which this game revolved. The Italians, from their Eritrean base, for their part desired Britain's active or passive support for increasing Italy's influence in Ethiopia, the goal being to unite Eritrea and Italian Somaliland. The British strategy regarding Italy always depended on Italy's willingness to support their plans for a dam. Ethiopia's emperor, for his part, wanted the British to support his demands for Eritrea, either as a trade-off for, or as compensation for, eventually backing British plans for Lake Tana. Both Mussolini and Haile Selassie knew that the British had a single key strategic interest in the region: the Blue Nile and the Tana dam.[3] I will explore these relationships more thoroughly in the subsequent discussion of Ethiopia.

Eritrea in exchange for a Nile dam

It is May 2011. One of the most used buildings for public gatherings in Asmara's centre is packed; people line the walls. They have come to hear me give a talk on Eritrea and the Nile, and how the country's history, according to my interpretation of it, cannot be understood without comprehending the strategy of the British Nile empire and the Ethiopian emperors' tactics for keeping the country unified and extending their empire's borders. This perspective, I realize, is one that few Eritreans are used to exploring, since the British policy has remained largely unknown, and the relevant diplomatic correspondence found in archives in London and Addis Ababa has been so little studied and analysed.

I begin by saying that the talk would be building on a section of my book *The River Nile in the Age of the British.* For that study I identified and read metre upon metre of boxes of documents and letters concerning Britain's Nile policy and the Horn of Africa, found in the archives of the British Foreign Office and subsequent Foreign and Commonwealth Office. All these documents gave a very clear impression of what Britain's overall interest in the region was, I told my audience. That interest was to secure London's political control over the use of the river in the entire river basin and more locally; to build a dam at Lake Tana on the Blue Nile. In particular, after the Egyptian revolution in 1919, after Egypt was given formal independence from London in 1922, and after the British exploited the Blue Nile by building the enormous cotton farm at Gezira in Sudan in 1925, the vision of a future dam at Tana under London's control gained even more strategic and economic significance. It would, it was thought, both enable Britain to expand Gezira and thereby benefit the textile capitalists in England, and also to strengthen London's hydropolitical power over an ever more water-thirsty Egypt.

London's strategy up until the mid-1920s was to win the Ethiopian emperor's support for this dam project, but the emperor dragged his feet (as the British diplomats described his behaviour). Eventually, it became obvious to the British representatives that the emperor was not satisfied with the offers they made him in exchange for the dam. During the interwar period, one British envoy to Addis Ababa after another sent frustrating reports home to London about Emperor Haile Selassie's obstinacy, apparent indifference, and indecision. Sometimes he simulated a lack of interest, something that irritated many of London's diplomats, and quite a few interpreted this as a kind of mix between apathy and laziness. Quite the contrary, however: it eventually turned out that the emperor had an unusually sharp memory and solid knowledge of the Nile, yet the British diplomats underestimated Selassie's diplomatic insight again and again.

The emperor's foreign policy goals during the interwar period were to keep Ethiopia unified, to oppose European plans to divide the country, and to acquire British backing for his desire to incorporate Eritrea into Ethiopia. The Eritrea question also functioned as a consolidating political project in an Ethiopia otherwise split along ethnic and religious lines. The way to attain these objectives, the emperor thought, was to exchange land for water. He was considering achieving territorial gains and guarantees by giving London the right to dam Lake Tana.

The British, however, never got the opportunity to support the emperor in his Eritrea ambitions, even if this had been their plan, since they were simultaneously involved in top-secret discussions with Mussolini in Italy regarding the possibility of securing their own interests in Ethiopia by increasing the pressure on the emperor through cooperation between London and Rome. In the latter half of the 1920s and into the 1930s, they bet that cooperation with Mussolini would yield them the dam. This European big-power politics thus helped guarantee Eritrea's continued independence from Ethiopia, by reinforcing its status as an Italian colony.

Then, in the mid-1930s, Italy invaded Ethiopia from their bases in Eritrea. The comprehensive war preparations helped augment the differences between the two neighbouring countries. In Eritrea a considerable market for wage labour had developed, in stark contrast to Ethiopia. Furthermore, 50,000 Eritrean soldiers were part of the Italian occupation forces. It was this fact that prompted the radical and leading African American intellectual, Marcus Garvey, to write his famous article in *The Black Man* in March/April 1937, where he denounced Haile Selassie as 'a negro slave master' because he fled to London, and he stated that in Africa 'it was black men fighting black men'. Rodolfo Graziani, head of Mussolini's invasion troops, sent the Eritrean soldiers into Addis Ababa first, and only marched in with his conquering Italian soldiers after he had confirmed that the Eritreans askaris had control.

After Britain declared war on Italy due to pre–Second World War events in Europe in 1939, London joined Haile Selassie and his supporters to chase away the Italians from Ethiopia. After a short and victorious military campaign, the Italians were thrown out of the entire Horn of Africa. At that point, the question immediately became, what should happen with Eritrea, since London was now also de facto ruler in that country? In London several alternatives were put on the table for discussion – perhaps the Muslim-dominated parts of the country could be merged with Sudan and the Christian parts with Ethiopia? Or, as was discussed in 1943: should Massawa and the northernmost parts of Tigray and Asmara be given to Ethiopia? Britain was now, however, a weakened world power. Both the United States and the Soviet Union were now emerging as new global payers, and a final decision about the future of Eritrea was postponed until the Second World War was over. The British were then given administration of Eritrea on the UN's behalf.

London could now fully disregard its agreements with Italy, and the other victorious powers did not have any real interest in preserving Eritrea as a single country. Both the United States and Great Britain had further signalled support for Haile Selassie's demand for Eritrea in exchange for his war effort and friendship with the Western powers. The British still had dam-building plans in Ethiopia, not least for geopolitical reasons. London needed tools they could use against an increasingly anti-British Egypt, and a Tana dam could still, they thought, be exploited as 'a pistol to Egypt's head'.

In 1952 the UN again debated the Eritrea question. Should the country be merged with Ethiopia, become an independent state, or a region with some form of autonomy within the Ethiopian empire? The UN committee opted for the solution that Great Britain and especially the United States were working: Eritrea would become an autonomous region within Ethiopia, and its ultimate decision to join would be decided by popular vote.[4] In the meantime, in 1953 the Americans built one of their most important listening stations on Eritrean soil, the Kagnew Station.

When the date for the popular vote on autonomy approached in 1962, agitation for full independence increased. Haile Selassie, however, cancelled the whole vote and transformed Eritrea, with general support from the big powers, into an Ethiopian province with a certain degree of self-governance.

The discussion following my lecture was energetic but not heated. I believe data from my archival research about Nile politics made it possible to give some understandable and even acceptable rationality to the policies of both the emperor and the British, and information that could help support a discourse about the past which is not imprisoned by too narrow a focus on only ethnic and political-ideological dimensions.

The river as metaphor and boundary

In 1962 Haile Selassie stood next to the Mareb River, the river forming the border between Eritrea and Ethiopia, and said, that by crossing the Mareb River they would remove the barrier that for so long had held the borders on each side of the river apart. As it turned out, he was catastrophically wrong, and many Eritreans saw it as an unilateral dissolution of the Eritrean parliament and an annexation of the country.

In 1994 I stood in the same place, on the bridge over the Mareb, or Gash as the river is called when it ends on the arid Sudanese plains. But I saw no river. There was no physical barrier to cross.

This was right after Eritrea, through a long drawn out war with Ethiopia, had become an independent country. I was there, among other things, to discover more about my home country, Norway's, unknown and unexpected role in Eritrea's history. Norway was the country on the UN Commission for Eritrea that, together with South Africa, most clearly supported Eritrea becoming part of Ethiopia in the 1950s. The Norwegian representative argued that Eritrea did not harbour the economic prerequisites for long-term independent development, and that the state would be torn apart by ethnic and religious conflict. Furthermore, the Norwegian diplomat argued, since an independent Eritrea meant that Ethiopia would lose its ocean access, this would be tantamount to asking for war at a later date. Then, thirty years later, through Norwegian Church Aid's leadership of a massive and extensive cross-border humanitarian assistance operation, supported by other European churches and countries, and implemented in the regions controlled by the Eritrean People's Liberation Front, Norway became a critical factor in this liberation movement's ability to become politically, economically and militarily so strong that they ultimately won the war for independence. The astonishing aspect of this radical change in policy was that Norway enacted this new role without a single discussion taking place regarding this new stance on the Eritrean question, or why this stance had changed – whether in government, in the expanded Committee on Foreign Affairs or in the national assembly. Norway simply followed what was regarded as a kind of necessary 'humanitarian commitment'. Influenced by the BBC's famous images from the Korem Camp, the public was concerned with helping those in need, whatever the political implications, and only gradually did it become evident that Norwegian Church Aid supported wholeheartedly the political aims of the Eritrean People's Liberation Front. Nothing indicates that anyone in the political leadership realized that the country was playing a not insignificant role in helping to support the establishment of a new state on the Horn of Africa and in the Nile basin.

The first time I went to Asmara was just after Eritrea had achieved independence, and when the relationship was still cordial between Eritrea and Ethiopia and between the two countries' new leaders, Isaias Afewerki and Meles Zenawi, who had fought shoulder to shoulder against the Ethiopian regime in the 1980s. The atmosphere was not only peaceful but congenial on the border running through the middle of the bridge. That was, however, just a few years before a new and more bloody war broke out between the two neighbouring countries.[5]

I told my driver he could have his cigarette and wait for me. I wanted to walk this river of stone, I explained. The sun was intense, and a hot afternoon breeze dried one's lips. The river held no water – just grey rocks, thousands of grey rocks, rippling across the landscape. The dry bed here was not due to climate change or to new dam structures upstream, or to any engineering projects. This border river had always dried up for several months every year, because that is how the river is, because that is how the weather here is.

As I walked across the dry, rocky depression that undulated through the scorched landscape, it struck me, or I realized properly for the first time, the way in which landscape may inform language's basic metaphors. The river as river is an image that people the world over, past and present, have constantly resorted to when emotions are described or social relationships explained. It has become an image of the eternal and of the fleeting, of the current of history and the power of the present, of intimacy and danger, of what is most beautiful and most terrifying, and its many contradictory functions have been used as an image of human consciousness. A telling insight for the enormously varied literature reflecting on the river as metaphor comes from the monumental and influential work by William James, *Principles of Psychology*, from 1890, where the author discusses the idea of 'stream of consciousness', in which 'every definite image in the mind is steeped [...] in the free water that flows around it'. The problem with psychology, according to James, is that it overlooks the fact that consciousness flows, it all the time runs away, like a river.[6] The river is also a much employed metaphor for the unconscious, because in the physical, outside world it obviously signals uncontrollable depths and carries with itself the burden and power of invisible and both controllable and uncontrollable forces. And, above all, ever since Heraclitus walked around asking if a person could enter the same river twice, the river has become an almost hackneyed symbol of the enigma of identity.

The problem with the Mareb River that I see and walk in, in such a context, and in relation to river metaphors, is that it does not run. It is dry. Therefore, it cannot symbolize the unconscious or consciousness, history's current, or what is eternal. The river is dry, although at another point in time of the year it will come cascading through the landscape. At certain times the Mareb's flood is indeed uncontrollable, whereas at other times it is nothing – just a dry depression in a landscape filled with rocks. The Mareb represents the very antithesis of precipitation-rich European rivers, which are characterized by their perennial flow; a fact that underscores that the river as metaphor must also vary from language to language. As I walk along the bed of the Mareb River, kicking small rocks, I formulate the following hypothesis: the fact that rivers vary was significant in the development of different languages' basic metaphors, but in ways no one has yet properly explored, even as every language will intervene in the relationship between humans and rivers and be important for how rivers, humans and the relationship between them will be understood.

Mareb's dry, rock-strewn ground is, therefore, not a fitting metaphor for either the unconscious or the conscious, but it can serve as a useful image of the region's climate vulnerability and a reminder that many would like to even out the river's seasonal variations.

An outcast among nations

In the years following its independence in 1993, Eritrea was gradually ostracized from the community of nations or, as the country's critics would have it, the country increasingly chose a greater self-imposed isolation. The government was condemned for its human rights violations, for supporting the Islamist organization al-Shabab in Somalia, and for playing a general destabilizing role in the Horn of Africa. The UN subsequently introduced sanctions against the country.

When I visited Asmara in 1994, an air of liberation and new-won freedom and independence still lay upon the city. People sat outside restaurants quietly discussing social issues and sipping a cup of coffee or a glass of beer into the late evening hours. It was not unusual to see the president walking down the street, unaccompanied by security guards, before he settled at a table and began talking to the people. There were hardly any cars in the streets, and the relaxed atmosphere struck me and many other visitors at the time. It did not take long, however, for the international aid representatives in Eritrea, the NGOs and UN employees, to come into conflict with the government and to begin levelling strong criticism against the new leadership.

Disagreements first arose in connection with the government's formal requirement that foreign organizations should register themselves with the responsible state office handling the relationship with international NGOs, and the government also insisted that it should be able to oversee their finances. The reasoning was that the state required this information to govern the country. The paradox was that the Eritrean government was strongly criticized by the NGO community for implementing the aid organizations' most important buzzwords about 'self-reliance' and that the 'recipients' should be in control. As it turned out, there was nothing the international aid system's representatives and most vociferous advocates opposed more strongly than exactly the adoption of the policy they officially and in general advocated.

The government's demands were denounced as authoritarian, as an unfortunate interference in 'the civil society', and so forth, whereas the government in Asmara had imposed no more formal requirements on the organizations than Western donor countries do on NGOs in their own countries. In 1994 I talked to representatives for these organizations in Eritrea as we were sitting at outdoor restaurants in the very comfortable highland climate, letting the capital's remarkable warm stillness enshroud us. They were all indiscriminately positive toward Eritrea's aim of becoming an independent sovereign nation. At the same time, all were unanimously critical of what they termed the state's authoritarian interference in their affairs. The foreign organizations refused to submit to such control; they insisted on their autonomy and that they had the right to do as they wished (as they in fact did in most other African countries), since they were looking upon themselves as acting on behalf of the poor people in the country. They wanted continued access to the toll-free import of goods, they did not want to be incorporated into the government's policies and priorities, and so forth, for they represented 'civil society' and 'democracy'.

The people responsible in Eritrea for the new state's effort at coordination of foreign aid were many of the same individuals to whom the organizations during the war had given millions of dollars, but back then they were simply recipients of aid in an emergency situation and had neither the time nor the need to control such help. Now, as state-builders, their situation was completely different: as representatives for a new state, they wanted to be able to decide what was best for the country, and thus reduce the power of the international NGOs. As the previous guerrilla soldiers who dealt with the NGOs told me when I interviewed them in the governmental offices, they thought theirs was both a logical and a necessary policy. And so the schism began to develop that ended with Eritrea becoming a pariah in international politics. Many of those who had helped the Eritreans now turned against them, and what created the first friction was that the recipients, who were supposed to be aided on their way to self-reliance, now wanted to determine how such aid should be used. Many of the foreign NGOs and their representatives I met, and who had spent so much energy and resources supporting Eritrea's struggle for independence, were surprisingly clueless regarding the region's history and strangely devoid of sympathy for Eritrea's strong imperative to feel and show that they were masters in what they finally could say was their country.

There can be no doubt that Eritrea under President Isaias Afewerki's leadership has undergone a remarkable transformation. All statistics indicate that few developing countries have been doing better when it comes to fighting AIDS, illiteracy and corruption. Eritrea is a land relatively poor in resources, and the country's productivity is affected by the fact that for many years they have organized the country as if they are at war with neighbouring Ethiopia. It is impossible to verify or falsify all the stories of torture, disappearances and examples of brutal repression that circulate about Eritrea. Obviously, many people have for decades been interested in tarnishing the country's reputation and all it stands for, and for a number of self-serving reasons, even as it is equally obvious that President Afewerki has adopted a steadily more authoritarian course, where more and more of what happens in the country depends upon his person and his decisions.

Eritrea has thus for decades been isolated; a closed, single-party state in a permanent not-at-war-not-at-peace condition. The fact that an increasingly larger number of young Eritreans after 2000 have been leaving their homeland illustrates growing disillusionment with the state of affairs, and that more and more people have come to the conclusion that the situation is unsustainable, even as the government has profited from all the Eritreans living abroad and sending money home to their families. Eritrea has also refused to participate to the same extent as the other countries in the Nile Basin Initiative in the wide-ranging cooperation project that was established in 1999, and which the World Bank and other countries have supported economically – a typical expression of Eritrean stubbornness and willingness to stand alone.

Troublemaker or peace ambassador?

It is June 2010 and Eritrea's president, Isaias Afewerki, is on a state visit to Egypt to discuss, among other things, the Nile. Many of the other upstream countries have just recently banded together in Entebbe, Uganda, on 14 May, against Egypt's will, to sign the new cooperative agreement for the river's use. According to Egyptian government newspapers, Isaias publicly suggested that Egypt declare war on Ethiopia. After all, he reportedly said, Ethiopia's development of the Blue Nile threatened Egypt's most precious interests.

I went to Asmara the year after to meet with President Afewerki, and before the interview I was shown around in the very modestly furnished President's Office, a building in Italian neoclassical style. As I looked, I tried to think through the policy options from Eritrea's point of view. There could be no doubt, I thought, that Eritrea had good reasons for seeking Egyptian friendship in its conflicts with Ethiopia. Nor would it be surprising if Egypt sought Eritrea as an ally in attempts at destabilizing Ethiopia, since a destabilized Ethiopia would be a weak Ethiopia, and a weak Ethiopia would not be capable of implementing large Nile projects. Those in Egypt who might consider an eventual military attack against Ethiopia would see the strategic benefit of having Eritrea as a close cooperative partner: the country is so situated that it can serve as a deployment base, as Italy found in the 1930s. The two countries, furthermore, share a 912-kilometre border in a fraught area that is difficult to oversee and control.[7] That Eritrea did not sign the new Nile Agreement together with the other upstream countries, effectively blocking a collective front from emerging, is something Egypt no doubt has viewed very positively, and for which Eritrea will expect something in return – for example, support in its conflicts with its neighbour. Eritrea acknowledged, of course, the fact that Ethiopia, for its part, had officially stated that the country would increase support for anyone who toppled Eritrea's president, as long as he refused to change his regional policy, which Ethiopia claimed was based on backing opponents of Ethiopia's government in both Somalia and in Ethiopia itself.

I met President Afewerki in the Italian-built palace where he entertains guests. He himself lives simply, in keeping with the liberation era's prescribed ethos. Despite rumours abounding in opposition circles that he was deathly sick and suffering from aphasia, the president seemed in fine shape to me. When I asked him what he meant in 2010 when he suggested that Egypt go to war with Ethiopia, he denied ever saying what the Egyptian newspapers claimed. He had never once encouraged Egypt to declare war on Ethiopia. He said: 'That is what makes the issue senselessness. Because why should you go to war against each other on behalf of whom, and what are the benefits of going to war? That's where this rhetoric has become very fashionable.' Whenever governments have internal problems, he said, then they 'will resort to these kinds of statements'.[8] To ally oneself with Egypt or Sudan due to the border conflict with Ethiopia would be naïve and simple. There was simply no point; it was, he argued, a meaningless policy.

The president obviously had no real reason to tell me the truth. Whatever he said was clearly meant as a diplomatic gesture, since the government-controlled media published the interview the following day. But even so, his arguments were logical and rational. The headlines from Cairo, on the other hand, given subsequent events, were most likely deliberate rumour-mongering. They could be interpreted as part of the former Egyptian elite's attempts to destabilize the situation upstream, even while creating the impression within Egypt that the Nile was threatened, and that the government was championing the Egyptian people's interests.

Even though the published statements from President Afewerki's state visit to Cairo in 2010 probably did not reflect exactly what was actually said, their publication was nonetheless a clear sign that regional Nile policies will draw Eritrea into the centre of the large and decisive struggle for power and influence over the river between Egypt and Ethiopia.

A surprise visit to Asmara

In July 2018, after years of a 'no-peace-no-war' relationship with Ethiopia, Asmara experienced what most observers would have thought was unthinkable just months earlier. On 8 July, the new Ethiopian prime minister, Abiy Ahmed, came to Asmara! He was warmly embraced by Isaias. The next morning, in the Eritrean capital, the two men announced that diplomatic and economic relations would resume between the two countries. What was called the 2018 Eritrea–Ethiopia peace summit was a reality.

This peace process had developed very fast. Only one month before, on 5 June, the executive committee of the ruling Ethiopian People's Revolutionary Democratic Front had announced its intention to accept and fully implement the 2002 ruling of the Eritrea–Ethiopia Boundary Commission. The decision came as a big surprise, probably to the government in Asmara, too, representing as it did a reversal of sixteen years of Ethiopian policy. In a statement, the Ethiopian ruling party called for Eritrea to reciprocate and implement the peace deal without preconditions. The Eritrean government did not comment on the Ethiopian offer for two weeks. On 20 June, the country's Martyr Day, Isaias gave a speech where he talked about 'two lost generations' of opportunity, and said that the government would send a delegation to Addis Ababa 'to gauge current developments [...] and to chart out a plan for continuous future action'.[9] Eritrea accepted the peace proposal.

Eritrea's position was well taken and widely praised. The US State Department, for example, in a breathtaking about-face, acting as if it had not until recently considered Isaias a pariah, applauded his 'courageous leadership'.[10] The peace deal could be seen as a triumph for the Eritrean leader, since it validated the Eritrean position and its insistence in the past that Eritrea had been illegally occupied by Ethiopia since the war ending in 2000. Moreover, the deal led to the cancellation of the UN Security Council's sanctions against Eritrea. It thus opened new opportunities for foreign investment, especially in the mining sector. The economy, which had been growing quite strongly in recent years, also received a welcome boost from the opening of the border (after a year it was again closed, due more to local, regional reasons and uncertainties in relation to the Tigrayan People's Liberation Front, the TPLF).

With the peace deal, Eritrea's government may have lost the excuse of Ethiopian hostility and UN sanctions to defend its authoritarian internal policies but it could, of course, with some justification, argue that its policies are justified, since it will take

Eritrea time to recover from a period of great adversity. Another factor should not be overlooked: the TPLF. They were against the deal. One reason in the first place for the peace initiative from Addis Ababa, and why they thought Eritrea would agree, was most likely that they were united in their stand against this still-potent mutual enemy, the TPLF. Isaias had in his 20 June speech been positive towards Ethiopia, but he was more concerned with 'the TPLF's toxic and malignant legacy', and his belief that what he called the TPLF 'vultures' would now work to impede positive change – both in the bilateral relationship and inside Ethiopia.[11] It is this political movement that controls the area along the Tekeze and the Badme area.

The ongoing and ever more complex rivalries among a constantly growing number of regional and global players for power and influence in the Horn of Africa and in the upstream countries of the Nile, will also continue to create problems and challenges for a future peaceful and friendly relationship between these two neighbours in the Nile basin.

To the Nile's water tower

I am flying east along the Blue Nile in the Sudan, over the Gezira Irrigation Scheme, and the enormous clay plain beneath us looks like a gigantic quilt in varying shades of green. Rectangle after rectangle of green plots, bordered and defined by canals drawn like arrow-straight brushstrokes, criss-crossing the landscape, stretch towards the horizon. In the afternoon sunlight the contrasts are underlined and strengthened; the mountains to the east and the desert to the north look extra-desolate, while the fields appear even more vibrant. The Gezira Scheme is a leftover from the British period and is now a national institution, but without the water and the silt that come from Ethiopia and the mountains in the east and which here, on this wide, flat plain, is slowly moved around in thousands of narrow channels, the huge scheme would not be possible. The plane is heading towards the mountains, towards the Nile basin's true source and reservoir.

It is only up close, amid the day-to-day happenings, in the ordinary life along the riverbanks, in the irrigation canals, or in the houses powered every evening by electricity from the Nile, where girls and boys do their lessons by the light of reading lamps, and where water is retrieved and dinner is cooked, that the river's concrete meaning in human life is visible, However, it is only from a distance that the Nile's complex, geopolitical potential and its structuring role as a historical actor becomes most evident and clearly observable.

Beneath me I can see the Blue Nile, which on average has delivered around 60 billion cubic metres of water to the Nile in Egypt every year. And on each side of it – the Atbara to the north and the Baro-Sobat to the south. The Atbara runs down from the border area between Eritrea and Ethiopia (there called Tekeze or Setit), carrying with it 12 billion cubic metres of water; the Baro-Sobat carries around 10 billion cubic metres of water annually, but much of its lost through the swamps in South Sudan. Around 90 per cent of all the water in Lake Nasser comes from the country towards which I am heading.

In the Ethiopian mountains the signs of approaching rain, and often of violent thunderstorms, are easy to discover. Rainbows bend clear colours against a black sky, and nature appears on the brink of a catastrophe. In the land of its birth, the Blue Nile does not play the role as of benefactor and life source, as it does in the Egyptian Delta, but, rather, it reappears with power and violence, as if the river itself is language of a mad, vindictive god.

The African winds shape the river. On their way from the South Atlantic, they cross the North African continent, absorbing the evaporation from rainforests and lakes; heavily laden, they blow over the oven-hot Sudan, until the winds abruptly strike the mountains of the Ethiopian highlands' cliffs, which rise, often precipitously, to three or four thousand metres above sea level. Rainfall amounts are a result of altitude variations and seasonal changes in the atmospheric pressure that controls the wind systems.

Of the more than 120 billion cubic metres of rain that falls on Ethiopia, only 3 per cent remains in the country. The rest flows down to the countries on the plains – to Somalia and Kenya to the south, but mainly with the Nile west and north. If Ethiopia had no volcanic peaks, and if the wind did not strike against them, so that every summer and autumn, from mid-June to September, rain rushes in powerful torrents from the sky, there would be no river hurrying snake-like towards the plainlands below, carrying with it the silt from mountains that through millennia transformed the desert hundreds of kilometres toward the north into one of the most fertile regions in the world. The wind, the rain and the mountains here shape Egypt by and through their faithful agency. After all, Ethiopia has not only sent down water but also the country itself – in the form of the silt that, together with the water, has made it possible to turn barren deserts into blooming, fruitful gardens.

The rain, which for thousands of years every autumn in the desert regions to the north has generated a process whereby nature is refreshed in the river's wake, meanwhile, arrives for Ethiopian farmers in the form of violent thunderstorms and chaotic downpours, transforming previously dry river beds and river valleys into areas that can now be cultivated, and a river that could not, until very recently, be tamed.

An overarching paradox that will dominate Ethiopia's future development irrespective of government is therefore this: only a tiny portion of the country is artificially irrigated, and, until recently, the country has only exploited less than 5 per cent of its hydropower potential. But still, Ethiopia is Africa's water tower. In the new millennium, the country's power needs have been rapidly increasing due to a quite high and stable economic development, at the same time as there have been reports about severely drought-stricken regions. At the beginning of the 2000s, Ethiopia had more than 80 million inhabitants; more, for the first time, than Egypt. In 2018 the estimated population in Ethiopia was 109 million as compared to 98 million in Egypt and 41 million in the Sudan, and in January 2020 Egypt reported that it had 100 million inhabitants. In 1950 the country had 18 million inhabitants; in 2050 the UN reckons that more than 170 million people will live there. The need to utilize the Nile for energy and irrigation will only become stronger and stronger, and Ethiopia's domestic policy, no matter who is in power, will to a steadily greater extent revolve around the validity of this paradox, and around how it might be solved.

Aksum and the highlands

Up until 1890 and Britain's establishment of the Nile basin as a political-strategic sphere of interest for the British Empire, acknowledged by the infamous Berlin Conference of 1884–5, the Nile was of marginal significance to Ethiopia's development.

Cultural influence from the outside, however, did not arrive via the river as a highway, as cultural diffusion has done in many other large river valleys, because as Burchart Heinrich Jessen, among others, confirmed at the very beginning of the new century: the river was not navigable. Nor was it possible to lay caravan routes up along its banks into Ethiopia. Instead, trade routes and cultural influence followed the back of the eastern plateau, from north to south, around where the Italian colonizers later built the so-called Strada Imperiale from Asmara to Addis Ababa. Along the line south, from Aksum and Adwa, were the centuries' old cultural centres of the Ethiopian Orthodox Church, places such as Lalibela, with its stone churches, and Debre Libanos.

The many stories about the origin and early history of Ethiopia were all written into the country's national epic, *Kebra Nagast* (*The Glory of Kings*), in the thirteenth and fourteenth centuries, and the epic also references this north–south connection. The first Kingdom of Aksum, or the Aksumite empire, was at its height in the fourth and fifth centuries CE, and ruled from the fringes of the Sahara in the west, across the Red Sea to the Arabian desert, including Mecca, in the east. It was converted to Christianity around 300 CE. Around 1270, a new dynasty was established in the Abyssinian highlands. According to *Kebra Nagast* this new dynasty were male-line descendants of the old Aksumite monarchs, and thus recognized as the continuing Solomonic dynasty. The ruler called himself King of Kings. This second Kingdom of Aksum ruled from the 1200s until the Islamic invasion in the 1500s.

The mythical history surrounding Ethiopian state formation and the Queen of Sheba goes like this. The queen was born in Aksum as the daughter of the local king, who was chosen king after he killed the dragon that had been terrorizing the population. The queen travelled north to Jerusalem with gifts of gold and ivory for Solomon, who was king over Jerusalem. The king said: 'A woman of such splendid beauty hath come to me from the ends of the world. What do I know? Will God give me seed in her?'[12] She lived in King Solomon's palace, became pregnant by him and gave birth to a son, Menelik. The night he was born, Solomon dreamed that a sun was shining over his land, but then it retreated to shine over the land of the Nile. Menelik later travelled to Jerusalem and was crowned King Menelik I of Ethiopia. Before leaving, he had copies made of Moses' stone tablets. He then used these copies to replace the originals, which he had taken and then brought back to Aksum. Solomon discovered the theft too late. He sent soldiers after Menelik and his men, but they turned back when Menelik's horses began running so fast that both they and the wagons were flying above the ground. When the company reached Tekeze, Archangel Michael protected them and they were once again set on the ground.[13] The Ethiopians were, so to speak, given stewardship of the stone tablets upon which Moses wrote the Ten Commandments, on behalf of humanity.

Kebra Nagast addresses what is crucial to a king's greatness: to possess the Tabernacle of Zion and to have an ancestor who has had a sacred pact with God. Representatives for what the literature terms the Solomonic state around 1270 argued that they could trace their lineage back to King Solomon of Jerusalem. The epic also works to substantiate the divine descent, via Adam to Solomon and thereafter to the Ethiopian royal house. As such, Ethiopia is a significant factor in God's plan for the world. The country, according to the Ethiopian Orthodox narrative, became Zion and the Ethiopians became God's chosen people.

This Ethiopian 'creation history' contributed to endowing traditional Ethiopian policy with a reservoir of religious meaning. Christianity became the court's and the country's religion in the fourth century CE. Ethiopia was at times a regional superpower, and it controlled, among other things, central parts of southern Arabia before Muhammed established Islam as the region's religion. Just as the founding and expansion of the Ottoman Empire at the Bosporus and the Black Sea weakened the Christian cultures to the East, in the Caucasus and in the Balkans, so Ottoman control over the Nile basin and the Red Sea also gradually limited Ethiopian Orthodox influence in the region. Ethiopian rulers, pressed as they were by the invasion of Muslim troops under Ahmad Gran in the 1500s, were aware of the danger, and they appealed for help. The Portuguese came to their rescue, and it was this Portuguese presence in Ethiopia that, among other things, made it possible for Jesuit monks in the 1600s to describe the Blue Nile's sources.

The classic conception of the Ethiopians as God's chosen people and the Nile as a sacred river – as the River of Paradise itself – for centuries played (as we shall see) a role in regional power politics. Even if the theme is now completely absent from the official debate in Ethiopia, there is no reason to believe it has been relegated for good to the scrapheap of history's dead ideas. It can be revived, because religion and politics are commonly woven together in the permanent tug of war between different ethnic groups, religious communities and countries in great international river basins. Structurally it is more interesting to note, however, that as the Ethiopians have become more and more involved in Nile politics, the country is becoming more and more oriented towards the east and the rest of Africa.

The moment's limitations

'You have to live as if every single moment might be your last', the pilot says in a loud voice as the helicopter abruptly lifts off from the small grass patch on the Ethiopian highlands with its kilometres-wide view on all sides. We fly low along the river's lonesome banks in the oppressively hot Blue Nile Gorge. Here the Nile runs in a great arc, like a prisoner of the great gorge; sometimes it circles around, but most often it cuts through the cliffs, flowing at the feet of deep chasms. For more than 500 kilometres the river is more or less inaccessible, since the chasms are sometimes a thousand metres deep. The Blue Nile has accurately been described as 'the Everest of rivers', and was branded as late as 1970 in an article on explorer history as 'the last unconquered hell on earth'.[14] In these regions, the Nile has for thousands of years lived its life alone, with no human face bending over it, and hardly an animal as companion. Here, the line it traces through the landscape has changed as little as the mountains contoured against the morning sky.

The pilot, who so cheerfully talked about every moment potentially being your last, and how you should live accordingly, has opened the helicopter door so I can see everything and, as he makes sure I am adequately buckled in, he is flying as though he thinks he is in a James Bond movie. We streak above the river, here and there just a few centimetres above the water's surface, with sheer cliff walls on both sides. The apprehension the pilot is consciously trying to produce in me makes the deserted mountains and river seen even more dramatic, not terrifying but alien and remote, for through the open door I watch the landscape as if it were in a film.

Since we never can know how what we say will affect others, the pilot, whom I've never seen before, has no clue that his statement immediately sets in motion a nagging, distracting train of thoughts. He is unaware, of course, that I am a historian and thereby often concerned with or thinking about time and the concept of time. For, what exactly is a moment, what is the past, what is the actual present, since even an experience (like flying in a helicopter over the Blue Nile), or an expression (like the pilot's haiku statement) can be studied as an historical phenomenon the moment it happens? How to comprehend the moment when I, staring through the door as the pilot rudely rolls the helicopter to the side, am surrounded by what has been 'eternally immutable', but which in the course of a few years will belong to the irretrievably past? A state leadership that considers the Nile's present as divorced from its history, or that views the river from the perspective of the present, or from the vantage point of just a few years, independent and isolated from the powerful processes of the long term that have shaped its possibilities, will make the so-called realist conception of the world as a place where the law of the jungle still prevails, into a self-fulfilling prophecy.

Compared with the river's persistence in these deep gorges, and its eternal, natural capacity to dig constantly deeper, I cannot avoid the thought, as I glimpse the pilot's profile beneath the headset and recognize how he enjoyed terrifying me as he once again twists the helicopter around and zips down to the river's surface, that the idea of thinking purely of the present moment or of today, is mannerism, is banal. And this is particularly the case along the Nile: if both state leaders and the general public in the Nile basin countries do not take a significantly long-term perspective regarding how the Nile can be controlled and shared, conflict will be unavoidable and the Nile might be destroyed. For our present is definitely only a passing moment in this river's long and eventful history.

Monastery island, the sea and the world's end

Lake Tana, out of which the Blue Nile flows, has long stood at a centre of power politics and diplomacy of world-historical proportions. The lake is 84 kilometres long and 66 kilometres at its widest, but it is exceptionally shallow, with an average depth of just 8 metres. The banks, with their palm trees and acacias, are also home to coffee bushes, whose red berries were brought here from Arabia.

The Tana region was both the political and religious centre of the Christian empire established on the Ethiopian highland between the collapse of the Zagwe dynasty in the fourteenth century and Gondar becoming a permanent centre early in the seventeenth century. Some twenty of the thirty-seven islands in Lake Tana house orthodox monasteries or churches. Two monasteries have great religious significance: Tana Kirkos and Daga Estifanos.

Tana Kirkos is an almost three-hour boat trip from Bahir Dar, the city on the Nile lake that Haile Selassie envisioned in the 1950s would be the country's new capital. After crossing it in a rented boat on a day when the lake was rough and grey, I arrive at the monastery island, which rises abruptly from the lake, almost cliff-like. The skipper calmly sets the boat ashore, and we are met by priests robed in long yellow capes. They walk along quietly, all of them equipped with a stick, and they speak softly to each other. Then they beckon to me: 'Come!' We walk up the steep path, and on the grassy stretch at the island's summit we pass a cluster of brown clay houses. A few monks are sitting on a tree trunk positioned between two trees. They gaze with expressionless faces across the lake that reflects the clouds in the sky. There is no radio here. No telephone. No electricity. Just the sound of insects and birds and human steps. I am immediately gripped by the island's distinctive mood. The atmosphere fits the legends – for example, how religious icons like Saint Yared taught the birds to sing, or the legend of Tekle Haymanot, who stood and prayed for eight years until he lost his foot. He is Ethiopia's most celebrated saint and is most often drawn or painted as an old man with wings and a single foot. There is also a well-known legend about the Virgin Mary here, who interceded on the Day of Judgement for the cannibal Belai, who had eaten seventy-two people but who repented and later gave water to a leper.

Tana Kirkos is the island where, according to myth, the stone tablets of Moses have been preserved for centuries, but it is also the island where the Virgin Mary, Jesus and Joseph lived for three months after travelling up the Nile in their flight from Herod. The monks here, say that you can see traces they left. One of them steps quickly in front of me while signalling that I should follow. On a high rocky outcrop atop a steep slope overlooking the lake, he shows it to me – clear marks he fervently claims are the footprints of Jesus and Mary. The monk steps eagerly to one tip of the rock and points out to me a tiny chapel that he says is built over marks on the ground left by Mary's dress when she sat there. 'You understand?' the monk asks. 'Jesus was five years old when he came to the island.'

The monks' story goes something like this. After the Virgin Mary, Jesus and Joseph had been driven to flight by Herod and had reached Egypt, they lived on a mountain in the desert for two years. One day Jesus pointed to a country, and when his mother asked what land it was, he said 'Ethiopia'. After that, the small family, accompanied by some invisible saints and five lions, began the march to Ethiopia. They walked through Eritrea on the way to Aksum before reaching a monastery north of Gondar. The lions remained there. The rest of the company eventually arrived at Marefit Mariam monastery, located on the edge of Lake Tana. From there they took a papyrus boat here to Tana Kirkos. One day an angel arrived to bid them return to Israel, but the Virgin Mary wanted to remain. In Israel she had been threatened and forced to flee, but here she had been met with hospitality, and therefore she did not wish to leave the island. A saint, however, convinced her that she must depart because Jesus was the son of God and he had to return to Israel to die on the cross for the sins of humanity. Before Mary and Jesus left, they bathed in Lake Tana, an event that obviously increased the lake's holiness. Then the Virgin Mary told the clouds: 'Bear us.' And it was in the clouds that she, Jesus, Joseph and their followers were carried back to Israel. As they left Ethiopia, they blessed the country, and that is why Ethiopia is so often mentioned in the Bible.[15] It is this event that apparently gave the lake its name. In the Geez language *tseane* means 'covered by', a reference to the clouds that transported the Virgin Mary and Jesus back to Israel. The name of the Blue Nile's chief reservoir, Lake Tsana or Lake Tana, thereby harbours deep Christian roots.

Lake Tana's fate has also been unfolded in an apocalypse scenario. The story goes like this. Within the lake is a sacred gold cross and a wealth of gold and silver that will not be discovered before *ferengis*, the white man, has drained and dried the lake. Then the Blue Nile will become a waterway flowing into paradise, which is Jerusalem. And then the Devil will stand and call to all the people. That will be the end of the world.[16]

An Ethiopian philosopher and cave dweller

North of Lake Tana, not so far from the newly constructed Tekeze Dam, is the cave of Zera Yacob, one of the foremost thinkers in Ethiopian history. In the seventeenth century, he lived there as a hermit for two years while developing his philosophy. Zera Yacob was the son of poor farmers in Aksum, and he studied sacred Christian texts when he was young.

Yacob sought refuge in the cave near Tekeze to escape accusations levelled at him by King Susenyos that he was an enemy of the Ethiopian Orthodox faith. Yacob subsequently said that he learned more living alone in that cave than living among the learned. This seventeenth-century thinker is one of the few African intellectuals whose philosophy has been preserved in writing. His renown today is due to Claude Sumner, a Canadian professor who moved to Ethiopia at the beginning of the 1950s. Sumner realized that the author of an already well-known Ethiopian book, *Reflections*, was not who everyone thought it was – the Italian Capuchin monk, Giusto d'Urbino, who had lived in Ethiopia in the nineteenth century – but rather Yacob. Sumner exemplifies the fact that an academic truly can play a crucial role: without him Yacob would have been forgotten, since there is no reason to believe that anyone else would ever have embarked on the same research venture.

Zera Yacob saw God as a lawgiver, providing laws on correct morality. Humankind, however, has free will to do wrong or right. Within Christianity and Islam, God can obviously give directives on what He prefers, but He will never deprive people of their free will and the ability to use their brains. As a result, Yacob says, God's laws are influenced by the people who interpret them – for example, by religious leaders. When these people interpret God's laws, they are rightfully exercising their free will. A problem, however, arises for those who follow the laws that have already been interpreted; they are being deprived or are depriving themselves of that same free will, because they are following other people's determinations of what is wrong and right.[17]

God created people to have mastery over their actions, so these become what they may – good or bad. These ideas fit a modern direction within theological moral theory that emphasizes the consequences of an action, and which sometimes makes the consequence of an action the criterion of, or test for, the degree of goodness or moral correctness.

I am walking along the shores of Lake Tana with the book, *Rationality of the Human Heart*, beneath my arm.[18] The text was devised in a cave in the Upper Nile basin about four hundred years ago, but parts of it seem astonishingly modern and rational. It contains a philosophical approach that, to the extent it is integrated into Ethiopia's and other countries' reflections regarding use of the Nile and the consequences that arise, can prove its ongoing relevance in a region where religious dogmatism and extreme versions of an ethic of conviction are on the advance.

Mass baptism in Bahir Dar

In the total darkness of the night, holding candles in their hands, the priest and monks chant a prayer in a monotone voice, and as the mood and the morning chill cause me to shiver, an annual ceremony is under way along Lake Tana's banks. With his face towards the lake and the sun, which rises slowly and casts a yellow-red gleam over the water, the trees and the people standing here at the Ura Kidane Meret monastery on Lake Tana's Zege Peninsula, the priest blesses the water and fills a brass pot. Draped in white sheet-like garments, one after another, the people who want to be rebaptized step forward, the old and the young, bend their heads beneath the pot, while the priest lets the holy Lake Tana water flow from the pot over their heads.

Timkat means immersion in Amharic, the language of the ethnic group that has dominated the Church here. The main ceremony takes place this morning, but the festival began yesterday afternoon. On Lake Tana's islands, in Bahir Dar and in most other places in Ethiopia, Timkat is celebrated in honour of the baptism of Jesus by John the Baptist in the Jordan River. This act is considered a baptism for humankind, an act of grace that functions as an instruction code for the entire world. The festival occurs on a certain date every year. Where it is physically possible, water from Lake Tana and the Blue Nile becomes the medium to connect the baptized with God, and in homage to the river's mythological, religious significance.

The mass baptism is an ancient tradition, and when Scotsman James Bruce travelled around Ethiopia around 1770, he described in detail how these ceremonies unfolded. Like many of the British explorers, Bruce was exceptionally focused on nakedness and gender, possibly because it helped to sell the books, as such nakedness would have been very unusual to the English reader at the time.

> The baptism [...] began at midnight, and the old tutor dipped every person under water, taking him by the head, saying 'I baptize thee in the name of the Father, of the Son, and of the Holy Ghost'. It was the most thronged at sun-rise and ended about nine o'clock; a long time for an old man to stand in frozen water. The number (as women were promiscuously admitted) could not be less than 40,000; so that even the nine hours this baptist-general officiated, he must have had exercise enough to keep him warm, if 40,000 (many of them naked beauties) passed through his hands.

[…]

The women were stark naked before the men, not even the rag about them. Without such a proper medium as frozen water, I fear it would not have contributed much to the interests of religion to have trusted a priest (even an old one) among so many bold and naked beauties, especially as he had the first six hours of them in the dark.[19]

Bruce related that people at that time believed in the Nile's spirit and called it 'the Everlasting God, Light of the World, Eye of the World, God of Peace, their Saviour, and Father of the Universe'. He also spoke with 'the Shum', the river priest, whose title was Kefla Abai, or 'Servant of the River'.

Returning by boat from the Zege Peninsula to Bahir Dar, we take a slight detour along the lake's outlet, which is surrounded by a swamp with tall papyrus plants. It is here the Blue Nile begins, surging over a cliff edge a few kilometres farther down to become one of Africa's most powerful and beautiful waterfalls. Suddenly, the motor stops – we are out of petrol. The shame-faced skipper acts quickly, and almost before we know it, he is in the water. While hippos float, snorting and threatening just a few metres away, and the most anxious of us can hear the approaching thundering falls in the distance, he takes the boat's rope between his teeth and pulls the vessel and us to safety, hails another boat that can supply petrol, and then sails on as if he swims away from hippos with a boat between his teeth every day.

In Bahir Dar the streets are packed: it is the Timkat Festival and there is an explosion of sounds, colours and voices. Flutes are blown. An odd assortment of instruments are struck. A replica of the Ark of the Covenant is carried from the main church to where the baptisms will take place. The procession from the main church in Bahir Dar surpasses all the others, and the priest who leads the ritual bears the replica Ark on his head; it is protected by a cloth worked in gold and silver, and the priests hold up ceremonial umbrellas to further protect it. Even though Bahir Dar lies right by the lake, the festival now takes place inside the city at Meskel Square. The square holds a baptismal pool – Bahire Timiket – with water blessed by the chief religious leaders before being sprinkled over the crowds. The Timkat Festival is a religious ceremony that historically has functioned as a confirmation of personal faith, but which also manifests the Church's power in society.

Lake Tana's role in the Orthodox Church's narratives and institutions has, therefore, not only had an impact on how people have related to the Nile and its water but also how the Nile itself has been tamed and developed. That is to say: the river's biography and its religious and ritual dimensions are also woven together here in complex ways – and always with high political consequences.

The sacred Nile and the Scot who posed as discoverer of the source

Gish Abay is the source of the Blue Nile, and it is also the name of a small place in the shadow of Mount Gish, located in the western part of Gojjam in Ethiopia's Amhara Region. Gilgil Abay, or the Little Nile, originates here and is the largest of the sixty or so rivers flowing into Lake Tana. The water here has always been regarded as sacred and has a legendary power.

The water's sacred nature is based on stories told in the Old Testament:

> A river watering the garden flowed from Eden; from there it was separated into four headwaters. The name of the first is Pishon; it winds through the entire land of Havilah, where there is gold. (The gold of that land is good; aromatic resin and onyx are also there.) The name of the second river is Gihon; it winds through the entire land of Cush.[20]

Before the Nile was called Abay, it was named Gihon. Gihon is one of the four rivers that flow from Heaven and from the Garden of Eden, and its source is Gish Abay. Orthodox tradition holds that when Adam and Eve lived in Paradise, Gihon was the river of life, and when humankind was expelled from there, Gihon flowed from Heaven to earth. Within this way of thinking the Blue Nile comes from Heaven.

The first Europeans to see the Blue Nile's or Gilgil Abay's source in Ethiopia were the Portuguese, sent there in 1541 together with Cristóvão da Gama, the son of Vasco da Gama, the Portuguese navigator who first found the sea route from Europe to India via the Cape of Good Hope. They played an important role in the battle that the Orthodox Church was waging against the advance of Islam and the Ottoman Empire's attempts to conquer Ethiopia. Exactly when the Portuguese saw the source of the Nile for the first time is unknown, since the event was not documented. What we do know is that the Jesuit priest, Pedro Páez, saw Gish Abay at the beginning of the seventeenth century. In *Itinerário*, written by the Jesuit missionary Jerónimo Lobo, the year is set at 1613, whereas James Bruce calculated that it must have been 1615. However, it was the Jesuit Athanasius Kircher, who published a Latin version of Páez's account, who came up with the date that has become 'official': 21 April 1618. Páez was the first to describe the site in his *History of Ethiopia*:

> Being in the suite of the Emperor and his army, I mounted this elevation, and examined all things with the utmost exactitude. I found there two circular springs, each four palms in diameter, and I beheld with pleasure what the Kings of Persia, Cyrus and Cambysses, Alexander and the famous Julius Caesar, had wished to see [...]. [T]he two eyes of the spring do not issue on the top of the mountain, but they disappear from view at the bottom of the ridge. [...] The second source is situated to the East, at about a stone's throw.[21]

In the five-volume work that James Bruce published in 1790, where he describes his travels from around 1770, Bruce wrote himself into world history by claiming to be the first European to see the source of the Blue Nile: 'It is easier to guess than describe the situation of my mind at that moment – standing in that spot which had baffled the genius, industry, and inquiry, of both ancients and moderns, for the course of nearly three thousand years. [...] Though a mere private Briton, I triumphed here, in my own mind, over kings and their armies.'[22]

According to Bruce, he had solved a 3,000-year-old mystery:

[The Nile's source] was the palm for three thousand years held out to all the nations in the world as a *detur dignissimo*, which, in my cool hours, I had thought was worth the attempting at the risk of my life, which I had long resolved to lose, or lay this discovery, a trophy in which I could have no competitor, for the honour of my country, at the feet of my sovereign, whose servant I was.

The Scotsman Bruce raised his glass to George III and the Virgin Mary in the same breath. The person he was truly toasting, however, was himself – that is to say, to the fact he had personally solved one of history's great riddles. Bruce's books emphasize how the impulse for discovery and the need for self-assertion can be two sides of the same coin. For, even if he did extend geographical knowledge of Ethiopia, he had made no new, great discovery; after all, he himself was aware that the Portuguese Jesuits had been there before him and had written about this in a book published in 1618, almost two centuries before his own. As such, Bruce's five volumes foreshadowed an entirely different Western literary tendency and tradition when it comes to Africa – one that orchestrates the author as a hero by staging him as the conqueror of the unknown and the exotic.

Gish Abay today is one of the Nile basin's few pilgrimage sites, and perhaps the only one of relative significance that is tied to the river itself. Only Ethiopian Orthodox Christians have access to the actual source. The idea is that non-believers will pollute the source, making the sacred water less sacred simply by virtue of who they are. At the source, shoes are also forbidden, and the source itself is covered by a green tent. Outside, people stand in long lines to receive the water handed to them from those within the tent, who pour the water into bottles. The water is first blessed by the priests. The water is itself holy, but the blessing makes it even more so. People believe it is potent enough to induce miracles for descendants up to seventy generations hence. It can also be used by people who cannot themselves come to Gish Abay, and people who are baptized in it will be cured of sin, sickness and misfortune.

The continuing, contemporary worship of the holiness of the water from the source, and the belief within the Christian Orthodox tradition that the Blue Nile is the river of Paradise, give the geopolitical power struggle about how the Nile should be used and controlled a potential religious dimension, which also extends into the future.

Prester John and the Virgin Mary govern the Nile

For about a thousand years stories have abounded regarding the way Ethiopia has used its location at the headwaters of the Nile to punish Egypt. During the Fatimid reign of Sultan al-Mustansir around 1089–90, it was speculated in Egypt whether Ethiopia had the power to influence the Nile's flow. During that year, the flood had failed with catastrophic results in Egypt. The author al-Makin reported that the sultan sent the Coptic Patriarch, Michael of Alexandria, to Ethiopia to implore the Ethiopians to restore the flood, which they subsequently did.[23] There is, however, a compelling reason to believe that this never actually happened, because back then the Ethiopians did not have the technological ability to control the flow.

Meanwhile, the belief or worry that the Ethiopians did have this capability was itself significant. In 1384 a certain Simone Sigoli visited Egypt, Sinai and Palestine, and he was told that the sultan paid taxes to Prester John in Ethiopia because he was the one who controlled the Nile's sluices. They stood only partially open, and to prevent Ethiopia from drowning Egypt, the Egyptians paid the emperor.

According to the British historian, Richard Pankhurst, the learned Venetian Alessandro Zorzi reported in the mid-1500s that the emperor could take the water from the Muslims, preventing it from reaching Cairo, but that he did not do so for fear that the Muslims 'would ruin the churches and the Christian monks who are in Jerusalem and those in Egypt of which there are many'. In Europe the myth was at least familiar from 1335 on, when Jacob of Verona travelled to Palestine and reported back on Ethiopia's power over the Nile.[24]

For centuries the Christians kept alive the idea that the Nile flood was one of the Virgin Mary's miracles. During one war between Christians and Muslims, Mary revealed herself and said that God had granted the Christian Ethiopian Emperor Dawit wisdom and power to change the Nile's course. That terrified the Muslims, and they declared they were not enemies of the Christians, at which point Ethiopia's king thanked Mary. In Miracle 268 of *Täamrä Maryam* (*Miracles of Mary*), the story is described as follows:

> And on this day at midnight Our Lady Mary, the holy twofold Virgin, bearer of God, appeared to the King of Ethiopia Dawit and she said to him: O ye beloved and beloved of my son Jesus Christ, and now I have asked my son on behalf of you that you will go and rescue my nation, the Christians, and thus He has granted and made even for you your way. Get up and go. And He will perform through your hand many miracles [. . .]. And God gave him wisdom and he stopped [the Nile] so that it did not descend into the land of Egypt, because there are no rains in the land of the people of Egypt; unless the water of [the Nile], which flows from Ethiopia, reaches them, they do not plough, they do not sow seed and they do not get water at all [. . .] And afterwards Dawit, King of Ethiopia said: Was it not said once: To restrain the water is like beginning a war, but the will of God, the Lord of the Christians, may come about.[25]

Occupation or agreement

When, at the end of the nineteenth century, the British established their control over the entire Nile basin, one question to present itself was: what to do with Ethiopia? London's strategists had no interest at all in the Blue Nile's religious dimension. They thought only of its economic and geopolitical significance, and, in contrast to what many historians have argued, from the 1880s onwards were completely aware that almost all the Nile's water came from Ethiopia.

Ethiopia was the ancient, mythical land of Prester John who, according to medieval European legends, governed a large Christian empire that was surrounded by Islamic states. This empire had a strong orthodox church that many Christians in the West long did not recognize as part of Christianity, and it had an imperial form of government with a long and deep historical ancestry. The country lagged far behind Europe in technology and science at the time when Europeans began to show interest in the region as part of the general European expansion into Africa. European observers who arrived there in the late 1800s and early 1900s often offered harsh critique. A typical example is James Baum in *Savage Abyssinia*. Baum claimed that, from his observations, the Ethiopians had not even developed weapons with which to kill wild animals; they had, he argued, contributed nothing to the progress of humankind.[26]

But when it comes to Ethiopia, it has been shown that descriptions of Africa written when the civilizing imperial zeal was at its strongest were often more a reflection of European ideologies and world views than the reality in Africa. Geographical conditions on the Ethiopian highlands were favourable to agriculture. With good rainfall it was possible to cultivate several times a year, almost whenever one wanted. The Aksum civilization has, among other things, left behind enormous monoliths testifying to both its technological competence and its social organization. In Aksum city today one can still see one of these monoliths, standing 33 metres high and weighing 517 tons. Obviously, it takes theoretical knowledge, practical ability and organizational talent to erect such structures. The same was true of the dam at Kohaito, which is almost 2,000 years old and is still in use, and the Mai Shum reservoir, or the Queen of Sheba's Bath as it has also been called. The Aksum civilization was a rain-based agricultural civilization and, naturally enough, progressed during periods of unusually good rainfall and declined when the rainfall was poor, so this part of the Ethiopian highlands is one of those places in the world where recurrent severe droughts have played an integral part in the people's history.[27] Aksum's advantage was that it was possible to dig wells, an idea reflected in the original meaning of its name: 'Well of the Chieftain'.

It turned out that London was not concerned with the fact that Ethiopia, with its Christian Orthodox background, its proximity to Islam's central regions, and its developmental potential, could prove the perfect country in which to spread European Christian civilization's values, nor was London concerned with the country's stage of development or general resources. Common, hegemonic descriptions of the imperialistic project are also not of much help here in understanding what happened. Colonialism's or imperialism's concrete policies cannot be analysed as if they are subject-less; as if they are a history without individual actors with aims and plans, So again, this theme also must be approached concretely: what did the most important British strategists think and do when it came to Ethiopia?

When the British leadership considered what to do regarding Ethiopia, one factor in their equation was that they already had military experience there. They had launched a famous raid into the country, a kind of premodern version of the Israeli Special Forces' 'Operation Entebbe' of 1971, when a hundred commando soldiers in the course of a night flew 4,000 kilometres in a transport plane from Israel to the White Nile's source in Uganda. The Popular Front for the Liberation of Palestine had landed a hijacked plane in Entebbe and they were holding Israeli hostages in it. The Special Forces rescued the hostages and killed the hijackers. In 1864 the British consul and several other Europeans in Ethiopia were kidnapped by Emperor Tewodros II and held prisoner at Magdala. All attempts to free the captives through negotiation failed. Finally, after the captives had been imprisoned for four years, Queen Victoria announced the decision to send a military expedition to rescue the hostages in August 1867, and the following year Sir Robert Napier entered Ethiopia with a force of 1,600 men. In a battle that countless books have narrated, the Magdala fortress was reached, attacked and stormed. Emperor Tewodros did not receive enough support from local warlords. He committed suicide rather than surrender. After Napier's troops had freed the captives and seized war spoils, and Ethiopia's leader had died by his own hand, they left the country. The British in 1868 had no urge to conquer Ethiopia either militarily or politically, nor any interest in doing so, a situation that had not changed by the century's end.

When Africa was divided among European powers in the 1880s and the Nile basin was acknowledged as a British 'sphere of interest', the British government did not want to occupy Ethiopia, the Nile's water tower, or to transform it into a colony. The British had only one – but overriding – interest there, and that was the water that the land sent down to Egypt. But to London it did not make sense to seize control of Ethiopia on that basis. Even as the Nile's hydrology was a central driving factor behind London's decisions to conquer Sudan and Uganda on the White Nile, that same hydrology was a chief reason that made conquering Ethiopia pointless. According to this way of reasoning, a fundamental fact was that most of the water from the Ethiopian plateau came surging down over a three-month period in the autumn. At this time of year, Egypt had more than enough water, and there was, furthermore, so much silt in the river that it could not be dammed from one year to the next or from one season to the next with existing dam-building technology. The cotton fields that earned the export profits that enabled Egypt to repay its debt to bankers in Europe, and that produced the raw materials for the Lancashire textile industries, needed water in spring and summer, and lay idle in the autumn.

London, therefore, instead opted for an agreement with Emperor Menelik II, whereby he surrendered control of the Nile system in his country and swore not to take a drop of water from the Nile without acquiring London's approval beforehand. Following in-depth correspondence with the emperor's Swiss adviser, London agreed that Ethiopia could exploit the water as a power source if this did not affect the river's water flow downstream, a point on which the British government was expressly clear. They also, they claimed, got a promise from the emperor that if Ethiopia ever sought to build dams on the Nile or on any of its tributaries, Ethiopia would first ask the British for aid and advice.[28]

Great Britain now controlled the Ethiopian Nile system politically, in full expectation that in the foreseeable future there it would be economically expedient and technologically possible to dam the Nile in Ethiopia but implemented by themselves in one way or another.

In exchange, the Ethiopian emperor received London's support for his expansionist policy towards other ethnic groups that bordered his empire's central regions. Menelik traded 'water for land', or sovereignty over the Nile for support in the widening of his territory. The emperor also viewed the British as a counterweight to other European states in their policy towards Ethiopia, particularly Italy, with whom they had just been at war, and famously beaten at the Battle of Adwa. In addition, there were lengthy discussions about Great Britain compensating Menelik for the water they used downstream, and occasionally staffers in London were sent to scour the archives to retrieve the pertinent documents. Based on the available source material, everything indicates that Menelik did not agree to this idea. He did not want to be accused of selling parts of his country for a sum of gold coins.

The treaty with Emperor Menelik II, which the British believed secured their diplomatic and strategic interests in Ethiopia, was signed in 1902. (Egypt still argues this agreement is valid and legally binding.) In the treaty, the Emperor agreed 'not to construct or allow to be constructed, any work across the Blue Nile, Lake Tsana, or the Sobat which would arrest the flow of their waters into the Nile' without London's approval. At the same time, and here the sources are clear, the British imperialists had one main objective in Ethiopia: to build a dam at the mouth of Lake Tana.

In keeping with this strategy, Lord Cromer in Egypt and the government in London stopped an initiative by a private British capitalist who already aimed to build such a dam in 1903.[29] The political leadership considered it too early to implement such a project; they did not want to needlessly challenge both Egypt and Ethiopia's emperor. And most importantly: the dam must be under the control of the British government and its imperial strategists. Thus, the British, under the leadership of Lord Cromer, adopted a diplomatic course where they planned, whether through argument, bribery or financial compensation, to enlist Ethiopia's support for building the dam.

This dam would serve multiple purposes. Controlling the Blue Nile's sources would give them a powerful tool to use against Egyptian nationalists. The British plan was as simple as it was brutal: if their position at Suez was threatened, they would threaten Egypt with their power over the Nile flow. (This Nile diplomacy was implemented in 1924 through the so-called Allenby ultimatum.) The dam would also fill an important economic role: after opening the Gezira scheme in Sudan in 1925, the British simply needed more water for their huge projects in the Nile basin.

The history of big hydropolitics regarding the dam at Lake Tana involved, as we have seen, Eritrea, London, the Sudanese government, Egyptian nationalists, Emperor Haile Selassie, American companies and, not least, eventually Mussolini. What remains quite unknown, however, is what role the struggle for the dam played in the prelude to the Second World War.

Rome and London's secret plot

From the middle of the First World War, Britain had sought support, whether passive or otherwise, from Ethiopia's leadership for their plans to build a dam at Lake Tana. They had tried it all. Bribes, or *bakshish*, as the Foreign Office bureaucrats called it, using the Arabic expression common to all north-east Africa. London even promised to return to Ethiopia the imperial crown the British had carted home after the Battle of Magdala. Heady with colonial power, they had repeatedly offered to give the emperor the Boma Plateau, which was part of Southern Sudan at the time, and they would help him with a port city on the Red Sea if that might prove useful to him. Emperor Haile Selassie 'dragged his feet', however, as the British formulated it, and he did so for many valid reasons. One of them was the interweaving of religion and politics when it came to the Nile waters; the emperor feared the Church's reaction if Lake Tana's water table was raised, since this would threaten the monastery islands. But most of all he wanted British support for his demands for Eritrea, something we have seen he did not receive.

Eventually, as London increasingly surrendered their hope that Addis Ababa would allow them to erect the Tana dam, they concentrated instead on enlisting the support of Italy and Mussolini. In fact, they established a top-secret diplomatic relationship with the Italian fascists for this purpose. It was incredibly important that these conversations in the 1920s about the Nile project and their speculations regarding plans for dividing Ethiopia into spheres of interest be kept in the deepest secrecy. They knew that reactions in Ethiopia and Egypt, in the world community and in the League of Nations, and not least, in the growing anti-colonial opinion in England and the United States, would be damning if the existence of these negotiations was leaked to the public. The British had already shot down vague Ethiopian plans to build a dam at Lake Tana, plans and projects that, according to the plans, would have been implemented by American companies in direct opposition to London's strategy. This was, of course, very worrying, since it would have undermined the logic of London's Suez strategy. At that point, the relationship with the emperor was, moreover, at its coldest. If London's plans for him and his country as discussed with the Italians were to be known publicly, it would hardly appear to be the 'finest hour' in British diplomatic history – as officials in the Foreign Office noted when they, among other things, decided not to deliver a letter the emperor had sent via the department to the British king George V, where the emperor simply asked the king to look after his daughter while she was visiting England.

And so, in the mid-1920s, Great Britain, with the deepest secrecy, entered into an agreement with Italy where, de facto, they divided Ethiopia between them. Italy would get the railway of its dreams, one connecting Eritrea with Italian Somaliland. And the Italians backed London's ambitions for Lake Tana.

The original note to the Italian government started with a statement; that Mussolini was well aware of the vital importance of the Blue Nile for irrigation purposes in Egypt and the Sudan, that he had been informed of the negotiations undertaken at Addis Ababa 'in order to obtain a concession from the Government of Abyssinia for the construction of a barrage at Lake Tsana by His Majesty's Government, acting in a fiduciary capacity for the Sudan Government and mindful of Egyptian interests in the matter', and that so far these negotiations had led to no practical result.

The original note then continues:

I have, therefore, the honour, under instructions from His Majesty's Principal Secretary of State for Foreign Affairs, to request your Excellency's support and assistance at Addis Ababa with the Abyssinian Government in order to obtain from them a concession for *His Majesty's Government* to construct a barrage at Lake Tsana, together with the right to *maintain a corridor road* for the passage of stores, personnel, &c, as *also the right to maintain an adequate establishment at the lake itself for the upkeep and protection of the dam.*

His Majesty's Government, in return, are prepared to support the Italian Government in obtaining from the Abyssinian Government a concession *to construct and run a railway from the frontier of Eritrea to the frontier of Italian Somaliland.* It would be understood that this railway, together with all the necessary works for its construction and for its running, would have *entirely free passage through the corridor road mentioned above.* [my italics][30]

The government in London declared at the same time that it was also prepared 'to recognize an exclusive Italian economic influence in the west of Abyssinia [the name for Ethiopia at the time] and in the whole of the territory to be crossed by the [...] railway', and promised 'to support all Italian demands for economic concessions in the above zone'.[31]

London and Rome believed they were being clever. Then the blow fell. The secret correspondence was leaked – by someone. Now, the whole world knew that together the British and Mussolini had engineered a top-secret plot against Ethiopia, a land highly respected internationally as the first independent African country in the League of Nations. The publication of these secret negotiations radically weakened London's position, both regarding Ethiopia and Egypt but also in opinion at home and among anti-fascists the world over.

London's response to this political crisis was to launch new, top-secret negotiations with Mussolini, the plan being to cobble together a more acceptable text, which they would then present as the original agreement. The document already leaked to the press would be described as a forgery. As it turned out, however, this was easier said than done. London could not, after all, alter the text more than was acceptable to Mussolini, because then he could create even greater problems for London by revealing that, in addition to everything else, the British had also attempted to cheat world opinion. After an intense tug of war, where Great Britain had the most to lose, Mussolini and London finally agreed upon a document they could send to the League of Nations, as if it were the original.

This diplomatic scandal and the attempts to repair the consequences gave Mussolini a potential chokehold on London. This would come in handy later, when Mussolini determined to invade Ethiopia and advance toward Lake Tana.

Mussolini at the lake

It was the morning of 3 October 1935, at the Mareb River on the border between Eritrea and Ethiopia. A force of around 100,000 soldiers, a great many of them so-called askaris, or Eritreans, together with 200 Italian journalists, was prepared for war. It was only awaiting orders from Il Duce. When the orders were received that morning, the Italian-led troops marched into Ethiopia, the country dubbed by the Italian press (among others) as a 'barbaric incompetence of a state', so that the invasion could be represented and justified as what would today might have been called a humanitarian intervention.[32]

This was Mussolini's war. He was prime minister and head of government, commander-in-chief of the fascist militia, leader of Italy's only political party and, since 1933, minister of war, navy, air force, colonies and foreign affairs. The occupation the Ethiopians had long feared had become a reality. The Italians would seize control of the entire Horn of Africa and, at the same time, exact revenge for their humiliating defeat at Adwa in 1896.

When news arrived that Italy had occupied Addis Ababa on the evening of 5 May 1936, there were scenes of wild jubilation among huge crowds in Rome. In his speech from the Palazzo Venezia balcony, the dictator proclaimed: 'During the thirty centuries of our history, Italy has known many solemn and memorable moments – this is unquestionably one of the most solemn, the most memorable. People of Italy, people of the world, peace has been restored.'[33]

The crowds refused to let him leave. Ten times Il Duce appeared on the balcony and waved. Young boys from the various fascist organizations sang the newly composed 'Hymn of the Empire'. The mood was electric. The occupation of Ethiopia was Mussolini's greatest hour as the leader of what he believed to be a resurrection of the Roman imperial tradition.

Mussolini had followed the Tana negotiations closely and personally since 1925. As Italian planes bombed Ethiopia and its soldiers marched toward Lake Tana's banks, the Italian ambassador proposed opening talks with Great Britain.

A dam and the prelude to the Second World War

On 9 May 1936, Mussolini announced that he had annexed Ethiopia, and that the King of Italy was now its emperor. Marshall Pietro Badoglio was appointed governor and viceroy, and was given all power in the country. Italian East Africa was a reality, or as it was known in Italian: Africa Orientale Italiana.

How would the world react? How would the League of Nations, the international organization established to protect the rights of smaller states to self-determination, handle Italy's occupation of Ethiopia? Emperor Haile Selassie, who was forced to flee his country and who spent the war's first years in solitude and poverty in Bath in England, addressed the world on 30 June 1936, speaking to the League of Nations as his country's legitimate leader: 'I noted with grief, but without surprise that three Powers, considered their undertakings under the Covenant as absolutely of no value.' He continued by saying that not only did they not support Ethiopia against Italy, but hindered Ethiopian soldiers fighting against Italian fascists. The emperor concluded by stating that the League of Nations would be committing suicide if it opted to comply with Italy in this situation, or as he said: 'Placed by the aggressor face to face with the accomplished fact, are States going to set up the terrible precedent of bowing before force?'[34]

The emperor would be proven right. The League of Nations under British and French leadership passed a very mild resolution. The British also allowed the Italians to use the airspace above Sudan and did not block the Suez Canal against transport of military materials, so Italy was encouraged to follow the path they were on. Hitler and the German Nazis, moreover, were closely watching the struggle against British imperialism in Africa and interpreted London's response as a sign of weakness and a green light to seize the Rhineland that same year. The League of Nations lost credibility as protector of smaller states, and the Second World War loomed definitively closer.

What would have happened, however, if the League of Nations had immediately sanctioned Italy? If Great Britain had closed the Suez Canal to all Italian transport and trade? That would have sent a clear message to all aggressors: war and occupation do not pay. It would have given the League renewed legitimacy. Most historians seem to agree that this lack of action after the 1936 occupation of Ethiopia brought war closer. Those same historians, however, also tend to regard British policy in this case as irrational: London had no interests in Ethiopia, the argument runs; there was nothing to prevent the country from condemning Italy. And yet they failed to do so.

Typical of this interpretation is the work of the very influential British historian, A.J.P. Taylor, who wrote in his *The Origins of the Second World War*: 'Italian conquest of Abyssinia would not affect Great Britain's imperial interests' – thereby concluding, like many others, that the British policy was irrational.[35] The weakness of this argument, however, is that the British did, in fact, have *hugely* central strategic interests in Ethiopia, though these would not be uncovered by seeking typical economic interests like capital exports, investment portfolios and the like. If one only looks for British investments, there is indeed nothing of significance to be found here, or as the British envoy in Ethiopia confidentially wrote to the British Foreign Secretary in 1931, there was no one in the City of London who would invest money in Ethiopia because there was nothing to gain there.

Meanwhile, it was Ethiopia's upstream position in the Nile basin that determined the country's fate, and that made it possible for Italy to occupy it without meaningful international protest. As London's Foreign Office noted early in 1934: 'if & when we do want to press for Tsana, we can obtain Italian assistance & point to our loyal fulfilment of our side of the 1925 bargain ... Tsana is so much our largest potential interest in Ethiopia in the near future that consideration of its abandonment seems at least premature.'[36]

The top-secret strategic report, prepared by the former governor-general of Sudan, Lord Maffey, regarding British policy in the region, was also very clear on what was important: 'In the event of the disappearance of Ethiopia as an independent state, His Majesty's Government should aim at securing territorial control over Lake Tana and a suitable corridor linking it to the Sudan.'[37]

The report concluded that London therefore had no reason to 'resist an Italian occupation of Ethiopia'. In 1938 the British entered a new agreement with Italy, announced on 16 April and called the Perth-Ciano Pact. The agreement sought to settle two major issues: the British recognized Italy's sovereignty over Ethiopia, and the Italians promised to help the British build their Tana dam, having already what the British called a 'finger in the Tana pie'. A separate protocol revolving around the dam was signed by Lord Perth on London's behalf and Count Ciano on behalf of Rome:

> The Italian Government confirm to the Government of the United Kingdom the assurance given by them to the Government of the United Kingdom on the 3rd April, 1936, and reiterated by the Italian Minister of Foreign Affairs to His Majesty's

Ambassador at Rome on the 31st December 1936, to the effect that the Italian Government were fully conscious of their obligations toward the Government of the United Kingdom in the matter of Lake Tsana and had no intention whatever of overlooking or repudiating them.[38]

The Italians had them fooled. The British did not receive the dam. And in Great Britain opposition to the agreement was so fierce that those responsible for it were forced from their ministerial posts. The Second World War was in the process of shifting the foundations of Britain's Nile strategy.

In 1941 London decided to drive Italy from Ethiopia by military means as part of their world war strategy. They allied themselves with the emperor, who was smuggled back into the Nile basin by the British military, and who in his autobiography describes entering the harbour at Alexandria, hiding in a stolen Italian boat before flying to Sudan. When the emperor landed in Wadi Halfa, the city on the Sudanese border with Egypt, in January 1941, he walked down to the Nile, placed his hands in the river, made a cup of them, then lifted them to his mouth and drank. It was an emotional moment for him because, as he told his English companions, it was an emblem of Ethiopia he was drinking.

The Cold War and hydropolitics

Right after Ethiopia was liberated from Italian occupation, the emperor invited the Americans to his country. London quickly realized that this was the beginning of the end of their strong position in Addis Ababa. The Americans could, namely, offer the emperor economic support for his infrastructure projects, whereas London was broke after the Second World War. Not long afterwards, Egypt, under Nasser's leadership, became increasingly anti-American. For this reason, Ethiopia became even more important to US African strategy. The US Bureau of Reclamation – the agency the United States has sent out into the world to implement large river projects that are in line with American political and economic interests – became very active along the Blue Nile in Ethiopia.

The Americans produced extensive reports and put forward comprehensive project proposals that would have made Ethiopia a Nile power. For Washington's part, publishing these reports at the time was most likely first and foremost a political manoeuvre; it was a clear way to inform Nasser in Cairo and his allies in Moscow that the Americans were positioned upstream and could encourage a Nile control policy in Ethiopia that would target Egypt and the new Aswan Dam. The reports were also Washington's message to the emperor that the Americans could offer him the technological and hydrological competence he required, and which the British had been unable to give him. In practice, however, nothing happened, in part because the emperor's regime had neither the necessary economic or political muscle nor the political will to radically fight against Ethiopia's underdevelopment, but also because the United States and the World Bank both insisted on agreements between the Nile countries prior to any dams being built. Still, the threat of dam-building upstream was a cheap but effective diplomatic strategy.

Then, early in the 1970s, Emperor Haile Selassie was overthrown. He had held Ethiopia together against intense European pressure to divide the country into spheres of interest, and he had conducted a Nile diplomacy that again and again had surprised Britain by its shrewdness. He had stopped the British from damming Lake Tana because he feared the local consequences as well as Britain's long-range goal to tie the region to Sudan, and because he did not receive adequate compensation.

His regime had neither the power nor the finances to implement any large Nile projects. In the 1920s, the emperor had, as previously mentioned, sought to ally himself with American firms in order to build a dam that would serve Ethiopia's interests at Lake Tana, but the British had helped to stop this initiative. What the British wanted to see least of all was that other powers were building dams upstream of the Sudan as this would, of course, undermine the entire Nile strategy they had forged in the 1890s, and which they largely followed until after the Second World War.

In 1974, on the evening of 11 September, the same date on which, two thousand years before, the Queen of Sheba supposedly returned to Ethiopia from Israel to establish the empire, Ethiopian television broadcast two programmes designed to prepare the public for the fact that the long line of Ethiopian emperors was to be ended. One programme concerned wealthy Ethiopians and the luxury and extravagance of the imperial court, and the other programme was concerned with Ethiopia's grotesque poverty and the people who were starving. The next day a small group of officers travelled to the imperial palace, where at 6.00 am they summoned Haile Selassie. He appeared before them in full uniform and was read a proclamation for his removal. Haile Selassie said that he accepted the decision, if it was best for the people. Then he was escorted from the palace, where a car awaited him. He was taken to a military headquarters. An hour later Radio Addis Ababa announced that Ethiopia had been liberated from Haile Selassie's repression. The Rastafari movement, most familiar in the West via Bob Marley, had lost their Jah or God. The word *Rastafari*, after all, stems from a combination of Ras, which means emperor or duke, and Tafari, which was Haile Selassie's birth name. The background for this particular faith includes the many mentions of Ethiopia in the Bible, and Haile Selassie's title as he was crowned emperor: King of Kings, Lord of Lords, Conquering Lion of the Tribe of Judah, Elect of God, and the Light of the World.

The emperor, who had once been viewed as Africa's liberator, the person who would overcome colonialism, was executed by Ethiopia's new rulers.

The new regime of Mengistu Haile Mariam obviously also understood that Ethiopia's development depended on increased Nile control. Now, at a time when the US-friendly Sadat was president of Egypt, Ethiopia was governed by the Soviet-friendly Mengistu regime and the Soviets were heavily involved in different types of aid projects within the country. At this point, the Ethiopians dusted off old ideas and developed new ones for exploiting the Nile. In the 1980s Ethiopia published plans suggesting that the country would claim half of the Blue Nile's water for its own development purposes. Rather than interpreting these as actual plans structured around projects realizable at the time, their publication should instead be viewed as a form of water diplomacy. The published plans were signals to Egypt and the United States that Ethiopia and the Soviet Union had a strong upstream card that could be used in the Cold War, which at that point was at its coldest.

The Mengistu regime's idea of moving large swathes of the population from dry areas of the country to regions where it was possible to carry out profitable agriculture was also tied to plans for increased Nile utilization in Ethiopia. The opposition to these relocation plans, however, turned out to be one of the most important causes behind the fall of the regime in the early 1990s.

The water tower to realize its potential

Few things illustrate the long history of the state of Ethiopia more clearly than the Queen of Sheba's Bath in Aksum. I especially enjoy the contrast between the barren, grey rock formation next to the bath, and the yellow Orthodox church standing in the shadow of a eucalyptus grove just at the stairs leading down to the bath, stairs used for long periods of time by the local population. The bath exemplifies that Aksum was a civilization that exploited water in different ways.

After about a day's car ride from Aksum, where the Orthodox Church has claimed that Moses' original stone tablets are preserved and where these are carried around in colourful processions once a year, our Landcruiser approaches the very facility that initiated a revolutionary transformation process that, in a period of just a few years, shifted power relations along the Blue Nile and also changed the developmental course of Ethiopia. With the 4,600-metre Simien Mountains looming in the distance, beyond the new, excellent and arrow-straight asphalt road over the tableland, we swing off the road and stop to chat with the guard at the Chinese barracks. Since we are expected, we leap straight into a five-course meal prepared by the camp's Chinese cooks, who have used ingredients brought with them from China.

It was in 2006 that I travelled to the Tekeze River, around the time the new dam's foundation was being laid, in order to see what, from a long time perspective, will be regarded as a site of critical historical significance. It was here that the first large Ethiopian Nile project was implemented, and where a huge wall of cement and concrete was about to be raised across the Tekeze tributary, as it cuts its way through the narrow mountain ravines. The dam functioned as a kind of test of Ethiopia's resolve and of the strength of the downstream states' reactions. Tekeze is one of the most important Nile tributaries, and it begins not too far from the famous churches at Lalibela, far inland on the Ethiopian plateau.

And while the Chinese engineer showed me sketches of the projected dam, bubbling with enthusiasm over the project for which he was technically responsible, we drove towards the dam site itself. There, straight across a deep cleft that forced the river into a narrow channel, was the foundation for what would become a concrete wall almost 200 metres high. I went down into the ravine, to feel both wall and the intense heat, and I talked to the American engineer who worked for a US company that had helped draft the plans, visited the power plant that was built into the mountain, and ventured to the cliff's edge to get a sense of the dam's enormous dimensions. The dam was completed in 2009.

Ethiopians had proven to themselves and to the wider world that they could tame the Nile. The political implications were far-reaching: if they could build this dam, they could in principle build more – which they have done, and at a furious pace, compared to what happened with the Nile in Ethiopia up until just a few years ago.

Without political stability and economic growth, this development could not have occurred. Stability, however, is not enough to explain the transformations that have taken place. Fundamentally, it is a deep, structuring history of technological development that has led to, and will lead to, a situation where the cards in future struggles on how the Nile shall be used most effectively, will repeatedly be dealt anew. The progress of dam-building technology, and the ability to channel water into pipes running through mountains and over great distances, will enable projects to be implemented that previously were the stuff of dream and fantasy.

The state of technology is no longer the decisive hindrance to using the Nile's water upstream. Now, it all rests on political will and economic capability.

Deep ecology, reflection and the river's sign

It is a few years later, in 2011. The Ethiopians have finished the Tekeze Dam. They have opened the Tana-Beles Project, which takes water from Lake Tana and channels it through a mountain tunnel to the valleys below the lake, in order to produce energy and provide artificial irrigation for agriculture. They have also set in motion several studies for new Blue Nile projects.

The discussion progresses loudly between Ethiopians, Norwegians, Britons and Italians regarding the dam that Ethiopia is in the process of building. The people around the table are hydrologists and dam builders, and enthusiasm for the Ethiopian plans is shared by all – not euphorically but matter-of-factly. No one here doubts that Nile control is a necessity. We sit in something like a pub, but since the rain has been drumming violently on the roof for hours, and the courtyard across which we walk to buy tea or beer has just about dissolved into an almost impassable, slippery path of mud, it has lost some of its charm.

Earlier in the day I stood on the mountainside over the Blue Nile, located far into the Ethiopian highlands, together with this same group of engineers and hydrologists. They had been asked by the Ethiopian government to outline the possibility for building one of the world's highest dams. Observing them as they pointed and discussed where the foundation should be placed, what form the dam should take, how high it could and should be, and which further studies were needed and should be implemented, it was easy to see they were experienced, and they also told me they had tamed rivers the world over. They approached the task without sentimentality, and our discussions made it very clear that they regarded themselves as a kind of vanguard of modernity.

As an outsider, as a characteristically powerless intellectual, I asked myself, as we discussed megawatts and sludge quantities and geological relationships: what would have happened in this country if there had been a popular movement propagating such deep ecological slogans as 'Let the river live'? How would such a philosophical school or idea have been received, had it been presented to the Nile basin countries?

Deep ecology is based on the idea that humankind is intimately integrated with nature; humankind and nature are one. Deep ecology is against all forms of anthropocentrism, defined as a world view where human values are regarded as the basis for, and source of, all values in general. According to itself, deep ecology therefore represents an alternative, often described using a water metaphor – 'going with the flow', as opposed to controlling nature, described as 'going against the flow'. Proponents of deep ecology must, therefore, if they are to argue according to principle, also oppose damming or controlling the rivers here, and claim that it is in the interest of Ethiopia just to let the flow go, untamed.

In terms of Ethiopia's current development situation, many people will tend to argue that deep ecology appears to be deeply reactionary, a kind of extremist way of thinking influenced by very specific historical and geographical relationships between humans and nature or between humans and rivers. Though it insists on breaking out of what is termed a Western, dualistic mentality, it rather reflects an attempt to total up experiences from a North European context, where rivers, if they are not already tamed, typically *appear* tamed and innocuous. Politically, the consequences of such a philosophy here would be that all the water surging down for a few months every year would have to be sent from Ethiopia to Sudan and Egypt because that is how the Nile's nature is. Such notions of deep ecology found no fertile soil here, among the Italian, Dutch, Ethiopian and Norwegian engineers, who regarded themselves not only as modernity's vanguard in Ethiopia, but also as soldiers in the army of people who will help develop Ethiopia, thereby reducing poverty. They were concerned with how the relationship between nature and humans could be changed in a way that would benefit the Ethiopians; that would entail a need to 'go against the flow'. To 'go with the flow' in Ethiopia, as Africa's water tower, would mean to forsake its own modernization; and the diplomatic text of the 1902 Agreement where Ethiopia promised not to reduce the flow of any of the Nile's tributaries, could be reinterpreted as an early, deep ecological oath regarding nature and the biosphere.

If one views the Nile as a living organism – and all living things strive to realize their objective, which in this sense must mean self-preservation, its form of fulfilment – then one must 'let the river live'.

Deep ecology claims that humankind has no right to reduce nature's rich diversity unless it is done to satisfy vital needs. The problem is that one cannot respect the Nile's innate life, or the principle of 'go with the flow', and at the same time, also satisfy 'vital needs'. Do such contradictions, and the absence of any clear criteria for what constitutes 'vital needs', undermine the relevance of deep ecology in such circumstances? Nile water is necessary to maintain life, and it is also necessary to prevent people and animals from dying from thirst or hunger. And, furthermore, the definition of what is a vital need where water and thus water control is concerned, will vary. It is difficult – after also attempting to draw a line based on a concern for biodiversity – to determine what is vital or not vital, especially when taking into account that power from a river tamed by pipes and turbines can be transported across society and, in principle, to other societies, also based on the their understanding of 'vital needs'.

Would a deep ecological movement among people in the Nile basin have doomed huge swathes of the region to perpetual poverty and to an eternal fate as slaves to the river's whims? Whatever the answer to that question, one thing is obvious: the philosophy appears remarkably provincial in its empirical basis, since its basic river metaphors are not able to handle real human–water relationships in large river basins, where gaps between water needs and water supply steadily increase.

Throughout history, dams have been an expression of the will of countries or peoples to improve their life situations. However, within the international development-aid system the idea that dominated for a long time was that a developing country, particularly one in Africa, could not handle this type of modern large-scale technology. Countless books and reports have been written about Africa's so-called 'white elephants' – that is, projects that, due to their technological level, were not suitable there – and that Africa, therefore, had to be developed with small-scale technology. What dominated was a world view, an ideology, that contributed to prevent countries from exploiting their water resources – arising not from what was in the interest of the countries, but from well-meaning prejudices.

Dominant ideological trends within international aid circles have argued that modern technology is unsuitable for Africa. When travelling to Africa for the UN in the 1980s, I was required to sit through an introductory course, organized by the national development agency and some hired anthropologists, where I would 'learn about African culture' in order to become a good aid worker.

One afternoon we were asked to squat in a ring on the floor. We were going to role-play and act as if we were meeting with African chieftains, under an acacia tree, obviously. The role of chieftain and 'elder' would shift around the circle. The basic idea was that by learning to listen to what 'the elders' said, we would understand Africa, and the true test of understanding was our refraining from suggesting anything that required modern technology; that is, we could suggest it, of course, but that would expose oneself as an idiot, that is to say, a technologist or an engineer. To suggest or even to discuss with the 'chief' the idea of a big dam was just unthinkable at the time. The main problem was not that we were asked to 'adopt a perspective' in line with the assumed local chieftain under the acacia tree, even if this obviously meant adapting to the status quo, but that development's actual dilemmas ceased to exist because the right answer was known beforehand, and alternatives were not only wrong but ridiculous. To avoid becoming part of this very embarrassing situation with its rehearsed dialogue, I suddenly stood up, gathered everything I had into a plastic bag, said I could not participate in this, and left the course – and my relationship to the aid milieu has never been the same.

Bob Geldof's Ethiopia: a land without rivers

Yet again I walked the short dirt road and the path up to the Blue Nile Falls to see how this wonderful place has lost its natural beauty and force since the Ethiopians in 2003 built a power plant there. After reading Bob Geldof's depiction of the same walk in his book *Geldof in Africa*, where this trip is described as exhausting, as a dangerous journey through the jungle, I think: the West is insatiable when it comes to stories of the White Man who, full of machismo, conquers this exotic, foreign continent – while in reality it is a nice, short stroll in a park-like landscape.[39]

This same Bob Geldof played an important role in, or rather functioned as a very powerful symbol of, the idea that Ethiopia is a helpless country, a country that, in its misery and poverty, is entirely dependent upon the White Man as its guide, helper and saviour. After the famine of 1984, which the BBC transformed into a strange world spectacle, laden with moral and ideological significance, and which Geldof used to mobilize an entire globe to aid Africa, descriptions and understanding of the country were long framed by an image of poverty, helplessness and aid dependence.

Few, if any, countries have become as imprisoned by the surrounding world's conceptions of it, as Ethiopia. For centuries it was Prester John's legendary country – barbaric, closed, unapproachable, but still exotic. At the end of the twentieth century Ethiopia became synonymous with drought, starvation and Western assistance. It did not help the Ethiopians that Abebe Bikila became the world's most iconic marathon runner and sprinted into history for all time when, running barefoot, he thrashed all the competition in Rome's streets in 1960 and again in Tokyo four years later. It would not have changed perceptions however many world-class runners they produced.

I visited Ethiopia for the first time at the beginning of the 1990s, and even though I had just written a book on the aid epoch's paternalistic views of developing countries and had read many books on the country's history, I was not prepared for what I experienced, simply because I was unable to think of the country without seeing before me the insistent TV images of starving and dying children.

It was May. The temperature was comfortable, just over 20°C. I drove around the countryside with a Sudanese friend. Just like that, we passed small groups of people dressed in white, sitting with their picnic baskets under trees, and they seemed to be all over the place; to the left and to the right, in front of us and behind us. Their laughter reached us like sounds from a dream world. When I returned home and talked about the nature, the mountains, the sun and the prosperity I had seen and admired in Ethiopia, I was criticized on a moral basis. Did I lack all human feelings? How could I be so blind to people's plight?

The droughts of the 1970s and 1980s and the TV cameras in the hunger camps had reduced Ethiopia to the utter symbol of world misery. This image, created by the rain's periodic absence and the media's presence, perverted conceptions of Ethiopia, which in the tourist brochures is justly advertised as having thirteen months of sun. The images of the development-aid era have been reproduced again and again since 1984. A heavy and growing aid and emergency relief system produces and reproduces these images. Every other year relief organizations proclaim that a new and worse drought than ever threatens millions with starvation, and they ask for donations of money to save lives.

It is these images that give emergency relief workers not only continued legitimacy within donor societies but also permanent employment. Ethiopia has suffered the fate of being the foremost staging ground of these Good Samaritans. Undoubtedly, it is true that parts of Ethiopia lie in a climate area where drought will certainly happen, even as agriculture is little developed. It has for years been one of the countries that has received the most aid relief on a regular basis. However, this is not simply on account of drought, but also because the government knows the political power of free food distribution. For the last couple of decades, the drought problems have been manageable.

Throughout the years, tales of a different Ethiopia have been met with opposition – and not just passive resistance but with active propaganda – because alternative images threaten a whole industry's livelihood, they rock the foundations of its basic self-conception and societal position, all of which rest upon the idea that the industry is making an indispensable and necessary difference.

Bob Geldof obviously did not create the conception that Ethiopia was dependent upon Westerners' will to give and care, upon outsiders' goodness, but he came to symbolize it as he and Midge Ure wrote, and sang with their friends, about an Ethiopia where 'nothing ever grows', and where 'no rain or rivers flow' and where they in this Christian country perhaps did not know 'it's Christmas time at all'.

The Renaissance Dam

In April 2011 Prime Minister Meles Zenawi of Ethiopia laid the foundation stone for a new gigantic dam, said to be the largest dam structure in Africa: 145 metres high and 1,800 metres wide. It would store 63 billion cubic metres of water, which would make this artificial lake twice as water-rich as Lake Tana. In 40°C heat, at the future dam site, Meles gave a speech to the Ethiopian people about this national project, which he promised would give Ethiopia a new and brighter future.

The idea of building a large dam on the Blue Nile was far from new. The site had already been identified as suitable decades before. Since then the dam had been on the drawing board in the state-run Ethiopian Electric Power Corporation under the code name 'Project X'. For a long time, the plans were kept secret. Then, in the spring of 2011, at the height of the Tahrir Square demonstrations, the Ethiopian government made the decision to build it publicly, first under the name the Millennium Dam, later rebranded as the Renaissance Dam. Prime Minister Meles declared: 'It is the largest dam we could build at any point along the Nile, or indeed any other river.' And he was careful to underline: 'Among the concerns we factored in when we made the decision to build the Nile Dam with our own resources, was to avoid any negative consequences for our neighbors.'[40]

The dam was the last and most ambitious initiative of a consistent Nile water policy followed by the government since the 1990s. It was, therefore, under Meles Zenawi – an erstwhile guerrilla soldier and staunch Marxist-Leninist, as guerrilla leaders tended to be in the 1970s and 1980s – that the country developed into a regional hydropolitical power. Meles and his political movement took control in 1991, following a few years of civil war against the Mengistu regime, and he implemented a policy that would transform Ethiopia, the river and power relations across the basin.

I met Meles Zenawi for the first time in 2005, and then again in the prime minister's office in Addis Ababa, in the spring of 2011, when he told me about the new project they were going to launch. What we talked about was, of course, the Nile issue. That was why I was there: to ask him about his opinions on the issue. He showed that he had a very good grasp of Nile hydrology and Nile politics, and his strategy was clear and remained basically the same throughout his period as prime minister. He explained his position regarding the 1902 Agreement: 'The issue is whether we can use some of this water', he said in 2005. 'The treaty does not bar us from doing so. The position of Ethiopia is that under international law we have the right to fair and equitable utilization of the water. Hopefully we will do so with the understanding and the support and cooperation with downstream countries. But in the end it is a question of our own survival'; thus in reality dismissing the validity of the Agreement.[41] It would turn out that he meant what he was saying and two years later Ethiopia started on the Tekeze Dam, and thereafter on the Tana-Beles Project. But the Renaissance Dam, which he informed me about in March 2011, overshadows everything.

When I asked him about consequences for the downstream countries, he insisted that Ethiopia wanted cooperation, and that the dam was also to their benefit, and that it would be a good thing for Sudan, in particular.

Meles completely dismissed the old policy of threatening to use the water weapon against Egypt. He said that:

Ethiopians used to threaten Egyptians that they would stop the flow of the Nile if the Egyptians, especially after the Arab invasion of Egypt, would not send the Patriarchs to Ethiopia. The Ethiopians of those days did not have any means of stopping the Nile, so the threat was more powerful than it should have been. I think the future is going to be – sooner or later – a policy of rationalism, but it will take some time before we completely discard the vestige of the past.

Under Meles Zenawi's leadership, Ethiopia's government became determined to realize its potential as an upstream power in the Nile basin. The country finally possessed the technological ability to stop the Nile's flow. So, for the first time in millennia, the Ethiopians are damming the river – in increasingly more places and with increasingly larger dams. Addis Ababa, however, has again and again argued that these projects are not meant to negatively impact downstream countries. On the contrary, Ethiopia claims that these projects are in the interests of Ethiopia and of other countries – they are win–win projects.

The prime minister was, however, very candid about what he saw as Egyptian threats and interference in order to stop them from doing what he described as the legal right and political duty to develop their country. He claimed that the Egyptian elite had again and again tried to destabilize Ethiopia by encouraging the populace 'to kill each other', as he put it, and by preventing Ethiopia from receiving foreign loans. Meles claimed that Egyptian leaders had written letters and demanded that donors and multilateral financial institutions refuse to support the project, and there can be no doubt that Egypt did conduct a frenzied diplomatic campaign to halt the dam. In response to what he regarded as Egypt's unfair opposition, Meles took a very surprising step: he went for securing the necessary funds from internal sources. His ambitious project was to mobilize the entire Ethiopian populace in an unprecedented campaign in order to self-finance the dam. The project was estimated at US$4.7 billion. The outcome of this national money-raising campaign would significantly impact power relations across the entire region. If it failed, it would be a huge defeat for the Ethiopian government and would undermine its legitimacy. In that case, it could take Ethiopia a long time to recover sufficiently to challenge Egypt's historical hegemony in the same way. He argued that the Egyptian elite had misused and misrepresented the threats against its water supply to retain power over its own people. Meles told me that he believed Egypt's downstream complex had been shaped by the Egyptian elite, as an instrument for furthering their own power and position. By convincing the country's inhabitants that their water source was threatened, the elite had succeeded in legitimizing its own autocratic policy. On behalf of the entire Egyptian population, the elite had staged itself as the champion of Egypt's water interests, as if it was the population's sole guarantee for keeping its lifeline.

This fear, Meles said, is based on a myth; Egypt's leadership and its people must understand that cooperation is the only way forward. So concluded the Ethiopian prime minister with all the clarity and conviction that made him the darling in certain policy circles on the international political scene, but which the Ethiopian opposition viewed as the rhetoric of someone who was himself an autocrat.

Donald Trump, the US and the Nile negotiations

Nine years on and still the Renaissance Dam prompts serious political clashes between Ethiopia and Egypt.

All the Ethiopian governments after Meles Zenawi passed away in 2012 have underlined that the most important national development project is the Renaissance Dam. It should turn the country into the powerhouse of East Africa, and it should electrify and unify the country. The construction of the dam has gone on without serious setback or interruption, but the date of the opening has gradually been shifted further into the future.

The project has met with political problems and resistance all the time, both externally and internally. In 2012 WikiLeaks published documents showing that Egyptian leadership apparently discussed plans in 2010 to attack the dam with bombers, but the idea was rejected by the Egyptian military. When the Egyptian president from the Muslim Brotherhood, Mohamed Morsi, and other political leaders were caught on camera talking about how to destabilize Ethiopia in order to stop the construction of the dam, Ethiopian conspiracy theories regarding Egypt's role in creating conflicts and wars in the Horn of Africa seemed to be confirmed. Morsi also talked openly about going to war in order to protect Egyptian interests in the Nile. After General Abdel Fattah al-Sisi came to power, Egypt's official Nile policy changed: Egypt accepted the dam, supported Ethiopia's decision to build it, but wanted negotiations about how it should be operated and filled. The latter point is, of course, very important to Egypt, because the faster the dam is filled, the less water the Nile will bring to Egypt during these years. The speed at which the dam's reservoir would be filled has thus been a permanent bone of contention. Filling began in 2020.

In the meantime, Ethiopia experienced a shocking death. In July 2018, Simegnew Bekele, the engineer in charge of the Renaissance Dam, was found shot inside a Toyota Land Cruiser, parked near a busy road at Meskel Square in the heart of Addis Ababa, and with a pistol in the car. The man who had been overseeing the project since the dam's construction began in 2011 had, according to the official explanation, shot himself. Simegnew had become – as chief engineer of what many called a national dream coming through – a national hero. He was the trustworthy, well-known and public face of the optimistic plans for a new Ethiopia; for a country that would no longer be known for famines and war but as Africa's powerhouse.

The chief engineer of the dam had come to the capital to give a news conference addressing concerns about delays in its construction, as well as allegations of corruption and mismanagement, not directed at him but at the state company involved in the project. The news of Simegnew's death prompted an outpour of grief in Ethiopia and a wave of theories about what had really happened. The project was further delayed and the new prime minister, Abiy Ahmed, declared that at the current pace of construction the dam might not be completed within ten years. These events were significant and alarming to Ethiopia's future and stability, because the dam is more than a dam of concrete. It has been hailed as the pride of Ethiopia, and as a project that had the potentials of unifying the country. In the time since Simegnew's death, continuing tensions between the country's complex patchwork of ethnic groups threaten the steady implementation of the project. Some activists argue still that the Balkanization of Ethiopia is inevitable, and in Ethiopia many blame Egypt for encouraging these divisions. Political instability means that the future of the project will be in jeopardy.

In 2019, Abiy Ahmed received the Nobel Peace Prize. He had become leader of the country in 2018, after the sudden resignation of Hailemariam Desalegn. Ahmed immediately freed many political detainees, lifted the state of emergency earlier than planned and, an important reason for the Nobel Peace Prize committee to award him the prize, he agreed to accept the border ruling by The Hague and to give the disputed territory back to Eritrea. He thereafter went to Asmara to declare, together with the president of Eritrea, the end of war between the two countries. After a few months in office he also appointed women to half of the ministerial posts. He came into power as the leader of the Oromo People's Democratic Organization, one of the four ethnically based parties that make up the ruling Ethiopian People's Revolutionary Democratic Front. By becoming prime minister, he ended what many in an ethnic-conscious Ethiopia will describe as twenty-seven years of ascendancy for Tigrayans, who in turn in the early 1990s had ended centuries of Amhara pre-eminence.

In his most prominent public appearance after winning the Nobel Peace Prize, Abiy Ahmed illustrated again the eternal importance of the Nile in regional geopolitics. He remarked in the Ethiopian parliament during a question-and-answer session: 'Some say things about use of force (by Egypt). It should be underlined that no force could stop Ethiopia from building a dam.' He continued: 'If there is a need to go to war, we could get millions readied. If some could fire a missile, others could use bombs. But that's not in the best interest of all of us'.[42] At the same time, negotiations on the dam proceeded. Egypt said that they had reached a deadlock, claiming that the Ethiopian delegation rejected all the proposals that took Egypt's water interests into account and presented one that lacked guarantees on how to deal with what they described as 'droughts that may occur in the future'. Ethiopia dismissed Cairo's assessment of the talks, arguing that it was 'completely false' that the talks ended in deadlock. In parliament Abiy stressed that his country was determined to complete the dam project, which was initiated by former leaders, because he regarded it as an excellent one.

Then, some few days later, Egypt succeeded in bringing in the United States and the World Bank, thus internationalizing the issue, a diplomatic route that Ethiopia has been firmly against, knowing that the United States and the World Bank would, at least to a certain extent, side with Egypt. Sisi talked with the US president, Donald Trump, and Trump decided to bring America's political and economic weight into the negotiations.

When Trump met with the delegations from Egypt, Ethiopia and the Sudan at the White House in November 2019, about a hundred years after the British, the Egyptians, the Ethiopians and the Sudan Government under the control of London tried to solve conflicts over dams on the Blue Nile, he suggested that he would like to 'cut the ribbon' at the inauguration of this Blue Nile dam.

The Ottoman Empire, the British Empire and the French Empire are all gone. But the contradictions among countries and regions in the Nile basin fundamentally shaped by the physical character of the river are still there. Nothing could underline the relevance of a long-term view on the history of the Nile more than the high-level negotiations that are taking place in Washington on the control and use of the Nile, and they are going on exactly the same days as I finish my biography on the river.

Whatever the result of these talks, they will cast long shadows into the future of hundreds of millions of people.

The End of the Journey

I am flying north over the Nile from Khartoum, towards the Mediterranean and in the direction of Europe. The last traces of sunset are gone. All is black. Beneath the plane lies the desert, unpopulated and empty. Just north of Khartoum only a few scattered lights are visible, all in a thin stripe towards the north. Then – and this is how I know we have reached Egypt – the lights eventually form denser and denser patterns, until they become a compact yellow blossom of light surrounded by intense darkness to the west and east – as well as to the north, for there lies the sea. Obviously, the Nile is not the only thread in the tapestry formed by the societies and economies of the Nile basin, but it is indisputably the most important thread.[1] Indeed, the darkness around that thin strip of light along the Nile through the deserts underscores that, in reality, it is *the only thread* holding the tapestry together.

The river of history and its future

The earliest evidence of human ancestors was found in the southern and eastern areas of this river basin, which covers a tenth of the African continent. It was here that they walked around four million years ago. 'Lucy' lived in Ethiopia, and by the Olduvai Gorge in the Serengeti within today's Tanzania wandered 'Nutcracker Man' and 'Handy Man'. Along a local river course, 3.5 million-year-old footprints have been discovered. Some of the oldest finds we have from societies that used various types of tools are 200,000 years old and originate from areas along the Nile in northern Sudan. It was also from regions along the Nile that, most likely, a few family groups wandered out to people the entire globe.

The Nile, as it flows today, appeared, probably, a little bit more than 15,000 years ago. After the Sahara dried out and became desert, and people had migrated from there towards the Nile Valley, it only took a few thousand years before the first attempts to exploit and use the river took place. That happened somewhere around 5,000 years ago, when primitive mounds of dirt and sand were built to contain the flood waters in the region that would later become Egypt. The most powerful of all ancient civilizations was based upon exploiting the river natural fluctuations and its water and silt, and the people along the riverbanks and in the Nile Delta created the most productive agriculture existing at that time. People and society adapted to the Nile's annual and seasonal variations, and based on this relationship between humans and river, life unfolded for about 3,000 years.

Then, 2,000 years before our time, a small water-lifting device came into more frequent use. This device made it possible to lift water from the river and from small artificial canals, and channel it over the desert sand. A few places could thus, even at that time, cultivate more or less all year round. However, for thousands of years it was almost exclusively in Egypt and, to a certain extent, in the Nubian portions of Sudan that the river was exploited for agricultural purposes. Throughout the rest of the basin, the water simply flowed by; it was fished, and in some places used for transport, and animals and people obviously drank from it – but the river as it ran through societies was largely nature's work; the waterscape was natural, untouched by human hand.

Such was the situation in 2,000 years – and humankind's relationship to the river remained basically unchanged.

Then dramatic events occurred, first in Egypt. In the mid-1800s, Muhammad Ali built a Nile barrage just north of the Delta. This raised the water level in the rivers and canals, and all at once the Delta could in many places be cultivated perennially. So came the British. They repaired and improved the barrage and carried out several hydraulic construction projects, the most important being the first Aswan Dam in 1902, built to improve Egypt's water supply during dry seasons. During the short period they ruled the Nile the British entered several agreements with the region's other political actors, agreements aimed at securing the water needs of Egypt. The initial British technological attack on the natural Nile was then followed up and carried to its utmost by the nationalist leader, Gamal Abd al-Nassar, when he pushed for the High Dam, which, when it was completed in 1971, transformed the mighty Nile into a government-controlled irrigation canal in Egypt.

In the mid-1920s, Sudan became a hydraulic state under British rule. Britain raised the Sennar Dam across the Blue Nile, and in 1954 they built the Owen Falls Dam at Lake Victoria's outlet in Uganda, both strongly opposed by Egyptian nationalists. Most of the basin, however, was still natural, or untamed, and so the situation remained up until the beginning of the 2000s.

Then, over the course of a few years, everything changed. All along its length the Nile became a river that suddenly most governments in the basin said they planned to control, tame and harness. The Toshka Project was launched in Egypt in 2002 – the idea was to build a new, artificially created Nile Valley in the Sahara by pumping Nile water there. In 2009, Sudan's President al-Bashir inaugurated the grand Merowe Dam just south of the Egyptian border. That same year, Ethiopia's prime minister opened the Tekeze Dam on a central Blue Nile tributary. The next year Tanzania's president launched the Shinyanga Project, a project that for the first time would pump water from Lake Victoria into the country's dry regions. Tanzania implemented a project that the British had stopped when, during the First World War, the Germans held power in the region and wanted water for their mining projects, and which Egypt just a few years earlier had threatened war in order to stop. In 2010, the leaders in Burundi, Tanzania and Rwanda also announced that together they would build a dam across the Rusumo Falls, while Kenya's political leadership laid out a plan that emphasized the need for using Nile rivers for water and irrigation in the country's poverty-stricken, western areas. Uganda also made it clear that the country's industrial revolution would be based on the energy inherent in the Nile waters, and thus required more Nile dams. This all happened the same year that representatives from the upstream countries, against Egyptian and Sudanese wishes, determined collectively to sign a new Nile Basin Agreement. Then, in March 2011, the Ethiopian government announced that they would build a gigantic new dam 600 kilometres long on the Blue Nile, the dam that soon was to be called the Renaissance Dam.

When tourists travel the Nile in a thousand years' time, they will, I would guess, be told stories about how our contemporary temples were the great dams. The Nile was in our time not honoured for religious reasons but for what it could create in terms of power and economic growth. Over just a few decades – after millennia of the Nile running free and unburdened by human interference – the river's face was radically altered, and society with it. Future tourists will, upon closer inspection of these Nile dam structures, discover that for the same reason that great architecture harbours no random lines and errant forms, so there is no chance that these gigantic hydro structures are somehow disconnected from the needs, desires and dominant conceptions of contemporary societies and their rulers.

They will also discover that the taming of the Nile with gigantic constructions – which overshadow the pharaonic memorials in size and grandeur, and which can fully compete with them in terms of aesthetics of power – meant being subjected to necessity in a completely different way, in the sense that their lines and form are also framed by the Nile's character, or its 'hydrological being'. Future tourists will be told histories and read books regarding the often perplexing, secretive and long undisclosed drama behind these modern Nile Valley temples.

Development in recent decades has been exceptional and revolutionary. Hardly any other international river basin has, over such a short time period and over such a large area, been more quickly or more radically transformed. After I have travelled around the different Nile countries and discussed issues with state leaders, experts and academics over the years, the impression is clear and unambiguous: the Nile is mentioned everywhere as a developmental prerequisite for, and as a potential eternal engine of, societal change and development. A Nile discourse marked by an understanding and acknowledgement of other countries' interests and needs has emerged, something that was not there to the same extent before the Nile Basin Initiative was launched at the end of the twentieth century. While dialogue and cooperation are emphasized, however, the principle is still largely first come, first served; the situation is characterized by what can be called hydrological anarchy, at the same time as state leaders work to strengthen cooperation and mutual understanding.

Given that it still is a fact that the resource is finite, the Nile cannot satisfy everybody's needs at any time. It is therefore positive that new water resources are constantly being discovered in the region: there are immense underground lakes beneath Egypt, Sudan and parts of Tanzania, a natural condition that will ease pressure on the river, though groundwater is much more expensive to utilize. The future of the entire region will therefore depend upon whether the countries can use the Nile in an optimal, expedient and cooperative manner.

A focus, therefore, on the legal, ethical or political aspects of Nile control alone will not create the climate necessary for lasting cooperation in the long term. An understanding for the river itself must be developed, a form of sympathetic solidarity with it and with all who live along its banks, based on knowledge of how the river runs from source to mouth, through swamps, forest and deserts, also considering the river's long, flowing and remarkably event-rich history. A Nile collaboration and a Nile solidarity must relate to, and overcome, the complex social and cultural differences between societies and between ethnic groups, but must also be rooted in a firm physical ground. This book is written in the conviction that, in a situation where the river's role becomes radically altered and the struggle surrounding its use increases, it is critical to collect and preserve its neglected myths and legends and to fight its continuous environmental degradation – to do everything that can boost understanding of and sympathy for this blue ribbon that binds hundreds of millions together into a common destiny, and which is woven into world history in thousands of ways. I have by writing it aimed at filling what can be called a 'meaning gap' regarding the understanding of, and the reflections about, the region's most important resource; a world river brimming with contemporary historical significance.

Predictions about the Great War for the Nile have abounded for years now. This has its reasons. President and Nobel Peace Prize winner Anwar al-Sadat of Egypt said in 1979 that Egypt would go to war if anyone took even a drop from the Nile. Prime Minister and Nobel Peace Prize winner Abiy Ahmed said in 2019 that Ethiopia was prepared to go to war for its right to build the Renaissance Dam. Alarmists have been numerous; and pessimistic warnings may make it easier to revert to what in political science studies of states' foreign policy have termed the 'law of the jungle'. The fact of the matter is that if everyone believes that the table is ringed with cheats or self-interested state leaders, everyone will take their liberties. There are alternatives, however, to war and to the strongest wielding unbridled control.

A long river like the Nile possesses resources that make it possible to conceive real win–win solutions, where the rhetoric of common interests *needs* not be a smokescreen for realizing one's own interests. Imagine three children arguing about who gets to have a drum. Thale demands the drum because she is the only one who can play it. Nikolai, for his part, argues that he should have it because he is so poor that he has no other toys. On the other hand, Christiane insists that the drum is hers because she is the one who made it. Who should get the drum? The answer is that there is no obvious 'right' answer to this question.[2] All three children can pose weighty ideological reasons for their viewpoint, and it will turn out that there is no single perfect form of social justice upon which all three can rationally agree to base themselves. Justice is a multidimensional, pluralistic concept that cannot be reduced to one single idea.

In the Nile basin there is no perfect form of justice upon which all parties can agree, nor any one ideal. To strive for the perfect agreement or perfect cooperative institution between basin countries will only delay solutions being found for the concrete problems surrounding Nile exploitation. Instead, it is necessary to seek those solutions that are realizable.

The sculpture in Rome

I am back in Italy, at Piazza Navona in the centre of Rome. Before the city is awake and just as the sun reaches the top of the stolen Egyptian obelisk in the middle of the fountain, I walk around it. This is the most beautiful expression of the Nile's position in the history of ideas in medieval Europe. Bernini's famous Fontana dei Quattro Fiumi, or the Four Rivers Fountain, was designed for Pope Innocent X and unveiled in 1651. The fountain symbolizes the Nile's distinctive place in the world views and beliefs of that time more clearly than any other artwork. At its centre is a large, Egyptian obelisk surrounded by four gigantic river gods. Typical for European mythology, the gods are depicted or represented as large, mature male figures. One river god, however, stands out. He is holding a cloth before his face. He does not know where he comes from, and we cannot look him in the eyes. This is the god of the Nile. Only the Nile had that mystical aura within Europe's seventeenth-century world view. For this river, so frequently mentioned in the Bible, described as the very River of Paradise, and providing the ancient Roman world with its granary, was one whose source and origin were still unknown. No one in Bernini's time knew the reason for its legendary fertility, but they understood that whoever controlled its water wielded great power.

Gradually, the Nile's secrets were uncovered. The sources are now known. Its hydrology has been mapped. And gradually, it has become even clearer that whoever controls the river has more power than ever. The struggle, therefore, concerning how the river should be exploited will affect regional and world development for decades and centuries to come.

The Nile is no longer a blindfolded mystery. Instead its biography is a wellspring of knowledge, not only of itself, but of Africa, the world, and of us.

Notes

Chapter 1

1 Some books that consider the relationship between Egypt and the development of Roman and Greek culture: Freeman (1996) *Egypt, Greece, and Rome: Civilizations of the Ancient Mediterranean*; Meyboom (1995) *The Nile Mosaic of Palestrina: Early Evidence of Egyptian Religion in Italy*; Roullet (1972) *The Egyptian and Egyptianizing Monuments of Imperial Rome*.
2 See fragment published in Allen and Amt (eds) 2003.
3 See Said 1993. There are a number of useful studies on the Nile's hydrology and physiography. For an overview, see Tvedt 2004b.

Chapter 2

1 For an early work on this subject see, for example, Mariette 1890. For a short guide, see Hewison 2008.
2 Forbes 1964–72.
3 There is extensive literature on the subject of ancient Egyptian world views. Some of the texts I have found to be the most interesting are: Anthes (1959) 'Egyptian Theology in the Third Millennium B.C.', *Journal of Near Eastern Studies*; Assmann (1995) *Egyptian Solar Religion in the New Kingdom: Re, Amun and the Crisis of Polytheism*; Blackman (1925) 'Osiris or the Sun-God?', *The Journal of Egyptian Archaeology*; Faulkner (1969) *The Ancient Egyptian Pyramid Texts* and (2007) *The Ancient Egyptian Coffin Texts*; Griffiths (1960) *The Conflict of Horus and Seth: From Egyptian and Classical Sources*; MacQuitty (1976) *Island of Isis: Philae, Temple of the Nile*; Trigger (2003) *Understanding Early Civilizations: A Comparative Study*; Wainwright (1963) 'The Origin of Storm-Gods in Egypt', *The Journal of Egyptian Archaeology*.
4 The Pyramid Texts are the oldest religious writings that modern scholars have from ancient Egypt. They were found on the tombs and walls of the pyramids at Saqqara, being from the time of Fifth and Sixth Dynasties of the Old Kingdom.
5 Today this mythology is not as easy to understand because it assumes that the pyramids, as burial chambers, are located directly on the riverbank. That is precisely where they were, however, 5,000 years ago. Up to the 1900s, the pyramids were reflected in the fluid, mystical divide between the two worlds. As the Nile was gradually tamed, however, the relationship between grave and river was terminated.
6 Herodotus 2008, II: Chapter 14.
7 Hawkes 1973: 318.
8 The three main rivers were the Pelusaic, the Sebennytic and the Canopic. See Hassan 1997.
9 Forster 1982. See also Marlow 1971 and Pollard and Reid 2006.
10 Russell 1962.

11 Aristotle n.d.: 294a 28–30.
12 Some historians claim that the boat was around 90 metres long and 15 metres wide, but this assumption is debated. Although no contemporaneous description of this boat exists, there is detailed information regarding large boats with ample space and magnificent ornamentation built by the same royal family 100 years earlier.
13 For a discussion and a description of this journey, see Hillard 2002.
14 Few people have had more biographies written about them than Cleopatra. This selection of texts provides a good impression of the role she played in her lifetime and the role she has assumed in subsequent myth creation: Chauveau (1997) *Cleopatra: Beyond the Myth* and (2000) *Egypt in the Age of Cleopatra*; Roller (2010) *Cleopatra: A Biography*; Tyldesley (2008) *Cleopatra: The Last Queen of Egypt*; Volkmann (1953) *Cleopatra: A Study in Politics and Propaganda*; Walker and Higgs (2001) *Cleopatra of Egypt: From History to Myth*.
15 Acts 7:22.
16 Exod. 7:20.
17 Isa. 19:21.
18 Mt. 2:13.
19 See: https://www.beliefnet.com/entertainment/2000/06/egypt-commemorates-journey-of-jesus-mary-joseph.aspx.
20 See, for example, Antes 1800: 78.
21 Ezek. 29:9–15.
22 Two books that generally discuss the Arab-Islamic conquest of Egypt, but which place little emphasis on the Nile question, are al-Sayyid-Marsot (2007) *A History of Egypt from the Arab Conquest to the Present* (covering that entire period in around 150 pages, but with particular weight placed on the period following Muhammad Ali) and Kennedy (2007) *The Great Arab Conquests: How the Spread of Islam Changed the World We Live In*.
23 This story is told, among other places, in Suyuti 1995: 129–30. There is also a video on YouTube with pictures, but here the story is rather different and has been jazzed up a few notches.
24 For a classic European description of Egypt in the early 1800s, see Lane 1836 [1908]. *Manners and Customs of the Modern Egyptian*.
25 al-Jabarti 1994, 2: 196 (which is conveniently cited in Lawson 2010).
26 Zarzeczny 2012: 78.
27 See, for example, Cole 2008 and Hamilton 2001.
28 See Chandler 1966.
29 See, for example, Cole 2008.
30 See, among many other books, Burleigh 2008.
31 Nelson's letter of 3 August 1798 written to *Dublin Penny Journal*. Cited in *Dublin Penny Journal*, Vol. 3–4 (Google Books): 389.
32 Cited in Jenkyns 2004: 92.
33 Warner 1960: 95.
34 See, for example, Brown 1994 and especially Willcocks 1889. For decades Willcocks was one of Britain's chief water-planners, though in the 1920s he was convicted for spreading information on the Nile's water flow contrary to what the British considered to be their interests.
35 Cited in Brown 1994: 129.
36 See Allin 1998.
37 See Tuchman 1956.

38 Discussed in Lewis 2002, footnote 67.

39 This story was told by Disraeli's adviser, who was known to be almost as gifted at storytelling as his boss. Historians later learned that the Rothschild family, a total of four times, had been given twenty hours to consider the request, and that the government had, at an earlier date, initiated a thorough analysis of the entire Suez Canal question. See Ferguson 1998: 299.

40 See Steegmuller 1983: 23.

41 See Northam, *The Collected Poems of Henrik Ibsen*, 7 April 2018. Available online: https://www.hf.uio.no/is/tjenester/kunnskap/ibsen-arkivet/tekstarkiv/ oversettelser/34498.pdf.

42 See https://web.archive.org/web/20150907222029/https://ebooks.adelaide.edu.au/i/ ibsen/henrik/peer/complete.html.

43 See Northam, *The Collected Poems of Henrik Ibsen*.

44 See, for example, Sawyer 2010.

45 In Caesar's *The Alexandrian War* (1955: 19):

> [...] in a short space of time the water nearer the contamination was entirely undrinkable, while that lower down was found to be relatively impure and brackish. This circumstance dispelled their doubts, and so great was the panic that took hold upon them that it seemed that they were all reduced to a most hazardous plight, and some asserted that Caesar was being slow in giving orders to embark.

46 See, for example, Bohannan 2010.

Chapter 3

1 Cited in Plinius Secundus 1962.

2 Russell 1831: 19–20.

3 El-Bashir 1983.

4 Ibn Battuta 1929: 50.

5 Ibid.

6 Quoted in Fischel 1967: 18–19.

7 Warner 2006.

8 See Lobo 1791: 36–7.

9 Shakespeare's *Antony and Cleopatra*, Act 2, Scene 7.

10 In ancient Egypt, the year had three seasons, all named after the Nile's different manifestations. *Akhet* was when the ground was under water, that is to say, irrigation season. *Peret* was the time of year when the land reappeared and it was the planting season (as a rule, the Nile returned to its normal river bed in November), and *shemu* was the season of water shortage and harvest.

11 It would take too much space here to reference all the literature behind the sections on the Nile and the struggle surrounding Nile exploitation from 1882 until today. Instead, I will refer to Tvedt 2004a and 2010, and Tvedt and Hovden 2008, where the extensive source material is listed and where all relevant books on the subject appear in different contexts. The exceptions to this bibliographical rule are works that I quote directly from.

12 Shelley's 'To the Nile'. Available online: http://www.poetryatlas.com/poetry/poem/471/ to-the-nile.html.

13 Cromer 1908, II: 130.
14 Ibid.: 146–7.
15 Cited in Sadat 1957: viii.
16 Nasser 1955.
17 R. Allen, Foreign Office to A.N. Cumberbatch, Cairo, 26 January 1953, FO 371/102843.
18 W.F. Crawford, Development Division, BMEO, c/o British Embassy, Beirut to J.C.B. Richmond, Middle East Secretariat, Foreign Office, 22 December 1952, FO 371/102784.
19 See Tvedt 2004a: 189–321.
20 Quoted in Heikal 1986.
21 Joesten 1960: 59.
22 See Danielson 1997.
23 Nightingale 1987: 32.
24 Homer 1996: 382–3.
25 Nightingale 1987: 78.
26 Flaubert 1979: 169.
27 Ibsen 1909: 423.
28 See the 1969 article by historian Ibrahim Amin Ghali.
29 Edwards 1877: 103.
30 Herodotus 2008, II: paras 35–6.
31 Cited in Tvedt 2004a: 25.
32 Letter from Cromer to Lansdowne, 15 March 1905, FO 407/164.
33 Herodotus 2008, II: para 29.
34 Sadat said: 'We depend upon the Nile 100 percent in our life, so if anyone, at any moment thinks to deprive us of our life we shall never hesitate [to go to war] because it is a matter of life or death' (Waterbury 1979: 78).
35 See *Egypt Independent*, 12 June 2012.
36 See, for example, Declan Walsh and Somini Sengupta, 'For Thousands of Years, Egypt Controlled the Nile. A New Dam Threatens That', *New York Times*, 9 February 2020, https://www.nytimes.com/interactive/2020/02/09/world/africa/nile-river-dam.html.
37 It sent shockwaves all over the Nile basin when President Morsi and other Egyptian politicians were caught on camera talking about covert attacks on Ethiopia; see: http://english.alarabiya.net/en/News/middle-east/2013/06/04/Egyptian-politicians-suggest-sabotaging-Ethiopia-s-new-Nile-dam.html.
38 Tvedt 2013: 196.
39 Cited in Margoliouth 1912: 255.
40 The first country was Saudi Arabia.

Chapter 4

1 Welsby 2006.
2 Adams 1977: 199.
3 Trevor-Roper 1964: 9.
4 Robinson 1925.
5 The narrative here relies heavily on Gershoni 2000 and his analysis and quotations from Huzayyin's work.
6 Quoted in Hill 1956: 247.
7 Baker 1866: 11.

8   An extensive number of historical studies deal with this question. For an overview of earlier and dominant explanations, see Robinson and Gallagher 1961 and 1981 (rev. ed.) for the most influential works. The 1981 edition contains two new chapters: as 'Explanation' and 'Afterthoughts'.

9   Wallis-Budge 1907, II: 254.

10 Crowfoot 1919: 183.

11 Holt 1967: 97.

12 Churchill 2005: 9.

13 Ibid.: 143.

14 Baker 1884b: 14.

15 Churchill 2005: 151.

16 Ferguson 2003: 375.

17 Foreign Office Memorandum, Murray, 4 January 1932, 'Memorandum on the Political Situation in Europe', FO 371/8972.

18 Lloyd 1906: 301.

19 For the following citations, see Jessen 1905 and 1906.

20 For information on Jessen's relationship to Amalie, see the note by Hans-Christian Oset in Borreminne: https://web.archive.org/web/20180421122435/http://borreminne. hive.no/aargangene/1998_99/21-amaliejessen.htm [in Norwegian].

21 Prayers of Consecration by the Rt Rev. Bishop Gwynne and the Mufti of the Sudan, 636/6/2, SAD, Sudan Archive, Durham University, England, cited in Tvedt 2004a: 112–13.

22 Ibid.

23 Fabumni 1960: 73.

24 Sudan Government 1945: 29, also cited more fully in Tvedt 2004a: 198.

25 See the book written by Churchill's private secretary, Shuckburgh 1986, cited in Tvedt 2004a.

26 https://reuters.screenocean.com/record/437664.

27 See, for example, *People's Daily Online*, 3 March 2009. Available online: http:// en.people.cn/90001/90778/90858/90866/6605330.html.

28 For a description of the project and its background, see Nazir and Desai 2001.

Chapter 5

1   Robertson 1974: 104.

2   Lyons 1906: 664.

3   Evans-Pritchard 1945: 64, also cited in Burton 1982: 477.

4   Lienhardt 1961: 104.

5   Bedri 1939: 125.

6   Lienhardt 1954. See also Burton 1982: 477.

7   Evans-Pritchard 1956: 31.

8   For an overview of this entire literature, see Tvedt 2004b.

9   Deng 1978: 133–4.

10 For African slavery in southern Sudan, see Sikainga 1989.

11 Searcy 2010.

12 Deng 1978: 133.

13 The Turkish-Egyptian expedition on the White Nile took place in 1840–1. The expedition travelled up the Sobat (for about 16 kilometres) and on to Gondokoro

(at today's Juba). An expedition in 1842 planned to travel even further upriver but was stopped by troops at Rejaf in today's South Sudan.

14 Evans-Pritchard 1971: 132.
15 Ibid.
16 Ibid.: 131.
17 Ibid.: 132.
18 Ibid.: 133.
19 Ibid.: 143.
20 See Waller 1874, II: 339.
21 Millais 1924: 86.
22 Wallis-Budge 1907: 314.
23 See Gallagher and Robinson 1953: 15 for this formulation. For a review of the discussion, see Tvedt 2010.
24 Ferguson 1922.
25 Deng 1978: 150–8.
26 Ibid.: 153.
27 Garstin 1899b, enclosed in a 'Despatch from Her Majesty's Agent and Consul-General at Cairo, and presented to both Houses of Parliament, June 1899'. A slightly different version published as 'Note on the Soudan' (1899a).
28 Garstin 1901.
29 Sir Hubert Huddleston to Sir Harold MacMichael, 6 February 1947, NRO, Khartoum.
30 See, for example, Director of Irrigation to Civil Secretary (in Khartoum), 19 October 1943 (Strictly Confidential), UNP 1/9/72, National Records Office, Sudan.
31 Jarvis 1937: 120.
32 Governor Upper Nile, 1928, Memorandum, Ch. 3: 3, National Records Archive, Sudan.
33 B.R. Marwood, Handing Over Notes, DC Bor District, UNP 1/51/13: 174, National Records Office, Sudan.
34 Collins 1969: 178.
35 Governor Equatoria, S. Freigoun, 2 December 1954, DAHLIA, Sudan Archive, Durham, England.
36 For a review of, and reference to, the dozens of reports that were written on the Jonglei Project in the 1970s, see Tvedt 2004b.
37 Executive Organ, National Council for the Development of the Jonglei Canal Area 1980: 6.
38 Ibid.: 18.
39 Ibid.
40 Hertzke 2004: 112.
41 See, among others, Mead 2006.
42 Hopper 1976: 202.

Chapter 6

1 Grant 1864: 196.
2 Speke 1863: 459.
3 Ibid.: 467.
4 Ibid.: 461.
5 Stanley 1878: 142.
6 Baker 1866: 308.

7 Ibid.: 308–9.
8 Ibid.: 313.
9 Stanley 1891: 291.
10 Stevenson 1932.
11 Herodotus 2008: 19–28.
12 See Telles 1710.
13 Cheesman 1968 [1936]: 13.
14 Perham and Simmons 1963: 14.
15 Stanley 1909: 296–7.
16 Eventually, as the British took control of Buganda, the Swahili word Uganda came to signify both the kingdom and the adjacent regions. Buganda continued, meanwhile, to exist as a protectorate and province and is today a kingdom within Uganda.
17 Kaggwa 1971: iv.
18 Speke 1863: 293.
19 Narrated in Moorehead 1960.
20 Low 1971: 6.
21 For some of their stories of the foreign European continent, see Muwanga 2005.
22 Cited in Dawson 1888: 225–7.
23 Ashe 1890: 227.
24 Siméon Lourdel, a French missionary in Uganda, wrote concerning Mwanga's stance to Charles Martial Lavigerie, a French cardinal and missionary leader in Africa, in November 1885, *Les Missions Catholiques* (1886), 314–15, cited in Robinson and Smith 1979: 100.
25 For this characterization, see Stock 1916.
26 Lord Lugard would be tied to the slogan 'indirect rule', which he later, among other things, employed while governing Nigeria with its 20 million inhabitants with an administration composed of around 200 British.
27 Lugard 1892: 827.
28 Baker 1884a.
29 Baker 1884b: 27–8.
30 Ibid.
31 Scott-Moncrieff 1895: 405.
32 Garstin 1909: 135.
33 Scott-Moncrieff 1895: 418.
34 Evans-Pritchard 1971: 134.
35 Baker 1866, I: xxi.
36 Ibid.: xi, 63, 218–19, 292, 43.
37 Churchill 1908: 56.
38 Ibid.: 126.
39 Ibid.: 118.
40 Ibid.: 93.
41 Ibid.: 97.
42 Ibid.: 123.
43 Ibid.: 123.
44 Ibid.: 155.
45 Hemingway 1935: 285.
46 Ibid.: 29.
47 This entire discussion of the Owen Falls Dam is based on comprehensive source material, which is provided in Tvedt 2004a, especially 154–89.

48 Hall to A. Creech Jones, Secretary of State for the Colonies, 3 March 1948, FO 371/69231. Quoted in Tvedt 2004a: 212.
49 Ibid.
50 Board of Trade, 'Note on Egyptian crops and water requirements', September 1956, FO 371/119063, quoted in Tvedt 2004a: 307.
51 Kyemba 1977: 53.
52 Ibid.
53 The magazine *DRUM*, January 1987.
54 In 1985 I sat and talked with a fully armed policeman at a roadblock in Nimule, the border town between Sudan and Uganda, as the unorganized Acholi army with its few trucks thundered across the border to Uganda to assume power in Kampala after Milton Obote. The Okello army quickly sprang to the defence and Museveni was that same year received as a liberating hero in Kampala and has occupied power in the country for almost thirty-five years.
55 This story is partly based on Behrend 1999. Quotes come from pp. 30–2.
56 Ibid.: 63.
57 https://www.youtube.com/watch?v=Y4MnpzG5Sqc&ab_channel=InvisibleChildren.
58 https://granta.com/how-to-write-about-africa/
59 'Troops Making Progress in Hunt for Kony', John Ryan, *USA Today*, 29 May 2012. https://web.archive.org/web/20140120020232/http://usatoday30.usatoday.com/news/world/story/2012-05-29/joseph-kony-hunt/55260364/1.
60 See for example Statement Of General Thomas D. Waldhauser, United States Marine Corps Commander United States Africa Command Before The Senate Committee On Armed Services, 13 March 2018.
61 Khareen Pech and David Beresford, 'Corporate Dogs of War Grow Fat Amid the Anarchy of Africa', *The Observer*, 16 January 1997.
62 Blackhall 2011: 157.
63 Holly Watt, 'Tory Donors' Links to Offshore Firms Revealed in Leaked Panama Papers', *The Guardian*, 4 April 2016.
64 See data in MacDonald 1919.
65 Uganda's water minister to the author in connection with an interview for a TV documentary on the Nile.
66 See Braudel 1995 for a very famous historical study, engaging with a multiplicity of temporalities, including the very long term.

Chapter 7

1   Buckley 1903: 353.
2   Naipaul 1979.
3   Cited in Ochieng' and Maxon 1992: 150.
4   Blixen 1937: 153.
5   Davidson 1959: 267.
6   Ibid.: 113.
7   Fanon 1963: 111.
8   Pringle 1893: 138–9.
9   *Washington Post*, 30 March 2008, 'Obama Overstates Kennedys' Role in Helping His Father'.
10 *The Standard* (Nairobi), 5 December 2011.

11 For this declaration, see my TV documentary, *The Nile Quest*, available on the
    YouTube channel Terje Tvedt's World History of Water'. Available online: https://www.
    youtube.com/channel/UCA6IbXwI8kF-GzputhX0dIQ.
12 Ibid.
13 See http://vision2030.go.ke/.
14 That this matter has received relatively little attention in overview works of the region
    does not mean that nothing has been written about it. See, for example, Moyse-Bartlett
    1956 and Wilson 1938.
15 See, for example, World Bank 1961: 16.
16 For a discussion of the Nyerere Doctrine see, for example, Makonnen 1984.
17 See Tvedt 2004a for quotations and sources.
18 *The Guardian*, 19 November 2001 and *The Daily News*, 12 November 2011.

Chapter 8

1   See Huntington 1968.
2   For an analysis of this, see Taylor 1994.
3   Rwanda Media Commission 2015.
4   See https://rsf.org/en/predator/paul-kagame-0.
5   For a description of Warren and his work, see Okeowo 2010.
6   See Wagner 2008.
7   Stoyan Zaimov, 'Rick Warren Guiding Rwanda's New Leaders, Calls Nation His 'Other'
    Home', *The Christian Post*, 21 March 2012. https://www.christianpost.com/news/
    rick-warren-guiding-rwandas-new-leaders-calls-nation-his-other-home.html.
8   https://www.nytimes.com/2010/08/28/world/africa/28congo.html.
9   For an unofficial translation to English, see https://www.ohchr.org/_layouts/15/
    WopiFrame.aspx?sourcedoc=/Documents/Countries/CD/DRC_MAPPING_
    REPORT_FINAL_EN.pdf&action=default&DefaultItemOpen=1.
10 See, for example, Hayes 1991 and Mowat 1987.
11 Mowat 1987: 365.
12 Kandt 1904.
13 Countless editions of Joseph Conrad's *Heart of Darkness* have been produced since it
    was first published in book form in 1902 (the story first appeared as a three-part
    feature in Blackwood's *Edinburgh Magazine* in 1899, and significant in our context, the
    year after the Battle of Omdurman).
14 Conrad 1990: 32.
15 Ibid.: 11.
16 Stanley 1878: 10.
17 Ibid.: 279.
18 For this citation and the next, see Abruzzi 1907.
19 Low 1904: 26.
20 See the title of the book: Stanley, Henry Morton 1878. *Through the Dark Continent or
    the Sources of the Nile around the Great Lakes of Equatorial Africa and Down the
    Livingstone River to the Atlantic Ocean.*
21 See, for example, Hochschild 1998.
22 Garstin 1904, 1905.
23 See note 30, Tvedt 2004a: 348.
24 For the text, see, for example: http://www.urome.be/fr2/reflexions/casemrepo.pdf.

25 Agreement between Great Britain and the Independent State of the Congo, modifying the Agreement signed at Brussels, 12 May 1894, relating to the Spheres of Influence of Great Britain and the Independent Sate of the Congo in East and Central Africa, signed at London, 9 May 1906. See: http://gis.nacse.org/tfdd/tfdddocs/40ENG.pdf.

26 Cf. Mt. 11:28: 'Come to me, all you who are weary and burdened, and I will give you rest.'

27 Stockwell 1978: 105. In 2013, the US State Department admitted that President Eisenhower had authorized the murder of Lumumba.

28 See De Witte 2001: xiii.

29 See Che Guevara 2011.

30 See Tshimanga 2010.

31 James Randerson, 'The Shifting River that is Making Uganda Smaller', *The Guardian*, 7 December 2010. Available online: https://www.theguardian.com/environment/2010/dec/07/climate-change-rerouting-semliki-river.

32 Ibid.

33 Stanley 1909: 412.

34 Quoted in Lemarchand 1970: 19.

35 'Opprørsleder tok imot Jesus etter kampanje', 1 January 2005. Available online: https://troensbevis.no/nyheter/93899-opprorsleder-tok-imot-jesus-etter-kampanje/.

36 See the TV documentary *The Nile Quest*. Available online: https://www.youtube.com/channel/UCA6IbXwI8kF-GzputhX0dIQ.

37 Mecklenburg 1910: 44.

Chapter 9

1 For an amusing book on this subject, see Denison et al. 2003.

2 It would occupy far too much space to reference individual works in this discussion, because the list is too long. The literature concerning the struggle for Ethiopia and Eritrea is almost as extensive as the literature on the Fashoda conflict in South Sudan. Meanwhile, the two research fields also share another trait: both overlook or do not sufficiently emphasize Britain's devised and comprehensive Nile strategy.

3 For a more comprehensive analysis of the geopolitical game surrounding Italy, Eritrea and Ethiopia, see Tvedt 2004a, especially 39–44, 113–36 and 247–60.

4 See, for example, Secretary of State John Foster Dulles's speech to the UN, cited in Selassie 1989: 37.

5 The bridge was destroyed during the last war between the two countries, but has since been repaired and is one of the many signs of an attempt to maintain a neighbourly relationship.

6 James 1890, I: 255.

7 In Egypt a number of key academics came out against Eritrea. They said that the Eritreans were stirring up trouble, and that Egypt's interests were not served by a war with Ethiopia but rather by economic cooperation.

8 Statements in the two-and-a-half hour TV documentary I made on the history of the Nile, called *The Nile Quest*. Available on Amazon.

9 'Eritrea Breaks Silence and Responds to Ethiopia Peace Overtures, Will Send Delegation', *Washington Post*, 20 June 2018.

10 US Embassy Eritrea. Statement by the Press Secretary on Progress Toward Peace Between Ethiopia and Eritrea, 22 June 2018. Available online: https://er.usembassy.

gov/statement-by-the-press-secretary-on-progress-toward-peace-between-ethiopia-and-eritrea/.

11 'Eritrean President Returns Favor, Visits Ethiopia as Hostilities Between the Countries Ease', *Washington Post*, 14 July 2018. Available online: https://www.washingtonpost.com/world/eritrean-president-returns-favor-visits-ethiopia-as-hostilities-between-the-countries-ease/2018/07/14/d28a7ed4-8684-11e8-8553-a3ce89036c78_story.html.

12 *Kebra Nagast* 1969: 28.

13 Ibid.: 67.

14 Blashford-Snell 1970: 43.

15 For a description of this, see, for example, Østigård and Gedef 2013 and Cheesman 1968 [1936]: 175, 188.

16 Told to Norden 1930: 215.

17 For a summary and discussion, see Sumner 1985.

18 Kiros 2005. The book was written by Zera Yacob and translated into English.

19 Bruce 1790, III: 328.

20 Gen. 2:10–14.

21 Cited in Beckingham and Huntingford 1954: 23–4.

22 Bruce 1790, III: 603–4.

23 Pankhurst 2000.

24 Van Donzel 2000.

25 Six 1999: 66.

26 Baum 1927: 54.

27 Butzer 1981: 471.

28 See Tvedt 2004a: 126-30, for a more specific analysis and discussion of this agreement. For more details regarding the correspondence, see FO 93/218, National Archives, London.

29 Again, for more details about this complex hydropolitical history, see Tvedt 2004a.

30 Graham to Mussolini 14 December 1925, Enclosure 1 in No. 1, Graham to Chamberlain, 1 January 1926, FO 371/11563. This version is the original version with the proposed changes in the text written by hand. Quoted also in Tvedt 2004a: 127, and there discussed in a much broader perspective.

31 This secret agreement is discussed in detail and analysed as an important part of the developments leading up to the collapse of the League of Nations in Tvedt 2004a: 113–36.

32 Woolbert 1935: 508.

33 Cited in Barker 1936: 129.

34 Haile Selassie, Appeal to the League of Nations, June 1936. Available online: https://www.mtholyoke.edu/acad/intrel/selassie.htm.

35 Taylor 1961: 89.

36 Foreign Office Minute, Wallinger, 5 June 1934, FO 371/18032. Maffey to Foreign Office, 18 June 1935, FO 371/19186, National Archives, London.

37 Report of Inter-Departmental Committee on British interests in Ethiopia, what was later called the Maffey-report, in Maffey to Foreign Office, 18 June 1935, FO 371/19186. See also Tvedt 2004a.

38 See Foreign Office 371/22010.

39 Geldof 2006.

40 See https://ethiopiangranddam.wordpress.com/2013/03/15/pm-meles-zenawi-speech-at-gerd-project-launch-on-april-2-2011/.

41 See the two interviews made with Meles Zenawi in my two documentaries: 'The Future of Water' (2007) and 'The Nile Quest' (2012), both available on Amazon video.

42 See 'Ethiopia's Nobel-Winning Leader Warns Egypt Over Dam', 22 October 2019. Available online: https://apnews.com/article/9deb28e2af6249198dde54160ff62c3b.

Chapter 10

1   For thousands of years the Nile has been considered the world's longest river, but recently some Brazilian and Peruvian researchers have challenged this assumption. They have discovered an Amazonian source farther south in Peru and have included it as part of the river. The international research community, has not yet reached a final conclusion (in part because it is impossible to define objectively what constitutes a river's beginning and end; water's very way of flowing through the landscape complicates this task). For the moment, the Nile is still regarded by most people as the world's longest river.
2   This example is taken from Amartya Sen's book *The Idea of Justice*.

References

Abruzzi, H.R.H. the Duke of, 1907. 'The Snows of the Nile: Being an Account of the Peaks, Passes and Glaciers of Ruwenzori', *Geographical Journal*, 29, 2: 121–46.

Adams, William Y., 1977. *Nubia: Corridor to Africa*. London: Allen Lane.

al-Jabarti, Abd-al-Rahman, 1994. *Abd al-Jabarti's History of Egypt* (ed. and trans. Thomas Philipp and Moshe Perlmann). Stuttgart: Franz Steiner Verlag.

al-Sayyid-Marsot, Afaf Lutfi, 2007. *A History of Egypt from the Arab Conquest to the Present* (2nd edn). Cambridge: Cambridge University Press.

Allin, Michael, 1998. *Zarafa: A Giraffe's True Story – From Deep in Africa to the Heart of Paris*. New York: Walker & Company.

Antes, John, 1800. *Observations on the Manners and Customs of the Egyptians: The Overflowing of the Nile and Its Effects, with Remarks on the Plague and Other Subjects*. London: John Stockdale.

Anthes, Rudolf, 1959. 'Egyptian Theology in the Third Millennium B.C.', *Journal of Near Eastern Studies*, 18, 3: 169–212.

Aristotle, n.d. *On the Heavens* (trans. J.L. Stocks). *The Internet Classics Archive*. Available online: http://classics.mit.edu/Aristotle/heavens.html.

Ashe, Robert Pickering, 1890. *Two Kings of Uganda; or, Life by the Shores of Victoria Nyanza, Being an Account of the Residence of Six Years in Eastern Equatorial Africa*. London: Sampson Low.

Assmann, Jan, 1995. *Egyptian Solar Religion in the New Kingdom: Re, Amun and the Crisis of Polytheism*. London: Kegan Paul.

Baker, Samuel W., 1866. *The Albert N'yanza: Great Basin of the Nile and Explorations of the Nile Sources*, 2 vols. London: Macmillan.

Baker, Samuel W., 1884a. 'An Interview with Sir Samuel Baker', *Pall Mall Gazette*, 'Extra' No. 8, 12 March, *Sudan Pamphlets*, 28.

Baker, Samuel W., 1884b. *In the Heart of Africa*. New York: Funk & Wagnalls.

Barker, A.J., 1936. *The Rape of Ethiopia*. New York: Ballantine Books.

Baum, James E., 1927. *Savage Abyssinia*. London: J.H. Sears.

Beckingham, C.F. and G.W.B. Huntingford, 1954. *Some Records of Ethiopia 1593–1646: Being Extracts from The History of High Ethiopia or Abassia by Manoel De Almeida. Together with Bahrey's History of the Galla*. London: Printed for the Hakluyt Society.

Bedri, Ibrahim Effendi, 1939. 'Notes on Dinka Religious Beliefs in Their Hereditary Chiefs and Rain Makers', *Sudan Notes & Records*, 22, 1: 125–31.

Behrend, Heike, 1999. *Alice Lakwena & the Holy Spirits: War in Northern Uganda 1985–97* (trans. Mitch Cohen). Oxford: James Currey.

Bermann, Richard A., 1931. *The Mahdi of Allah*. London: Putnam.

Blackhall, Sue, 2011. *Simon Mann: The Real Story*. London: Pen & Sword Military.

Blackman, Aylward M., 1925. 'Osiris or the Sun-God? A Reply to Mr Perry', *The Journal of Egyptian Archaeology*, 11, 3/4: 201–9.

Blashford-Snell, J.N., 1970. 'Conquest of the Blue Nile', *The Geographical Journal*, 136, 1: 42–60.

Blixen, Karen, 1937. *Out of Africa*. London: Putnam.

Blount, Henry, 1638. *A Voyage into the Levant: A Briefe Relation of a Journey, Performed by Master Henry Blunt Gentleman, from England by the Way of Venice, into Dalmatia, Sclavonia, Bosnah, Hungary, Macedonia, Thessaly, Thrace, Rhodes and Egypt, Unto Gran Cairo*. London: Andrew Crook.

Bohannon, John, 2010. 'Climate change: The Nile Delta's Sinking Future', *Science*, 327, 5972: 1444–7.

Braudel, Fernand, 1995. *The Mediterranean and the Mediterranean World in the Age of Philip II, volume 1* (trans. Siân Reynolds). Berkeley, CA: University of California Press.

Brown, Nathan J., 1994. 'Who Abolished Corvée Labour in Egypt and Why?', *Past & Present*, 44, 1: 116–37.

Bruce, J., 1790. *Travels to Discover the Source of the Nile, in the Years 1768, 1769, 1770, 1771, 1772, and 1773*, 5 vols. London: J. Ruthven.

Buckley, R.B., 1903. 'Colonization and Irrigation in East Africa Protectorate', *The Geographical Journal*, 21, 4: 349–71.

Burleigh, Nina, 2008. *Mirage: Napoleon's Scientists and the Unveiling of Egypt*. New York: Harper Perennial.

Burton, John W., 1982. 'Nilotic Women: A Diachronic Perspective', *The Journal of Modern African Studies*, 20, 3: 467–95.

Butzer, Karl W., 1981. 'Rise and Fall of Axum, Ethiopia: A Geo-Archaeological Interpretation', *American Antiquity*, 46, 3: 471–95.

Caesar, Julius, 1955. *The Alexandrian War*, Loeb Classical Library. Cambridge, MA: Harvard University Press.

Casati, Gaetano, 1891. *Ten Years in Equatorial Africa and the Return with Emin Pasha*. London: Frederick Warne.

Chandler, David G., 1966. *The Campaigns of Napoleon*. New York: Simon & Schuster.

Chauveau, Michel, 1997. *Cleopatra: Beyond the Myth* (trans. David Lorton). Ithaca, NY: Cornell University Press.

Chauveau, Michel, 2000. *Egypt in the Age of Cleopatra: History and Society under the Ptolemies* (trans. David Lorton). Ithaca, NY: Cornell University Press.

Che Guevara, Ernesto, 2011. *Congo Diary: The Story of Che Guevara's 'Lost' Year in Africa*. Lancing: Ocean Press.

Cheesman, R.E., 1968 [1936]. *Lake Tana and the Blue Nile: An Abyssinian Quest*. London: Frank Cass.

Churchill, Winston S., 1908. *My African Journey*. London: Icon Books.

Churchill, Winston S., 2005. *The River War: An Historical Account of the Reconquest of the Sudan*. London: Prime Classics Library.

Cole, Juan, 2008. *Napoleon's Egypt: Invading the Middle East*. London: Palgrave Macmillan.

Collins, Robert O. (ed.), 1969. *The Partition of Africa: Illusion or Necessity?* New York: John Wiley.

Conrad, Joseph, 1990. *Heart of Darkness*. New York: Dover Publications.

Cromer, Earl of, 1908. *Modern Egypt*, 2 vols. London: Macmillan.

Crowfoot, J., 1919. 'Angels of the Nile', *Sudan Notes and Records*, 2, 3: 183–97.

Danielson, Virginia, 1997. 'The Voice of Egypt': Umm Khulthūm, Arabic Song, and Egyptian Society in the 20th Century*. Chicago: University of Chicago Press.

Davidson, Basil, 1959. *Old Africa Rediscovered*. London: Victor Gollancz.

Dawson, E.C. (ed.), 1888. *The Last Journals of Bishop Hannington Being Narratives of a Journey through Palestine in 1884 and a Journey through Masai-Land and U-Soga in 1885*. London: Seeley.

De Witte, Ludo, 2001. *The Assassination of Lumumba* (trans. Ann Wright and Renée Fenby). London: Verso.

Deng, Francis M., 1978. *Africans of the Two Worlds: The Dinka in Afro-Arab Sudan.* Khartoum: University of Khartoum.

Denison, Edward, Guang Yu Ren and Naigzy Gebremedhin, 2003. *Asmara: Africa's Secret Modernist City.* London: Merrell.

Edwards, Amelia B., 1877. *A Thousand Miles up the Nile.* London: Longmans, Green and Co.

El-Bashir, Ahmed, 1983. *The United States, Slavery and Slave Trade in the Nile Valley.* Lanham, MD: University Press of America.

Evans-Pritchard, E.E., 1945. *Some Aspects of Marriage and the Family Among the Nuer.* Lusaka: Rhodes-Livingstone Institute.

Evans-Pritchard, E.E., 1956. *Nuer Religion.* Oxford: Oxford University Press.

Evans-Pritchard, E.E., 1971. 'Sources with Particular Reference to Southern Sudan', *Cahier d'Études africaines*, 11, 41: 121–79.

Executive Organ, National Council for the Development of the Jonglei Canal Area, 1980. *Jonglei Canal: A Development Project in the Sudan.* Khartoum: National Council for the Development of the Jonglei Canal Area.

Fabumni, L.A., 1960. *The Sudan in Anglo-Egyptian Relations, 1800–1956.* London: Longman.

Fanon, Frantz, 1963. *The Wretched of the Earth* (foreword by Jean-Paul Sartre). New York: Grove Press.

Faulkner, R.O., 1969. *The Ancient Egyptian Pyramid Texts.* Oxford: Clarendon Press.

Faulkner, R.O., 2007. *The Ancient Egyptian Coffin Texts.* Oxford: Aris & Phillips.

Ferguson, Niall, 1999. *The House of Rothschild: The World's Banker, 1849–1998, Vol. II.* New York: Penguin Books.

Ferguson, Niall, 2003. *Empire: How Britain Made the Modern World.* London: Allen Lane.

Ferguson, V.H., 1922. 'The Holy Lake of the Dinkas', *Sudan Notes and Records*, 5: 165–9.

Fischel, Walter, 1967. *Ibn Khaldūn in Egypt: His Public Functions and his Historical Research, 1382–1406 – A Study in Islamic Historiography.* Berkeley, CA: University of California Press.

Flaubert, Gustave, 1979. *Flaubert in Egypt: A Sensibility on Tour: A Narrative Drawn from Gustave Flaubert's Travel Notes & Letters* (trans., ed., intro. Francis Steegmuller). London: Penguin.

Forbes, J.R., 1964–72. *Studies in Ancient Technology*, 9 vols, Vol. 2. Leiden: Brill.

Forster, E.M., 1982. *Alexandria: A History and a Guide.* London: Michael Haag.

Fossey, Dian, 1983. *Gorillas in the Mist.* Boston, MA: Houghton Mifflin.

Freeman, Charles, 1996. *Egypt, Greece, and Rome: Civilizations of the Ancient Mediterranean.* Oxford: Oxford University Press.

Gallagher, John and Ronald Robinson, 1953. 'The Imperialism of Free Trade', *The Economic History Review*, Second Series, 6, 1: 1–15.

Garstin, William E., 1899a. *Note on the Soudan.* Cairo: Ministry of Public Works.

Garstin, William E., 1899b. *Report on the Soudan: HMSO Parliamentary Accounts and Papers*, No. 112: 925–51. London.

Garstin, William E., 1901. *Despatch from His Majesty's Agent and Consul-General Cairo Enclosing a Report as to Irrigation Projects on the Upper Nile.* London: Foreign Office, Blue Book, Egypt No. 2.

Garstin, William E., 1904. *Report upon the Basin of the Upper Nile with Proposals for the Improvement of that River.* Cairo: Ministry of Public Works.

Garstin, William E., 1905. 'Some Problems of the Upper Nile', *The Nineteenth Century and After*, 58, 343: 345–66.

Garstin, William E., 1909. 'Fifty Years of Nile Exploration and Some of Its Results', *The Geographical Journal*, 33, 2: 117–47.

Garvey, Marcus, 1937. 'The Failure of Haile Selassie as an Emperor', Editorial, *The Black Man*, March/April.

Geldof, Bob, 2006. *Geldof in Africa*. London: Arrow.

Gershoni, Israel, 2000. 'Geographers and Nationalism in Egypt: Huzayyin and the Unity of the Nile Valley, 1945–1948', in Haggai Erlich and Israel Gershoni (eds), *The Nile: Histories, Cultures, Myths*, 199–219. London: Lynne Rienner.

Ghali, Ibrahim Amin, 1969. 'Touristes romains en Égypte et égyptiens à Rome sans le Haute Égypte', *Cahiers d'histoire Égyptienne*, 11: 43–62.

Grant, James A., 1864. *A Walk Across Africa or Domestic Scenes from my Nile Journal*. Edinburgh: Blackwood and Sons.

Green, Matthew, 2008. *The Wizard of the Nile: The Hunt for Africa's Most Wanted*. Northampton, MA: Olive Branch Press.

Griffiths, J.G., 1960. *The Conflict of Horus and Seth: From Egyptian and Classical Sources*. Liverpool: Liverpool University Press.

Hamilton, Jill, 2001. *Marengo: The Myth of Napoleon's Horse*. London: Fourth Estate.

Hassan, Fekri A., 1997. 'The Dynamics of a Riverine Civilization: A Geoarchaeological Perspective on the Nile Valley, Egypt', *World Archaeology*, 29, 1: 51–74.

Hawkes, Jacquetta, 1973. *The First Great Civilizations: Life in Mesopotamia, the Indus Valley, and Egypt*. New York: Alfred A. Knopf.

Hayes, Harold, 1991. *The Dark Romance of Dian Fossey*. London: Chatto & Windus.

Heikal, Mohamed H., 1986. *Cutting the Lion's Tail: Suez Through Egyptian Eyes*. New York: Deutsch.

Hemingway, Ernest, 1935. *Green Hills of Africa*. New York: Charles Scribner's Sons.

Hemingway, Ernest, 1954. 'The Christmas Gift', *Look*, 20 April and 4 May, 18, 8 and 18, 9.

Hepburn, Katharine, 1987. *The Making of The African Queen or How I Went to Africa with Bogie, Bacall and Huston and Nearly Lost My Mind*. New York: Alfred A. Knopf.

Herodotus, 2008. *The History of Herodotus: Volume I* (trans. G.C. Macaulay). *Project Gutenberg*. Available online: https://www.gutenberg.org/files/2707/2707-h/2707-h.htm.

Hertzke, Allen D., 2004. *Freeing God's Children: The Unlikely Alliance for Global Human Rights*. Lanham, MD: Rowman & Littlefield.

Hewison, R. Neill, 2008. *The Fayoum: History and Guide*. Cairo: American University in Cairo Press.

Hill, Richard, 1956. 'The Search for the White Nile's Source: Two Explorers Who Failed', *The Geographical Journal*, 122, 2: 247–50.

Hillard, T.W., 2002. 'The Nile Cruise of Cleopatra and Caesar', *The Classical Quarterly*, 52, 2: 549–54.

Hobsbawm, Eric, 1983. *The Invention of Tradition*. Cambridge: Cambridge University Press.

Hochschild, Adam, 1998. *King Leopold's Ghost: A Story of Greed, Terror and Heroism in Colonial Africa*. Boston, MA: Houghton Mifflin Harcourt.

Holt, P.M., 1967. *A Modern History of the Sudan: From the Funj Sultanate to the Present Day* (3rd edn). London: Weidenfeld and Nicolson.

Homer, 1996. *The Iliad* (trans. Alexander Pope). Eugene, OR: Wipf and Stock.

Hopper, W. David, 1976. 'The Development of Agriculture in Developing Countries', *Scientific American*, 235, 3: 197–205.

Huntington, Samuel P., 1968. *Political Order in Changing Societies*. New Haven, CT: Yale University Press.

Ibn Battuta, 1929. *Travels in Africa and Asia 1325–1354* (trans. and ed. H.A.R. Gibb). London: George Routledge and Sons.

Ibsen, Henrik, 1909. *Efterladte Skrifter, vol. I, Digte 1847–1896, Prosastykker 1841–1898; Taler 1879–1891; Ungdomsdramaer 1849–1860*. Kristiania: Gyldendalske boghandel.

Ibsen, Henrik, 1986. *The Collected Poems of Henrik Ibsen* (trans. John Northam), Oslo: Norwegian University Press.

Ibsen, Henrik, 2012. *Peer Gynt*. CreateSpace Independent Publishing Platform.

James, William, 1890. *Principles of Psychology*. New York: Henry Holt.

Jarvis, C.S., 1937. *Oriental Spotlight*. London: John Murray.

Jenkyns, Richard, 2004. *Westminster Abbey*. London: Profile Books.

Jessen, B.H., 1905. 'South-Western Abyssinia', *The Geographic Journal*, 25, 2: 158–71.

Jessen, B.H., 1906. *W.N. McMillan's Expeditions and Big Game Hunting in Southern Sudan, Abyssinia and East Africa*. London: Merchant Singer and Co.

Joesten, Joachim, 1960. *Nasser: The Rise to Power*. Westport, CT: Greenwood Press.

Joinville, Jean de, pub. between 1305 and 1309. *Histoire de Saint Louis (Life of Saint Louis)*. Fragment published in S.J. Allen and Emilie Amt (eds), 2003. *The Crusades: A Reader*, 343–7. Peterborough, ON: Broadview Press.

Kaggwa, Apolo, 1971. *The Kings of Buganda* (ed. M.S.M. Kiwanuka). Kampala: East African Publishing House.

Kalfatovic, Martin R., 1992. *Nile Notes of a Howadji: A Bibliography of Travelers' Tales from Egypt, from the Earliest Time to 1918*. Metuchen, NJ: Scarecrow Press.

Kandt, Richard, 1904. *Caput Nili: Eine Empfindsame Reise zu den Quellen des Nils*. Berlin: Dietrich Reimer.

Kebra Nagast, 1969. *A Modern Translation of the Kebra Nagast: The Glory of Kings* (ed. Miguel F. Brooks). Kingston, Jamaica: LMH Publishing Co.

Kennedy, Hugh, 2007. *The Great Arab Conquests: How the Spread of Islam Changed the World We Live In*. Boston, MA: Da Capo Press.

Kiros, Teodros, 2005. *Zara Yacob: Rationality of the Human Heart*. Lawrenceville, NJ: Red Sea Press.

Kyemba, Henry, 1977. *A State of Blood: The Inside Story of Idi Amin*. New York: Ace Books.

Lane, Edward William, 1836 [1908]. *Manners and Customs of the Modern Egyptians*. London: Society for the Diffusion of Useful Knowledge / J.M. Dent & Co.

Lawson, Fred H., 2010. 'Nile River Flows and Political Order in Ottoman Egypt', in Terje Tvedt and Richard Coopey (eds), *Rivers and Society: From the Birth of Agriculture to Modern Times*, Vol. II, Series II in Terje Tvedt (Series Editor), *A History of Water*, 203–21. London/New York: I.B. Taurus.

Lemarchand, René, 1970. *Rwanda and Burundi*. London: Pall Mall Press.

Lewis, Bernard, 2002. *What Went Wrong? The Clash Between Islam and Modernity in the Middle East*. London: Weidenfeld and Nicolson.

Lienhardt, R.G., 1954. 'The Shilluk of the Upper Nile', in C. Daryll Forde (ed.), *African Worlds: Studies in the Cosmological Ideas and Social Values of African People*, 138–93. London: Oxford University Press.

Lienhardt, R.G., 1961. *Divinity and Experience: The Religion of the Dinka*. Oxford: Clarendon Press.

Lloyd, Albert B., 1906. *Uganda to Khartoum: Life and Adventures on the Upper Nile*. London: T. Fisher Unwin.

Lobo, Jeromino, 1791. *A Short Relation of the River Nile, Of its Source and Current; Of its Overflowing the Campagnia of Aegypt, 'till it runs into the Mediterranean; And of Other Curiosities* (trans. Peter Wyche). London: Printed for the Royal Society, MDCLXIX.

Low, Donald Anthony, 1971. *The Mind of Buganda: Documents of the Modern History of an African Kingdom*. Berkeley, CA: University of California Press.

Low, Sidney, 1904. 'Henry Morton Stanley'. *Cornhill Magazine*, New Series 17: 26–42.

Lugard, F.D., 1892. 'Travels from the East Coast to Uganda, Lake Albert Edward and Lake Albert', *Proceedings of the Royal Geographical Society and Monthly Record of Geography*, New Monthly Series, 14, 12: 817–41.

Lugard, F.D., 1893. *The Rise of Our East African Empire*, 2 vols. Edinburgh: W. Blackwood & Sons.

Lyons, H.G., 1906. *The Physiography of the River Nile in the Basin*. Cairo: National Printing Department.

MacDonald, Murdoch, 1919. *Nile Control: A Statement of the Necessity for Further Control of the Nile to Complete the Development of Egypt and Develop a Certain Area in the Sudan, with Particulars of the Physical Conditions to be Considered and Programme of the Engineering Works Involved, Vol. 2*. Cairo: Government Press.

MacQuitty, William, 1976. *Island of Isis: Philae, Temple of the Nile*. London: MacDonald and Jane's.

Mahfouz, Naguib, 1993. *Adrift on the Nile*. New York: Doubleday.

Mailer, Norman, 1975. *The Fight*. New York: Brown, Little.

Maistre, Xavier de, 1825 [2005]. *A Journey Around My Room*. London: Hesperus Classics.

Makonnen, Yilma, 1984. *The Nyerere Doctrine of State Succession and the New State of East Africa*. Arusha: Eastern Africa Publications.

Margoliouth, D.S., 1912. *Cairo, Jerusalem, and Damascus: Three Chief Cities of the Egyptian Sultans* (illus. W.S.S. Tyrwhitt). New York: Dodd, Mead & Co.

Mariette, Auguste, 1890. *Outlines of Ancient Egyptian History* (trans. and ed. M. Brodrick). Available online: www.forgottenbooks.org.

Marlow, John, 1971. *The Golden Age of Alexandria: From its Foundation by Alexander the Great in 331 BC to its Capture by the Arabs in 642 AD*. London: Gollancz.

Mauss, Marcel, 1925. *Essai sur le don: forme et raison de l'échange dans les sociétés archaïques* [*The Gift: Forms and Functions of Exchange in Archaic Societies*]. Paris: L'Année Sociologique / Presses Universitaires de France.

Mead, Walter Russell, 2006. 'God's Country'. *Foreign Affairs*, September/October. Available online: https://www.foreignaffairs.com/articles/united-states/2006-09-01/gods-country.

Mecklenburg, A.F., 1910. *In the Heart of Africa*. London: Cassel.

Meyboom, P.G.P., 1995. *The Nile Mosaic of Palestrina: Early Evidence of Egyptian Religion in Italy*. Leiden: E.J. Brill.

Millais, John G., 1924. *Far Away up the Nile*. London: Longmans.

Milner, Alfred, 1892. *England in Egypt*. London: E. Milner.

Moorehead, Alan, 1960. *The White Nile*. London: Hamish Hamilton.

Mowat, Farley, 1987. *Woman in the Mists: The Story of Dian Fossey and the Mountain Gorillas of Africa*. New York: Warner Books.

Moyse-Bartlett, Hubert, 1956. *The King's African Rifles: A Study of the Military History of East and Central Africa, 1890–1945*. Aldershot: Gale & Polden.

Muwanga, J.S.B, 2005. *On the Kabaka's Road for Uganda: A Contribution to the Positive Mind of Buganda*. Kampala: LDC Publishers.

Naipaul, V.S., 1979. *A Bend in the River*. London: Deutsch.

Nasser, Gamal Abdel, 1955. *Egypt's Liberation: The Philosophy of the Revolution.* Washington, DC: Public Affairs Press.

Nazir, Osman A. El and Govind D. Desai, 2001. *Kenana: Kingdom of Green Gold – Grand Multinational Venture in the Desert of Sudan.* London: Kegan Paul.

Ngũgĩ wa Thiong'o, 1967. *A Grain of Wheat.* London: William Heinemann.

Nightingale, Florence, 1987. *Letters from Egypt: A Journey on the Nile, 1849–50* (ed. Anthony Sattin). New York: Weidenfeld & Nicolson.

Norden, Hermann, 1930. *Africa's Last Empire: Through Abyssinia to Lake Tana and the Country of the Falasha.* London: H.F. & G. Witherby.

Ochieng', W.R. and R.M. Maxon, 1992. *An Economic History of Kenya.* Nairobi: East African Educational Publishers.

Okeowo, Alexis, 2010. 'Rick Warren in Rwanda', *Foreign Affairs*, 18 August. Available online: http://nplusonemag.com/rick-warren-in-rwanda.

Orwell, George, 1934. *Burmese Days.* New York: Harper and Brothers.

Østigård, Terje and Abawa Firew Gedef, 2013. *The Source of the Blue Nile: Water Rituals and Traditions in the Lake Tana Region?*, Newcastle upon Tyne: Cambridge Scholars Publishing.

Pankhurst, R., 2000. 'Ethiopia's Alleged Control of the Nile', in H. Erlich and I. Gershoni (eds), *The Nile: Histories, Cultures, Myths*, 25–37. Boulder, CO: Lynne Rienner.

Perham, Margery and J. Simmons, 1963. *African Discovery: An Anthology of Exploration.* London: Faber and Faber.

Petherick, John, 1861. *Egypt, the Soudan and Central Africa: With Explorations from Khartoum on the White Nile to the Regions of the Equator, Being Sketches from Sixteen Years' Travel.* London: William Blackwood and Sons.

Petherick, John and K.H. Petherick, 1869. *Travels in Central Africa, and Explorations of the Western Nile Tributaries.* London: Tinsley Brothers.

Plinius Secundus, Gaius (Maior), 1962. *Natural History*, 10 vols (trans. D.E. Eichholz). Cambridge, MA: Harvard University Press.

Pollard, Justin and Howard Reid, 2006. *The Rise and Fall of Alexandria: Birthplace of the Modern Mind.* New York: Viking.

Pringle, J.W., 1893. 'With the Railway Survey to Victoria Nyanza', *Geographical Journal*, 2, 2: 112–39.

Robertson, James, 1974. *Transition to Africa: From the Direct Rule to Independence.* London: C. Hurst.

Robinson, Artur E., 1925. 'The Conquest of the Sudan by the Wali of Egypt. Part I', *Journal of the Royal African Society*, 25, 97: 47–58.

Robinson, David and Douglas Smith, 1979. *Sources of the African Past: Case Studies of Five Nineteenth-Century African Societies.* New York: Africana.

Robinson, Ronald and John Gallagher (with Alice Denny), 1981 [1961]. *Africa and the Victorians: The Official Mind of Imperialism* (expanded 2nd edn). London: Macmillan.

Roller, Duane W., 2010. *Cleopatra: A Biography.* New York: Oxford University Press.

Roullet, Anne, 1972. *The Egyptian and Egyptianizing Monuments of Imperial Rome.* Leiden: Brill.

Russell, Bertrand, 1962. *History of Western Philosophy.* London: George Allen & Unwin.

Russell, Michael, 1831. *View of Ancient Egypt with an Outline of its Natural History.* Available online: www.forgottenbooks.org.

Rwanda Media Commission, 2015. *The State of Media Freedom in Rwanda.* Kigali: RMC. Available online: https://rsf.org/sites/default/files/6_5_2015_ib_-_final_report_on_state_of_the_media_freedom_in_rwanda_00.00.pdf.

Sadat, Anwar El, 1957. *Revolt on the Nile* (trans. Thomas Graham). London: Allan Wingate.

Said, Edward, 1978. *Orientalism*. New York: Vintage Books.

Said, Rushdi, 1993. *The River Nile: Geology, Hydrology and Utilization*. Oxford: Pergamon Press.

Sawyer, Ralph D., 2010. 'Aquatic Warfare Historic China', in Tvedt, Terje, Graham Chapman and Roar Hagen (eds), *Water and Geopolitics in the New World Order*, Vol. II, Series II, 111–37, in Terje Tvedt (Series Editor), *A History of Water*. London/New York: I.B. Tauris.

Scott-Moncrieff, C., 1895, 'The Nile', *Royal Institution of Great Britain*, Proceedings 14 (25 January): 405–18.

Searcy, Kim, 2010. *The Formation of the Sudanese Mahdist State: Ceremony and Symbols of Authority, 1882–1898*. Leiden: Brill.

Selassie, Bereket Habte, 1989. *Eritrea and the United Nations*. Trenton, NJ: Red Sea Press.

Sen, Amartya, 2009. *The Idea of Justice*. Cambridge, MA: Belknap Press.

Shakespeare, William, 1607. *Anthony and Cleopatra*. Available online: http://shakespeare.mit.edu/cleopatra/full.html.

Shaw, George Bernard, 1901. *Caesar and Cleopatra. Project Gutenberg*. Available online: http://www.gutenberg.org/files/3329/3329-h/3329-h.htm.

Shuckburgh, Evelyn, 1986. *Descent to Suez: Diaries 1951–56*. London: Weidenfeld and Nicolson.

Sikainga, Ahmad Alawad, 1989. 'The Legacy of Slavery and Slave Trade in the Western Bahr al-Ghazal, 1850–1939', *Northeast African Studies*, 2, 2: 75–95.

Six, Veronika, 1999. 'Water, the Nile, and the Tä'amrä Maryam: Miracles of Virgin Mary in the Ethiopian Version', *Aethiopica*, 2: 53–68.

Speke, John Hanning, 1863. *Journal of the Discovery of the Source of the Nile*. Edinburgh: Blackwood and Sons.

Stanley, Henry Morton, 1878. *Through the Dark Continent or the Sources of the Nile around the Great Lakes of the Equatorial Africa and Down the Livingstone River to the Atlantic Ocean, Vol. 1*. New York: Harper.

Stanley, Henry Morton, 1891. *In Darkest Africa or the Quest, Rescue and Retreat of Emin, Governor of Equatoria*. New York: Charles Scribner's Sons.

Stanley, Henry Morton, 1909. *The Autobiography of Sir Henry Morton Stanley* (ed. Dorothy Stanley). Boston, MA: Houghton Mifflin Company.

Steegmuller, Francis (trans. and ed.), 1983. *Flaubert in Egypt: A Sensibility on Tour*. London: Michael Haag.

Stevenson, Edward L. (ed. and trans.), 1932. *Geography of Claudius Ptolemy*. New York: New York Public Library.

Stock, Eugene, 1916. *The History of the Church Missionary Society: Its Environment, Men and Work*. London: Church Missionary Society.

Stockwell, John, 1978. *In Search of Enemies: A CIA Story*. New York: W.W. Norton.

Sudan Government, 1945. *The Advisory Council for the Northern Sudan: The Proceedings of the First Session, held at the Palace, Khartoum, 15–18 May 1944*. Khartoum: McCorquodale.

Sumner, Claude, 1985. *Classical Ethiopian Philosophy*. Addis Ababa: Central Print.

Suyuti, Jalal ad-Din as-, 1995. *The History of the Khalifahs Who Took the Right Way*. London: Ta-Ha.

Taylor, A.J.P., 1961. *The Origins of the Second World War*. New York: Atheneum.

Taylor, Christopher C., 1994. *Sacrifice as Terror: The Rwandan Genocide of 1994*. Oxford: Berg.

Telles, Balthazar, 1710. *Travels of the Jesuits in Ethiopia: Containing I: The Geographical Description of All the Kingdoms and Provinces of the Empire. . . II: Travels in Arabia Faelix. . . III: An Account of the Kingdoms of Cambate, Ginqiro, Alaba and Dacali Beyond Ethiopia in Africa Never Travelled into by Any but the Jesuits.* London: Printed for J. Knapton et al.

Trevor-Roper, Hugh, 1964. *The Rise of Christian Europe.* London: Thames and Hudson.

Trigger, Bruce G., 2003. *Understanding Early Civilizations: A Comparative Study.* Cambridge: Cambridge University Press.

Tshimanga, Raphael M., 2010. 'The Congo Nile: Water Use, Policies and Challenges', in Terje Tvedt (ed.), *The River Nile in the Post-Colonial Age: Conflict and Cooperation in the Nile Basin Countries*, 73–92. London/New York: I.B. Tauris.

Tuchman, Barbara W., 1956. *Bible and Sword: England and Palestine from the Bronze Age to Balfour.* New York: New York University Press.

Tvedt, Terje, 2004a. *The River Nile in the Age of the British: Political Ecology and the Quest for Economic Power.* London/New York: I.B. Tauris.

Tvedt, Terje, 2004b. *The Southern Sudan: An Annotated Bibliography*, 2 vols (2nd edn). London/New York: I.B. Tauris.

Tvedt, Terje (ed.), 2010. *The River Nile in the Post-Colonial Age: Conflict and Cooperation in the Nile Basin Countries.* London/New York: I.B. Tauris.

Tvedt, Terje, 2013. *A Journey in the Future of Water* (trans. Richard Daly). London/New York: I.B. Tauris.

Tvedt, Terje and Eirik Hovden, 2008. *A Bibliography on the River Nile*, 3 vols. Bergen: BRIC.

Tyerman, Christopher, 2006. *God's War: A New History of the Crusades.* Cambridge, MA: Belknap Press of Harvard University Press.

Tyldesley, Joyce, 2008. *Cleopatra: The Last Queen of Egypt.* New York: Basic Books.

Van Donzel, Emery, 2000. 'The Legend of the Blue Nile in Europe', in Haggai Erlich and Israel Gershoni (eds), *The Nile: Histories, Cultures, Myths*, 121–38. Boulder, CO: Lynne Rienner.

Volkmann, Hans, 1953. *Cleopatra: A Study in Politics and Propaganda* (trans. T.J. Cadoux). London: Elek Books.

Wagner, C. Peter, 2008. *Dominion! How Kingdom Action Can Change the World.* Grand Rapids, MI: Chosen Books.

Wainwright, G.A., 1963. 'The Origin of Storm-Gods in Egypt', *The Journal of Egyptian Archaeology*, 49, 1: 13–20.

Walker, Susan and Peter Higgs (eds), 2001. *Cleopatra of Egypt: From History to Myth.* London: British Museum.

Waller, H. (ed.), 1874. The Last Journals of David Livingstone in Central Africa from 1865 to his Death, Vol. 2, 2 vols. London: John Murray.

Wallis-Budge, E.A., 1907. *The Egyptian Soudan, Vol. II.* London: Gilbert and Rivington.

Warner, Nicholas, 2006. *The True Description of Cairo: A Sixteenth-Century Venetian View.* Oxford: Arcadian Library.

Warner, Oliver, 1960. *The Battle of the Nile.* London: B.T. Batsford.

Warren, Rick, 2002. *The Purpose Driven Life.* Grand Rapids, MI: Zondervan.

Waterbury, John, 1979. *The Hydropolitics of the Nile Valley.* Syracuse, NY: Syracuse University Press.

Welsby, Derek A., 2006. 'Settlement in Nubia in the Medieval Period', in I. Caneva and A. Roccati (eds), *Acta Nubica: Proceedings of the X International Conference of Nubian Studies, Rome, 9–14 September 2002*, 21–43. Rome: Libreria dello Stato.

Werne, Ferdinand, 1848. *Expedition to Discover the Sources of the White Nile, in the Years 1840, 1841*, 2 vols. London: R. Bentley.

Willcocks, William, 1889. *Egyptian Irrigation*, 2 vols. London: E. & F.N. Spon.

Wilson, C.J., 1938. *The Story of the East African Mounted Rifles*. Nairobi: East African Standard.

Woolbert, Robert Gale, 1935. 'Italy in Abyssinia', *Foreign Affairs*, 13, 3: 499–508.

World Bank, 1961. *The Economic Development of Tanganyika: Report of a Mission Organized by the International Bank for Reconstruction and Development at the Request of the Governments of Tanganyika and the United Kingdom*. Washington, DC: International Bank for Reconstruction and Development.

Zarzeczny, Matthew D., 2012. *Meteors that Enlighten the Earth: Napoleon and the Cult of Great Men*. Newcastle upon Tyne: Cambridge Scholars Publishing.

Index of Names